Management Theory and Practice

Sixt

Management Theory and Practice

Sixth Edition

Gerald Cole

THOMSON™

Australia • Canada • Mexico • Singapore • Spain • United Kingdom • United States

Management theory and practice, sixth edition

Copyright © Gerald Cole 2004

The Thomson logo is a registered trademark used herein under licence.

For more information, contact Thomson Learning, High Holborn House, 50-51 Bedford Row, London WC1R 4LR or visit us on the World Wide Web at:
http://www.thomsonlearning.co.uk

British Library Cataloguing-in-Publication Data
A catalogue record for this book is available from the British Library

ISBN 1-84480-088-1

First edition published by Continuum 1979
Second edition published by Continuum 1982
Third edition published by Continuum 1988
Fourth edition published by Continuum 1992
Fifth edition published by Continuum 1996
This edition published by Thomson Learning 2004
Reprinted 2004 (twice) by Thomson Learning

Typeset by YHT Ltd, London
Printed in the UK by Ashford Colour Press, Gosport, Hampshire

CONTENTS

Aims of the book

The aim of the book is to provide, in one concise volume, an accessible introduction to the principal ideas and developments in management theory and practice. The book also aims to stimulate further reading and thinking about the subject of management by signposting a wide range of books and articles, and by providing opportunities for discussion and comment on important issues arising from the text. The examination questions are also useful in this respect, encouraging readers to set out their ideas in response to typical examination-type questions, and comparing their answers with the suggested answers that are supplied.

Approach

Since management is a rather eclectic subject, drawing its subject matter from a variety of sources, the material in the book is presented in relatively short chapters with numbered paragraphs for easy reference. Chapters are grouped by topic and arranged in a logical sequence, so that whilst the subject matter is wide-ranging, and sometimes quite complex, it is possible to see some development of the body of knowledge that we call 'management'. Each group of chapters has its own list of questions for discussion or homework, and most also have one or two examination questions. The book can be used as a class-based textbook or as a practice manual for independent self study. The short glossary is intended to reinforce some of the definitions referred to in the main text, and may be especially helpful to overseas students unfamiliar with British practices.

How to use the book effectively

The basic elements of the book are the fifty-two short chapters that are grouped into fourteen topics, which form the major building blocks of the subject. This enables readers to focus on particular topics, or to work through them all systematically, depending on need or preference. The questions at the end of each group can be used to check understanding of earlier chapters, or to raise issues with tutors and/or fellow students. Such questions can also be used by tutors to encourage students to apply the results of their reading to their own organisations, or to develop their own ideas as to how management ought to be practised.

The reading lists are founded on the many other texts referred to in the book, and it is hoped that readers will seek out these other texts, old and new, in order to see for themselves how key ideas have been expressed or developed by important writers on management. In this respect the current book is a guide to the works of other writers, and an encouragement to wider reading.

The examination questions at the end of the groups of chapters are provided with suggested answers intended to give students guidance in handling such questions. There are also questions without suggested answers in the book.

NOTES ON THE SIXTH EDITION

This new edition expands and updates earlier material. Given the speed of developments in information technology, the chapter on this topic (Chapter 30) has been completely rewritten. Other chapters that have also been substantially revised include Chapter 15 on the international aspects of management, and Chapter 50 on individual employment rights. Topics that have been expanded include corporate governance and the role of directors, business ethics, organisation culture, and strategy.

The overall structure of the book remains the same as the previous edition.

Any constructive suggestions for changes in the future are welcomed by the publisher.

Gerald Cole
Sussex, England
November 2002

ACKNOWLEDGEMENTS

The author would like to express thanks to the following for permission to reproduce past examination questions:

Chartered Association of Certified Accountants (ACCA)
Chartered Institute of Management Accountants (CIMA)
Institute of Bankers
Institute of Chartered Secretaries & Administrators
Institute of Administrative Management
Institute of Marketing

I am very grateful to my elder daughter, Nichola, for her help with the index.

GLOSSARY OF MANAGEMENT TERMS

The following list provides a brief guide to some of the more common examples of management terminology in use in the United Kingdom today. It may be especially helpful for overseas students with little knowledge of British management practices. Most of the examples quoted are dealt with more fully elsewhere in the text.

ACAS Advisory, Conciliation and Arbitration Service; an independent body established by statute to provide an impartial service to prevent or resolve disputes (individual or collective) at work.

Added Value A measure of productivity, expressed in financial terms, which indicates the effects of the workforce on the sales revenue of the business; it is usually expressed as the value of sales less the cost of purchases.

Arbitration A device for settling disputes where the parties concerned fail to agree; the key feature is that the person (or persons) arbitrating takes the decision for the parties. (See also Conciliation and Mediation.)

Basic Pay Pay which is guaranteed from one period to the next; it excludes bonus earnings, overtime etc.

Behavioural Science The study of the individual and the group in the working environment; subjects of study include motivation, communication, organisation structure, decision-systems, and organisational change; as a science it is still in the development stage, relying considerably on the contributions of psychology and sociology.

Benchmark Jobs In job evaluation, these are the representative sample of jobs which are precisely written up and measured so as to provide a satisfactory range and standard of jobs upon which to base the evaluation of the remainder.

Benchmarking Comparing the organisation's standard of performance in one or more key aspects of strategy (or operations) in terms of that of a first-class competitor or comparable organisation.

Benefits Items such as pensions, sickness payments, company cars etc, which are additional to earnings; sometimes known as 'fringe benefits'.

Blue-collar Worker A manual worker as opposed to a white-collar worker (clerical, administrative, managerial etc).

Bonus A payment in addition to basic pay; may be given for a variety of reasons, eg for attendance, for dirty conditions and for payment-by-results; can apply to managers as well as to employees.

Bridlington Agreement Refers to the TUC's own procedure for the avoidance of disputes between unions; its principal body is the Disputes Committee. (See also TUC.)

Business Process Re-engineering A method of raising organisational efficiency by questioning every stage of key operational processes to see if they still achieve what is required of them in terms of cost, quality, service and speed.

CBI Confederation of British Industry. The principal employers confederation in the United Kingdom.

Certified Trade Union A trade union, which, under procedures originating from the Employment Protection Act, 1975, has been granted a certificate of independence by the Certification Officer.

Change Agent A third party, invariably a trained behavioural scientist, who acts as a catalyst in bringing about change by means of an organisation development programme; usually an external consultant, but may be an internal specialist. (See also Organisational Development.)

Check-off Arrangement whereby the employer deducts union dues from the wages of employees in the union, and pays them over to the union(s) concerned.

Clocking on/Clocking off Recording the times of arrival or departure of employees by means of a clock-operated franking machine; used mainly in manufacturing; clocking offences invariably invoke severe disciplinary action.

Coaching A method of providing on-the-job training for an employee in which an experienced and skilled individual helps a colleague to apply knowledge and skills in practice.

Codes of Practice Refers (i) to guidelines on employee relations matters issued by ACAS; and (ii) to guides issued by the appropriate Minister under the Health and Safety at Work etc Act, 1974 and others; they are not legally enforceable in their own right, but may be used in evidence at a court or tribunal.

Collective Agreements The results of collective bargaining are expressed in agreements; these are principally procedure agreements and substantive agreements; they are not legally enforceable in the UK. (See also Procedure Agreements and Substantive Agreements.)

Collective Bargaining The process of negotiating wages and other working conditions collectively between employers and trade unions, it enables the conditions of employees to be agreed as a whole group instead of individually.

Communications Essentially the process by which views and information are exchanged between individuals or groups; usually refers to the system of communication in use, but can also mean personal skills of communication.

Conciliation Attempts by a third party to promote agreement between the original parties in dispute; unlike in arbitration, a conciliator does not aim to take any decision himself, but attempts to find common ground which may lead to a settlement between the parties themselves. (See also Arbitration and Mediation.)

Convenor A senior shop steward elected by fellow stewards to represent them at meetings with other unions or with management; may be full-time in a few establishments.

Corporate governance The process by which business enterprises regulate the way in which their directors are appointed, paid and removed; it includes measures to ensure that the company accounts are reported in a fair and transparent way; it also requires attention to the ethics of conducting a public business.

Corporate Planning Company-wide planning process involving the setting or modification of objectives, and the short and long-term plans for achieving them.

CRE Commission for Racial Equality; monitors effects of Race Relations Act, 1976.

Culture The predominant value-system or ethos of an organisation; usually a mixture of implicit beliefs/values and explicit statements.

Delayering Reducing the number of layers (levels) in a job hierarchy. (See also Downsizing.)

Delegation The process of assigning duties to subordinates to enable them to act within the authority granted to them; delegation does not take away the ultimate accountability of the senior person.

Differentials Differences in earnings between groups of workers, usually based on skills, responsibility or custom and practice.

Disciplinary Procedure A set of rules or guidelines for dealing with instances of bad behaviour or rule-breaking amongst employees; the most common sanctions are warnings, suspensions and dismissals.

Discrimination Usually refers to unfair treatment of an individual or group on grounds of their sex or race.

Dismissal The termination of an employee's contract of employment either by the employer, or by the employee himself in circumstances where the employer's conduct justifies such a step (constructive dismissal); dismissal may be with or without notice.

Downsizing Reducing the scale of an organisation, especially in terms of reducing the headcount/labour force. Often accompanied by delayering. (See also Delayering.)

Earnings The total monetary remuneration received by an employee, including overtime, commission, bonuses etc.

EAT Employment Appeal Tribunal set up under the Employment Protection Act, 1975, to hear appeals from industrial tribunals; usually consists of a High Court Judge and two lay persons, experienced in industrial relations matters, from either the employers' or the trade unions' point of view.

Email Electronic mail – world-wide system of communicating messages using the global network of computer servers known as the Internet.

Employee Benefits Usually refers to pensions, sick pay schemes, company cars and other major additions to basic pay. (See also Perks.)

Employers' Association An organisation of employers set up for the purposes of collective bargaining and/or for advising and assisting members with industrial relations problems; some also deal with trading interests as in a 'trade association'.

Empowerment Granting employees more discretion over how their jobs are done or their responsibilities fulfilled. Similar to, if not same as, delegation. (See also Delegation.)

EOC Equal Opportunities Commission, set up under the Sex Discrimination Act, 1975, to monitor the whole field of sex discrimination.

EPA Employment Protection Act, 1975.

Flexitime Flexible working hours: A system enabling employees to vary their working hours in a particular period, provided they do attend during certain 'core hours', eg 1000 hours – 1600 hours.

Foreman An employee who supervises the work of others, usually in a factory, but is not considered to be of managerial status. (See also Supervisor.)

Glass Ceiling Expression used to denote a subtle barrier to women's promotion to senior posts in an organisation, and usually implying that it is kept in place by men's innate prejudice against women in senior management positions.

Globalisation The implementation of an international business strategy based on the idea that the sourcing and manufacturing of goods, or the provision of services, can be undertaken in almost any part of the world to take advantage of cheap labour, ready access to raw materials, lower taxation or other cost advantages.

Glocalisation An expression coined to describe efforts by multinational businesses to achieve international standards across their world-wide subsidiaries, whilst at the same time respecting local practices and taking them into account.

Go-slow Sanction imposed by trade union members which involves restrictions on work-output and productivity.

Grapevine Refers to the informal and unofficial channels of communication in an organisation.

Grievance Complaint made by an employee about wages, conditions of employment, or the actions of management; most organisations have a special procedure for handling grievances.

Hawthorne Effect Term used to describe changes in the productivity and morale of employees as a direct result of management interest in their problems; improvements may arise *before* management takes any action as such; the term originates from the famous studies in the United States in the 1920s at the Hawthorne works of the Western Electric Company.

Hygiene Factor An element of work motivation concerned with the environment or context of the job, eg wages, status, security etc; to be distinguished from motivators, eg achievement recognition etc. Lack of attention to hygiene factors can lead to dissatisfaction with the job; based on a theory by F. Herzberg. (See also Motivators.)

Incentives Payments made to employees over and above their basic pay in order to encourage them to increase production; the payments are made on results achieved.

Increment Refers to an increase within a pay scale, usually of a fixed amount and paid annually; incremental scales are especially common in the public services.

Induction The process of introducing a new employee into his job with the aim of integrating the newcomer as quickly and effectively as possible.

Industrial Democracy Term with a variety of meanings, but generally understood to mean any system at work that provides employees with opportunities for sharing in the major decision-making processes of the enterprise. (See also Worker Director/Two-tier Board.)

Industrial Tribunals Tribunals set up originally to hear appeals against training levies; their scope has increased considerably since 1971 to include unfair dismissal, sex discrimination etc. Now known as Employment Tribunals.

Internet An international network of computers, cables and satellite links that enables individuals to communicate worldwide through their personal computer or workplace server.

Job A set of tasks or responsibilities grouped together under a particular title.

Job Description A statement of the overall purpose and scope of a job, together with details of its tasks and duties; the description is a product of job analysis.

Job Enlargement The horizontal increasing of job responsibility, ie by the addition of tasks of a similar nature to be distinguished from job enrichment.

Job Enrichment The process of vertically increasing the responsibilities of a job, by the addition of motivators, eg more discretion, improved job interest etc.

Job Evaluation A technique for determining the size of one job compared with another, and the relationship between the two; job evaluation schemes can broadly be divided into analytical and non-analytical; the technique forms the basis for wage and salary administration.

Key Result Area Term used especially in management by objectives; refers to those areas of a person's job that make the biggest impact on end results. (See also Management by Objectives.)

Labour Turnover Percentage figure which indicates the rate at which employees move in and out of employment with the organisation; usually expressed as follows:

$$\frac{\text{Number of employees left during year}}{\text{Average number employed during year}} \times 100$$

Line and Staff A reference to an organisational configuration which embraces line functions, which contribute directly to the provision of goods or services, and staff functions, which contribute indirectly by supporting the line functions; should be distinguished from Line and Functional organisation structures, in which functional, ie staff specialist, managers can exercise considerable power over other managers, including line managers.

Lock-out Situation where, as a result of industrial conflict, an employer closes down the business, or part of it, either temporarily or permanently.

Long-range Planning Similar to corporate planning; depending on the industry concerned, long-range could mean two years or ten years; the technique is vital for highly capital intensive industries. (See also Corporate Planning.)

Management by Objectives An approach to management which aims to integrate the organisation's objectives with those of individuals; it involves the reduction of overall objectives into unit and individual objectives; in the UK the approach is associated with John Humble. (See also Key Result Area.)

Management Development A systematic process for ensuring that an organisation meets its current and future needs for effective managers; typical features include manpower reviews, succession planning, performance appraisal and training.

Manpower Planning A technique aimed at securing and improving an organisation's human resources to meet present and future needs; three principal stages can be distinguished: evaluation of existing resources, forecast of future requirements and, finally, action plan; increasingly referred to as Human Resource Planning.

Marketing Mix The particular combination of marketing variables offered to a market at any point in time; the principal variables are usually grouped by reference to product, price, promotion and distribution.

Matrix Management A system of management operating in a horizontal as well as vertical organisation structure, where, typically, a manager reports to two superiors – one a departmental/line manager and the other a functional/project manager.

Mediation A process whereby a third party makes specific proposals to both sides in a dispute in order to promote a mutually acceptable solution; some-times regarded as a 'half-way house' between conciliation and arbitration. (See also Arbitration and Conciliation.)

Mentoring process whereby a senior or experienced person is assigned to guide and assist a junior person in their development at work; a mentor is not someone in a position of formal authority over the person being mentored.

Method Study An aspect of Work Study; its object is to see whether a job is being performed in the most efficient and economical manner; it normally precedes work measurement. (See also Work Study.)

Mission Statement A statement of an organisation's overriding purpose or vision for the organisation. Usually expressed in general terms, but tends to suffuse the organisation's culture.

Motivators Factors leading to job satisfaction and high employee morale; highlighted in F. Herzberg's theory of motivation; motivators are important in job enrichment programmes. (See also Hygiene Factors.)

Negotiations Term used to describe the bargaining between employers and trade union representatives on the subject of terms and conditions of employment; the object of the negotiations is to obtain mutual agreement to improved conditions. (See also Collective Bargaining.)

Network Analysis A set of techniques used to plan and control complex processes and activities on the basis of a network diagram; two commonest examples are CPM (Critical Path Method) and PERT (Programme Evaluation and Review Technique).

O&M Organisation and Methods; a term used for the techniques employed in Method Study and Work Measurement when applied in an office situation for the purpose of improving clerical procedures.

OR Operational Research – a scientific method which uses models of a system to evaluate alternative courses of action with a view to improving decision-making.

Organisation Development A systematic process aimed at improving organisational effectiveness and adaptiveness on the basis of behavioural science knowledge; typical stages in an OD programme include analysis, diagnosis, action plans and review, an external third party assists the process. (See also Change Agent.)

Outsourcing The practice of delegating to some outside specialist work that had previously been supplied in-house (such as salary administration, computer maintenance).

Overtime A period of work, in excess of normal or standard hours, which is paid at an enhanced rate.

Pay Policy Refers to Government intervention in collective bargaining by means of pay ceilings or other restraints on the negotiation of employment conditions.

Performance Appraisal The process of assessing the performance of an employee in his job; appraisal can be used for salary reviews, training needs analysis and job improvement plans, for example.

Performance Management Any system for improving management effectiveness by means of standard-setting, appraisal and evaluation; combines informal day-to-day aspects with formal appraisal interviews and goal-setting.

Perks Short for perquisites – incidental benefits allowed to an employee, eg tips, gifts from customers, use of telephone etc; not as formal nor as important as 'Employee Benefits'. (See also Employee Benefits.)

Picketing Trade union activity where groups of workers in dispute with their employers attend at their own place of work for the purpose of peacefully persuading other workers not to leave or enter the premises for work; the persons in attendance are the pickets, and the area they are picketing is called the picket line.

Procedure Agreement A collective agreement setting out the procedures to be followed in the conduct of management–union relations with particular reference to negotiating rights, union representatives, disputes and grievance procedures. (See also Substantive Agreement.)

Quality Control An activity in manufacturing industries which aims to establish quality standards, check that they are being adhered to, take corrective action where necessary, and set improved standards where possible.

Recognition Issue A situation where an employer and a trade union disagree about the extent to which the employer is prepared to recognise the union for the purposes of collective bargaining; unions may seek the help of ACAS, but employers are not obliged to grant recognition. (See also ACAS.)

Redundancy The loss of a job on the grounds that it is no longer required or no longer available at a particular place of employment; it is regarded as a form of dismissal.

Seven Point Plan A guide to selection interviewing, enabling interviewers to assess candidates under seven headings: physical make-up, attainments, general intelligence, special aptitudes, interests, disposition and domestic/family circumstances.

Shop Steward A union member elected by colleagues to represent them to management in their place of work; shop stewards are appointed under, and work within, their union rules; they are not full-time, nor are they paid for their union work. (See also Convenor.)

Stress The physical symptoms of ill-health caused by excessive pressures in the workplace or elsewhere and leading to reduced job performance; how far an individual succumbs to stress is determined mainly by personality, and the extent to which they are confident of their ability to overcome the pressures.

Substantive Agreement A collective agreement dealing with terms and conditions of employment, eg wages, hours of work, holidays etc. (See also Procedure Agreement.)

Supervisor A person who directly supervises the work of others, eg as a foreman (see above); a senior supervisor may in turn directly supervise the work of other supervisors, eg as a works superintendent; supervisors provide the main link between the organisation's workgroups and the management.

SWOT Analysis A systematic way of analysing (a) the strengths and weaknesses of the organisation's internal situation, and (b) the opportunities or threats posed by the external environment.

Synergy The extent to which investment of additional resources produces a return which is proportionally greater than the sum of the resources invested; sometimes known as the $2 + 2 = 5$ effect.

Theory X Theory about motivation, expounded by D. McGregor, which suggests that people are lazy, selfish, unambitious etc, and need to be treated accordingly; managers who act in accordance with this view may be dubbed 'Theory X Managers'; this theory contrasts with Theory Y – the optimistic view of people.

Theory Z An expression coined by an American, W.G. Ouchi, as a result of studying Japanese success in manufacturing industry to denote a process of organisational adaptation in which the management of an enterprise concentrates on coordinating people, not technology, in the pursuit of productivity.

Trade Union An organisation of employees whose principal purpose is to negotiate with employers about terms and conditions of employment and other matters affecting the members' interests at work. (See also Certified Trade Union.)

Training Needs Analysis A rational approach to assessing the training or development needs of groups of employees, aimed at clarifying the needs of the job and the needs of individuals in terms of training required.

TUC Trades Union Congress – the principal national body for the coordination of trade union activities in the UK; its role is mainly political and economic lobbying on behalf of the trade unions as a whole; it has no direct power over individual unions. (See also Bridlington Agreement.)

Two-tier Board Refers to the Continental practice of dividing the Board of a Company into a Supervisory Board, the senior body, and a Management Board, the executive body; contrasts with the unitary (i.e. single) Board, as in the UK.

Unfair Dismissal A statutory definition of dismissal now part of the Employment Protection (Consolidation) Act, 1978; the Act states that every employee shall have the right not to be unfairly dismissed; remedies for unfair dismissal must be pursued via an industrial tribunal, which may award compensation or reinstatement or re-engagement.

Value Analysis A term used to describe an analytical approach to the function and costs of every part of a product with a view to reducing costs whilst retaining the functional ability; sometimes known as value engineering.

Worker Director An employee of a company who is elected to serve as a director on the Board; such directors are invariably non-executive and may also lack any representative capacity; where a two-tier Board exists, worker directors sit on the Supervisory Board; this form of worker participation has not yet taken root in the UK. (See also Two-tier Board.)

Work Measurement A technique of Work Study designed to establish the time for a qualified worker to carry out a specified job at a defined level of performance. (See also Method Study and Work Study.)

Work Study A term describing several techniques for examining work in all its contexts, in particular those factors affecting economy and efficiency, with a view to making improvements; the two most common techniques of Work Study are Method Study and Work Measurement. (See also Method Study and Work Measurement.)

World Wide Web A system of communication between computers, or servers, enabling documentary, sound and video forms of information to be passed between them on the Internet, using a form of software known as global hypertext devised by British physicist, Tim Berners-Lee.

Part One

MANAGEMENT THEORY

The two short opening chapters in this section of the book provide an overview of developments in management theory (Chapter 1), together with some discussion of key terms, especially that of 'management' (Chapter 2). The theoretical framework for Part One (Chapters 1–11) is based on the idea that management activities can best be analysed in terms of four essential groups of activities, namely planning, organising, motivating and controlling. Whilst this approach omits some aspects of management, it nevertheless simplifies the study of the theoretical basis of the subject.

CHAPTER 1

Developments in Management Theory 1910–2000

Introduction

1. The earliest contributors to our understanding of management theory included practising managers as well as social scientists. More recent theorists have tended to be academics or management consultants. The early theorists can be divided into two main groups – the practising managers, such as Taylor and Fayol, and the social scientists, such as Mayo and McGregor. The practising managers tended to reflect upon, and theorise about, their personal experiences of management with the object of producing a set of rational principles of management which could be applied universally in order to achieve organisational efficiency. The resultant 'theories' of management were concerned primarily with the structuring of work and organisations, rather than with human motivation or organisation culture, for example. The label generally ascribed to these theorists is 'Classical', or, in some cases, 'Scientific Managers'. Their approaches were generally prescriptive, ie they set out what managers ought to do in order to fulfil their leadership function within their organisation.

2. The social scientists, by contrast, were academics, whose starting point was research into human behaviour in the workplace. At first most of their studies were also linked to concerns about efficiency, including the effects of physical working conditions on employees. Subsequent theorists were more interested in the human factor at work, and thus concentrated their attention on issues such as employee motivation, interpersonal communication and leadership style. Their focus was as much on individual satisfaction as on the efficient use of resources. Typical labels that have been assigned to these early social scientists include 'Human Relations theorists' and 'Social Psychological School'. They were concerned primarily with social relationships and individual behaviour at work.

3. Another group of social scientists, whose work was grounded in the idea of organisations as social systems, produced a more comprehensive view of the behaviour of people at work based on the interaction of a number of variables, such as structure, tasks, technology and the environment. Later theorists of this school were given the label

3

'Contingency theorists', since their ideas were based on what was appropriate in given circumstances, ie where the effect on people of one variable was contingent on its relationship with one or more others.

4.   The most recent theorists of management, such as Mintzberg, Porter, Peters and Moss Kanter, have usually taken a strategic perspective, involving several key organisational factors. These have embraced such factors as organisation mission, vision, culture and values, organisational structure, leadership, the external environment, and customer satisfaction (including both internal as well as external customers). Not surprisingly, these approaches build on the work that has gone before. They generally adopt a comprehensive view of organisations, and in many ways may be regarded as modern exponents of contingency theory. Their concern has been to predict which conditions are the most likely to produce organisations capable of meeting the competing demands of their various stakeholders. The contribution of the academics among them has been more objective than that of the management consultants (eg Peters), who are inclined to be prescriptive in their approach.

Classical Theories

5.   The classical approach to management was primarily concerned with the structure and activities of formal, or official, organisation. Issues such as the division of work, the establishment of a hierarchy of authority, and the span of control were seen to be of the utmost importance in the achievement of an effective organisation. The two greatest exponents of classical theories were undoubtedly Henri Fayol (1841–1925) and F.W. Taylor (1856–1915). Between them these two practising managers laid the foundations of ideas about the organisation of people at work and the organisation of work itself. At first these ideas were developed separately, Fayol in France and Taylor in the United States. By the 1930s their work was being promoted and developed by writers such as L.F. Urwick and E.F.L. Brech on both sides of the Atlantic. The work of these contributors to classical theories of management is described in Chapter 3.

Bureaucracy

6.   While Fayol and Taylor were grappling with the problems of management, a German sociologist, Max Weber (1864–1924), was developing a theory of authority structures in which he identified a form of organisation to which he gave the name 'bureaucracy'. The distinguishing features of a bureaucracy were a definition of roles within a hierarchy, where job-holders were appointed on merit, were subject to rules and were expected to behave impartially. Weber's ideas and their impact on modern organisation theory are discussed in more detail in Chapter 4.

Human Relations and Social Psychological Schools

7.   The fundamental idea behind the human relations approach to management is that people's needs are the decisive factor in achieving organisational effectiveness. The leading figure of human relations was Professor Elton Mayo, whose association with the so-called 'Hawthorne Studies' between 1927 and 1932 provided an enormous impetus to considerations of the human factor at work. A summary of the Hawthorne Studies and their impact on industrial psychology is contained in Chapter 5.

8.   Many of the issues raised by Mayo and his colleagues were taken up in the post-war years by American social psychologists. An early major influence here was Abraham

Maslow's work on motivation based on a hierarchy of human needs, ranging from basic physiological needs (food, sleep etc) to higher psychological needs, such as self-fulfilment. Other important contributors included McGregor, Argyris, Likert and Herzberg. The work of these theorists and the results of their researches are covered in Chapter 5. Later theorists of motivation (eg Vroom) are summarised in Chapter 6.

Systems and Contingency Approaches

9.   By the late 1960s another group of theories began to challenge the dominance of human relations and psychology. These were theories that viewed organisations as complex systems of people, tasks and technology. The early work on this approach was conducted by British researchers from the Tavistock Institute of Human Relations, who, despite their title, recognised that human or social factors alone were not the most important consideration in achieving organisational effectiveness. They recognised that organisations were part of a larger environment with which they interacted and in particular were affected by technical and economic factors just as much as social ones. They coined the phrase 'open socio-technical system' to describe their concept of a business enterprise. An 'open' social system is one that interacts with its environment, eg a commercial enterprise, a 'closed' social system is self-contained, eg a strict monastic community. This approach is described in greater detail in Chapter 9.

10.   Arising out of the open systems approach is an essentially pragmatic 'theory' which argues that there is no one theory at present which can guarantee the effectiveness of an organisation. Management has to select a mix of theories which seem to meet the needs of the organisation and its internal and external pressures at a particular period in its life. This has been termed a contingency approach to management. Notable exponents of this approach are Pugh and colleagues in the United Kingdom, and Lawrence and Lorsch in the United States. A summary of their work appears in Chapter 10.

Modern Approaches to Management

11.   The emphasis in management theorising over the last twenty years has been on organisational effectiveness with its focus on *strategic* issues. This emphasis implies more than just efficiency, which is concerned with *'doing things right'*. Effectiveness is primarily a question of *'doing the right things'* even more than performing them efficiently. Thus, the concerns of modern theorists have been topics such as developing strategic mission and implanting organisational values/culture (ie doing the right things) as well as on managing change, promoting total quality management, achieving organisational excellence, facilitating personal empowerment and optimising stakeholder relationships. Some of the leading ideas in these areas of interest are described in Chapter 11.

Conclusion

12.   The task of management is carried out in the context of an organisation. Over the past eighty years or so the development of coherent theories to explain organisational performance has moved away from approaches that relied purely on a consideration of structural or human relations issues in favour of more comprehensive perspectives. Early ideas about management were propounded at a time when organisations were thought of as machines requiring efficient systems to enable them to function effectively. The emphasis, therefore, was on the efficient use of resources, especially human resources, in the service of a mechanistic model of organisations. Later theorists modified this approach by taking account of social and environmental as well as technical factors in the workplace. Their emphasis was

as much on employee satisfaction as on organisational effectiveness. Modern approaches to the analysis of organisational effectiveness do not necessarily rule out the ideas put forward by earlier theorists, but emphasise that they must be evaluated in the context of an organisation's overriding need for flexibility in responding to change in its external and internal environment, in order to meet the competing demands of all its various stake-holders – customers, suppliers, employees and shareholders etc.

CHAPTER 2

Definitions of Management

Introduction

1.   Not unexpectedly, the variety of approaches to the theoretical background of management has produced a number of versions of what is meant by such key words as 'management' and 'organisation'. This chapter looks at the most typical interpretations of such words, and offers some explanations.

The Meaning of Management

2.   There is no generally accepted definition of 'management' as an activity, although the classic definition is still held to be that of Henri Fayol. His general statement about management in many ways still remains valid after more than eighty years, and has only been adapted by more recent writers, as shown below:

> 'To manage is to forecast and plan, to organise, to command, to coordinate and to control.'
>   H. FAYOL (1916)[1]

> 'Management is a social process… the process consists of… planning, control, coordination and motivation.'
>   E.F.L. BRECH (1957)[2]

> 'Managing is an operational process initially best dissected by analysing the managerial functions…The five essential managerial functions (are): planning, organising, staffing, directing and leading, and controlling.'
>   KOONTZ and O'DONNELL (1984)[3]

> 'Five areas of management constitute the essence of proactive performance in our chaotic world: (1) an obsession with responsiveness to customers, (2) constant innovation in all areas of the firm, (3) partnership – the wholesale participation of and gain sharing with all people connected with the organisation, (4) leadership that loves change (instead of fighting it) and instils and shares an inspiring vision, and (5) control by means of simple support systems aimed at measuring the "right stuff" for today's environment.'
>   T. PETERS (1988)[4]

The definitions proposed by Brech, Koontz and O'Donnell represent changes of emphasis rather than principle. For example, Fayol's use of the term 'command' is dropped in favour of 'motivation' (Brech), or 'directing and leading' (Koontz & O'Donnell). Tom Peters' view of management, by comparison, shifts the emphasis away from describing what management is about and stresses what it is that managers need to do. Nevertheless, even his enthusiastic prescriptions for dealing with chaos are tempered by references to 'participation' (ie motivating), 'leadership' and 'control'.

3. It has to be recognised that the above definitions are extremely broad. Basically, what they are saying is that 'management' is a process that enables organisations to set and achieve their objectives by planning, organising and controlling their resources, including gaining the commitment of their employees (motivation). Over the past twenty years, several writers (eg Stewart, Mintzberg) have attempted to move away from this generalised approach towards a more detailed and behaviour-oriented analysis of what managers actually do.

4. Mintzberg (1973)[5], for example, in reporting his major study of managerial work, highlights a number of key roles that seem to appear regularly in such work. He describes these roles as 'organised sets of behaviours identified with a position', and gathers them into three main groupings, as follows:

Interpersonal roles	Informational roles	Decisional roles
Figurehead	Monitor	Entrepreneur
Leader	Disseminator	Disturbance handler
Liaison	Spokesman	Resource allocator
		Negotiator

Recognisable though these ten role-models may be, they are still defined very generally, and there is the additional problem that some of them apply equally to non-managerial jobs (eg monitor, negotiator).

5. Stewart (1994)[6], in reviewing efforts to define management, shows how difficult it is to produce a sufficiently focused and yet comprehensive answer. She points out that in fact there is not just one but three categories of management position: the first level entails a direct responsibility for other people, the second entails a responsibility for other managers, and the third entails responsibility for multiple functions (the 'general manager'). In each of these situations the job-holder is faced with some crucial concerns:

- learning what it means to be a manager at that level (ie what role has to be played)

- learning how to improve the ability to judge others (because one is going to have to rely on others as work and tasks are delegated)

- learning to understand more about one's own capacities and weaknesses

- learning how to cope with stress

6. Stewart considers that managerial jobs, in particular, are affected by the extent of, and the relationship between, the following:

- the core of the job (ie the personal responsibilities of the jobholder which cannot be delegated), which she terms the 'demands' of the job

- the 'constraints' of the job (eg limited resources)

- the 'choices' available to the job-holder by way of different work from another person (eg different amounts of time spent on operational as opposed to strategic matters).

In her research Stewart found that managerial jobs could vary considerably in the size and impact of each of these three factors.

7. The search for a comprehensive definition of 'management' that is not over-generalised still proceeds. In the meantime, this book deals with management as a collection of activities involving planning, organising, motivating and controlling (see below). This approach is helpful in enabling the work of management to be analysed for study purposes.

Administration

8.   At this point it will be helpful to distinguish the concept of 'management' from that of 'administration'. At one time these concepts were more or less inter-changeable. Fayol himself used the French word *administration* to mean what we now would understand as 'management', in his original treatise on the subject, and so did Lyndall F. Urwick (see next chapter). For the last forty years or so, however, the term 'management' has been understood as encompassing much more than 'administration', which has tended to be understood as the narrower process of developing and maintaining *procedures*, eg as in office administration. That is to say 'administration' is seen primarily as an aspect of organising. 'Management', by comparison, is also concerned with planning, controlling and motivating staff.

Organisations

9.   Whatever view is preferred concerning the definition of management, it is clear that it can only be discussed realistically within the context of an organisation. Brech (1965)[7] once described organisation as 'the framework of the management process'. It must be recognised, however, that this 'framework' can be described in several different ways. The first distinction is between the use of the word 'organisation' to describe the *process* of organising, and its use to describe the social entity formed by a group of people. Organisation as a *process* is dealt with later (Chapters 22 et seq). Organisation as a *social entity* is what we are concerned with in this chapter.

10. As yet there is no widely accepted definition of an organisation. Nevertheless, as the following quotations suggest, there are some commonly accepted features of organisations such as *purpose, people and structure.*

> 'Organisations are intricate human strategies designed to achieve certain objectives.'
> ARGYRIS (1960)[8]

> 'Since organisations are systems of behaviour designed to enable humans and their machines to accomplish goals, organisational form must be a joint function of human characteristics and the nature of the task environment.'   SIMON (1976)[9]

> 'Organisations are systems of inter-dependent human beings.'   PUGH (1990)[10]

> 'Organisations are set up to achieve purposes that individuals cannot achieve on their own. Organisations then provide a means of working with others to achieve goals ... likely to be determined by whoever is in the best position to influence them.... A key characteristic of organisations is their complexity.'   STEWART (1994)[11]

11. Like discussions about management theory, approaches to organisation theory tend to follow the pattern of classical, human relations and systems perspectives. The *classical approach* concentrates attention on the organisation structure and all that is required to sustain it (organisation charts, procedures, communication channels etc). Brech and Urwick are good examples of writers who see organisations in this way.

The *human relations* approach, by comparison, says, in effect, that people *are* the organisation. Therefore it is vital to give first consideration to issues of group and individual needs before such other issues as structure, authority levels, and decision-making, for example. Job enrichment is a typical example of a human relations approach to organisational design.

The *systems approach* aims to describe organisations in terms of open systems, responding to external and internal influences in developing, and ultimately achieving, their objectives.

Key areas of attention for systems theorists include the relationship between formal and informal (or unofficial) organisations, the external environment, the question of boundaries, the organisation's culture and the impact of technology.

Finally, the *contingency approach* aims to develop systems theory by balancing a number of key organisational variables within a given context (both external and internal). This latter approach is the one that is adapted by practically every modern theorist in their search for the optimum organisational profile – structure, strategy, staffing etc.

Relationship between Management and Organisation Theory

12. Over the past thirty years the impact of the behavioural sciences on the study of people at work has led to the ascendancy of organisation theory over purely management theory. Management is no longer seen as *the* controlling factor in work organisations. Instead it is seen as a *function* of organisations. Its task is to enable the organisation's purposes to be defined and fulfilled by adapting to change and maintaining a workable balance between the various, and frequently conflicting, pressures at work in the organisation.

13. Handy (1993),[12] sums up the new relationship very neatly. In a discussion on the role of the manager, he suggests that the key variables a manager has to grapple with are:

- people
- work and structures
- systems and procedures.

These variables cannot be dealt with in isolation but within the constraints of an environment in which Handy sees three crucial components.

- the goals of the organisation
- the technology available
- the culture of the organisation (its values, beliefs etc).

All six factors mentioned interact with each other, and change in one of them will inevitably lead to change in one or more others. To manage successfully is to balance these factors in a way that meets the needs of the organisation at a particular period in time, which is essentially a contingency approach to management.

The Process of Management

14. The systems approach to organisations (see Chapter 9), is based on the three major elements of *inputs, throughputs/conversion*, and *outputs*. The process of management is concerned with all three of these elements, and especially with the conversion processes of organisations. As Drucker (1955)[13] first put it, over forty years ago, management is concerned with the 'systematic organisation of economic resources' and its task is to make these resources productive. The following paragraphs introduce the idea of management as a conversion process, describe its principal elements and emphasise that management is oriented towards results as well as towards action.

15. Management is not an activity that exists in its own right. It is rather a description of a variety of activities carried out by those members of organisations whose role is that of a 'manager' ie someone who either has formal responsibility for the work of one or more persons in the organisation or who is accountable for specialist advisory duties in support of key management activities. These activities have generally been grouped in terms of

planning, organising, motivating, and *controlling* activities. These groupings describe activities which indicate broadly what managers do in practice, primarily in terms of their inputs. They apply to supervisory and junior management positions as well as to middle and senior management roles.

16. The groupings of management activities can be summarised as follows:

- **Planning**   Deciding the objectives or goals of the organisation and preparing how to meet them.

- **Organising**   Determining activities and allocating responsibilities for the achievement of plans; coordinating activities and responsibilities into an appropriate structure.

- **Motivating**   Meeting the social and psychological needs of employees in the fulfilment of organisational goals.

- **Controlling**   Monitoring and evaluating activities, and providing corrective mechanisms.

These traditional groupings – the POMC approach – are the ones chosen to represent the framework for this book. It is appreciated that they do not tell the whole story about what constitutes management, but they are a convenient way of describing most of the key aspects of the work of managers in practice.

17. Before moving on to look at each of these groupings in detail, it will be useful to consider some of the shortcomings of the POMC approach, in order to make allowance for it in the chapters that follow. As stated above, the approach focuses on the *actions* (inputs) of managers rather than on *results* (outputs). It also ignores the role elements of a managerial job, and does not take into account the different levels of management job.

18. Firstly, let us turn to the question of results. One particularly influential writer on the subject of managerial effectiveness, Professor Bill Reddin of the University of New Brunswick, considers it essential for the job of management to be judged on output rather than by input, and by achievements rather than by activities. In his book *Managerial Effectiveness* (1970)[14], he argues that we tend to confuse efficiency with effectiveness. Efficiency is the ratio of output to input. However, although 100% efficiency can be obtained by high output in relation to high input, the same result can be achieved where both output and input are *low*. Effectiveness, as Reddin defines it, is the extent to which a manager achieves the *output* requirements of his position. This assumes that the outputs have been identified and made measurable. Examples of differences between 'efficient' managers and 'effective' manages, according to Reddin, are that 'efficient' managers seek to solve problems and reduce costs, whereas 'effective' managers seek to produce creative alternatives and increase profits. On this basis the POMC approach is more concerned with efficiency than 'effectiveness'.

19. It has to be recognised that the POMC approach is essentially a leader-centred approach to management. It does not take account of the variety of roles that managers can be called upon to play. We saw above that Mintzberg's analysis of managerial roles identified seven key roles, which clearly encompass more than just planning, organising, motivating and controlling. Other crucial, albeit lower-key roles, include liaison activities and disturbance-handling, for example. Kotter (1996)[15] takes the view that, where change is concerned, success is mostly down to *leadership* rather than *management*. The former in his view enables change to happen, often with long-term results. The latter enables predictability and order, and can produce short-term results. Kotter believes that there is too much emphasis on *managing* organisations, and too little on providing them with *effective leadership*.

Planning

20. Planning is an activity which involves decisions about *ends* (organisational aims/objectives), *means* (plans), *conduct* (policies), and *results*. It is an activity that takes place against the background of (1) the organisation's external environment, and (2) the organisation's internal strengths and weaknesses. Planning can be long term, as in strategic and corporate planning, or short term, as in the setting of annual departmental budgets. Long term usually implies a time horizon of about five years, although this may be ten or twenty years in certain industries (oil extraction, pharmaceuticals etc). Short term can be any period from the immediate future (crisis management) up to about one year. Chapters 16–21 describe the major aspects of planning.

Organising

21. Plans have to be put into operation. This involves detailed organisation and coordination of tasks and the human and material resources needed to carry them out. A key issue here is that of formal communications. Various aspects of organising are dealt with in Chapters 22–27.

Motivating

22. We consider some of the most significant theories of motivation in Chapters 5 and 6. The motivating activities of managers, however, are essentially practical in their intent for, in setting plans and executing them, managers have to gain the commitment of their employees. This is primarily a question of leadership, or style of management, and Chapter 7 outlines the principal options available to managers in practice.

Controlling

23. Controlling activities are concerned essentially with measuring progress and correcting deviations. The basic functions of control are:
- to establish standards of performance
- to measure actual performance against standards
- to take corrective actions where appropriate.

Control activities act as the feedback mechanism for all managerial activities. Their use is, therefore, crucial to the success of management. Key aspects of control are discussed in Chapters 28–30.

References

1. Fayol, H. (1949), *General and Industrial Management*, Pitman.
2. Brech, E.F.L. (1957), *The Principles and Practice of Management*, Longman.
3. Koontz, H. & O'Donnell, C. (1984), *Management* (8th edition), McGraw-Hill.
4. Peters, T. (1988), *Thriving on Chaos – Handbook for a Management Revolution*, Macmillan.
5. Mintzberg, H. (1973), *The Nature of Managerial Work*, Harper & Row.
6. Stewart, R. (1994), *Managing Today and Tomorrow*, Macmillan.
7. Brech, E.F.L. (1965), *Organisation – the Framework of Management* (2nd edition), Longman.
8. Argyris, C. (1960), *Understanding Organisational Behaviour*, Tavistock.
9. Simon, H. (1976), *Administrative Behaviour* (3rd edition), Collier Macmillan.
10. Pugh, D. (ed.) (1990), *Organisational Theory: Selected Readings* (3rd edition), Penguin.

11. Stewart, R. (1994), *Managing Today and Tomorrow*, Macmillan.
12. Handy, C. (1993), *Understanding Organisations* (4th edition), Penguin.
13. Drucker, P. (1955), *The Practice of Management*, Heinemann.
14. Reddin, W. (1970), *Managerial Effectiveness*, McGraw Hill.
15 Kotter, J.P.(1996), *Leading Change*, Harvard Business School Press.

Questions for Discussion/Homework

1. What do you understand by the terms 'management' and 'organisation'? Explain, using your own words.

2. Broadly in what ways does a classical approach to organisations differ from a human relations approach?

3. What are the key organisational variables that might confront a manager in a typical organisation? Which are more likely to need frequent revision, and why?

4. What is the advantage to the student of management of considering *managerial roles* rather than *managerial functions* in analysing the process of management?

5. Why do you think the current emphasis on satisfying the customer leads organisations to adopt particular management priorities?

Examination Question

As this has been an introductory section, most of the questions it raises occur with greater relevance in the next group of chapters. However, one very general question on the role of management is listed below for practice purposes. An outline answer will be found in Appendix 2.

EQ 1   Organisations employ various resources (eg finance, raw materials, people, plant and equipment) in order to achieve objectives. Discuss the role of management in an organisation and assess the relative importance of management as a resource.

(ICSA MPP)

The two chapters in this section describe, and comment on, the main ideas of the leading classical theorists.

Chapter 3 firstly outlines the ideas put forward by Henri Fayol, then describes the work of F.W. Taylor and the so-called Scientific Management School, and finally describes how Lyndall F. Urwick and E.F.L. Brech adapted and extended classical ideas in the period after the Second World War.

Chapter 4 outlines the theory of bureaucracy, with particular reference to the formative work of Max Weber.

CHAPTER 3

The Search for Principles of Management

Introduction

1.   The search for universally applicable principles of management began in the industrial heartlands of Europe and America in the last years of the nineteenth century. This chapter firstly describes the most important ideas on management propounded by the Frenchman, Henri Fayol, at the beginning of the twentieth century. Particular attention is paid to his definition of management, and to his general principles of management, which may then be compared with similar principles proposed by other classical writers. The chapter continues with an account of F.W. Taylor's ideas concerning 'scientific management' in the workplace, together with some brief references to other individuals who shared his viewpoint. The chapter ends with summaries of the ideas of two latter-day scientific managers, L.F. Urwick and E.F.L. Brech, who developed many of the ideas of Fayol and Taylor in the period following the Second World War.

Henri Fayol

2.   Henri Fayol, (1841–1925) the celebrated French industrialist and theorist, began his working life as a young mining engineer at the age of nineteen. He spent his entire working life with the same company, rising to Managing Director at the age of forty-seven, and only retiring after his seventy-seventh birthday! Under his leadership the company grew and prospered despite its near-bankrupt state when he took over. His entrepreneurial successes won him considerable fame and popularity, and when, in 1916, he published his major work on management, he ensured himself a place in the annals of industrial history.

3.   The publication of 'Administration industrielle et generale' in 1916 brought to light the distillation of a lifetime's experience of managerial work. The best-known English translation is the one by Constance Storrs, published by Pitmans under the title of 'General

and Industrial Management' in 1949[1]. The foreword to this translation was provided by none other than L.F. Urwick (see below). Urwick questioned the appropriateness of the title, in which the French *'administration'* had been translated as 'management'. His fear was that with such a title Fayol's work would be seen as relevant only to industry, whereas, in Urwick's view, it was just as applicable to central and local government as well. History has shown that he need not have worried, since Fayol's ideas have had a major influence on the world of organisations.

Fayol's Definition of Management

4.   Fayol prefaced his famous definition of management by stating what he considered to be the key activities of any industrial undertaking. He outlined six such key activities, as follows:

❶   Technical activities, eg production.

❷   Commercial activities, eg buying and selling.

❸   Financial activities, eg securing capital.

❹   Security activities, eg safeguarding property.

❺   Accounting activities, eg providing financial information.

❻   Managerial activities, eg planning and organising.

Fayol accepted that the first five were already sufficiently well known, but recognised at the outset that the sixth group of activities would require further explanation for his readers. Whilst the other activities were all interdependent to some extent, there was no single one which was concerned with broad planning and resourcing. It was vitally necessary to isolate these last mentioned activities, said Fayol, and it is these to which he gave the name 'managerial'.

5.   To manage, said Fayol, is to 'forecast and plan, to organise, to command, to coordinate and to control'. He saw forecasting and planning as looking to the future and drawing up a plan of action. Organising was seen in structural terms, and commanding was described as 'maintaining activity among the personnel'. Coordinating was seen as essentially a unifying activity. Controlling meant ensuring that things happen in accordance with established policies and practice. It is important to note that Fayol did not see managerial activities as exclusively belonging to the management. Such activities are part and parcel of the total activities of an undertaking. Having said this, it is equally important to point out that Fayol's general principles of management take a perspective which essentially looks at organisations from the top downwards. Nevertheless, they do have the merit of taking a comprehensive view of the role of management in organisations. Thus, Fayol's analysis has more far-reaching implications than F.W. Taylor's ideas on scientific management, which were centred on the shop floor.

Fayol's Principles of Management

6.   In his book Fayol lists fourteen so-called 'principles of management'. These are the precepts which he applied the most frequently during his working life. He emphasised that these principles were not absolutes but capable of adaptation, according to need. He did not claim that his list was exhaustive, but only that it served him well in the past. The fourteen 'principles' listed below in Figure 3.1 are given in the order set out by Fayol, but the comments are a summary of his thinking on each point.

1.	Division of work	Reduces the span of attention or effort for any one person or group. Develops practice and familiarity.
2.	Authority	The right to give orders. Should not be considered without reference to responsibility.
3.	Discipline	Outward marks of respect in accordance with formal or informal agreements between firm and its employees.
4.	Unity of command	One man one superior!
5.	Unity of direction	One head and one plan for a group of activities with the same objective.
6.	Subordination of individual interests to the general interest	The interest of one individual or one group should not prevail over the general good. This is a difficult area of management.
7.	Remuneration	Pay should be fair to both the employee and the firm.
8.	Centralisation	Is always present to a greater or lesser extent, depending on the size of company and quality of its managers.
9.	Scalar chain	The line of authority from top to bottom of the organisation.
10.	Order	A place for everything and everything in its place; the right man in the right place.
11.	Equity	A combination of kindliness and justice towards employees.
12.	Stability of tenure of personnel	Employees need to be given time to settle into their jobs, even though this may be a lengthy period in the case of managers.
13.	Initiative	Within the limits of authority and discipline, all levels of staff should be encouraged to show initiative.
14.	Esprit de corps	Harmony is a great strength to an organisation; teamwork should be encouraged.

Figure 3.1. Fayol's Principles of Management.

7.   Fayol's General Principles have been adopted by later followers of the classical school, such as Urwick and Brech. Present day theorists, however, would not find much of substance in these precepts. From our present day view point, the following general comments may be made.

1.   The references to division of work, scalar chain, unity of command and centralisation, for example, are descriptive of the kind of formal organisation that has come to be known as bureaucracy. Fayol, in true classical fashion, was emphasising the structural nature of organisations.

2.   Issues such as individual versus general interests, remuneration and equity were considered very much from the point of view of a paternalistic management. Today, questions concerning fairness, or the bona fide conflict of interests between groups,

15

have to be worked out jointly between management and organised labour, often with third party involvement by the State.

3. Although emphasising the hierarchical aspects of the business enterprise, Fayol was well aware of the need to avoid an excessively mechanistic approach towards employees. Thus references to initiative and esprit de corps indicated his sensitivity to people's needs as individuals and as groups. Such issues are of major interest to theorists today, the key difference being that whereas Fayol saw these issues in the context of a rational organisation structure, the modern organisation development specialist sees them in terms of adapting structures and changing people's behaviour to achieve the best fit between the organisation and its customers.

4. Fayol was the first to achieve a genuine theory of management based on a number of principles which could be passed on to others. Many of these principles have been absorbed into modern organisations. Their effect on organisational effectiveness has been subject to increasing criticism over the last twenty years, however, mainly because such principles were not designed to cope with modern conditions of rapid change, flatter structures, and increased employee participation in the decision-making processes of the organisation.

F.W. Taylor and Scientific Management

8. The following paragraphs summarise the key ideas of the pioneers of 'Scientific Management' – F.W. Taylor, Frank and Lilian Gilbreth and H. Gantt – and comment on the main consequences of their work.

9. Frederick Winslow Taylor (1856–1915), like Fayol, was one of the early practical manager-theorists. Born in Boston, Massachusetts, in 1856, he spent the greater part of his life working on the problems of achieving greater efficiency on the shop-floor. The solutions he came up with were based directly on his own experience at work, initially as a shop-floor worker himself and later as a manager. His career began as an apprentice in engineering. Having served his time, however, he moved to the Midvale Steel Company, where, in the course of eleven years, he rose from labourer to shop superintendent. It was during this time that Taylor's ideas of 'scientific management' were born. In 1889 he left Midvale to work for the Bethlehem Steel Company, where he consolidated his ideas and conducted some of his most famous experiments in improving labour productivity. Taylor was keen to pass on his ideas to others, which he achieved through his writings, most notably 'The Principles of Scientific Management' published in 1911[2]. After his death, his major works were collected together and published as 'Scientific Management' in 1947[3]. He did not meet Henri Fayol and it is possible that he did not know of Fayol's analysis of management.

The Setting for Scientific Management

10. The last twenty years or so of the nineteenth century were a time for facing up to the often ugly realities of factory life. From the employers' point of view, efficiency of working methods was the dominant issue. The gathering pace of the industrial revolution in the Western world had given rise to new factories, new plant and machinery; labour was plentiful. The problem was how to organise all these elements into efficient and profitable operations.

11. It was against this background that Taylor developed his ideas. He was passionately interested in the efficiency of working methods. At an early stage he realised that the key to

such problems lay in the systematic analysis of work. Experience, both as a worker and as a manager, had convinced him that few, if any, workers put more than the minimal effort into their daily work. He described this tendency as *'soldiering'*, which he subdivided into *'natural'* soldiering, ie Man's natural tendency to take things easy, and *'systematic'* soldiering, ie the deliberate and organised restriction of the work-rate by the employees. The reasons for soldiering appeared to Taylor to arise from three issues:

❶ Fear of unemployment.

❷ Fluctuations in the earning from piece-rate systems.

❸ Rule-of-thumb methods permitted by management.

Taylor's answers to these issues was to practise 'scientific management'.

The Principles of Scientific Management

12. Taylor recognised that the measures he was proposing would appear to be more than just a new method – they would be revolutionary! He stated at the outset that 'scientific management' would require a complete mental revolution on the part of both management *and* workers.

13. In its application to *management*, the scientific approach required the following steps:

• Develop a science for each operation to replace opinion and rule-of-thumb.

• Determine accurately from the science the correct time and method for each job.

• Set up a suitable organisation to take all responsibility from the workers except that of actual job performance.

• Select and train the workers.

• Accept that management itself be governed by the science developed for each operation and surrender its arbitrary power over worker ie cooperate with them.

14. Taylor saw that if changes were to take place at the shopfloor level, then *facts* would have to be substituted for opinion and guesswork. This would be done by studying the jobs of a sample of especially skilled workers, noting each operation and timing it with a stop-watch. All unnecessary movements could then be eliminated in order to produce the best method of doing a job. This best method would become the standard to be used for all like jobs. This analytical approach has come to be known as Work Study, the series of techniques now utitilised all over the world (see Chapter 40).

15. In Taylor's time the most usual practice at the work organisation level was for the management to leave working methods to the initiative of the workers – what Taylor called rule-of-thumb. His suggestion that managers should take over that role was certainly new. Not only that, it was controversial, for he was deliberately reducing the scope of an individual's job. Contemporaries said it turned people into automatons. Taylor argued that the average worker preferred to be given a definite task with clear-cut standards. The outcome for future generations was the separation of planning and controlling from the doing, or the fragmentation of work. McGregor's Theory X assumptions about people (see Chapter 5) are essentially a description of the managerial style produced by Taylor's ideas. In the last decade or so, ideas such as job enrichment and work design have been put into practice precisely to combat the fragmentation effects of years of Taylorism. Another comment of Taylorism is that the gradual de-skilling of work has been accompanied by a rise in educational standards, thus tending to increase worker-frustration even further.

16. Taylor felt that everyone should benefit from scientific management – workers as well as managers. He disagreed with the way most piece-rate systems were operated in his day, as the practice was for management to reduce the rates if workers earnings went up beyond an acceptable level. Taylor's view was that, having *scientifically* measured the workers' jobs and set rates accordingly, then efficient workers should be rewarded for their productivity without limit. The difficulty for most managers was that they lacked Taylor's expertise in measuring times and had to resort to arbitrary reduction in rates where measurements had been loose.

17. So far as the *workers* were concerned, scientific management required them to:

- Stop worrying about the division of the fruits of production between wages and profits.

- Share in the prosperity of the firm by working in the correct way and receiving wage increases of between 30% and 100% according to the nature of the work.

- Give up their ideas of soldiering and cooperate with management in developing the science.

- Accept that management would be responsible, in accordance with the scientific approach, for determining what was to be done and how.

- Agree to be trained in new methods, where applicable.

18. One of Taylor's basic theses was that adoption of the scientific approach would lead to increased prosperity for all. It was, therefore much more important to contribute to a bigger cake than to argue about the division of the existing cake. Needless to say this kind of approach did not receive much favour with the trade unions at the time. Taylor saw them as a decidedly restrictive influence on issues such as productivity. In his view wages could now be scientifically determined, and should not be affected by arbitrary factors such a union power or management whim. His own experience had shown how considerable were the increases in earnings achieved by workers adopting their part of the scientific approach.

19. In terms of work-organisation, the workers were very much under the control of their management in Taylor's system. Taylor felt that this would be acceptable to them because management's actions would be based on the scientific study of the work and not on any arbitrary basis. It would also be acceptable, argued Taylor, because of the increased earnings available under the new system. He claimed that there were rarely any arguments arising between management and workers out of the introduction of the scientific approach. Modern experience has unfortunately shown Taylor's view to be considerably over-optimistic in this respect. The degree of trust and mutual cooperation, which Taylor felt to be such an important factor in the success of scientific management, has never been there when it mattered. As a result, although workers' attitudes towards Work Study have often been favourable, the ultimate success of work-studied incentive schemes has always been rather limited owing to workers' feelings that the management was attempting to 'pin them down' and to management's feelings that the workers had succeeded in 'pulling the wool over their eyes' concerning the timing of key jobs.

20. In support of his Principles, Taylor demonstrated the benefits of increased productivity and earnings which he had obtained at the Bethlehem Steel Works. He described to his critics an experiment with two shovelers – 'first-class shovelers', in his words – whose efforts were timed and studied. Each man had his own personal shovel, which he used regardless of the type of ore or coal being shifted. At first the average shovel load was about 38 pounds and with this load each man handled about 25 tons of material a day.

The shovel was then made smaller for each man, and the daily tonnage went up to 30. Eventually it was found that with smaller shovels, averaging about 21 pounds per load, the daily output rose even higher. As a result of this experiment, several different sizes of shovel were supplied to the workforce to enable each man to lift 21 pounds per load whether he was working with heavy ores or light coals. Labourers who showed themselves capable of achieving the standards set by the two 'first-class' shovelers were able to increase their wages by 60%. Those who were not able to reach the standard were given special training in the 'science of shovelling'.

21. After a three-year period, Taylor and his colleagues reviewed the extent of their success at the Bethlehem Works. The results were impressive: the work of 400–600 men was being done by 140; handling costs per ton had been reduced by half, and as Taylor was quick to point out, that included the costs of the extra clerical work involved in studying jobs; and the labourer received an average of 60% more than their colleagues in neighbouring firms. All this was achieved without any kind of slave-driving which was no part of scientific management, at least so far as Taylor was concerned.

Scientific Management after Taylor

22. Three important followers of scientific management were Frank and Lilian Gilbreth together with Henry Gantt. All made significant contributions to the study of work.

23. The husband-and-wife team of Frank and Lilian Gilbreth, who were somewhat younger than the pioneering Taylor, were keenly interested in the idea of scientific management. In his now famous Testimony to the House of Representatives Committee in 1912[4], Taylor describes how he was first approached by Frank Gilbreth who asked if the principles of scientific management could be applied to bricklaying. Some three years later Gilbreth was able to inform Taylor that as a direct result of analysing, and subsequently redesigning, the working methods of typical bricklayers, he was able to reduce the number of movements in laying bricks from 18 per brick to 5 per brick. The study of task movements, or 'motion study' as it was known, was a development of Taylor's ideas and represented the Gilbreths' major contribution to basic management techniques.

24. A particular feature of the Gilbreths' work was its detailed content. 'Measurement' was their byword, and the Science of Management, as they put it, consisted of applying measurement to management, and of abiding by the results. They were convinced that is was possible to find the 'one best way' of doing things, and there is no doubt that they went a long way towards the ideal. As employers, the Gilbreths practised what they preached. They laid down systematic rules and procedures for the efficient operation of work, and insisted that these be kept to. In return, the employees were paid well above competitors' rates, and, into the bargain were freed from unnecessary effort and fatigue. With this approach, the separation of the planning from the doing was complete. The employees had no discretion whatsoever once the scientific process had determined how the job should be done. Although these ideas were challenged at the time, they could not be ignored by the new industrial age and its obsession with ideas of efficiency. Whilst few people were prepared to undertake the sheer details of the Gilbreths' methods, the basic techniques caught on, and today (as Method Study) they represent one of the key measures used by managements to organise and control working methods in a wide range of industries.

25. Two examples of the recording techniques used by the Gilbreths are 'therbligs' and process charting. Therbligs (Gilbreth spelt backwards, in effect) are the basic elements of on-the-job motions and provide a standardised basis for recording movements. They

include such items as: search, find, grasp, assemble and inspect. A few items cover periods when no motion may be in evidence such as: wait-unavoidable, rest and plan. The most usual list of therbligs contains 18 items, and may be accompanied by appropriate symbols and colours to aid recording. Examples of Therbligs are shown below in Figure 3.2.

Symbol	Name	Colour
⬭	Search	Black
⬭	Find	Grey
→	Select	Light Grey
⋂	Grasp	Red
⌂	Hold	Gold
		Ochre

Figure 3.2 Therblig symbols.

Flow process charts were devised by the Gilbreths to enable whole operations or processes to be analysed. In these charts five symbols were utilised to cover Operation, Transportation, Inspection, Delay and Storage.

Flow chart symbols used in the flow process charts are shown in Figure 3.3.

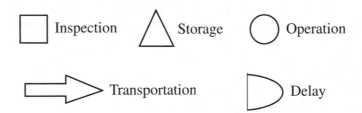

Figure 3.3 Flow chart symbols.

Henry Gantt

26. Gantt was a contemporary and colleague of Taylor's at the Bethlehem Steel Company. Whilst accepting many of Taylor's ideas on scientific management, Gantt felt that the individual worker was not given enough consideration. Although Taylor himself was not a slave-driver in any way, his methods were used by less scrupulous employers to squeeze as much production as possible out of their workforce. This was particularly true in respect of piece-rate systems. Gantt introduced a payment system where performance *below* what is called for on the individual's instruction card still qualified the person for the day-rate, but performance of *all* the work allocated on the card qualified the individual for a handsome bonus. Gantt discovered that as soon as any one worker found that he could achieve the task, the rest quickly followed. Better use was made of the foremen, because they were sought after by individuals who needed further instruction or help with faulty machines. As a result, supervision improved, breakdowns were minimised and delays avoided by all concerned. Eventually individual workers learned to cope on their own with routine prob-

lems. Gantt's bonus system also allowed for the men to challenge the time allocated for a particular task. This was permitted because Gantt, unlike the Gilbreths, did not believe that there was a *'one best way'*, but only a way *'which seems to be best at the moment'*. Gantt's approach to scientific management left some discretion and initiative to the workers, unlike those of his colleague, Taylor, and of his fellow theorists, the Gilbreths.

27. Although it was his ideas on the rewards for labour that made Gantt a notable figure in his day, he is best remembered nowadays for his charts. The Gantt chart was originally set up to indicate graphically the extent to which tasks had been achieved. It was divided horizontally into hours, days or weeks with the task marked out in a straight line across the appropriate numbers of hours or days etc. The amount of the task achieved was shown by another straight line parallel to the original. It was easy from such a chart to assess actual from planned performance. There are many variations of the Gantt chart in use today, and an example is given below:

Period	Week 1	Week 2	Week 3	Week 4
Planned Output	1000 units	1000 units	1000 units	1000 units
Actual Output	850 units	900 units	1000 units	1100 units
Weekly Actual				
Cumulative				

Figure 3.4 Gantt chart.

Comments on the Scientific Management School

28. The *benefits* arising from scientific management can be summarised as follows:

- Its rational approach to the organisation of work enabled tasks and processes to be measured with a considerable degree of accuracy.
- Measurement of tasks and processes provided useful information on which to base improvements in working methods, plant design etc.
- By improving working methods it brought enormous increases in productivity.
- It enabled employees to be paid by results and to take advantage of incentive payments.
- It stimulated managements into adopting a more positive role in leadership at the shop-floor level.
- It contributed to major improvements in physical working conditions for employees.
- It provided the foundations on which modern work study and other quantitative techniques could be soundly based.

29. The *drawbacks* to scientific management were principally the following:

- It reduced the worker's role to that of a rigid adherence to methods and procedures over which he had no discretion.
- It led to the fragmentation of work on account of its emphasis on the analysis and organisation of individual tasks or operations.
- It generated a 'carrot-and-stick' approach to the motivation of employees by enabling pay to be geared tightly to output.

- It put the planning and control of workplace activities exclusively in the hands of the management.

- It ruled out any realistic bargaining about wage rates since every job was measured, timed and rated 'scientifically'.

30. Whilst it is true that business and public organisations the world over have benefited from, and are continuing to utilise, techniques which have their origins in the Scientific Management movement, it is also a fact that, in the West at any rate, a reaction against the basic philosophy of the creed has taken place. Tasks and processes are being re-integrated, the individual is demanding participation in the key decision-making processes, management prerogatives are under challenge everywhere by individuals and organised groups alike. Yet, as Chapter 15 points out, Japanese companies in particular have taken up many of the beneficial aspects of scientific management and combined them with other approaches to produce a highly successful production system (see Theory Z).

31. On balance, the most important outcome of scientific management was that it stimulated ideas and techniques for improving the systematic analysis of work *at the workplace*. It also undoubtedly provided a firm launch-pad for a wide variety of productivity improvements in a great range of industries and public services.

32. Its major disadvantage was that it subordinated the worker to the work system, and so divorced the 'doing' aspects of work from the planning and controlling aspects. This led to:

- the creation of boring, repetitive jobs;

- the introduction of systems for tight control over work; and

- the alienation of shop-floor employees from their management.

L.F. Urwick

33. Lyndall F. Urwick was an enthusiastic and prolific writer on the subject of administration and management. His experience covered industry, the Armed Forces and business consultancy. He was strongly influenced by the ideas of Henri Fayol, in particular. He was convinced that the only way that modern Man could control his social organisations was by applying principles, or universal rules, to them. In one of his best-known writings – 'The Elements of Administration' – published in 1947[5] he set out numerous principles which, in his view, could be applied to organisations to enable them to achieve their objectives effectively. Like other classical writers, Urwick developed his 'principles' on the basis of his own interpretation of the common elements and processes which he identified in the structure and operation of organisations. On this basis, the principles represented a 'code of good practice', which, if adhered to should lead to success in administration, or management as we would call it today.

34. In 1952 Urwick[6] produced a consolidated list of ten principles, as follows:

❶ The Principle of the Objective – the overall purpose or objective is the raison d'être of every organisation.

❷ The Principle of Specialisation – one group, one function!

❸ The Principle of Coordination – the process of organising is primarily to ensure coordination.

❹ The Principle of Authority – every group should have a supreme authority with a clear line of authority to other members of the group.

⑤ The Principle of Responsibility – the superior is absolutely responsible for the acts of his subordinates.

⑥ The Principle of Definition – jobs, with their duties and relationships, should be clearly defined.

⑦ The Principle of Correspondence – authority should be commensurate with responsibility.

⑧ The Span of Control – no one should be responsible for more than 5 or 6 direct subordinates whose work is interlocked.

⑨ The Principle of Balance – the various units of the organisation should be kept in balance.

⑩ The Principle of Continuity – the structure should provide for the continuation of activities.

35. As a statement of classical organisation theory, Urwick's list would be difficult to better, concentrating as it does on mainly structural issues. Compared with Fayol's Principles of Management, Urwick's list is less concerned with issues such as pay and morale, for example. Its emphasis is very much on getting the organisational *mechanisms* right.

36. There is no doubting the rational appeal of Urwick's 'principles', especially in relation to the internal environment of the organisation. Organisations, however, do not operate in a vacuum. They have to interact with their external environment. That is to say they are open systems. Where modern studies have found weaknesses in Urwick's 'principles' is precisely on this point. The 'principles' tend to assume that it is possible to exert control over the issues mentioned, but many current trends in Western society, in particular, run directly counter to several of the 'principles'. For example, attitudes towards greater sharing of authority at work are likely to clash with the Principle of Authority and the Principle of Correspondence. Similarly, attitudes towards the reintegration or enrichment of jobs will conflict with the Principle of Specialisation, the Principle of Definition and the Span of Control.

37. Organisations are not self-contained. They have to respond to the pressures of an external environment – social, political and economic. Urwick's 'principles', therefore, are not capable of being introduced easily into modern organisations. They can be, and are, adopted with modification in several cases, but will always be suspect because they fall into the category of 'what ought to be' rather than 'what actually is' in terms of the realities of organisations today.

38. Urwick's ideas in general achieved considerable popularity with business organisations on both sides of the Atlantic because of their commonsense appeal to managers. In more recent times, however, Urwick's emphasis on purpose and structure has not been able to provide answers to problems arising from social attitudes, external market pressures and rapidly changing technology. His ideas are now a little anachronistic. They prescribe part, but only part, of what is needed for organisational health.

E.F.L. Brech

39. E.F.L. Brech wrote widely on management and organisation issues. Whilst sharing Urwick's concern with the development of principles, or general laws, of management, Brech was also concerned with the development of people within the organisation. His approach was basically a classical one, but tempered to some extent by the prevailing human relations theories of the 1950s and 1960s. He saw management as a process, a

social process, for planning and regulating the operations of the enterprise towards some agreed objective, and carried out within the framework of an organisation structure. Key issues for Brech in the formation of the structure were:

- Defining the responsibilities of the management, supervisory and specialist staff.
- Determining how these responsibilities are to be delegated.
- Coordinating the execution of responsibilities.
- Maintaining high morale.

40. Brech's own list of principles of organisation overlapped considerably with those of Fayol and Urwick. It was less dogmatic in approach than the others, but was nevertheless concerned with the division of responsibilities, lines of communication, unity of command and the allocation of authority, to give just a few examples. Fundamentally, in his view, the principles exist to maintain a balance between the delegation of managerial responsibility throughout the organisation and the need to ensure unity of action as well.

41. In his last writings (1975)[7], Brech regretted that there was still no general agreement about a fundamental body of principles of management. Until such principles are developed, he argued, it will be impossible for management to gain recognition as a science, or indeed as a profession. He believed that such principles, or basic *laws of management*, could be deduced from an analysis of the nature of the management process, and this is what he himself attempted in the footsteps of Fayol, Urwick and others. However, he conceded that the development of principles would probably be acceptable only on the basis of first-hand research into management practices – a view which would undoubtedly have pleased researchers such as Rosemary Stewart (1994)[8], Henry Mintzberg (1973)[9], and others who believe that it is primarily through research into managerial behaviour that a body of relevant knowledge or fundamental truths may emerge.

42. Brech's writings on principles are much more directed towards helping practising managers become more effective in their roles, than towards contributing to a general body of knowledge concerning the theory of management. In this respect his own contribution is that of a thoughtful management consultant aiming to improve management practice rather than that of an objective research worker seeking to test out hypotheses. Seen in this light, Brech's contribution has been considerably influential, especially in management training and development.

References

1. Fayol, H. (1949), *General and Industrial Management*, Pitman.
2. Taylor, F.W. (1911), *The Principles of Scientific Management*, Harper & Bros.
3. Taylor, F.W. (1947, *Scientific Management*, Harper & Row.
4. Taylor, F.W. (1912), *Testimony to the House of Representatives Committee*.
5. Urwick, L.F. (1947), *The Elements of Administration*, Pitman.
6. Urwick, L.F (1952), *Principles of Management*, Pitman.
7. Brech, E.F.L. (1975), *Principles and Practice of Management,* 3rd edition, Longman.
8. Stewart, R.(1994), *Managing Today and Tomorrow*, Macmillan.
9. Mintzberg, H. (1973),*The Nature of Managerial Work*, Harper & Row.

CHAPTER 4

Max Weber and the Idea of Bureaucracy

Introduction

1.   'Bureaucracy' is a term with several meanings, and this has led to genuine misconceptions about what it truly means. The most common meanings are as follows:

*   Bureaucracy is *'red tape'*, ie an excess of paperwork and rules leading to gross inefficiency. This is the pejorative sense of the word.

*   Bureaucracy is *'officialdom'*, ie all the apparatus of central and local government. This is a similar meaning to red tape.

*   Bureaucracy is an *organisational form* with certain dominant characteristics, such as a hierarchy of authority and a system of rules.

2.   In this chapter the term 'bureaucracy' is interpreted as an organisational form. The object of the chapter is to describe and discuss this important and all-pervading form of organisation, with particular reference to the fundamental work of Max Weber.

Max Weber

3.   Max Weber (1864–1920) spanned the same period of history as those early pioneers of management thought, Fayol and Taylor, to whom we have already referred. Unlike them, however, Weber was an academic – a sociologist – and not a practising manager. His interest in organisations was from the point of view of their authority structures. He wanted to find out why people in organisations obeyed those in authority over them. The observations and conclusions from his studies were first published in translation from the original German in 1947[1]. It was in this publication that the term *'bureaucracy'* was used to describe a rational form of organisation that today exists to a greater or lesser extent in practically every business and public enterprise.

4.   In his analysis of organisations, Weber identified three basic types of legitimate authority: traditional, charismatic and rational-legal authority. Before describing these, it will be helpful to understand what he meant by the expression 'legitimate authority'. Firstly, the concept of authority has to be distinguished from that of power. Power is a unilateral thing – it enables one person to *force* another to behave in a certain way, whether by means of strength or by rewards. Authority, on the other hand, implies acceptance of rule by those over whom it is to be exercised. It implies that power may only be exercised within limits agreeable to subordinates. It is this latter situation to which Weber refers when he talks about legitimate authority.

5.   The three types of legitimate authority described by him can be summarised as follows:

*   **Traditional authority** – where acceptance of those in authority arises from tradition and custom (eg as in monarchies, tribal hierarchies etc).

*   **Charismatic authority** – where acceptance arises from loyalty to, and confidence in, the personal qualities of the ruler.

- **Rational-legal authority** – where acceptance arises out of the office, or position, of the person in authority, as bounded by the rules and procedures of the organisation.

It is this last-mentioned form of authority which exists in most organisations today, and this is the form to which Weber ascribed the term 'bureaucracy'.

Bureaucracy

6. The main features of a bureaucracy, according to Weber, are as follows:

- A continuous organisation of functions bound by rules.
- Specified spheres of competence, ie the specialisation of work, the degree of authority allocated and the rules governing the exercise of authority.
- A hierarchical arrangement of offices (jobs), ie where one level of jobs is subject to control by the next higher level.
- Appointment to offices are made on grounds of technical competence.
- The separation of officials from the ownership of the organisation.
- Official positions exist in their own right, and job holders have no rights to a particular position.
- Rules, decisions and actions are formulated and recorded in writing.

7. The above features of bureaucratic organisation enable the authority of officials to be subject to published rules and practices. Thus authority is legitimate, not arbitrary. It is this point more than any other which caused Weber to comment that bureaucratic organisation was capable of attaining the highest degree of efficiency and was, in that sense, the most rational known means of carrying out *'imperative control over human beings'*.

8. Weber felt that bureaucracy was indispensable for the needs of large-scale organisation, and there is no doubt that this form of organisation has been adopted in one way or another by practically every enterprise of any size the world over. The two most significant factors in the growth of bureaucratic forms of organisation are undoubtedly *size* and *complexity*. Once an organisation begins to grow, the amount of specialisation increases, which usually leads to an increase in job levels. New jobs are created and old jobs redefined. Recruitment from outside becomes more important. Relationships, authority boundaries and discipline generally have to be regulated. Questions of control and coordination became all-important. Thus a small, relatively informal, family concern can suddenly grow into quite a different organisation requiring new skills and new attitudes from its proprietors.

9. Although size almost inevitably implies complexity, there are also issues of complexity for smaller organisations. These can arise out of the requirements of sophisticated modern technology, for example. In such an environment specialised and up-to-date skills are required, the span of control has to be small, questions of quality control are vital and last, but by no means least, a keen eye needs to be kept on the competition. Add to all these points the rules and regulations of governments and supranational bodies, such as the European Union and the General Agreement on Tariffs and Trade (GATT), and the result is a highly complex environment, which can only be controlled in a systematic form of organisation. Indeed, one of the challenges to modern managements is to maintain a 'lean' organisation in such circumstances.

Bureaucracy after Weber

9.   Weber's contribution to our understanding of formal organisation structures has been a major one. No subsequent discussion or debate on this topic has been possible without reference to his basic analysis of bureaucratic organisation. Nevertheless, without disputing the basic proposition that bureaucracy is the most efficient means of organising for the achievement of *formal* goals, several researchers since Weber have established important weaknesses in the bureaucratic model. These researchers have identified a number of awkward side-effects or *'dysfunctions'* of bureaucracy. These can be summarised as follows:

❶ Rules, originally designed to serve organisational efficiency, have a tendency to become all-important in their own right.

❷ Relationships between office-holders or roles are based on the rights and duties of each role, ie they are depersonalised, and this leads to rigid behaviour (predictability).

❸ Decision-making tends to be categorised, ie choices are previously programmed and this discourages the search for further alternatives, another form of rigidity.

❹ The effects of rigid behaviour are often very damaging for client or customer relations and also for management–worker relationships; customers are unable to obtain tailor-made services, but have to accept standardisation; employees have to work within a framework of rules and controls which has been more or less imposed on them.

❺ Standardisation and routine procedures make change and adaptation difficult when circumstances change.

❻ The exercise of *'control based on knowledge'*, as advocated by Weber, has led to the growth of experts, whose opinions and attitudes may frequently clash with those of the generalist managers and supervisors.

10. One particularly well-known follow-up to Weber's theories was conducted by an American sociologist, Alvin Gouldner. He studied the effects of introducing a bureaucratic system into an organisation which had been very informal and indulgent in its management style. The head office of a small gypsum company had appointed a new manager to made the plant more efficient. His new approach led to the replacement of informal methods of working by formalised procedures such as work study and production control. These changes were resented by the workforce and the eventual outcome was a *reduction*, rather than an increase, in the efficiency of operations. In studying this situation Gouldner (1955)[2] identified three different patterns of bureaucracy operating within the one organisation. These were as follows:

❶ **Mock Bureaucracy.** This expression was applied by Gouldner to situations where the rules and procedures were imposed by an outside body (eg Head Office) and where they were either ignored, or were merely paid lipservice to, by the employees concerned. In this situation a separate set of 'rules' (ie their own!) was developed by these employees.

❷ **Representative Bureaucracy.** In this case the rules were followed in practice because both management *and* employees agreed on their value.

❸ **Punishment-centred Bureaucracy.** This description was applied to situations where either the management or the employees imposed their rules on the other. Disregard of the rules was seen as grounds for imposing sanctions. Each side considered its rules as legitimate, but there was no common position.

11. Weber's thinking on bureaucracy was dominated by his view of how rational it was. Gouldner by contrast helped to indicate that opinions and feelings are also a key ingredient in the success of a bureaucratic form of organisation. Whereas Weber emphasised the structural aspects of organisation, Gouldner emphasised behaviour. He saw that rules not only generated *anticipated* responses eg obedient behaviour, but also *unanticipated* responses, eg minimum acceptable behaviour. Therefore, in any one organisation, there will be a tendency to respond to the rules in any one of the three ways described above, depending on how and why the rules were introduced.

12. Handy (1993)[3] describes bureaucracies as *'role cultures'* based on logic and rationality. In the role culture, power comes from position power ie the authority of the office, as determined by rules and procedures. Such a culture offers security and predictability to its members, but can be frustrating for those who are ambitious and results-oriented. Handy sees bureaucracy as a Greek temple, based on the firm pillars of its speciality departments and ideally constructed for stability. Its very stability is a drawback in times of change. The Greek temple is not designed for adaptability.

13. However one chooses to describe a bureaucracy, there is little doubt that it is by far the most frequent form of organisation in society, and the question that has to be asked is not so much 'is this organisation a bureaucracy?' as 'to what extent is this organisation a bureaucracy?' The evidence seems to suggest that there is something of the Greek temple in every organisation!

References

1.   Weber, M. (1947), *The Theory of Social & Economic Organisation*, The Free Press.
2.   Gouldner, A. (1955), *Patterns of Industrial Bureaucracy*, The Free Press.
3.   Handy, C. (1993), *Understanding Organisations*, 3rd edition, Penguin.

Questions for Discussion/Homework

1.   What difficulties might confront a manager today, if he or she tried to implement Fayol's principles of management as they were originally stated?

2.   What common features do you see between Fayol's principles of management and Weber's description of bureaucracy?

3.   How would you summarise the principal effects of 'scientific management' on (a) managers, and (b) employees?

4.   Why is it difficult to implement **principles** of management along the lines suggested by Fayol, Urwick and Brech, for example?

5.   Discuss the main advantages and disadvantages of the ideal-type of bureaucracy, as described by Weber.

Examination Questions

The following contains a typical cross-section of questions taken from the major examining bodies, selected for their relevance to the subject matter of this Section. Outline answers to these questions can be found in Appendix 2.

EQ 2   'Attempts to bring scientific methods into management merely show what an inexact art management really is'. Discuss.

(ACCA)

EQ 3   Critically evaluate the contribution of the classical/traditional school of management theorists to our understanding of organisation.

(CIMA)

EQ 4   Does the work of F.W. Taylor have any relevance to modern marketing management?

(Inst. of Marketing)

Whereas the exponents of classical theory were principally concerned with the *structure* and *mechanics* of organisations, the human relations and social psychological theorists focused on the *human factor* at work. These latter were invariably academics – social scientists – interested in people's behaviour in the workplace. They were particularly interested in human motivation, group relationships and leadership. Chapter 5 introduces the concept of 'motivation', and describes the famous Hawthorne Studies conducted in the United States almost seventy years ago. A brief outline of the ideas of Mary Parker Follet follow, then the chapter continues with an outline of the ideas of several early contributors to motivation theory, in the 1950s and 1960s, notably Abraham Maslow, Douglas McGregor, Frederick Herzberg, Rensis Likert, Chris Argyris and D.C. McClelland. Chapter 6 summarises the work of later theorists, including Victor Vroom's so-called 'expectancy theory', and the contributions of E.A. Locke, A. Kelley and B.F. Skinner.

CHAPTER 5

Motivation – The Early Theorists

Introduction

1.   The chapter begins with an explanation of the basic concept of *motivation*, and follows this with a summary of different models of motivation put forward by Schein (1988)[1]. This is followed by an account of the celebrated Hawthorne Studies, conducted in the USA some seventy years ago. The chapter continues with an outline of the work of a number of American social scientists, namely Mary Parker Follett, Abraham Maslow, Douglas McGregor, Frederick Herzberg, Rensis Likert, Chris Argyris and D. C. McClelland.

The Concept of Motivation

2.   Human motivation studies aim, in essence, to discover what it is that triggers and sustains human behaviour. A working definition of motivation is as follows:

> 'Motivation' is the term used to describe those processes, both instinctive and rational, by which people seek to satisfy the basic drives, perceived needs and personal goals, which trigger human behaviour. (Cole, 1995, p.119)[2]

Not all theorists focus on the *process* of motivation. In fact, most of the early theorists were interested in the drives and/or needs of people at work, ie the *content* aspects of motivation.

3.   A very basic and simplified model of motivation is shown in Figure 5.1. This suggests that a stimulus, such as hunger (physical) or the desire for company (social) gives rise to a response. This response takes the form of some kind of behaviour, which leads to an outcome, which is either satisfactory or unsatisfactory. Where the behaviour is appropriate, satisfaction is achieved. Where it is not, the stimulus remains in the form of frustration, and the process begins again.

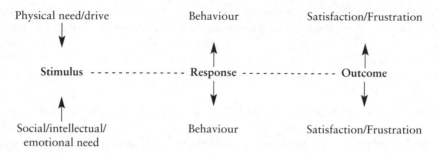

Figure 5.1. A basic model of motivation

4. Understanding human motivation is a complex matter. Sometimes a person's motives may be clear to him, but quite puzzling to others. In other situations both the individual and those affected by his behaviour understand what is driving him. In some situations, especially where stress is involved, the individual concerned may be totally unaware of his motives, whereas others may see them quite clearly. It is important for those in managerial and supervisory positions to be aware of these issues, and to take account of their own prejudices in this area of their work. This is because our efforts to understand others are coloured by our attitudes towards them and the assumptions we make about their behaviour. If we assume that a particular group of workers is hardworking and reliable, we tend to treat them with respect and trust; if, however, we see them as lazy and unreliable, we are likely to treat them as requiring close control and supervision.

5. Schein (op. cit.) propounded a classification of managers' assumptions about people based on a review of earlier approaches to motivation. His classification follows a broadly chronological pattern as follows:

- **Rational-economic model.** This view of human motivation has its roots in the economic theories of Adam Smith in the 1770s. It suggests that the pursuit of self-interest and the maximisation of gain are the prime motivators. According to Schein, this view places human beings into two main categories: (1) the untrustworthy, money motivated, calculative masses, and (2) the trustworthy, more broadly motivated moral elite whose task it is to organise and control the masses. Such an approach is evident in the work of Taylor and the Gilbreths, and the entrepreneurs of mass production techniques.

- **Social model.** In the 'social model', Schein drew heavily on the conclusions of the Hawthorne researchers. This view sees people as predominantly motivated by social needs – the need for personal relationships. The implication for managers is that an emphasis on attending to people's needs over the needs of the task will lead to greater productivity as well as higher morale. Such a view, according to Schein, needs to be treated with some reservations.

- **Self-actualising model.** This concept is based on Maslow's theory of human needs (see below), which whilst allowing for the influence of other needs, stresses the individual's need for self-fulfilment as the prime motivator. The implication for managers is that people need challenge, responsibility and autonomy in their work if they are to work effectively. There is some research evidence to support such a view, especially amongst professional and highly skilled employees.

- **Complex model.** Schein proposes this model of motivation as being fuller than the earlier models. It presupposes that understanding people's motivation is a complex business in which several interrelated factors are at work. Managers in this situation need to be sensitive to a range of possible responses to employee motivation against differing work and team environments. Schein himself prefers to see motivation as a form of 'psychological contract' between the organisation and its employees, based on their respective expectations of each other's contribution. Ultimately, the relationship between an individual and his or her organisation is both interactive and interdependent.

6. Schein's classification helps us to relate the major approaches to management theory with the concept of motivation, the basis of which is that human motives are directed towards desired ends, and that behaviour is selected consciously or sometimes instinctively, towards the achievement of those ends. Differing opinions have emerged as to what these ends are, and how they are best met in the work situation. Several of the most well-known theories are outlined in the following paragraphs, commencing with the findings arising from the research carried out by Mayo, Roethlisberger and Dickson in the so-called Hawthorne Studies.

The Hawthorne studies

7. Professor Elton Mayo is usually associated with the social research carried out at the Hawthorne plant of the Western Electric Company in Chicago, USA, between 1927 and 1932, and named the Hawthorne Studies. In these studies, the emphasis was on the *worker* rather than on work. Unlike Taylor and the scientific managers, the researchers at Hawthorne were primarily concerned with studying people, especially in terms of their social relationships at work. Their conclusions were that people are social animals – at work as well as outside it – and that membership of a group is important to individuals. Group membership leads to establishment of informal groups within the official, formal, groupings as laid down in the organisation structure.

8. These conclusions gave rise to the idea of social man (now the social model) and to the importance of human relations. Elton Mayo has been described as the founder of the human relations movement, whose advocates stressed the need for managerial strategies to ensure that concern for people at work was given the highest priority. This movement, if it can be described as such, spanned the period from the mid-1920s to the mid-1950s, after which there was a gradual trend away from the social model, and its close relation the self-actualising model, towards the complex model, where people operate in highly variable organisational environments.

Elton Mayo

9. Elton Mayo (1880–1949) was an Australian by birth, a psychologist by training, and, according to some, a natural PR man by inclination! At the time of the Hawthorne studies he was Professor of industrial research at the Harvard Graduate School of Business Administration. He was already involved in a study of issues related to fatigue, accidents and labour turnover at work when he was approached by executives of the Western Electric Company for advice. The company, which prided itself on its welfare facilities, had begun a number of studies into the effects of lighting on production and morale. It had discovered, to its surprise, that the groups of workers who were the subject of study improved their productivity whether their lighting was improved or not. Clearly some factor other than the impact of physical improvements was at work. The company management decided to call in the experts.

10. Their decision was to bring considerable fame to Mayo, in particular. His popularisation of the results of the Hawthorne Studies (Mayo, 1933),[3] made an enormous impact at

the time. The social model was seen as a rebuttal of the ideas of scientific management, with its emphasis on the task and the control of work. Subsequent decades have also been greatly influenced by the findings at Hawthorne, and most of the credit has gone to Mayo.

11. The studies were carried out over several years in a number of different stages, as follows:

First Stage (1924–1927). This was conducted by the company's own staff under the direction of Messrs Pennock and Dickson. As mentioned above, this stage was concerned with the effects of lighting on output. Eventually two groups of comparable performance were isolated from the rest and located in separate parts of the plant. One group, the control group, had a consistent level of lighting; the other group, the experimental group, had its lighting varied. To the surprise of the researchers, the output of both groups increased. Even when the lighting for the experimental group was reduced to a very low level, they still produced more! At this point Pennock sought the help of Mayo and his Harvard colleagues.

12. **Stage two** (1927–1929). This stage became known as the Relay Assembly Test Room. The objective was to make a closer and more detailed study of the effects of differing *physical* conditions on productivity. At this stage, it is important to note, there was no deliberate intention to analyse *social relationships* or *employee attitudes*. Six women workers in the relay assembly section were segregated from the rest in a room of their own. Over the course of the experiments the effects of numerous changes in working conditions were observed. Rest pauses were introduced and varied, lunch times were varied in timing and in length. Most of the changes were discussed with the women before being implemented. Productivity increased whether the conditions were made better or worse. Later studies included altering the working week. Once again output increased regardless of the changes. By the end of stage two the researchers realised they had not just been studying the relationship between physical working conditions, fatigue, monotony and output, but had been entering into a study of employee *attitudes* and *values*. The women's reactions to the changes – increased output regardless of whether conditions improved or worsened – has come to be known as 'the Hawthorne Effect'. That is to say the women were responding not so much to the changes as to the fact that they were the centre of attention – a special group.

13. **Stage three** (1928–1930). Before the relay assembly test had come to an end, the company had decided to implement an interview programme designed to ascertain employee attitudes towards working conditions, their supervision and their jobs. The interviews were conducted by selected supervisors, initially on a half-hour, structured basis. Eventually the interview pattern became relatively unstructured and lasted for ninety minutes. Despite this, the numbers interviewed reached over 20,000 before the programme was suspended. The wealth of material gained was used to improve several aspects of working conditions and supervision. It also became clear from the responses that relationships with people were an important factor in the attitudes of employees.

14. **Stage four** (1932). This was known as the bank wiring observation room. In this study fourteen men on bank wiring were removed to a separate observation room, where, apart from a few differences, their principal working conditions were the same as those in the main wiring area. The aim was to observe a group working under more or less normal conditions over a period of six months or so. The group was soon developing its own rules and behaviour – it restricted production in accordance with its own norms; it short-circuited the company wage incentive scheme and in general protected its own sectional interests against those of the company. The supervisors concerned were powerless to prevent this situation. The group had clearly developed its own unofficial organisation, run

in such a way that it was able to protect itself from outside influences whilst controlling its internal life too.

15. **Final stage** (1936). This stage was commenced some four years after stage four because of the economic difficulties of the depression. This final stage was based on lessons learned from the earlier studies. Its focus was firmly on employee relations and took the form of personnel counselling. The counsellors encouraged employees to discuss their problems at work and the results led to improvements in personal adjustments, employee-supervisor relations and employee-management relations.

16. The official account of the Hawthorne studies was written not by Mayo but by a Harvard colleague (Roethlisberger) and one of the company's own researchers (Dickson). Their detailed descriptions[4] of the research did not appear until 1939, some time after Mayo had already put the spotlight on the Studies in his popularised account published six years earlier.

17. There have been many criticisms of the way the Hawthorne Studies have been interpreted. Mayo's references to them were included in writings, which propounded *his* theories about Man and industrial society. As a result, his use of the studies was biased towards his own interpretation of what was happening. For the official evidence one must look to Roethlisberger and Dickson. Modern researchers point out that their Hawthorne colleagues overlooked important factors in assessing their results. They also adopted some unreliable methods for testing the evidence in the first place. However, everyone is agreed that the Hawthorne Studies represented the first major attempt to undertake genuine social research. Important lessons were learned, and, perhaps even more importantly, many questions were raised by these studies.

18. The main conclusions to be drawn from the Hawthorne researches are:

- Individual workers cannot be treated in isolation, but must be seen as members of a group.
- The need to belong to a group and have status within it is more important than monetary incentives or good physical working conditions.
- Informal (or unofficial) groups at work exercise a strong influence over the behaviour of workers.
- Supervisors and managers need to be aware of these social needs and cater for them if workers are to collaborate with the official organisation rather than work against it.

19 The Hawthorne experiment began as a study into *physical* conditions and productivity. It ended as a series of studies into *social* factors: membership of groups, relationships with supervision etc. Its most significant findings showed that social relations at work were every bit as important as monetary incentives and good physical working conditions. They also demonstrated the powerful influence of groups in determining behaviour at work. By modern standards of social research, the Hawthorne studies were relatively unsophisticated in their approach. Nevertheless, they represented a major step forward for the social sciences in their study of work organisations. Also, by their model of 'social man', they did much to further the humanisation of work.

Mary Parker Follett

20 The ideas of Mary Parker Follett (d. 1933) were so far ahead of her time that most of them were ignored. The fact that she was a woman, trying to speak out in a man's world, was undoubtedly another factor. In her principal work on the workplace, published after her death, *Dynamic Administration* (1941)[5], she took forward the work of the Hawthorne

researchers by concluding that human problems were not just important, but were *central* to the success of organisations. In particular, she argued the case for giving greater, not less, responsibility to people at work. She was aware of the importance of teamwork, and the role of the leader, which she saw in holistic and shared terms. The leader's role was to envision the future and to empower others to achieve that future. She herself did not use the modern expression *empowerment*, but that is clearly what she meant. Her idea of leadership meant gaining others' collaboration and respect, and reconciling conflicts. Such a leadership approach depended on the interaction of leader and followers, and her ideas on the significance of followers pre-dated Fiedler (see Chapter 7) by thirty years.

21. Follett's view of conflict was that there were basically three ways of dealing with it: by domination, by compromise, or by integration. Today we would refer to her integration as a 'win-win' solution. Domination implies a 'win-lose' outcome, and compromise a 'lose-lose' situation, in which neither side is content. She was strongly against the notion that conflict was a matter of 'either-or', as this meant that alternative solutions were restricted from the outset. Today, Follett's ideas are being acknowledged, as writers and historians look back across the twentieth century, free from the prejudices of her contemporaries, and with the detachment of historical hindsight, as in Graham (1995)[6].

22. The concept of social man dominated the thinking of social researchers and practising managers alike in the wake of the Hawthorne studies. The emphasis on the employee's social and belonging needs, as opposed to the needs of the task, continued throughout the 1930s, and 1940s until the mid 1950s. If more attention had been paid to the ideas of Mary Parker Follett in those years, we might have moved forward earlier from the era of social man towards that of self-actualising man.

23. This is a suitable point to introduce what many commentators have described as the *social psychological school* of motivation. The emphasis is still on people as the most crucial factor in determining organisational effectiveness, but people who have considerably more than just physical and social needs. The dominant concept here is that of self-actualising man, and the influential contributors here are the American social scientists Abraham Maslow, Douglas McGregor, Frederick Herzberg, Rensis Likert, Chris Argyris and D.C. McClelland.

Maslow's Hierarchy of Needs

24. Maslow's studies into human motivation led him to propose a theory of needs based on an hierarchical model with basic needs at the bottom and higher needs at the top, as in Figure 5.2. This theory made a considerable influence on developments in management theory during the 1950s/60s due partly to the simplicity of the model and partly to the identification of higher-level needs.

25. The starting point of Maslow's hierarchy theory, first published in 1954[7], is that most people are motivated by the desire to satisfy specific groups of needs. These needs are as follows:

- **Physiological needs** – needs for food, sleep, sex etc.
- **Safety needs** – needs for stable environment relatively free from threats.
- **Love needs** – needs related to affectionate relations with others and status within a group.
- **Esteem needs** – needs for self-respect, self-esteem and the esteem of others.
- **Self-actualisation needs** – the need for self-fulfilment.

Figure 5.2 Hierarchy of needs.

26. The second, and most central, point of Maslow's theory is that people tend to satisfy their needs systematically, starting with the basic physiological needs and then moving up the hierarchy. Until a particular group of needs is satisfied, a person's behaviour will be dominated by them. Thus, a hungry person is not going to be motivated by consideration of safety or affection, for example, until after his hunger has been satisfied. Maslow (1961)[8] later modified this argument by stating that there was an exception to the rule in respect of self-actualisation needs. For this group of needs it seems that satisfaction of a need gives rise to further needs for realising one's potential.

27. Maslow's theory provided an early useful framework for discussions about the variety of needs that people may experience at work, and the ways in which their motivation can be met by managers. One criticism of the theory is that systematic movement up the hierarchy does not seem to be a consistent form of behaviour for many people. Alderfer (1972)[9], for example, argued that individual needs were better explained as being on a continuum, rather than in an hierarchy. He considered that people were more likely to move up and down the continuum in satisfying needs at different levels. He concluded that there were really only three major sets of needs – existence needs (ie the basics of life), relatedness needs (ie social and interpersonal needs), and growth needs (ie personal development needs). Drucker (1974)[10] commented that Maslow had not recognised that when a want was satisfied, its capacity to motivate was changed. An initially satisfied want that was not sustained could, on the contrary, become counter-productive and act as a disincentive.

D. McGregor – Theory X and Theory Y

28. Like Schein's classification of managers' assumptions about people, McGregor's Theory X and Theory Y[11] are essentially sets of assumptions about behaviour. In proposing his ideas, McGregor pointed to the theoretical assumptions of management that underlie its behaviour. He saw two noticeably different sets of assumptions made by managers about their employees. The first set of assumptions regards employees as being inherently lazy, requiring coercion and control, avoiding responsibility and only seeking security. This attitude is what McGregor termed *Theory X*. This is substantially the theory of scientific management, with its emphasis on controls and extrinsic rewards. Schein's rational-economic model (see para 5 above) is very similar to that of Theory X.

29. McGregor's second set of assumptions sees people in a more favourable light. In this case employees are seen as liking work, which is as natural as rest or play; they do not have

to be controlled and coerced, so long as they are committed to the organisation's objectives. Under proper conditions they will not only accept but also seek responsibility; more, rather than less, people are able to exercise imagination and ingenuity at work. These are the assumptions of *Theory Y*. They are closely related to Maslow's higher-level needs and to Schein's self-actualising model.

30. Theory X and Theory Y have made their greatest impact in the managerial world rather than in the academic world. The two labels have become part of the folklore of 'management style', which will be looked at in the chapter on leadership (Chapter 7). They do help to identify extreme forms of management style, but there is a danger that they may be seen only as polar extremes representing an *either/or* style. In real-life a blend of the two theories is more likely to provide the best prescription for effective management.

Herzberg's Motivation-Hygiene Theory

31. Herzberg's studies (1959)[12] concentrated on satisfaction at work. In the initial research some 200 engineers and accountants were asked to recall when they had experienced satisfactory and unsatisfactory feelings about their jobs. Following the interviews, Herzberg's team came to the conclusion that certain factors tended to lead to job satisfaction, whereas others led frequently to dissatisfaction (see Figure 5.3). The factors giving rise to satisfaction were called *motivators*. Those giving rise to dissatisfaction were called *hygiene factors*. These studies were later (1968)[13] extended to include various groups in manual and clerical groups, where the results were claimed to be quite similar.

32. The most important *motivators*, or satisfiers, to emerge were the following:

- achievement
- recognition
- work itself
- responsibility
- advancement.

Herzberg pointed out that these factors were intimately related to the *content* of work, ie with its intrinsic challenge, interest and the individual responses generated by them.

33. The most important *hygiene factors*, or dissatisfiers, were as follows:

- Company policy and administration.
- Supervision – the technical aspects.
- Salary.
- Interpersonal relations – supervision.
- Working conditions.

Herzberg noted that these factors were more related to the *context*, or environment, of work than to its content. When in line with employee requirements, such factors could smooth the path of working life, but in a *taken-for-granted* way. When these factors were out of line with employees' expectations, they could be a source of difficulty and complaint, and definitely provided grounds for dissatisfaction at work. This lack of a positive aspect to these factors led Herzberg to call them 'hygiene' factors, because whilst they contributed to the prevention of poor psychological health, they did not make a positive contribution to employees' sense of well being, at least not in any lasting way.

34. The key distinction between the motivators and the hygiene factors is that whereas motivators can bring about *positive* satisfaction, the hygiene factors can only serve to

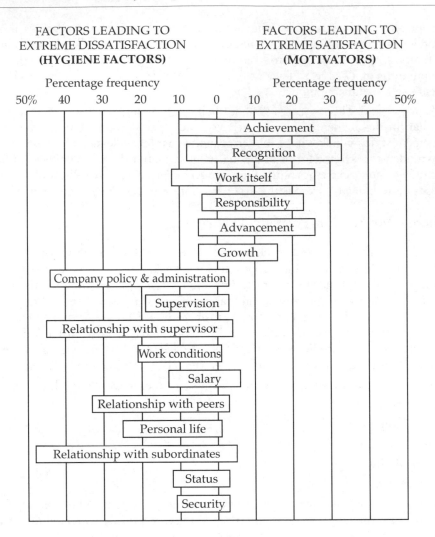

FACTORS LEADING TO
EXTREME DISSATISFACTION
(HYGIENE FACTORS)

FACTORS LEADING TO
EXTREME SATISFACTION
(MOTIVATORS)

Percentage frequency

Percentage frequency

50% 40   30   20   10   0   10   20   30   40   50%

Achievement
Recognition
Work itself
Responsibility
Advancement
Growth
Company policy & administration
Supervision
Relationship with supervisor
Work conditions
Salary
Relationship with peers
Personal life
Relationship with subordinates
Status
Security

Note: The *length* of each 'box' denotes the frequency with which the factor occurred in the situations described by the respondents. The overlap of the boxes across the centre line indicates:

a)   that motivators have their *negative* aspects, eg lack of achievement can lead to dissatisfaction; and

b)   that hygiene factors have their *positive* aspects, eg salary can be a source of satisfaction.

Figure 5.3. Factors affecting job attitudes.

prevent dissatisfaction. To put it another way, if motivators are absent from the job, the employee is likely to experience real dissatisfaction. However, even if the hygiene factors are provided for, they will not in themselves bring about substantial job satisfaction. Hygiene, in other words, does not positively promote good health, but only acts to prevent ill health.

35. If we apply Herzberg's theory to the ideas and assumptions of earlier theorists, it is possible to see that Taylor and colleagues were thinking very much in terms of hygiene factors (pay, incentives, adequate supervision and working conditions). Mayo, too, was placing his emphasis on a hygiene factor, namely interpersonal relations. It is only when we consider the ideas of the neo-human relations school that motivators appear as a key element in job satisfaction and worker productivity.

36. Herzberg's motivation-hygiene theory was generally well received by practising managers and consultants for its relatively simple and vivid distinction between factors inducing positive satisfaction and those causing dissatisfaction. It led to considerable work on so-called *job enrichment* – ie the design of jobs so that they contain a greater number of motivators. The approach here is basically to counter the effects of years of Taylorism, in which work was broken down into its simplest components, and over which there was no responsibility for planning and control. Herzberg's ideas were less well received by fellow social scientists, mainly on grounds of doubt about (a) their applicability to non-professional groups and (b) his use of the concept of 'job satisfaction', which they argued is not the same thing as 'motivation'.

Rensis Likert

37. Likert's contribution to the concept of motivation, and its applicability to the world of work, came mainly from his work as Director of the Institute of Social Research at the University of Michigan, USA. These so-called 'Michigan studies' were described by Likert (1961)[14], in a text in which he theorised about high-producing and low-producing managers. The former, according to his research, were those who achieved not only the highest productivity, but also the lowest costs and the highest levels of employee motivation. The latter, by comparison, produced higher costs and lower employee motivation.

38. The researches indicated that the high-producing managers tended to build their success on interlocking and tightly knit, groups of employees, whose cooperation had been obtained by thorough attention to a range of motivational forces. These included not only economic and security motives, but also ego and creativity motives (self-actualisation, in Maslow's terminology). Another key feature noted by the Michigan researchers was that, although the high-producers utilised the tools of classical management – work study, budgeting etc – they did so in a way that recognised the aspirations of the employees, by encouraging participative approaches.

39. A dominant theme in Likert's discussion of these 'new patterns of management' is the importance of supportive relationships. Management can achieve high performance when employees see their membership of a work group to be 'supportive', that is to say when they experience a sense of personal worth and importance from belonging to it. High-producing managers and supervisors tended to foster just such relationships with, and within their groups.

40. The idea of supportive relationships is built into Likert's view of the ideal organisation structure. Supportive relationships lead to effective work groups which can interact with other effective groups in an overlapping form of organisation. In this form of structure certain key roles perform a 'linking pin' function. A head of a section, for example, is a member not only of his own group but also of his superior's group. His superior, in turn, is a member of a further group higher up the organisational hierarchy, and so on. Such an organisation still has the basic shape of a classical organisational pyramid, but operates in practice on the basis of interlocking teams, instead of separate specialisms. This form is shown diagrammatically in Figure 5.4.

41. In reviewing his work on motivation, leadership and organisation structures, Likert distinguished between four separate systems, or styles, of management. These are founded on a number of differing assumptions about human behaviour and are useful to compare with Schein's classifications and McGregor's theory X – theory Y. The four systems are as follows:

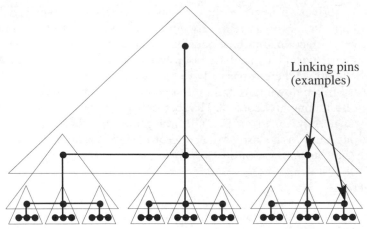

Linking pins
(examples)

Figure 5.4 Overlapping group form of organisation.

1 **Exploitative-authoritative** where power and direction come from the top downwards, where threats and punishment are employed, where communication is poor and team-work non-existent. Productivity is mediocre.

2 **Benevolent-authoritative** is similar to the above but allows some upward opportunities for consultation and some delegation. Rewards may be available as well as threats. Productivity is fair to good but at the cost of considerable absenteeism and turnover.

3 **Consultative** where goals are set or orders issued after discussion with subordinates, where communication is both upwards and downwards and where teamwork is encouraged, at least partially. There is some involvement of employees, as a motivator. Productivity is good with only moderate absenteeism etc.

4 **Participative-group** is the ideal system. Under this system, the keynote is participation, leading to commitment to the organisation's goals in a fully cooperative way. Communication is good both upwards, downwards and laterally. Motivation is obtained by a variety of means. Productivity is excellent and absenteeism and turnover are low.

42. System 1 above corresponds closely to Schein's rational economic model and McGregor's theory X. System 2 can be considered as a similar, but softer, approach. System 3 is fairly close to the idea of the social model. System 4 is more like Schein's self-actualising model and very close to the idea of theory Y. System 1, at one extreme, is highly task oriented, whilst system 4 is highly people oriented at the other.

Chris Argyris

43. Professor Argyris was a contemporary of Likert's. His initial interests, while at Yale University, were in the relationship between people's needs and the needs of the organisation. He suggested that the reason for so much employee apathy was not so much because of laziness, but rather because people were being treated like children. This led to what he called the *immaturity-maturity theory*[15], which suggests that the human personality develops from immaturity to maturity in a continuum, in which a number of key changes take place. These are as follows (Figure 5.5).

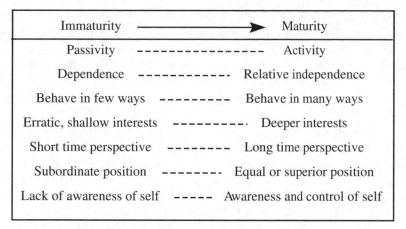

Immaturity	⟶	Maturity
Passivity	- - - - - - - - - - - -	Activity
Dependence	- - - - - - - - - - -	Relative independence
Behave in few ways	- - - - - - - -	Behave in many ways
Erratic, shallow interests	- - - - - - - -	Deeper interests
Short time perspective	- - - - - - -	Long time perspective
Subordinate position	- - - - - - -	Equal or superior position
Lack of awareness of self	- - - -	Awareness and control of self

Figure 5.5 Immaturity-Maturity Theory.

44. Against the above model of maturity, Argyris sets the features of the typical classical organisation: *task specialisation, chain of command, unity of direction* and *span of control*. The impact of this type of organisation on individuals is that they are expected to be passive, dependent and subordinate ie they are expected to behave immaturely! For individuals who are relatively mature, this environment is a major source of frustration at work. This frustration leads to individuals seeking informal ways of minimising their difficulties such as creating informal organisations that work against the formal hierarchy.

45. The lessons for motivation are important. For the more we can understand human needs, the more it will be possible to integrate them with the needs of organisations. If the goals of the organisation and the goals of individuals can be brought together, the resulting behaviour will be cooperative rather than defensive or downright antagonistic. Argyris's ideas, therefore, favour a self-actualisation model of man with some of the attributes of complex man too.

Achievement Motivation

46. Whilst many social psychologists have studied *common* factors in human motivation, others have focused on *differences* between individuals. One such researcher, whose work is well known, is D.C. McClelland[16] of Harvard University. He and his team drew attention to three sets of needs in particular, as follows:

- the *need for achievement* (n-Ach)
- the *need for power* (n-Pow)
- the *need for affiliation,* or belonging (n-Aff).

McClelland isolated n-Ach as a key human motive, and one that is influenced strongly by personality and by environment.

47. Persons with a high need for achievement tend to have the following characteristics:

- Their need for achievement is consistent.
- They seek tasks in which they can exercise personal responsibility.
- They prefer tasks which provide a challenge without being too difficult and which they see as within their mastery.
- They want feedback on their results.

- They are less concerned about their social or affiliation needs.

McClelland's conclusion was that the need for achievement is developed more by child-hood experiences and cultural background than by purely inherited factors. If this is correct it has important implications for management and supervisory training. If the need for achievement is influenced primarily by environmental factors, then clearly it is possible to develop training programmes designed to increase the achievement motive in the employees concerned.

48. The major disadvantage of persons with high n-Ach is that, by definition, they are task oriented and less concerned with relationships. These characteristics are not always suitable for those whose responsibility is to get work done through people – ie managers and supervisors. This may not be a problem for an entrepreneurial figure in a small organ-isation, but what of the high achiever working in a typical industrial or commercial bureaucracy? In the latter case high n-Ach can be frustrated by the constraints imposed by delegating responsibility. Nevertheless, McClelland's ideas were important as a contribution to our understanding of motivation at work, and how the concept of n-Ach might be applied in practice.

References

1. Schein, E.H. (1988), *Organisational Psychology* (3rd edition*)*, Prentice-Hall.
2. Cole, G.A. (1995), *Organisational Behaviour*, Continuum.
3. Mayo, E. (1933), *The Human Problems of an Industrial Civilisation*, Macmillan.
4. Roethlisberger, F.J. & Dickson, W.J. (1939), *Management and the Worker*, Harvard University Press.
5. Follett, M.P. (1941), *Dynamic Administration*, Harper Bros.
6. Graham, P. (ed.) (1995), *Mary Parker Follett – Prophet of Management: A Celebration of Writings from the 1920s*, Harvard Business School Press.
7. Maslow, A. (1954), *Motivation and Personality*, Harper & Row (re-issued in 1970, 1987).
8. Maslow, A. (1961) *Towards a Psychology of Being*, Van Nostrand Reinhold (re-issued in 1998 by John Wiley).
9. Alderfer, C. (1972), *Existence, Relatedness and Growth*, Collier Macmillan.
10. Drucker, P. (1974), *Management: Tasks, Responsibilities, Practices*, Heinemann.
11. McGregor, D. (1960), *The Human Side of the Enterprise*, McGraw-Hill.
12. Herzberg, F. (1959), *The Motivation to Work* , (2nd edition) John Wiley.
13. Herzberg, F, (1968), *Work and the Nature of Man*, Staples Press (GB).
14. Likert, R. (1961), *New Patterns of Management*, McGraw-Hill.
15. Argyris, C. (1957), *Personality and Organisation*, Harper & Row.
16. McClelland, D. (1961), *The Achieving Society*, Van Nostrand.

CHAPTER 6

Motivation – Later Theorists

Introduction

1. The motivation theories put forward in the previous chapter have been labelled 'content theories' of motivation, because they focus on the needs, drives or triggers of human behaviour in the workplace. This chapter examines some of the ideas proposed by

those whose focus is mainly on the process of motivation rather than its content. Not surprisingly, these theories tend to be called 'process theories' of motivation. One of the most well known of these is so-called Expectancy Theory, which is the first to be outlined. This is followed by a brief consideration of other later theories of motivation, including the following: Equity Theory, Goal Theory, Attribution Theory, Reinforcement Theory, and an analysis of Japanese motivational practices given the name of 'Theory Z'.

Expectancy Theory

2.   The development of this theory of motivation has been based on the work of the American, V.H. Vroom[1], during the 1960s. A key point of his theory is that an individual's behaviour is formed not on objective reality but on his or her subjective perception of that reality. The core of the theory (see Figure 6.1) relates to how a person perceives the relationships between three things – effort, performance and rewards. Vroom focused especially on the factors involved in stimulating an individual to put effort into something, since this is the basis of motivation. He concluded that there were three such factors, each based on the individual's personal perception of the situation. These were:

❶   **Expectancy,** ie. the extent of the individual's perception, or belief, that a particular act will produce a particular outcome.

❷   **Instrumentality,** ie the extent to which the individual perceives that effective performance will lead to desired rewards.

❸   **Valence,** ie the strength of the belief that attractive rewards are potentially available.

This approach to the concept of human motivation, with its emphasis on the psychological *mechanisms* that trigger effort, is quite different from that of the content theorists whose work was described in the previous chapter.

3.   The basic model developed by Vroom, indicating the components of effort that can lead to relevant performance and appropriate rewards, can be summarised in Figure 6.1.

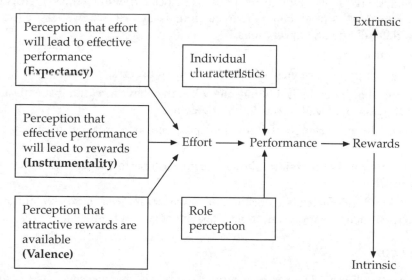

Figure 6.1. Expectancy Theory.

4.   It is important to note that Vroom distinguishes 'valence' from 'value'. He does so by defining the former in terms of the *anticipated* satisfaction the individual hopes to obtain from the outcome or reward, and by defining 'value' in terms of the *actual* satisfaction

obtained by the individual. According to Vroom the three factors – Expectancy, Instrumentality and Valence – combine together to create a driving force (**Force**), which motivates an individual to put in effort, achieve a level of performance, and obtain rewards at the end. Vroom suggested that **Force** was a multiple of **Expectancy** and **Valence** (encompassing Instrumentality) in the formula:

$$\text{Force} = \text{Expectancy} \times \text{Valence (or } F = E \times V)$$

5.   Effort alone, however, may not necessarily lead to effective performance. Other factors are involved, such as the individual's own characteristics (personality, knowledge and skills) and the way in which he perceives his role. For example, the prospect of promotion could be seen by a newly-appointed employee as an attractive prospect (valence), but his expectancy of gaining promotion could be low, if he perceives that promotion is attained primarily on length of service. In such a situation, performance does not lead to rewards, so effort in that direction is not seen as worthwhile. In any case, effort does not necessarily lead to effective performance, if the individual has insufficient knowledge and skills, or if his perception of his role does not equate with that of his superior, for example.

6.   Other factors which are not shown may also affect performance, eg constraints of the job, organisation style etc. Effort, therefore, does not always result in effective performance. It is also true that effective performance may not always lead to the rewards anticipated by the individual. Nevertheless, on both counts, it is not the reality which spurs on the individual, but the prospect of effective performance and /or desirable rewards. It is the individual's perception of the situation that is the vital part of this theory.

7.   Rewards may be put into two categories – (1) *intrinsic* and (2) *extrinsic*. Intrinsic rewards are those gained from fulfilling higher-level personal needs, such as self-esteem and personal growth. The individual can exercise a degree of personal control over these. Extrinsic rewards, by comparison, are those provided by the organisation, and thus outside the control of the individual, such as pay, promotion and working conditions. Several research studies have suggested that the rewards associated with intrinsic factors are more likely to be perceived as producing job satisfaction. The extrinsic rewards are less likely to come up to the individual's expectations.

8.   The main features of Expectancy Theory are:

- it takes a comprehensive view of the motivational process.
- it indicates that individuals will only act when they have a reasonable expectancy that their behaviour will lead to the desired outcomes.
- it stresses the importance of individual perceptions of reality in the motivational process.
- it implies that job satisfaction follows effective job performance rather than the other way round.
- it has led to developments in work redesign, where emphasis has been laid on intrinsic job factors, such as variety, autonomy, task identity and feedback.

Equity Theory

9.   The basis of Equity Theory, in a work context, is that people make comparisons between themselves and others in terms of what they invest in their work (inputs) and what outcomes they receive from it. As in the case of Expectancy Theory, this theory is also founded on people's *perceptions*, in this case of the inputs and outcomes involved. Thus, their sense of equity (ie fairness) is applied to their *subjective* view of conditions and not

necessarily to the objective situation. The theory states that when people perceive an unequal situation, they experience *'equity tension'*, which they attempt to reduce by appropriate behaviour. This behaviour may be to act positively to improve their performance and/or to seek improved rewards, or may be to act negatively by, for example, working more slowly (cf. Taylor-type soldiering) on the grounds of being under-rated or under-paid.

10. Robbins (1993)[2], in a review of research, suggests that when people perceive an inequitable situation for themselves they can be predicted to make one of six choices:

❶ change their inputs (eg, not exerting as much effort)

❷ change their outcomes (eg, individuals paid on a piece-rate basis increase their pay by producing a higher quantity of units even if of a lower quality)

❸ distort their perceptions of self (eg, 'I used to think I worked at a moderate pace but now I realise I work a lot harder than everyone else.')

❹ distort perceptions of others (eg, 'X's job isn't as desirable as I first thought.')

❺ choose a different reference point (eg, 'I may not be doing as well as my brother, but I'm doing better than our father did at my age.')

❻ 'leave the field' (ie, quit their job!)

11. Equity Theory suggests that people are not only interested in rewards as such, which is the central point of expectancy theory, but they are also interested in the *comparative* nature of rewards. Thus, part of the attractiveness (valence) of rewards in a work context is the extent to which they are seen to be comparable to those available to the peer-group. Such thinking, however, is best applied to *extrinsic* rewards, such as pay, promotion, pension arrangements, company car and similar benefits, since they (a) depend on others for their provision, and (b) have an objective truth about them. Equity theory cannot apply in the same way to *intrinsic* rewards, such as intrinsic job interest, personal achievement and exercise of responsibility, which by their very nature are personal to the individual, entirely subjective, and therefore less capable of comparison in any credible sense.

12. Nevertheless, so far as extrinsic rewards are concerned, managers would be well advised to reflect on the ideas of Equity Theory, especially in recognising that subjective perceptions are extremely powerful factors in motivation. As Jaques (1961)[3] discovered more than thirty years ago, questions of equitable payment in relation to the discretion or autonomy available to an individual in the job are a key factor in achieving a sense of fairness at work. In a subsequent handbook for managers (1964)[4] he commented that:

> '...individuals privately possess common standards as to what constitutes fair payment for given levels of work... These norms of fair payment are relative; ie they indicate what differentials in payment are felt to be fair in relation to differentials in levels of work.'

The 'felt fair' factor is essentially a restatement of 'individual perception of fairness'.

Goal Theory

13. The thinking behind Goal Theory is that motivation is driven primarily by the goals or objectives that individuals set for themselves. Unlike Expectancy Theory, where a satisfactory outcome is the prime motivator, Goal Theory suggests that it is the goal itself that provides the driving force. Locke (1968[5]) first proposed the idea that working towards goals was in itself a motivator. His research indicated that performance improved when individuals set specific rather than vague goals for themselves. When these specific goals were demanding, performance was even better. General exhortations to *'do one's best'* appear to be less effective than identifying *specific* targets and aiming for them.

14. Goal theorists (eg Locke & Latham, 1988[6]) also argue that an individual's motivation is enhanced when feedback on performance is available. Other important factors include goal-commitment (ie the extent to which the individual is committed to pursuing the goal even when things get rough), and self-efficacy (ie the perception that one has the ability to achieve the goal). Goal commitment is likely to be enhanced when goals are made public and when they are set by the individual rather than imposed externally. Clearly, the concept of goal 'ownership' is important here. A major aspect of management-by-objectives (eg Humble, 1967)[7] is the intention that the process should attempt to harmonise individual and company goals. Self-efficacy is rather like the quality noted by McClelland (1961[8]) as being at the core of those with a high n-Ach, ie a belief that they were capable of achieving their goals, which were set at a realistic, though challenging, level (see previous chapter).

Attribution Theory

15. Attribution Theory suggests that we judge other people's behaviour by attributing meaning to their behaviour in the light of perceived internal or external forces. Internally caused behaviour is perceived to be under the control of the individual, ie they have made a *choice* in selecting the behaviour. Externally caused behaviour results from *environmental* forces that are perceived to influence people's behaviour (eg organisational rules, machinery breakdown etc), and over which the individual has little or no control. Kelley (1972)[9] suggests that when people make attributions, they do so with three major criteria in mind:

- **Distinctiveness**, ie how distinctive or different is the behaviour? How untypical?
- **Consensus**, ie how far is the behaviour typical of others in the same situation?
- **Consistency**, ie how consistent is the behaviour over time? Or is this an unusual piece of behaviour?

16. Application of the theory to an issue such as an individual's lateness for work might result in the following thinking:

	Distinctiveness	Consensus	Consistency
Internal Attribution	Individual is considered to dislike work	Other people are usually on time	Individual is frequently late
External Attribution	Individual is not usually late to work	Other employees were also late	Individual is rarely late

In the case of the internally caused behaviour, we would be likely to draw the conclusion that this person was an unmotivated individual who disliked his job, and therefore 'chose' to be late. Where the behaviour was seen as essentially caused by external factors, we would be likely to conclude that this was a one-off event caused by circumstances outside his control, such as a major traffic hold-up en route to work.

17. Attribution Theory is as much an issue of perception between individuals as a theory of motivation. Nevertheless, by providing another way of looking at people's behaviour, it can add to our understanding of the motivational process. The theory clearly has connections with Achievement Theory, since people attributed with primarily internal sources of behaviour have strong similarities with those showing high n-Ach needs (ie belief in their own internal strengths). People attributed with external causes of behaviour are likely to

see their working lives dominated by external forces, such as the production system, actions of management etc.

Reinforcement Theory

18. Whereas Attribution Theory has strong links with ideas about human perception, Reinforcement Theory, as applied to motivation, has major connections with learning theory, and especially the work of the behaviourist, B.F. Skinner (1974)[10]. The Reinforcement Theory of motivation suggests that a given behaviour is a function of the consequences of earlier behaviour. Thus, it is argued, all behaviour is determined to some extent by the rewards or punishments obtained from previous behaviour, which has the effect of reinforcing current actions. In this sense all behaviour is caused by *external* sources, since we can have little control over the consequences of our actions. So, if an individual's efforts to contribute new ideas to a team are consistently met with an indulgent but apathetic approach by the management (ie negative reinforcement), then the individual is likely to be discouraged from making further suggestions, and may even seek to change his or her job. Where, by comparison, the individual is encouraged to share new ideas and help to develop them (ie positive reinforcement), then the person is likely to generate even more ideas.

19. Strict Reinforcement Theory would argue that an individual's own understandings, emotions, needs and expectations do not enter into motivation, which is purely about the *consequences* of behaviour. However, modifications of the theory (eg Social Learning Theory) do allow for the effect of individuals' perceptions of the rewards/punishments obtained by others as a contributor to motivation. Thus, an employee is not just affected by the consequences of his own actions at work, but is able to infer 'appropriate' behaviour from what he sees as the consequences for others of their behaviour. Reinforcement Theory is not basically concerned with what motivates behaviour, or how, and is not strictly a theory of motivation. It is more concerned with control of behaviour (ie power over others).

20. Supporters of Reinforcement Theory (eg Jablonsky & De Vries, 1972)[11] offer some important guidelines to those intending to use it as a motivating tool in the workplace. Typical suggestions include the following:

- Positively reinforce desired behaviour
- Ignore undesirable behaviour, so far as possible
- Avoid using punishment as principal means of achieving desired performance
- Provide reinforcement as soon as possible after the response
- Apply positive reinforcement regularly
- Assess positive and negative factors in the individual's environment
- Specify desired behaviour/performance in quantifiable terms

The underlying assumption behind this approach is that people are there to be controlled, and that management's task is to provide the 'right' conditions to encourage high performance. This is not quite such a negative view of people as is suggested by McGregor's Theory X (see previous chapter), but Reinforcement Theory is not too far removed from that concept of human motivation.

Theory Z – The Japanese Approach

21. The reference in the previous paragraph to McGregor's Theory X is timely, for it leads us into the last 'theory' in this chapter – 'Theory Z'. This describes an approach to

employee motivation based on Japanese management practices. The phrase was coined by an American exponent of Japanese approaches to management, W. Ouchi (1981)[12], who used it to describe attempts to adapt Japanese practice to Western firms.

22. Over the course of the past two decades considerable attention has been given to the success of Japanese manufacturing industries. One of the key factors in their success, according to Ouchi, has been their approach to their management of resources, especially people. Among the key features of Japanese industrial organisations, notes Ouchi, are the following personnel-related factors:

- there is a high degree of mutual trust and loyalty between management and employees

- career paths are non-specialised with life-long job rotation as a central feature of career development

- decision-making is shared at all levels

- performance appraisal is long-term (ie the first appraisal takes place 10 years after joining the company)

- there is a strong sense of *collective* responsibility for the success of the organisation, and cooperative effort rather than individual achievement is encouraged

23. Although Ouchi recognises that many of the features of Japanese management cannot be translated into Western industrial society, he believes that certain features can be applied in a Western context. The move from the present hierarchical type of organisation to a Theory Z type organisation is a process which, says Ouchi:

'...has the objective of developing the ability of the organisation to coordinate people, not technology, to achieve productivity'.

24. In his view this requires a 'new' philosophy of managing people based on a combination of the following features of Japanese management:

1 lifelong employment prospects

2 shared forms of decision making

3 relationships between boss and subordinate based on mutual respect.

This step requires the following strategy:

- The adoption of a 'top-down' approach, based on a definition of the 'new' philosophy agreed and supported by the organisation's top management.

- The 'new' philosophy should embrace the ideas of security of employment, shared decision making, career development, team spirit and acknowledgement of individual contribution within the team.

- The implementation of the new approach should be carried through on the basis of consultation and communication with the workforce and with full training support to develop relevant skills for managers, supervisors and their teams.

25. Despite the participative management style implied by the above theory, it is important to note that the Japanese have taken up many of the ideas of F.W. Taylor (see Chapter 3), but, in contrast to Western industrialised nations, they have emphasised the importance of the human resource element in achieving production efficiency using Taylor's methods. In Japan today engineering is held in the highest esteem, and there is a marked production orientation in the workplace. The situation in Britain, for example, is rather different. Taylorism is seen as discredited, mainly on the grounds that it has led to the disintegration of work and loss of job satisfaction. Engineering, therefore, has a low status compared with other professions. Robert Cole (1979)[13] reported in a study entitled 'Work, Mobility

and Participation' that in terms of specialist management functions, Japanese firms ranked production and personnel highest, whereas British firms chose accounting and finance.

26. The acceptance of Taylorist approaches to manufacturing has enabled the Japanese to capture an enviable place in world markets for their manufactured goods. It is not that the Japanese are particularly innovative, but they have found the secret of achieving a standard of production control which ensures a consistently excellent product. This standard has been achieved because of thorough attention to human resource issues as well as to questions of technology, quality and cost control. Backed by financial policies aimed at long-term growth rather than short-term profits, and a worldwide view of product marketing, Japanese manufacturing companies have set a high standard for their competitors to follow.

27. Critics of Japanese manufacturing companies have pointed to the slow processes of decision-making, the lack of risk-taking, the reliance on a myriad of small firms and part-time employees, the docile nature of the trade unions, and the imprisoning effect of lifetime employment in one company. It is precisely because of such criticisms that Japanese management practices have to be adapted if they are to be employed successfully elsewhere. The whole point of Theory Z, as Ouchi himself was at pains to point out, lies in the *adaptation* of Japanese approaches to Western production methods.

28. In a Work Research Unit report (1984)[14], comparing British and Japanese production methods, the representative of Thorn EMI Ferguson, manufacturers of colour televisions and associated equipment in Britain, drew a number of conclusions about the relative situation of his company vis-à-vis the Japanese TV factories visited. He concluded that, in terms of *production technology*, his company was unsurpassed by any of the Japanese companies visited. In *labour flexibility* terms, the Japanese were well ahead, principally because of the use of part-time employees (25–30% of the total workforce) and the high turnover of the predominantly female workforce. Very high *volumes* of colour televisions were produced in each of the Japanese factories, considerably in excess of the British company's output. It was also noticed that where the Japanese had a very limited range of models, the British firm had about two hundred in production. In terms of 'Personnel policy' there were important differences. The Japanese policy was directed at maximising the contribution of each employee through exhortation, training, job rotation, use of quality circles and individual counselling. The emphasis on learning about, and being committed to, the company culture was striking. The British approach to Personnel policy usually emphasised rewards and employee support mechanisms rather than employee attitudes and output.

29. The Thorn representative concluded that:

> 'If the delegation came back with one single message, it would be that competing in design technology and production technology with the Japanese is not enough. To survive in the long term we must compete in the field of employee commitment'.

Suggestions made by the representative, which might be said to be his version of Theory Z, were as follows:

❶ eliminate artificial status barriers (ie permit 'harmonisation')

❷ restructure work as to allow individuals to undertake meaningful roles and thus offer the opportunity to contribute positively to company success

❸ develop training for management succession

❹ improve communications in each direction, especially on issues such as company performance, policies and future prospects

⑤ encourage greater individual responsibility for work, quality and environment

⑥ introduce major improvements in factory housekeeping.

30. What is significant, in the context of British manufacturing, is that the ideas of Theory Z are not new. Indeed many well-known firms have practised them for years. What has happened in Japan is that the will has existed to put them into practice *on a grand scale*, and therein lies the difference. This, of course, is a matter of operational strategy rather than motivational practice. In the final analysis, however, this is what the application of a good theory is all about – to produce a practical and effective means of solving a continuing problem, in this case, how best to motivate one's employees.

References

1. Vroom,V. (1964), *Work and Motivation*, Wiley.
2. Robbins, S.P. (1993), *Organizational Behaviour*, 6th edition, Prentice-Hall.
3. Jaques, E. (1961), *Equitable Payment*, Heinemann.
4. Jaques, E. (1964), *Time-Span Handbook*, Heinemann.
5. Locke, E.A. (1975), 'Personnel Attitudes and Motivation', in Rosenzweig, M. & Porter, L. (eds), *Annual Review of Psychology*, Palo Alto.
6. Locke, E. & Latham, G.P. (1988), *A Theory of Goal-setting and Task Performance*, Prentice-Hall.
7. Humble, J. (1967), *Improving Business Results*, McGraw-Hill.
8. McClelland, D. (1961), *The Achieving Society*, Van Nostrand.
9. Kelley. H. (1972), 'Attribution in Social Interaction', in Jones, E et al (eds), *Attribution: Perceiving the Causes of Behavior*, General Learning Press.
10. Skinner, B.F. (1974), *About Behaviourism*, Random House.
11. Jablonsky, S. & De Vries, D. (1972), 'Operant conditioning principles extrapolated to the theory of management', in *Organisational Behaviour and Human Performance, 14*.
12. Ouchi, W. (1981), *Theory Z*, Addison-Wesley.
13. Cole, R.E. (1979), *Work, Mobility and Participation: a Comparative Study of American and Japanese Industry*, University of California.
14. Work Research Unit (1984), *Learning from Japan*, WRU.

NB Extracts from several of the theories referred to in this chapter and the previous chapter may be found in Vroom, V.H. & Deci, E.L. (1992), *Management and Motivation*, 2nd edition, Penguin.

Questions for Discussion/Homework

1. What are the needs or motives most frequently referred to by the leading theorists of human relations? In what ways is it possible to group these needs?

2. Give examples of tangible and intangible goals and suggest how a person might seek to achieve them.

3. What are the similarities between Schein's description of the Rational-Economic Model, McGregor's Theory X and Likert's System 1 (Exploitive-Authoritative)?

4. What is the 'Hawthorne Effect'? What are the implications of this for those undertaking research into human behaviour in the workplace?

5. Why were the Hawthorne Studies considered to be so important in their time?

6. In what ways has Maslow's concept of self-actualisation been taken up by other theorists?

7. What are the essential differences between motivators and hygiene factors in Herzberg's theory of motivation.

8. How can an understanding of the need for achievement be of use to managers in industry and commerce?

9. In what respects is Expectancy Theory novel in its approach to motivation at work?

10. In what ways can human beings contrive to come to terms with a work situation that appears not to be satisfactory to them? Give examples to illustrate your answer.

11. What is 'Theory Z', and to what extent can its underlying assumptions be transferred to non-Japanese manufacturing companies?

Examination Questions

The following questions are selected for their relevance to this section, and, in some cases, to the section on classical theories as well. Outline answers can be found in Appendix 2.

EQ 5 Discuss the major features and significance of ... the Hawthorne experience at Western Electric ...

(ACCA – part of an either/or question)

EQ 6 Compare the approaches taken by the classical/traditional theorists with the human relations/resources theorists, in understanding the nature of organisations.

(CIMA)

EQ 7 *'People only come to work for money'.* Discuss.

(IOB)

EQ 8 Motivation of subordinates is an important aspect of a manager's job.

1. What do you think motivates a person to work well?

2. What steps can a manager take to motivate his subordinates?

(ICSA MPP)

This section of the book examines some leading concepts in the related fields of leadership and group behaviour. Chapter 7 describes a number of different ways of looking at leadership, discusses the tensions between concern for the task and concern for people, and summarises a number of important theories of leadership. Chapter 8 looks at crucial aspects of the workplace behaviour of people in groups, and examines some features of the working of groups, including the effect of competition and the task of team-building.

CHAPTER 7

Leadership – Theory and Practice

Introduction

1. The crux of every management job lies in the job-holder's capacity to obtain the commitment of people to the objectives of the organisation, which is another way of saying 'to exercise appropriate leadership'. Leadership is a concept which has fascinated humankind for centuries, but only in recent years has any kind of *theory* of leadership emerged. This chapter describes and comments on a number of the theoretical and practical aspects of leadership in the work situation. A review of the main theories of leadership is followed by a discussion of the alternative styles of leadership available, in practice, to a person in a management or supervisory position.

2. Before attempting a working definition of 'leadership', it would be appropriate to reflect briefly on the various types of leader which have been identified, and to consider some of the practical difficulties arising from these. The most important types of leader are as follows:

❶ the **Charismatic** leader, who gains influence mainly from strength of personality, eg Napoleon, Hitler, Churchill, Robert Maxwell and others. The difficulty with charismatic leadership is that few people possess the exceptional qualities required to transform all around them into willing followers! Another issue is that personal qualities, or traits, of leadership cannot be acquired by training, they can only be modified by it.

❷ the **Traditional** leader, whose position is assured by birth, eg kings, queens and tribal chieftains. This is another category to which few people can aspire. Except in the small family business, there are few opportunities for traditional leadership at work.

❸ the **Situational** leader, whose influence can only be effective by being in the right place at the right time, eg the butler in J.M. Barrie's 'The Admirable Crichton'. This kind of leadership is too temporary in nature to be of much value in a business. What is looked for is someone who is capable of assuming a leadership role in a variety of situations over a period of time.

❹ the **Appointed** leader, whose influence arises directly out of his position, eg most managers and supervisors. This is the bureaucratic type of leadership, where legitimate power springs from the nature and scope of the position within the hierarchy. The problem here is that, although the powers of the *position* may be defined, the job-holder may not be able to implement them because of weak personality, lack of adequate training or other factors.

⑤ the **Functional** leader, who secures their leadership position by what he or she does, rather than by what they are. In other words, functional leaders adapt their behaviour to meet the competing needs of the situation. This particular type will be looked at more closely later on in the chapter.

⑤ the **Principle-centred** leader, whose approach to leadership is influenced by moral and ethical principles, involving considerations of equity, justice, integrity, honesty, fairness and trust. This approach is associated with the ideas of Stephen Covey (see below).

3. Leadership, then, is something more than just an aspect of personality, tradition, opportunism or appointment. It is intimately connected with actual behaviour and attitudes towards oneself and others. Although leadership may involve empowering others, and sharing the leadership burden in many respects, it nevertheless cannot abdicate its final responsibility for a group's results. Any leader, ultimately, must accept personal responsibility for success or failure. The way in which the leadership is carried out is influenced strongly by cultural factors (see Chapter 13), and this is an important consideration for top management given the extent of globalisation in many industries. For present purposes, we can define 'leadership' as follows:

> Leadership at work is a dynamic process whereby one individual in a group is not only responsible for the group's results, but actively seeks the collaboration and commitment of all the group members in achieving group goals in a particular context and against the background of a particular national culture.

The suggestion that leadership is a dynamic process implies that there is no 'one best way' of leading – leadership is essentially about striking the right balance between the needs of people, task and goals in a given situation. If a football team is behind at half-time, the club manager's talk to the team is likely to be much tougher than the upbeat speech he gave it just before kick-off! Before the start his object would have been to encourage and show confidence; at half-time he would be pointing out weaknesses, insisting on tactical changes, and urging the team to do better.

4. The main variables in the leadership process can be illustrated as follows (Figure 7.1):

LEADER	TASK/ GOALS
● Skills	Group goals
● Principles	Individual goals/ targets
● Knowledge	Relative complexity
● Personality	
GROUP MEMBERS	**SITUATION/ ENVIRONMENT**
● Skills	Internal dynamics of group
● Needs	Cultural issues
● Motivation	External pressures
	Resources available

Figure 7.1 The key leadership variables.

The critical variable in the above is the leadership role. Using his or her skills and knowledge, drawing on personal qualities and adhering to principles of integrity and trust, a leader has to make the best of the other three variables. Perhaps all three might be favourable at a particular time, but the likelihood is that one or other of task, group members and situation will be problematic, and thus the leader will be challenged. The task facing the leader and the group may be complex, and there will always be the need to consider individuals' goals or targets within the overall objective. The group members themselves may not always have the best blend of knowledge and skills, and they may need motivating to achieve the overall objective. There will always be issues of group morale to be considered, as well as the needs of individuals. Finally, the situation or environment, both internal and external, is important. The interactions within the group and with the leader are major factors affecting outcomes. Cultural traditions may need to be considered where the group is not homogeneous. There will always be external pressures of one kind or another that may not be favourable to group progress, and there may be problems with insufficient resources to support the group in its efforts. The art of good leadership is to be able to make the best use of all the variables even when they are unfavourable. If they are very unfavourable, part of the leader's role is to seek help on behalf of the group. Thus, a very important aspect of leadership is to recognise one's own dependence on others.

Theories of leadership

5.   Ideas about leadership in management roles range from the 'ideal' approaches of scientific management, the human relations and social psychological schools, and Covey's principle-centred leadership to the pragmatic approaches of the contingency theorists. The leading theories of leadership that have been proposed over the past fifty years are generally classified under 'trait theories', 'style theories' and 'contingency theories'. These will be examined briefly in turn, followed by a summary of Covey's ideas on principle-centred leadership.

Trait Theories

6.   As we saw earlier, in the discussion of classical management ideas, the debate was usually led by practising managers who were strong characters in their own right. Part of their success was undoubtedly due to personal qualities, and it is perhaps not surprising that the earliest studies that were undertaken into leadership focused their attention on the *qualities* required for effective leaders. Handy (1993)[1] mentions that by 1950 over 100 studies of this kind had been undertaken, but that the number of common traits or characteristics identified by the researchers was only 5% of the total! It has proved an impossible task to identify the particular traits or characteristics that separate leaders from non-leaders. Of those traits which do appear more frequently, intelligence, energy and resourcefulness are perhaps the most representative and these are certainly mentioned in Covey's ideas of 'principle-centred' leadership (see below).

Style Theories

7.   The interest in the human factor at work which was stimulated by the researchers of Human Relations, and taken up by the social psychologists who followed them, led logically to an interest in leadership as an aspect of *behaviour* at work, rather than of personal characteristics. Since the 1950s, in particular, several theories about leadership, or management, style have been put forward. These have tended to be expressed in terms of authoritarian versus democratic styles, or people-orientation versus task orientation. In some

cases, despite acknowledged inconsistencies in the theories themselves, style theories have led to quite useful devices for improving training for leadership. A selection of the best-known style theories is discussed below.

8. **Authoritarian-Democratic.** Three examples of this approach to management style are as follows:

❶ D. McGregor's Theory X manager – tough, autocratic and supporting tight controls with punishment-reward systems – the authoritarian. The contrasting style is that of the Theory Y manager – benevolent, participative and believing in self-controls – the democrat. These styles flow from the assumptions about people that are the original basis of Theory X and Theory Y (see Chapter 5).

❷ Rensis Likert's four management systems:

> System 1   the exploitive-authoritative system, which is the epitome of the authoritarian style.
>
> System 2   the benevolent-authoritative system, which is basically a paternalistic style.
>
> System 3   the consultative system, which moves towards greater democracy and teamwork.
>
> System 4   the participative-group system, which is the ultimate democratic style.

Likert's ideas were discussed in Chapter 5.

❸ Tannenbaum and Schmidt's model of a continuum of leadership styles, ranging from authoritarian behaviour at one end to democratic behaviour at the other, as illustrated in Figure 7.2 below

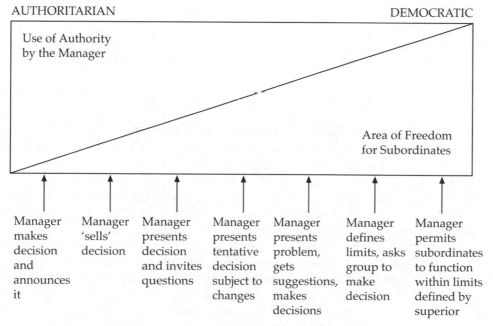

Figure 7.2 A continuum of leadership styles.
(adapted from Tannenbaum and Schmidt, Harvard Business Review, 1957)[2]

The implication behind the above three approaches is that managers have a basic choice between being either authoritarian or democratic, and that the best style – the ideal – is a democratic one. In practice, the either/or choice proposed by the theorists may be somewhat artificial. Much will depend on the other elements of the leadership situation, as in Figure 7.1 above. In some circumstances an authoritarian style could be more effective than a democratic style, and vice versa. The suggestion that a democratic style is generally preferable to an authoritarian one has been criticised on the grounds that whilst this may apply to current trends in Western industrialised nations, it need not apply at all in other cultures. The main weakness of these approaches is that they place too much emphasis on the *leader's* behaviour to the exclusion of the other variables in leadership, such as the internal dynamics of the group, the nature of the task, and the competencies of group members.

10. **People-Task Orientations.** Examples of approaches utilising *two* of the leadership variables – people and tasks – are as follows:

- **The Michigan Studies** – these studies, which were first reported in 1950[3], analysed a number of variables between managers of high-productivity groups and managers of low-productivity groups. The object was to see if any significant differences could be identified, thus providing some clues to leadership behaviour. In many respects (age, marital status etc) there were no such differences between the two groups. However, one significant difference was noticed, and this was that the supervisors in charge of the high-producing groups tended to be employee-oriented while their opposite numbers in the low-producing groups tended, ironically, to be production-centred. The employee-oriented supervisors paid more attention to relationships at work, exercised less direct supervision and encouraged employee participation in decision-making. Production-oriented supervisors were more directive and more concerned with task needs than people needs. The two different orientations appeared to represent different ends of the same continuum, as shown in Figure 7.3.

Figure 7.3 The Michigan continuum.

- **The Ohio Studies** – these studies were conducted during the 1950s[4]. Like the Michigan studies shortly before, they were concerned to describe leadership behaviour. The basis of the initial research was a Leader Behaviour Description Questionnaire of some 150 items. When the responses to this questionnaire were analysed two distinct groupings of behaviour emerged. These were defined as 'Consideration' and 'Initiating Structure'. Consideration described behaviour that was essentially relationships-oriented or considerate of employees' feelings. Initiating structure referred to behaviour concerned with the organisation of the work processes, including communication channels, allocating tasks etc. Unlike in the Michigan studies, the Ohio team's conclusion was that the two dimensions of Consideration and Initiating Structures were *separate dimensions*. It was shown to be possible for a supervisor to score high on both dimensions. This finding was developed by Robert Blake and Jane Mouton in their concept of the Managerial Grid[5] (see Chapter 46).

- **The 3-D Theory** – this approach, by Professor Reddin of New Brunswick University, Canada, takes the Blake-type grid a stage further and introduces a three-dimensional perspective[6]. This adds considerably to the flexibility of leadership styles by including the factor of effectiveness in the dimensions. Reddin's Grid (Figure 7.4), is able to consider aspects of the *situation* in which leadership is exercised, as well accounting for the concern for people (Relationship Oriented – RO) and the concern for production (Task Oriented – TO). The basic Grid together with the eight styles which spring from it are as shown in Figure 7.4.

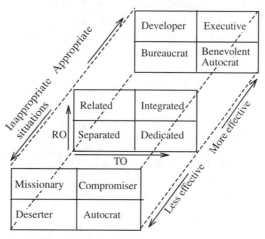

Figure 7.4 Reddin's 3-D Theory.

Reddin describes the central grid as the set of basic styles available in the light of the Relationship and Task orientations. So, for example, a manager who is high on people and low on task has a *basic* style that is Related. However each basic style has two alternative *management* styles arising from it, depending on whether the style is appropriate to the leadership situation or not. Appropriate leadership tends to be more effective, ie achieves the output requirements of that particular managerial job. Thus, a Related style that is used appropriately is called Developer, whilst an inappropriate style is called Missionary. The concept of effectiveness, added to the dimensions of relationships and task orientations, makes up the three-dimensional perspective. Unlike the Blake Grid, which has only one effective style (9,9), the Reddin Grid has four effective styles. Like the Blake Grid, however, Reddin's ideas have not been validated by research, and whilst useful for the purposes of management development, are not an authoritative answer to the question of what is effective leadership.

- **The Harvard Studies** – as a result of studying small-group behaviour, Harvard researchers[7] identified two distinct groups of leaders: task leaders and socio-emotional leaders, who were mutually exclusive. A person could not be a task leader and a socio-emotional leader as well. The task leader showed a concern for the structuring of activities, whereas the socio-emotional leader showed concern for supportive relationships. These two types of leader corresponded closely to the types defined by the Ohio studies, ie Initiating Structure and Consideration, but, unlike those studies, the Harvard results suggested that the two dimensions were mutually exclusive.

Contingency Approaches

11. **Functional, or Action-centred Leadership**. This concept of leadership was developed in the United Kingdom by Professor John Adair[8]. It is based on the theory that leadership is more a question of appropriate behaviour than of personality or of being in the right place at the right time. Adair's model of leadership (Figure 7.5) incorporates the concern for task and concern for people that has featured in all the theories which we have just mentioned. The functional model, however, distinguishes the concern for *individuals* from the concern for *groups*, and stresses that effective leadership lies in what the leader *does* to meet the needs of task, group and individuals. This takes the functional model nearer to the contingency approaches of modern theorists, whose concern is with the variety of factors – task, people and situation – which have a direct bearing on leadership and leadership styles.

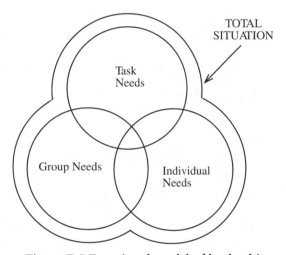

TOTAL SITUATION

Task Needs

Group Needs

Individual Needs

Figure 7.5 Functional model of leadership

12. The key features of the functional model can be summarised as follows:

- Task, Group and Individual Needs are fulfilled in the context of a total leadership situation. The circumstances of each situation affect the priority which attaches to each area of needs. An effective leader is one who is aware of these priorities and who can act in accordance with them. For example, in a situation of great urgency, task needs must predominate over group and individual needs. In another situation, such as the re-building of a football team, it is group needs which must come first, then individual needs, with task needs last. The model thus encourages a flexible style of leadership, which may be relatively task-oriented *or* group-oriented *or* individual-oriented, depending on circumstances.

- Task functions, directed towards task needs, include activities such as the setting of objectives, the planning of tasks, the allocation of responsibilities and the setting of appropriate standards of performance.

- Group maintenance functions, directed towards group needs, include activities such as team-building and motivation, communication, discipline, and acting as group representative to others outside the boundaries of the unit.

- Individual maintenance functions, directed towards the needs of individuals, include activities such as coaching, counselling, motivation and development.

13. Adair's concept of leadership is basically a contingency theory of leadership. It stresses that the leader's behaviour in relation to task, group and individual needs has to be related to the overall situation and, therefore, has to be adaptive.

14. **Contingency Leadership.** The first theorist to use the label 'contingency' explicitly was F.E. Fiedler (1967[9]) Fiedler named his leadership model 'the leadership contingency model'. In his view, group performance is contingent upon the leader adopting an appropriate style in the light of the relative favourableness of the situation. According to Fiedler, the three most important variables in determining the relative favourableness of the situation are:

1 Leader–member relations

2 Degree of structure in task and

3 Power and authority of the position

These three situational variables can produce eight possible combinations of situation, of which the most favourable to the leader is when (1) he has good leader–member relations, (2) the task is highly structured, and (3) he has a powerful position. By comparison, the least favourable conditions are when (1) he is disliked, (2) the task is relatively unstructured and (3) he has little position power.

15. On the topic of leadership style, Fiedler sees the two main choices as between 'relationship-motivated' and 'task-motivated'. Applying these styles to the range of situations possible, Fiedler found that task-motivated leaders tended to perform most effectively in situations which were either very favourable or very unfavourable. Relationship-motivated leaders tended to perform most effectively in situations that were intermediate in terms of favourableness. Fiedler's theory is another step towards the development of a comprehensive contingency theory of leadership. It is probably at its weakest on the issue of leadership style, but its greatest value lies in its attempt to distinguish and evaluate the key situational variables that influence the leader's role.

Principle-centred leadership

16. Leadership, according to Covey (1992)[10], can be contrasted with *management* and described as follows:

> 'Leadership deals with direction – with making sure that the ladder is leaning against the right wall. Management deals with speed… Leadership deals with vision – with keeping the mission in sight – and with effectiveness and results. Management deals with establishing structure and systems to get those results…
>
> Leadership focuses on the top line. Management focuses on the bottom line. Leadership derives its power from values and correct principles. Management organises resources to serve selected objectives to produce the bottom line.
>
> …management and leadership are not mutually exclusive; in fact… leadership is the highest component of management.'

(Principle-Centred Leadership p.246)

17. Covey's view of leadership is based on the idea that effectiveness in a social role, such as management, depends on how far a person keeps to certain principles of behaviour. He argues that the extent to which leaders recognise, and keep to, principles such as fairness, justice, integrity, and trust, determines their progress towards survival and stability, or to disintegration and destruction. He sees these principles as universal, objective and self-evident, just like the principle of gravity. He contrasts *principles* with *values*, which he

argues are subjective, internal and derive mainly from our culture. The key issue, as Covey sees it, is for people is to align their values to the 'correct' principles, of which there are four: *trustworthiness*, *trust*, *empowerment* and *alignment*.

18. *Trustworthiness* is essentially about a person's character and competence. We trust people for their honesty and reliability, that is for their character or integrity, and for their ability to carry out a role effectively, which is competence. *Trust*, in the sense of putting one's trust in others, is essential to effective team working and other personal relationships at work. A lack of trust is a major cause of failure in businesses and public sector alike. *Empowerment* is the enabling of teams and individuals to assume responsibility for achieving the results they have agreed. It enables people to respond to the trust vested in them by their senior managers, who need to become sources of help, not measurers of performance. Where empowerment is practised, organisational structures and systems can be realigned, so that there is little hierarchy, a wide span of control and flexible systems. *Alignment* is the process of constantly reviewing the situation in the light of external conditions and the implementation of the other three principles.

19. Covey is effectively introducing a moral element into the practice of management. He identifies eight discernible characteristics of people whom, based on study, observation and personal experience, he would describe as 'principle-centred leaders'. These characteristics reflect many of the traits referred to in para. 6 above. They are as follows:

- Principle-centred leaders are continually learning – they read, listen, question, develop new skills and interests, for 'the more they know, the more they realise they don't know'.

- They are service-oriented – they think of others, they need to serve.

- They radiate positive energy – they are cheerful, pleasant, upbeat in their outlook.

- They believe in other people – they believe in the unseen potential of people, even when others are being negative or critical, and do not bear grudges.

- They lead balanced lives – they have wide interests, an active social life, are open in their communications, and can laugh at themselves; they are not extremists.

- They see life as an adventure – they live life to the full, and because they are secure in themselves, they look forward confidently to new experiences.

- They are synergistic – they tend to improve nearly every situation they get into, and act as catalysts in times of change; in negotiations they focus on optimum results for both sides rather than mere compromise.

- They exercise for self-renewal – they engage in activities that exercise emotional and spiritual dimensions as well as the physical and mental aspects.

20. Covey's principles are essentially aimed at improving one's *own* outlook and personal competency, rather than about how to manipulate other people and situations in order to attain goals. They are intended to encourage an entirely new way of seeing the managerial role. In the work situation Covey sees the principles of *trustworthiness, trust, empowerment* and *alignment* operating at four different levels:

- *personal* (the relationship with oneself, where trustworthiness is the key principle)

- *interpersonal* (interaction with others, where trust is the key principle)

- *managerial* (getting a job done with others, where empowerment is the key principle)

- *organisational* (building teams, developing structures, strategies and systems, where alignment is the key principle).

He argues that principle-centred leadership has to be grounded in all four levels. In other words the principles cannot be applied in a vacuum but have to be related to the people and tasks comprising the situation in which the leader has to operate. In the current conditions of downsizing, restructuring and delayering in many businesses and public-sector operations, people in leadership positions, according to Covey, are more likely to be successful if they adopt the principles he advocates. Covey's work on leadership further develops ideas introduced in his widely read text *The Seven Habits of Highly Effective People* (1992), which is referred to in Chapter 27.

Summary

21   A comparison between the various leadership theories is shown in Figure 7.6, which concludes this chapter.

Source	Title (if any)	Characteristics	Dimensions
D McGregor	Theory X/ Theory Y	authoritarian versus democratic	'either/or'
R Likert	Systems 1–4	authoritarian versus democratic	'either/or'
Tannenbaum & Schmidt	Leadership Continuum	authoritarian versus democratic	'either/or'
Michigan Studies	–	employee-centred v production-centred	'either/or'
Ohio Studies	–	'consideration' and 'initiating structure'	both
Blake & Mouton	Managerial Grid	'concern for people' and 'concern for production'	both
W Reddin	3-D Theory	relationships and task orientations; effectiveness	all three
Harvard Studies	–	'task leaders' vs 'socio-emotional leaders'	'either/or'
J Adair	Functional Theory	task, group and individual needs; adaptive behaviour	multiple
F E Fiedler	Theory of Leadership Effectiveness	'favourableness of the situation'; adaptive behaviour	multiple
S. Covey	Principle centred	adoption of key moral principles	multiple

Figure 7.6 Summary of leadership theories

References

1.   Handy, C. (1993), *Understanding Organisations* (3rd edition), Penguin.
2.   Tannenbaum, R. & Schmidt, W. (1958), 'How to Choose a Leadership Pattern', in *Harvard Business Review* (Mar/Apr).
3.   Likert, R. (1961), *New Patterns of Management*, McGraw-Hill.

4. Vroom, V. (1983), 'Leadership', in Dunnette, M. (ed.) *Handbook of Industrial and Organisational Psychology*, Wiley.
5. Blake, R. & Mouton, J. (1984), *The New Managerial Grid III*, Gulf Publishing.
6. Reddin, W. (1970), *Managerial Effectiveness*, McGraw-Hill.
7. Bales, R.F. (1951), *Interaction Process Analysis*, Addison-Wesley.
8. Adair, J. (1973), *Action-centred Leadership*, McGraw-Hill.
9. Fiedler, F. (1967), *A Theory of Leadership Effectiveness*, McGraw-Hill.
10. Covey, S. (1992) *Principle-Centred Leadership*, Simon & Schuster.

CHAPTER 8

Groups and Group Behaviour

Introduction

1. The study of groups in work situations has been an important activity of behavioural scientists ever since the pioneering work of the Hawthorne Researchers over fifty years ago. The outcome of numerous studies into different aspects of the behaviour of groups is a considerable store of useful and practicable knowledge about the working of groups. Typical areas of research have included the study of group effectiveness, inter-group competition, and group cohesiveness.

2. The most important factors in the behaviour of groups are as indicated in Figure 8.1.

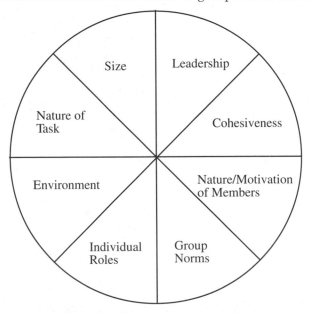

Figure 8.1 Key factors in group behaviour.

Previous chapters have dealt with various aspects of leadership, tasks and environment, and whilst these factors cannot be ignored, this chapter focuses attention on the other factors, such as group norms, group cohesiveness and roles within groups. It concludes with a summary of recent research into teams and team building.

3. Groups at work are formed as a direct consequence of an organisation's need to differentiate itself. Differentiation, or specialisation, involves not only the breaking down of the organisation into functions, but also the formation of groups to support the tasks assigned to those functions. A group is basically a collection of individuals, contributing to some common aim under the direction of a leader, and who share a sense of common identity. Thus, a group is more than an aimless crowd of people waiting in an airport lounge or at a busstop. A group has some central purpose, temporary or permanent, and a degree of self-awareness as a group. In the work situation, most tasks are in fact undertaken by groups and teams, rather than by individuals. Groups are also widely used for solving problems, creating new ideas, making decisions and coordinating tasks.

These group functions are what the organisation itself needs to fulfil its purpose. However, individuals themselves need groups. Groups provide stimulus, protection, assistance and other social and psychological requirements. Groups, therefore, can work in the interests of organisations as a whole as well as in the interests of individual members.

4. One of the earliest distinctions to be made between groups (arising from the Hawthorne investigations) was between formal and informal groups. Formal groups were those set up by the management of an organisation to undertake duties in the pursuit of organisation goals. Some writers have described formal groups as official groups, to avoid the confusion that can arise when describing groups operating in an informally structured organisation (eg an organic type of organisation). Such groups may be informal in the sense that they have few rules, enjoy participative leadership and have flexible roles. Nevertheless they are completely official. What is meant by informal organisations are those groupings which the employees themselves have developed in accordance with their own needs. These, of course, are unofficial. Every organisation has these unofficial groups, and research has shown how important they are for organisational effectiveness.

Group Norms & Group Cohesiveness

5. A useful way of looking at the development of groups was devised by B. Tuckman (1965)[1], who saw groups as moving through four key stages of development. Later (1977)[2] he added a fifth stage. The final model can be summarised as follows:

Stage 1 **Forming**. Finding out about the task, rules and methods; acquiring information and resources; relying on the leader.

Stage 2 **Storming**. Internal conflict develops; members resist the task at the emotional level.

Stage 3 **Norming**. Conflict is settled, cooperation develops; views are exchanged and new standards (norms) developed.

Stage 4 **Performing**. Teamwork is achieved, roles are flexible; solutions are found and implemented.

Stage 5 **Adjourning**. Group disperses on completion of tasks.

6. Group norms can be seen to develop at Stage 3 in the above analysis. Norms, in this context, are common standards of social and work behaviour which are expected of individuals in the group. Once such norms have been developed, there are strong pressures on people to conform to them. Norms are influenced by organisational factors such as policies, management style of superiors, and rules and procedures. They are also influenced by

individual employees, whose standards may or may not be in line with those of the official organisation. For example, a group norm for the young men in an engineering workshop could be to follow a fashion of wearing long hair. This could conflict with organisational norms concerning the safety of employees in the workplace. Another example of a conflict between official and unofficial group norms can be drawn from a situation where a group itself decides to operate a certain level of output over a given time, regardless of targets set by the management in their search for increased efficiency and productivity. The ideal situation, from an organisation's point of view, is attained when the *unofficial* norms of the group are in harmony with the *official* norms of the organisation. There is no doubt that part of the leadership role of a manager is to secure this harmony in his or her own section.

7.   Tuckman's analysis of group development can be compared with that of Woodcock (1979)[3,] who has made a particular study of teams and their development. Woodcock also sees a four-stage sequence of development as follows:

❶ The Undeveloped Team   Feelings are avoided, objectives are uncertain, the leader takes most of the decisions.

❷ The Experimenting Team   Issues are faced more openly, listening takes place, the group may become temporarily introspective.

❸ The Consolidating Team   Personal interaction is established on a cooperative basis, the task is clarified, objectives agreed and tentative procedures implemented.

❹ The Mature Team   Feelings are open, a wide range of options considered, working methods are methodical, leadership style is contributory, individuals are flexible and the group recognises its responsibility to the rest of the organisation.

8.   The key point made by these analyses of team or group development is that effectiveness (see below) is an outcome which develops over time, as the group begins to understand what is required of it and how it can utilise the knowledge, skills and attributes of the individual members in fulfilling group and individual goals. On the way to achieving effectiveness, groups will undoubtedly face uncertainty, if not conflict, but these processes have to be seen as necessary costs of achieving both harmony and purposeful behaviour.

9.   Group cohesiveness refers to the ability of the group members to stick together. It also applies to the ability of a group to attract new members. A very cohesive group will demonstrate strong loyalty to its individual members and strong adherence to its established norms. Individuals who cannot accept these norms are cast out from the protection of the group. The sending of individuals 'to Coventry' as a result of some dispute within the group is an example of this behaviour. As Tuckman's analysis shows, cohesiveness develops over time. A newly-formed group has little cohesiveness.

10. There are several factors which can help cohesiveness to develop in a group. These include the following:

• similarity of work

• physical proximity in the workplace

• the work-flow system

• structure of tasks

• group size (smaller rather than larger)

• threats from outside

- the prospect of rewards
- leadership style of the manager
- common social factors (age, race, social status etc)

In general, the reasons why people do develop into closely knit groups are threefold: because of those things they have in common, because of pressures from outside the group, and because of their need to fulfil their social and affiliation needs.

Group Effectiveness

11. Group effectiveness has to be considered in at least two dimensions – effectiveness in terms of task accomplishment, and effectiveness in terms of the satisfaction of group members. Clearly, the official organisation view of effectiveness is more concerned with output, efficiency and other benefits, than with satisfying the needs of individuals. By comparison, an individual's view of effectiveness is more concerned with personal success in his role and personal satisfaction from being a member of a team. Looking at the issue in ideal terms, effectiveness is achieved when the needs and expectations of the organisation are one and the same as those of individuals.

12. In his classic work, 'The Human Side of Enterprise' (1960), Douglas McGregor[4] provided a perceptive account of the differences between effective and ineffective groups. A summary of the most important features he noted appears below:

Effective groups	Ineffective groups
1. Informal, relaxed atmosphere.	1. Bored or tense atmosphere.
2. Much relevant discussion with high degree of participation.	2. Discussion dominated by one or two people, and often irrelevant.
3. Group task or objective clearly understood, and commitment to it obtained.	3. No clear common objective.
4. Members listen to each other.	4. Members tend not to listen to each other.
5. Conflict is not avoided, but brought into the open and dealt with constructively.	5. Conflict is either avoided or is allowed to develop into open warfare.
6. Most decisions are reached by general consensus with a minimum of formal voting.	6. Simple majorities are seen as sufficient basis for group decisions, which the minority have to accept.
7. Ideas are expressed freely and openly.	7. Personal feelings are kept hidden and criticism is embarrassing.
8. Leadership is not always with the chairman, but tends to be shared as appropriate.	8. Leadership is provided by chairman.
9. The group examines its own progress and behaviour.	9. The group avoids any discussion about its own behaviour.

McGregor's view of effective groups corresponds to Tuckman's Stages 3 and 4, ie Norming and Performing. The features of ineffective groups are closer to Tuckman's Stage 2, ie Storming. A difference between McGregor and Tuckman seems to be that the former sees some groups as fixed in their poor behaviour, whereas the latter implies that groups tend to move out of the ineffective stages into more effective behaviour.

13. The major influences on group effectiveness can be broken down into two main categories:

❶ Immediate constraints, eg group size, nature of task, skills of members, and environmental factors.

❷ Group motivation and interaction.

The basic difference between the two categories is that (1) represents *things that cannot be changed in the short-term*, and that (2) represents *behaviour that (potentially) can be changed in the short-term*. Let us now look at key points in each of these categories.

Immediate Constraints

14. There are four particularly influential constraints. These are as follows:

❶ Group size – small groups tend to be more cohesive than larger groups; small groups tend to encourage full participation; large groups contain greater diversity of talent.

❷ Nature of task – in work-groups, the production system, including the type of technology used, has a major effect on groups, eg high-technology plant often disperses employees into isolated couples incapable of forming satisfactory groups. Where group tasks are concerned with problem-solving, decision-making or creative thinking, different member talents may be required along with a variety of leadership styles. A further aspect of task is the time factor, ie urgency tends to force groups to be task and action-oriented.

❸ Membership – the personalities concerned, the variety of knowledge and skills available cannot be changed overnight. A knowledgeable group, skilled at group working, are much more likely to succeed in their tasks, than an inexperienced group. Equally a group with a wider range of talents in its midst tends to be more effective than a group with a narrow range of talents.

❹ Environmental factors – these include physical factors, such as working proximity, plant or office layout. In general, close proximity aids group identity and loyalty, and distance reduces them. Other environmental issues include the traditions of the organisation and leadership styles. Formal organisations tend to adopt formal group practices. Autocratic leadership styles prefer group activities to be directed. More participative styles prefer greater sharing in groups.

The important point about these immediate constraint is that they establish the scenario for the operation of the group. If the expectations and behaviour of the members match this scenario, then the group will tend to perform very effectively. By contrast, if there is a considerable mis-match, the chances of the group succeeding in its objectives will be slight.

Group Motivation and Interaction

15. Group motivation – the level of motivation in the group will be a decisive factor in effectiveness. High motivation can result from members' perception of the task, and their role in it, as being of importance. Standards of performance are essential to motivation, together with adequate and timely feedback of results. Individuals also need to feel satisfied with membership of the group. Where these features are absent, motivation will tend to be low.

16. Group interaction – this depends mainly on factors such as leadership, individual and group motivation, and appropriate rules and procedures. As we saw in the previous chapter on Leadership, the key to success in leadership is to obtain the best 'mix' of attention to task and attention to people, taking the total situation into account. The ability of the leader in a group to obtain the commitment of his team to achieving the task (team spirit) will result in a high degree of collaboration. Where interaction is high people tend to be more open, and more comfortable with the pursuit of the task. All groups need

some modus operandi. This might consist of a few simple rules and procedures to control decision-making and conflict, for example. Alternatively, as in formal committees, quite complex procedures may apply in order to encourage or control interaction.

17. The items discussed here are essentially about actual behaviour in a group. This behaviour is part of a dynamic, or constantly changing, process within the group, which can be influenced by individuals in response to issues that have occurred whilst undertaking the task. Thus, even where the immediate constraints impose tight restrictions on behaviour the group can still be effective if individuals can be motivated to work together to achieve their objectives.

Group Behaviour & Group Roles

18. An area of considerable interest to behavioural scientists for many years has been the process of interaction within groups. This area of study was first opened up by Professor Kurt Lewin in the United States in the mid 1940s with the use of so-called 'T-groups' as a device for the study of inter-personal relations within groups. The T-group approach is based on unstructured, leader-less groups whose 'task' is to study their own behaviour and provide feedback to individual group members. The emphasis in such groups is on the 'here and now' situation and the thoughts and feelings generated by it. Each group is aided by a tutor or consultant, whose task it is to help the group with the feedback aspects. As a basis for developing information about the working of groups, the T-group method has been immensely useful. As a practical training method, however, the approach has proved less than popular on account of the threats posed to individuals by the exposure of their beliefs, attitudes and feelings to people with whom they have to work.

19. Coverdale training is another approach aimed at throwing light on the behaviour of group members. The name is derived from the author of this approach, which is based on examining group processes during the progress of a series of practical tasks. Unlike T-groups, Coverdale exercises are structured events. Having discussed questions of how the initial task was planned and organised and how people felt about it, the experience is utilised to improve task effectiveness and member satisfaction for the next exercise, and so on until the series of tasks is completed. By using practical tasks as a vehicle for the real issue of assessing group interaction, much of the threatening nature of group process analysis disappears. Unlike in T-groups, the tutor, or trainer, plays a key role in briefing the group for its tasks and in directing the development of feedback by means of questions and comments at the end of each exercise.

20. Other approaches, designed to make people aware of their behaviour in groups, use questionnaires and rating scales to enable participants to record their feelings, perceptions and ideas about the group and its behaviour. Among such approaches is the Managerial Grid of Blake and Mouton, which is shown in Chapter 46.

21. One of the most useful attempts to develop categories of behaviour, especially verbal behaviour, in groups was that of R.F. Bales (1950)[5]. In several studies of small groups, Bales and his colleagues were able to generate a list of frequent behaviour categories to enable them to observe behaviour in a way that was relevant and consistent. Some examples of the categories were as follows:

- Shows solidarity
- Agrees
- Gives suggestion
- Gives opinion

- Asks for orientation
- Asks for suggestion
- Shows antagonism.

These categories were grouped according to whether they furthered the task functions or whether they aided inter-personal relations, or socio-emotional functions, as Bales called them.

22. Bales' ideas have been adapted by a number of British researchers, notably Rackham and Morgan (1977)[6], who have used their version as the basis for improving skills in inter-personal relationships. Their list utilises the following categories of possible behaviour in groups:

- Proposing (concepts, suggestions, actions)
- Building (developing another's proposal)
- Supporting (another person or his concepts)
- Disagreeing
- Defending/attacking
- Blocking/Difficulty stating (with no alternative offered)
- Open behaviour (risking ridicule and loss of status)
- Testing understanding
- Summarising
- Seeking information
- Giving information
- Shutting out behaviour (eg interrupting, talking over)
- Bringing in behaviour (involving another member).

Experience in the use of such categories can enable observers of group behaviour to give constructive and relevant feedback to group members, instead of rather generalised or anecdotal descriptions of what has appeared to have taken place.

23. Categories of behaviour are a key element in distinguishing roles in groups. Feedback to groups can help the members to see what kind of role they played in the proceedings. Role is not quite the same as position (or job). The latter is concerned with the duties and rights attached to a particular job title. The former is concerned with *how* the job is performed, and is affected by the expectations of superiors, of organisational policies, of colleagues and subordinates as well as the expectations of the job-holder himself. This web of relationships has been called the role-set.

24. In any group activity a number of roles are likely to be performed – for example, the roles of 'leader', 'peacemaker', 'ideas person', 'humorist' and 'devil's advocate' to name but a few. In informal groups roles may emerge in line with individual personality and know-how. In formal groups many roles are already defined, such as chairman, secretary, visiting expert and others. Sometimes members of a group experience a conflict of roles. For example, a union representative may feel a conflict between his or her need to fulfil a spokesman role for constituents, and the need to act responsibly as an employee of the company. Sometimes the chairman of a committee stands down temporarily from the chair in order to express a deeply felt personal view about an issue in which he or she has an interest. This action prevents undue role conflict on the question of impartiality from the chair.

25. Roles are influenced considerably by organisation cultures. In one organisation managers may be expected to take a directive style in the management of their subordinates. Anything in the form of participation would be viewed as weak management. In another organisation the dominant climate could well be democratic and participatory. In this kind of organisation a directive style would be seen as quite out-of-place. Some organisations operate different cultures in different departments. Production departments, for example, tend to be task-oriented and directive in style, whereas research and development departments tend to be more considerate of people's needs, and less directive.

Competition between Groups

26. So far we have been discussing behaviour *within* groups. Another important aspect of group behaviour is *intergroup* relations. Since every organisation is made up of a number of different groups of employees, the question of collaboration between groups is vital for obtaining an overall balance in the social system. As Lawrence and Lorsch were at pains to point out (see Chapter 10) integration is as crucial to organisational success as differentiation. Breaking an organisation down into smaller units (work groups), in order to cope adequately with the diversity of tasks that face it, creates opportunities to develop task interests and special know-how, but, at the same time it also creates rivalries and competing interests which can be damaging to the organisation's mission.

An understanding of the consequences, good and bad, of intergroup competition can, therefore, be of considerable help to an organisation's management.

27. The first systematic study of intergroup competition was made many years ago by Sherif and colleagues[7] in the United States. They organised a boys' camp in such a way that two deliberately-created groups were formed for the experiment. Various devices were used to encourage the development of separate identities between the two groups. As the camp progressed, a number of interesting changes took place both within and between the groups.

Within groups   Collections of individuals, with no special ties with each other, grew into closely-knit groups; the group climate changed from being play-oriented to work-oriented, and leadership tended to become more autocratic; each group became more highly structured and put a much greater emphasis on loyalty and conformity.

Between groups   Each group began to see the other group as 'the enemy', hostility between groups increased whilst communication between them decreased; stereotyped opinions of the other side began to emerge, especially negative stereotypes.

28. A further aspect of the Sherif study concerned the effects of winning or losing in an intergroup competition. This again provided some fascinating material for the researchers. Winning tended to maintain or even strengthen group cohesiveness, but reduced the motivation to fight; winning also caused a move away from task-orientation towards greater concern for individual needs. Losing tended to lead to a disintegration of the group, and the search for scapegoats both within and outside the group; tasks needs became even more important to the loser; losing, however, forced groups to re-evaluate their view of themselves and eventually come to a more realistic assessment of what changes were required to make the group effective.

29. Intergroup competition, as was noted above, has its advantages and disadvantages. The prime advantages are that a group develops a high level of cohesiveness and a high regard for its task functions. The main disadvantages are that groups develop competing or conflicting goals, and that intergroup communication and cooperation breaks down. Since the Sherif study, several researchers have followed up with studies of conflict resolution between groups. The general conclusions are that to reduce the negative side-effects of intergroup competition, an organisation would need to:

❶ encourage and reward groups on the basis of their contribution to the organisation as a whole, or at least, to large parts of it, rather than on individual group results;

❷ stimulate high interaction and communication between groups, and provide rewards for intergroup collaboration;

❸ encourage movement of staff across group boundaries for the purposes of increasing mutual understanding of problems; and

❹ avoid putting neighbouring groups into a situation where they are competing on a win-lose basis for resources or status, for example.

30. Not all conflict is harmful. On the contrary, disagreement is an essential element in working through problems and overcoming difficulties. The conflict of ideas when put to the service of organisation or group goals is in fact the sign of a healthy organisation. What is to be avoided is the point-scoring conflict that develops between groups who see their relative success and status vis-a-vis their neighbours as being more important than the pursuit of the common good.

Teams & Team-Building

31. A team, according to Adair (1986)[8], is more than just a group with a common aim. It is a group in which the contributions of individuals are seen as complementary. Collaboration, working together, is the keynote of a team activity. Adair suggests that the test of a good (ie effective) team is:

> 'whether ... its members can work as a team while they are apart, contributing to a sequence of activities rather than to a common task, which requires their presence in one place and at one time.'

What we have described in this chapter are the key variables that determine the relative effectiveness of groups in achieving their goals and satisfying the needs of their members. These variables have to be addressed if there is to be any chance of building a successful team.

32. What, then, are the characteristics of effective teamwork?

Research suggests that they are as follows:

- clear objectives and agreed goals
- openness and confrontation
- support and trust
- cooperation and conflict
- sound procedures
- appropriate leadership
- regular review
- individual development

- sound intergroup relations.

Adair emphasises the importance of careful selection of team members. They key factors here for individuals are not only technical or professional competence, but also the ability to work as a team member, and the possession of 'desirable personal attributes' such as willingness to listen, flexibility of outlook, and the capacity to give and accept trust.

33. Long-term research into management team-skills has been carried out by R.M. Belbin and colleagues (1981)[9]. The result showed that a manager's team behaviour fell into one or more of eight fairly distinct team roles, as follows:

• **Chairman**	An individual who can control and coordinate the other team members, who recognises their talents but is not threatened by them, and who is concerned with what is feasible rather than what is exciting or imaginative.
• **Shaper**	This is another leader role, but one in which the role-holder acts much more directly to shape the decisions and thinking of the team.
• **Innovator**	This type of person provides the creative thinking in a team, even if a concern for good ideas over-shadows his ability to be sensitive to other people's needs.
• **Monitor/Evaluator**	The strength of this role lies in the holder's ability to analyse issues and suggestions objectively.
• **Company Worker**	Whilst the first four roles provide the major inspiration and leadership, this role provides for implementation of ideas by the role-holders' ability to translate general ideas and plans into practice.
• **Team Worker**	This role meets the needs of the team for cohesiveness and collaboration, for role-holders tend to be perceptive of people's needs and adept at supporting individuals.
• **Resource Investigator**	A person in this role looks for resources and ideas outside the team with the aim of supporting the team's efforts.
• **Completer**	This is an individual whose energies are directly primarily to the completion of the task, and who harnesses anxiety and concern towards getting the job done on time and to a high standard.

34. Individual managers are likely to be predisposed to behaving in one predominant role, even though they may show tendencies towards others. The dominant role is closely linked to particular reasoning abilities and personality characteristics, but is also affected by the priorities and processes of a manager's job. An effective team is one that is likely to have a range of roles present in its make-up. Belbin concluded that the ideal team would be composed of one Chairman (or one Shaper), one Innovator, one Monitor Evaluator, and one or more Company Workers, Team Workers, Resource Investigators or Completers. Since ideal conditions are rarely present, managers have to build their teams from amongst the people they have, and encourage a greater degree of role flexibility. However, a

manager can benefit from understanding the distinctions between the roles and making an assessment of the role-strengths of his own staff. Knowing what to expect, as well as what *not* to expect, from colleagues enables the manager to head-off potential tensions or even group breakdown.

References

1. Tuckman, B. (1965), 'Developmental sequence in small groups', in *Psychological Bulletin*, 63.
2. Tuckman, B. & Jensen, N. (1977), 'Stages of Small Group development Revisited', in *Group and Organisational Studies* (Vol 2).
3. Woodcock, M. (1979), *Team Development Manual*, Gower.
4. McGregor, D. (1960), *The Human Side of Enterprise*, McGraw-Hill.
5. Bales, R. F. (1950), *Interaction Process Analysis*, Addison-Wesley.
6. Rackham, N. & Morgan, T. (1977), *Behaviour Analysis in Training*, McGraw-Hill.
7. Sherif, M. et al. (1961), *Intergroup Conflict and Cooperation – The Robbers' Cave Experiment*, University Book Exchange.
8. Adair, J. (1986), *Effective Teambuilding*, Gower.
9. Belbin, R.M. (1981), *Management Teams – Why they Succeed or Fail*, Butterworth Heinemann.

Questions for Discussion/Homework

1. Why is it unhelpful to talk of leadership in terms of qualities? What would supply a more practicable answer to the question 'what is leadership?'?
2. In what ways might the following influence a leader's style of leadership:
    a.   his or her subordinates?
    b.   the tasks to be performed? and
    c.   the situation?
3. What do you see as the advantages of Reddin's 3-D Theory over the Managerial Grid of Blake and Mouton?
4. Discuss the concept of 'dimensions of leadership' with reference to the work of McGregor, Likert, Reddin and the studies made by the researchers at Michigan and Ohio.
5. What are the most important factors to take into account when assessing the behaviour of groups in an industrial or commercial setting?
6. How are group norms established, and why are they sometimes in conflict with the norms of the organisation as a whole?
7. What roles would you expect to see played in:
    a.   effective groups?
    b.   ineffective groups?
8. What are the implication of Belbin's research for team development or team building?

Examination Questions

The following questions are selected for their relevance to this section, and, in some cases, to the section on classical theories as well. Outline answers can be found in Appendix 2.

EQ 9 The word leadership is sometimes used as if it were an attribute of personality, sometimes as if it were a characteristic of certain positions within an organisation, and sometimes as an aspect of behaviour. Discuss.

(ICSA MPP)

EQ 10 Discuss the evidence which suggests that in order to be effective, a manager can and should be flexible in the choice of his managerial style.

(ICMA OMM)

EQ 11 List the factors influencing effective teamwork. Take four of the factors and write a short paragraph on each.

(IOB Nature of Mgt.)

The dominance of first the Classical School and second the Human Relations/Social
Psychological Schools has been overtaken by a more comprehensive approach to the study
of management in organisations. This more recent approach views the organisation as a
system of interrelated sets of activities which enable inputs to be converted into outputs.
The approach, which is described in more detail below, enables theorists to study key
elements of organisation in terms of their interaction with one another and with their
external environment. Whereas, in the past, the explanations were in terms of structures or
people, now it is possible to identify theories which seek to explain or predict organisational behaviour in a multi-dimensional way by studying people, structure, technology and
environment at one and the same time.

The most recent formulations of systems theories tend to be labelled contingency theories
because they emphasise the need to take specific circumstances, or contingencies, into
account when devising appropriate organisational and management systems. Chapter 9
introduces the concept of 'systems' as applied to organisations, and describes some of the
major developments in the growth of systems theory while Chapter 10 summarises developments in contingency theories.

CHAPTER 9

Organisations as Systems

Introduction

1.   This chapter defines the characteristics of open social systems and summarises the
current theoretical position as a prelude to a discussion of the ideas of several outstanding
theorists who have contributed to the growing understanding of organisations as systems.

Definitions and Characteristics

2.   Put at its simplest, a system is a collection of interrelated parts which form some
whole. Typical systems are the solar system, the human body, communication networks
and social systems. Systems may be 'closed' or 'open'. Closed systems are those, which, for
all practical purposes, are completely self-supporting, and thus do not interact with their
environment. An example would be an astronaut's life-support pack. Open systems are
those which *do* interact with their environment, on which they rely for obtaining essential
inputs and for the discharge of their system outputs. Social systems (eg organisations) are
always open systems, as are biological systems and information systems. A basic model of
an open system can be shown diagrammatically as in Figure 9.1.

Figure 9.1 Basic model of an open system.

3.   The three major characteristics of open systems are as follows:

•   they receive inputs or energy from their environment

•   they convert these inputs into outputs

•   they discharge their outputs into their environment.

In relation to an organisation, the inputs include people, materials, information and finance. These inputs are organised and activated so as to convert human skills and raw materials into products, services and other outputs which are discharged into the environment, as shown in Figure 9.2.

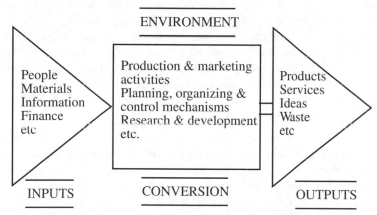

Figure 9.2 The organisation as an open system.

4.   A key feature of open systems is their interdependence on the environment, which may be relatively stable or relatively uncertain at a particular point in time. This feature is of considerable importance to business enterprises which need to adapt to the changing fortunes of the market place if they are to flourish. A classification of environments is given later in the chapter.

5.   Most systems can be divided into sub-systems. For example, the human body – a total system – encloses a number of major sub-systems, such as the central nervous system and the cardiovascular system, to name but two. Organisations have their sub-systems as well, eg production, marketing and accounting sub-systems. The boundaries between sub-systems are called interfaces. These are the sensitive internal boundaries contained within the total system, and they will be referred to again shortly. In the meantime it is important to consider a few points about system boundaries. An organisation's boundaries are defined as much by corporate strategy as by actual fact. This is not so for all systems, In physical or biological systems, the boundaries are there to be seen, and there is no problem distinguishing one motor vehicle, or one human being, from another, for example. In such systems it is also easy to identify boundaries between the total system and its sub-systems. For example, the gearbox of a motor vehicle is a clearly recognisable sub-unit of the whole vehicle. In the same way the cardiovascular system in the human body is a recognisable

sub-system of the whole body. These boundaries are matters of fact. For organisations the issue is not quite so straightforward.

6. The point is that the boundaries of an organisation are not visible, for the boundaries of a social system are based on *relationships* and not on things. Thus while certain factual elements, such as physical location, do have some impact on an organisation's boundaries, it is the results of management decisions, ie *choices*, that really determine where the organisation ends and the environment begins. Similarly, while the physical presence of machinery, for example, may partly determine some of the internal boundaries of the organisation, it is ultimately a matter of corporate, or departmental, strategy which decides where the production system begins and where it ends.

7. In any organisation, some employees work consistently at the *external* boundary. These are the people who have to deal with the inputs and the outputs to the system, eg those responsible for raising capital, purchasing from suppliers, identifying customer requirements etc and those responsible for sales, distribution etc. Other employees work consistently on *internal* boundaries, ie at the interfaces between the various sub-systems of the organisation. These people may be responsible for the provision of services to others in the organisation, eg management accountants, personnel officers, office service managers etc. They may be responsible for integrating activities, eg managers and supervisors. In fact, it is becoming increasingly recognised that *'boundary management'* is of vital importance to the effectiveness of those in managerial and supervisory roles. Boundary management in this context means establishing and maintaining effective relationships with colleagues working in neighbouring sub-systems.

8. Whilst organisations are open social systems, taken as a whole, their sub-systems may be either open or closed. Production sub-systems and accounting sub-systems tend to be closed systems, ie they are relatively self-contained and are affected in ways which are usually predictable. Marketing and R & D (research and development) activities tend, on the other hand, to work best in open systems ie where they can be aware of, and adapt to, key influences in the external environment. In the main, closed systems are required for stability and consistency, whereas open systems are required for unstable and uncertain conditions. Closed systems are designed for efficiency, open systems for survival. The early Classical theorists were expounding a closed systems approach. Developments in Human Relations, by contrast, were biased towards open systems. The modern consensus appears to be that both types are necessary for the maintenance and growth of successful organisations.

9. One of the most useful attempts to summarise the complexities of organisations as open systems has been that of the two American academics, Katz and Kahn (1966)[1]. They identified the common characteristics of such open systems as follows:

- Importation of energy and stimulation, eg people and material.

- Throughput or conversion eg the processing of materials and organising of work activities.

- Output, eg of products or services.

- Cyclic nature, eg the returns from marketing the output enable further inputs to be made to complete the cycle of production.

- Negative entropy. Entropy is the natural process by which all things tend to break down or die. Developing negative entropy means importing more energy etc than is required for output, and then storing it to enable survival in difficult times, eg firms building up their reserves.

- Feedback. Negative feedback, in particular, enables the system to correct deviations. Organisations tend to develop their own thermostats!

- Steady state. This refers to the balance to be maintained between inputs flowing in from the external environment and the corresponding outputs returning to it. An organisation in steady state is not static, but in a dynamic form of equilibrium.

- Differentiation; eg the tendency to greater specialisation of functions and multiplicity of roles.

- Equifinality. This word was coined by an early systems theorist, L. von Bertalanffy, in 1940. It means that open systems do not have to achieve their goals in one particular way. Similar ends can be achieved by different paths and from a different starting point.

10. The Katz and Kahn summary utilises a number of specialised systems terms (eg negative entropy and equifinality) which are beyond the scope of a general management text. What is important to grasp at this stage is that the input–conversion–output model, as shown in Figure 9.2, now needs to be expanded to take in the key factors of feedback and steady state. The result of including feedback from output to input is to produce a so-called *'closed loop'* system. A closed loop system is basically a self-regulating system, such as a thermostat in a heating system or, to take a business example, a budgetary control system in a departmental operating plan. In each case, information fed back to the input side of the system enables corrective changes to be made to keep the system on course, ie in a steady state. The revised model of the organisation as an open system can now be drawn as in Figure 9.3.

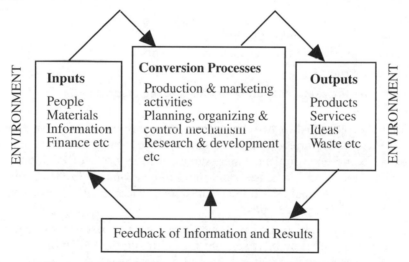

Figure 9.3 The basic cycle of the organisational system.

11. The revised model shows the consequences of the outputs as information and results. The information can take many forms, eg sales volumes, new orders, market share, customer complaints etc, and can be applied to control the inputs and conversion processes, as appropriate. The results are the revenues and profits which are fed back into the organisation to provide further inputs, and so ensure the survival and growth of the system. An adaptive system, such as the one described above, is sometimes referred to as a 'cybernetic' system. The term *'cybernetics'* in this context means the study of control and communication in the animal and the machine. Cybernetics was made famous by Norbert Wiener in the late 1940s, but is still very much a developing science. The essence of a

cybernetic system is self-regulation on the basis of feedback information to disclose a shortfall in performance against standards and to indicate corrective action.

Developments in Systems Theories

12. As we have seen in previous chapters, the dominant theories of organisations prior to the 1960s were (1) the classical/traditional school, who saw organisational design as a rational structure, or mechanism, which could be imposed on people, and (2) the human relations, or social psychological school, who saw organisations primarily in terms of the needs of the individuals in them. The theorists of human relations set out to humanise the workplace, and this they did, but at the expense of studying the organisation as a whole. They did not address themselves sufficiently to several major problems that can arise in practically every organisation, for example the problem of dealing with the tensions between the requirements for structure and the needs of people. Questions of conflict tended to be dealt with in terms of avoiding it by attention to motivation and leadership. A further difficulty in the human relations approach was its emphasis on the practical application of ideas rather than on the conceptual development of organisational theory. This is not to deny the usefulness, to practising managers in particular, of the propositions of human relations, but it suggests the need to look elsewhere for a fuller explanation of behaviour in organisations.

13. This is where we have to turn to theorists who see organisations as complex social systems, responsive to a number of interdependent and important variables. The key variables that are of greatest interest to those adopting a systems approach to organisations are as follows:

- People – as individuals and in groups
- Technology – in terms of the technical requirements of work
- Organisation structures
- Environment – the external conditions affecting the organisation

Whereas earlier theorists looked at individual variables in isolation, the theorists of systems study the relationship between two or more of them. Initially, the Tavistock researchers, for example, looked at the relationships between people and technology, and between structure and environment. Later studies, such as those of Pugh and colleagues, have developed a more comprehensive and multi-dimensional approach, utilising all the above variables. The principal developments in systems theories of organisation design are discussed in the following paragraphs.

14. The researches, so far, have indicated that there is no one best way of designing organisations to meet their current objectives. On the contrary, the evidence seems to suggest that the variables are so volatile that only a 'contingency' approach can prove practicable. This suggests that organisations can only be made viable when steps are taken to adapt them to a particular set of prevailing conditions. Naturally, this approach appeals more to theorists than practising managers, who must feel daunted by the need to be eternally adaptive. Nevertheless, it offers the best prospect to date of achieving the optimum organisation design. Before looking at contingency approaches it is necessary to describe some of the earlier contributions to systems theory as applied to organisations, commencing with the Tavistock researchers.

The Tavistock Group

15. The Tavistock Institute of Human Relations in London has been engaged in various forms of social research for over fifty years. Despite its title, the Institute has made its reputation for its contribution to *systems* theory. In particular, Trist and Bamforth introduced the concept of *'socio-technical' systems* (1951)[2] and A.K. Rice and F.E. Emery promoted several important ideas relating to open-systems theory and types of environment.

16. The Trist and Bamforth studies into changes in the method of extracting coal in British pits took place in the 1940s. The researchers were interested in the effects of mechanisation on the social and work organisation at the coal-face. Before mechanisation, the coal had been extracted by small, closely knit teams working as autonomous groups. They worked at their own pace, often isolated in the dark from other groups. Bonds established within groups became important outside work as well as during the shift. Conflicts between competing groups were frequent and sometimes violent, but were always contained. This was the system which operated before the coal-cutters and mechanical conveyors were introduced. It was called the *shortwall method*.

17. The mechanised coal-face was completely different. It consisted of a long wall which required not small groups, but groups of between forty and fifty men plus their supervisors. These men could be spread out over 200 yards, and they worked in a three shift system. The new system, known as the *longwall method*, was essentially a mass-production system based on a high degree of job specialisation. Under the former shortwall method, each team had provided all the skills required, but in the longwall arrangement the basic operations were separated between the shifts. So, for example, if the first shift cut the coal from the face, the second shift shovelled it into the conveyor, and the third shift advanced the coal-face along the seam. Even within each shift, there was a high degree of task specialisation.

18. The social consequences of the new method, arising from the breakdown of the previously closely-integrated social structure were: increased haggling over pay, inter-shift competition for the best jobs, the seeking of scapegoats in other shifts, and a noticeable increase in absenteeism. The results of the radical change in working methods and the miners' adverse response to them, led Trist and Bamforth to the conclusion that effective work was a function of the *inter*dependence of technology (equipment, physical layout and task requirements) and social needs (especially relationships within groups). It was not sufficient to regard the working environment as *either* a technical system *or* a social system. It was a combination of the two: a *socio-technical system*.

19. Eventually a so-called *'composite longwall method'* was developed which enabled the needs of the social system to be met, whilst at the same time utilising the benefits of the new mechanised equipment (the technical system). Tasks and working arrangements were altered so that the basic operations could be carried out by any one shift, and so that tasks within each group were allocated by the members. Payment was changed so as to incorporate a group bonus. The outcome of the composite methods was increased productivity, reduced absenteeism and a lower accident rate.

20. Alongside the coal-mining studies mentioned above, the reputation of the Tavistock group was also assured by A.K. Rice's (1958)[3] studies into the calico mills at Ahmedabad, India. In his book Rice elaborated on key aspects of systems theory as applied to organisations, two of which are selected for inclusion here: his concept of systems, and his views on work design.

21. Rice saw any industrial system (eg a firm) as an open system, importing various items from its environment, converting them into goods, services and waste materials, and then exporting them into the environment. Within the total system of the firm, he suggested, there existed two main systems: an operating system and a managing system. The operating system deals with the import, conversion and export of the product or service, while the managing system deals with the control, decision-making and communication aspects of the total system. Each system can have one or more sub-systems, which is why it is necessary to develop the managing system, so as to coordinate the interaction of all the systems and sub-systems.

22. Rice's view of systems can be compared usefully with those of Handy (1993)[4], writing some years later. Handy describes and comments on, not only the operating system but also the *adaptive, maintenance and information systems* in activating the various parts of the total organisation. It is these last three which come closest to making up the managing system formulated by Rice. On balance, the more modern analysis is the clearer of the two in helping to establish the prime focal points of the managing system.

23. The studies at Ahmedabad produced, among other things, some interesting conclusions about the design of work. These can be summarised as follows:

- Effective performance of a primary task is an important source of satisfaction at all levels of work.
- The capacity for voluntary cooperation is more extensive than is often expected.
- There is great benefit in allowing individuals to complete a whole task.
- Work groups of eight seem to have the best chance of success for achieving group tasks.
- There is a clear relationship between work effectiveness and social relations.
- Where group autonomy has been established, unnecessary interference by supervisors will be counter-productive.

24. The above findings have been incorporated into current ideas on the design and re-design of work, so as to meet social and psychological needs of employees as well as the requirements of changing technology. They also share much common ground with Herzberg's ideas of motivation and job enrichment.

25. The final example of the work of the Tavistock Group relates to another key factor in systems theory – the nature of the environment. Emery and Trist (1965)[5] were the first to produce a classification of environments. They described four types of environment as follows:

❶ **Placid, randomised.** This represents a relatively unchanging and homogeneous environment, whose demands are randomly distributed.

❷ **Placid, clustered.** This environment too, is relatively unchanging, but its threats and rewards are clustered. So, for example, in a monopoly situation an organisation's failure or success depends on its continued hold over the market.

❸ **Disturbed, reactive.** In this environment there is competition between organisations, and this may include hindering tactics.

❹ **Turbulent field.** This describes a dynamic and rapidly changing environment, in which organisations must adapt frequently in order to survive.

26. Emery and Trist were particularly interested in the last type, the turbulent field. This is an area where existing formal, or bureaucratised, structures are ill-suited to deal with their

environment. According to the writers, more and more environments are becoming turbulent, and yet organisation structures are not becoming correspondingly flexible. This important point is referred to in the next chapter – see the summary of the 'mechanistic-organic structures' concept introduced by Burns and Stalker (1961)[6].

27. The field of management and organisation theory has been poorly served, in general, by British writers and theorists. The outstanding exception to this situation has been the work of the Tavistock Group, whose contribution to our understanding of organisations as open social systems has been fundamental and worldwide.

Katz & Kahn

28. Reference was made to these two researchers earlier. Their view of organisations has had a considerable influence on the developments of systems approaches to organisation theory. Katz and Kahn saw social structures as essentially contrived systems, where the forces that hold them together are psychological rather than biological. Social systems are seen to be more variable than biological systems and are more difficult to study because they have no easily recognisable boundaries. They have a structure, but it is *a structure of events* rather than of physical parts. Nevertheless Katz and Kahn set out to describe their view of social systems and their related sub-systems. They followed similar lines to Rice in advocating an open system approach, in which they identified five sub-systems at work in organisations.

29. The five sub-systems they identified can be summarised as follows:

❶ **Production or Technical sub-systems.** These are concerned with the accomplishment of the basic tasks of the organisation (production of goods, provision of services etc).

❷ **Supportive sub-systems.** These are the systems which procure the inputs and dispose of the outputs of the production sub-system. They also maintain the relationship between the organisation as a whole and the external environment.

❸ **Maintenance sub-systems.** These are concerned with the relative stability or predictability of the organisation. They provide for the roles, the rules and the rewards applicable to those who work in the organisation.

❹ **Adaptive sub-systems.** The first three systems above serve the organisation as it is. The adaptive sub-systems by comparison are concerned with what the organisation might become. They deal with issues of change in the environment, eg as in marketing, and research and development.

❺ **Managerial Sub-systems.** These comprise the controlling and coordinating activities of the total system. They deal with the coordination of substructures, the resolution of conflict, and the coordination of external requirements with the organisation's resources. An important managerial sub-system is the authority structure which describes the way the managerial system is organised for the purposes of decision-making and decision-taking.

30. Other key features of social organisations, according to Katz and Kahn, are roles, norms and values. Roles differentiate one position from another, and require a standardised form of behaviour. The network of roles constitutes the formal structure of the organisation, and the formalised role system. Roles limit the effects of the incumbent's personality on performance in the position. This idea is very much in line with Weber's view of the rational, and impersonal, conduct of an office. In fact, Katz and Kahn describe bureaucratic structures as the clearest examples of their definition of social organisation.

31. While roles help to differentiate the activities of the organisation, norms and values help to integrate behaviour. Norms, or standards of behaviour, are closely associated with roles, because they specify role behaviour in terms of expected standards. For example, an office manager would be expected to conform to certain norms relating to dress, time-keeping and honesty, to name but three responsibilities. Values are more generally held beliefs; they represent the ideology of the organisation – 'its culture' (see Chapter 13). Loyalty to the organisation is an example of a value.

32. Katz and Kahn have provided us with a useful way of looking at organisations as systems. Their descriptions of the major sub-systems of organisation, together with the pattern of roles which are inextricably linked with them, represent an important step forward in understanding the complexities of the nature of organisations.

References

1. Katz, D. & Kahn, R.L. (1966), *The Social Psychology of Organisations*, Wiley.
2. Trist, E.L. & Bamforth, K. (1951), 'Some Social and Psychological Consequences of the Longwall Method of Coal-getting', in *Human Relations*, Vol 4. No 1.
3. Rice, A.K.(1958), *Productivity and Social Organisation*, Tavistock.
4. Handy, C. (1993), *Understanding Organisations* (3rd edition), Penguin.
5. Emery, F.E. & Trist, E.L (1965), 'The Causal Texture of Organisational Environments', in *Human Relations*, Vol. 18, No. 1.
6. Burns, T. & Stalker, G. M. (1961), *The Management of Innovation*, Tavistock.

CHAPTER 10

Contingency Approaches to Management

Introduction

1. There is no clear distinction between the systems approach and the contingency approach to the management of organisations. The latter has developed out of the findings of the former. A systems approach highlights the complexity of the interdependent components of organisations within equally complex environments. A contingency approach builds on the diagnostic qualities of the systems approach in order to determine the most appropriate organisational design and management style for a given set of circumstances. Essentially the contingency approach suggests that issues of design and style depend on choosing what is the best combination, in the light of prevailing (or forecast) conditions, of the following variables: (a) the external environment, (b) technological factors, and (c) human skills and motivation.

2. The label 'contingency approach' was suggested by two American academics, Lawrence and Lorsch (1967)[1]. Their important contribution to this approach will be summarised shortly. Other writers referred to in this chapter, and who have adopted a contingency approach, are British: Joan Woodward is noted for her important studies into

the effects of technology on structure and performance; Burns and Stalker introduced the concept of mechanistic and organic types of structure and discussed them in relation to the environment; finally, the so-called Aston group (Pugh, Hickson et al.) have made some interesting studies into several of the technology-structure variables in organisations.

3.   Unlike the Classical and Human Relations approaches to the management of organisations, the contingency approach does not seek to produce universal prescriptions or principles of behaviour. It deals in relativities, not absolutes. It is essentially a situational approach to management. The contingency approach does not turn its face against earlier approaches, but adapts them as part of a 'mix' which could be applied to an organisation in a particular set of circumstances. The following paragraphs look at several important research studies which have dealt with two or more elements of this 'organisational mix'.

Lawrence & Lorsch

4.   These two Harvard researchers set out to answer the question what kind of organisation does it take to deal with various economic and market conditions. They were concerned, therefore, with structure and environment as the two key variables in their study. Initially Lawrence and his colleague studied the internal functioning of six plastics firms operating in a diverse and dynamic environment. The results in these six firms were then compared with two standardised container firms operating in a very stable environment, and two firms in the packaged food industry, where the rate of change was moderate.

5.   The major emphasis of their study was on the states of differentiation and integration in organisations. Differentiation was defined as more than mere division of labour or specialisation. It also referred to the differences in attitude and behaviour of the managers concerned. These differences were looked at in terms of:

- their orientation towards particular goals, eg issues of cost reduction are more important to production managers than to sales or research managers.

- their time orientation, eg sales and production managers have short-term orientations while research managers have long-term orientations.

- their interpersonal orientation, eg production managers tend to be less relationship-oriented than sales managers.

- the relative formality of the structure of their functional units, eg the highly formalised production departments with their many levels, narrow span of control and routine procedures as contrasted with the relatively informal and flat structures of the research departments.

6.   Integration was defined as the quality of the state of collaboration that exists among departments. It was seen to be more than a mere rational or mechanical process, as in the Classical approach. Integration was a question of interrelationships, in the final analysis, said Lawrence and Lorsch. Inevitably the differences of attitude referred to in paragraph 5 above would lead to frequent conflicts about what direction to take. These conflicts were not catered for adequately in the Classical theories. A key interest of the two researchers, therefore, was to assess the way conflict was controlled in organisations.

7.   In approaching their studies, Lawrence and Lorsch took the view that there was probably no one best way to organise. What they could hope for was to provide a systematic understanding of what states of differentiation and integration are related to effective performance under different environmental conditions.

8.   Effective performance was judged in terms of the following criteria:

- change in profits over the past five years,
- change in sales volume over the same period,
- new products introduced over the period as a percentage of current sales.

As it turned out, the firms selected for study encompassed a range of performance from high through medium to low performance when set against the chosen criteria.

9. The main conclusions that Lawrence and Lorsch arrived at were as follows:

- The more dynamic and diverse the environment, the higher the degree of both differentiation and integration required for successful organisation.
- Less changeable environments require a lesser degree of differentiation, but still require a high degree of integration.
- The more differentiated an organisation, the more difficult it is to resolve conflict.
- High-performing organisations tend to develop better ways of resolving conflict than their less effective competitors. Improved ways of conflict resolution lead to states of differentiation and integration that are appropriate for the environment.
- Where the environment is uncertain, the integrating functions tend to be carried out by middle and low-level managers; where the environment is stable, integration tends to be achieved at the top end of the management hierarchy.

10. The research referred to above was based on a very small sample of firms, it relied on some rather subjective information, and several of the measures employed have been criticised as unreliable by subsequent researchers. Despite the criticisms, the Lawrence and Lorsch study represented a most important step forward in the search for a theory of organisations that could take account of the major variables affecting the structure of successful organisations.

Burns & Stalker

11. Another famous study of the environment-structure relationship was conducted by Burns and Stalker during the 1950s in Scotland and England. Some twenty firms in the electronics industry were studied from the point of view of how they adapted themselves to deal with changing market and technical conditions, having been organised to handle relatively stable conditions. The findings were written up in 'The Management of Innovation' published in 1961[2].

12. The researchers were particularly interested in how management systems might change in response to the demands of a rapidly changing external environment. As a result of their studies, they came up with two distinctive 'ideal types' of management system: *mechanistic* systems and *organic* systems. The key features of both systems are summarised below.

13. Mechanistic systems are appropriate for conditions of stability. Their outstanding features are as follows:

1. a specialised differentiation of tasks, pursued more or less in their own right,
2. a precise definition of rights, obligations and technical methods of each functional role,
3. an hierarchical structure of control, authority and communication,
4. a tendency for vertical interaction between members of the concern,
5. a tendency for operations and working behaviour to be dominated by superiors,
6. an insistence on loyalty to the organisation and obedience to superiors.

14. By contrast, organic systems are appropriate for conditions of change. Their outstanding features can be summarised as follows:

❶ individual tasks, which are relevant to the total situation of the concern, are adjusted and re-defined through interaction with others,

❷ a network structure of control, authority and communication, where knowledge of technical or commercial aspects of tasks may be located anywhere in the network,

❸ a lateral rather than vertical direction of communication through the organisation,

❹ communications consist of information and advice rather than instructions and decisions,

❺ commitment to the organisation's tasks seen to be more important than loyalty and obedience.

15. Burns and Stalker did not see the two systems as being complete opposites, but as polar positions between which intermediate forms could exist. They also acknowledged that firms could well move from one system to the other as external conditions changed, and that some concerns could operate with both systems at once. They stressed that they did not favour one or other system. What was important was to achieve the most appropriate system for a given set of circumstances – a perfect expression of the contingency approach!

16. The Burns and Stalker study was influential in the design of the Lawrence and Lorsch study mentioned earlier. Clearly, mechanistic systems are closely related to considerations of states of differentiation, and organic systems have much in common with the concept of integration. It is interesting to note, however, that whereas Burns and Stalker see organic systems as being more appropriate to changing conditions than mechanistic ones, their American counterparts see *both* systems as crucial to coping with diversity. The more dynamic and diverse the environment, the higher the degree of both differentiation and integration, say the Americans. Differentiation involves several of the features of the mechanistic systems, which Burns and Stalker see as being ill-adapted to conditions of change. This points to one of the major criticisms made against the mechanistic versus organic approach – it assumes that change can best be effected by organic types of structure, when this is not at all certain. Large organisations, however great their commitment to delegation, involvement and communication between groups, have to maintain a high degree of structure and formality, even when confronted by periods of change.

Joan Woodward

17. The Woodward studies[3], conducted by a small research team from the South East Essex College of Technology during the period 1953–1958, were initially aimed at assessing the extent to which classical management principles were being put into practice by manufacturing firms in the area, and with what success. Information on various aspects of formal organisation was collected from 100 firms. About half the firms had made some conscious attempt to plan their organisation, but there was little uniformity. In terms of structure, for example, the number of levels of management varied between two and twelve, and spans of control (the number of persons directly supervised by one superior) ranged from ten to ninety for first-line supervisors. The conclusions drawn by the team were that there was little in common amongst the most successful firms studied, and there was certainly no indication that classical management principles were any more likely to lead to success than other forms of organisation. At the time this was considered to be rather disconcerting, given the popularity of classical ideas.

18. Having had no positive conclusions from the first part of their studies, Woodward's team turned their attention to the technological data they had collected. The question they posed was as follows: is there any relationship between organisational characteristics and technology? In attempting to answer this question, the team made a lasting contribution to the theory of organisations by establishing the key role of technology as a major variable affecting organisation structures.

19. Their first step was to find some suitable form of classification to distinguish between the different categories of technology employed by the firms concerned. Three main categories were eventually selected as follows:

❶ Unit and Small Batch Production. This included custom made products, the production of prototypes, large fabrications undertaken in stages, and the production of small batches.

❷ Large Batch and Mass Production. This encompassed the production of large batches, including assembly-line production, and mass production.

❸ Process Production. This included the intermittent production of chemicals in multi-purpose plant, as well as the continuous flow production of liquids, gases and crystalline substances.

20. When the firms in the study were allocated to their appropriate categories, and then compared by their organisation and operations, some discernible patterns began to emerge. For example, it was seen that process industries tended to utilise more delegation and decentralisation than large-batch and mass production industries. This was just one aspect of the link between technology and organisation structure. Others included the following:

- the more complex the process, the greater was the chain of command, ie there were more levels of management in the process industries than in the other two categories.

- the span of control of chief executives increased with technical complexity ie the number of people directly responsible to the chief executive was lowest in unit/ small-batch production firms and highest in process production.

- by contrast with the point above, the span of middle management decreased with technical complexity, ie fewer people reported to middle managers in process production than in large-batch/mass production firms, who in turn had fewer people than in unit/small-batch production.

21. As well as the differences mentioned above, there were also some interesting similarities. For example:

- the average number of workers controlled by first-line supervisors was similar for both unit/small-batch and process production – and these were noticeably fewer in number than for mass production situations.

- another similarity between unit/small-batch and process production was that they both employed proportionately more skilled workers than mass production categories.

- Woodward's team also found that firms at the extremes of the technical range tended to adopt organic systems of management, whereas firms in the middle of the range, notably the large-batch/mass production firms, tended to adopt mechanistic systems.

22. Having established some definite links between organisational characteristics and technology, Woodward's team turned their attention to the relationship, if any, between these two factors and the degree of business success (profitability, growth, cost reductions achieved etc). What they found was that the successful firms in each category were those whose organisational characteristics tended to cluster around the median figures for their

particular category. So, for example, a process production firm would be better served by a taller, narrower structure backed up by an organic system of management rather than by a flatter, broader structure operated mechanistically. On the other hand, a mass-production firm would appear to benefit from a flatter, broader structure, operated in a mechanistic way. Firms in either category which did not have their appropriate characteristics would tend to produce less than average results.

23. Woodward concluded that the predominance given to the Classical theorists, especially in respect of the application of their ideas in practice (span of control, unity of command, definition of duties etc), only made sense when seen in terms of large-batch/mass production processes. Classical ideas did not seem appropriate for other categories of production. Her researches strongly suggested that not only was the system of production a key variable in determining structure, but that also there was a particular form of organisation which was most suited to each system.

24. This contingency approach is very much in line with the conclusions reached by Lawrence and Lorsch. Woodward's conclusions also confirm the criticism of the Burns and Stalker study which has been made previously (see para. 16 above). From her studies it would seem that mass production firms could not cope successfully with change if they adopted an organic system, ie an inappropriate system, according to her evidence.

The Aston Group

25. The so-called Aston group – Pugh, Hickson and others – now dispersed, but originally at the University of Aston, Birmingham, began a major study into various aspects of structure, technology and environment in the late 1960s. Unlike the earlier studies of Woodward and Trist and Bamforth, for example, which did not break technology down into more than one variable, the Aston study attempted to discern the basic elements of technology by gathering data on several possible dimensions. These included features such as operating variability, workflow integration and line control of the workflow. Many of the results of the Aston study did not accord with those of the Woodward studies. One explanation put forward was that the Woodward studies were conducted into mainly smaller firms, while the Aston study had included several large companies. This was significant because Pugh and his colleagues had concluded that the impact of technology on organisation structure must be related to size. In small organisations they said, technology will be critical to structure, but in large organisations other variables will tend to confine the impact of technology to the basic operating levels.

26. The importance of the Aston group is that they have adopted a multi-dimensional approach to organisational and contextual variables, ie they have attempted to develop the idea of an 'organisational mix' which can be applied to an organisation at a particular point in time in order to achieve successful results. This essentially contingency approach has provided the basis for further research into what represents the ideal structure for an organisation in the light of a particular grouping of circumstances.

27. The Aston study[4] distinguished six primary variables of *structure* and considered them against a number of *contextual* variables. The structural variables were as follows:

1 Specialisation (of functions and roles).

2 Standardisation (of procedures and methods).

3 Standardisation of employment practices.

4 Formalisation (extent of written rules, procedures etc).

5 Centralisation (concentration of authority).

6 Configuration (shape of organisation).

These variables were considered in a number of different contexts including the following:

1 Origin and history.

2 Ownership (owner-managers, shareholders, parent company etc).

3 Size of organisation.

4 Charter (ie number and range of goods/services).

5 Technological features (in several dimensions).

6 Interdependence (balance of dependence between the organisation and customers, suppliers, trade unions etc).

28. Among the conclusions reached by the Aston team was the relevance of size to the structural variables. As an organisation grows beyond the stage at which it can be controlled by personal interaction, it has to be more explicitly structured. Larger size tends to lead to:

1 more specialisation,

2 more standardisation,

3 more formalisation but

4 less centralisation.

Overall, the conclusion of the researchers was that it was possible to predict fairly closely the structural profile of an organisation on the basis of information obtained about the contextual variables.

Conclusion

29. The table below (Figure 10.1) summarises the principal systems and contingency approaches to organisation and management theory. The dates refer to the first publication of the relevant theory or research report.

Date	Research/theory	Theorist(s)
1951	Socio-technical systems	Trist & Bamforth
1958	Open systems/work design	A.K. Rice
1961	Mechanistic/Organic management systems. Environment and structure	Burns & Stalker
1965	Technology and structure	Woodward
1965	Types of environments	Emery & Trist
1966	Systems approach to organisations	Katz & Kahn
1967	Environment and structure. Contingency theory of organisations	Lawrence & Lorsch
1968/9	Environment, technology and structure – multi-dimensional approach	Pugh, Hickson and others

Figure 10.1

References

1. Lawrence, P.R. & Lorsch, J.W. (1967), *Organisation and Environment*, Harvard University Press.
2. Burns, T. & Stalker, G.M. (1961), *The Management of Innovation*, Tavistock.
3. Woodward, J. (1965), *Industrial Organisation – Theory and Practice*, OUP.
4. Pugh, D.S. & Hickson, D.J. (1976), *Organisational Structure in its Context: The Aston Programme I*, Gower Publishing.

Questions for Discussion/Homework

1. What are the major differences, in each case, between the approach of the systems theorists and those of (a) the Classical theorists, and (b) the Human Relations theorists?

2. Why are 'open ' systems so called ?

3. What sub-systems do you see in the organisation in which you work or study? Are these sub-systems open or closed?

4. What are the essential elements of a socio-technical system?

5. In what ways is the concept of 'integration' important for organisations?

6. How would you summarise the principal contributions to organisation and management theory of:

   a.   Joan Woodward's Essex studies and

   b.   The Burns and Stalker studies?

7. In what ways could the Aston group's study be said to have furthered understanding about the analysis of organisations?

Examination Questions

Questions relating to this section appear to be growing increasingly popular with examiners. A representative sample across a wide range of examining bodies is included below. Outline answers may be found in Appendix 2.

EQ 12 Discuss the major features and significance of ... the coal-mining research of the Tavistock Institute in the 1940s in Britain.

(ACCA—part of an either/or question)

EQ 13 'There is no one best way of designing an organisation!' Discuss.

(IOB Nature of Management)

EQ 14 Comment on the contingency approach to organisation structures.

(IAM POC)

EQ 15 Identify the principal factors that might influence the design of the structure of an organisation.

(ICMA OMM)

EQ 16 a. What are the main features of a bureaucratic organisation?

   b. How effectively do bureaucratic organisations respond to changing circumstances in the environment?

(ICSA MPP)

Part One ends with a single short chapter which outlines a number of key issues facing modern organisations, and identifies a selection of the theorists who are helping practising managers address these issues. All the issues referred to are dealt with in various chapters throughout the rest of the book.

CHAPTER 11

Modern Approaches to Management

Introduction

1.   Interest in the management of organisations is as lively at the beginning of the twenty-first century as it was over the previous seventy years. The search for better and more efficient ways of utilising people's knowledge and skills in providing goods and services has never been stronger. The desire to understand the external world of the organisation, and to learn how best to cope with change in the environment is as challenging now as it ever was. The appreciation of the importance of human skills, ingenuity and motivation has grown, not diminished, with the arrival of new technologies. Micro-electronic technology itself is transforming possibilities for Third World businesses to compete more competitively with businesses in the developed nations. What, perhaps, has changed is the recognition that there will be an increasing international and multicultural dimension to both large and smaller business corporations, as they seek to find skilled labour or low-cost production facilities. The global economy is not too far away, as the various regional groupings begin to develop their own infrastructure, as in the European Union and the Asia-Pacific Rim.

2.   This short chapter summarises some of the current issues for management at the start of the new millennium, and identifies leading exponents of management theory whose ideas over the past quarter century have led us to the present position. The work of these theorists will be discussed in more detail in subsequent chapters.

The Background to Modern Management

3.   The strategic importance of management to national economies has grown considerably over the last quarter of a century. This is largely on account of the increasing demands for higher living standards among national populations, together with a desire amongst developing economies to trade on more equal terms with their well-established counterparts in Europe, Japan and the North American continent. The principal factors involved in these changes include:

•   the rapid advance of micro-electronic technology, which has revolutionised many of the processes by which goods and services are made available to customers

- the increased ability of firms to compete with each other due to the benefits of new technology and a sufficiency of trained labour
- the entry into world markets of new low-cost manufacturing firms from Asian countries who are successfully challenging established Western firms
- the increased expectations of customers for quality and variety in consumer goods and personal services
- the massive improvements in world-wide communication systems, especially the development of the Internet, leading to better and more timely information for buyers, sellers and middlemen/agents
- the greater inter-connectedness of the world's peoples due to increased trade and cultural contact (eg via tourism and the Internet), and by growth in air travel and transportation

4.   The respected American economist, Lester Thurow (1998)[1], suggests that all industrial nations are now seeking market share in essentially the same range of industries. These include micro-electronics, bio-technology, computers, telecommunications, civil aviation, robotics, machine tools and software. No longer are nations thinking in terms of their dominant former industries, such as farming, oil production, shipbuilding and heavy chemicals. In this new age, Thurow sees competitive advantage springing primarily from the knowledge and skills of the workforce.

5.   What issues are raised for business organisations by this expanding economic activity throughout the globe? The following are issues that have been identified in management theories promoted during the latter part of the last century:

- the importance of establishing a vision, or mission, for the organisation
- the clarification of organisational purpose and goals
- the development of shared values in the organisation (ie 'culture')
- the continuing need for leadership that can see beyond the bounds of what is, to what might be
- the development of organisation structures that permit flexibility of action, but with relative stable core systems
- the development of multi-skilled employees with relevant knowledge, skills and competence
- the optimisation of employee contribution through job challenge and empowerment
- the continuing need to anticipate changes in the external environment – customers, competitors, suppliers, technological, economic and political trends
- the improvement of internal communication and decision-making channels
- the use of new technology to communicate more effectively with markets and individual customers
- the management of change in and about the organisation
- the development of standards of excellence throughout the organisation
- the development of a global strategy in the light of international trade
- the need to balance global control and universal standards with the culture and practices of the local business unit.

6.   In diagrammatic form, the above issues can be seen in relation to each other, as in Figure 11.1:

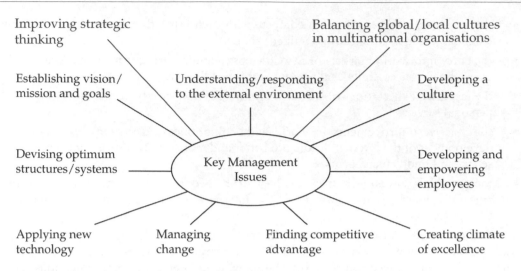

Figure 11.1 Key management issues – 1970 to 2000.

7.   Of course, a diagram as in Figure 11.1 over-simplifies the situation, but it does help to break down the complexity of the challenge facing management, where each issue feeds off, or contributes to, the others. Thinking about strategy, and devising a relevant mission and accompanying goals, triggers the kind of culture that will mark out the organisation in the marketplace. The drive towards creating a climate of excellence forms a key part of that culture. The external environment plays a pivotal role, because customers, competitors, suppliers, local communities and other external stakeholders all exert a crucial influence on how the management will seek to achieve competitive advantage. Internally, the abilities and attitudes of employees, and the way in which their contribution is optimised is critical. The manner in which people are treated, the exploitation of new technology, and the pressures arising from the external marketplace, are all aspects of the challenge of managing change. On top of all these factors are the organisational structures and systems that are a major part of the organisation's fabric, linking all the various parts and processes together in a whole tapestry of organisational activity. Increasingly, for many firms, there is the issue of balancing global/international standards with those of local business units in differing cultures.

Modern Management Theorists

8.   Most of the contributors to the theory and practice of management nowadays are academics with strong research backgrounds, and most are from the USA. Of the practitioners, almost all are practising management consultants, indeed most also hold positions in American universities. There are few who can be compared to Henri Fayol and F.W.Taylor, in the early part of the century, who were genuinely practising managers first and management thinkers second.

9.   Throughout this book there are examples of the work and thinking of these modern theorists. For the purposes of this introductory chapter, the leading theorists are listed below (Figure 11.2) in terms of their dominant areas of interest.

Key management issue	Major contributors to theory
1 Establishing vision	Peters, T. & Waterman, R.
2 Managing the environment	Porter, M.E.; Kotler, P.
3 Developing culture	Mintzberg, H.; Hofstede, G.; Moss Kanter, R.; Schein, E.
4 Devising structures and systems	Mintzberg, H.; Peters, T.; Hammer, M. & Champy, J.; Handy, C.; Morgan, G.
5 Developing/empowering employees	Peters, T.; Kotter, J.P.
6 Applying new technology	Hammer, M & Champy, J.
7 Managing change	Moss Kanter, R.; Peters, T.; Kotter, J.P.
8 Finding competitive advantage	Porter, M.
9 Improving strategic thinking	Hamel, G. & Prahalad, C.; Mintzberg, H.
10 Creating excellence	Peters, T. & Waterman, R.; Goldsmith, W. & Clutterbuck, D.
11 Modifying national cultures in multinational corporations	Hofstede, G.; Trompenaars, F. & Hampden-Turner, C.
12 Developing learning and knowledge in the workplace	Senge, M.

Figure 11.2 Key issues and Principal Theorists.

10. As stated earlier, there are further discussions of the work of the above contributors to management theory and practice in subsequent chapters. Key works that will be referred to include the following:

Goldsmith, W. & Clutterbuck, D. (1984), *The Winning Streak*, Penguin.
Hamel, G. & Prahalad, C.K. (1994), *Competing for the Future*, Harvard Business School Press.
Hammer, M & Champy, J. (1993), *Reengineering the Corporation – A Manifesto for Business Revolution*, Nicholas Brealey.
Handy, C. (1993), *Understanding Organisations*, Penguin.
Hofstede, G. (1980), *Culture's Consequences: International Differences in Work-related Values*, Sage Publications.
Hofstede, G. (1997), *Cultures and Organisations*, McGraw-Hill.
Kotler, P. (1996), *Principles of Marketing* (7th edition), Prentice-Hall.
Kotter, J.P. (1996), *Leading Change*, Harvard Business School Press
Mintzberg, H. (1979), *The Structuring of Organisations: A Synthesis of the Research*, Prentice-Hall.
Mintzberg, H. (1983), *Structure in Fives*, Prentice-Hall.

Morgan, G. (1986), *Images of Organisation*, Sage Publications.
Moss Kanter, R. (1983), *The Change Masters*, Unwin Hyman.
Peters, T. & Waterman, R. (1982), *In Search of Excellence*, HarperCollins.
Peters, T. (1988), *Thriving on Chaos – a Handbook for a Management Revolution*, Macmillan.
Porter, M.E. (1985), *Competitive Advantage: Creating and Sustaining Superior Performance*, The Free Press.
Porter, M.E. (1990), *The Competitive Advantage of Nations*, The Free Press.
Senge, P. (1990), *The Fifth Discipline*, Century Business.
Trompenaars, F. & Hampden-Turner, C. (1997), *Riding the Waves of Culture* (2nd edition), Nicholas Brealey.

Questions for Discussion/Homework

1. To what extent is micro-electronic technology a key factor in triggering change in the way companies compete in a global marketplace?

2. Why are international firms concentrating their attention on developing a vision, creating a climate of excellence, and 'empowering' their employees?

Part Two

MANAGEMENT IN PRACTICE

Having examined some of the key theoretical aspects of management, we now turn to the practice of management. This section of the book considers some of the important contextual issues that lie behind the day-to-day operation of work organisations. Chapter 12 outlines the main types of business organisation, with an emphasis on limited companies and introduces the idea of 'corporate governance'. Chapter 13 considers aspects of organisational values-building, ie the development of corporate culture. This is followed in Chapter 14 by a consideration of key issues raised for women in management. The assumption in this text is that there is nothing to separate the sexes when it comes to managing a team of people. However, given the amount of prejudice against women in managerial positions, it is necessary to point to some of the evidence surrounding women's performance as managers. Chapter 15 rounds off the contextual issues by briefly considering some international aspects of management.

CHAPTER 12

Business Organisations and Corporate Governance

Introduction

1.   The subject-matter of this book is management. Many of the management issues touched upon are common to every kind of organisation, be it business, state enterprise, public service, non-profit-making charity or private club. However, the full range of management theory and practice occurs mainly in what we call 'business organisations'. This chapter describes the main legal characteristics of such organisations.

2.   A *Business* organisation, in contrast to a public service organisation or a charity, exists to provide goods or services usually at a profit. Making a profit may not necessarily be the sole aim of a business, but it is certainly what distinguishes it from a non-business organisation. In Britain, business organisations are mainly to be found in the private sector of the economy, which has grown in recent years as a number of State-owned corporations have been privatised. The business organisations we are concerned with here range in size from the one-man business, or sole trader, through partnerships between two or more people working in collaboration, to large public limited companies (plc's) employing thousands of staff in a variety of locations. There are also cooperative enterprises, notably in retail distribution, but also in manufacturing on a small scale.

3.   The most common types of business organisation are as follows:

- limited companies
- sole traders
- partnerships
- cooperatives

Society, through Parliament and the Courts, sets standards of behaviour for all these types of business.

These standards are made public by means of legal requirements and judicial interpretations. The following paragraphs summarise the principal legal features of these businesses, together with the main advantages and disadvantages for the parties concerned.

Limited Companies

4. When a limited company is formed, it is said to have become 'incorporated', ie endowed with a separate body, or person. The corporation so formed is treated in English law as a separate entity, independent of its members. The corporation, or 'company', as it is generally called, is capable of owning property, employing people, making contracts, and of suing or being sued. Another important feature of a company is that, unlike a sole trader or a partnership, it does have continuity of succession, as it is unaffected by the death or incapacity of one or more of its members.

5. The key feature of a 'limited' company is that, if it fails it can only require its members (shareholders) to meet its debts up to the limit of the nominal value of their shares. The principle of legally limiting the financial liabilities of persons investing in business ventures was introduced by Parliament in the 1850s to encourage the wealthy to give financial support to the inventors, engineers and others who were at the forefront of Britain's Industrial Revolution. Without the protection of limited liability, an investor could find himself stripped of his home and other personal assets in order to meet debts arising from the failure of any company in which he had invested his money.

6. Since the turn of the twentieth century, various Company Acts have laid down the principles and procedures to be followed in the conduct of business organisations. Such legislation has been intended to minimise the risk to suppliers and customers as well as to shareholders, and to a lesser extent employees, arising from gross mismanagement of, or deliberate restriction of information about, a company. The legislation of recent decades has now been consolidated into one Principal Act – the Companies Act, 1985 – as amended by the Companies Act, 1989.

7. Limited liability companies fall into two categories:

❶ public limited companies (plcs)

❷ private limited companies.

The Memorandum (see Para. 8) of a plc must state that the company is a public company (ie its shares are available for purchase by the public) and the company name must end with the words 'Public limited company'. A private limited company by comparison may not offer its shares to the public, and is even restricted in the transfer of its shares between the private shareholders. The name of a private limited company must end with the word 'Limited'. Both kinds of company must have at least two members and one director. Once registered under the Companies Act, a private company can begin trading without further formality. A public limited company has to obtain a certificate of trading from the Registrar of Companies. All limited companies have to fulfil certain procedures before they can be incorporated. These include the filing of two particularly important documents: (a) the Memorandum of Association and (b) the Articles of Association.

8. The Memorandum of Association must supply the following information:

• the company's name

• the location of the registered office

• the objects or purpose of the company

• a statement that the liability of members is limited

- the amount of share capital, together with the numbers and class of shares
- a declaration of association in which the initial members (subscribers) express their desire to form a company and to take up shares.

The details contained in the Memorandum are available for public inspection. Persons considering doing business with a company, or wishing to purchase shares in it, can therefore consult the register before deciding whether to take the risks involved.

9.   The Articles of Association are aimed at regulating the internal affairs of the company, and set out the rules for such matters as:

- entitlement to membership of the company
- the appointment of directors
- the role of the company secretary
- the conduct of general meetings of shareholders/ members
- the conduct of board meetings
- the requirements for minutes of board and general meetings
- the keeping, publishing and auditing of the company's accounts.

10.   The main advantages of limited liability can be summarised as follows:

- in the event of failure of the business, shareholders are protected against the loss of more than the nominal value of their shareholding
- the separate legal person of the company exists independently of the members
- shares (in plc's) are readily transferable
- wider share-ownership is encouraged
- companies are required to submit annual returns to the Registrar, and these are available for public inspection.

11.   The disadvantages are primarily as follows:

- precisely because liability is limited, it may be difficult for small companies to borrow as extensively as desired, since banks and other financial institutions may be unable to recover their funds if the business fails.
- there are considerable legal procedures involved in setting up a company, as well as the procedures incurred in publishing the various financial accounts of the company.

Company directors

12.   The directors of the company are, in law, its agents, and are accountable for the conduct of the company's affairs. They are appointed by the shareholders/ members to use their best endeavours to achieve the company's objects. Every director has a duty to act honestly in the best interests of the company, to avoid possible conflicts of interest, and not to make a personal profit from the directorship other than what the company is prepared to pay by way of salary and fees, for example. A director also has a duty of skill and care in the performance of his or her duties. Directors may be executive, having operational as well as strategic responsibilities, or non-executive, having only board responsibilities. Executive directors are usually full-time employees, whereas non-executives usually work part-time for one or two days a month. Some non-executive directors serve on several different boards, and this has raised questions as to whether there should be restrictions on the number of such posts held by any one individual.

13. In the UK the typical company board is a unitary board composed of a majority of executive directors with a small number of non-executives. A few companies, especially those that are not-for-profit businesses, may have a majority of non-executive directors. The law does not distinguish between the two types, and they bear the same legal responsibilities. This situation is presently under scrutiny in the light of recent scandals, where non-executive directors have been implicitly criticised for not exercising a more critical influence over their executive colleagues. Their role as independents in raising critical questions about means, as well as ends, is seen as providing an essential monitoring influence on the way a company is run.

14. In particular, non-executive directors are being encouraged to take the leadership of key board committees, such as the audit and remuneration committees. This means they, rather than their executive colleagues, are monitoring the company's financial audits and setting the remuneration of the board members. There are a few who argue that the UK's so-called unitary boards are *de facto* two-tier boards, where one section is composed of full-time executive directors, fully in the picture about what is happening in the company, whilst the other, smaller, section comprises the part-time non-executives, who are remote from most of the day-to-day events in the company. Whether present discussions will lead to the development of formalised two-tier boards, such as in most European companies, is a matter of conjecture. If that were to be the case, then the law would need to spell out more specifically the difference in duties between the two types of director. At present the law makes no such distinction.

15. The principal director is usually the chairman of the board, who may be full or part-time. The senior executive director is the person who holds the title of managing director or chief executive officer (CEO) and who is responsible for overall day-to-day operations, as well as for board duties. The CEO is responsible for implementing policies and strategy, as well as for helping to formulate them. He, or she, is responsible for building and motivating the senior management team, and for installing appropriate systems to ensure the smooth-running of the business. The chief administrative officer of the board is the company secretary, who is responsible for ensuring that the legal requirements for running meetings, appointing directors, voting and other procedures, are adhered to. The company secretary may, or may not, be a director. In a small company the CEO may act as company secretary.

16. Directors' responsibilities include determining, and subsequently monitoring, the company's strategic goals and the policies under which they are to be achieved. They are also responsible for preparing and publishing the company's financial accounts for the shareholders/ members. These accounts (see Chapter 51) have to include the balance sheet, showing the company's assets and liabilities as at the end of the trading year. They must include a profit and loss account (or income and expenditure account), showing the income received from trading activities, the cost of sales, the amount of profit, taxation, dividends paid and profits retained in the business. Most accounts also include a cash flow statement.

17. All such accounts are required to be audited by an external and independent firm of accountants, which has to state that the accounts represent 'a true and fair view of the state of affairs of the company'. Otherwise, the auditors have to qualify the accounts. It is the responsibility of the directors to recommend the appointment of the company's auditors, and to satisfy themselves that the latter are fulfilling their duties properly. In particular, directors need to pay attention to the way the company treats such issues as depreciation, stock valuation and financial provisions, which are open to being fudged. In the light of recent accountancy scandals, where auditors have apparently connived at dubious reporting

practices, aimed at presenting an overly optimistic picture of a company's financial health, there are moves to improve corporate governance. These include strengthening the monitoring role of non-executive directors on the board, and requiring that the auditing firm is truly independent of any other services that it may be offering to the client company.

Corporate Governance

18. The manner in which company directors promote and control their company's operations, that is the way they exercise their stewardship, is not just a matter of interest to their shareholders/members, but is a matter of public interest too. In the UK a number of codes of good practice have been developed over recent years, following criticisms of the behaviour of some boards and individual directors. In 1992, the Cadbury Report looked especially at the division of responsibilities between chairmen and chief executives, and argued against the two roles being held by the same person. In 1995 the Greenbury Report examined directors' pay and made a number of recommendations. In 1998 the Hampel Committee conducted a far-ranging examination of corporate governance, which led to what is now known as the Combined Code[1], which establishes basic principles of good governance and sets out a code of best practice.

19. Some important examples of the areas of governance covered by the Code are summarised as follows:

- Every listed company should be headed by an effective board, which should lead and control the company. The board should meet regularly and should have a formal schedule of matters reserved to it for decision; directors should bring an independent judgement to bear on issues of strategy, performance, resources and standards of conduct; directors should receive appropriate training on first appointment, and as necessary thereafter.

- There are two key tasks at the top of every public company – the running of the board (the chairman's role), and the executive responsibility for the operation of the company's business (the chief executive's role). There should be a clear division of responsibilities between the two roles, so as to ensure a balance of power and authority, and thus avoid a situation where one person has unfettered powers of decision.

- The board should have a balance between executive and non-executive directors, with at least one third from the latter. The majority of non-executives should be independent of the management and free of business relationships that could interfere with their independence.

- There should be a formal and transparent procedure for the appointment of directors, and all directors should offer themselves for re-election every three years.

- Levels of remuneration should be sufficient to attract and retain the directors needed to run the company successfully, but should not be excessive. Part of the pay of executive directors should be in the form of performance-related elements.

- The board should use the Annual General Meeting (AGM) to communicate with individual investors and encourage their participation (by use of proxy/ postal voting as well as by attendance).

- The board should present a balanced and understandable assessment of the company's financial position and prospects.

- The board should maintain a sound system of internal control, which should be reviewed annually, and reported to the shareholders.

- The board should establish an audit committee of at least three non-executive directors with the task of reviewing the scope of the audit, and the independence and objectivity of the auditors. Where the latter supply a substantial amount of non-auditing services (such as consultancy), the committee should ensure that they can continue to act objectively in their audit role.

20. Such a code cannot guarantee that fraud or sharp practice will never take place. Nor can it prevent accounts from being 'massaged' to present a better-than-actual set of results, but it can help to improve standards generally in the area of corporate governance, and by encouraging transparency it can help shareholders to ask pointed questions in cases where certain results appear to have been fudged.

Sole Traders

21. The sole trader is the simplest form of business organisation – one person in business on his own. The legal requirements for setting up such a business are minimal, but the owner is fully liable for any debts incurred in running the business, since the owner literally *is* the business. Ownership and control are combined. All profits made by the sole trader are subject to income tax rather than the corporation tax levied on company profits. Apart from the need to maintain accounts for controlling the business and for dealing with the Inland Revenue, there are no formal accounts to be published.

22. The main advantages of operating as a sole trader are:

- the formalities for starting up are minimal
- complete autonomy to run the business as the individual wishes
- the profits of the business belong to the trader
- various business expenses are allowable against income tax
- no public disclosure of accounts (except to Inland Revenue).

23. The main disadvantages are as follows:

- the sole trader is entirely responsible for the debts of the business
- the individual as owner and manager has to be responsible for all aspects of the business (marketing, product development, sales, finance etc).

Partnerships

24. A partnership exists when at least two, and usually not more than twenty, persons agree to carry on a business together. The Partnership Act, 1890, defines a partnership as a relationship which 'subsists between persons carrying on a business in common with a view to profit'. The legalities required to set up a partnership are minimal, although it is advisable to have a formal Partnership agreement drawn up by a solicitor. Such an agreement can specify the rights and obligations of individual partners, and can make provision for changes brought about by death or retirement of partners. As with a sole trader, the members of a partnership are owners of its property and liable for its contracts. Therefore they are fully responsible for meeting their debts to third parties. Partners are not automatically entitled to a salary for the services they provide for the partnership, but are entitled to their proper share of the profits of the business. However, many agreements do allow for salaried partners.

25. Many partnerships, and some sole traders, have been converted into limited companies because of the perceived benefits of incorporation. Most professional persons, and

especially accountants and solicitors, maintain partnership as their form of business in order to preserve the principle of individual professional accountability towards the client.

26. The main advantages of partnership are:

- few formalities required for starting up
- sharing of partners' knowledge and skills
- sharing of management of business
- no obligation to publish accounts (except for Inland Revenue purposes)
- sharing of profits (or losses!) of business.

27. The disadvantages are primarily these:

- each partner is liable for the debts of the partnership, even if caused by the actions of other partners
- risk that the partners may not be able to work together at a personal level
- the death or bankruptcy of one partner will automatically dissolve the partnership, unless otherwise provided for in a partnership agreement.

Cooperative Enterprises

28. Small groups of people who wish to set up business along explicitly democratic lines and with the benefit of limited liability, can choose to establish a cooperative. This kind of business has been a feature of British commercial life for well over a hundred years, at least so far as distribution is concerned. These distribution cooperatives were essentially consumer-cooperatives in which the profits of the business were given back to consumers in dividends based on the amount of their purchases over a given period. The modern trend in cooperatives is towards producer-cooperatives in which individuals benefit not only as investors but as employees in the business. There are more than 700 such worker-cooperatives in Britain at the present time.

29. The promotion of cooperatives has been encouraged by recent governments in Britain, and a Cooperative Development Agency has been established since 1978 to provide advice and assistance to those considering setting up such a business.

30. The legislation governing cooperative enterprises is the Industrial & Provident Societies Act, 1965, which requires that in lieu of Memorandum and Articles, every cooperative shall have a set of rules approved by the Registrar of Friendly Societies. The rules must embrace the following principles:

- each member must have equal control on the 'one person, one vote' principle
- members must benefit primarily from their participation in the business, ie as employees as well as investors
- interest on loan or share capital has to be limited
- surplus ('profit') must be shared between members in proportion to their contribution (for example, by number of hours worked or wage level), or must be retained in the business
- membership must be open to all who qualify.

For the principle of limited liability to apply to the members, the cooperative must be registered, in which case a minimum of seven members is required.

31. The main advantages of cooperative enterprise are:

- provides opportunity for genuine pooling of capital between a group of people
- encourages active collaboration between all sections of the workforce
- enables decisions to be made democratically
- provides rewards on an equitable basis among those involved
- provides limited liability (if registered).

32. The disadvantages are mainly:

- there is less likelihood of a level of profitability and growth that could be achieved by a limited company
- as with partnerships, relationships can deteriorate, especially when some members are seen to be making a smaller contribution than the rest
- democratic decision-making can lead to lengthy discussions before action is taken
- members who are not truly dedicated to the democratic ethos of the business, may find themselves at odds with the openness of communication and decision-making.

CHAPTER 13

Developing an Organisation Culture

Introduction

1.   It is difficult to escape from the influence of 'the organisation culture' in any consideration of how organisations work. For example, as noted in Chapter 22 below, in the discussion of the various factors that contribute to, and are influenced by, organisation structures, the issue of culture has to be taken into account. In essence the culture of an organisation is its dominant pattern of shared beliefs and values. Morgan (1986)[1], from a sociologist's perspective, describes it as:

'Shared meaning, shared understanding and shared sense-making...'

Handy (1993)[2], looking at organisations as a management consultant, points out that:

'...anyone who has spent time with any variety of organisations ... will have been struck by the differing atmospheres, the differing way of doing things, the differing levels of energy, of individual freedom, of kinds of personality.'

2.   The important point about culture is that whilst there may be striking differences *between* organisations, there is a shared understanding *within* them. The culture does not become established until this shared understanding achieves a dominance in the collective thinking of the members of the organisation. Having said this, it also has to be accepted that within any single (dominant) culture, there are usually subcultures, which operate at a lower level of influence. As Morgan puts it:

'Just as individuals in a [national] culture can have different personalities while sharing much in common, so too with groups and organisations ....

Organisations are mini-societies that have their own distinctive patterns of culture and subculture ... Such patterns of belief or shared meaning...can exert a decisive influence on the overall ability of the organisation to deal with the challenges that it faces.' (p.121)

3.   The dominant culture that develops in an organisation is primarily the product of the aims and methods of its founders, or their successors in senior management, combined with their interaction with a variety of internal and external forces. Figure 13.1 illustrates some important interrelationships that both produce, and are deeply affected by, the organisation's culture.

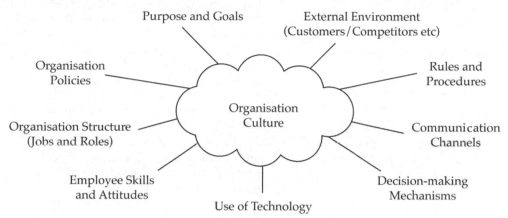

Figure 13.1 Key interrelationships between culture and other aspects of an organisation

4.   The purpose and goals of the organisation initially trigger the kind of culture that the founders or their successors want to see (their 'vision'). The extent to which they achieve this culture depends as much on the other factors as on their own leadership and charisma. The external environment will play a significant role, since customers, competitors, suppliers and other external stakeholders will all exert some influence on what the organisation chooses to do, and how it will do it. Internally, the abilities and attitudes of employees, especially managers, will be critical. The nature of the technology available, and the way it is implemented in the organisation, will also play a part in the development of culture. And, of course, on top of all these factors are the organisational structures, mechanisms and procedures that are a major part of the organisation's fabric. The latter analogy is illuminating because it is helpful to think of the culture as being woven in between all the other factors, linking them together and producing a whole tapestry.

Ideas about Culture

5.   Handy (op. cit.), in discussing the issue of organisation culture, highlights some of the alternative types of culture favoured by many organisations. He identifies four main types of culture (Figure 13.2), which help to illustrate the point he makes above when commenting on the differences between organisations.

6.   Handy's model considerably simplifies the reality of organisation culture, which more likely than not is composed of elements of *all four types*. He himself admits that his typology is impressionistic and imprecise, commenting that 'A *culture cannot be precisely defined, for it is something that is perceived, something felt.*' (p 191). Nevertheless, he raises some key aspects of culture, which are very significant, such as:

Type	Metaphor	Characteristics
Power Culture	A web	Control/power emanate from the centre; very political and entrepreneurial; resource power and personal power predominate. This culture serves the figure-head and the leader.
Role Culture	The Greek temple	Classical structure; bureaucratic nature; roles more important than the people who fill them; position power predominates, and expert power tolerated. This culture serves the cause of structure.
Task Culture	A net	The focus is on completing the job; individuals' expertise and contribution are highly valued; expert power predominates, but both personal and position power are important; the unifying force of the group is manifested in high levels of collaboration.
Person Culture	A cluster or galaxy	A loose collection of individuals – usually professionals – sharing common facilities but pursuing own goals separately; power is not really an issue, since members are experts in their own right. This type of culture serves the individual.

**Figure 13.2 Four types of culture in organisations
(based on Handy)**

- how are power and/or control handled by the organisation – centralised? diffused throughout the organisation?

- what type of power is respected in the organisation – personal power (charisma)? resource power (gatekeepers)? position power (bureaucrats)? expert power (the technical whizz-kids)?

- what working methods are preferred – individualistic? collaborative? competitive?

- do people have to fit the structure or does the structure serve the people?

- whose interests are best served by the dominant culture – the leaders? the key position holders? the individual? selected groups?

- what about other stakeholders, such as customers, suppliers, shareholders?

7. On the question of how to define the term 'culture', Schein (1992)[3], in his leading text on culture and leadership, comments that:

> 'The word **culture** has many meanings and connotations. When we apply it to groups and organisations, we are almost certain to have conceptual and semantic confusion because groups and organisations are also difficult to define unambiguously ... In talking about organisational culture ... I often find we agree "it" exists and "it" is important ... but that we have completely different ideas of what "it" is.' (p.8)

Schein argues that superficial models of culture should be avoided in favour of *'deeper, more complex anthropological models'*, since culture is the result of a complex group learning process, in which leaders play a key role.

8. Schein extends our understanding of the term when he comments that culture is generated not only by sharing values and traditions, but even more by sharing the *assumptions* that emerge about the best way of handling problems. He puts it as follows:

'A pattern of shared assumptions that the group learned as it solved its problems of external adaptation and internal integration ... and therefore to be taught to new members as the correct way to perceive, think and feel in relation to those problems.'

In this definition culture is a deep-rooted phenomenon which exists at several different levels. Not only are there the overt signs of culture, which he calls the *artefacts* of culture, such as policy statements and important rituals, but also the underlying values that these signs imply.

9.   Many commentators would stop there and say that the underlying values are the basis of culture. Schein, however, goes further. He argues that at this second-tier level the values are still being put to the test – they are what he describes as *espoused values*, and therefore may, or may not, be practised throughout the organisation. We could say at this level that individuals may experience a certain amount of 'lip-service' being paid to selected values. Attention to customer care, for example, may be a value that is proclaimed in mission statements and departmental objectives, yet may be put on one side when the organisation is busy, or when some other operational factor demands managers' attention. According to Schein's perception of culture, it is only as these second-tier values become absorbed into the organisation's subconscious, and become implicit assumptions about behaviour, that they truly deserve to be termed its *culture*. Thus, in this example, attention to customer care becomes so much a way of behaving that no one would compromise it, even when operational difficulties occured.

10.   Hofstede (1997)[4], discussing culture and organisations, describes culture as a form of mental programming – patterns of thinking, feeling and doing learned from childhood. He sees culture as a collective phenomenon derived from shared experiences in the same social environment, and which distinguishes one group of people (or organisation) from another. Culture can modify the way we express our basic human nature – our physical and psychological functions – for example in the way we show fear or anger. It can also modify our own personality, which derives partly from inherited factors and partly from what we learned and experienced in childhood. Hofstede reminds us that a group's culture manifests itself in a variety of ways through *symbols*, *heroes*, *rituals* and *values*.

11.   *Symbols* are external signs of things that have a special meaning for those who share the culture. They may be pictures, objects, styles of dress or such things as particular words or gestures. Hofstede considers symbols to be the outer layer of culture, for which he uses the analogy of an onion – a multi-layered vegetable. *Heroes* represent the next layer. These are people (dead or alive) who are looked up to in the culture, and who serve as models for acceptable behaviour. *Rituals*, according to Hofstede, are collective activities that are considered as socially essential. Rituals include ways of greeting strangers, public and religious ceremonies, and also many business meetings. Symbols, heroes and rituals are visible, and essentially are the culture practices. What they do not show, but only imply, are the meanings attached to these practices. It is these meanings which lead us to the core of the 'onion', which is formed by the group's *values*.

12.   Hofstede sees values as broad tendencies to prefer certain things over others. Values, he argues, have a plus and a minus side, such as evil versus good, ugly versus beautiful, and abnormal versus normal. Values are acquired very early in life, tend to become hidden in the person's unconscious and can only be inferred from the way the person acts. In trying to interpret people's values, it is important to distinguish between what they may think is *desirable* (what they think should apply to everyone), and what they personally *desire* (for themselves). Desirable things tend to have an absolute standard applied to them, which means they are seen to be either right or wrong, and are part of the group's ideology. Desired things are concerned more with practical matters, with people's wants, and the

standards applied are likely to be statistical, indicating the choices actually made by the majority.

13. The culture that lies at the heart of Hofstede's onion is not a homogeneous collection of values, for it is itself made up of a number of different layers, including national aspects, regional, class and generation. In many modern societies these different subcultures are frequently in conflict with each other, and employers have to take such potential conflicts into account in their personnel/human resource policies. Issues concerning the effect of national cultural differences on employment are discussed in Chapter 15 as part of the examination of Hofstede's (1980)[5] earlier research into how national differences were manifested in the workplace of a large multinational corporation, namely IBM.

14. In subsequent research into the effects of culture on organisations, Hofstede (1990)[6] found that the major cultural differences between organisations lay in their practices (symbols, heroes, rituals) rather than in their *values*. The research, which was on a much smaller scale than the IBM study, covered twenty organisational units in two European countries (Denmark and the Netherlands), and examined their cultural practices in terms of six dimensions, as follows:

1. **Process-orientation versus results orientation** (whether the organisation culture favoured a concern for *means* as opposed to a concern for *results*).

2. **Employee-orientation versus job orientation** (whether the organisation culture favoured a concern for *people* versus an emphasis on completing the *job*).

3. **Parochial versus professional** (whether the individual employees identified themselves with their local organisation or saw themselves as professionals hired for their skills; in the former culture, loyalty centred on the local organisation, in the latter, it centred on professional pride (competence).

4. **Open (social) system versus closed (social) system** (whether the organisation culture favoured an openness to newcomers and outsiders, or had an inward-looking, almost secretive attitude towards its members; on this dimension national cultural differences emerged, with the Danes generally favouring openness, whilst the Dutch preferred closed groups).

5. **Loose control versus tight control** (whether the culture favoured strict adherence to matters of costs and timeliness, or preferred a more relaxed approach to these issues).

6. **Normative versus pragmatic approach to customers** (whether the culture expected people to conform to rules in respect of customers, procedures and ethics, or to act flexibly in order to meet customers' wants or achieve targets).

15. Broadly, the results showed that four of the above dimensions (1, 3, 5, 6) were closely related to the business or industry that the organisations represented. Thus, the key factors of task and markets were very influential in locating units along each dimension. Manufacturing operations and large office organisations, for example, showed a particular concern for *processes*, whilst research and development organisations and service units were more concerned with *results*. Those using traditional technology in their tasks tended to be *parochial*, whilst those employing high-tech equipment had a *professional* orientation. On the control dimension, pharmaceutical units and those engaged in the financial sector exercised *strict controls*, whereas units engaged in innovative activities favoured *loose controls*. Interestingly, both the police departments surveyed favoured loose controls, demonstrating their need to give officers on the ground a fair degree of discretion in their fight to maintain law and order. Nevertheless, those units engaged in implementing laws or operating under monopoly conditions tended towards a *normative* approach to their

public, whilst service units and those operating in very competitive markets were *pragmatic* in their approach.

16. Neither of the remaining two dimensions were much affected by task and market, and were more likely to be a product of the founder's attitude towards people, or, in the case of open or closed systems, by national preferences. Hofstede comments that the six dimensions of culture are not prescriptive. In other words there are no intrinsically good or bad positions, and he begs to differ with the Peters & Waterman (1982)[7] view of the norms required for 'excellence' (see Chapter 24 paragraph 19).

17. Two other major recent contributors to thinking about organisation cultures are Trompenaars & Hampden-Turner (1997)[8]. Their researches into this field across job, company and national boundaries reached three major conclusions. These were (1) there is no 'one best way' of managing and organising; (2) it is very important for managers to recognise and understand their own culture, and how cultural differences occur; and (3) cultural insights are vital in understanding the tension between local cultures and global issues in international companies. Most of their discussions were focused on *national* cultural differences, and are summarised later (see Chapter 15). However, their general comments about *organisation* culture are worth mentioning here.

18. They stress that culture is fundamentally a matter of shared meanings, which influence our priorities, our actions and our values. So, in work organisations the meanings that people assign to such concepts as 'the organisation', together with its structure, practices and policies, are defined by their culture. There are no universal laws of organising for optimum results. Instead there are only ways of assessing how people in different cultures make sense of their experiences. Throughout the second half of the twentieth century various solutions have been put forward to enable organisations to perform more effectively – *management by objectives, total quality management, business process reengineering*, and *performance management*, to name but a few – but most of such ideas have been rooted firmly in North American and North-West European cultures. It has been shown that they do not work if merely transplanted from one national culture to another.

19. It should be noted that, even within the European Union, whose development is having an important influence on changing the national cultures of its members, it is clear that there are many areas of life where uniformity cannot be imposed. Individual governments have to be given time to introduce novel systems, such as a common currency, and in other cases, such as driving on the left or right, member states are allowed to maintain national traditions.

20. In examining the impact of national cultures on organisation culture, Trompenaars and colleague identified four types of corporate culture derived from two key dimensions: *person*-orientation versus *task*-orientation, and preference for an *egalitarian* versus an *hierarchical* structure. Using these two dimensions, they produced a typology of four alternative types of culture, as shown in Figure 13.3.

Briefly the four types of culture can be summarised as follows:

- The *family*, where the dominant culture is one of paternalism, and where power is exercised through the members rather than over them. Nevertheless, there is no question that the leader knows best! This culture is similar to Handy's (op. cit) *power culture*.

- The *incubator*, by contrast, dislikes hierarchy and encourages equality. Relationships are spontaneous and creativity is highly respected. This type is close to Handy's *person culture*.

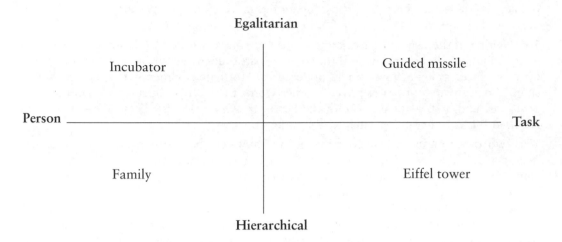

Figure 13.3 Four corporate cultures (based on Trompenaars & Hampden-Turner, 1997)

- The *guided missile* is a culture that thrives on successful teamwork in solving problems. Its people pride themselves on their professionalism. This culture is similar to Handy's *task culture*.

- The *Eiffel Tower* culture, as might be expected, is the one that embodies bureaucracy. The emphasis on task and roles within a defined hierarchy place this example on a par with Handy's *role culture*.

21. Of course, any typology is of necessity an over-simplification, and this is recognised by all the reputable writers on organisation cultures and management. The useful aspect of a typology, however, is that it emphasises the principal distinguishing features of alternative scenarios. It can also help managers to identify their own situation, and perhaps to become more sensitive to the alternatives that may be present in their customers, suppliers or other stakeholders.

Recognising a culture

22. When all has been said and done about the theoretical side of culture, the practical question remains: 'Where, and how, do managers come to recognise the dominant culture in their organisation?' Where should they look, and what questions should they ask? As Figure 13.1 shows, there are several factors that are both a source of culture, and a manifestation of it. Examples of some of the ways in which managers learn about their culture are shown in the following list:

Source/means	Examples
• Organisation mission statement	'To be the best and most successful company in the airline industry' *(British Airways)* 'We are committed…to a process of development by peaceful means which aims to help people, especially the poor and under-privileged, regardless of the politics or style of regime under which they live…' *(Oxfam)*
• Corporate aims	'To provide overall superior service and good value for money in every market segment in which we compete' *(British Airways)*

		'Simplicity, frugality and avoidance of waste will be elements in our corporate lifestyle…' *(Oxfam)*
•	**Policy statements**	'We do not discriminate against anyone on any grounds. The sole criterion for selection for promotion is the suitability of any applicant for the job…' *(Marks & Spencer)*
		'We will compete vigorously but fairly in the marketplace; we will not seek to use our market position in a way that unfairly disadvantages our competitors' *(British Telecommunications)*
•	**Organisational rituals**	Formal address to staff by Managing Director or other senior manager. Induction programmes for newcomers. Retirement parties/leaving speeches. Reward ceremonies for key sales staff.
•	**Organisation logos**	British Standards Institution kite-mark. Company logos (eg BMW/ICI/Virgin). Other logos (eg Red Cross). Brand names (eg Mars, Coke, MS-DOS).
•	**Procedures/rules**	Standard operating procedures/software for production-line or clerical routines. Rules about dress, hairstyles, jewelry etc. Safety procedures.
•	**Management attitudes**	How far do the *senior* management achieve consistency of values throughout the organisation? How far do *middle* management reinforce, or perhaps contradict, official organisation policy/practice? To what extent are *informal* cultures permitted (eg in terms of specific alternative practices)?
•	**Peer-group attitudes**	How far does the employee's own work-team conform to, or work against, the official company procedures?
•	**Training staff attitudes**	How far do training staff attitudes reflect official company policies, styles and procedures in their induction and other training courses/activities?
•	**Organisation structure**	What messages are given out by the way work is organised and responsibility shared out? How well, and in what ways, does the structure facilitate, or hinder, day-to-day communications between employees?
•	**Technology**	What is the status of technology in the organisation? How are people expected to deal with it? Who are the organisation's technocrats?

23. Employees are, of course, not the only group who are affected by an organisation's culture. They are the most likely recipients of the culture, as well as helping to shape it. However, there are other stakeholders who are affected by it. Indeed, that powerful group of stakeholders called 'customers' not only experience the culture from the outside, but are even

more influential in its development than the employees who have to live and work in it! Customers experience what it is like to be treated as a customer by the organisation. For some the experience will be entirely beneficial; for others it may be a mixture of benefits and disappointments; and for yet others the experience may be entirely negative. Their relative experiences will be gained through two major sources, the end product, or service, which they have sought, and the way it has been delivered to them. Customers' responses to the organisation will help to form (or reform) its culture by exerting the pressure of their buying preferences. In today's markets, where there is a high degree of competition between suppliers of goods and services, the customer's wishes are seen as paramount by many organisations. Thus, they will adapt their cultural norms in order to meet their customers' requirements.

24. Depending on their relative power in a particular situation, the behaviour of stakeholders such as suppliers, creditors (eg banks), and competitors may also influence the organisation's culture. Competitors, in particular, can introduce changes into their marketing strategy and organisation, which not only change their own culture, but also contribute to change in others, who may be forced to follow their lead in order to retain market share. For example, there is much change in the UK insurance market at present, and many firms are seeking to merge with others in order to gain access to a wider customer base, and to take advantage of corporate-wide computer systems to reduce their operating costs. A few old-established firms are attempting to resist the trend of joining up with competitors. This is because they have a different culture as a result of being owned by their policy-holders (having so-called 'mutual' status) rather than by shareholders. If they were to become limited companies, their profits would be partly paid to shareholders instead of being paid mainly as bonuses to policy-holders. Mutual companies tend to have lower operating costs than limited companies at present, although this advantage could be lost if successfully-merging competitors are able to reap the benefits of scale. Similar considerations apply in other areas of financial services, where several building societies are considering becoming banks, or are selling out to banks, and thus changing their mutual status. This would almost certainly affect their current culture, as would the launch into a far wider financial services market (eg comprising not just mortgages, but banking and other services).

25. An awareness of the culture of their organisation is important for managers, since one of their tasks is to ensure that the values and assumptions around which the culture grows are passed on to their staff. Managers also need to be aware of the effect of the culture on their own work and their own values, since they are in a position to bring about changes in the culture. They experience at first hand the effects of technology, systems of work, people's reactions, the structure of jobs, decision-making channels and so on, and are thus able to see where obstacles are occurring, and may need to be removed. Morgan[1] (*op. cit.*) reckons that managers cannot control culture '*in the way that many management writers advocate*' because it is so diffuse. He also sees it as a very complex phenomenon:

> 'When we are observing a culture, whether in an organisation or in society at large, we are observing an evolved form of social practice that has been influenced by many complex interactions between people, events, situations, actions, and general circumstance. Culture is always evolving.' (p.139)

So, an organisation adopting one of the types of organisation culture identified earlier in this chapter is unlikely to hold on to it for ever. A combination of external and internal events will eventually bring about change, and a new culture will emerge.

References

1. Morgan, G. (1986), *Images of Organisation*, Sage.
2. Handy, C. (1993), *Understanding Organisations*, (3rd edition), Penguin.
3. Schein, E. (1992), *Organisational Culture and Leadership,* (2nd edition), Jossey-Bass.
4. Hofstede, G. (1997) *Cultures and Organisations*, McGraw-Hill.
5. Hofstede, G. (1980) *Cultures, Consequences: Influential Differences in Work-related Values*, Sage Publications.
6. Hofstede, G., et al (1990), 'Measuring Organisational Cultures: A Qualitative and Quantitative Study across Twenty Cases,' in *Administrative Science Quarterly 35/2*.
7. Peters, T. & Waterman, R. (1982), *In Search of Excellence: Lessons from America's Best Run Companies*, Harper & Row.
8. Trompenaars, F. & Hampden-Turner, C. (1997). *Riding the Waves of Culture* (2nd edition), Nicholas Brealey Publishing.

Further Reading

Hickson, D.J. & Pugh, D.S. (1995), *Management Worldwide – The Impact of Societal Culture on Organisations around the Globe*, Penguin.

CHAPTER 14

Women in Management

Introduction

1.   In recent years nation-states in many parts of the world have been attempting to improve the status of women in their society. An important element in national policies is the improvement of women's access to a wider range of jobs, including those at a managerial level. Many nations, Great Britain included, have introduced legislation to prevent unfair discrimination against women in the workplace. Such legislation (see Chapter 50) in itself cannot bring about the changes sought by governments, but it can serve to influence male attitudes towards the role of women at work.

2.   There is still much progress to be made, especially in relation to the appointment of women to middle and senior management roles. It has been estimated (Davidson & Cooper, 1993)[1] that, in the UK, women hold less than 5% of senior management posts, and perhaps some 26% of all managerial-type positions. This is in a situation where they make up more than 40% of the total workforce. This chapter examines some of the key issues involved in the employment of women as managers in the workplace. The solution to these issues lies principally in bringing about a massive cultural change in organisations in respect of most of the practices referred to elsewhere throughout this book, for there is hardly any aspect of management practice which could not benefit from a greater involvement by women.

The Social Background

3.　Attitudes towards the role of women as homemakers and/or career people vary from one society to another. Some societies emphasise the woman's role as wife, mother and homemaker. Their attitudes are generally biassed against women taking on anything other than relatively low-level, part-time work. Education for women in such circumstances tends to be geared towards these assumptions about a woman's role. By comparison, the expectations of *men* as breadwinners are high, and thus social action is geared to the education, training and support of men in employment. In such a situation the chances of women being able to gain management positions are poor, except in occupations such as infant teaching, nursing and social work, where women are employed in a professional capacity.

4.　In the UK, major efforts have been made over the past two decades to remove obstacles to women's career development. Legislation such as the Sex Discrimination Act, 1975, and Equal Pay Act,1970, is aimed at encouraging greater fairness towards women at work. Other efforts to improve the lot of women employees include such developments as WISE (Women into Science and Engineering) and Opportunity 2000 – a programme launched in 1991 with the purpose of 'increasing the quality and quantity of women's participation in the workforce by the year 2000'. Since these various developments, but not necessarily because of them, women have begun to take a more active role in management. An official survey (1993)[2] showed that women held about 33% of positions described as Manager or Administrator, but that many of these positions were in traditionally female occupations. In the most senior roles, as already mentioned, women lag far behind men, and well out of proportion even to their presence in middle management.

5.　Why are women so poorly represented at management levels? Several reasons have been put forward, including:

- the social attitudes mentioned above
- the conflict of combining work with family responsibilities
- lack of provision of creche/nursery facilities for working mothers
- the traditional structuring of work which is based on men's needs for full-time work and a career as principal breadwinners
- the need of many women for part-time or temporary work in order to juggle work with their domestic responsibilities – for children, when they are younger, and for elderly relatives when they are older
- the assumptions of many male managers that women are not interested in promotion and/or a full-time career
- the need for many women to have extended career breaks precisely to bring up children and/or care for elderly relatives
- the lack of effective social networks at senior and middle management levels
- the dominance of male values in organisation cultures

6.　In the face of such difficulties, women have to find coping strategies. Flanders (1994)[3] identifies eight different working patterns adopted by women, ranging from continuous full-time work with no career break, or with just short maternity breaks, through a wide variety of part-time forms of employment to self-employment. As if these were not enough, her list does not include being a full-time homemaker! Her conclusion is that:

> 'Women are therefore far more likely than men to require a job which allows them flexibility. Career breaks to have children or look after elderly relatives are an inevitable part of many women's working lives...'(p.5)

The clear implication here is that, if women are to make greater progress in obtaining managerial posts, work must be restructured to allow for greater flexibility of working – including part-time work for managers, agreed career breaks, improved arrangements for the reintroduction of women managers into the management hierarchy following a break, and other facilitating measures.

7.   Work structuring is not the only problem for women. Male prejudice is another. Flanders points out that, whilst past experience helps us to decide how to act in the present, it is nevertheless important to see if that experience is still valid. Men, in particular, she argues, need to examine their current attitudes towards the employment of women managers, since these attitudes may not always be based on sound evidence of a woman's performance. Typical myths, or prejudices, she identifies include the following:

- 'women dislike power, or are afraid of it'
- 'women lack leadership qualities, especially assertiveness'
- 'women are insufficiently ruthless in the workplace'

There is very little evidence to justify such prejudices, and they cannot be used fairly to discriminate against women in management. However, they do exist, and until they are overcome women will continue to be at a considerable disadvantage in their search for a fairer share of management positions.

Sex Differences at Work

8.   Many of the myths about women's needs, wants and capabilities arise from the assumptions that men make about women in the workplace. Research into sex differences at work has tended to focus on identifying physical, cognitive and motivational differences between men and women. Some studies have also examined differences in leadership styles and attitudes towards work. As a general rule, and taking a wide range of studies into account, most of the research indicates that there are few important differences between the performance of the sexes at work, especially in situations where they are able to compete on equal terms.

9.   Where sheer *physical* strength is involved men are invariably superior to women, being generally taller, larger and more muscular. However, the occasions nowadays when purely physical strength is called for are very rare in the work environment, and thus the physical differences between the performance of men and women are scarcely relevant. When it comes to *mental*, ie *cognitive*, skills, there are noticeable differences between the sexes, but these are linked to particular aspects of intelligence, and not to differences in overall intelligence. Colwill (in Vinnicombe & Colwill, 1995)[4], reviewing recent research, and reporting on her own studies, comments in relation to *verbal* skills that: '*Among adults, men tend to have an edge in the solving of analogies, but women outperform men in most other verbal tests, including vocabulary, anagrams and verbal fluency.*' (p.25) She notes that *visual-spatial ability* – important for engineers, architects and air crew, for example – is higher among men than women. So too is *advanced mathematical ability*, although at *lower* levels of performance there is little difference between the sexes.

10. Colwill's own research suggests that, even though women are verbally superior to men, the styles of communication they adopt are devalued at work. She found that women tended to be more polite than men, had a strong tendency to qualify their statements, and tended to use disclaimers (eg '*I know this may sound silly, but couldn't we adopt a strategy of...*). Such deference to others seems to be taken as a sign of weakness, especially by men, whom she found typically listen less than women, interrupt more, and use more aggressive

language. Colwill comments that '... *the verbal styles associated with women's speech are not only devalued; there is evidence that they are devalued more for women than for men ... The research shows ... that women who use ... disclaimers are seen as less intelligent and less knowledgeable ... than women who do not use these 'feminine' styles ... [and] ... less intelligent and less knowledgeable than men who do use them'* !(p.29)

This kind of evidence from recent research helps to indicate the deeply-ingrained male dominance of the work environment. It is not just a question of men's prejudice against women in management roles, but their sheer lack of experience – over decades, if not centuries – of women in responsible roles in the workplace. This is a reflection of organisational culture (see Chapter 13), where the leadership culture of work has been established by men for men. For this cultural tradition to change men and women have to listen and learn from each other.

11. On the topic of women and organisation culture, Marshall (1993)[5] has some interesting comments to make:

> 'I see male and female values as qualities to which both sexes have access ... Women and men are, then, both the same and different. Until recently many researchers have emphasised similarities to win women acceptance in employment. But this theme of equality for similarity has distorted many women's lives and left organisational cultures largely unchanged by the inclusion of women.'

She distinguishes, it should be noted, not between male and female as such, but between their *values* as follows:

Male values	Female values
self-assertion	interdependence
separation	cooperation
control	receptivity
competition	merging
focused perception	acceptance
rationality	awareness of patterns, wholes and contexts
clarity	emotional tone
discrimination	being
activity	intuition
	synthesising

12. Marshall argues that Western society has given predominance to male values, which have shaped its organisations, its language and its cultural norms. This leads, she claims, to assumptions that when they *are* perceived as different to men, women are considered to be inferior – '*Female characteristics and values, such as emotions, intuition, and interdependence, are denied legitimacy and are covertly or actively suppressed.*' Sadly, the same could be said of most human societies.

13. On the issue of women and leadership, Eagly & Johnson (1990)[6], conducted a literature review involving 370 comparisons of styles between men and women managers. The conclusions they drew from all the studies they investigated can be summarised as follows:

❶ women generally adopted a more democratic or participative style compared with men who tended to prefer an autocratic or directive style

❷ in contrived settings (eg assessments) men tended to be more task-orientated than women, but in ordinary work situations there were no noticeable differences in task-orientated styles between the sexes

③ in contrived settings (eg assessments) women tended to be more interpersonally orientated than men, but again in the ordinary workplace, no such difference emerged

Overall, there were fewer differences of leadership style in the workplace than might have been expected, but one consistent difference did remain – women managers were much more likely to adopt a democratic/participative style than their male counterparts. Ironically, such an approach to leadership is the one most favoured by modern management gurus, most of whom are men!

14. There have been numerous research studies into possible differences between men and women in such aspects of workplace behaviour as motivation, attitudes to work, ability to motivate teams, and in work performance generally. The overall results demonstrate clearly that on these points there are no major differences between the sexes. What, therefore, can be done by organisations and by individuals to allow women to make a full contribution to work activities?

Women in the Workplace – Breaking through the Glass Ceiling

15. The difficulties faced by women, in attempting to break into what has been, and still is, mainly a man's world, has been referred to as 'the glass ceiling', an analogy which attempts to describe the subtly transparent barrier that prevents women from gaining access to the more senior roles in their organisations. Given the nature of the male dominance over the workplace, what can organisations do to achieve greater fairness for women and a better balance of the sexes in managerial roles?

16. There are several possible actions that can be taken at an organisational level to provide a fairer framework of working conditions. These are more likely to succeed (ie to be fully accepted by both sexes) if they are open both to men and women, thus avoiding possible charges either of favouring men or of patronising women. Possible steps that may be taken include:

- Going beyond merely supporting the often minimal requirements of legislation (eg in terms of sex discrimination)
- Increasing part-time opportunities for permanent staff
- Permitting flexible working hours, where this approach can be accommodated within the usual demands of the job
- Making job-sharing available, where this may be practicable, given the demands of the job
- Enhancing training opportunities for potential managers, especially in such aspects of work as leadership skills, assertiveness and time management
- Provide personal development opportunities in form of secondments, special projects and other opportunities to undertake new challenges and extend experience in managerial roles
- Developing awareness training for senior management towards the benefits of women managers
- Introducing career breaks
- Providing, or paying for, creche facilities for employees with family responsibilities
- Ensuring that individuals' accrued rights (eg to pensions, holidays etc) are not disadvantaged merely because the job-holder is a part-time employee or has had gaps in their service with the organisation

17. Although many of the above steps focus on practical aspects of employment conditions, they are nevertheless sending powerful messages to the members of the organisation as a whole. Effectively, what attention to the above implies is a cultural change in the organisation. McDougall & Briley (1994)[7] point out that change in general, and change in equal opportunities in particular, requires 'a sound and accepted reason for initiating such change' (p.22). They go on to suggest that there are increasing external pressures on organisations to reconsider women's roles in the work-place, which are likely to supply the sound and accepted reasons just referred to. The pressures are giving rise to a number of organisational imperatives, including:

- the introduction of flatter organisation structures requiring a broader range of skills from each employee

- the demand for managers in flatter organisations to encourage flexibility of working

- an increased dependence on team-working in organisations – a situation which seems likely to favour *women* managers, since it requires participative leadership styles

- the move to increase individual employees' discretion over their work (*'empowerment'*) creates opportunities for more women to experience the exercise of authority

- the use of objective external standards in work (eg via NVQs/Investors in People etc) enables women to compete with men on equal terms in demonstrating their competence in the job

- the career structures of the past are no longer available, as organisations change their job structures with increasing frequency within flatter overall structures, thus causing men as well as women to experience job changes, periods of unemployment, temporary work and the development of a portfolio of jobs as they progress through their working lives; career breaks for women in such circumstances are less likely to be seen as an obstacle to women's employment, and more a fact of life for everyone.

18. McDougall & Briley conclude that cultural change in itself may not be enough. What is required is that the cultural change should contain an explicit commitment to equal opportunities. This clearly requires the support of top management, including statements to the effect that *'The specific contributions that...the increased representation of women in management positions can make should be identified and communicated to all employees.'* (p.94). It also requires the investment of sufficient resources to achieve the change programme, which should include a training and education strategy for women trainees and line managers, and, most importantly, *'systems and structures to support the change (for example, including equal opportunities as a key result area for managers).'* (p.94).

19. The provision of fairer work structures and employment conditions, combined with real attempts to introduce a culture that operates both male and female values, can only work for women if they are prepared to take advantage of these improvements. Schein (1968)[8], many years ago described three ways in which people could respond to their organisation's efforts to enforce compliance with its values and expectations, that is, to conform to its culture. They could take three stances:

❶ they could *conform* by accepting the organisations values and norms

❷ they could *rebel* by rejecting these values and norms, and take the consequences, which might be positive, but are more likely to lead to resignation or dismissal

❸ they could engage in *'creative individualism'* by accepting certain key values and norms of the organisation, but ignoring others; clearly this is easier to do in some functions than others.

20. The last two of the above methods of coping with a hostile culture are likely to lead to a considerable degree of role conflict, and the third method requires a measure of personal toughness. Marshall (1993)[5] suggests that there are four alternative ways open to women to enable them to cope with their organisation's culture, and especially in what she terms *'high-context, male-dominated cultures'*:

- Stage A – **Muted**. *'The individual does not see organisational cultures as male-dominated. These managers say they want to be treated as people rather than as women … Typically they will argue that being a woman has made no difference to their working life or career progress … for the majority I believe it is largely a process of denial.'* This stage seems to represent Schein's conformity stance.

- Stage B – **Embattled**. *'The first response to this recognition of basic inequality is often anger … Her highly reactive behaviour may well cause problems in relationships … She may become isolated. One choice will be whether to label herself as 'a feminist' – a label seldom welcomed in organisations … This is … an inherently unstable coping pattern.'* This stage seems to be closer to Schein's rebellious stance.

- Stage C – **Rebellious**. *'These people are 'offensive' in at least two senses. They attack inequality … they challenge what others take for granted … To speak out in this way, individuals need a robust sense of self and of their values … (they) may need the support of like-minded women and men to affirm their interpretations in a world that generally disconfirms or rejects them … Despite the challenge people in this position offer the domiant culture, they are also constrained by what is acceptable.'* This stage could represent an overlap between Schein's rebellious stance and the creative individualism.

- Stage D – **Meaning-making**. Women adopting this approach do so on the basis that women have equal power with men in the organisation in terms of shaping the culture. The individual is flexible in her perspectives, but this pattern of coping *'requires high levels of personal and contextual awareness.'* This awareness involves inquiring into purposes and assumptions, not unlike the approach being adopted in business process reengineering (see Chapter 21 below). Marshall comments that ' … *women managers I meet are talking about processes of organisational change and looking for strategies with these subtle characteristics. The collaboration and mutual development potentially involved fit well with female values … This manager is combining aspects of the female and male principles and using contextual sensitivity to shape as well as adapt.'*

21. Marshall acknowledges that reaching Stage D requires a leap of faith. It also involves *'withdrawing consent and collusion from the processes that affirm men as dominant power-holders.'* Adopting this position is likely to create 'organisational turbulence' which the person will have to handle. Marshall concludes that this last stage offers more choices about strategies and criteria for success, but admits that *'No pattern is… inherently effective.'* Nevertheless, her analysis of possible choices for women managers clarifies the position in which they presently find themselves, and suggests at least one positive step forward. Ultimately, however, it is men's attitudes that have to change if women are to become 'empowered' in the way that most senior managers are empowered.

References

1. Davidson, M. & Cooper, C. (eds) (1993), *European Women in Business and Management*, Paul Chapman.
2. *Labour Force Survey, 1993*. HMSO

3. Flanders, M. (1994), *Breakthrough – The career woman's guide to shattering the glass ceiling*, Paul Chapman.
4. Vinnicombe, S. & Colwill, A. (1995), *The Essence of Women in Management*, Prentice-Hall.
5. Marshall, J. (1993), 'Patterns of Cultural Awareness: Coping Strategies for Women Managers', in Long, C. & Kahn, S. (eds), *Women, Work and Coping*, McGill-Queens University.
6. Eagly, A. & Johnson, B., 'Gender and leadership style: A meta-analysis', in *Psychological Bulletin* Vol. 108, No. 2 (1990), p 233–256.
7. McDougall,M. & Briley, S. (1993), *Developing Women Managers*, HMSO.
8. Schein, E.H. (1968), 'Organisational Socialisation and the Profession of Management', in *Industrial Management Review,9, No.2.*

CHAPTER 15

The International Context of Management

Introduction

1.   Few business organisations in any major trading nation can afford to ignore the international dimension of their work. For more than fifty years, large US companies such as Ford, General Motors, Coca Cola, Texaco and others systematically established operations in other countries, such as the UK, bringing their own know-how, management attitudes and business styles. During the last thirty years many important Japanese companies have also established production and marketing operations overseas, especially in the UK, and in so doing have succeeded in introducing a number of their production methods and personnel practices to the British workforce. More recently a number of other Asian companies have begun investing in overseas operations. South Korea and Malaysia have companies such as Daewoo Electronics, and Samsung having a firm presence in the UK. There are more than 120 S. Korean companies operating in Britain – the highest proportion of South Korean investment in the European Union. Trade between nations has been a feature of vibrant human societies ever since the time of the Phoenicians. What is different today is that such trading is conducted on a truly world-wide scale, and is not only about exchanging goods and services, but also of producing them in the trading partners' own economy. Aided by means of telecommunication undreamed of by our ancestors, the truly global economy is beginning to emerge. This is a development that has enormous implications for businesses that decide to become not just multinational but global. Business and management practices increasingly have to account for cultural differences as well as differing legal and compliance regimes in different nation-states.

2.   There are many factors contributing to the increasingly international dimension of management practice. Some of the most significant include:

*   the moves towards political and economic cooperation in major world regions, such as Europe and the Pacific Basin

*   the gradual reduction of tariff barriers and other obstacles to free trade world wide

- the desire of national governments to expand their economies by achieving higher levels of employment at home as a result of inward investment

- the response by national governments to offset the adverse effects of industry restructuring (for instance in coal and steel) by attracting alternative industries funded in part by overseas nations

- the competitive advantage to be obtained from manufacturing in a low-cost economy compared with traditional manufacturing bases

- the opportunity of gaining a foothold in a major economic grouping, and thus overcoming possible trade restrictions or tariff barriers

- the opening up of major new markets in Asia and the Far East

- the sheer competitiveness of markets for key goods and services leading large companies to decide to invest strategically in consumer nations

- the necessity for international collaboration in the manufacture of multi-million dollar projects in industries such as launching global communication satellites, civil aircraft production and oil exploration

- the huge advances which have been made in international communications (for example, via electronic mail, satellite communications, facsimile transmissions and the Internet)

- the increased opportunities available for transporting goods from one part of the world to another at economic prices via pipelines, bulk carriers, container ships and air cargo.

3. The rest of this chapter is devoted to an overview of three major developments in the international context of management in the UK – first, the growing influence of the European Union, both as a market and as a legal framework for business; second, the impact of Japanese practices on British industry; third, the implications of differing national cultures for multinational businesses.

The European Union

4. The significance for British business of membership of the European Union can be judged from the size of the EU market. In 1997 the EU was the world's leading exporter, greater even than the United States and almost twice as large as Japan. As an importer of goods and services the EU was second to the USA. Its most important trading partners are the USA, Switzerland and Japan with significant contributions from China, Russia, Norway, Taiwan, Poland and South Korea. However, because the EU is composed of fifteen separate national economies, which have considerable disparities between them, the political, legal and economic framework of the Union is aimed at harmonising conditions between one nation and another. Britain's participation in the EU means that its own laws (and customs) are gradually changing to conform to EU guidelines, laws, codes of practice and administrative decisions.

5. Although individual countries are permitted to retain some local practices (the notion of *subsidiarity*), the overall intention of the underlying legislation (the Treaty of Amsterdam, 1997) is to work towards the harmonisation of business and economic practices between all the EU nations. The key issue for every nation is how to balance local (national) customs with acceptance of European-wide policies and practices. This issue, which has been termed *glocalisation* (Trompenaars et al, 1997, p.3), is one that is likely to become increasingly important for companies seeking global expansion with a genuinely multicultural workforce.

121

6.   Whereas, in other parts of the world, regional co-operation is by means of trade agreements, the European model, as evident in the EU, is intended to achieve close *political* union, as well as to develop trade internally and with the world-wide community. Already, the laws of the EU take precedence over those of its members on several issues affecting the management of people (for example, regarding equal opportunities). Under EU law, an *Article*, for example from the *Treaty of Amsterdam 1997*, is directly binding on member states, and a *Directive* requires a member to introduce its own legislation, whilst not being directly binding.

The Social Charter

7.   The Treaty of Amsterdam effectively consolidated the effects of earlier legislation (such as the Maastricht Treaty), and further encouraged the development of guideline agreements, such as the so-called 'Social Charter', which aims to provide a general standard for improved living and working conditions for workers in the EU. Initially, the UK government opted out of the original Charter on the grounds that it was too prescriptive in areas such as works councils, hours of work and some aspects of social benefits. Management organisations in Britain also had reservations about the charter, especially regarding the harmonisation of employee relations matters. However, in 1998 the newly elected Labour government decided to sign up to the Charter, and UK labour law is gradually being adapted to meet the Charter's standards in those cases where the present law falls short.

8.   The main principles underlying the Social Charter can be summarised as follows:

* social aspects of the developing European Market must be accorded the same importance as the economic aspects

* the promotion of employment and the reduction of unemployment are key priorities

* the completion of the Market must offer EU citizens improvements in the social sphere, particularly in relation to freedom of movement within the Community, living and working conditions, social protection, education and training

* in social policy any discrimination on grounds of sex, race, ethnic origin, religion or belief, disability, age or sexual orientation should be avoided.

9.   Within these broad aims there are several specific rights conferred on EU citizens. Although there have been reservations among the management professions concerning the prescriptive nature of some elements of the Charter, there has also been an acknowledgement that most of it represents 'good practice'. The effect on managers throughout the EU will certainly be felt in the implementation of revised terms and conditions of employment that will be expected of their organisations. The Charter, which embraces twelve major aspects of employment rights, is entitled The Community Charter of Fundamental Social Rights for Workers. Examples of all the principal rights are illustrated in the following list:

❶   **The right to freedom of movement**
* Every citizen of the EU will have the right to freedom of movement throughout the territory subject to certain restrictions relating to public order or health.
* A citizen shall be able to engage in any occupation or profession on the same terms as those applied to nationals of the host country ...

❷   **Employment and remuneration**
* All employment shall be fairly remunerated whether by law, collective agreement or other practice.

- A decent wage shall be established especially at the basic level.
- Every individual shall have free access to public placement services.

③ **Improvement of living and working conditions**
- A maximum duration of working time will be established.
- Improvements should also cover seasonal, part-time and temporary workers as well as issues such as night work and shift work.
- Every worker shall have the right to annual paid leave and to weekly or other agreed rest period.

④ **Right to social protection**
- All workers, whatever their status, and whatever the size of their undertaking, shall enjoy adequate levels of social benefits proportional, where appropriate, to their length of service, pay and personal contribution to the social security system.

⑤ **Freedom of association and collective bargaining**
- Employers and workers shall have the right to form associations for the defence of their economic and social interests, and to have the right to join or not to join such associations.
- Employers' and workers' organisations shall have the right to make collective agreements under the conditions laid down by national legislation and practice
- The right to resort to collective action in case of a dispute shall include the right to strike, subject to national regulations and collective agreements
- Appropriate levels of conciliation, mediation and arbitration procedures should be encouraged to facilitate settlements.

⑥ **Right to vocational training**
- Every EU worker shall have the opportunity to continue his/her training during working life.
- Every EU citizen shall have the right to enrol for occupational training on the same terms as nationals in the country where the course is held.

⑦ **Right of men and women to equal treatment**
- Equal treatment for men and women shall be assured, and equal opportunities developed, especially in relation to remuneration, access to employment, social protection, education and training, and career development.
- Such action shall imply the development of facilities to enable those concerned to reconcile their occupational and family obligations more easily.

⑧ **Right of workers to information, consultation and participation**
- Information, consultation and participation for workers must be developed taking account of national laws and practices.

⑨ **Right to health protection and safety at the workplace**
- Every worker must enjoy satisfactory health and safety conditions.

⑩ **Protection of children and adolescents**
- The minimum employment age shall not be lower than the minimum school-leaving age, and, in any case, not lower than 15 years.
- Young employees must receive equitable remuneration in accordance with national practice.

- The duration of work must be limited and night work prohibited for those under 18 years.

- Following the end of compulsory education, young people must receive initial vocational training of sufficient duration during working hours.

⑪ Elderly persons

- Every person in retirement shall be able to enjoy a decent standard of living.

⑫ Disabled persons

- All disabled persons shall be entitled to additional measures aimed at improving their social and professional integration.

10. Many of the above rights are already contained within UK law and/or collective agreements. Most are within the scope of collective bargaining agreements between employers and employees, and could be introduced, or extended, by the parties concerned. Some rights, for example relating to social security, are the responsibility of the government, which must act before employers can introduce the appropriate improvements. It is clear that the EU model goes far beyond making mere trade agreements between members. It is building a massive regional economy for the European continent, and also acting as a vehicle for the achievement of political ends, such as the distribution of wealth and protection of the elderly, within its members. As global links increase, other regional trade groups in the world will be looking at the European experience with much interest over the next decade or two.

Japanese Companies

11. The phenomenal success of Japanese enterprises in securing such a significant proportion of world trade over the past thirty years has been of particular interest world wide. In the UK, this interest has been sharpened by the considerable investment in the economy by major Japanese firms, entering key industries, such as motor manufacturing and electronics. Whilst taking advantage of investment incentives offered by the British government, and the range of skills offered by British workers, companies such as Toyota, Honda and Panasonic have introduced several of their own personnel and production practices. These have been adapted to the British context and have gained the acceptance of the managers and workers concerned. New practices in relation to production methods, quality control and management-worker attitudes have been successfully introduced, for example by the Nissan motor company in the north-east of England, once an area well known for its coal, steel and shipbuilding.

12. The success of Japanese corporations both at home and overseas has stimulated a great deal of enquiry about the reasons for their success. Some of the most important reasons are mentioned below. However, as the world moved towards the end of the second millennium, the Japanese economy faltered and then experienced a sharp decline. Large international companies such as Panasonic saw their profits drop by more than half during the last four years of the century. Many such companies had to shed core staff, mainly by means of early retirement. Wages and prices fell. Banks faced an increase in bad debts, and were less inclined to invest in developing businesses. The outlook for the start of the third millennium was one of considerable challenge. Interestingly, whereas some Japanese electronics companies in the UK were cutting back, others, especially in motor manufacturing, were achieving excellent results.

13. Over the last thirty years a number of myths have grown up around the success of Japanese industry, and today these are being put to the test. Some of the arguments that

have been put forward are discussed later in this chapter. There are at least five important differences between Japanese and British industrial concerns. The first general difference between Japanese and British companies lies in the way they are funded. In Japan, there is much less reliance on shareholders for the funding of business. Instead the major banks play the greater role in providing funds. One result of this is that the board of directors is more powerful than the shareholders' meeting. The board determines the long-term strategy of the company, appointing an executive board made up of senior directors, which concentrates on short-term, operational issues. Most Japanese directors have line responsibilities, and this gives the executive board a strong production emphasis. However, this emphasis has to be seen against the background of state-supported fiscal, and research-and-development, policies aimed at encouraging long-term planning, based on a close analysis of previous performance statistics.

14. The second difference is that the trade unions in Japan are *company* based rather than *occupationally* based, as in Britain, or *industry* based, as in Germany. The company-based approach to trade union organisation reflects a unitary attitude towards employee relations rather than the pluralistic attitude that typifies British employee relations (see Chapter 49). Thus, in Japan employees are only able to join their company union, whose primary aim will be to achieve lifetime job security for its members, and ensure, in collaboration with the management, the success and efficiency of the company, upon which everyone depends. This contrasts strongly with a British trade union, which is not dependent on any one company, and indeed has to show that it is *independent* to obtain official listing. The emphasis in British trade unions is on protecting and promoting the *members'* interests, even though in practice this implies support for the employment opportunities offered by the business concerned. Nevertheless, an example of British practice prevailing over Japanese occurred in October 2001, when the Honda motor company at Swindon finally recognised the engineering union (AEEU). The situation came about after the union had sought a recognition ruling from the Central Arbitration Committee (see Chapter 49), during which it had to prove that at least 10% of the employees were already union members. Once the figure was independently proven, the Company agreed to recognise the AEEU. For the previous sixteen years a company union had represented the workforce. The company is nevertheless one of the most effective motor manufacturers in Europe.

15. The third difference between UK and Japanese practices is that, at least until recently, personnel policies in Japanese firms have been based on a number of traditional assumptions about work, which imply a loyalty to the company, and identification with its products and ultimate success. In other words there is a strong adherence to company culture (see Chapter 13 above). These key assumptions that lie at the root of Japanese employee relations have been as follows:

- the workforce will be composed of a core labour force supported by casual or part-time employees (mostly women)
- lifetime employment will be offered to core workers only
- retirement of core workers at age 55 is insisted on
- career paths for core workers are non-specialised, and job flexibility is a key feature of all work
- pay is based on seniority
- considerable attention is paid to employee selection and training
- collaboration and team working are seen as essential

- the culture is egalitarian in which single-status predominates (at least for core workers)
- promotion is invariably from within the workforce.

16. Fourthly, the organisation structure of Japanese companies, whilst hierarchical, is much less dependent on formal, bureaucratic authority than on group consensus and individual expertise. Decision-making processes in Japanese firms tend to be focused on defining questions rather than on finding solutions. Thus, as all levels of the organisation are involved in this process, so an overall consensus on problems and priorities emerges. This consensus approach tends to reinforce feelings of loyalty and commitment from all concerned.

17. Fifthly, meticulous attention is paid to production planning and quality issues. Particular points of interest here include:

- quality control is seen as the responsibility of every employee not just supervisors or quality control specialists.
- the widespread use of discussion groups called *quality circles* enables employees at every level to participate in the achievement of high standards of quality
- an overall sense of teamwork and commitment to company business goals is encouraged
- training is seen as a necessary ingredient in the task of bringing individual employees up to a state of readiness to influence quality in the workplace
- employees are expected to accept complete job flexibility after training is completed
- use of key statistical data in discussions about quality and efficiency at shop-floor level
- employees are required to understand what statistics are available and how they can be interpreted.
- most recruits to Japanese firms have to work their way up from the shop-floor level, so there is a shared experience of life at this level for all managers and supervisors.

Japanese Management Practices in Britain

18. How have Japanese management practices been adapted in the context of employee relations in the UK? Typical features of employment conditions in Japanese-owned companies in Britain are as follows:

- Each company will only grant 'recognition' with full negotiating rights to one union (for example, AEEU at Toshiba, Nissan and Honda). Of course, in the UK context these are independent trade unions not company unions.
- Terms and conditions of collective agreements are held to be binding on both sides.
- There is a 'no-strike' clause in procedure agreements.
- In the case of a dispute which cannot be resolved internally, there is resort to 'pendulum arbitration' (an external arbitrator has to decide in favour of one side or the other, with no compromise).
- Single status applies (all employees are staff, receive annual salaries and share the same facilities).
- Selection is rigorous and training is thorough (for example, new recruits sent to Japan for part of their basic induction and job training).
- Full participation in company as well as shop-floor decisions is expected as well as encouraged by management.

- Great attention is paid to the quality of work and the efficiency of systems.

19. Japanese firms investing in Britain have undoubtedly been able to take advantage of a situation that was favourable to them. Unemployment in the areas selected for investment was high, enterprise grants were made available from government, and trade union power was weakened by the threat of unemployment. However, it is clear that such firms eventually won the support of their workers, who demonstrated their ability to collaborate positively with Japanese styles of management to produce quality products. It is interesting to note that many of the practices mentioned in the previous paragraph, such as single status and commitment to teamwork, were by no means new to British managements, and had been promoted by organisations such as the Industrial Society for many years earlier. Other practices such as single union agreements, flexible working and no-strike clauses are more recent, and have arisen from changes in employment law over the past fifteen years (see Chapters 49–50). The pay off for the Japanese companies involved is that they have been able to provide themselves with regional manufacturing bases from which to launch their products into the huge EU market.

Myths about Japanese Industry

20. In his book about doing business in Japan, Rice (1995)[2] looked to the future by noting that Japan was certainly changing, but that certain truths that have remained constant for several hundred years 'can be safely assumed to have relevance for a few more at least'. He quoted in particular the idea of group consciousness predominating over the individual consciousness, and the fact that people would still tend to spend their entire careers with one company. He also predicted that there would be no structural down-turn in the Japanese economy brought about by changes in traditional values. This viewpoint is being tested strongly at the start of the new millennium, as major Japanese companies are struggling to offset the effects of a slump in world trade.

21. Matsumoto (2002)[3], describing how he sees the new Japan, refers to seven stereotypes about Japanese behaviour that he believes can now be seriously questioned. Six of these are related to work. He argues that the *collectivist approach* to work issues is not proven, as Hofstede (1980)[4] hinted several years ago. Matsumoto also disagrees that the *interdependent self concept*, where the self is seen as merging with others, is as dominant now as it was in earlier times. He argues along the same lines when considering the idea of *high versus low interpersonal consciousness*, where awareness of and response to others comes before awareness of one's own needs. On the issue of *tight versus loosely controlled emotions*, he argues that the typical stereotype does not apply, even though it is true that Japanese do tend to express their emotions in terms of their context. Matsumoto agrees that the idea of the Japanese employee as a *loyal salaryman* is partly true, but less so for those employed in large corporations, who are demonstrating their desire for a balanced work/home/leisure life. On the associated stereotype of *lifetime employment*, Matsumoto thinks that this is becomingly increasingly less true. He quotes surveys showing that the number of companies offering lifetime employment has dropped from about 27% in 1990 to just under 10% in 1999. Graduates recruited from university are projected to fall from 89% in 1998 to about 81% in 2003. Matsumoto concludes that 'Japanese business culture, like its mainstream societal culture, is going through a major transition ... the changes we are witnessing are not just a fad ... they are representative of the broader changes in culture and society that are occurring in Japan today' (p.79).

22. The broad changes taking place in Japanese society are symptomatic of the effects of growing international collaboration between nations and cultures. The necessities of inter-

national trade, and the increased awareness of alternatives via the Internet, both help to promote evolutionary change, especially in nations where ancient traditions no longer seem to provide the answers to modern-day problems of earning a living, raising a family and generally contributing to society. Dominant national cultures will always be influential in decisions about what is important in the workplace, and how resources should best be utilised, as evidenced by Hofstede, Trompenaars and others (see section below), but it is also inevitable that some adaptations will occur as the result of international collaboration.

Multinational Enterprises

23. Investment by foreign companies in Britain has been undertaken by large business corporations rather than small companies, and this is typical of internationalisation in business. The American writer Korth (1985)[5] sees four stages of internationalisation, ranging from domestically based, reactive trading with foreign countries to full-blooded multinational operations on a global scale. Only in the later stages of international trading do companies actually invest in foreign countries. Such investment plays an important part in the shaping of company business strategy, even though headquarters is still in the home country. Full multinational status is likely to confine the influence of headquarters to that of a holding company, as it is the international divisions that are responsible for the success of the company's overall product-market strategies.

24. The size of multinational organisations is enormous, many of them have total sales well in excess of the Gross National Product of many of the world's nations. World Bank statistics of comparisons between multinational enterprises and national GNPs show, for example, that large oil firms such as Exxon and Shell are larger in economic terms than nations such as South Africa, Austria and Argentina, and substantially greater than nations such as Greece, Bulgaria and Egypt. Other large multinationals include General Motors, British Petroleum, Ford and IBM.

25. The sheer size (and wealth) of multinationals means that they can have a significant effect on host countries. Most of the effects are beneficial, and they include:

- capital investment in major economic activities
- creation of jobs across a broad spectrum of knowledge and skills
- stimulating demand for education and training in the economy
- releasing wider range of products/facilities to local customers
- the introduction of new or scarce skills
- installation of state-of-the-art technology
- facilitates trade between host nation and others
- improvements in the nation's balance of payments
- improves prospects of a higher standard of living for the nation's population
- potentially adds to the nation's pool of skilled/highly qualified personnel.

26. Nevertheless, there are some potential disadvantages, for example:

- the power of multinationals over national economies, due to the extent of their investment in the host nation, cannot be denied, as it is always open to such international enterprises to remove their operations to another country at relatively short notice, which is a powerful sanction on the host country
- local politicians may compromise on employment conditions or environmental considerations in order to retain the benefits of the multinational organisation

- multinationals may always pose a threat to new indigenous rivals in the marketplace, thus holding back the development of strong national enterprises able to compete with foreign competitors.

International and Cultural Differences in Managing Organisations

27. In a classic study into cultural differences in national values between employees of a multinational business organisation, Hofstede (1980)[6] investigated value differences between over 11,000 employees in a single multinational company (IBM) operating in 40 countries. Culture, according to Hofstede, 'determines the identity of a human group in the same way as personality determines the identity of an individual' (p.26). In his view *values* are the building blocks of a *culture*, a term he applies exclusively to the characteristics of a *society*, using the expression *sub-culture* to refer to organisations, professions and families. Basically, Hofstede's study focused on the influence of *national culture* on the *sub-culture of organisations*, as elicited from questioning, and observing, the employees of a large multinational corporation.

28. From his data, Hofstede selected four key dimensions (and later identified a fifth) against which to differentiate contrasting values and attitudes towards work-related issues in each of the various national cultures. These dimensions can be summarised as follows:

- **Individualism versus collectivism** – this dimension distinguishes *individualism* as a national attribute that favours people looking to themselves and their families as their first priority, and *collectivism* as an attribute that expects people to give loyalty to, and find protection in, the wider group.

- **Power distance** – this refers to the extent to which different cultures accept different distributions of power within the society; a *high power distance* society accepts wide differences of power between those at the top of society and those at the bottom; a *low power distance* society sees power as being shared much more equitably, leaving less of a power gap between the top and the bottom ranks.

- **Uncertainty avoidance** – this is concerned with the extent to which a society is able to tolerate uncertainty and therefore feels less need to avoid it (*low avoidance*) or where uncertainty is not tolerated, people feel threatened by it and therefore seek to avoid it (*high avoidance*).

- **Masculinity versus femininity** – this rather provocative dimension distinguishes between those nations that prefer assertiveness and materialism (*masculinity*) and those concerned more with relationships and the welfare of others (*femininity*).

29. Hofstede found that, when comparing the results obtained from the forty countries against the criteria of the framework, it was possible, using the technique of statistical cluster analysis, to allocate them to eight 'cultural clusters', each of which had a particular profile of characteristics under the four dimensions. These clusters were labelled according to *geographical* area (Asian, Near Eastern, Germanic and Nordic) or *language* (Latin and Anglo) and can be summarised as in Figure 15.1.

30. Hofstede's initial research stimulated other culture-related studies, and a fifth cultural dimension was isolated in association with Canadian researcher Michael Bond (1988)[8], whose research was conducted from a Chinese perspective. This fifth dimension was as follows:

- **Long-term versus short-term orientation** – this refers not just to expectations of results, but also to attitudes towards savings and investment, towards social pressures 'to keep up with the Joneses', and towards respect for tradition.

I – More developed Latin
High power distance
High uncertainty avoidance
High individualism
Medium masculinity
Belgium   France
Argentina   Brazil
Spain
(Italy)

II – Less developed Latin
High power distance
High uncertainty avoidance
Low individualism
Whole range of masculinity
Columbia   Mexico
Venezuela Chile
Peru
Portugal

III – More developed Asian
Medium power distance
High uncertainty avoidance
Medium individualism
High masculinity
Japan

IV – Less developed Asian
High power distance
Low uncertainty avoidance
Low individualism
Medium masculinity
Pakistan   Taiwan
Thailand   Hong Kong
India   Philippines
Singapore

V – Near Eastern
High power distance
High uncertainty avoidance
Low individualism
Medium masculinity
Greece
Iran
Turkey
(Yugoslavia)

VI – Germanic
Low power distance
High uncertainty avoidance
Medium individualism
High masculinity
Austria
Israel
Germany
Switzerland

VII – Anglo
Low power distance
Low-medium uncertainty avoidance
High individualism
High masculinity
Australia   Canada
Great Britain
Ireland
New Zealand
USA
(South Africa)

VIII – Nordic
Low power distance
Low-medium uncertainty avoidance
Medium individualism
Low masculinity
Denmark   Finland
Netherlands
Norway
Sweden

Figure 15.1 Cultural clusters arising from Hofstede's research.
(adapted from Hofstede[2] 1980, p 336)

Countries that scored high on long-term orientation included China, Taiwan, Japan, and South Korea. Countries in the lower third of the scale included Canada, Great Britain, USA, Australia and Germany.

31. Hofstede concluded from his researches that it is impractical to produce a unified managerial approach that can be adopted world wide to meet the needs of individuals and groups, their structures and the requirements of change. A contingency approach is called

for in these circumstances. This implies that organisation structures, management styles, organisation cultures and programmes of change have to be *adapted* to the dominant cultural attributes of the host nation. This finding is of major significance to multinational organisations and others that employ or collaborate with nationals of a foreign country. For example, the Japanese companies that have invested in the UK have learned to work with British managers and workers by accepting their high sense of individualism, but at the same time seeking compromise on uncertainty avoidance. Such international collaboration may well hold important clues to future developments, as each nation's managers learn to adapt their cultural values in the light of their experience of working together.

32. The most significant feature of Hofstede's research is that it draws attention to five crucial areas of human behaviour at work where there are likely to be substantial differences in cultural assumptions (see Chapter 13 above), and therefore quite different ways of approaching the management of people. In essence these five areas of difference can be re-stated as follows:

- different attitudes towards the sharing of power and status, and what alternative structures, management styles and other manifestations these may lead to
- differences in the extent to which uncertainty is tolerated, and thus the degree of risk likely to be acceptable, especially in novel situations
- differences in the value put on team work as opposed to individual effort and achievement, leading to alternative ways of structuring work and roles, and rewarding people
- different attitudes towards 'success' and how it should be obtained, giving rise to different goals (for example, personal success or the common good), and different ways of achieving them (such as personal drive and assertiveness versus harmonious relationships and collaborative methods)
- differences in the extent to which a long-term rather than a short-term view is taken concerning business results, the use of resources, the pressures for change, and the setting aside of funds (investment) for future needs.

33. More recent studies of international cultural differences have been conducted by Trompenaars and Hampden-Turner (1997)[9], who have grouped the major differences around *seven* dimensions, the first five adapted from much earlier work by the American sociologist, Talcott Parsons (1951)[10], and two other dimensions derived from their ongoing research. Their seven dimensions are:

- **Universalism versus particularism** – the extent to which rules predominate over relationships, which asks the question 'is keeping to the rules more important than loyalty to others?' Universalists are concerned with consistency, equality and adherence to the rules, whereas particularists are less concerned with abstract rules, but take account of people's needs in particular circumstances.
- **Communitarianism versus individualism** – the extent to which the community's needs are placed before those of individuals, or, in the case of work situations, where the team effort is considered as more important than individual efforts.
- **Neutral versus emotional** – the extent to which interactions are detached and objective (neutral) or whether the expression of emotions is permitted.
- **Diffuse versus specific** – the extent to which interpersonal relations are seen as involving the whole person or merely the person as customer, supplier or other specific role; the former approach sees building relationships as central to business dealings, the latter focuses on the facts of the matter.

- **Achievement versus ascription** – the extent to which a person is judged by what they do (have achieved) or on the basis of who they are (age, gender, business connections); in an achievement culture, a new recruit is more likely to be asked *what* they studied and *what* degree they obtained, whereas in an ascriptive culture they are more likely to be asked *where* they went to university, and *how much* they enjoyed it.

- **Sequential versus synchronic notions of time** – the extent to which people view time in a linear fashion as one event after another, or as something that links the present with both the past and the future; those with a sequential orientation prefer to do one thing at a time, and are very punctual, whereas those with a synchronic orientation can do several things (successfully) at once, and are less concerned with punctuality.

- **Inner-directed attitude towards the environment versus an outer-directed attitude** – the extent to which an individual sees the natural environment as something to be controlled, or harnessed, rather than recognising that the self is part of that environment and can embrace it; the former view sees the world as a machine, the latter as an organism.

34. The dimensions used in the two sets of research described above are mostly quite different. Only on the *individual–collective* dimension is there a complete overlap. Perhaps two others have some characteristics in common, but interestingly, even on attitudes towards *time*, the researchers examined different aspects of the issue – in one case, *long versus short-term*, and in the other *sequential versus synchronic*. The outcome is that we can add a further six areas of difference to the five already mentioned in paragraph 32 above. The six additional areas can be summed up as follows:

- different attitudes towards rules and consistency
- differences in the extent to which emotions are allowed to influence decisions and personal interactions
- differences in the extent to which relations with others are seen narrowly (in specific terms), or broadly, as whole persons
- differences in the way people are judged, whether mainly on what they have achieved, or by what kind of person they are
- differences in the extent to which matters are dealt with sequentially rather than being able to carry out several tasks at about the same time
- differences in how the environment is perceived, whether as a machine to be controlled, or as an organism of which people are a part.

Businesses operating in a truly global market will need to be prepared to deal with at least eleven important differences between the national cultures involved. Much of the challenge in the future will lie in reconciling, or adapting, these differences in order to achieve the best results from a multinational workforce.

35. Trompenaars and Hampden-Turner (1997)[11] recognise that their seven sets of opposing attitudes need to be reconciled if international collaboration is to take place, and the truly 'global economy' emerge. For each of the seven, they propose ways of mediating the unhelpful effects that can arise when the two cultural attitudes clash. So, in the case of *universalism versus particularism*, their argument runs along the following lines: 'Yes, we need to apply rules universally to ensure equity and consistency, but we do not want to be too rigid and bureaucratic, so we want people to adapt to circumstances, where appropriate, but we must avoid chaos, or losing our sense of direction, so we need to apply some rules and procedures, thus completing the circle.'

By acknowledging both the positive and negative features of their dimensions, they can ask questions aimed at encouraging managers to take an adaptive stance towards them in the light of their own national cultural preferences.

36. In applying their ideas to the subculture of organisations, Trompenaars and colleague proposed a two-dimensional approach to corporate culture, based on an *equality-hierarchy* dimension, and a *task orientation-person orientation* dimension. This work is summarised in Chapter 13 above in the discussion on organisation cultures.

Theory Z (Ouchi)

37. Ouchi (1981)[12], whose ideas have already been outlined in a discussion of motivation theory (Chapter 6), made an early contribution to the discussion of cultural differences and whether they could be transferred. Ouchi's studies into the differing characteristics of Japanese and American organisations were principally to see if selected practices from Japanese industry could be translated to the USA. His primary concern was with identifying aspects of practice that could be adapted. Among his findings, Ouchi discovered the following differences in the behaviour of Japanese and American organisations, most of which have been mentioned earlier in this chapter:

Japanese organisations - - - - - - - - - - - - - - - **American organisations**

1. Offer *lifetime* employment - - - - - - - - - - - Offer (generally) *short-term* (core workers only) - - - - - - - - - - - - - - - - - employment

2. Promote from *within* - - - - - - - - - - - - - - - Recruit from *outside*

3. Career paths are *non-specialised* - - - - - - - - Generally *specialised* career paths

4. *Shared* decision-making - - - - - - - - - - - - - *Individual* decision-making

5. *High* degree of mutual trust/loyalty - - - - - - - *Varying* degrees of trust/loyalty between managers and employees - - - - - - - - between the two sides

6. Importance of *collective* responsibility - - - - - *Individual* responsibility for results

7. *Long-term* performance appraisal - - - - - - - - *Short-term* performance more important

8. Success seen in terms of *cooperative* - - - - - - Success seen in terms of *individual* efforts achievements

38. Ouchi proposed 'theory Z' as a means by which American companies could imitate certain features of the Japanese approach to managing people. He argued that American firms could make changes in the following areas of human resource management:

- they could offer more secure employment prospects and better prospects of a career

- they could extend employee participation in decision-making

- they could place greater reliance on team spirit and on recognising the contribution of individuals to team effort

- they could encourage greater mutual respect between managers and their staffs.

Such an approach, he argued, had be supported from the top, and required appropriate consultation measures, and a substantial training commitment, especially for managers. Looking back over the twenty years since Ouchi's ideas were put forward, it is true that many of his suggestions have been put into practice in the USA, especially in those companies seeking 'excellence' (see Chapter 11). However, Ouchi's analysis was carried out at a time when the Japanese economy was flourishing, and more core workers could be employed. With the economic downturn that came just before the end of the millennium, the implicit promise of security of employment, and a lifetime career, was severely under strain in Japan. It is less likely to feature in the future given the world economic and competitive environment.

References

1. Trompenaars, F. & Hampden-Turner, C. (1997), *Riding the Waves of Culture*, Nicholas Brealey.
2. Rice, J. (1995), *Doing Business in Japan*, Penguin Books.
3. Matsumoto, D. (2002), *The New Japan*, Intercultural Press/ Nicholas Brealey Publishing.
4. Hofstede, G. (1980), *Culture's Consequences: International Differences in Work-related Values*, Sage Publications.
5. Korth, Christopher M. (1985), *International Business, Environment and Management*, 2nd edition, Prentice-Hall.
6. Hofstede, G. (1980), op. cit.
7. Hofstede, G. (1997), *Cultures and Organizations*, McGraw-Hill.
8. Hofstede, G. &, Michael Harris Bond (1988), 'The Confucius connection: from cultural roots to economic growth', in *Organizational Dynamics*,16, 4, 4–21.
9. Trompenaars, F. & Hampden-Turner, C. (1997), op.cit.
10. Parsons, T. (1951), *The Social System*, Free Press.
11. Trompenaars, F. & Hampden-Turner, C. (1997), op. cit.
12. Ouchi, W. (1981), *Theory Z: How American Business can Meet the Japanese Challenge*, Addison Wesley.

Questions for Discussion/Homework

1. What is the significance of limited liability to the following stakeholders:

   (a) shareholders?   (b) creditors?   (c) bankers?

2. For what overall purpose are companies obliged to make public their constitution and activities?

3. How would you describe the benefits of partnership over sole tradership?

4. Why do some people prefer to establish a registered cooperative enterprise rather than, say, a private limited company?

5. In what ways might an organisation's policies and procedures both reflect and help to shape the organisation's culture?

6. What are the *visible* aspects of an organisation's life that might lead an interested outsider to get an idea of its culture?

7. What practical steps could be taken by organisations to significantly improve women's chances of obtaining (a) middle management posts, and (b) senior posts at board level?

8. What arguments would you put forward in your organisation in favour of giving women employees greater opportunities for promotion and personal development? How would you counter arguments that women are not interested in promotion and career development?

9. To what extent do Japanese management practices in the UK represent what might be considered as 'good management practice'?

10. In Hofstede's terms, what issues of work structuring and management style would an *Anglo* business (eg British) need to consider if opening up a manufacturing plant in a *more developed Latin* country (eg France)?

11. Select four differing cultural attitudes to the organisation of work, and discuss their implications for a multinational company.

Examination Question

An outline answer to this question can be found in Appendix 2.

EQ17 Describe and explain the recognised types of business enterprises. What are some of their advantages and disadvantages when seen from the viewpoint of a proprietor or manager?

(ACCA)

The following six chapters provide a basic introduction to the fundamental management activity of planning. No enterprise can be undertaken in a vacuum. It must have some purpose in mind, and the means to at least make a start towards achieving that purpose. Planning, in essence, is a process concerned with defining *ends*, *means* and *conduct* at every level of organisational life. It is a management activity, which begins by defining the aims and objectives of the organisation, ie *ends*. Planning is also about taking steps (*making plans*) to agree on the resources, ie the *means*, by which the aims and objectives may be fulfilled. Part of this process includes deciding the policies, which will guide the implementation of the plans, ie the manner in which the organisation will *conduct* itself. Planning is an essentially cyclical and an ongoing process, in which aims and objectives are regularly reviewed, and where the progress of plans are subject to frequent review and updating in the light of results. The time perspective of planning is the *future* rather than the present or the immediate past.

Chapter 16 summarises some of the key issues involved at the strategic level of planning, where decisions are taken about the primary vision, goals, competitive situation, and resourcing of the organisation. Chapter 17 looks in a little more detail at some of the practical implications of setting goals, objectives and policies. Chapter 18 outlines some important aspects of setting performance standards in the planning process. Chapter 19 examines some basic decision-making processes, and Chapter 20 summarises the planning aspects of the organisation's human resources. Finally, Chapter 21 considers some aspects of 'grass-roots' planning aimed at improving the ability of the organisation to deliver its goals.

CHAPTER 16

Strategic Aspects of Management

Introduction

1.   As noted in the introduction to this section, planning is a process that takes place at every level of the organisation. As Mintzberg (1994)[1] points out in his robust critique of planning, the term 'planning' implies *formal* planning, which is an activity that breaks down issues, rationalises them and attempts to articulate them. It is an analytical process, even though its ultimate aim is synthesis in the form of coherent proposals. Mintzberg is unhappy with this machine view of planning, especially in relation to strategy making, and argues that organisations can consider their future (plan) without engaging in a formal planning process. Conversely, they can engage in formal planning procedures, yet not consider the future! Ultimately, he sees planning as servicing the strategy formulation process by contributing both to the inputs and outputs of the strategy itself. The lesson to be drawn from Mintzberg's criticisms is that a mechanistic view of the planning process does not tell us everything that is going on in the internal positioning of the organisation in its environment. Nevertheless, for study purposes, it can be very helpful to use mechanistic

models, as they can help to identify the most important issues involved in the planning process.

2.　Most managers are involved in planning at an operational level, engaged in the detailed formulation and review of plans, usually in the form of specific targets and budgets. This operational perspective will be examined later in Chapters 18 and 20. The focus of this present chapter is firmly on the broad, strategic perspective of management. This is the prime responsibility of the board of the company, who are accountable for securing the future of the enterprise, as well as enabling the business to thrive. The principal distinctions between strategic and operational levels of planning are illustrated in simplified form in Figure 16.1.

Strategic planning
Prime accountability: company board/ top management.
Prime focus: company mission, long-term goals, effectiveness.
Major concerns: competitive position, company values, business success (growth in assets, turnover and profits),establishing appropriate financial controls.
Time scale: up to 10 years.

Operational planning
Prime accountability: senior/ middle management.
Prime focus: achieving targets, optimising resources, efficiency.
Major concerns: budgets, sales/ production targets, harnessing technology, human resource management, performance measurement, quality issues, feedback.
Time scale: 1–2 years

Figure 16.1 Differences between strategic and operational planning

3.　Figure 16.1 shows that the prime focus of strategy is effectiveness in the long term, which means making the best choices for the future, whereas operations are primarily concerned with the efficient use of resources in achieving short-term targets. *Effectiveness* is about doing the right thing; *efficiency* is about doing things right. Strategy is concerned with positioning the business in the market, establishing a reputation with customers, employees and other stakeholders. It is concerned with long-term growth and with the stewardship of resources. Those making strategy need to know they are in control of the business. Operational managers, by comparison, are concerned with the efficient delivery of goods and services. Their horizons are the present and the immediate future, as they attempt to make the best use of employee skills, operating procedures and technology in servicing their customers.

4.　Ohmae (1982)[2], the Japanese author of a major text on strategy, comments that 'What business strategy is all about … is, in a word, competitive advantage. Without competitors, there would be no need for strategy, for the sole purpose of strategic planning is to enable the company to gain, as efficiently as possible, a sustainable edge over its competitors.' Such a view is understandable given the highly competitive situation that Japan found itself in at that time. The theme of competitive advantage was also taken up at about the same time by the American academic, Michael Porter, whose work will be discussed shortly. However, it must be said that strategy is more than just a question of gaining competitive advantage, important though that is. Strategy is also about setting standards of behaviour, developing a corporate culture, setting goals in relation to other stakeholders, such as the company's own employees, its suppliers and its shareholders. Companies increasingly have to decide how they are going to serve community interests as well, so there is more to strategy than trying to beat the competition.

5.   At its simplest level, strategic management is designed to ensure that those running a business enterprise are giving proper attention to the following crucial matters:

- setting an overall vision, or mission, for the organisation – a task that should be required only infrequently

- establishing the fundamental long-term aims of the business in relation to its key stakeholders and the competition – again an infrequent task

- establishing the policies that will guide the implementation of decisions, and provide standards of integrity and public accountability – infrequent

- reviewing, and adapting as necessary, the decision-making and other mechanisms designed to support the strategy-making process – an ongoing task

- setting the key product-market, resourcing, quality and other targets arising from the basic long-term aims – a task required at least annually

- ensuring appropriate team structures and staff competencies to enable business operations to function efficiently and effectively – an ongoing challenge

- establishing appropriate monitoring procedures to enable relevant feedback to be supplied to every level of the enterprise – ongoing.

6.   Strategic management is a complex process involving considerable interplay between its component parts. The ultimate aim is not just to optimise the enterprise's competitive and other goals but also to achieve the best alliance between people, structures and resources within the organisation's own boundaries. Although initiated by top management, and ultimately their responsibility, the process is one in which all personnel eventually play their part. The rest of this chapter discusses some of the major issues of strategic management, based on the work of a selection of the leading theorists on this topic.

7.   The strategic dimension of management has grown in importance over the last thirty years, due to the increasing complexity of modern business organisations. Important contributing factors include:

- the increased expectations of customers for the quality and variety of consumer goods and personal services

- the rapid advance of micro-electronics, which has revolutionised the processes by which goods and services are made available to customers

- the increased ability of firms to compete with each other due to the benefits of new technology, and a sufficiency of trained labour

- the entry into world markets of new low-cost manufacturing firms from Asian countries, which are successfully challenging established Western firms

- the greater concern among nations for protecting the natural environment, leading to the development of alternative materials, components, energy sources etc

- a greater emphasis on consumer rights (in terms of safety, product reliability, level of service etc), leading to increased pressure on companies from legislation at local/regional level

- the improvement in world-wide communication systems, enabling better and more timely information to be available prior to decision-making, for buyers, sellers and middlemen/agents

- the greater interconnectedness of the world's peoples, not only in their trading and commercial activities (as in multinational corporations), but also in political and economic terms (for example, the European Union (EU), Oil Producing and Exporting Countries (OPEC), General Agreement on Trade and Tariffs (GATT))

- the growth of truly multinational corporations, embodying both supranational and local cultures and value systems.

8. The scenario thus presented to many industrial and commercial enterprises is a complex one, requiring attention to the longer-term view and the broader perspective. Strategic thinking has to address such questions as:

- What is our core business? Where are our core markets?

- Do we wish to continue with these?

- Where do we want to be in 5, 10 or 20 years time?

- What are the prospects for growth in the business?

- What resources are we likely to require to sustain growth?

- What threats are we likely to face in our operating environment?

- How can we gain and/or retain a competitive advantage over others?

- How do we plan for the future, yet retain the ability to adapt flexibly in the face of short-term problems?

9. Such questions indicate the principal challenges to the top management of an organisation, for it is their task to ensure that the business has a healthy and prosperous future. This chapter will concentrate on the positive aspects of strategic management, which is planning for growth and development. However, it should not be forgotten that there are situations where the strategy is one of survival. For example, where a business is in decline, the issues are how to make the operation viable, and if rationalisation is called for, how to reduce the impact on the local community. In such cases governments themselves often have to intervene in order to mitigate the effects of unemployment, and attract new employers into the area.

Theories about Strategy

10. The remainder of this chapter outlines some of the ideas proposed by leading consultants and academics, who have studied concepts of strategy and strategic management, developing their ideas from the results of their research into real business enterprises. Many of the issues deal with the problem of reconciling the conflicting forces present in the formulation and implementation of strategy. Others focus on developing corporate goals and objectives, or how to devise a viable internal structure. Yet others focus on the demands of the external world, and their implication for the business. Ultimately, the challenge of strategic management is to orchestrate all these diverse elements into an overall plan for the success of the enterprise.

11. An important early definition of strategy was provided by the American business historian, Alfred D. Chandler (1962)[3], as follows: '(strategy is) the determination of the basic long-term goals and objectives of an enterprise, and the adoption of courses of action and the allocation of resources necessary for carrying out these goals'. Note that Chandler sees strategy as combining goal setting and the planning/action elements required to achieve goals. A key element in Chandler's study of large corporations was the link between strategy and organisational structure. In his view, structure follows strategy,

implying that the adoption of a strategy has inevitable implications for the kind of structure that is needed to deliver the aims and goals embedded in it. Thus, according to Chandler, a growing organisation passes through a number of phases of development. From being a single-location, single-product and single-entrepreneur business, it may grow by geographic expansion or by vertical integration (buying into suppliers or distributors). It may then proceed to functional divisionalisation (with separate divisions for production, marketing etc), and finally to diversification (by introducing new product-markets) in a multi-divisional organisation structure.

12. Another writer, Kenneth Andrews[4], also combines goal-setting with the policies and plans needed to achieve the goals. He distinguishes between corporate strategy, which defines the business(es) the company is to compete in, and business strategy, which determines how the company will compete in a given business. Thus the latter strategy is subordinate to the former, although both are seen as the outcomes of strategic management. Andrews' view of corporate strategy is that it is a pattern of decisions, which represent 'the unity, coherence and internal consistency of a company's strategic decisions that position a company in its environment and give the firm its identity, its power to mobilise its strengths, and its likelihood of success in the marketplace.'

13. By comparison with the above two viewpoints, H.I. Ansoff, some of whose ideas are referred to in Chapter 19, prefers to separate goals, or what he calls objectives, from strategy. However, he envisages a close relationship between the two in which an objective (end) is followed by a strategy (means), which is evaluated and may lead to a revision of the original objective. In order to realise a strategy, Ansoff argues that three types of decisions need to be made. These are strategic, administrative and operating decisions. The first are decisions about product-market aims, the second are decisions about the organisational infrastructure and the third are decisions about budgeting, scheduling and other matters concerned with controlling resources.

14. As one contribution to the debate about strategies (means) Ansoff[5] suggested a matrix of product-market alternatives, which has become widely used. In basic terms the matrix offered the following alternatives (Figure 16.2):

	Present Products	New Products
Present Markets	Market Penetration	Product Development
New Markets	Market Development	Diversification

Figure 16.2 Ansoff's product-market growth strategies.

What the matrix suggests is four growth strategies based on remaining with present products and/or markets, or moving into new products and/or markets. Firms choosing to stay in present markets with current products are basically presented with a strategy of market penetration (ie going for increased market share); those looking for new products in present markets will focus on developing appropriate new products or brands; those aiming to take existing products into new markets will concentrate on sustaining market development activities; and, finally, those firms which intend to develop new products in new markets will pursue a strategy of diversification. This last option is developed by Ansoff to include further alternatives such as horizontal diversification (ie sideways extension into same type of markets with related products), vertical integration (ie upwards or downwards extension into markets/products covered by suppliers, wholesalers etc) and conglomerate diversification, which refers to new products in an unrelated technology and with a new type of market.

15. In a later work (1984) Ansoff[6] redefined strategic management as follows:

'...a systematic approach for managing change which consists of:
1. positioning of the firm through strategy and capability planning;
2. real-time strategic response through issue management;
3. systematic management of resistance during strategic implementation.'

The second item refers to the need to respond quickly to sudden or unanticipated changes in external forces (eg unexpected government policies, trade union sanctions etc) and to adapt the strategic plan to accommodate or minimise the effect of these. The third item shows Ansoff's concern with the possibility of a lack of acceptance by other stakeholders (eg employees or customers) of the changes being pursued in the plan.

16. Another set of alternative strategies that has been put forward is contained in the Boston Consulting Group's (BCG) matrix – named the 'portfolio framework' (see Figure 16.3). This matrix is based on three major variables: a firm's relative market share, the growth rate of its market(s) and the cash flows (negative or positive) generated by the firm's activities. The matrix yields four alternative outcomes for a firm, expressed somewhat idiosyncratically as Stars, Cash Cows, Dogs or Question Marks. Stars are businesses that have a high market share in an expanding market and could be profitable, but where there may be a negative cash flow because of the need to keep up investment to keep pace with market growth. Cash Cows are businesses which have a high share of a slow-growing market and which are usually very profitable and generate a positive cash flow. Dogs are businesses with a low share of a slow-growing market and may produce either a modest positive cash flow or an equally modest negative one. Question Marks are those businesses which have a low share of a fast-growing market and which require considerable investment to keep up with the growth in the market, thus producing negative cash flow. Yet it is precisely these businesses which may have the potential to exploit the growing market and go on to achieve greater market share, healthy cash flow and adequate profitability. Eventually a successful Question Mark can turn into a Star and then into a Cash Cow. However, this outcome depends on an appropriate strategy including adequate funding.

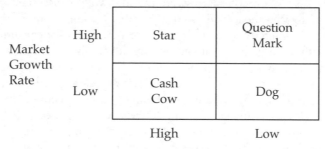

Figure 16.3 Outline of the Boston Matrix (Boston Consulting Group)

17. The BCG matrix has been widely used in the United States despite the criticisms that the names given to each of the possible outcomes are simplistic and misleading. Dogs, for example, may appear as rather mediocre businesses from the matrix, whereas in reality they may have far more potential for growth, cash flow and profitability than they are given credit for. Also Cash Cows may be regarded as ripe for milking, ie to fund Question Marks, for example, whereas they may benefit from further investment themselves.

Nevertheless, the BCG matrix does enable strategists to reflect on some of the important issues for their firms and may encourage them to consider a wider range of options than previously.

Competitive Advantage

18. A different approach to developing corporate strategy has been proposed by M.E. Porter (1980)[7], who has taken competitive advantage as his focus. As an engineer and economist, Porter is concerned with the impact of the external environment on the firm. He sees five major influences (forces) on a firm's ability to compete (see Figure 16.4), comprising not only existing competitors in the industry, but also potential rivals (new entrants), the threat of substitute products, the bargaining power of buyers and the bargaining power of suppliers. These forces are represented schematically as follows:

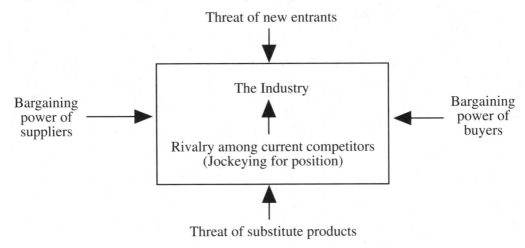

Figure 16.4 Outline of Porter's schema of competitive forces.

19. Porter's five forces can be utilised by firms in their formulation of strategy, and especially in their assessment of their strengths and weaknesses (see SWOT analysis, Chapter 17). Any analysis is most likely to begin with an examination of the firm's industry competitors. At a time of intense rivalry (eg as in the private motor car industry following a period of deep economic recession) competitors are advertising strongly, offering incentives to buyers (interest free credit, free membership of breakdown services etc) and devising ways of differentiating their products ('lean-burn' engines, safety air-bags etc). Firms have to consider how they are going to respond to, or counter, these immediate threats to their sales from rivals. In such a case, suppliers are in a relatively weak position in relation to the firm, since their sales are dependent on the end product (ie new motor cars) being sold. If a car manufacturer is stock-piling vehicles this is bad news for its suppliers.

Buyers, conversely, are in a strong position in these circumstances and can thus drive a harder than usual bargain with dealers (eg looking for a good trade-in price, extra accessories, free delivery etc). Substitute products are not going to be an issue in the above situation, since buyers can pick and choose. However, it would be possible in other circumstances for potential customers to give up motoring in favour of a motor bike or pedal cycle, for example. Given the intensity of the competition in this case, with low profit margins all round, new entrants to the industry are unlikely, as the costs of entering would be high and the returns low.

20. Porter specifically considers the issue of entering new markets and lists seven major barriers to market entry, which can be summarised as follows:

❶ Economies of scale, ie newcomers have to come in on a large scale or accept inevitable cost disadvantages. (This factor alone is likely to deter most would-be entrants, unless they can buy their way into the market by purchasing a firm already active in it.)

❷ Product differentiation, ie newcomers have to find ways of overcoming existing brand loyalties in order to get their own product/brand accepted.

❸ Capital requirements, ie the need to invest considerable sums of money in a new venture, much of which will be unrecoverable (eg start-up losses, advertising, research & development). (This is another huge disincentive to newcomers, unless they have cash surpluses from a Cash Cow business or some other possibility of raising the initial capital resources.)

❹ Switching costs, ie the initial costs of machinery, equipment and other first-time resources required to enable the firm to switch into the new market.

❺ Lack of access to distribution channels, ie the newcomer must work his way into existing distribution channels (eg dealer networks, wholesalers etc) or establish brand new ones. (See Chapter 34 for discussion of distribution channels.)

❻ Cost disadvantages regardless of size, ie newcomers will always tend to have certain cost disadvantages compared with established firms, who will have gained experience in the market, may have access to proprietary technology, and favourable locations, and may also benefit from government subsidies; new entrants may have none of these advantages.

❼ Government policy, ie through licensing and legal regulation, governments can limit or even prevent newcomers from operating in the industry. (Typical licensed industries in the UK include road transport, oil exploration and retail alcohol sales.)

21. Porter's work on competitive advantage has been very influential. His ideas are not without their critics, however, and other commentators have pointed to the lack of reference to issues of the legality and ethics of the barriers described in Porter's list. Also in the schema of the five forces, there are no explicit references to other stakeholders in the firm's environment, especially the community at large, and employees. When Porter talks of buyers and suppliers he does so in terms of their power (or, by implication, lack of it) and avoids any issues regarding the obligations that firms might have in determining their strategy in the market-place.

Other Theories of Strategy

22. Further insights into the nature of strategy have been provided by Hofer and Schendel (1986)[8], who are particularly interested in the adaptations that successful firms make with their environment (survival of the fittest) compared with unsuccessful firms. They are also keen to emphasise the difference between effectiveness and efficiency, where effectiveness refers to the extent to which an organisation achieves what it has set out to achieve (actual versus desired *outputs*), and efficiency refers to the ratio between *outputs and inputs*. In their experience, Hofer and Schendel concluded that when firms adapt to events in their *external* environment, the results are more likely to make an impact on effectiveness, whereas when they adapt their structures and ways of working (ie responding to the *internal* environment), the impact is more likely to be felt on efficiency. On a day-to-day

basis managers are mostly interested in efficiency, but so far as strategic management is concerned it is effectiveness that is the more important, and this implies attention to the external environment of the business.

23. Hofer and Schendel prefer to separate goal-setting from strategy formulation, and they see strategy as a pattern 'of present and planned resource deployments and environmental interactions that indicates how the organisation will achieve its objectives'. For them strategy is clearly to do with means rather than ends. They conclude that strategy has four components, which can be summarised as follows:

1. Scope or domain, ie the extent of the organisation's interactions with its environment. (This could be represented by its product-market position, for example.)

2. Resource deployments, ie both past and present resource and skill deployments that help to achieve organisational goals; these are also referred to as the organisation's 'distinctive competences'.

3. Competitive advantages, ie the unique competitive position developed by an organisation through its pattern of resource deployment and scope decisions.

4. Synergy, ie the total effect sought by the organisation through all its strategic decision-making. (Synergy is usually expressed as the 2+2=5 effect, ie the sum is greater than the total of the parts.)

24. Finally, we outline some of the ideas of two other American researchers, Thompson and Strickland (1990)[9], who suggest that there are five tasks of strategic management, which they see as bringing together (a) the setting of the overall mission or goals of the organisation, (b) the establishing of business objectives, and (c) the strategy required to achieve the first two. The five tasks can be summarised as follows:

*   Task 1 is to define the overall business and develop a mission (or principal goal)

    NB This is essentially an entrepreneurial task involving vision, risk and judgement.

*   Task 2 is to break down the mission statement into specific performance objectives (both long-range and short-range).

    NB This task is also entrepreneurial, and may be considered as an element of a corporate strategy by those who do not separate goal/objective-setting from strategy. Thompson and Strickland, however, only see this task as a separate objectives-setting exercise.

*   Task 3 is the crafting of a strategy, ie the *'pattern of organisational moves and managerial approaches used to achieve organisational objectives ... and mission.'*

    NB At this stage the activities are those of business planning in support of the goals and objectives, and will be concerned both with effectiveness and efficiency.

*   Task 4 is to implement and execute the strategy.

    NB This stage will be more concerned with team leadership, efficiency and other operational matters.

*   Task 5 is to evaluate, review and adjust the implementation activities, as necessary.

    NB A key consideration at this point is organising the feedback of the results of the review, and the model described by Thompson and Strickland allows for feedback to connect with every previous task.

25. The model proposed by Thompson and Strickland is useful for the way it shows the links between top-level strategy formulation and lower-level strategy implementation, which leads neatly to the next chapter, which is essentially concerned with examples of corporate objectives and business planning.

26. Pascale (1991)[10], in a critique of current strategic practices, especially those overtly aimed at gaining 'excellence', argues that there is no one best way of managing strategically. Strategic thinking has to embrace both old and new ways of thinking. He prefers people to think in terms of 'and/also' rather than 'either/ or'. He sees a number of contextual shifts in management, for example as follows:

From exclusive reliance on:	To include as well:
A machine view of organisation, emphasising 'hard' dimensions (structure, systems).	An organic view, emphasising 'soft' dimensions (people, skills).
Manager-dominated leadership.	Managers as facilitators of empowered employees.
Concern for content and specific techniques.	A concern for process and a holistic approach.
Solving problems at all costs.	Solving problems in due course.
Resolving tension.	Maintaining constructive tension.
'Truth' based on laws and principles.	'Truth' as an approximation, ambiguity acceptable.

27. Pascale argues that the choices managers make need not be restricted to the current 'fad' (fashionable theory), but depend on the context in which decisions have to be made. Managers need a new mind set in his view. He suggests that there are three main factors in determining organisational stagnation or renewal. These can be summarised as follows:

Fit   This refers to the internal consistency (or otherwise!) of the organisation's structure, priorities and practices.

Split   This concerns measures taken to delegate and decentralise.

Contend This refers to a management process, which aims to harness tensions and contradictions rather than suppress them.

In order to juggle with the conflicting needs of fit, split and contend, managers need to employ a transcendent approach to strategy, which recognises that 'disequilibrium is a better strategy for adaptation and survival than order and equilibrium'. Pascale clearly believes that managers should live dangerously, as well as thoughtfully!

28. A final comment on strategy can be left to Hamel & Prahalad (1994)[11], whose research into the success of some smaller businesses competing against large international enterprises showed that the ability to foresee new opportunities was crucial. They conclude that the goal of strategy has to include transforming an industry, not just improving an organisation; strategic thinking has to show that incremental change is not enough –

quantum leaps are required! Businesses that are not seeking out, and preparing for, a new future are doomed to failure. The researchers suggest that the quest for competitiveness, in the long-term, depends more on the capacity to reinvent industries and regenerate strategies, than on restructuring (including downsizing) or reengineering, which are aimed mainly at becoming smaller, leaner and more efficient, in the short to medium term. Most firms, in their experience, only consider reinvention or regeneration after they have failed to slow corporate decline through restructuring and reengineering. Success in the future will only come from being a pioneer in the industry, not from benchmarking performance against successful competitors.

29. How can a business organisation orient itself towards competing for a future that does not exist at present, or only partially so? Hamel & Prahalad suggest that the following questions might help to move firms into the new way of thinking:

1 Where is the competitive challenge to be found?

- In reengineering, or in regeneration?
- In transforming the organisation, or in transforming the industry?
- In competing for market share, or in competing for future opportunities?

2 How do we find the future?

- Through learning, or through forgetting?
- Through market positioning, or by developing foresight?
- By developing strategic plans, or by reviewing strategic architecture?

3 How do we mobilise for the future?

- By aligning ourselves with our present strategy, or by developing a strategy that stretches our imagination and sense of risk?
- By seeing strategy in terms of resource allocation, or as resource accumulation for an uncertain future?

4 How do we get to the future before others?

- By being competitive within our present industry, or by aiming to shape our industry in the future?
- By competing for product leadership, or competing for leadership in core competencies?
- By competing as a single entity, or by developing coalitions?
- By maximising the number of new product successes, or by maximising learning about new markets?
- By minimising time taken to reach market, or by minimising time to achieve the global market?

By asking their questions in this way, Hamel & Prahalad hope to encourage managers to think more broadly than previously, and challenge some of the assumptions they have made in the past. Before managers can learn to take risks, however, they have to understand the basics of strategic management, which is the concern of the following chapters in this section.

References

1. Mintzberg, H. (1994), *The Rise and Fall of Strategic Planning*, Prentice-Hall.
2. Ohmae, K. (1982), *The Mind of the Strategist*, McGraw-Hill.
3. Chandler, Alfred D. (1962), *Strategy and Structure*, MIT Press.

4.   Andrews, Kenneth R. (1987), *The Concept of Corporate Strategy*, (3rd edition), Richard D. Irwin.

5.   Ansoff, H.I. (1965), *Corporate Strategy*, McGraw-Hill.

6.   Ansoff, H.I. (1984), *Implanting Strategic Management*, Prentice-Hall International.

7.   Porter, M.E. (1980), *Competitive Strategy: Techniques for Analyzing Industries and Competitors*, The Free Press.

8.   Hofer, C.W. & Schendel, D. (1986), *Strategy Formulation: Analytical Concepts*, West Publishing Company.

9.   Thompson, Arthur & Strickland, A.J. (1990), *Strategic Management: Concepts and Cases*, Richard D. Irwin.

10.   Pascale, R. (1991), *Managing on the Edge*, Penguin.

11.   Hamel, G. & Prahalad, C.K. (1994), *Competing for the Future*, Harvard Business School Press.

CHAPTER 17

Objectives, Policies and Organisational Ethics

Introduction

1.   Planning, as was noted in the introduction to this section, involves decisions about ends (objectives) as well as means, and decisions about conduct as well as results. The objectives set for an organisation will be determined mainly by the view of its owners or senior management as to what is its prime purpose. Thus, the objectives of a business organisation will be based around concepts such as profitability, customer service, shareholder satisfaction and employee motivation. The objectives of a public service are likely to focus on the efficient delivery of a service (eg health or education) to the community. The clarification and definition of key objectives is vital for any organisation, since these are what provide it with a sense of direction and a mission.

2.   One way of looking at strategic management is from the perspective of corporate planning. This has been described variously as a technique, a style of management, or a process. It is probably best to think of it as a process which enables an organisation to identify the following:

*   what it is there for, and what are its principal objectives

*   what are its current strengths and weaknesses

*   what opportunities and threats are posed by its external environment

*   what is the basis of its long-term plans (resourcing etc)

*   what is the context of its short-term plans (annual budgets/rolling plans etc)

*   what are the key performance standards that it is seeking to achieve

*   what rules of conduct/ethical principles it is prepared to support

Clearly, there is much which is similar to, if not the same as, the process of strategic management. It is mainly a question of how widely or narrowly one interprets the concept of strategy.

3.   Corporate planning with its organisation-wide perspective is not the same as long-range planning, which usually focuses on one part of an organisation at a time. A further distinction is that long-range planning looks at the future selectively, whereas corporate planning looks at it comprehensively. The chapter outlines the process of corporate planning, and aims to show the relationship between corporate objectives, policies and ethical statements, and operating plans, as illustrated in diagrammatic form in Figure 17.1.

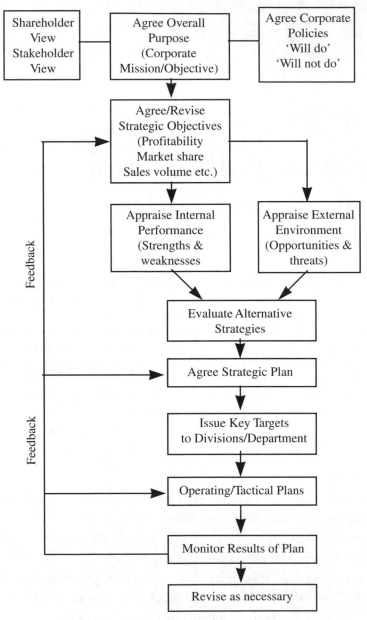

Figure 17.1 An outline of corporate planning.

Corporate Objectives

4.   A major part of corporate planning is the business of setting corporate objectives. Such objectives are usually of two kinds – those that state the overall objective or purpose of the organisation – its mission – and those that set out the organisation's long-term strategic aims. An example of an overall purpose for a business organisation could be *'To grow a successful business for the benefit of customers, employees, shareholders, suppliers and the community in which the company operates'*. A similar example for a public service could be *'To provide an efficient, responsive and considerate revenue collection service for the state'*. Overall objectives tend to be stated in general terms, and are intended to be relatively permanent. They are often accompanied by statements which declare how the organisation intends to conduct itself in the pursuit of its purpose. These are the principal policy statements of the organisation, and will be discussed shortly.

5.   Strategic objectives or aims are set out in similar terms to the overall purpose. They focus on the fundamental purpose of particular parts of the organisation, eg marketing, personnel, finance etc. Their time horizon is usually at least five years, so inevitably such objectives have to be written up in fairly general terms. If they are specific and highly quantifiable they are not strategic objectives, but operational, or tactical, objectives. However, strategic objectives should be stated in such a way that it is possible to see whether they have been achieved or not. For example, a strategic objective for the Personnel function in an organisation could be 'To ensure that the organisation's needs for sufficient and suitable manpower are met over the next five years'. Such a statement says nothing about the different types of skills that may be needed, nor does it say anything about relative numbers. Nevertheless, it would be quite possible after the period concerned to assess whether Personnel had met their long-term aim. A marketing example could be 'To meet the organisation's need for information and advice concerning (a) its markets (existing and potential); (b) its competitors and (c) its economic environment'. This kind of broad statement indicates one of the principal reasons why a Marketing Department exists, ie to provide market research and market intelligence for the organisation.

6.   Strategic objectives are normally set for all the major functions of the organisation, and taken together they sum up what business the organisation intends to be in during the foreseeable future. Such objectives cover areas such as markets (or community served), product or service development and profitability or efficiency.

7.   Strategic objectives will be influenced strongly by the views of the directors of the organisation. The shareholders may decide that all such objectives shall be related firmly to the return on capital. This has been called the *shareholder theory of the firm*. In the case of a business enterprise, the owners will be concerned with setting objectives relating to the return on shareholders' capital, earning per share and profit, for example. In the case of a State-owned corporation, the emphasis will be more on providing an efficient service within the limitations of the funds allocated by Parliament. Another theory of the firm has been called the *stakeholder theory*. This suggests that the beneficiaries of the organisation are not only the shareholders, but also the customers, suppliers, employees and the public at large. Where this theory is held, strategic objectives are set not only for the good of the business, but also for the good of these other groups as well. An example would be where a pharmaceutical company sets objectives relating to the safety aspects of its products, both in relation to its own employees and to its consumers. Apart from small, owner-managed, enterprises, most organisations tend to adopt the stakeholder theory, if only in response to external pressures.

Policies

8.   Once an organisation has established its corporate objectives, it can begin to say in what manner it intends these to be achieved. Policy statements are made to indicate to those concerned just what the organisation will, and will not, do in pursuance of its *overall* purpose and objectives. Such statements are one expression of the organisation's culture and belief system. Policies are not the same as objectives or plans, even though they are frequently confused with them. Objectives state an aim or goal, ie they are *ends*; plans provide a framework within which action can take place to attain objectives, ie they are *means*; policies, on the other hand, are neither ends nor means, they are *statements of conduct*. Policies cause managers to take actions in a certain way, they are not actions in themselves. Policies both reflect and contribute to the organisation culture.

9.   A major factor affecting policy is the attitude of the organisation's owners. Those taking the shareholder view will tend to adopt a narrower range of policies than those holding the stakeholder view. Organisation policy is affected also by the attitudes of the society in which it operates. Thus national laws and local customs all play a part in determining an organisation's policies. Examples of different kinds of policies are as follows:

*   A high-street retail chain will only sell goods under its own brand-name.

*   The same retail chain will concentrate its buying in British markets.

*   A shipping company will not permit its vessels to sail under a flag of convenience.

*   A newspaper group will not interfere with the freedom of its editors to decide what shall be included in their own papers, subject to the laws of libel and indecency, for example.

*   A manufacturing company will take account of its consumers' safety needs when using its products, regardless of whether or not legislation exists for health and safety.

*   An international motor manufacturing company will source up to 80% of its suppliers from the host nation.

Some of the above policies state what the organisation will do, and some state what it will positively not do. Some policies relate to marketing issues, others relate much more to ethical and philosophical issues. The variety can be considerable, but the intention is the same: to guide the organisation's managers in the conduct of its affairs.

Ethics

10. Ethical codes go further than most policy statements in that they are focused on matters of right and wrong (eg refusing to engage in industrial espionage or refusing to turn a blind eye to the discovery of a possible health risk in one of their products) rather than just on standards of behaviour (eg courtesy towards customers and suppliers). The Chartered Institute of Management[1] defines codes of ethics as *'a set of moral principles or values, used by organisations to steer the conduct both of the organisation itself and its employees, in all their business activities, both internal and in relation to the outside world.'*

Thus a code applies individually as well as collectively to the organisation's members, and affects its internal affairs as well as those with its external stakeholders. Codes, as opposed to straightforward policy statements, have the advantage of providing explicit guidance on key moral issues that might arise during the course of the organisation's activities. However, they must be strongly supported from the top to retain credibility, and may prove difficult to live up to!

11. An example of an ethical code can be found in the official Principles of the Movement of the International Red Cross/Red Crescent organisation. The Principles include the following:

> **Impartiality**
> We care for all victims regardless of the side to which they belong...
> **Neutrality**
> We take initiatives but we never take sides...
> **Voluntary Service**
> We work round the clock but never for personal gain...
> **Universality**
> We respect Nations but our work knows no boundaries...'
>
> [Source: British Red Cross, 'Care in Crisis', 1996]

It is made quite clear to Red Cross/Red Crescent workers what these ground rules are. This enables all their staff to work internationally with complete impartiality to relieve human suffering in whatever quarter. Naturally, working for a charitable organisation is usually prompted by altruistic motives, so employees are already inclined to take the moral high ground in their work.

12. Most ethical issues in business organisations tend to be dealt with within the terms of existing policies rather than in specific codes of ethics. Examples of recent policy statements in two large British companies are as follows:

> 'We will compete vigorously but fairly in the marketplace; we will not seek to use our market position in a way that unfairly disadvantages our competitors.'
>
> (British Telecommunications plc)
>
> 'Everyone should have full and fair consideration of all job vacancies for which they offer themselves as suitable applicants. We do not discriminate against anyone on any grounds. The sole criterion for selection for promotion in the Company is the suitability of any applicant for the job...'
>
> (Marks & Spencer plc)

13. Ethics in business has come under the spotlight recently after the accounting scandals at Enron and World.Com, where massive frauds were discovered, despite the attentions of the companies' auditors. Such high-profile cases help to focus greater attention on the rights and wrongs of conducting an enterprise. In a growing number of companies one answer is to develop a code of ethics to give guidance to staff on how to conduct themselves in areas of work, which may not always be black and white. Issues that may have to be faced include bribery and corruption, the suppression of safety failures in products, and the remuneration of directors. There also has to be a confidential system to enable staff to report possible ethical breaches without harassment from those involved, especially if the culprits are senior to the 'whistle blower'. A code of practice in such matters can be helpful.

14. The Institute of Business Ethics[2] in the UK recommends twelve steps for implementing an ethical code. These can be summarised as follows:

- integrate the code into the company's value-system (its mission, policies etc)
- ensure that the code is endorsed by top management
- circulate the code to all employees
- advise employees (a) how to deal with a potentially difficult ethical choice, and (b) how to react to a possible breach of the code
- give all staff the chance to respond to the content of the code
- introduce a requirement that managers state that they understand and apply the code in practice

- introduce a procedure for regular reviews of the code and for revisions, where necessary
- consider making adherence to the code a matter of contract for employees (and hence of discipline)
- provide training in relevant issues if they arise from implementation of the code
- translate code into local languages, where appropriate
- distribute copies of the code to suppliers and customers to encourage their compliance
- reproduce the code in the company's annual report, so that shareholders and the public may know about the company's position on ethical matters.

15. The principal aspects of a business that are likely to produce moral dilemmas include:

- the way certain activities or decisions are reported in the annual accounts, such as depreciation measures, special contingencies and provisions
- the gaining of sales contracts in highly competitive markets, where inducements or trade offs may be suggested
- the acquisition of competitors' plans, designs and other critical information by under-hand means (industrial espionage)
- the deliberate suppression of facts that might compromise the safety or effectiveness of a product.

It has to be said, however, that there is often a fine line between what is, and what is not, acceptable conduct in business negotiations, especially in situations where there are no statutory restraints. The existence of a code of practice in ethics, supported by top management and made a natural feature of a company's culture, will enable better distinctions to be made between what is acceptable business practice and what is sharp practice.

16. Other ethical issues may arise from the exploitation of women or child labour either directly, or by suppliers. Multinational enterprises, in particular, may have to confront local practices involving vulnerable groups working long hours for low wages. There are also many environmental matters that can be directly influenced for good or worse by business corporations. The world is increasingly endangered by pollution, destruction of rainforests and other ecosystems, and the problem of global warming. The boards of large enterprises can contribute positively to alleviating such problems by minimising pollution, reducing waste and developing eco-friendly methods of production. In some cases they are encouraged to act positively by national laws and international agreements, but where no such laws or agreements exist, the responsibility for creating a healthier environment lies with the leaders of such enterprises and the ethical standards they adhere to.

Social Responsibility

17. One important area for policy development is that of 'social responsibility', which we shall now consider. Being *socially responsible* implies playing more than just an economic role in society. Increasingly, firms are being expected by society to play a direct role in meeting community needs in the Arts and education, in health and environmental matters, and in social welfare, in addition to their roles as employers and producers. In response to the pressure to be 'socially responsible', many firms have developed their own social or community programmes. These are aimed at demonstrating that corporate organisations are just as capable as individuals of being 'good citizens'.

18. There are two ways of encouraging commercial enterprises to develop a sense of social responsibility:

❶ they can be forced by law, or

❷ they can be persuaded voluntarily.

In Britain, as in most other states, the law plays an important, though not dominant, role in regulating the relationships between firms and their various stakeholders. So, for example, there are laws designed to protect the community from less welcome effects of commercial activities, such as industrial pollution, unsightly building developments and hazardous products. However, when we are discussing 'social responsibility' we are generally referring to *voluntary* measures undertaken by firms as part of their wider role in society.

19. Most firms are likely to operate their social responsibility programmes from the point of view of enlightened self-interest. By contributing to those activities which, even in prosperous countries, are never sufficiently funded by the state, a firm can ensure that its reputation is maintained in society. In previous centuries, it was wealthy landowners and princes who patronised the arts and social welfare. Today such patronage is exercised by large business enterprises. As in previous times, patronage can bestow a number of benefits on the patron, notably the establishment of a high reputation for good works.

20. Individual company motives for engaging in social responsibility programmes range from the highest altruism to the most calculating self-interest. Historically, firms owned by Quakers (eg Rowntree, Cadbury) have pursued such programmes for altruistic reasons. Most firms generally do not aspire to such unselfish heights, but have a mixture of motives for patronising community activities.

21. An example of one entrepreneurial company's attitude towards social responsibility is provided by STC plc (formerly Standard Telephones & Cables) as follows:

- To be an economic, intellectual and social asset to the local community, the nation, the EEC, and the world as a whole.

- To respect the environment and to be sensitive to the interests of people living in the neighbourhoods in which we have plants.

- To encourage people to fulfil their personal sense of duty to the community as well as their objectives within the Company.

- To help in finding solutions to national problems by contributing knowledge and talent.

- To conduct the Company's affairs with honesty and integrity. People at every level will be expected to adhere to high standards of business ethics, and the Company will comply with the spirit as well as the letter of the law.

- To pursue a policy of equality of opportunity whereby all personnel actions will be administered regardless of race, colour, religion or sex.

(STC – The Best Company Book, 1983)

22. In what way do statements such as the above get translated into action? At the present time, there are several types of community activity that UK commercial enterprises support. The most typical of these are as follows:

- work creation schemes
- welfare programmes
- support for educational institutions
- support for the arts
- contributions to overseas aid

Large companies tend to operate separate funding arrangements for those activities which are predominately 'charitable' (altruistic) and those which are 'promotional' (enlightened self-interest). Charitable donations, usually to welfare and educational programmes, are made from distinct charitable funds or foundations. Promotional activities (see Chapter 33, para 31), mostly involving the arts or sport, are paid for out of the organisation's operating budgets.

23. Specific examples of activities engaged are:

- Work Creation — London Enterprise Agency set up in 1979 to help small business start-ups. Funding and advice provided jointly by IBM, Marks & Spencer, Barclay's Bank, Midland Bank, BP, Shell and United Biscuits.

- Welfare — J. Sainsbury, the grocery firm, have established a 'Good Neighbour Scheme' whereby money from a central charitable fund is donated to local projects in support of a 'theme of the year' (eg Youth, Mentally Handicapped). Sainsbury's policy, as a high street retailer is to give major support to local as well as to national activities. Other high street firms have adopted a similar approach.

- Education — Support for specific universities, eg Oxford (the Nuffield Foundation) and Nottingham (Boots). Support for specific forms of research, eg cancer, mental health.

- Arts — Financial subsidies to the Royal Philharmonic Orchestra by the Bankers Trust Company, the Woolwich Equitable Building Society and others.

- Overseas Aid — Television programmes sponsored by the broadcasting media and a wide variety of others in support of particular appeals (eg Band-Aid appeal for Ethiopia).

24. An unusual case, where a business organisation is obliged by law to make over a substantial proportion of its income to charitable and other community purposes, is exemplified by Camelot plc, which operates the British National Lottery. Under the present conditions of its franchise, Camelot has to devote 28% of its revenue to the community ('good causes') as well as paying a 12% Lottery Duty and corporation tax on its profits.

Business Plans

25. Business planning follows on from the setting of the organisation's key objectives and policies. Plans essentially state how the organisation intends to move forward over a given period, usually between 1 and 5 years. At the head of such planning is the strategic, or corporate, plan which identifies the direction which the organisation is to take over the next 2–5 years, or in some cases up to 10 years, and the resources that are to be deployed to ensure that the plan is put into effect. The resources are generally expressed in financial terms sufficient to cover anticipated expenditure on people, buildings, machinery etc. Because of the number of variables at work in the external environment, most business organisations tend to work on a rolling five year plan basis, in which only the next year's budgets are expressed in detailed terms, and the remaining four years are set out in flexible terms allowing for a range of unexpected contingencies. Thus, in Figure 17.1, the time-scale of the item shown as 'Agree Strategic Plan' is likely to be between 2 and 5 years, whilst the item shown as 'Operating/Tactical Plans' will be the current/forthcoming year's detailed statements of anticipated expenditure and income (where relevant).

26. In order to decide which product-market, competitive and other strategies to adopt, business organisations have to consider two major questions:

❶ What is the organisation's *current performance*, especially in terms of its major strengths and weaknesses?

❷ What factors in the *external environment* might affect the organisation's proposed plans for the future?

One way of assessing the evidence for these two questions is to conduct what has been called a 'SWOT analysis'. This is essentially a review of the organisation's major internal strengths, weaknesses, together with an assessment of those opportunities and threats in the external environment which are likely to make an impact on strategic choices. Such an analysis lends itself to the 'brainstorming method' of tackling problems, since individual managers and their advisers can consider the situation separately and then combine their thinking to stimulate discussion about (a) the nature of the issues facing the organisation, and (b) their importance as likely determinants of future strategy.

27. A simple SWOT analysis based on a typical UK supermarket chain is illustrated in Figure 17.2.

Internal Factors	
Strengths	**Weaknesses**
Widespread coverage	Substantial reliance on part-time employees
Light and airy stores	Overcrowding of stores at peak times
Ample parking	Reliance on regular transport of products
Attractive new developments	from regional cold store
Wide range of goods	Profitability at risk from price reductions on
Reputation for freshness of food	certain key goods
In-store services (eg pharmacy/post office)	
Competitive pricing on many products	
Convenient locations	
Petrol station	
Excellent cash flow	
No quibble cash-back guarantee	
Provision of local bus service (free)	
External Environment	
Opportunities	**Threats**
Attract bank/building society cashpoints	Local competition from other major
Encourage use of bottle banks	supermarket chains
Provide space for mobile library	Price-cutting by competitors
Community projects (eg computers for schools)	Failure to obtain planning permission for
Open new stores in viable locations	new developments
Source new suppliers (home/overseas)	

Figure 17.2 SWOT analysis for a major supermarket chain.

28. Current internal performance is usually assessed in terms of key performance ratios, such as sales turnover, net profit, output per head and other ratios (see Chapter 28 below). In a SWOT analysis, however, managers will be encouraged to make qualitative judgements about performance based on their assessment of customer satisfaction (eg as in the supermarket example above), and other key issues such as employee motivation, workflow

processes, impact of on-the-job learning and other non-quantifiable elements in the total performance of the organisation.

29.   The appraisal of the *external* environment follows a similar approach, except that here the two headings employed are *opportunities* and *threats*. In this case, the organisation's planners are assessing the likely impact on organisational objectives of technological, economic, political and social trends, together with the activities of competitors. Taking the last-mentioned factor first – the competition – this is always a potential threat to a supermarket chain, which is operating in a highly competitive marketplace, and is vulnerable to price-cutting and novel in-store developments which it might find hard to match. To take another example, supposing a firm has been first in the field with a mass-production light-weight battery car for urban use, what opportunities does this lead give them and what threats might be posed by other manufacturers? One opportunity might be to offer competitors the possibility of producing the vehicle under licence, another might be to seek some joint production and marketing facility. A major threat could be the manufacture of cheaper varieties of such a car by overseas competitors with lower labour costs and/or the benefits of improved production technology. Another example, taking economic trends into consideration, could be the opportunities and threats posed by an organisation's dependence on oil. In this situation there might be no opportunities other than seeking alternative forms of energy, whereas the threats could be fundamental to the future existence, let alone growth, of the organisation.

30.   The next step following a SWOT analysis is usually to develop a list of alternative corporate strategies which will form the basis for the final corporate plan. Organisations develop strategies along two lines: (a) those aimed at producing *actions* to fulfil objectives, and (b) those aimed at ensuring the *resources* to support these actions. Strategies therefore tend to be developed (a) in terms of products, services and markets where actions (or sometimes no actions) will be required, and (b) in terms of size, structure, financing and staffing, where resources are the issue. Typical corporate strategies could be as follows:

❶   Expand into new markets with existing products (or services)

❷   Continue to maintain market share in existing markets with existing products, ie a 'no change' strategy

❸   Add to product base or range of services by acquisition of a competitor

❹   Seek long-term, low-interest loans from European Bank/World Bank for redevelopment projects

❺   Reorganise company into separate profit centres

❻   Divest non-core businesses (eg in a group or conglomerate).

31.   It can be seen that such strategies point the direction in which an organisation is to move over the medium term. They are sufficiently clear to be evaluated in terms of whether they have been achieved or not, but they are not so specific that they tie down the organisation to meeting what could be impossible long-term targets in conditions of uncertainty. Specific targets can only be set for short-term purposes, say of up to one year. Such targets form part of the operational or tactical plans worked out by departments and divisions to meet the demands of the master plan. Examples of operational plans include marketing, production and human resource plans.

32.   This leads us on to one of the final stages of corporate planning: the issue of key targets in a year-on-year format to the various departments and divisions of the organisation. Some targets may be expressed in budget form, indicating, for example, sales revenue,

direct and indirect costs, and trading profit. Others may be expressed in alternative measures of performance, such as:

- output per employee
- percentage utilisation of machines
- percentage increase in market share
- costs as a percentage of sales.

Once targets have been set, they are monitored and revised as necessary. If revisions are made the whole plan is rolled forward as a consequence. Thus the long-term perspective is maintained, but the entire plan is kept up-to-date.

Conclusion

33. Business planning at corporate/strategic level is a continuing process by which the long-term objectives of an organisation may be formulated, and subsequently attained, by means of long-term strategic actions designed to make their impact on the organisation as a whole. Corporate planning also involves deciding the policies, or code of conduct, of the organisation in pursuit of its objectives. Thus business aims and ethical considerations are brought together.

References

1. Institute of Management Checklist No. 028, *Codes of Ethics*, Institute of Management Foundation.
2. Le Jeune, M. & Webley, S. (1998), *Company Use of Codes of Business Conduct*, Institute of Business Ethics.

CHAPTER 18

Performance Standards in Management

Introduction

1. Managers have tended to be judged on their performance in one of three principal ways:

1 in terms of business outcomes (turnover, profits, return on investment etc), in cases where they are directors or senior managers

2 in terms of their agreed departmental/unit objectives, as agreed under some system of management by objectives – an approach especially favoured for middle management levels

3 in terms of how they have performed generally in carrying out their responsibilities, as stated or implied in their job descriptions, and where performance is assessed as much on the individual manager's *input* into the job as on any outcomes he or she has achieved.

These models of assessing performance have not always been effective, especially in the case of middle management. In recent years there has been a growing interest in the development and assessment of managerial competencies as a means of setting managerial performance standards and assessing people against them. This short chapter focuses on items 2 and 3 above by outlining two approaches that are widely used in modern business and public service organisations. These are Management by Objectives and Competency-based Management.

Management by Objectives (MbO)

2.   The phrase 'management by objectives' (MbO) was first coined by Peter Drucker[1] in the 1950s, in his classic book 'The Practice of Management'. He saw it as a principle of management aimed at harmonising individual manager goals with those of the organisation. In Britain, the leading exponent of MbO, Humble (1971)[2] sees MbO as a means of integrating organisational goals, such as profit and growth, with the needs of individual managers to contribute to the organisation and to their own self-development. A system of management by objectives, therefore, seeks to achieve a sense of common purpose and common direction amongst the management of an organisation in the fulfilment of business results.

3.   The most important features of MbO are:

❶   it focusses on *results* (system outputs) rather than on *activity* (system processes).

❷   it develops logically from the corporate planning process by translating corporate and departmental objectives into individual manager objectives.

❸   it seeks to improve management performance.

4.   Not surprisingly, in view of the business pay-offs claimed for it, MbO was first employed in business enterprises, with the principal intention of improving profitability and growth. Its apparent success in these intentions, together with the improvements in managerial effectiveness and motivation led to its introduction into the public services. Here, too, important successes have been recorded but in terms of reliability and efficiency of services as well as of management morale.

The Framework of MBO

5.   The link between corporate objectives and the strategic plan was shown in the previous chapter (Figure 17.1). The link between the strategic plan and a system of MbO, together with the respective time-spans, can be shown as in Figure 18.1.

The diagram demonstrates how objectives at the front-line of the organisation's operations flow logically from the overall strategic plan for the organisation. In systems terms the MbO activities are a key part of the conversion processes of the organisation. Linked as it is with the strategic plan of the organisation, MbO can only be operated successfully with top management's approval and support.

6.   The Key Results referred to in Figure 18.1 are derived from an analysis of the individual manager's job, in which key result areas are identified and key tasks drawn up from them. These are worked out by agreement between the individual manager and his or her superior. The resulting job description, unlike one that merely describes job activities, sets out the job in terms of its most vital, and potentially most productive, responsibilities. These are the responsibilities that produce the biggest returns for the job, and usually there are no more than eight or nine of these for a managerial position. It is from the key tasks

TIME-SPAN

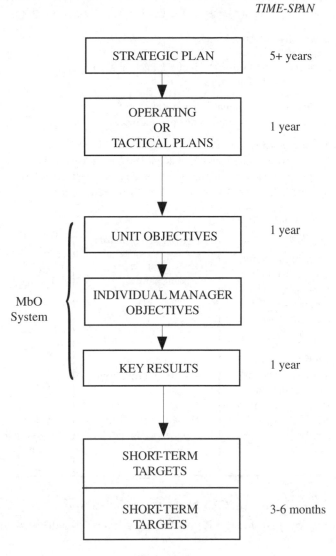

Figure 18.1

that the short-term targets are developed. These targets serve as the focus for immediate and short-term priorities in the job. Figure 18.2 sets out the format of a typical MbO-type of job description and gives some examples of the kind of information one could expect to find in it.

7.   Note that each Key Task has one or more performance standards against which it can be measured over a period of time (usually one year). These standards should express satisfactory performance and not necessarily *ideal* performance. They are usually expressed in terms of end-results and qualified in some way, eg in respect of time, quality and quantity. The column for Control Data ensures that consideration is given to the *evidence* against which performance can be checked. Once such a job description is completed, it is possible to use it as the basis for short-term targets to form part of what Humble calls a Job Improvement Plan.

```
Job Title: Branch Manager (Retail Chain)      Date: Jan 2000

Reporting to: Area Manager

Own staff:  65 Full-time (incl. 12 Section Managers)
            45 Part-time

Scope of Job:  Annual Branch Revenue £x
               Average Sales per sq. ft. £x

Overall Purpose of Job:
To achieve Revenue targets in accordance with Area budget
by providing and maintaining an attractive and reliable retail
service that meets customer needs in the locality.

Key Result Areas:
```

Key Tasks:	Performance Standards	Control Data
Prepare and gain acceptance for Branch revenue targets as contribution to Area budget	Targets accepted without major amendments	Area Budget
Set recruitment levels and standards for guidance of subordinate managers etc. etc.	(a) Branch fully staffed throughout year	Weekly staff report
	(b) Staff turnover not to exceed 20% per annum	Area Personnel Figures

Figure 18.2 An MbO-type job description.

8.   A Job Improvement Plan for the Retail Branch Manager could be developed as shown in Figure 18.3.

The Job Improvement Plan is very much an *action* document. It sets out the actions which need to be taken in the short-term in order to ensure that the Key Tasks are fulfilled to the required standard. In each case the appropriate Key Task is identified and the priority actions are set alongside it together with a target date. The time-scale of short-term actions is usually one month to one quarter, although some improvement plans may be spread over a six-month period. In fast-changing situations it may be better to set improvement plans at more frequent intervals than in situations of relative calm market activity.

8.   One of the most attractive elements of MbO for top managements has been its emphasis on setting standards and specifying results for all managers at the operating level of the business. In the past only those in functions such as production and sales were subject to anything like measurable performance standards. Now, with MbO, it was possible to quantify, or at least *qualify*, the efforts of specialist managers as well. The performance standards, which are set as a measure of the degree of achievement of key tasks, are expressed in terms of quantity, where this is practical, or in terms of some agreed

Key Task	Actions Planned	Target Date	Notes
Branch revenue targets	Set up meeting with Area Manager to achieve improved checkout facilities at rear of store in light of major extension of public car-park	Within one month	Brief Checkout Manager beforehand
	Hold coaching sessions on revenue target-setting for all newly appointed Section Managers	By end of next quarter	
Recruitment levels/ Standards	Arrange meeting between Area Personnel Officer and all Section Managers on all the implementation of new staff induction procedures etc. etc. etc.	Within one month	

Figure 18.3 Job Improvement Plan for a quarterly period.

judgement of what could be reasonably expected, ie some qualitative measure. Examples of the two broad categories of measurement are as follows.

Quantitative

a. Increase sales of product X by 20% in next 12 months.

b. Staff turnover not to exceed 30% in any year.

c. Stocks not to exceed budgeted levels.

d. Previous month's Budget figures for actual against target results to be ready for distribution within two weeks of the start of the following month.

Qualitative

a. Vacancies for Branch Manager posts to be filled by internal promotion.

b. Budget is to be accepted by the directors.

c. All supervisors able to operate grievance procedure without incurring trade union complaints.

d. Conclude productivity agreements with the trade unions which realise genuine cost savings to the Company.

9.   An MbO system enables managers to see how well they are performing in the key areas of their jobs. It also provides a basis for realistic discussions between managers and their superiors concerning progress in these key areas. This brings us to another important aspect of MbO – appraisal and review. As the initial objectives-settings phase is hammered

out jointly between the individual managers and their superiors, so the results obtained are jointly reviewed. The precise way the reviews are conducted by superiors will depend on the relationship they have with their staff and on their preferred management style. Some managers undoubtedly use the performance standards and improvement plans as sticks with which to beat their subordinates. Others prefer a joint problem-solving approach where the emphasis is on how to make things better. The ideal is that reviews should:

1 focus on *performance* rather than personality,

2 concentrate on *improvement for the future* rather than on criticism of the present,

3 be genuinely *participative*.

10. MbO allows for two types of review – Performance Review and Potential Review. The Performance Review is concerned with the individual managers' results in the key areas of their *present* job, as discussed in the preceding paragraph. The Potential Review is concerned with managers' anticipated abilities to succeed *in their next job*. This assumes, of course, that the organisation concerned has a management development plan into which such a Potential Review can fit as part of management succession planning. For further information on the subject of management development, see Chapter 46.

11. The principal stages of an MbO system can now be summarised, as shown in Figure 18.4.

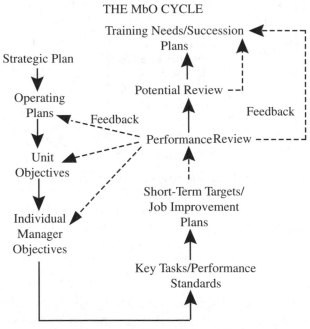

Figure 18.4 The MbO cycle.

The cycle of events demonstrates the links between the organisation's strategic plan, the objectives and key tasks of individual managers, and the vital review of performance which provides important feedback for other parts of the system. The Performance Review provides feedback to the operating system (plans and objectives), and to the training and development system (training needs and succession plans). The Potential Review feeds back to the training and development system.

12. Reference was made earlier to management succession planning and the contribution to it of the Potential Review. Management succession plans are drawn up to ensure that

vacancies created by career moves, death, retirement and other reasons, are capable of being filled internally. Most plans provide for immediate temporary successors to certain key posts as well as identifying long-term successors to such posts. This is to ensure that a sudden death does not bring a particular function to a halt whilst a long-term successor is sought to replace the deceased member of staff.

13. If the organisation is intent on using MbO as a *system* of management rather than as a limited *technique* for improving manager-productivity, then it will indeed see training and development as a key factor in the total system. In fact, one of the great advantages claimed for MbO is that it provides an ideal basis for the analysis of managerial training needs. Once managerial jobs have been written up in terms of their key results and required standards of performance, it is clearly easier to identify those areas of the job, if any, where an existing job-holder is falling short of the required level of performance. It should then be possible to identify shortfalls due to gaps in the individual's knowledge and skills, which hopefully can be overcome by suitable training. This particular topic is dealt with later in Chapter 44.

Competency Models of Management

14. Whilst there has been some argument, even confusion, about the meaning that should be ascribed to the word 'competence', it is generally agreed that it is concerned with a person's *performance* at a task. Thus, as a concept, it is closely related to the idea of *'skill'*, or, more precisely, *'skill at'* performing some task. The expression 'competent', however, is more likely to be employed in a holistic way to imply an individual's *overall capability to undertake certain work* rather than just their ability to perform certain aspects of their work to an acceptable standard. A term often used to describe the detailed aspects of an individual's job performance is 'competency' (ie this person has shown competency in so-and-so), and what is looked for in individuals is a range of 'competencies'.

15. The definition of competence adopted by the UK's Employment Department is as follows:

> ' the ability to perform activities within an occupation or function to the standards expected in employment'.

Underlying this definition is an employment-led model of job competence expressed in terms of four interrelated components:

❶ **Task skills,** ie the performance of relevant tasks

❷ **Task management,** ie the skills required to manage a group of tasks within a job

❸ **Contingency management skills,** ie the skills required to respond to breakdowns in routines and procedures

❹ **Job/Role environment,** ie skills in responding appropriately to the wider aspects of the job or role (eg dealing with people).

16. When examining ways of describing *management* jobs in competency terms, it was found necessary to use a further model in order to describe other competencies that were also important. This further model, known as the Personal Competence model, focuses on the personal behaviour of the job-holder in carrying out his or her work. The model (eg Fowler, 1994)[3] is based on four sets of personal competencies as follows:

❶ **Planning** to optimise the achievement of results

❷ **Managing others** to optimise results

❸ **Managing oneself** to optimise results

❹ **Using intellect** to optimise results.

17. These sets of competencies are very general, and therefore each set is broken down into a number of *personal dimensions*, for example:

- **Planning**   – *'Setting and prioritising objectives'*
                                  – *'Monitoring and responding to actual against planned activties'*

- **Managing oneself** – *'Managing personal emotions and stress'*.

Each dimension is then further analysed under a number of specific associated behaviours, which means the job requirements are described in detailed terms.

18. One of the most influential contributors on the topic of generic competencies is that of Boyatzis (1982)[4] who identified twelve competencies that, in his view, distinguished superior from average managers in terms of performance. The twelve characteristics, which as can be seen are expressed in very general terms, were as follows:

- concern with impact
- diagnostic use of concepts
- efficiency orientation
- proactivity
- conceptualisation
- self-confidence

- use of oral presentations
- managing group processes
- use of socialised power
- perceptual objectivity
- self-control
- stamina and adaptability

19. In the late 1980s the so-called 'Management Charter Initiative' (MCI) was established to examine and develop occupational standards for managers, primarily with a view to rationalising the range of educational and training qualifications for managers, although this was subsequently broadened to encompass other issues such as job design and performance appraisal. Standards, in this context, were expressed in terms of *units* and *elements of competence* supported by appropriate *performance criteria* and statements of context (*'range statements'*). The challenge in such initiatives is to find generic standards of competence that can be applied to managers in a range of middle management roles. In other words, it is more important to understand what it is that enables managers to achieve acceptable, or even excellent, performance in their work, than to be able to describe what precisely they should be doing. Previous standards focused more on what managers were expected to do, rather than on what generic capabilities they should possess. The current standards[5] are described in more detail in Chapter 46 below. They have been used both as a means of enabling managers to achieve a vocational qualification (NVQ/SVQ), and as an aid to improving management performance by utilising the 'best practice' benchmarks embodied in the standards.

References

1.   Drucker, P. (1954), *The Practice of Management*, Heinemann.
2.   Humble, J. (1971), *Management by Objectives*, Management Publications/BIM.
3.   Fowler, B. (ed) (1994), *MCI Personal Competence Model: Uses and Implementation*, Research Report No. 24, Employment Department.
4.   Boyatzis, E. (1982), *The Competent Manager: A Model for Effective Performance,* Wiley.
5.   Management Standards Centre, Management Standards, H.M.S.O.

CHAPTER 19

Decision-making in Organisations

Introduction

1.   Decision-making is an accepted part of everyday human life. As individuals we may make decisions on the spur of the moment or after much thought and deliberation, or at some point between these two extremes. Our decisions may be influenced by emotions, by reasoning or by a combination of both. As members of groups we may find ourselves making decisions on a group basis, where our own views and feelings have to be tested and argued with the other members. In organisations, people with managerial roles are expected, among other things, to make decisions as an important part of their responsibilities. In this chapter we are concerned with managerial decision-making. That is to say we are concerned with behaviour that is designed to cause things to happen, or not to happen, as the case may be. Whilst it may be affected by feelings and interpersonal relationships, managerial decision-making tends to be rational in its approach. Considerable time and effort may be spent in assessing problems, developing alternative solutions and evaluating their consequences before arriving at an agreed decision. Certain types of decision-making can be made easier and faster by means of special techniques, some of which are referred to briefly later in the chapter.

Decision Processes: A Theoretical Model

2.   An analysis of the way decisions are made in organizations results in the sequence of events shown in Figure 19.1.

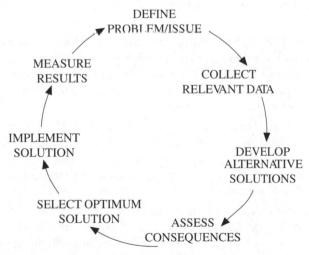

Figure 19.1 Decision model

This sequence indicates a rational approach that can be applied to the business of reaching decisions in organisations. It commences by seeking to ask the right questions, continues by encouraging creative answers, and concludes by ensuring that the chosen solution is monitored and evaluated.

3.   There are several important issues raised by a model such as the one we have described. These can be summarised as follows:

- The technical *quality* of the decision, ie doing the right thing, has to be distinguished from the *acceptability* of the decision by the parties involved, ie doing things right.

- Both the development of alternatives and the selection of an optimum solution will be limited considerably by the organisation's objectives and policies, and by the attitudes of managers and other employees.

- The assessment of the possible consequences of proposed solutions is a step that is frequently given insufficient attention.

- The model makes no allowance for the time factor. Clearly, however, it favours decision-making for the future rather than decision-making for immediate problems.

Types of Decisions

4.   Decisions can range from those of a vital, once-for-all nature to those of a routine and relatively trivial nature. They can be immediate in their effect or they can be delayed. A decision to move a computer manufacturing enterprise out of mainframe computers into micro-computers is clearly a major long-term commitment of a strategic kind. H.I. Ansoff (1965; 1987)[1] sees management as having three principal decision areas: strategic, operating and administrative. This seems to be a useful way of separating out the major categories of decisions, and the descriptions which follow adapt several of Ansoff's ideas.

5.   **Strategic Decisions.** These are the basic, long-term decisions which settle the organisation's relationship with its environment, notably in terms of its product or service and its markets. These are the decisions which set the principal goals and objectives of the organisation. Also included here would be the major policy statements of the organisations. Such decisions tend to be non-routine and non-repetitive. They are usually complex, especially in terms of the number of variables which have to be considered before final choices are made.

Operating Decisions. These are the short-term decisions which settle issues such as output levels, pricing and inventory levels. Fewer variables are involved in the decision-making process, and the decisions themselves are routine and repetitive by nature. Operating decisions tend to receive priority over others because of the sheer weight of their volume plus their ability to show results in the short-term.

Administrative Decisions. These decisions arise from, and are subject to, the conflicting demands of strategic and operational problems. They are essentially concerned with settling the organisation's structure, eg by establishing lines of authority and communication. The use of 'administrative' in this context is narrower than the more usual meaning of the word, as defined in Chapter 2.

6.   A final distinction that can be made between types of decision concerns so-called programmable and non-programmable decisions. A programmable decision is one capable of being worked out by a computer, ie the variables are quantifiable and the decision rules can be clearly stated. These criteria would certainly apply to numerous operating decisions. By contrast, a non-programmable decision is one which cannot be quantified in the same way, and where human judgements have to be made. This would be the case for all strategic decisions, for example.

Decision-making Tools

7.   Figure 19.1 showed the key steps that can be identified in the decision-making process. In recent years several techniques have been developed to aid the processes of problem-definition, of devising solution options and of evaluating their possible consequences. Since the majority of decisions have to be made in conditions of relative risks and uncertainty, any techniques which can help predict the future are worth having. In earlier centuries men of power looked to soothsayers, prophets or gipsies for an indication of the future. Nowadays we can look to the combined efforts of mathematicians, statisticians and computer specialists to help us forecast possible outcomes.

8.   One of the most significant sets of tools now available for decision-makers is that of OR (Operational Research). This encompasses a collection of techniques which apply scientific methods to complex problems in organizations. In particular, OR involves the use of scientific models, or conceptual frameworks, to represent real situations. The models utilize mathematical and statistical terms to express the variables involved in a decision. Particular OR techniques include Network Analysis, Risk Analysis and Statistical Decision Theory. The chief benefits of such techniques are that they assist with the analysis of problems and the development of solutions. Further information can be found in Chapter 28.

9.   Whilst it is not necessary for detailed examples of OR techniques to be supplied, it would be useful to outline the basic approach of such techniques. The procedure which follows is clearly influenced by general systems theory. The basic steps are shown in Figure 19.2

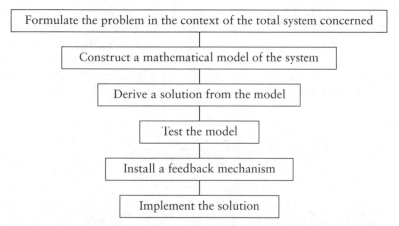

Figure 19.2 Operational Research.

10.   The principal advantage of such an approach is that it seeks to define and solve problems in their organisational context. It is important to appreciate that the approach is utilised to *assist* decision-making. OR techniques in themselves do not implement decisions. What they can do is to provide managers with information and options which can lead to qualitatively better decisions being taken.

11.   Another increasingly useful tool for management decision-makers is the so-called 'decision tree'. This is basically a conceptual map of possible decisions and outcomes in a particular situation. It is useful in cases where a manager is required to make a number sequential decisions ie where earlier decisions will affect later ones. A simple decision tree is shown in Figure 19.3.

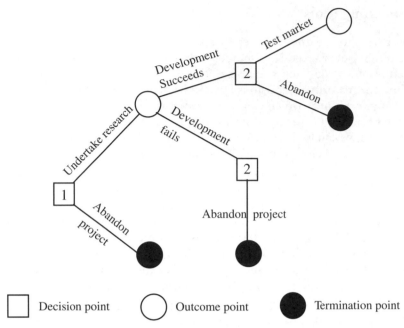

□ Decision point	○ Outcome point	● Termination point

Figure 19.3 R & D Decision tree.

12. Such a diagram focusses attention on outcomes or consequences as well as decisions. It is customarily built on three key features of decision-making: (i) a decision point, (ii) one or more outcomes, and (iii) a termination point. Outcomes can be further elaborated in terms of their probability and their anticipated pay off. It is also possible to add a time dimension to the whole diagram, so that in Figure 19.3 the period from decision point 1 to decision point 2 could be one year. These additional features all help to make the use of decision trees a salutary exercise for managers.

References

1. Ansoff, H.I. (1965), *Corporate Strategy* (revised 1987), McGraw-Hill.

CHAPTER 20

Human Resource Planning

Introduction

1. Human resource planning (HRP), like any other form of planning, is a means to an end. In this case the end is to secure the human resources of the organisation in order to achieve corporate objectives. In organisations that have adopted a corporate planning or strategic approach to HRP, an overall assessment will have been made of the current strengths and weaknesses of the employee situation. This assessment will have led, where necessary, to a number of long-term proposals for HRP aimed at securing sufficient

numbers and categories of suitable employees to undertake the task of producing the organisation's goods or services to the standards expected by the end-users. Even organisations that rarely plan far ahead usually have to make some assessment of their present employee situation, so as to ensure that an appropriate range of skills is available for all the mainstream activities of the organisation. This chapter assumes that a systematic and planned view of HRP is the norm.

2. Whatever the nature of the organisation, if it is of a size where changes in the workforce will have a significant effect on business results, then it will need some kind of human resource planning activity. In this book human resource planning is defined as:

'a rational approach to the effective recruitment, retention, and deployment of people within an organisation, including, when necessary, arrangements for dismissing staff.'

HRP is, therefore, concerned with the flow of people through and sometimes out of the organisation. It is, however, not a mere numbers game. On the contrary, effective HRP is considerably more concerned with the optimum deployment of people's knowledge and skills, ie *quality* is even more important than quantity.

3. Before moving on to look at the various stages of HRP, it is worth considering the questions which such planning aims to answer. These can be summarised as follows:

- What kind of people does the organisation require and in what numbers?
- Over what time-span are these people required?
- How many of them are employed by the organisation currently?
- How can the organisation meet any shortfall in requirements from *internal* sources?
- How can the organisation meet the shortfall from *external* sources?
- What changes are taking place in the external labour market which might affect the supply of human resources?

4. In responding to these questions, HRP is essentially concerned with four major activities:

❶ analysing the existing human resource situation

❷ forecasting future demands for people

❸ assessing the external labour market and forecasting the supply situation

❹ establishing and implementing human resource plans.

We shall now look at these major activities in more detail.

The Human Resource Planning Process

5. Human resource planning can only make sense when seen in relation to business objectives. The basic demand for people springs from the organisation's need to supply goods or services to its customers. In this sense, HRP is a resourcing activity. However, it is also a fact that these resources in themselves have a vital influence on organisational objectives. For example, a firm may be unable to pursue its expansion plans in a new market because it is unable to find enough suitably trained personnel to carry them through. So, information arising from the HRP process produces feedback which may cause other business plans to be cancelled or amended.

6. In its simplest form, human resource planning can be depicted as shown in Figure 20.1.

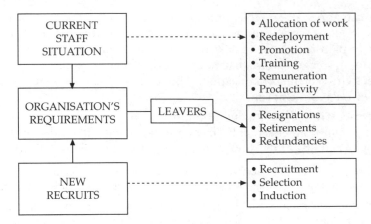

Figure 20.1 Personnel decisions and human resource requirements.

Even this simple model of the process indicates the ramifications of human resource planning, and emphasises the qualitative aspects of it. HRP is clearly not just concerned with numbers. Plans for training, redeployment, promotion and productivity all indicate the importance of getting the right staff in the right jobs, as well as in the right numbers.

7.   Figure 20.1 shows the flow of people through the organisation, and identifies some of the key actions that need to be taken at the operational level. This is the kind of model that almost every organisation can utilise. However, larger or more complex organisations need a more strategic approach at the outset. Such an approach would incorporate the four major activities mentioned earlier in paragraph 4, but would link them into the overall business planning activity of the organisation. Thus, a more appropriate and comprehensive model for this situation would be as shown in Figure 20.2.

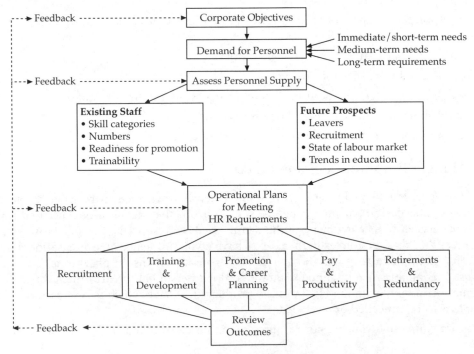

Figure 20.2 The human resource planning cycle.

Demand for Human Resources

8.   In the light of Figure 20.2 we can look at the key features of each of the major stages of the HRP cycle, starting with the demand for human resources. This is a more or less continuing demand in any organisation. It has its short-term aspects, ie the clearly-defined requirements for specific skills, or positions, which need to be filled in the context of existing plans. This usually means periods of up to about 6–9 months. It also has medium-term (9–18 months) and long-term (18 months – 5 years) aspects, in line with the market and financial targets of the corporate plan. A longer-term view of HRP is essential for ensuring that the organisation is supplied with skills which take time to be developed. Most professional jobs, for example, require a training period of three to five years before the trainee can claim even the basic competencies of the profession. If an organisation decides to develop its own staff, it needs to look ahead for at least five years from the time the first recruits are appointed. If the organisation decides it will not train its own special-ists, but buy them in from the market-place, then it has to be reasonably assured of the availability of trained people in the labour force at the time they will be required.

Supply of Labour

9.   This leads us on to the question of the supply of labour, which is the next major stage in the cycle of events. Any analysis of the supply of labour must commence with the existing state of the organisation's personnel. Answers need to be sought to such questions as:

*   What categories of staff do we have?
*   What are the numbers in each category?
*   What about age and sex distribution within the categories?
*   What skills and qualifications exist?
*   How many staff are suitable for promotion or re-deployment?
*   How successful are we in recruiting particular categories of staff?

These are important questions for both immediate and future needs. If, for example, a contraction of the business was planned, it might be an advantage to have an ageing work-force. Equally, if *expansion* was planned in the same business, an ageing workforce would be a definite disadvantage, and the organisation would need to draw heavily on the national labour market.

10.   When considering the existing supply of human resources available to the organisa-tion, we are not just considering the numbers and categories at a particular point in time. We are also considering (1) the organisation's ability to continue to attract suitable recruits into its various operations, and (2) the rate at which employees are leaving the organisa-tion. Can the organisation count on filling vacant posts satisfactorily when it goes into the market-place? Are some posts more difficult to fill than others, and can anything be done about this? What about leavers? Why are they moving out – retirements? seeking better opportunities elsewhere? pregnancy? dismissal? redundancy? Some organisations rely on a high fallout rate of employees to enable fresh recruits to be brought in at regular intervals. Other organisations expect a considerable degree of stability among their workforce, and build this expectation into their planning assumptions.

11.   The analysis of the existing supply of human resources must also take into account the *potentialities* of existing staff to undertake other roles in the organisation. There are

considerable variations in the policies of organisations concerning career development. Some offer no real prospects for increased variety or responsibility at work. Others claim career development as the high-spot of their reputation as employers. Clearly firms that take the latter view can call on far greater internal resources for meeting change than those in the former category. Increasingly, nowadays, organisations are seeking job flexibility across all job categories – manual, clerical, technical etc. – and are insisting on a multi-skilled workforce. This strategy serves the interests of organisations who wish to 'grow their own' flexible workforce.

12. Having considered its existing supply of human resources, an organisation will know the shortfall in its requirements for the future. If we assume that the organisation cannot meet its future needs internally, then it must look to the external labour market. There are a number of important issues here. For example:

- What is the overall employment situation likely to be in the course of the next five years?
- How is this situation likely to affect our local labour market?
- What competition for personnel is likely?
- Are there any trends in the educational sector which might affect our recruitment plans?
- Are there factors in our corporate plans which might speed up the voluntary leaving rate?

13. The answers to these questions will indicate the likely prospects of meeting future personnel needs from external sources. Skilled labour is usually a scarce resource in most advanced industrialised nations, but the situation has changed with relatively large-scale unemployment, and even a surplus of some skills. These changes do not happen overnight. Thus, firms that are planning ahead for their requirements can offset some of the worst affects of acute shortages, or surpluses, of labour arising from economic changes over which they have no control. Another example of the need to recruit externally is when changes in technology or production processes bring about changes in the number and types of employees required. Improved technology can lead to redundancies and/or more boring jobs for machine operators on the one hand, whilst leading to more jobs for skilled maintenance technicians on the other.

14. Once the organisation has assessed its supply position in relation to its requirements, it can then draw up plans to meet these requirements. Since people are probably *the* most volatile resource available to the organisation, the best plans will be those which have the greatest flexibility. Most human resource plans are developed on a rolling five year basis, which means that forecasts for next year and the succeeding years in the cycle are updated every year in the light of this year's out-turn. Detailed plans for securing sufficient and suit-able employees for current needs are laid for a one-year period in line with current budgets. Less detailed plans are laid for the five year period, but at least major contingencies are prepared for in line with the organisation's corporate strategy.

15. Whether long- or short-term, the plans for securing the workforce will usually include consideration of the following:

Recruitment:
How do we ensure our anticipated needs for replenishing or adding to our workforce? By increasing traineeships and apprenticeships? Or by recruiting trained and experienced people? How much provision should be made for recruiting part-timers and contract staff? What steps should be taken to promote the organisation in schools, colleges and universi-

ties? What use, if any, should we make of recruitment consultants? What improvements could be made to our selection procedures?

Training and Development:

What job and professional training should be provided to prepare new and existing staff to fulfil their roles satisfactorily? Should we concentrate on in-company or in-service training, or should we send people on external courses? What special programmes need to be established to deal with re-training, or up-dating? How can induction procedures be improved? How best can multi-skilling be encouraged by means of work-place training?

Promotion, Redeployment & Career Planning:

How can internal procedures be improved so as to facilitate the movement of staff to jobs where they can exercise greater, or different, responsibilities? What new succession plans need to be drawn up for key management and supervisory roles? How well is training linked to career development? How can job interest/career challenge be maintained in a flatter organisation structure?

Pay & Productivity:

What steps must be taken to ensure that pay and incentives are sufficient to attract, retain and encourage our workforce? What are the cost limits on pay? How can we make best use of high-cost groups of key employees? In what ways can labour costs be paid for out of improved output per employee, or other productivity indicators? How best can pay be related to performance?

Retirements & Redundancy:

What provision should be made for those reaching retirement age? What inducements may be needed to be provided to encourage older employees to consider opting for early retirement? What arrangements should be made for dealing with planned redundancies? How should retirements and redundancies be phased over the course of the year? What are the estimated costs of these plans?

16. Human resource planning is essentially a corporate activity. It cuts across all the divisional and departmental boundaries of an organisation. It is an activity which claims the attention of all managers. It is not the preserve of any one group of specialist managers (eg personnel), even though such specialists may well play a key coordinating role in the implementation and review of HR plans. So, as we turn to the final stage of the HRP cycle – the review – we can see this as a responsibility in which all managers share. Major reviews of progress will usually take place once a year, when revisions may be made to the subsequent years of the five-year planning cycle. There will also be reviews carried out half-yearly, or quarterly, by the specialist coordinators in the organisation. The principal vehicle of the monitoring process will be budget statements, probably expressed in terms of headcounts, or wage and salary costs.

17. Human resource planning review activities are important for generating feedback information. This information tells the organisation not only how well it is achieving its HR plans, but also points the way to necessary changes that must be made at one or more points in the cycle. Some changes need only be made at the tactical level, ie to amend next year's operational plans. Others may have to be made at the highest strategic level, ie where plans for 5, or even 10, years ahead must be amended. Thus, the cycle of events depicted in Figure 20.2 comes full circle.

CHAPTER 21

Work Structuring, Job Design and Business Process Re-engineering

Introduction

1.   This chapter examines some of the key issues involved in designing work for people, and outlines several important approaches that have been adopted in the search for the best ways of combining people's needs and aspirations with the constraints and opportunities offered by technology and work processes. Some of these approaches, such as Job Enrichment and Autonomous Work Groups, have been employed for a quarter of a century. Others, including Business Process Re-engineering, have only been tried in recent times.

Work Design

2.   One of the major legacies of 'Scientific Management' (see Chapter 3) has been that work has generally been designed around technology and technical processes, rather than attempting to fit the latter around the needs and preferences of employees and their managers. Thus, the most important criteria for designing work have tended to include the following:

- maximising the degree of job/task specialisation
- minimising the time required to do a specific job/task
- minimising the level of skill required to perform the job/task
- minimising the learning/training time in the job
- maximising the use of machines and technology
- minimising the individual worker's discretion over how the job/task should be done.

3.   Despite the theoretical arguments in favour of simplifying industrial jobs, it is clear that Britain and many other industrial nations have experienced far fewer benefits than expected. The principal reason seems to be that people are not willing to be subjugated to machines. This unwillingness to cooperate with what has been described as the 'engineering approach to job design' has manifested itself in high labour turnover, absenteesim, lateness and poor attention to quality.

4.   The pressures on manufacturing organisations to reverse the trend towards work simplification have come from two main sources:

❶ high manufacturing costs due to low productivity

❷ demands for increased control over the pace and method of working by employees themselves.

A further pressure has also been applied by researchers and academics working in the field of social psychology. Studies into motivation and job satisfaction (see Chapters 5–6 above) have demonstrated vividly that employees at all levels seek some degree of self-control and self-direction at work.

Boredom at Work

5.   If we are to be able to redesign jobs to adapt technology to meet the motivational needs of employees, then it is important to know what employees find demotivating about their work. Some useful evidence has been provided by Guest and colleagues (1978)[1] in a study of boredom amongst three contrasting groups of employees: insurance workers, civil servants and manufacturing workers. The following factors were found to make a significant contribution to people's view of boredom:

- Constraints in the job – having to carry out certain tasks which the management saw as essential, but which employees found uninteresting (eg form-filling, figurework).

- Meaningless tasks – tasks which had to be done regardless of whether they were thought to be a waste of time by the employee.

- Lack of interest and challenge – clerical workers, in particular, found undemanding tasks such as filing and form filling very boring.

- Repetition – repetitive tasks were seen as a major source of boredom for production workers.

- Never-ending nature of the job – the public sector staff said that boredom arose from the lack of any sense of completion of the task; however much work was achieved in a day, there was always more to come.

6.   Boredom and lack of interest at work are not just caused by factors in the work itself. Two other factors, especially, play an important role:

❶ individual differences

❷ compensatory activities.

Whilst some generalisations can be made about people's perception of boredom, researchers have found that individual viewpoints vary considerably. Differences in the physical, mental and emotional make-up of individuals lead to differing levels of need, differing abilities and differing responses to stress. The extent to which individuals may be able to offset boring factors in their work depends partly on what compensatory activities are available. These may be of a work or a non-work kind, such as having a different task to handle (work) or having a meal-break (non-work) of sufficient length to allow for relaxation, shopping etc.

7.   Flexitime is one answer to the problem, as it enables employees to have greater control over the way they switch their time between work and non-work activities. Typically, a flexitime system identifies a non-negotiable part of the working day called 'core time' and a negotiable part called 'flexible time'. Core time is usually 10:00–12:00 and 14:00–16:00. The arrangement works well in those situations where employees can commence their work, or break it off, without disrupting the general workflow. The system is not normally suited to assembly-line situations.

Job Design and Job Satisfaction

8.   An organisation which has made a particular study of work design is the Work Research Unit of the Department of Employment. In an occasional paper, Sell (1983)[2] suggested that the following characteristics were crucial if a job is to satisfy human needs:

- a degree of autonomy over the way tasks are to be achieved

- individuals being responsible for their own work, and for the resources they use (eg equipment)

- an element of variety should be present in the job, so as to permit variations in task, pace and method
- longer rather than shorter work cycles
- task repetition reduced to a minimum
- arrangements to be made to provide feedback on job performance
- wherever practicable, the job should enable the completion of a complete item
- some degree of social contact should be available to the job-holder
- learning opportunities to be built into the job, so as to provide an element of challenge, as well as the opportunity to extend individual's repertoire of knowledge and skills
- roles should be clear, so that job-holders and others know what is expected from the job
- every job should have some definite goals to aim for.

9. Currently, there are three main approaches to achieving increased job satisfaction at work through task restructuring. These are:

- job enrichment
- job enlargement
- autonomous work groups.

Each of these approaches embodies several, if not all, of the characteristics referred to in the previous paragraph. There are, of course, other methods of enhancing employee job satisfaction, for example by improving consultation and/or permitting participation in decision-making, but here we concentrate on the three principal approaches.

Job Enrichment

10. The term 'job enrichment' is usually applied to the vertical extension of job responsibilities. It implies taking tasks from those both senior and junior to the job-holder in order to enable a job-holder to have more responsibility than before. Herzberg (see Chapter 5) saw job enrichment in terms of building motivators into a job. His view was that opportunities for achievement, recognition and responsibility need to be included in a person's job. For example, if a sewing machinist's job is expanded from being responsible for stitching one part of a garment, to the stitching of a whole garment with additional responsibility for the training of newcomers, then the job may be considered enriched.

11. One of the difficulties associated with job enrichment is that it will lead to changes throughout a job hierarchy. Some job-holders may find that their jobs are threatened by a job enrichment programme. Supervisors, in particular, may find that many of their duties have been handed down to members of their team. Any attempt at job enrichment must take account of such consequential changes on the overall structure of jobs.

12. The main benefits of job enrichment for individual employees are felt in terms of increased job satisfaction resulting from increased intrinsic rewards in the job (see Expectancy Theory, Chapter 6). Organisations tend to benefit by a reduction in overhead costs caused by absenteeism, lateness, lack of attention to quality and other negative features of poor morale.

Job Enlargement

13. Job enlargement, in contrast to job enrichment, is the horizontal extension of jobs, that is to add extra tasks of the same level as before. To put it another way, it is *'to add one undemanding job to another!'* To take the example of the sewing machinist again. Her job could be enlarged by giving her shirt collars to stitch as well as blouses. Job rotation (the switching from one undemanding job to another undemanding job) is a form of job enlargement. Such a step does increase job variety to a certain extent, and may create more meaningful tasks. What it does not achieve is any real increase in responsibility. The approach nevertheless has many supporters, not least because it often works in practice to bring about improved morale and/or productivity.

Autonomous Work Groups

14. The idea behind autonomous work groups is that job satisfaction and hence employee morale can be enhanced if employees work together in a group to achieve their production goals. An autonomous group is a self-organised work group which is held responsible for the rate and quality of its output. This approach to work design resulted from the efforts of the socio-technical systems theorists from the Tavistock Institute (see Chapter 9). The first reported autonomous work groups were those established in the British coalmining industry under the 'composite longwall method'. Subsequent experiments in Norway and Sweden, especially the work at the Volvo car plant, have shown that such groups can improve quality and reduce overheads as well as providing greater job satisfaction for the employees concerned.

15. Autonomous group working may not prove effective over a period of years. For example, in a case study reported by the Work Research Unit (1982)[3], a British clothing manufacturer, who introduced the practice of 'self-organised work groups' in 1973, found that after three or four years some of the machinists wanted to return to the original system of single working. By 1980 the self-organised groups had virtually disappeared! The reasons for the reversal of the autonomous group approach were seen to be as follows:

- The women concerned were able to broaden and develop their skills, but some became noticeably more efficient than others in the group, and this caused frustrations to appear; efficient workers felt held back by the less efficient workers, while the latter felt the pressure on them from their workmates

- The group payment system did not meet the needs of the more efficient workers in a manner that was possible with the earlier piecework system.

- The group system carried the seeds of its own destruction, because it stimulated problem-solving, versatility and efficiency of working among all the members of the group, and once the best machinists were fully proficient, they no longer needed the group.

- The technology involved in this case – individual sewing machines – did not require group working as a necessary element in the production process, unlike the assembly of a motorcar, for example.

16. The above case demonstrates the importance of individual differences both in terms of ability and of need. Fortunately for the management concerned the improved versatility and efficiency of the women working on their own led to less work-in-progress and more styles of garment being worked on at any one time. Productivity and quality did not suffer, and overall the outcome seemed to be one of mutual satisfaction. However, what started

out as an experiment into autonomous groups working ended up as an exercise in job enrichment!

Difficulties in Work Design

17. Individual jobs are essentially a collection of tasks. These tasks are generated primarily by the needs of the organisation, as made explicit by line managers who are confronted by a number of different pressures from marketing, financial and personnel colleagues. To a manager at the operational end of the business, every job represents some sort of compromise between conflicting pressures, arising mainly from the following:

- the need to meet the customer's specification
- the need to meet financial targets
- the operating requirements of the machinery involved
- the nature of the production process
- the requirements for stocking materials
- the delivery arrangements
- the motivational needs of employees.

18. In the light of the above pressures, it is not surprising that job redesign is rarely considered by the majority of firms, on account of the complexity of the problems at precisely the point where the product is being manufactured (or the service delivered), and where disruptions have an immediate effect. The approach likely to be taken by a typical production manager, for example, is to focus on the *technical specification* of the product, and how it is to be met within the cost, time and quality constraints imposed by senior management. Thus work is organised primarily to achieve accuracy, reliability, uninterrupted workflow, consistency of quality and the containment of costs. Only after these considerations have been met is the manager likely to consider *employee* needs. The extent to which he or she may defer to demands for increased job satisfaction will depend as much on the relative bargaining power of the employees as on any magnanimity on the manager's part!

19. A further factor to be considered when looking at the above pressures is that new technology (see Chapters 30 and 41) has all the potential to deal comprehensively with the complexities of modern production systems, and to do so with very little need for an interface with human beings. Where people are working in a computerised production system, they will tend to be integrated into the technical system rather than the other way round. Fewer operators, but with newer skills, will be the order of the day.

Business Process Re-engineering

20. In recent years much attention has been focused on an approach to greater business efficiency known as 'Business Process Re-engineering' (BPR). The term 're-engineering' was first applied to businesses in a seminal work by Hammer & Champy (1993) [4] whose definition of BPR is as follows:

> 'Re-engineering ... is the fundamental rethinking and radical redesign of business processes to achieve dramatic improvements in critical contemporary measures of performance, such as cost, quality, service, and speed.'(p.32)

They underline what they see as the radical nature of this approach. They argue that it is vital, under modern conditions of customer expectations, intense competition and the pervasive nature of change, to move away from the familiar attention to tasks and structure in order to focus on *business processes*. Taking a systems perspective, the authors describe processes as *'a collection of activities that takes one or more kinds of input and creates an output that is of value to the customer'*. Typical processes of this kind include ordering, buying, manufacturing, product development, delivery and invoicing.

21. In rethinking a key business process, such as ordering, a company employing the BPR approach has to put its existing arrangements mentally to one side, and then question everything about the process – for example, how the customer orders, what it is he wants, why he wants it that way, who deals with the customer, how, and in what order. The idea is to go back to basic principles and completely rethink the process in question. According to Hammer & Champy, the re-engineering process tends to lead to the following changes in the way work is undertaken:

- several jobs or tasks becoming combined with related jobs/tasks

- workers become more involved in decision-making (ie empowerment increases)

- the various steps in a process being performed in accordance with the needs of the next process rather than in some predetermined linear form

- processes having several versions to deal with differing customer requirements

- work is performed where it makes most sense (ie normal boundaries do not apply)

- a reduction in the number of checks and controls insisted on during the process

- the minimisation of reconciliations (eg of orders) between customers and suppliers

- a single person as point of contact with the customer ('empowered' customer service representatives)

- hybrid centralised/decentralised operations prevail (where the centralised operation is often in the form of a shared database).

22. Hammer & Champy also note that a number of important changes are likely to occur in structural forms and employee behaviour, as a result of introducing BPR. These include the following:

- work structures move away from functional departments towards process teams

- jobs tend to be made up of a range of tasks (ie *multi-dimensional*) instead of being a collection of simple tasks

- employees are empowered to act in ways that were previously controlled by rules

- 'empowerment' implies a willingness, and an ability, to accept greater responsibility for work outcomes

- preparation for work implies a greater emphasis on *education* (ie to understand the 'why' of the job) rather than on *training* (which is usually directed at the 'how' of the job)

- the focus for performance and payment shifts from activities to results (expressed in terms of the value created for the customer)

- advancement within the organisation is more likely to be based on the ability to undertake the work rather than on performance in the current job – the emphasis is on change rather than on rewards

- a culture change will occur in which the typical employee will see the customer as more important than the boss

- organisational structures are likely to become flatter and less hierarchical

- senior executives assume the role of culture leaders rather than financial 'score-keepers'.

23. Hammer & Champy see the role of information technology (IT) in BPR as crucial, because it can facilitate the re-engineering process. The key to the exploitation of IT in this context lies not so much in its ability to allow organisations to conduct their *present* operations more efficiently, but to open up *other* uses of IT to enable new goals to be achieved and new systems to be discovered. Thus, IT enables the re-engineering process to fulfil its primary goal of introducing radical change, since the raison d'etre of BPR is *innovation* rather than automation. The introduction of such examples of IT as the personal computer, the photocopier, fax machine, electronic mail facilities and the digital mobile phone, have demonstrated that IT has a potential far beyond the applications that its innovators first imagined. Such technology 'catches on' when mass populations realise that they too can benefit from its uses at work and at home. However, in the first place someone has to engage in some lateral thinking in order to develop an idea and then bring it as a product to the marketplace. The exponents of BPR would claim that this is one of its key features, ie it encourages lateral thinking about work processes, forcing people to think outside their normal frame of reference.

A Critique of BPR

24. Coulson-Thomas and colleagues (1994)[5] have challenged several of the claims made for BPR by such proponents as Hammer & Champy. As a result of their continuing European-wide study of business restructuring, the authors have begun to offer a more balanced view of what BPR can and cannot do, and to place its contribution in the context of other forms of radical change, such as Total Quality Management (TQM) (see Chapter 29) and culture change (see Chapter 24). The authors do accept that BPR has benefits:

> 'The benefits of BPR largely derive from thinking, organizing and acting horizontally, ie in terms of cross-functional processes, rather than vertically in terms of specialist functions and departments. Radical improvements result from challenging assumptions, breaking down barriers, innovative uses of technology, introducing new ways of working, changing relationships and re-drawing traditional boundaries. What is sought could be a longer term increase in capability and competitiveness.' (p.29)

25. They claim, however, that much of what passes for BPR is not so much process re-engineering but *process simplification*, the primary differences being that the latter tends to be incremental rather than revolutionary, is process-led rather than vision-led, and works within existing frameworks rather than by challenging them. Another conclusion drawn by the authors is that BPR, as practised, makes people work harder rather than smarter. It can be used as a cover for 'downsizing' the organisation (ie reducing the headcount as efficiently as possible) with its negative foci of cost reduction and getting more productivity out of the staff who remain. In this context people become victims of BPR rather than its beneficiaries. The drive to please the *external* customer can lead not just to a different perception of the individual's boss, but also to a lesser regard for those colleagues who represent the employee's *internal* customer base.

26. Talwar (1994)[6] identifies a range of re-engineering practices, some of which focus on work structures, and some which are more concerned with strategic change. Those which focus on work structuring are as follows:

- **process improvement** – this is the basic level of change, which is both local and limited, and *'is not re-engineering in the truest sense of the word'*.

- **process re-engineering** – a broader approach, which challenges existing processes, and involves *'the fundamental rethinking ... of an end-to-end process'*.

Those which go well beyond work structuring into the realm of organisational change are the following:

- **business re-engineering** – this is a strategic approach to organisational change, which implies *'greater emphasis on appraisal and redesign of the entire business architecture'*.

- **transformation** – a radical approach in which the business itself may be reinvented.

- **ongoing renewal** – the consequence of transformation in which the organisation's changed mind-set becomes *'part of the organisation's DNA...'*

27. Talwar concludes that re-engineering can do *'untold and lasting damage to the organisation when used rashly and indiscriminately as a blunt cost cutting tool'*, but that it is at its most powerful when *'it is used as a critical element in the fundamental rethinking and redesign of the business itself – not just its processes'*.

In his view, therefore, much of the impact of BPR is in fact outside the scope of work design, and is more applicable to strategic management and organisational change.

28. Hammer & Champy (1994)[7], in a postscript to their main argument, answer some of the criticisms that have been made of their approach. They admit, for example, that *'Re-engineering and TQM are neither identical nor in conflict; they are complementary'*, and on the topic of downsizing they comment that *'Whilst some employees may lose their jobs as a result of a corporate re-engineering program, re-engineering itself is a process for reorganising work, not eliminating workers.'* Also they recognise that those organisations that have successfully re-engineered their structure and processes have to accept that there will be a need for recurring re-engineering in the future – *'Our long-term goal must be to institutionalize a capacity for re-engineering in our companies, so that they view change as the norm rather than as an aberration.'*

Conclusion

29. Redesigning jobs is not easy. Changes in one part of a job hierarchy are bound to bring about changes elsewhere. Change may be welcome in one group, but not in another. This is likely to cause tensions between groups. Individuals may initially welcome change, but then feel less enthusiastic if related job conditions (pay, re-training etc) do not meet their needs. Once expectations are raised, there is no going back! Supervisory staff may feel particularly threatened by any form of job redesign, but will expect to benefit ultimately.

30. However, when work can be redesigned effectively, the rewards are twofold. For *individuals*, there is the opportunity to find personally challenging and satisfying work. For *firms*, there is the opportunity to achieve lower costs, better quality and improved productivity through a more effective match between the needs of people and the requirements of technology.

31. The approach to work structuring and job design embodied in some aspects of Business Process Re-engineering focuses on key business processes rather than on tasks and operational structures in designing work. This may lead to job losses for some, but also to more interesting and challenging jobs for others. Organisations employing BPR may enjoy reduced costs of production and improved relations with their customers.

References

1. Guest, D. et al (1978), *Job Design and the Psychology of Boredom*, Work Research Unit.
2. Sell, R. (1983), *The Quality of Working Life*, WRU Paper, Department of Employment.
3. White, G.C. (1982), *Technological Change and Employment*, WRU Occasional Paper No. 22, Department of Employment.
4. Hammer, M. & Champy, J. (1993), *Reengineering the Corporation – A Manifesto for Business Revolution*, Nicholas Brealey.
5. Coulson-Thomas, C. (ed) (1994), *Business Process Re-engineering: myth and reality*, Kogan Page.
6. Talwar R. (1994) 'Re-engineering – A Wonder Drug for the 90s?', in Coulson-Thomas (ed), *Business Process Re-engineering: myth and reality*, Kogan Page.
7. Hammer, M. & Champy, J. (1994), *Reengineering the Corporation – A Manifesto for Business Revolution*, revised edition, Nicholas Brealey.

Questions for Discussion/Homework

1. What issues need to be resolved by managers undertaking a strategic review of their organisation?
2. What are the benefits of corporate planning for an organisation?
3. What are policies, at whom are they directed, and why are they of importance to organisations?
4. In what ways might the corporate objectives of a local authority differ from those of a merchant bank (or similar commercial enterprise)?
5. Why may it be advantageous to consider Management by Objectives as a system of management rather than as a management technique?
6. In your own words, describe the sequence of events which lead to successful decision-making, illustrating your answer with an example taken from an organisation you are familiar with.
7. What is the part played by the following activities in human resource planning:

   (a) recruitment? (b) promotion?

8. Why is human resource planning especially important to an organisation in a period of change?
9. What practical difficulties are managers likely to face when attempting to redesign work and jobs?
10. How might the concept of Business Process Re-engineering be distinguished from other approaches to work design? Give examples to illustrate your answer.

Examination Questions

The questions selected cover much of the subject matter of this section. Outline answers can be found in Appendix 2.

EQ18 What are the major steps in the decision-making process? Identify and explain the key considerations in each step.

(IOB NOM)

EQ19 Why is it necessary for companies to establish and periodically review their objectives? What objectives should a business aim to achieve?

(Inst. of Mktg. Business Organisation)

EQ20 Describe what you understand by a system of management by objectives. What do you think are the advantages and disadvantages of such a system?

(IOB NOM)

EQ21 Manpower planning is an important aspect of the work of a Personnel Manager.

a. What is manpower planning?
b. Why is it necessary?

(Inst.of Mktg. Business Organisation)

If *planning* is considered as providing the route map for the journey, then *organising* is the means by which you arrive at your chosen destination. Plans, as we saw earlier, are statements of intent, direction and resourcing. To put intentions into effect requires purposeful activity, and this is where the organising function of managment comes in. Organising is concerned, above all, with *activity*. It is a process for:

❶ determining, grouping and structuring activities

❷ devising and allocating roles arising from the grouping and structuring of activities

❸ assigning accountability for results

❹ determining detailed rules and systems of working, including those for communication, decision-making and conflict-resolution.

It is important here to repeat a point made earlier (Chapter 2 paragraph 9), and make the distinction between *'organising'* and an *'organisation'*. The former, as we have just noted, is a *process*; the latter is a *social grouping*. The process, however, can only be explained in the context of the social grouping. If we take a systems view of an organisation, ie as an open social system receiving inputs from the environment, converting them and discharging the outputs back into the environment, then *organising* is essentially one of the conversion processes. It is one component of the total social system.

The next six chapters concentrate on key aspects of the *process* of organising. In particular, Chapter 22 deals with the structural aspects of organisations, Chapter 23 highlights the issues of delegation and empowerment, Chapter 24 considers key aspects of the management of change, Chapter 25 looks at the implementation of change, Chapter 26 reviews formal communications in organisations, and Chapter 27 deals with time management.

CHAPTER 22

Organisation Structures

Introduction

1.   The study of organisation structures is still a developing field. It has been a major source of interest for classical theorists (see Chapter 3), the inspiration for Weber's theory of bureaucracy (Chapter 4), and a key element in the work of the theorists of complex organisation – the contingency school (Chapter 10). More recently it has been the focus of fresh thinking about organisation structures by the Canadian academic, Henry Mintzberg. This chapter summarises the issues of structure facing modern organisations, and identifies the most important practical options available to senior management.

2.   An organisation structure, according to Mintzberg (1979)[1] is:

'the sum total of the ways in which it divides its labour into distinct tasks and then achieves coordination between them.'

This is a succinct way of describing the point made earlier by Lawrence and Lorsch (1967) who pointed out (Chapter 10) that most organisations are in a state of tension as a result of the need to be both differentiated and integrated. Once an organisation has grown beyond the point when the owners can exercise direct control, then some degree of differentiation, or specialisation, is inevitable. This at once requires some steps to be taken to ensure sufficient coordination of the new structure. Thus, most organisations have to face up to a number of crucial questions about the kind of structure that will best sustain the success of the enterprise.

3.   The most frequent questions that need to be addressed are as follows:

- to what extent should we encourage the specialisation of roles?
- what degree of standardisation should be imposed on behaviour and methods, or, to put it another way, what degree of discretion (empowerment) should be allowed to individual job-holders?
- how much formality should be encouraged?
- how many levels of authority should we establish?
- to what extent should decision-making be centralised or decentralised?

There is no perfect answer to any of these questions, but there are a number of viable options, which, taken together, can produce an optimum design for an organisation. As pointed out elsewhere (Cole, 1995)[2], an organisation structure is a concept that is used to describe something that is intangible:

> '...an intangible web of relationships between people, their shared purposes, and the tasks they set themselves to achieve those purposes.'

4.   Two approaches to the analysis of organisation structures that have been put forward in recent years are those of Handy (1993)[3] and Mintzberg (1983)[4]. Handy, in looking at organisations in terms of their cultures, identified four structures that supported the cultures he was describing. These four structures are imaginatively described as follows:

- the **web structure**, where power is centralised in the hands of a few key individuals, and which is suited to small organisations
- the **Greek temple**, which is based on functional specialisms and defined roles, and is generally seen as a bureaucracy
- the **net**, which is essentially a matrix organisation, in which project teams are coordinated by line and functional units, and where the emphasis is on the task
- the **cluster**, or **galaxy**, which is constructed around relatively independent and self-supporting individuals, such as in a professional practice of some kind (doctors, architects, accountants etc).

In practice, it is likely that organisations will comprise more than one of the above models, even though one may predominate.

5.   In a less imaginative but pragmatic manner, Mintzberg (1983) developed his rational concept of an organisation as composed of five segments (Figure 22.1), summarised as follows: A *'strategic apex'* comprising the chief executive and directors; then, proceeding down the operational line, a *'middle line'* of operational management, followed by the *'operating core'* of those directly involved in supplying the firm's goods and services; on either side of the operational line (traditionally called *'the line'* in classical thinking) are (i) the *'technostructure'* comprising functional specialists and advisors, and (ii) the *'support staff'*, who provide corporate services (and who in classical terms would be seen as *'staff'* employees).

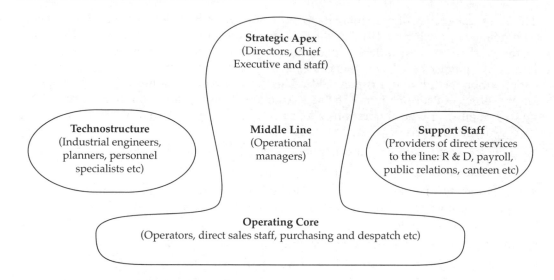

Figure 22.1 The basic parts of organisations – Mintzberg's model.

6.   Mintzberg's model looks, on the surface, as though it is the hierarchical model we associate with bureaucracy, but he uses it flexibly to develop five different configurations of structure. His synthesis of the research on organisations produces a set of five clusters, or configurations, that provide the focal points for the study of organisations. These configurations reduce the separate influences of key organisational features into manageable concepts that can be used in the study of organisations. In Mintzberg's own words *'In each structural configuration, a different one of the coordinating mechanisms is dominant, a different part of the organisation plays the most important role, and a different type of decentralisation is used.'* The five configurations are as follows:

❶ **Simple Structure** (basically no structure)

❷ **Machine Bureaucracy** (dominated by technical/specialist priorities)

❸ **Professional Bureaucracy** (dominated by skills of core staff)

❹ **Divisionalised Form** (dominated by products/outputs)

❺ **Adhocracy** (shared dominance of core staff and support services).

7.   Mintzberg analysed each configuration in terms of the organisation's prime coordinating mechanism, its key part, the main design parameters, and certain contingency factors. The analysis can be summarised as shown in Figure 22.2.

8.   By reviewing the implications of the five-configuration model, an organisation's senior management can consider the alternatives open to them, identify those parts of the organisation that are most likely to be affected by them, and design the appropriate parameters. They can consider these aspects of organisation design against the contingency factors (eg size, age of business, state of external environment) that typify their organisation. The Aston Group (Chapter 10) had shown earlier, for example, that organisational growth tended to lead to greater *specialisation*, more *standardisation* (ie of procedures, methods, personnel practices) and more *formalisation* (ie written rules etc), but *less centralisation*. What Mintzberg's ideas about configuration demonstrate is that particular sets of mechanisms and design features lead to identifiable forms of organisation structure – the configuration.

Configuration	Prime Coordinating Mechanism	Key Part of Organisation	Main Design Parameters	Contingency Factors
❶ Simple Structure ('non-structure')	Direct supervision	Strategic apex	• Centralisation • Organic	• Age: young • Technical: simple • Environment: simple/ dynamic
❷ Machine Bureaucracy	Standardisation of work processes	Techno-structure	• Behaviour formalisation • Specialisation • Centralisation	• Age: old • Size: large • Technical: simple & regulated • Environment: stable/external control
❸ Professional Bureaucracy	Standardisation of skills	Operating core	• Training • Horizontal specialisation • Decentralis-ation	• Environment: complex • Technical: simple, non-regulated
❹ Divisionalised Form	Standardisation of outputs	Middle line	• Unit grouping (markets) • Performance control	• Environment: diversified mkts • Age/size: old/large • Power: middle managers
❺ Adhocracy	Mutual adjustment	Support staff Operating core	• Liaison devices • Organic • Unit grouping (functional/ markets)	• Age: young • Technical: automated • Environment: complex/ dynamic

Figure 22.2 Structural configurations (Mintzberg).

Key Organisational Variables

9.   The key organisational issues, or variables, that feature time and time again in discussions about what determines organisation structures are basically as follows :

❶   **Purpose/Goals** (ie the fundamental aims and goals of the group)

❷   **People** (ie those who make up the organisation)

❸   **Tasks** (ie those basic activities that are required to achieve organisational aims and goals)

❹   **Technology** (ie the technical aspects of the internal environment)

❺   **Culture** (ie the dominant values guiding the organisation)

6 **External Environment** (ie the external market, technological and social conditions affecting the organisation's activities)

10. In diagrammatic form these key variables can be set out as shown in Figure 22.3.

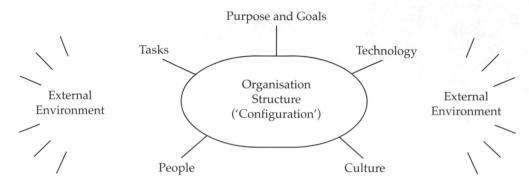

Figure 22.3 Major variables in establishing organisation structure.

11. In considering the above model, it is important to bear in mind that it can only offer a simplification of the nature of the processes involved in creating an organisation structure. It cannot, for example, indicate the weight that each factor might carry in a given situation, nor can it illustrate any 'chain reaction' arising from the interaction of one factor with another. However, it can show the basic factors involved, and point to the fact that they have to be seen in relation to each other. This is important because it enables us to analyse the concept of organisation structure as an intangible web of interrelationships. Finally, it must be noted that any emergent structure that develops will *itself* exert an influence on the other factors in the model. Thus the whole process of organisational interaction is a dynamic process, in which change and adaptation in one part of the model will have a knock-on effect somewhere else in a more-or-less restless cycle of change.

12. When undertaking any enterprise, the design of a suitable structure must begin with some idea of what the organisation is there for, and where it intends to go. In other words, the *prime purpose*, or raison d'etre, of the group plays a key role in directing the members towards the kind of structure they need. In making this step the group must take account of their *external environment*, ie the market or client groups they are intending to reach, the technological, economic, legal and political background, and the nature of that environment in terms of change or stability. The next step is likely to be to identify the *key tasks* that must be accomplished if the group is to succeed in its purpose. This leads on to a consideration of *people,* especially the skills and talents of current members, and the identification of any gaps in their portfolio of skills and knowledge, which may have to be filled by training, or the employment of newcomers. The question of *technology* will also have to be addressed. What production systems are already in operation, or planned? What equipment will be necessary? What are the demands of new software systems on people and work processes? How well do existing staff cope with new technology? Lastly, there is one other important variable, which must be taken into account, and that is the organisation's *culture* (or value system).

13. Each of the variables is affected to a lesser or greater extent by its companions, and in practice the thinking processes involved in designing a structure would not be nearly so tidy as the diagram suggests. Nevertheless, the six variables identified will have to be juggled at one time or another if an effective structure is to emerge. Given the dynamic nature of organisations, it is always likely that there will be pressures to adapt the structure

somewhere in the organisation, even if not overall. Thus structuring and re-structuring is a continual process in the life of many organisations.

Common Forms of Organisation Structure

14. There are a number of alternative ways of deploying the intangible webs of relationships that make up an organisation structure. Five of the most common forms of structure that have been 'designed' are as follows:

❶ **Functional organisation** – based on groupings of all the major business functions, eg production, marketing, finance, personnel.

❷ **Product-based organisation** – based on individual products, or product ranges, where each grouping carries its own functional specialisms.

❸ **Geographical organisation** – centred around appropriate geographical features, eg regions, nations, subcontinents.

❹ **Divisionalised structure** – usually based on products, or geography, or both, and with certain key functions such as planning and finance reserved for headquarters.

❺ **Matrix structures** – based on a combination of functional organisation with project-based structures, and thereby combining vertical and lateral lines of communication and authority.

These five grouping of activities are considered in the following paragraphs, commencing with *functional organisation*.

15. In a functional organisation structure, tasks are linked together on the basis of common functions. Thus, all production activities, or all financial activities, are grouped together in a single function which undertakes all the tasks required of that function. A typical chart of a functional organisation is as shown in Figure 22.4.

Figure 22.4 Functional organisation structure.

The main advantages of functional organisation are that by grouping people together on the basis of their technical and specialist expertise, the organisation can facilitate both their utilisation and their coordination in the service of the whole enterprise. Functional grouping also provides better opportunities for promotion and career development. The disadvantages are primarily the growth of sectional interests which may conflict with the needs of the organisation as a whole, and the difficulties of adapting this form of organisation to meet issues such as product diversification or geographical dispersement. Functional structures are probably best suited to relatively stable environments.

16. Another frequent form of grouping is by product. This is a popular structural form in large organisations having a wide range of products or services. In the National Health Service, for example, the key groups of employees – medical, nursing, para-medical and hotel services – are dispersed according to the service they provide, eg maternity, orthopaedic, surgical, psychiatric and other services. By comparison, a large pharmaceutical company could be organised as shown in Figure 22.5.

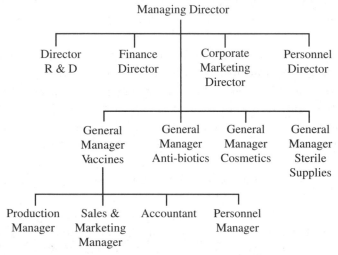

Figure 22.5 Example of a product-based structure.

The advantages of a product organisation as shown are that it enables diversification to take place, it can cope better with problems of technological change by grouping people with expertise and their specialised equipment in one major unit. The main disadvantage is that each General Manager may promote their own product group to the detriment of other parts of the company. In this situation top management must exercise careful controls, without at the same time robbing the product managers of their motivation to produce results.

17. Another familiar form of organisation structure is the one grouped on a geographical basis. This is usually adopted where the realities of a national or international network of activities make some kind of regional structure essential for decision-making and control. An example of this form of organisation is shown in Figure 22.6.

As in a product organisation, the geographically based organisation tends to produce decentralised activities, which may cause additional control problems for the senior management. Hence it is usual with such structures to find groups of senior *functional* managers at headquarters in order to provide direction and guidance to line managers in the regions or product groups.

18. With increasing complexity and size, many companies are opting for a mixed structure, which may combine the benefits of two or more of functional, product and geographical forms of organisation. Two such mixed structures will be looked at briefly: divisionalised structures and matrix structures. In the case of a divisionalised structure, the organisation is divided up into divisions on the basis of products and/or geography, and each division is operated in a functional form, but with certain key functions retained at

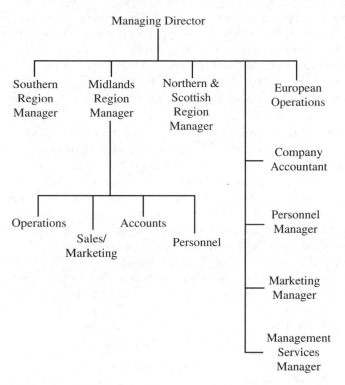

Figure 22.6 Geographically-based structure for a road transport company.

company headquarters (eg planning, finance and personnel policy). This is a common organisational form for highly diversified firms operating in more than one country. Figure 22.7 shows an example of a divisionalised structure in a British pharmaceutical company, operating worldwide.

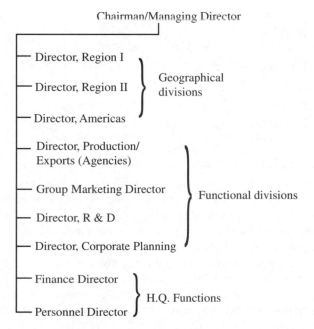

Figure 22.7 Divisionalised structure

191

19. In this example, the regions act very much like self-standing companies, producing and marketing the products developed by the parent company. Research and development activities and key corporate standards are controlled worldwide via the functional divisions, whilst the headquarters division provides group policy in key areas such as finance and personnel. A balance can, therefore, be maintained between necessary corporate control from the centre and desired divisional independence at the regional and functional levels.

20. Matrix structures are organisational forms which have come about as a result of coordination problems in highly complex industries such as aircraft manufacture, where functional and product types of structure have not been able to meet organisational demands for a variety of key activities and relationships arising from the required work processes. A matrix structure usually combines a functional form of structure with a project-based structure, as demonstrated in Figure 22.8. Thus, in a two-year project to produce a modified version of a standard aircraft, one project manager will coordinate, and be held accountable for, the work to be undertaken by the project team, and he will be the person who deals on a regular basis with the client. However, in addition to reporting to his own senior *line* manager on progress with the project as a whole, he will also report on specialist matters, such as design issues, to one or more *functional* managers, depending on the complexity of the project. The functional managers provide technical expertise and organisational stability. The project manager provides the driving force and the day-to-day control required to steer the project through during its relatively temporary lifetime.

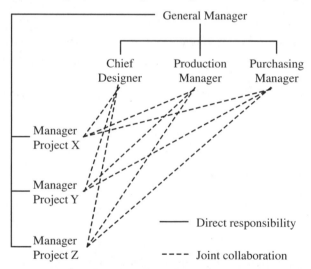

Figure 22.8 Typical matrix structure (engineering industry)

21. The main feature of a matrix structure is that is combines lateral with vertical lines of communication and authority. This has the important advantage of combining the relative stability and efficiency of a hierarchical structure with the flexibility and informality of an organic form of structure. A matrix form focuses on the requirements of the project group, which is in direct contact with the client. It helps to clarify who is responsible for the success of the project. It encourages functional managers to understand their contributive role in the organisation's productive efforts, and thus offsets one of the principal disadvantages of the purely functional form, ie individual empire-building by the functional heads. However, like all organisational form, matrix structures do have their disadvantages. The most important are:

- the potential conflicts that can arise concerning the allocation of resources and the division of authority as between project groups and functional specialists;

- the relative dilution of functional management responsibilities throughout the organisation; and

- the possibility of divided loyalties on the part of members of project teams in relation to their own manager and their functional superiors.

Despite these disadvantages, the matrix form probably offers us the best answer to date to the issue of handling the tension between the need to differentiate and the need to integrate the complex activities of modern organisations.

Centralisation and Decentralisation

22. The inevitable push towards specialisation in all but the smallest of organisations leads to the diffusion of authority and accountability. The need to structure activities develops logically into the need to allocate appropriate amounts of authority to those responsible for undertaking those activities. As we have seen in the organisation charts in this chapter, the issues are as much about power and authority as they are about grouping activities and deploying key roles. Thus, every organisation of any size has to consider how much authority to delegate from the centre, or the top. Only the small entrepreneurial organisation can sustain what Handy calls the 'power culture' where effective authority is firmly retained at the centre. Most organisations have to decide how, and how much, to delegate to managers and others throughout the job hierarchy.

23. The concept of centralisation, as it is being considered here, is not referring to the *physical* dispersal of an organisation, but to the dispersal of the *authority to commit the organisation's resources*. The physical deployment of an organisation may or may not reflect genuine power sharing. In our definition, therefore, a highly decentralised organisation is one in which the authority to commit people, money and materials is widely diffused throughout every level of the structure. Conversely, a highly centralised organisation is one where little authority is exercised outside a key group of senior managers. In practice, some functions are more easily decentralised than others. The production and marketing/sales functions are more amenable to extensive delegation than the planning function and R & D, for example. So, even highly decentralised organisations tend to reserve certain key functions to the centre. As well as planning and research, it is usually the finance and personnel functions that are least decentralised, because of the need to maintain procedural consistency and legal and other standards.

24. The advantages of decentralisation are chiefly:

- it prevents top-management overload by freeing them from many operational decisions and enabling them to concentrate on their strategic responsibilities

- it speeds up operational decisions by enabling line units to take local actions without reference back all the time

- it enables local management to be flexible in their approach to decisions in the light of local conditions, and thus be more adaptable in situations of rapid change

- it focuses attention on to important cost and profit-centres within the total organisation, which sharpens management awareness of cost-effectiveness as well as revenue targets

- it can contribute to staff motivation by enabling middle and junior management to get a taste of responsibility, and by generally encouraging the use of initiative by all employees.

25. The main disadvantages of decentralisation are:

- it requires an adequate control and communication system if major errors of judgement are to be avoided on the part of operational management

- it requires greater coordination by senior management to ensure that individual units in the organisation are not working against the interests of the whole

- it can lead to inconsistency of treatment of customers, clients or the public, especially in service industries

- it may encourage parochial attitudes in subsidiary units, who may be inclined to look more to their own needs than to those of colleagues in the organisation

- it does require a plentiful supply of capable and well-motivated managers, able to respond to the increased responsibility which decentralisation brings about.

26. On balance, the advantages outweigh the disadvantages, but this is principally because of the enormous pressures on modern business organisations to concede more and more authority to staff at executive and specialist levels, not to mention the pressures for shop-floor participation in the decision-making processes of the company. It is worth recalling at this point the University of Aston study's conclusion[5] (see Chapter 10, paragraph 28) that large size tends to lead to less centralisation, but relatively *more* specialisation, *more* rules and *more* procedures.

Organisation Levels

27. The emphasis so far in this chapter has been on vertical aspects of organisation structures. Let us now turn to some of the horizontal aspects, and in particular to the question of how many levels are appropriate between the top and bottom layer of an organisation. Organisations can be flat or tall in relation to their total size. The main features of a flat organisation are shown in Figure 22.9.

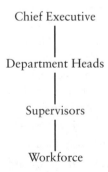

Chief Executive

Department Heads

Supervisors

Workforce

Figure 22.9 Chart of a flat organisation structure.

28. Flat organisations tend to have the following characteristics:

- centralised authority
- few authority levels
- wide span of control.

However, in recent times, as flatter structures are becoming more common, there have been major efforts to delegate authority throughout the system by empowering workforce teams in a way that was not thought possible, or desirable, some years ago.

29. A structure as flat as the one shown in Figure 22.9 would apply, generally, only to a

small organisation, say of up to about 500 employees. Most organisations, whether business enterprises or public services, find that a flat structure produces a span of control (ie the number of subordinates directly controlled by a superior) that is unmanageable for most managers/supervisors. This issue is dealt with in greater detail in the next chapter, but, clearly, wide spans of control create more opportunities for mis-managing people than do narrow spans. A flat organisation is less likely to provide career development opportunities than a taller structure. On the other hand, a flat organisation has fewer problems of communication and coordination, does encourage delegation by the managers involved, and can motivate rank-and-file employees to take greater responsibility for their output.

30. An example of a tall organisation structure is shown in Figure 22.10.

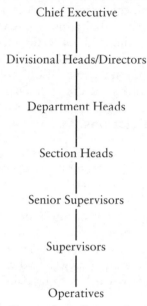

Chief Executive

Divisional Heads/Directors

Department Heads

Section Heads

Senior Supervisors

Supervisors

Operatives

Figure 22.10 Chart of a tall organisation structure.

31. Tall organisation structures tend to have the following characteristics:

- decentralised authority
- many authority levels
- narrow spans of control.

The above structure shows a typical number of levels for an organisation of about 5000 employees. Research evidence suggests that as an organisation increases in size, so it tends to hold down the number of levels. Thus, an organisation of 10,000 employees might still have seven levels, as in Figure 22.10, and certainly would not exceed eight. The advantages of tall structures arise mainly from their ability to sustain a very high degree of specialisation of functions and roles. They can also provide ample career and promotion opportunities for employees. Their principal disadvantages are connected with long lines of communication and decision-making. Thus tall structures seem to go hand in hand with formality and standardisation, which may discourage initiative and risk-taking at operational levels.

32. The major factors in determining the number of levels for any one organisation are likely to be:

- size of the operation
- nature of operation, especially in relation to the complexity of production

- the dominant management style.

As we have seen in the above discussion, size is one of the most important factors influencing organisations towards relatively flat or relatively tall structures. As a general rule, the smaller the organisation, the more likely it is to have no more than three or four levels, and the larger it is, the more likely it is to have seven or eight levels. However, factors such as the technology employed can offset the influence of size alone. Woodward's studies[6], to which we referred in Chapter 10 (paragraphs 17–24) suggested strongly that the type of production process had a direct impact on the span of control of managers at different levels. Mass production operations, for example, appeared to derive more benefit from a flatter structure, with wider spans of control, than from a taller, narrower structure. Management style also has a significant effect on structure. Organisations with a definite policy of increasing managerial responsibility for results will tend to adopt structures that consciously encourage decision-making and innovation at lower levels, ie they will tend to adopt the flatter structure to minimise the length of the chain of command. Conversely, organisations that do not, or cannot, decentralise decision-making, perhaps for safety reasons, will tend to settle for a taller structure with narrow spans of control.

Line & Staff: Functions & Relationships

33. There is sometimes a confusion between the terms 'line', 'staff' and 'functional' when these expressions are used to describe structural aspects of organisation. One of the main reasons for this confusion undoubtedly stems from the attempt to promote classical 'principles' in complex organisational structures which are often far from classical in themselves. For example, the classical concept of 'unity of command' – for each person, one superior – is just not practicable in organisations where the legal, financial, personnel and technological implications of the line processes can only be dealt with by diffusing authority *across* the management hierarchy as well as down it. This is not to reject the classical view out of hand, but to say that it has to be considerably qualified in the light of modern organisational complexity.

34. The terms 'line' and 'staff' are usually understood in two senses: firstly, as *functions* contributing to organisation objectives (Figure 22.11), and, secondly, as *relationships* of authority (Figure 22.12). Taking these meanings in order, we can summarise the most frequent views that have been expressed about 'line' and 'staff'.

Line	Staff
Functions contribute *directly* to the provision of goods and services to the customer.	Functions contribute *indirectly* to goods and services by supporting the line.
Typical line functions are **production** and **sales**.	Typical staff functions include **purchasing, accounts, legal** and **personnel**.
Seen as the *primary* functions of the organisation.	Seen as the *secondary* functions of the organisation.
Line functions *act*.	Staff functions *think*.

Figure 22.11 Line and staff as functions.

35. In terms of relationships of authority, 'line' and 'staff' can be more effectively distinguished if 'staff' is sub-divided into service and functional as shown in Figure 22.12.

Line	Staff	
	Service	Functional
Direct authority over others. Part of the role of every manager and supervisor. Line authority is the essence of the chain of command. Line relationships *TELL* Line authority is invariably qualified by functional authority.	Advisory only. Seen as authority without responsibility. Service relationships *SELL*	Direct authority over others *in respect of specialist functions only.* Functional relationships also *TELL*, but only *AS PRESCRIBED.*

Figure 22.12 Line and Staff as Relationships of Authority.

36. It makes more sense to consider line and staff in terms of authority relationships, where there are *real* differences, rather than in terms of functions, where it is highly arguable to state that some functions are primary and other secondary. The key point about functions is that every organisation is a complex blend of functions that are dependent each on the other. Almost every comment made in Figure 22.11 concerning *functions* can be challenged. No wonder there is confusion! It is much more productive to concentrate attention on line and staff as an issue of differences of authority between one type of manager and another.

37. *Line authority* is the simplest to understand as well as to agree about. It is the authority that every manager exercises in respect of his or her own subordinates. Thus specialist managers, such as chief accountants and personnel managers, exercise line authority over their own staff. In this role they are not different from so-called line managers, such as production managers and sales managers. Line authority, then, is not dependent on line *functions*. It is the central feature of the total chain of command throughout the entire organisation structure.

38. *Staff authority*, as such, is a misleading concept altogether. It begins to make more sense when divided into two further concepts, those of *'service'* and *'functional authority'*, as suggested above. Unlike for line authority, the concept of staff authority is derived from the staff function, and this does relate it to the advisory and service functions of the internal structure of an organisation. However, because of the very interdependence of all the key functions in a modern organisation, one must distinguish between those aspects of the staff function that merely provide services (eg costing, recruitment, market research etc), and those that provide key standards of performance for all other sections of the organisation (eg setting and monitoring company accounting procedures, installing and controlling industrial relations procedures etc). When looked at in this way, it is probably best to forget the term 'staff authority' altogether in favour 'functional authority', which is the former stripped of its servicing aspects, but made much more powerful in respect of standards in the particular function.

39. *Functional authority*, unlike line authority, is not exercised by every manager. It can only be exercised by managers of specialist functions, and it consists of the right to order

others, including other managers, as to what to do, and how to do it, *in relation to agreed aspects of their own particular specialism*. So, for example, the Finance Director of a company is not only responsible (ie accountable) for the conduct of the financial matters, but also has the authority to insist that line managers and others adhere to the company's established financial procedures and policies. With the complexity of modern business, it is not practicable for senior line managers to divert their attention away from operational duties in order to attend to the design and implementation of financial, personnel and other procedures. Thus, the use of functional authority is a very real part of organisations today. Naturally, the existence of such authority detracts from the power of line managers to exercise their own discretion as widely as they would like, but, given the pressures imposed on organisations by their external environment, it is only by having strong specialist guidance that line managers can fulfil their responsibilities in the ways demanded by customers, employees and other stakeholders. What has to be avoided, however, is turning line managers into puppets, operated by functional masters at the centre.

40. Ironically, perhaps, the very *power* of functional specialists arises from the operation of another classical idea – that of the 'principle of correspondence' (see Chapter 3, paragraph 34). This states that *authority* should be commensurate with *responsibility*. It will be useful to consider for a moment the differences between these three concepts.

Authority is the legitimate power to act in certain ways; it is rarely granted carte blanche; it emanates from the top, and can be delegated to subordinates. Relatively few people in an organisation are endowed with authority.

Responsibility is the obligation to perform certain functions on behalf of the organisation; responsibility may range from the very specific to the very broad; it is commonly called accountability; unlike authority it cannot be delegated. Every job-holder has some level of responsibility for their work.

Power. Both of the above concepts can be distinguished from power, which is the ability to implement actions, regardless of considerations of formal authority or responsibility. Charismatic individuals, for example, may have no formal authority conferred on them, but nevertheless can exercise power over others and lead them into actions that might be against the organisation's interests. Managers in situations where such behaviour occurs will have the authority to put a stop to rebellious or obstructive actions, but may not necessarily have the power to do so. Given the potential problems associated with the misuse of power, the current affection in some organisations for the concept of 'empowerment' (see the following chapter) is rather ironical. Effectively, 'empowerment' in the present context is not to do with power but rather refers to 'enhanced responsibility'.

References

1. Mintzberg, H. (1979), *The Structuring of Organisations – a Synthesis of the Research*, Prentice-Hall.
2. Cole, G.A. (1995), *Organisational Behaviour*, DP Publications.
3. Handy,C.(1993), *Understanding Organisations*, (4th edition), Penguin Business.
4. Mintzberg, H. (1983), *Structure in Fives: Designing Effective Organisations*, Prentice-Hall.
5. Pugh, D. & Hickson, D. (1976), *Organisational Structure in its Context*, Gower.
6. Woodward, J. (1963), *Industrial Organisation – Theory and Practice*, OUP.

CHAPTER 23

Delegation and Empowerment

Introduction

1.   As we saw in the previous chapter, one of the central issues of organisation design is the question of how to create the best balance between control from the centre and delegation throughout the rest of the system. This chapter examines some of the factors surrounding delegation, including questions of span of control and the current concept of 'empowerment'. In the previous chapter, delegation was considered in organisation-structure terms, especially in terms of centralisation versus decentralisation. This was taken to mean the degree to which the authority to commit resources was diffused throughout the organisation by means of the formal allocation of roles within a structure. This chapter considers delegation at the more personal level as the transfer of authority between one individual and another, ie as a *management* issue rather than an organisational one.

2.   Discussion about delegation and empowerment are centred around issues of authority, responsibility/accountability, and power. It is worthwhile reminding ourselves what these different concepts mean. The distinctions that are usually made between them are as follows:

❶   **Authority** is a right conferred on some members of an organisation to act in a certain way over others. Authority is rarely arbitrary, and thus there are always constraints on an individual manager's ability to act. Authority can be regarded as a defined amount of power granted by the organisation to selected members – directors, managers, specialist personnel and supervisors. French & Raven (1958)[1], in a classic analysis of power in various forms, described this type of power as *legitimate power*.

❷   **Responsibility** is a concept that refers to the legitimate expectation of a level of perfor mance that a senior person has of his or her subordinates or team members. Another word for responsibility is *'accountability'*, which in some respects is a more helpful term, since it implies that one person is accountable to another for a given task. In fulfilling their responsibilities, a person may delegate (ie hand down) some of their own authority to act, but they cannot pass off their responsibility (accountability). This is why there is always an element of risk attached to delegation, for if things go wrong, the delegator cannot blame the person to whom he or she assigned certain tasks. The delegator alone is accountable to the superior, not the team member.

❸   **Power** is essentially the ability to effect change in other people so that they do what you want. When used on its own, the term 'power' implies unfettered control over others. Power in this sense is usually unauthorised, and is described as arbitrary or *coercive* power (French & Raven). Only when power is restrained within defined parameters can it be called 'authority'.

❹   **Empowerment** is a currently fashionable phrase with several meanings attached to it, ranging from delegation to job enrichment. In this chapter 'empowerment' will be taken to signify an approach to managing people which permits team members to exercise greater decision-making on day-to-day matters in their work. It is thus more concerned with issues of *authority* rather than power, as defined above.

Delegation

3.   Delegation is essentially a power-sharing process in which individual managers transfer part of their legitimate authority to subordinates/team members, but without passing on their own ultimate responsibility for the completion of the overall task which has been entrusted to them by their own superiors. The fulfilment of practically every task in an organisation requires a certain amount of authority or the right to act in a certain way. The fact is that if a job-holder is to carry out the responsibilities attached to their job successfully, they must have the rights that go with the job, especially the right to take certain decisions (authority), and the right to possess adequate resources with which to complete the job. As the old classical management idea put it, *'authority should be commensurate with responsibility'*. In practice, it would be self-defeating if employees were to be assigned responsibilities, but given no rights to enable them to achieve them.

4.   In the process of delegating tasks with their commensurate authority, it is important to ensure that the amount of authority is defined, or prescribed, in an unequivocal way. The principal options open to a manager, ranging from tight to loose control, are shown in Figure 23.1.

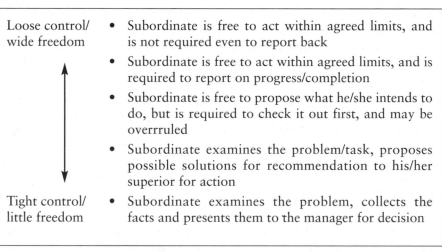

Figure 23.1 Delegation – the main options.

5.   Delegation does not come easily to most managers. It takes time, effort and confidence in one's team members to explain what is wanted and then let them go away and do it, whilst trusting that they will not disappoint you. Insecure managers are less likely than confident individuals to take the risk of giving their staff greater freedom to act. An insecure person will tend to delegate at the lower end of Figure 23.1. However, there are ways in which delegation can be made 'safer' for managers. After all, even confident and experienced managers will not want to take unnecessary risks. Good practice in delegating in situations where either the manager is new, or the team is newly formed, is likely to include the following principles:

- ensure that the objective to be achieved is made clear

- indicate the standard of performance that is required (what, when etc)

- decide what level of authority to grant

- allocate adequate resources (staff, equipment, expenses etc)

- ensure that clear reporting arrangements are made

- encourage subordinate to request further help if needed
- inform subordinate that early mistakes will be used as learning opportunities
- ensure that the task is completed according to agreed standards
- provide any advice or further resourcing that may be required if the task has proved to be more difficult than anyone had first anticipated
- thank the individual for their efforts.

6. If a manager is to be judged mainly on the performance of their team in work of a specialised or highly professional nature, for example, then it is reasonable to grant that person the authority to select and appoint their own staff, and to be able to remove any who are unsatisfactory. Authority could be granted in several different ways. Where the manager had the full confidence of his or her superiors, the authority is likely to be as follows:

- Complete authority to recruit staff within budget limits (costs and/or headcount)
- Authority to appraise own staff within the scope of company procedures
- Authority to transfer, or dismiss, employees who turned out to be unsuitable.

7. Where the manager was less experienced, it is likely that a more qualified form of delegation would be granted, as follows:

- Authority to select final candidates subject to approval by their superior
- Authority to appraise staff within procedures
- Authority to recommend unsatisfactory staff for transfer or dismissal.

Few managers, however senior, have carte blanche in the exercise of their authority. Modern organisations have developed policies and procedures to circumscribe the limits of authority at whatever level it may be granted. The art is to balance the legitimate use of power with the risks associated with it and the need to motivate managers to perform at their best for the organisation.

8. The reasons for delegation are mainly practical, but some are idealistic. Practical reasons include:

- Senior managers can be relieved of less important, or less immediate, responsibilities in order to concentrate on more important duties
- Delegation enables decisions to be taken nearer to the point of impact, and without the delays caused by frequent reference upwards
- Delegation gives managers the opportunity to experience decision-making and the consequences of their decisions
- Delegation encourages managers to learn how to cope with responsibility
- Delegation enables organisations to meet changing conditions more flexibly, especially at the boundaries of their system
- Delegation contributes to staff development and motivation.

9. Idealistic reasons for delegation include:

- delegation is a 'good thing' for individual growth, and contributes to staff morale
- delegation is *the sine qua non of empowerment*' (Peters, 1988)[2]
- delegation helps to enrich individuals' jobs and humanises work.

Most organisations find the need to delegate forced on them by circumstances, especially the pressures on managers to concentrate on environmental issues rather than on internal problems. However, the best practice is to be found in organisations that use delegation positively as an important employee motivator as well as a means of facilitating effective decision-making throughout the enterprise.

Span of Control

10. One of the major questions which has to be faced when considering the practical aspects of delegation is how many subordinates, or team members, can be managed effectively by any one manager or supervisor. This is the classical management issue of the so-called *'span of control'*, ie the number of employees reporting directly to one person. In practice spans can vary between one and forty or more subordinates directly supervised, although the most likely range is between three and twenty. Smaller spans tend to be found among managerial, professional and technical groups. Here factors such as cost, the complexity of work and the need to deal adequately with the problems of people, who may themselves be managers of others, require a closer involvement by superiors in the total operation of their units. Towards the bottom end of the organisational hierarchy, where routine tasks are being carried out by employees who have no subordinates themselves, it is practicable to have much larger spans.

11. Various writers and theorists have made proposals about the best span of control. The first of these was a French management consultant, V.A. Graicunas, who wrote a famous paper on this topic in 1933. Graicunas attempted to demonstrate mathematically the increase in the number of relationships arising from each increase in the number of subordinates reporting to the manager. For example, with just one subordinate, the total number of possible relationships was still one, but for two subordinates it rose to six relationships. By the time six subordinates were supervised, the total number of relationships rose to 222. The formula which Graicunas developed to produce these figures was as follows:

$$R = n(2^{n-1} + n - 1)$$

where R is the number of relationships and n is the number of subordinates.

12. This concept of the span of control is a very theoretical one, of course, and bears no relationship to what happens in practice. The value of Graicunas's idea is that it draws attention to the potentially rapid increase in the complexity of management and supervisory roles when the span of control rises beyond a certain point. Others who have put forward views on the span of control include L.F. Urwick (1952)[3]. Among his Principles of Management (see Chapter 3 above), he included the span of control, which he believed should not exceed five or six subordinates *whose work interlocked*. The italics emphasise Urwick's thinking that it is the *complexity* of work that determines the optimum span. Where the work being undertaken by subordinates is relatively self-contained, then larger spans are possible.

13. The whole question of spans of control is linked to top management's views about the number of levels they should have in their organisation. If a flat organisation is preferred, then larger spans are an inevitable consequence, especially for middle managers. If a tall structure is preferred, then spans can be smaller. Any final decision has to be a compromise between these opposing consequences. Other important influences on the size of the spans in an organisation or unit include:

- the level of ability of management ie are they capable of producing results with spans of a certain number?
- the level of knowledge and experience of the subordinates concerned, eg well-trained and experienced staff require less supervision than those without training and experience;

- the complexity of the work of the unit and the degree of change to which it is subject, ie the more complex and more fast-changing the work, the more necessary it is to install narrow spans of control;

- the costliness of possible mistakes by individuals in the unit;

- the degree of hazard or danger associated with the work, eg work on oil-rigs or in biochemical laboratories requires special attention to safety procedures.

14. An early example of a company which tried to take account of the variables at work in deciding spans of control was the Lockheed Company in the USA. In the 1960s they developed a method of 'span evaluation' which allocated weightings and points to different degrees of key variables in delegation. These variables were as follows:

1 Similarity of functions   In a range from identical through to similar to fundamentally distinct.

2 Geographic contiguity   Together or dispersed.

3 Complexity of functions   In a range from simple repetitive to highly complex and varied.

4 Direction and control   From minimum supervision and training to constant close supervision.

5 Coordination   From minimum relation to others to extensive mutual non-recurring relationships.

6 Planning   From minimum scope and complexity to extensive effort in areas and policies not chartered.

Few organisations have gone to the lengths that Lockheed did, but the work provided some useful focal points for clarifying important aspects of managing people that have to be taken into account in establishing the levels of delegation which are possible in a given situation.

Empowerment

15. 'Empowerment' was defined earlier as an approach to managing people which permits team members to exercise greater decision-making on day-to-day matters in their work. In a review of ideas about empowerment, Clutterbuck (1994)[4] refers to a number of different definitions of the concept. These range from empowerment being treated as a *cultural* exercise in which people are encouraged to take personal responsibility for improving the way they do their work, through delegating responsibility for decision-making as far down the line as possible, to the *'controlled transfer of power from management to employee in the long-term interest of the business as a whole'* (p.13).

16. Clutterbuck considers that organisations have been pressed into delegating more widely, and with more worthwhile work, because of the following trends in organisations:

- requirement to be more responsive to the marketplace

- reduction in number of levels in structures – so-called de-layering

- need for lateral collaboration and communication among work teams with minimal supervision

- need for top management to stand back from day-to-day issues in order to concentrate on longer-term (strategic) issues

- need to make best use of all available resources (especially human resources) to maintain and improve competitiveness

- pressure to meet the higher expectations of a better-educated workforce
- the development of 'learning organisations', ie where continuous improvement of peoples' performance is encouraged, individually and in work teams.

17. As with delegation, empowerment can be implemented at a number of different levels, ranging from relatively simple and routine matters to involvement in policy-making. Clutterbuck refers to four general areas where empowerment techniques may be applied. These are as follows:

- the **knowledge base**, eg extending people's knowledge/skills in job-related matters (as in work design), or, in the case of professionals, *reducing* the focus of the work to enable expertise to be developed
- **discretion over tasks** (when, how, design), eg by delegating more widely to the extent of creating self-governing teams
- **involvement in policy-making**, eg from use of referenda and cascade briefings to participation on boards of directors
- **organisational change**, eg encouraging suggestions for change in other functions/departments, and developing cross-functional quality improvement teams (ie another lateral approach).

18. Examined under these headings, empowerment seems to be an umbrella term covering a number of human resource management activities referred to elsewhere in this book, such as job design, job enrichment, employee participation and business process re-engineering. In the present context, it is best seen as a qualitative approach to the delegation of authority throughout an organisation, combining both practical and idealistic values about the best use of people at work.

References

1. French, J. & Raven, B. (1958), 'The Bases of Social Power', in Cartwright, D. (ed), *Studies in Social Power*, Institute for Social Research.
2. Peters, T. (1988), *Thriving on Chaos: Handbook for a Management Revolution*, Macmillan.
3. Urwick, L.F. (1952), *The Elements of Administration*, Pitman.
4. Clutterbuck, D. (1994), *The Power of Empowerment*, Kogan Page.

CHAPTER 24

Managing Change: Key Concepts

Introduction

1. To change something implies altering it, varying or modifying it in some way. Organisations change, or adapt, what they want to achieve and how. Some organisations change mainly in response to external circumstances (reactive change); others change principally because they have decided to change (proactive change). Some organisations are conservative in outlook, seeking little in the way of change, other are entrepreneurial in outlook, ever seeking new opportunities and new challenges. Some organisations are so constructed (even constricted!) that change, ie adaptation, is a slow and difficult process;

others are designed with an in-built flexibility, enabling adaptation to take place regularly and relatively easily. Over thirty years ago Burns and Stalker[1] conducted their famous enquiries in the management of innovation (see Chapter 10), when they identified mechanistic and organic types of organisation. Their organisational types have been confirmed time and time again by subsequent researchers, and current exponents of organisational change, such as Tom Peters and Rosabeth Moss Kanter, also make reference to these two basic organisational forms in their writings.

2.   Change does not always imply *innovation*, ie introducing something new, something novel, but this is the aspect of change most attractive to researchers and consultants. Innovation, therefore, forms the focus for most of this, and the following, chapter. However, there are some general points that can be made about the concept of organisational change. The first is that change is a process which is rarely contained by functional or specialist boundaries. Change in one part of an organisation invariably affects people and processes in another part. As Figure 24.1 illustrates, organisational change can influence, and be influenced by, several important features of organisational life – the organisational mission and strategy, its structure, products and processes, its people and culture, and the nature of the technology employed. These features of the organisation are themselves affected by the nature of the external environment.

Figure 24.1 Organisational change and key organisational features.

3.   A second important point about change is that it can be triggered by any number of external and internal factors. *External* triggers may include:

*   changes in demand for the organisation's products or services (eg as a result of changing consumer preferences, action by competitors, government etc)

*   threatening tactics of competitors (eg by aggressively cutting prices or producing an advantageous enhancement to a product or service)

*   arrival of a newcomer with a competing product or service

*   takeover of the business by a more powerful enterprise

*   merger of the business with another

*   failure of a key supplier to meet the organisation's requirements

*   changes in the terms of trade (eg currency exchange rates, tariffs etc)

- inability to attract sufficient numbers of skilled employees

- development of new technologies now available for application

- political changes (eg new labour laws, changes in company law, taxation etc).

An important point concerning these external triggers is that some are less predictable than others, and therefore less open to planned (ie proactive) change.

4.   *Internal* triggers, which should, in theory, be more predictable indicators of change, include the following:

- planned changes in strategy as a result of revised mission or goals (themselves largely influenced by *external* considerations)

- efforts to introduce cultural changes (eg in management style, collaborative working etc)

- need to improve productive efficiency/make better use of resources

- need to improve the quality of products or services

- need to respond to the development of potential new products/services devised by R&D or marketing departments

- need to improve standards/systems for dealing with suppliers

- need to deploy people (the human resources) where they are most effective.

5.   In facing up to these internal triggers of change, managements have to plan how they will respond to them. Some potential changes will have been announced well beforehand, and in these cases planning is taken care of proactively. Some changes will, however, be brought about by a crisis of some kind (eg the failure of a new product or supplier or even a key manager). In these latter cases, it may be impossible to plan in any detail, but only to respond reactively and urgently. Where key individuals or products are concerned, however, well-organised enterprises will usually have a fall-back position in the shape of a 'contingency plan'. This may not be the ideal response, but at least it will prevent a crisis from turning into a tragedy of major proportions.

6.   Other general issues concerning organisational change include resistance to change, the use of key individuals as agents of change, and the costs of implementing change. It is vital that managers planning changes should acknowledge that some resistance will be unavoidable. Individuals at every level in the organisation are potentially liable to feel threatened by change, and thus change must be 'sold' to those affected by it. This issue is examined later in the chapter. The subject of change agents is dealt with in the next chapter. Finally, in this introduction to change, the question of costs must be briefly addressed. All change will incur some *direct* costs (eg equipment costs, relocation costs, recruitment costs, and possible redundancy payments). There will also be *indirect* costs, such as communicating the changes to employees, providing appropriate training, and temporarily redeploying key managers and staff on change projects. A final comment on costs is that it may be important for an organisation to consider what might be the costs of *not* introducing proposed changes.

7.   We can now turn to some of the ideas about the concept of change that have been put forward by leading academics and consultants, whose researches into change in organisations have produced a clearer picture of the issues and possible solutions to them.

Rosabeth Moss Kanter

8.   In her in-depth study of 10 major US companies, which also drew on related research

in another 100 American business enterprises, Moss Kanter (1984)[2] identified two quite different ways in which companies approached innovation. One approach, which she called the *'integrative'* approach described firms that dealt holistically with problems, were willing to try out new ideas, prepared to push the organisation to its limits, and generally saw change as an opportunity rather than a threat. The other approach, by contrast, compartmentalised its problem-solving, saw the organisation as a collection of segments rather than as organic whole, dealt with change within segments/compartments and was unwilling to alter the balance of overall structure. This approach she called *'segmentalist'*. It became clear to her that *innovation*, which she sees as more than the introduction of new products and new technology, but also the implementation of new ideas and practices, was much better handled by integrative companies than by the segmentalists.

9.   The most important motive for innovation in a business enterprise is, according to Moss Kanter, to improve the organisation's ability to meet and satisfy customer needs. For companies to become integrative they need to develop three new sets of skills:

❶   **Power skills** – ie skills in persuading others to invest time and resources in new (and risky) initiatives

❷   **Skills in managing problems** arising from team-working and employee participation

❸   **An understanding of how change is designed** and constructed in an organisation.

These are points which are taken up by several other writers, including Peters, whose ideas will be referred to shortly.

10.   In dealing with issues of resistance to change and overcoming inertia, which she calls *'roadblocks to innovation'*, Moss Kanter suggested a number of possible actions, which can be summarised as follows:

❶   As a prerequisite to change, top management must be personally committed to supporting innovation and must learn to think integratively

❷   A *'culture of pride'* should be encouraged within the organisation, in which achievements are highlighted and where experienced innovators serve as consultants to other parts of the organisation

❸   Access to power sources (management committees etc) should be enlarged to improve support for innovatory experimental proposals

❹   Lateral communication should be improved. Cross-functional links should be developed, and staff mobility should be encouraged

❺   Unnecessary layers of hierarchy should be reduced (ie a flatter structure should be aimed for) and authority should be pushed downwards (*'empowerment'* of staff)

❻   Information about company plans should be more widespread and given as early as possible to enable people to contribute to change before decisions are made (eg by means of task-forces, problem-solving groups etc).

Resistance to Change

11.   There is not much point in *'change for change's sake'*, and most people need to be persuaded of the need to change. Some people fear it. The reality is that every human grouping has some forces within it which keep it together and provide it with stability, and others which provide it with a reason to change or adapt. Kurt Lewin (1951)[3] illustrated the dilemma neatly with his classic notion of *'Force-field theory'*. This theory suggests that all behaviour is the result of an equilibrium between two sets of opposing forces (what he

calls *'driving forces'* and *'restraining forces'*). Driving forces push one way to attempt to bring about change; restraining forces push the other way in order to maintain the status quo. The basic Force-field model is as shown in Figure 24.2.

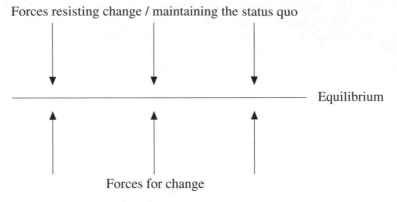

Forces resisting change / maintaining the status quo

Equilibrium

Forces for change

Figure 24.2 Force-field theory.

12. Generally speaking, human beings tend to prefer to use driving forces to bring about change. They want to 'win' by exerting pressure on those who oppose them, but, as Lewin's model suggests, the more one side pushes, the more the other side resists, resulting in no change. The better way of overcoming resistance, therefore, is by focusing on the removal, or at least weakening, of the objections and fears of the resisting side. Thus the initial policy should be not 'How can we persuade them of *our* arguments for change?', but rather 'What are *their* objections/fears, and how can we deal with them?'

13. Lewin developed a three-stage approach to changing behaviour, which was later adapted by Edgar Schein (1964)[4]. This comprises the following steps:

1. **Unfreezing existing behaviour** (ie gaining acceptance for change)
2. **Changing behaviour** (ie adopting new attitudes, modifying behaviour) – this usually requires a change agent
3. **Refreezing new behaviour** (ie reinforce new patterns of thinking/working).

The unfreezing stage is aimed at getting people to see that change is not only necessary but desirable. The change stage is mainly a question of identifying what needs to be changed in people's attitudes, values, and actions, and then helping them to acquire ownership of the changes. The role of a change agent (ie a person who is responsible for helping groups and individuals to accept new ideas and practices) is crucial at this stage. The refreezing stage is aimed at consolidating and reinforcing the changed behaviour by various support mechanisms (encouragement, promotion, participative management style, more consultation etc).

14. One of the principal ways in which organisations can bring about planned change is by means of an Organisation Development programme, which will be described briefly in the next chapter. Another approach which has received considerable attention is called 'Action Research'. This is a collaborative approach to change in which people work in groups (either their own work-teams, or cross-functional groups) in order to analyse a problem situation and suggest ways in which it might be tackled. Action groups usually follow a five-stage sequence, as shown in Figure 24.3.

15. The two principal attractions of action research are (1) that it is problem-oriented rather than solution-oriented, and (2) that it actively involves employees in issues of importance to their work and thus gains their cooperation in bringing about change. Also, due to

its essential grounding in 'real' issues, it is easier to 'sell' to senior management than many other change methods.

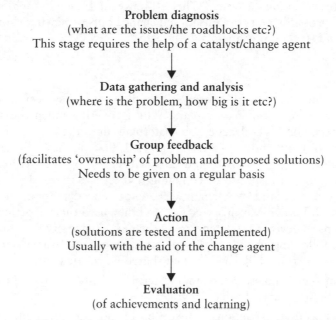

Problem diagnosis
(what are the issues/the roadblocks etc?)
This stage requires the help of a catalyst/change agent

Data gathering and analysis
(where is the problem, how big is it etc?)

Group feedback
(facilitates 'ownership' of problem and proposed solutions)
Needs to be given on a regular basis

Action
(solutions are tested and implemented)
Usually with the aid of the change agent

Evaluation
(of achievements and learning)

Figure 24.3 An Action Research methodology.

16. Another approach to change – business process re-engineering – has already been mentioned (Chapter 21 above). Suffice to say here that, whatever the criticisms of BPR, it has re-focused particular attention on certain key issues of change notably by:

- challenging current assumptions about work processes, collaborative approaches etc
- focusing on changing processes rather than structures or tasks
- suggesting that lateral work processes are crucial
- stressing the multidimensional nature of jobs under modern conditions
- pointing to the interdependence of work processes
- facing up to the need to empower employees in re-engineered processes and organisations
- stressing the role of the customer as the ultimate beneficiary of BPR
- highlighting the facilitating role of information technology (IT) in improving business processes.

17. Talwar (1994)[5], in his model of the range of re-engineering practices (see Chapter 21), includes some practices which focus on strategic change, and are especially relevant to the subject-matter of this chapter. These are the BPR practices which go well beyond work structuring into the realm of organisational change. They are the following:

- **business re-engineering** – as stated earlier, this is the strategic approach to organisational change, where *'the entire business architecture'* of the enterprise is restructured; this approach is more akin to Organisation Development, which is discussed in the next chapter.
- **transformation** – this is a radical approach in which the business itself may be reinvented, and lies more in the realm of strategic management, in which the very raison d'etre of the organisation is subject to scrutiny and reappraisal.

- **ongoing renewal** – this is effectively the process of sustaining the consequence of trans-formation, in which the organisation's changed mind-set becomes, as Talwar puts it, *'part of the organisation's DNA…'*. This is a powerful biological analogy to use in this context, and probably most organisational change falls somewhat short of this degree of cultural and structural change.

Tom Peters

18. The way in which 'successful' companies handle change has been a focus of interest for a number of researchers in recent years. Whilst covering much the same ground as Moss Kanter, Peters, and his colleague Bob Waterman, used the concept of 'excellence' as the central feature of their study of 43 of the largest US companies[6]. 'Success' was defined as a mixture of above average growth and financial return together with a reputation for continuous innovation in response to changing market situations. It was not meant to imply perfection. Peters and Waterman were experienced management consultants, working for the well-known McKinsey & Co, and they used their experience of analysing client organisations to devise a model for use in their excellence survey. This model focused attention on the following characteristics of business organisations: structure, strategy, systems, management style, skills, people, and shared values (ie culture).

19. As a result of their studies, Peters and Waterman identified eight attributes of excel-lence, which can be summarised briefly as follows:

❶ They have a bias towards action, ie once a problem is identified and analysed, people are expected to come up with solutions

❷ They listen to their customers – customer service is foremost

❸ They encourage internal autonomy and entrepreneurship (and are prepared to tolerate the inevitable failures that will occur)

❹ Employees are held in high esteem, but in a performance-conscious environment; expectations are high

❺ They emphasise the organisation's basic values (culture) and demonstrate their commitment to them

❻ They stick to what they know (acknowledging that what they know increases over time)

❼ Complex structures are avoided; divisionalised structures are the most likely; corpo-rate/headquarters staff are kept to the minimum

❽ Control is loose yet tight; it is loose in that decision-making is pushed downwards, but tight in that certain core values/practices are insisted upon (eg attention to quality, information feedback etc)

20. One other important conclusion reached by Peters and Waterman was that there was invariably one strong individual at work in the crucial early stages of developing the culture of excellence. In encouraging others to take up the cause of excellence, and thus increase the number of people willing to take up the key leadership role, Peters has written subsequently on the subject of excellence. In his book, *Thriving on Chaos* (1987)[7], he proposes some prescriptions for managing change, innovation and survival. The title of the book is intended to show that the external environment is turbulent and unstable, and managements have to develop a suitable strategy for change if they and their firms are to survive and win. He proposes 45 prescriptions for excellence, although comments that excellent firms probably don't believe so much in excellence as in constant improvement and constant change.

21. His 45 prescriptions are developed under five different headings, of which the first is *Creating Total Customer Responsiveness*. Here he suggests that firms should concentrate on finding appropriate market niches – differentiation is the order of the day. Having found the niche, meet the customer's needs with top quality products/services, provide superior service, develop responsiveness, become internationalist and create uniqueness (make your product or service stand out among the competition). Listening to customers is a vital element here; others include making more positive use of manufacturing and marketing functions. Such attributes are those which have already been adopted by many leading Japanese firms, and some are featured in Deming's Fourteen Points for Quality (see Chapter 29).

22. Peters' second heading is *Pursuing Fast-Paced Innovation*. The main point here is that innovation should be pursued in small starts. Big firms have to tackle innovation as if they were small firms. Thus there is an incremental approach to change – little by little but ever onward. Innovations should be tested (piloted) before introduction; success should be rewarded and used as a model for others; failures should be tolerated, especially what he calls 'fast failures', since there is much to be learned from failure. Overall, the organisation should aim to create a corporate capacity for innovation.

23. The third heading is *Achieving Flexibility by Empowering People*. This word 'empowerment' is also used by Moss Kanter. It implies allowing, indeed encouraging, employees at all levels to share in the decision-making processes of the organisation. Thus firms should do all they can to create opportunities for people to participate fully in the running of the operation, providing incentives, recognising successes, providing training and reducing the amount of supervision and other traditional controls. These policies are again features of many Japanese companies.

24. The fourth heading is entitled *Learning to Love Change: A New View of Leadership at All Levels*. This is mainly about management style. It proposes that managers should be single-minded about their pursuit of key values in order to provide a stability of purpose and vision, but should be willing to listen, to delegate and to defer to the front line (ie a participative style). Many of the ideas in this section overlap with those of the earlier one on empowerment.

25. The last heading is concerned with *Building Systems for a World Turned Upside Down*. This is concerned mainly with control systems, and Peters' exhortation is to measure what is important (eg product quality, customer satisfaction as well as financial situation) and keep the measures as simple as possible. He suggests that a new look should be taken at such controls as Management by Objectives, Employee Appraisal and Job Descriptions with a view to encouraging self-control and flexibility. Information, Authority and even Strategic Planning should be decentralised (ie bottom-up planning), and, surprisingly, he proposes that organisational goals should be conservative, by which he means not timid goals but achievable ones. This fits in with his idea of incremental steps towards change. Finally, on the issue of trust, he urges everyone to practice total integrity, ie an honest living-up to commitments both inside and outside the firm.

26. Peters' book, as summarised above, has the sub-title *Handbook for a Management Revolution* and it is true that may of the ideas and practices that he and other current exponents of innovation, quality management and corporate excellence are proposing are destined to bring about the collapse of many mechanistic forms of organisation and many Theory X approaches to people management. What is notable about these proposed changes in the management of organisations is:

❶ Decentralisation is likely to increase

2 Decision-making is likely to be diffused throughout the organisation (ie empowerment practice will increase)

3 Stability will be maintained chiefly through vision and values (ie company culture)

4 Innovation will be encouraged, but in manageable amounts, on a more or less continuous basis

5 Mistakes will be dealt with as positive forms of learning

6 Corporate decisions and strategies will be directed fundamentally at serving the customer

7 This sense of the customer will be employed *within* firms (ie where each employee is seen as the customer of another)

8 Whilst mistakes and failures will be accepted as part of the drive towards excellence, the emphasis on total quality will be stronger as the organisation strives to 'get it right first time'

9 The overall impact on organisation structures will be a move away from mechanistic forms in favour of organic structures.

27. The management of innovation and change is a challenge to every person in an organisation. For management it is particularly important to develop positive attitudes towards change and to support these by means of appropriate learning and action. In a highly competitive marketplace made even more complex by the activities of governments and pressure groups of all kinds, firms must adapt or die.

References

1. Burns, T. & Stalker, G. (1966),*The Management of Innovation,* Tavistock.
2. Moss Kanter, R. (1984), *The Change Masters – Corporate Entrepreneurs at Work*, Allen & Unwin.
3. Lewin, K. (1951), *Field Theory in Social Science,* Harper.
4. Schein, E. (1951), 'The Mechanics of Change', in Bennis, W.G. et al (eds), *Interpersonal Dynamics,* Dorsey Press.
5. Talwar, R. (1994), 'Re-engineering – A Wonder Drug for the 90's?' in Coulson-Thomas (ed), *Business Process Re-engineering – myth or reality*, Kogan Page.
6. Peters, T. & Waterman, R. (1982), *In Search of Excellence: Lessons from America's Best-Run Companies*, Harper & Row.
7. Peters, T. (1988), *Thriving on Chaos – Handbook for a Management Revolution*, MacMillan.

CHAPTER 25

Implementing Change: Organisation Development

Introduction

1. So far we have looked at organisations in two principal ways in this book: firstly in terms of the theoretical choices of organisational type and structure (Chapters 3, 4, 9 &

10), and secondly in terms of alternative structures (Chapter 22). This chapter will now consider the problem of dealing with organisational change. The study of how organisations try to adapt to changing conditions, whether internal or external, is a development of the last decade or so. The phrase which has been coined to describe the conscious process of adapting to change is 'organisation development'.

2. At this point it will be helpful to devise a working definition of organisation development (or OD) as follows:

> 'Organisation development is a strategy for improving organisational effectiveness by means of behavioural science approaches, involving the application of diagnostic and problem-solving skills by an external consultant in collaboration with the organisation's management'.

Several important points can be made about this definition. *Firstly*, OD is an organisation-wide process; it takes an essentially systems view of the organisation. *Secondly*, it utilises the techniques and approaches of the behavioural sciences, ie psychology, social psychology, and sociology, insofar as they relate to the study of people at work in organisations. *Thirdly*, OD involves the intervention of an external third party in the shape of a 'change agent' trained and experienced in behavioural science applications in the work situation. This person is usually an academic or experienced consultant, employed for a temporary period, or sometimes a member of a corporate department, seconded to a subsidiary unit or division. Last, but not least, OD is aimed at *organisational* effectiveness, ie it is something more than *management* development; it is as concerned with changing structures and decision processes as it is with changing people's behaviour. OD, therefore, has something of the flavour of corporate planning about it, and would certainly be an important element in getting corporate plans implemented in times of change.

3. A key feature of any OD process is the relationship built up between the change agent and his client group. It is essential that a collaborative relationship is developed, otherwise the process will never get off the ground. In practice, collaboration means being open with one another, having a high degree of trust, and being prepared to work through conflict in a constructive way. By definition, OD is about change, and change can be painful, especially when it involves people's attitudes, beliefs and self-image. Those involved in the process have to acknowledge the implications of collaboration, if they are genuine about improving their organisation.

4. The rest of this chapter considers some of the major questions surrounding OD – when is it utilised? what are the key stages in an OD programme? what is the role of the change agent? what are the major approaches which have been adopted so far? and finally, what are the benefits to organisations and individuals?

5. When is OD utilised? The most likely answer is when the senior management of an organisation come to recognise that the key components of the organisational system are not working harmoniously together. In other words, when the complex mix of objectives, people and structure is failing to produce the fruits of organisational activity, then is the time to consider re-vitalising the entire enterprise. The diagnostic stage of the OD process, which will be described shortly, invariably commences with a review of the objectives and key tasks of the organisation or sub-unit concerned. It continues with an assessment of the relationships between people (eg team-work, collaboration between sections/departments, leader–group relationships etc), and finally investigates the organisational structure itself. Such a searching self-analysis will not be undertaken lightly by an organisation, but many business enterprises have embraced the risks involved in order to ensure their survival and growth in the face of significant change. This situation could be due to rapid expansion of

the business, or radical changes in markets or technology, or to internal social pressures for change (eg demands for less autocratic or paternalistic styles in favour of more participation). Whatever the reason for adopting a programme of organisation development, the answers it is expected to produce will be fundamental ones for the future of the organisation.

OD Programmes: The Key Stages

6.   There is no one best way of introducing and designing an OD programme. Nevertheless, certain patterns of treatment have developed over recent years, and the following sequence of events would not be untypical:

- **Preliminary Stage.** The senior management team discuss the scope and implications of OD with the external third party (the 'change agent'). This will include discussion about the aims of a possible programme and the means by which it might be achieved. It will also include a consideration of the possible implications for the organisation arising from the implementation of a programme. It will also define the nature of the relationships between the third party and the organisation's management, ie whether the third party is to play the role of an expert, a catalyst for new ideas, educator, or some other agreed role.

- If agreement is reached about the idea of commencing an OD programme, the next stage is **Analysis and Diagnosis.** This is the stage where the third party usually takes the initiative by designing appropriate methods for obtaining relevant information (eg interviews, surveys etc) and by proposing a strategy for putting these into operation with the full backing of the management team. An example of the kind of questions which may be put to management staff, in particular, are shown in Figure 25.1. The information obtained should clarify the problems facing the organisation, and build up a picture of staff attitudes and opinions, as well as supplying some important suggestions as to how the problems might be solved. On the basis of the information received, the management team aided by the third party agree their diagnosis of the situation.

- The third stage, is **Agreement about Aims of the Programme.** The management team, in close collaboration with the third party, agree what are to be the aims and objectives of the programme. These aims could be to improve profitability, secure a share of a new market, improve staff motivation or other desired improvement. To these ends, specific objectives would be required, such as 'to achieve the restructuring of the company along matrix lines over a period of eighteen months' and 'to obtain the full commitment of all management staff to an open and democratic style of leadership' or 'to reduce substantially the number of customer complaints about after-sales service'. With aims and objectives firmly established, the next stage can be initiated – action plans.

- **Action Planning.** The organisation's problems have been analysed, a diagnosis of the overall situation has been made, agreement has been reached about the aims and objectives of the exercise. Now comes the moment for planning the content and the sequence of the activities designed to achieve the aims of the programme. Much of the tactics at this stage will be influenced by the third party, whose skills and expertise in behavioural matters will be brought to bear on the manner of introducing the various OD activities. These activities will be examined more closely in a moment. All that need be said now is that they are much wider in scope than management development or other forms of personnel development.

- **Evaluation and Review.** Once the plans have been put into action, it is very important that they should be monitored at frequent intervals by the management team and their third party colleague. Difficulties and misunderstandings are bound to occur, and

---

KEY TASKS

(a) List the four most important tasks in your Department/Section:

1 . . . .

2 . . . .

3 . . . .

4 . . . .

(b) How do you know how well you are doing in relation to your most important key task?

☐ FORMAL FEEDBACK (Committees, reports, etc)

☐ INFORMAL FEEDBACK (calls, notes, gossip, etc)

☐ OTHER MEANS . . . .

(c) How long is it before you know how well you are doing in relation to this key task?

☐ IMMEDIATELY   ☐ FEW WEEKS

☐ FEW MONTHS   ☐ YEARS

☐ NEVER

(d) If a wrong decision about the key task was to be made today, when would its effects be noticeable?

☐ ALMOST   ☐ AFTER A
   IMMEDIATELY   FEW WEEKS

☐ MONTHS   ☐ YEARS

☐ NEVER

STRUCTURE-ENVIRONMENT

(a) How appropriate is the structure of your organization in terms of fulfilling its purpose?

☐ VERY APPROPRIATE   ☐ QUITE APPROPRIATE

☐ NOT VERY   ☐ NOT SURE
   APPROPRIATE

If you don't think it appropriate, why? . . . .

. . . .

(b) How is your organization basically divided? (Tick all that apply)

☐ PRODUCT   ☐ REGION

☐ MARKET   ☐ BUSINESS FUNCTION

☐ MANAGERIAL   ☐ TECHNICAL

☐ NOT SURE

(c) What are the three most important outside pressures to which your organization must respond?

1 . . . .

2 . . . .

3 . . . .

Figure 25.1 Part of an Organisational Diagnosis questionnaire.

these must be registered as soon as possible and dealt with just as quickly. If a particular activity is having adverse results, it will have to be amended or even dropped from the programme. From time to time, more substantial reviews of progress towards the aims and objectives of the exercise will be required, and this often leads on to a further and final stage as follows.

- **Revised Aims and Plans.** In the light of a major review, it is possible that some important revisions of aims may be necessary, for which a further sequence of plans will be required. At the end of the programme, the third party leaves the scene and the management team get on with the task of running a more successful business.

The Role of Third Party

7. The success of any OD programme depends very largely on the part played by the external third party, or change agent. The change agent is at the centre of the entire OD process. If he is unable to build a firm relationship between himself and the management team concerned, or if he fails to establish his credibility with a range of other groups, his chances of obtaining the degree of commitment required will be slim. Conversely, if he gains trust and respect both as a person and as a skilled adviser, he has the best possible basis for achieving his own contribution to the aims and objectives of the programme.

8. The role of the third party is, in practice, a multiple one. It would be more correct to speak of the *range* of roles required by the third party. These roles range from the highly directive, leader type of role to a non-directive counselling role. In the first mentioned role, the third party will tend to prescribe what is best for his clients; at the other extreme he will tend to reflect issues and problems back to his clients without offering any judgement himself. In between these extremes are several other possible roles, as indicated in Figure 25.2.

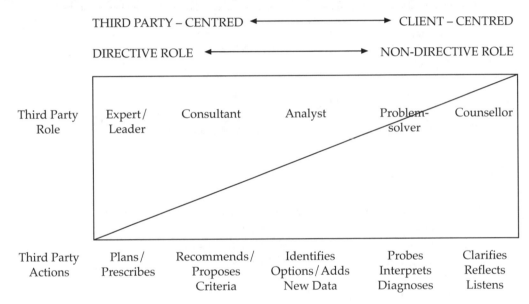

Figure 25.2 Range of roles for third party.

9. Experience with OD programmes suggests that particular qualities, values and abilities are necessary for change agents. These can be summarised as follows:

- Qualities of intellect and personality are important, in particular the ability to listen diagnostically, and to apply rational approaches to problems and situations; also a mature outlook in terms of an awareness, and acceptance, of personal strengths and weaknesses.

- Values that include a preference for interpersonal relations based on mutual trust and liking, for team-work rather than competitiveness, and for conflict to be handled openly and constructively.

- Abilities required are not only those associated with behavioural science knowledge, but more general skills such as interviewing skills, presentation skills and the ability to establish and maintain comfortable relationships with a wide cross-section of people.

10. This combination of attributes suggests that OD change agents will not always be readily available. It takes a certain kind of person to be able to make the contribution to

joint problem-solving and decision-making that is required in OD. Academics are not always suitable because many find it hard to apply theory to practice. Business consultants are often unsuitable because they feel that they must give *expert* guidance in order to justify their fee. What is really required is someone who can positively help a group of clients to help themselves and then fade gracefully into the background.

Major Approaches in Organisation Development

11. This part of the chapter considers the *means* by which OD programmes are carried out. Most of the activities in a programme can be classified in three ways:

1. those aimed at changing people's behaviour
2. those aimed at changing organisation structures
3. those aimed at problem-analysis.

Examples of typical activities for each of these three classifications are briefly described below.

12. Activities designed to change behaviour at work include the following:

- **Coaching and counselling** activities, designed to help *individuals*, and usually on a one-to-one basis
- **Team-building** activities, designed to improve *team* relationships and task effectiveness
- **Inter-group activities,** designed to improve the level of collaboration between interdependent groups
- **Training and development** activities, designed to improve key areas of employee knowledge and skill, and involving a range of participative learning methods.

13. Activities aimed at changing structures include:

- **Role analysis** – ie focusing on what is expected of people rather than on their present job description, and devising new configurations of jobs and tasks
- **Job re-design/job enrichment** – reassessing current jobs in terms of their range and type of tasks, reallocating tasks and redefining jobs, including vertical job enlargement.

14. Activities aimed primarily at problem-analysis include:

- **Diagnostic activities** utilising questionnaires (see Figure 25.3), surveys, interviews and group meetings
- **Planning and Objectives-setting activities**, designed to improve planning and decision-making skills
- **Process consultation,** where the third party helps clients to see and understand the human processes that are taking place around him (eg leadership issues, communication flows, competition between individuals or groups, power struggles etc)
- **Business Process Re-engineering** – examining key business processes from a questioning point of view (see Chapter 21).

15. Of the three groups of activities, those concerned with problem-analysis are the most frequently used, which is to be expected in the light of the need to assess the size and shape of the problems confronting the organisation at the time. The other two groups of activities cannot usefully be activated before the initial diagnostic effort has taken place. Nevertheless, practically every OD programme highlights problems of human relations, if not of organisation structure, and consequently there is invariably a need for two or three of the behaviour-changing exercises.

Organisational Health Checklist

The twelve statements below describe various key aspects of an organisation. The boxes alongside each statement contain four alternative responses.

You are asked to consider *your own organisation* and select the response that, in your opinion, is the nearest to the truth. Circle the preferred response and enter the number in the Score column.

Statement	Strongly agree	Partly agree	Slightly disagree	Strongly disagree	Score
Employees in this organisation know what its objectives and aims are.	1	2	3	4	
The organisation structure helps us achieve our objectives and aims.	1	2	3	4	
Communications in the organisation are clear.	1	2	3	4	
Relations between managers and their staff are usually harmonious.	1	2	3	4	
People in this organisation have a good team spirit.	1	2	3	4	
People are always encouraged to try out new ideas in the organisation.	1	2	3	4	

Figure 25.3 Part of an employee opinion questionnaire.

Benefits of Organisation Development

16. The most significant benefits of an OD programme are as indicated below. The relative importance and relevance of any one benefit obviously depends on the needs of the organisation at the commencement of the programme. However, in general terms, the benefits of OD can be summarised as follows:

• it enables an organisation to adapt to change in a way that obtains the full commitment of the employees concerned

- it can lead to organisation structures that facilitate employee cooperation and the achievement of tasks
- it releases latent energy and creativity in the organisation
- it can improve understanding of organisational objectives by employees
- it can improve decision-making processes and skills
- it provides opportunities for management development in the context of real organisational problems
- it may stimulate more creative approaches to problem-solving throughout the organisation
- it usually increases the ability of management groups to work as teams.

Difficulties in implementing change

17.   In case those pursuing a change programme such as Organisation Development begin to see it primarily in mechanistic 'what to do' terms, Kotter (1996)[1], reminds them that it is the *manner* in which the programme is driven that is the more important. He identifies eight typical mistakes made by senior management in relation to organisational change:

❶   They allow too much complacency

❷   They fail to create a sufficiently powerful guiding coalition

❸   They underestimate the power of vision (the sense of an end-goal)

❹   They greatly under-communicate the vision to be attained

❺   They permit obstacles to stand in the way of the vision (NB Covey's 7 Habits)

❻   They fail to create short-term wins

❼   They declare victory too soon

❽   They neglect to anchor changes in the organisation's culture.

The result of such errors is to reduce the positive effects of new strategies or schemes, producing fewer outcomes over a longer than expected period with greater costs than forecast.

18.   Kotter's answer to the above problems is to establish an eight-stage process of creating major changes, as follows:

❶   Create, and sustain, a sense of urgency about the future

❷   Create and empower a leadership team (a 'guiding coalition')

❸   Develop an end-goal (a 'vision') and a strategy for achieving it

❹   Constantly communicate the new vision and set out what changes in behaviour are required

These first four stages are intended to '*help defrost a hardened status quo*' (p.22). These are followed by the introduction, and rooting, of new practices, such as:

❺   Empowering employees to help change happen by removing obstacles, such as restrictive organisation structures, lack of necessary skills, inflexible managers and unimaginative rewards systems.

❻   Generating some benefits in the short-term ('short-term wins'), so that people can see some tangible improvements on the way to achieving the end-goal.

❼   Consolidating short gains and producing more change by continuing the actions taken in point five above, introducing new projects and bringing in more people who are committed to the changes that are sought.

8. Embedding the new approaches in the organisation's culture ('anchoring') so as to avoid eventual regression into previous practices. This implies adapting the culture from some earlier model and being prepared to adapt again and again.

19. Kotter's conclusion, based on a wide experience of working with organisations, is that without proper attention to the eight major processes of creating change, no organisation will reap the kind of rewards that it looked for at the outset when establishing its vision for the future. Clearly, the approach advocated by Kotter cannot be implemented overnight. It seeks to achieve a revolution in the way an organisation is led and managed, and in how it sees itself, and this takes time. However, for any change to have a chance of success it is essential to have not only an ideal to aim for (a vision), but also an ideal framework for guiding those responsible for achieving that vision.

Reference

1. Kotter, J.P.(1996), *Leading Change*, Harvard Business School Press

---

CHAPTER 26

Communication in Organisations

Introduction

1. The issue of communication is a vital one for any organisation. It is worth considering for a moment what is the meaning of so important a concept. Communication is the process of creating, transmitting and interpreting ideas, facts, opinions and feelings. It is a process that is essentially a sharing one – a mutual interchange between two or more persons. In organisations, communication is generally dealt with in terms of the following:

- the *content* of communication (factual information, discussion points, formal notices etc)
- the *form* of communication (memos, reports, bulletins etc)
- the *media* of communication (face-to-face, written reports/memos, emails, fax, telephone, audio-visual etc)
- the *skills* of communication (report-writing, chairing meetings, interviewing, telephone selling etc)
- the *organisation* of communication (formal channels of communication, committee structure, authority levels, communication procedures, disciplinary issues etc).

2. These five aspects of communication are the basis of *formal* communications in the organisation. That is the system as set down by the management, often in agreement with employees, by which individuals within the organisation will normally communicate with their colleagues. There are always unofficial, or *informal*, methods of communication within organisations, usually described as the 'grapevine', which refers to information passed on by individuals with no authority, and which gives rise to rumour and gossip. Sometimes such informal communication represents strongly felt opinions from amongst the workforce, and may eventually be recognised as legitimate, and be placed in the formal

communication chain. This chapter is concerned only with *formal* communications. These, effectively, have to deal with answering the following key issues:

- What do we need to communicate?
- To whom do we need to communicate?
- How should we communicate?
- When or how often should we communicate?

The Flow of Communications in Organisations

3. The communications network of most organisations consists of vertical lines of communication providing upwards and downwards means of transmitting information, with a few integrating mechanisms such as committees built across these lines. Some organisations also provide lateral lines of communication, which are seen as having equal importance with the vertical. As we saw in the discussion of the work of Burns and Stalker (Chapter 10, paragraph 10), mechanistic (bureaucratic) organisations tended to adopt vertical lines of communication and interaction, whereas organic organisations tended to adopt lateral lines. We saw, also, that matrix-type structures contained both vertical and lateral lines of communication (Chapter 22, paragraph 20).

4. **Vertical communication**. The greatest tendency in most organisations is for communication to be thought of in terms of vertical interaction. In particular, management communicates policies, plans, information and instructions *downwards*, and employees communicate ideas, suggestions, comments and complaints *upwards*. The downwards communication is achieved by means of the management chain, while the upwards communication is achieved by work-group meetings, by joint consultation machinery and by grievance procedures. Vertical communication tends to be dominated by what flows in the downward direction.

5. **Lateral communication**. The flow of information *across* the organisation is rarely comparable with the vertical flow. However, every organisation has to make *some* arrangements for coordinating the efforts of more than one department or section, and this may be done by means of interdepartmental meetings or committees. This is a rational and controlled approach to the problem of integration. It represents about the least that organisations can do to set up lateral lines of communication. Where an organisation is more organic in its operation, it tends to make greater use of lateral flows of information between people in the same specialisms or working on similar tasks, for example. Much of the information flowing between such groups is highly technical or task-orientated and facilitates cooperation between groups. Such information is only passed up the line if it is of particular significance, or where it comes under the category of 'need to know' for the manager concerned. Organisations which operate a system of 'management by exception' are able to make wider use of lateral forms of communication compared with organisations whose management insist on being kept fully in the picture all the time. Managing by exception implies a high degree of delegation, where, once responsibilities have been fixed and standards of performance agreed, the managers concerned will only ask for information if (a) there is a problem or (b) it is time for a periodic review of progress.

6. Research work that has been carried out on groups at work suggests that, for simple problems, the quickest and most accurate results will be obtained by means of centralised (leader-dominated) channels of communication. Conversely, for complex problems, the most acceptable results are likely to come from decentralised communication channels, where there is greater encouragement to share facts, views and feelings. The most frequent channel-alternatives that have been tested are shown in Figure 26.1.

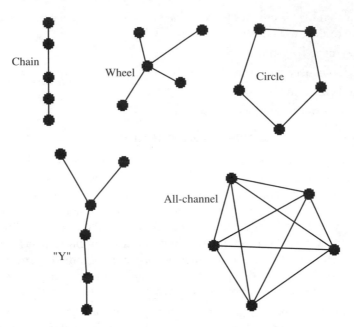

Figure 26.1 Communication networks.

In Figure 26.1, the wheel represents the most centralised communication channel with its obvious leader or coordinator at the centre of relationships. By contrast, the circle and, especially, the all-channel networks rely on decentralised channels with shared leadership. The chain and 'Y' networks are basically hierarchical and not decentralised. Organic organisations would show a preference for all-channel networks, mechanistic organisations would tend to use the chain, the 'Y' and the wheel.

The Content of Communication

7.   Whether information is supplied in written, electronic or audio-visual forms its essential purpose is to convey some message. In a work organisation the message is usually factual, supplying information about internal policies and procedures, reporting on issues, or providing details of meetings. Typical examples of such communications range from formal statements of new policies, minutes of joint employee-management meetings, reports to senior management, health-and-safety notices, and staff vacancies. Some communications are intended to promote questions and discussion, perhaps prior to some new management initiative or the annual round of negotiations with trade unions. Others are aimed specifically at consultation, in order to obtain employees' viewpoints and opinions about proposed changes. Generally, the content of communications is open to public view, at least so far as the organisations' employees are concerned. There will also be communications that are restricted in their circulation and are not intended for the public domain. These may include discussion papers circulated to board members or senior staff, reports received from external consultants, draft budget documents, and negotiating strategies prior to pay and salary negotiations. Confidential documents are more likely to be issued in hard copy form (ie paper) rather than electronically (eg as an electronic file attached to an email), because the former is more secure.

The Form of Communication

8.   This brings us on to the form in which communications are sent. These have not changed much over the past decades. Internal memos, letters, formal reports, minutes of

meetings, statements of accounts, invoices, bulletins and a variety of notices are still the principal form of communications, and have been unaffected by changes in technology. And, of course, we must not overlook the countless conversations that take place between individuals as they grapple with problems and situations at work. Written forms of communication tend to be more considered than face-to-face forms, and have a permanence that is lacking in the latter, which are usually spontaneous. Written forms are less susceptible to misinterpretation and, being visible, are less easy to deny, or qualify, than oral communications. This is one reason why written minutes of meetings are so important, because they attempt to capture the spoken words and put them on record. Written forms, of course, take longer to prepare, and are only as good as the powers of expression of the writer. Oral communication, whilst transient, nevertheless has the advantage of enabling the communicator to see the immediate non-verbal reactions of the recipient, such as facial expression, gestures and body posture.

Communication Media

9.   Until the last decade of the twentieth century most internal communications would have been conducted in face-to-face meetings or by telephone, or presented in hard copy written format. These methods of communicating are still vital but have been enhanced by the arrival of electronic media, especially electronic mail (email) but also including fax messaging, video links via computer and other forms of interactive audio-visual media. What the electronic revolution has enabled is communication on a faster and more global basis than before. Items of news or information can be sent to colleagues on the other side of the world in an instant, such is the effectiveness of the Internet and its associated benefits.

Communication Skills

10.   The quality of communications in any organisation is as good as the people who contribute to the process. It takes skill to write a good report or lead an effective meeting. It takes skill to sell services over the telephone or interview prospective staff. Sometimes there is tendency to assume that these skills are present in everybody, and that people just need a little practice to improve them. Most business enterprises soon discover that this attitude is not enough – staff need to be trained to develop appropriate skills. Fortunately, any communication skill that is improved is likely to remain with the individual for the rest of his life, because communication is a need we can exercise in every interpersonal relationship we encounter. There are three areas of communication where skills are particularly called for: report writing, chairing meetings and giving presentations. We shall examine key points relating to each of these.

Report Writing

11.   In a work organisation the commissioning of a report is a frequent response to dealing with a problem that has occurred, or an issue that needs to be faced. Asking for a formal report gives those concerned the opportunity to delegate the essential fact finding and analysis to another member of staff before they themselves are required to make a judgement on the matter. The first skill of report writing is to understand what sources of information and data are worth consulting in order to provide the basic material for the report. Some of the required information will be available in written form from internal and external sources. Other information must be gleaned from interviews with appropriate

personnel. Some information may be available via the Internet. Whatever the outcome, one thing is sure – the report writer will end up with far more information than can be put into his or her report. A process of distillation must take place before any kind of summary material can emerge. This is often the most difficult part of writing a report because it forces the writer to decide what to put in the final document and what to leave out.

12. Once the raw material has been refined to the point where it can be considered suitable for inclusion in the report, the writer must then decide how to present the information. At this stage, meeting the needs of the readers must be the foremost requirement. What are these? The first need surely is for clarity of expression, closely followed by logic of argument. Readers will want to be able to see readily the thrust of the report and the evidence that supports it. They will want to know what the implications of the research are, and to see some alternative solutions for dealing with them. Report writers are not usually expected to come up with one right answer, but it is very helpful if they can point to possible scenarios that will stimulate ideas in the readers. The point of most reports is to provide evidence and argument that will enable other people to make better decisions.

13. Experience has shown that the headings that are likely to be helpful to report writers when considering how to set out their findings are as follows:

Title of report
(chosen by the report's author)

Terms of reference
(as given by the person/group requesting the report)

Executive summary
(a one or two page summary of key points
in cases where the report is lengthy
or complicated)

Introduction
(setting the scene; spelling out aims;
explaining the methodology)

Main findings
(reporting the main facts)

Implications of the findings
(may be combined with Findings)

Conclusions drawn
(in the light of findings and implications)

Recommendations or proposals

Name of author
(often omitted in internal reports!)

Date of report
(essential)

Appendices
(supplementary or illustrative
material to support main findings)

A clear, well-argued report will be received far better than one that is over-complicated and badly expressed, however relevant its content. Staff who can write good reports are well sought after in work organisations from chief executives down to junior managers.

Chairing Meetings

14. All managers are called upon to chair meetings at some time or another. Senior managers, in particular, may find that most of their time is taken up in this way but even junior managers will be called upon to conduct meetings of their own team. Learning how best to manage a meeting is an important skill, and one that can be improved by training and subsequent experience. Of course there are always exceptional individuals who consistently have the capacity to bring out the best in a group, but these are a minority. Most managers have to work at chairing a meeting and there are a few important guidelines that, if followed carefully, will enable them to do so relatively successfully. Pointers for formal committees are referred to later, but for less formal management meetings helpful guidelines are likely to include the following:

> Ensure there is an agenda
> Be as well briefed as possible beforehand
> Bring relevant reports/documents
> Explain purpose of the meeting
> Set out any procedures to be followed
> Where possible take account of personality
> and experience of group members
> Encourage participation/ questions/ ideas
> Summarise progress as appropriate
> Ensure list of action points where appropriate

Giving Presentations

15. **Giving Presentations**. Most managers are called upon from time to time to make a presentation to their colleagues or their superiors. Presentations are widely used in selling situations, and in management planning exercises; they are also used when formally introducing major reports or when introducing new ideas or proposals to colleagues. There are three key elements in any presentation:

- Preparation
- Content
- Delivery

Preparation is a vital prerequisite for any presentation. The person making the presentation needs to consider the *content* of his talk and its *delivery*. So far as content is concerned, this is primarily a question of considering what to include and what to leave out, taking into account the needs and prior knowledge of the audience. Top management groups, for example, are mainly interested in the salient features of an idea or proposal, together with a summary of its principal benefits and disadvantages. Operational levels of management generally require more detailed information and will respond to a more technical approach than their senior counterparts.

The question of *how* to deliver the presentation again depends largely on the nature of the audience. Some groups will not be satisfied with anything less than a brilliant display of wit and ingenuity, others will be quite satisfied with a low-key, but extremely relevant, demonstration. One point that is always helpful, whatever the audience, is the use of visual aids. There is hardly a presentation that does not benefit enormously from visual illustration. Visual aids that are most frequently employed include flipcharts, overhead transparencies, films (video and cine) and models or physical examples of an item. Increasingly, now, organisations are using computer-generated displays, such as Powerpoint, to illustrate key points in management presentations.

16. A code of good practice in the making of presentations could be as follows:

❶ Consider your audience and their needs.

❷ Assemble your facts and ideas in the light of (1) above and taking account of the complexity of the material.

❸ Develop sufficient and suitable visual aids.

❹ Consider what other information should be made available (drawings, specifications, reports etc).

❺ Tell your audience what you are going to tell them, tell them, and then tell them what you have told them!

❻ Be enthusiastic about the subject (unless this would be completely inappropriate, eg the announcement of a new redundancy plan).

❼ Be natural, ie if you are a quiet person, then be *quietly* enthusiastic.

❽ Maintain eye contact with your audience.

❾ Be prepared for questions both during and at the end of your presentation.

Barriers to Communication

17. There are numerous barriers to communication, and some of the most important ones are discussed briefly below:

•   Individual bias and selectivity, ie we hear or read what we want to hear or see. People are often unaware of their bias until it is brought to their attention. Much of the bias is to do with cultural background and personal value-systems.

•   Status differences, ie subordinates may well read more than was intended into a *superior's* message. By contrast, superiors may listen less carefully to information passed up the line by subordinates. People at all levels may be reserved about passing information upwards, in case they incur criticism. One of the reasons for the relative failure of the 'open door' policy of communication adopted by many managers is that it relies on subordinates overcoming both their natural reserve and the status barriers of the organisation.

•   Fear and other emotional overtones can cloud the communication message. If a person has bad news to pass on, which is almost certain to upset the recipient, they will tend to avoid the whole truth and be content to pass on part of the message only. This issue of emotional barriers is particularly relevant in the handling of grievances. Angry people do not make good listeners, and thus any manager dealing with a deeply-felt grievance must allow for a period of 'cooling off' before expecting to make any headway with a solution. Indeed, it is now recognised that it is precisely in the area of the emotions that human beings appear to be worst at sharing, ie communicating. Not surprisingly, this is an area of attention in Organisation Development programmes, especially in relation to how conflict can be handled in a team.

- Lack of trust is another important barrier to effective communication. If we are not sure of someone, we tend to hold back in our communication with that person. This mistrust may arise because of doubts about the recipient's motives or his ability to grasp what is being said.

- Verbal difficulties are a frequent source of confusion and misunderstanding. These may arise because of the sheer lack of fluency on the part of the sender, or because of the use of jargon (specific application of words in technical and professional contexts), or perhaps because of pitching the message at too high a level of understanding. In terms of written words, the barriers are usually those associated with long-windedness, ie a failure to get to the point quickly and concisely.

- Other important barriers to communication include information overload (where a person is overloaded with memos, reports, letters, telephone messages etc), inadequate machinery for communication (committees, briefing groups, joint consultation meetings etc) and sheer lack of practice in the skills of communicating.

18. Overcoming, or at least reducing the effects of, barriers to communication mainly consists in finding answers to the issues raised in the paragraph above. Improvements in communication can be made by adopting a strategy of (i) ensuring that employees are made aware of communication problems, (ii) setting up appropriate machinery for communication (upwards, downwards and laterally), and (iii) training employees in relevant techniques of communication. Particular mechanisms which have been widely adopted include:

❶ Downwards communication

- Briefing Groups (where team leaders brief their immediate staff about events).
- Staff Meetings (where all staff in one unit or from one site are brought together).
- Bulletins, Notices and Circulars.

❷ Upwards communication

- Joint Consultation Committees (where management and staff meet to consult about issues).
- Suggestions Schemes.
- Trade union channels (via shop stewards, negotiating committees etc).
- Grievance Procedure.

❸ Lateral communication

- Interdepartmental Committees
- Special Project Groups.
- Coordinating Committees.

Note: The Employment Act, 1982, now requires companies of more than 250 employees to include in their Directors' Report a statement showing what arrangements have been made to encourage greater employee involvement in the affairs of the company by means of information, consultation, share ownership etc.

Committees in Organisations

19. Committees abound in practically every kind of organisation. They are an integral part of the operation of every public sector organisation, and are almost as popular in the

private sector. What are committees? The first thing that can be said about them is that they are *formal* groups with a chairman, an agenda and rules of conduct. Committees invariably have a specific task or set of tasks to achieve. These tasks are frequently, although not always, associated with decision-making. In fact, many committees are expressly forbidden from reaching decisions, eg joint consultative committees and advisory committees. Some committees meet regularly, eg monthly senior officers' committee in a public authority or a quarterly planning committee in a manufacturing company. Others meet for ad hoc purposes only, eg committees of enquiry set up by Parliament or steering committees set up to monitor short-term projects.

20. As was stated above, committees are formal groups. The formality of a committee is expressed by the following features:

A chairman (or chairperson), who is responsible for ensuring (a) that the committee is conducted in accordance with the rules, and (b) that it is supplied with the necessary resources, particularly with the written information it requires to carry out its work effectively.

A secretary, who is responsible for taking the minutes of meetings, sending out the agenda and other papers, and generally acting as the administrative link with the members.

An agenda, which sets out the agreed subject-matter of the meeting. Part of the chairman's job before the meeting is to approve the agenda, over which he or she usually has the final word. The agenda enables committee members to know what is to be discussed, and in what order, and this enables them in turn to prepare adequately before the meeting.

The minutes of the meeting, which are the official record of what has taken place. They serve to remind members of important issues or decisions that were debated at the time. Since they have to be agreed by the members as a true and correct record, they are a reliable source of information both to members and outsiders alike. In local authority committees and joint union-management committees, for example, the minutes are made public for the benefit of ratepayers or union members, as the case may be.

Committee Papers and Reports, which provide the committee with the quality of information, which will enable it to make well-informed decisions or proposals. Reports, for example, may be purely factual, or both factual and analytical. Yet others may be innovative and imaginative. Whatever their contents and presentation, their aim is the same, ie to provide relevant information, ideas and suggestions as the focal points for the discussion of agenda items.

Rules of procedure, which are designed to promote the smooth-running of a committee and to ensure that consistency and fair-play are maintained. Such rules include procedures for:

- speaking in a debate,
- proposing motions,
- voting,
- adding emergency items to the agenda, and
- other issues relating to the operation of the committee as a communication medium.

The rules enable both sides in an argument to state their case, they help to minimise the effect of bullying tactics, and they ensure that a proper record of the proceedings is kept.

21. In the light of all this formality, what are the benefits and disadvantages of committees? The advantages can be summarised as follows:

Advantages

- Precisely because they are *organised* groups, committees can undertake a larger volume of work than individuals or very small groups working in isolation.

- Decisions or proposals are based on a *group* assessment of facts and ideas, and not just on one powerful individual's preferences.

- Committees can encourage the pooling of special know-how and talents possessed by individual members.

- Committees are very useful for achieving coordination and collaboration between work groups.

- Committees act as a useful focal point for information and action within organisations.

These advantages are particularly important in two respects. *Firstly*, the sheer size and complexity of modern organisations make it increasingly impossible for isolated individuals or small groups to meet the decision-demands of their organisations. *Secondly*, the growing pressures from all sections of the workforce for a greater say in the decision-making processes of their organisations are creating expectations that decision-making will become more open and democratic. Committees are likely to be even more in demand as a result of these two factors.

22. However, it would be unrealistic to gloss over the disadvantages of committees as communication media. The main disadvantages are as follows:

Disadvantages

- Decision-making is an altogether slower process when dominated by committees. It is also true that committee decisions may often represent compromise solutions rather than optimum solutions.

- Managers may be tempted to hide behind committee decisions, where these have proved unpopular, and thus abdicate their personal responsibility.

- Committees sometimes have a tendency to get bogged down in procedural matters, which reduces the time available for the discussion of substantive issues.

- Committee work demands certain skills. Members who are unsure of themselves or unskilled in committee practice tend to leave the initiative to the 'good committee-men'.

- Committees do not exist between meetings, and thus cannot act quickly and flexibly to meet sudden changes in a situation.

On balance, committees are probably best suited to large-scale bureaucracies and organisations which have a high degree of public accountability. Smaller-scale enterprises, on the other hand, would probably benefit more from the greater flexibility obtainable from less formal processes of decision-making, such as informal management meetings and temporary project groups.

CHAPTER 27

Time Management and Personal Effectiveness

Introduction

1.   So far in this section on Organising, we have been considering organisational and group issues. Ultimately, however, the effectiveness of organisations comes down to the effectiveness of individuals, which is the concern of this chapter. The management of time is an issue which is fundamental to job performance. In the past (see Scientific Management, Chapter 3) attention to the relationship between time and job performance was restricted to manual workers, and then, by means of Organisation and Methods, to clerical workers. The consideration of time utilisation for managerial and professional grades has not received much attention until recently. Current approaches are based on the assumption that personal effectiveness at work is primarily a function of the individual's management of his or her time.

2.   Much of the subject matter of this chapter overlaps with those dealing with such issues as leadership, delegation and communication. The interest in time management as a topic of attention in its own right has drawn together these other issues. The main factors affecting a person's use of time are set out in Figure 27.1.

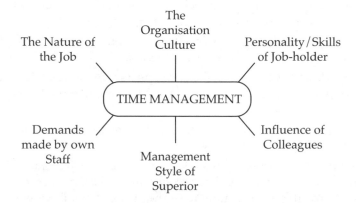

Figure 27.1 Main factors affecting time management.

These factors and the key issues arising from them form the subject of the rest of the chapter.

Key Issues in the Use of Time

3.   The principal issues of time management can be grouped under three headings:

*   those related to the nature of the job
*   those related to the personality and attributes of the job-holder
*   those related to the people who make up the job-holder's role-set.

Nature of the Job

4.   The nature of a person's job is fundamental to the amount of control over time that is both desirable and necessary. For example, a person whose job involves regular contacts with others is always going to be under greater pressure from interruptions than someone whose work is of a solitary nature. Similarly, a person who is employed in a new and developing job is more likely to suffer from conflicting priorities and unpredictable events than someone working in an established position, where predictability and routine are the order of the day.

5.   An important issue for any job-holder is the identification of the priorities in the job. In cases where Management by Objectives (see Chapter 18) or some form of target-setting is practised, then individuals will have had experience of identifying and working towards priorities, or key result areas, in the job. However, by far the great majority of managerial and professional employees do not work under such systems, and are therefore unused to a systematic approach to prioritising key tasks.

6.   A useful method is to encourage individuals to identify (a) the tasks they alone are responsible for, and (b) the tasks that either require the greatest effort, or produce the greatest return. Once individuals have identified what they see as their key tasks or responsibilities, they can discuss these with their immediate boss or with a job counsellor. Often a training course in the company of colleagues provides a useful stimulus to this form of diagnostic activity.

7.   It is not enough, however, just to consider job priorities. It is also important to consider what the individual job-holder has to do in order to fulfil them. Some jobs call for administrative skills and a sound knowledge of organisation procedures, others demand social skills and a sensitivity to people-needs, and yet others require technical and specialist knowledge and the ability to apply it. Individuals, therefore, need to examine the processes associated with their jobs.

8.   A well-tried method of obtaining information about job processes is that of keeping a detailed time-diary, in which the individual records his or her work activities every day for a week or a month, for example. The simplest form is one listing the day in half-hour intervals alongside which are spaces for the job-holder to record what has happened, eg writing letters, conducting a meeting, travelling to a client, conducting an interview, answering the telephone etc. Job-holders are frequently surprised at how little time they have to themselves at work, as well as at the number of interruptions they accept.

Typical Time-wasters at Work

9.   Whilst a high level of interaction between people at work can normally be considered as a healthy phenomenon, there are nevertheless potential disadvantages for any one individual's personal effectiveness. These arise from the following:

*   prolonged, or unnecessary, meetings with colleagues
*   interruptions from own staff, colleagues or boss (however well-intentioned)
*   idle conversations (in the sense of casual chit-chat)
*   unnecessary memos and other paperwork.

A further problem is that of time lost due to travelling between jobs. It is not easy to overcome such lost opportunities for effective working, but some ways will be discussed later.

Personal Attributes of the Job-holder

10. A person's ability to make best use of their time depends to a considerable extent on their personality and inclinations. For example, a naturally assertive person will be better equipped to deal with people who trespass on their time than someone who is naturally rather inoffensive. There are other important differences in personal attributes and styles, for example:

- some people work best early in the day, whilst others work best later in the day
- some people like to pace out their work effort, whilst others prefer to concentrate their efforts into short, intensive periods
- some people can only deal with one issue at a time, whereas others can juggle with several simultaneously
- some people are task-oriented whereas others are people-oriented
- some people like to delegate as much as possible, where others prefer to keep tasks to themselves
- some people are tidy and methodical, others are untidy and disorganised
- some individuals are more skilled or experienced than others

11. In the final analysis an individual will find that better use of time will probably come about by developing personal strengths and attempting to off-set weaknesses, in a word *self-discipline.*

The Job Context

12. The context of a person's job consists of:

- the members of his or her role-set (boss, own staff, colleagues etc)
- the physical surroundings (office, location of others etc)
- the culture of the organisation (the dominant values that prevail).

The implications of these three will be considered briefly.

13. The people who work alongside an individual – their role-set (see Figure 27.2) – are always an important influence on that person's use of time. An interfering boss, for example, can be very disrupting. By contrast, a boss who is an effective delegator can be a positive source of help in identifying job priorities. Subordinates' abilities to work effectively on their own, rather than seeking advice from their manager all the time, can enable the latter to work on personal tasks without undue interruptions. Colleagues can be a frequent cause of wasted time, especially when they call into your office at a time when they themselves are less busy, or want a short break from what they are working on. Senior or experienced members of any group will find that they are regularly sought out by junior members wishing to clarify a point or discuss an immediate problem. All these activities have their benefits, but at the cost of any one individual's time.

14. In these days of continuous job improvement and just-in-time methods of supplying line units (see Chapter 38 below), each person in an office, factory or wherever is being encouraged to regard workmates and colleagues as 'customers'. This adds extra pressure on people to deliver their particular service on time as well as effectively to their role-set. A basic role-set for a manager in touch with both external customers/clients, and internal 'customers' is shown in Figure 27.2.

Figure 27.2 Role set for customer service manager.

15. Given the prime importance of the external customer or client to the organisation as a whole, it is likely that the manager in this case will often have to respond reactively, and sometimes even immediately, to customers who are directed towards him or her. It is well-nigh impossible for such a job-holder to fob off this kind of interruption to planned activities. Some customers will be referred by the line departments, and again the same considerations will tend to apply. In this example, the manager's best tactic would be to ensure that his or her own manager and staff respect the demands of the outside world and thus will adapt their expectations of the role-holder's priorities accordingly. The reference to Training and Personnel staff is made because customer complaints usually point to some deficiency in training or personnel, or both, and this normally requires the Customer Services Manager to alert the former concerning possible shortfalls among the staff.

16. Physical surroundings may help or hinder a person's efforts to make better use of his or her time. Clearly, if you do not have an office, then there are no real physical barriers that you can erect between you and all those who, however well-intentioned, wish to interrupt your work. Those who do have an office of their own can always shut the door, even at the risk of a certain amount of unpopularity. Whilst an 'open door' policy for staff communication is generally recommended, there are still occasions when it would be better to suspend this policy temporarily in the interests of personal work efficiency. The location of furniture and equipment can also affect the use of time. For example, if the photocopier and the computer terminal are on different floors to your office, or are at the opposite end of the building, then a good deal of time can be wasted walking to and from these machines. Currently, one of the most persuasive arguments for introducing computerised work-stations (see Chapter 30) is one of time-saving.

17. Another major physical influence on an individual's work pattern is that of travelling. The location of colleagues, customers and suppliers invariably means that an individual has to spend some time in travelling between appointments. This time can often be completely wasted, unless, for example, the individual travels by train or has a chauffeur-driven car, in which case it is possible to carry out work tasks whilst travelling.

18. The final aspect of the job context that we shall consider is the organisation culture. Some cultures favour strict adherence to procedures and protocol, which discourages informal contacts and 'short cuts'. Others encourage an open access policy on all aspects of communications, which can be very stimulating but also very wasteful of individual time. Organisations that set great store by accuracy and quality are implicitly requiring their members to take more time over their work, compared with organisations who are always working to tight deadlines and thus have to risk the occasional error or inaccuracy. In yet other organisations, the speed with which decisions are reached is more important than the thoroughness of those decisions. Such an attitude clearly has considerable implications for an individual's personal work standards.

19. There are several ways in which managers can improve their own and others use of time. These are broadly the following:

- by personal priority and action planning
- by target-setting
- by negotiation with key members of their role-set
- by delegating tasks to own team members
- by developing appropriate skills (eg faster reading, writing, handling meetings, and being assertive)
- by developing an appropriate strategy for self-development.

20. Personal priority and action planning entails sitting down with one's superior, and subsequently one's work-team, in order to agree job priorities, and in particular those things that the others will look to you for completing. Prioritising implies having a clear idea of the principal responsibilities of the job. It may lead to people setting targets for their own staff and for themselves, perhaps along the lines of those indicated earlier in Chapter 18. Managers always do well to consider the '80-20' Rule – that is identifying the 80% of their activities that are only likely to produce 20% of the required outcomes, and focusing on the 20% of the job that delivers 80% of the results. Time allocated to work by individuals tends to follow the sheer volume of activities involved in it rather than to be geared to their relative importance. Personal planning in management jobs also requires some time being set aside for reflection – a period in which further priorities and alternative actions can be *thought about* before being put to superiors and/or own staff.

Delegation

21. Delegation as an issue in management was considered earlier (Chapter 23). In the context of this chapter one or two points bear repeating. The art of successful delegation does not come easily to managers, and many have all too often done something themselves instead of delegating it because '*I could do it quicker myself*'. It does indeed take time, effort, and confidence (in oneself as well as in one's team members) to delegate properly. It is necessary to explain what is wanted, answer any questions the staff may have, supply them with any resources they need (especially time!), before letting them go away and carry out what is required. An insecure manager will tend to delegate less readily than a confident manager. However, delegation can be made 'safer' for all managers if they take a few simple precautions.

22. Good practice in delegating includes ensuring the following:

- clear objectives/expected outcomes are set
- standards of performance are established (ie what constitutes successful completion of the task, including reference to the time-scale)
- appropriate authority is granted (ie the extent of empowerment)
- adequate resources are allocated (staff, equipment, expenses and time)
- clear reporting arrangements are made
- team members are encouraged to seek help when needed
- team members are informed that early mistakes will be used as learning opportunities
- the task is completed according to the agreed standards
- those concerned are thanked for their efforts.

23. The first step is to explain what is required of the employee concerned, both in terms of what is to be achieved and to what standard. Unless the person concerned is extremely inexperienced or the task truly warrants it, the manager should not normally explain in detail *how* the job should be done. It will be enough to give general guidance initially and then be available to assist if necessary. This gives the subordinate an opportunity to learn from the experience. Part of the help that the manager must supply is to define the limits of the person's authority to commit the organisation's resources (eg people, materials and money). Any authority delegated can only be within the authority of the manager himself. The next stage is for the manager to devise a simple control procedure for ensuring that progress is being made and that any difficulties are identified and dealt with. Part of this control procedure will embrace an opportunity for counselling, or coaching, the employee. In some cases special training may be required as part of the resourcing involved. In order that the delegation is seen to be taken seriously, the manager should ensure that the task is completed, or the responsibility fulfilled, to an acceptable standard. If a task is delegated, but then forgotten by the manager, the credibility of the process comes into question. Finally, the employee should be thanked.

Assertiveness

24. Assertiveness can contribute to the better use of managers' time by enabling them to deal more effectively with interruptions. Turner (1983)[1] defines assertion as *'the capacity to express our ideas, opinions or feelings openly and directly without putting down ourselves or others'.*

Recently, attention has been given not only to identifying assertive rights, but also to training people in assertiveness. Assertive rights are based on the fundamental notion that each individual adult is the ultimate judge of his or her own behaviour. It implies taking personal responsibility for one's actions.

25. The right to say 'no' is difficult for most people to accept. They feel that they ought not to say 'no' because it is uncooperative, selfish etc. Assertiveness training attempts to emphasise the importance for individual rights of the capacity to say 'no' without feeling guilty about it, and points out that in saying 'no' we are rejecting the *request* not the person. Making better use of one's personal rights can enable managers to fend off many of the interruptions inflicted on them by others, and thus create more space for themselves at work. Similar considerations apply to the right not to feel obliged to take responsibility for other people's problems. In this case managers can learn by assertiveness training to improve their ability to tactfully, but firmly, pass back to colleagues, team members and even superiors, problems which are the latter's responsibility.

26. Assertive rights have been identified (eg Back & Back, 1991)[2] by a number of commentators, and can be summarised as follows:

• I have as much right to my own opinions as others have of theirs

• I am entitled to ask others for help (knowing they are entitled to refuse)

• I am entitled to say 'No!', and to do so without explanation, if need be

• I am entitled to make mistakes

• I am entitled to change my mind, and to do so without giving reasons unless I choose to

• I do not have to accept responsibility for other people's feelings, or problems

• I am entitled to say that I do not know something, or feel inadequate

- I do not have to be manipulated by others.

27. Saying 'No!' to people is difficult for many managers, especially if the person applying the pressure is their superior. Some senior managers are inclined to forget that their own managers have pressing or important problems of their own to confront. They seem unaware that they are invading their team member's space, and see only their own problem. Refusing to be drawn into someone else's problem is not easy at first, especially when the problem is brought suddenly into one's work as an interruption, and you are being asked to respond right away. The important point about assertiveness is that the space-invasion problems you personally are facing, are likely to be experienced by *your* own staff and colleagues at some time or another. So, learning how to deal with others also enables you to see how they might deal with *you* in similar circumstances!

28. Possible assertive responses to one's superior manager, depending on the nature of the issue, could include the following:

- I am in the middle of this work you gave me earlier, and would have to leave it to deal with the question you have just put to me. Do you want me to change my priority, in which case I will have to put this work to one side?

- To be honest with you, it would be very inconvenient to take time out at the moment to deal with your request. I would prefer to look at it later, if that is alright by you.

- I am in the middle of a meeting with some of my own staff at this moment, but will be free to talk to you in about an hour's time.

- I am in some difficulty with your request to turn my attention to X, do you mind if I complete what I am finishing off at the moment?

Here the person trying to handle their superior's interruptions is being honest about the effect that the boss is having on their current duties or activities, and flagging this up to the manager concerned without being either defensive or submissive. Atkinson (1988)[3] makes the point that to succeed in saying 'No!' to people, especially when you are doing so politely, you have to be prepared to repeat your message over time in order to convince others that you really mean what you say.

Personal Communications Skills

29. A manager's use of time can be made more productive if personal communication skills are improved. In paragraph 19 above, we mentioned three particular aspects: faster reading, report writing and handling meetings. We shall look at these very briefly in turn.

30. **Reading skills** – being selective in reading is probably as important as being able to read faster. Managers need to be able to identify:

- what is essential reading?

- what is essential and urgent?

- what is essential but not immediate?

- what is of marginal use/interest?

If a manager has to do a lot of reading in his or her job, then there are specific courses aimed at improving a person's speed in reading.

Report writing – one of the key tasks of every manager is to present ideas, impressions and proposals in writing. A knowledge of the basic strategy involved in drawing up a report will help a manager to make better use of the time incurred (see previous chapter).

Handling meetings – many managers find themselves at a meeting of one kind or another several times a day. To use the time spent on meetings more effectively a number of simple questions can be asked:

- is a meeting necessary to deal with this issue? (ie could a telephone call, fax or a memo suffice?)
- what is the purpose the meeting?
- how can we prepare for this meeting?
- how can we ensure that the meeting is going to be worthwhile to those attending?
- how long should the meeting last?
- who should be invited to attend?
- how will action points be captured and dealt with?

Personal Effectiveness

31. Much of what has just been said about time management and assertiveness boils down to personal effectiveness. In his influential text on highly effective people, Covey (1994)[4] comments that *'In the last analysis, what we are communicates far more eloquently than anything we say or do.'* His answer is to go beneath the superficial aspects of what he terms the Personality Ethic (attributing success to public image, social skills, positive mental attitudes etc) in order to uncover the Character Ethic (success founded on such qualities as integrity, patience, courage, sense of justice etc). Covey argues that whilst the elements of the Personality Ethic are indeed important, they are nevertheless secondary. The primary elements of human success, the foundation of all human actions, are all based on the Character Ethic – those qualities, fundamental truths even, that are found the world over regardless of race or social conditioning: fairness, integrity, honesty, dignity etc. He then proposes what he calls the Seven Habits of Highly Effective People, which allow individuals to fully experience themselves and their sense of self-worth, and thus enable them to deal effectively with others from a position of quiet inner strength.

32. Covey describes habits as internalised principles and patterns of behaviour, which he sees as the product of knowledge, skills and personal desire or motivation. The Seven Habits highlighted by him have the effect of moving an individual person from dependence (*'I need you'*) through independence (*'I can do this'*) to interdependence (*'We can do this – and create more than our combined efforts'*). The seven habits can be summarised as follows:

❶ Be proactive – take responsibility as well as the initiative

❷ Begin with the end in mind – where do you want to go, what do you want to be, what do you want to achieve?

❸ Put first things first – identify your real priorities in the light of the end you wish to achieve (thus enabling you to say no to what is not important)

❹ Think win/win – look for the gain that *all* parties can get from relationships, solutions, negotiations etc

❺ Seek first to understand...then to be understood – develop listening skills, think before you act, and try to understand others before trying to make yourself understood.

❻ Synergise – become creative (*'1+1 may equal 8, 16 or even 1,600'*)

❼ Sharpen the saw – ie constantly make time for renewal based on personal reflection, physical, spiritual and emotional replenishment (keeping fit in every department of your life).

33. Covey's ideas have ended this chapter on time management and personal effectiveness. However, if the seven habits were to be adopted by managers as a means of underpinning the achievement of personal and work-related goals, then the earlier suggestions in the chapter could all play a part in a total programme of self-development and personal success.

References

1. Turner, C. (1983) *Developing Interpersonal Skills*, Further Education Staff College.
2. Back, K & Back, K. (1991), *Assertiveness at Work*, Pitman.
3. Atkinson, P.E. (1988), *Achieving Results through Time Management*, Pitman.
4. Covey, S.R. (1989), *The Seven Habits of Highly Effective People*, Simon & Schuster.

Questions for Discussion/Homework

1. A national, single-product manufacturing company is about to take over a smaller, but more diversified, rival, which has one-third of its productive capacity overseas. Advise the managing director of the new group about the alternative organisation structures which could best serve the company's increased size and scope. State the pros and cons of each alternative.

2. In what ways are line and functional authority similar, and in what ways are they different? What is the basic difference between line and functional authority and so-called staff authority? Give examples of each of the different kinds of authority.

3. What differences would you expect to find in the spans of control in the following situations:

   a. routine mass-production process?

   b. central research department of an electronics company? and

   c. large tax and financial planning consultancy?

4. How might a policy of empowering employees lead to more than just finding better ways of delegating tasks?

5. Taking an overall view of Organisation Development, how would you describe its salient features to the top management team of either a commercial enterprise, or a public sector undertaking?

6. What are the most frequent barriers to communication, and how can they be overcome?

7. How would you describe the benefits of more effective time-management for persons in management positions?

8. In what ways could you argue that Covey's Seven Habits suggest a new way forward for achieving personal success?

Examination Questions

The subject matter of this section is extremely popular with examiners in most of the professional examinations. The following examples are very typical of the questions asked. Outline answers may be found in Appendix 2.

EQ 22 Describe the phases of a typical Organisation Development programme.

(ICMA OMM)

EQ 23 What would you expect to be the results of a mismatch between delegated authority and responsibility?

(ACCA Business Mgt.)

EQ 24 What do you understand by the phrase 'matrix organisation'? In what kinds of organisations and situations would you expect matrix organisation to apply? *Give reasons for your answer.*

(ICSA MPP)

EQ 25 What factors would influence your decision to delegate work to a subordinate? What are the major barriers to delegation?

(IOB NOM)

The control function in management rounds off the POMC process referred to at the outset of this book. Once the planning, organising and motivating activities are under way, then they must be monitored and measured, ie controlled. The primary aim of the control function of management is to measure performance against aims, objectives and standards with a view to enabling corrective actions to be taken, where necessary, to keep plans on course. Control is essentially a question of developing feedback systems throughout the organisation. It may be implemented both quantitatively and qualitatively.

There are three chapters in this section of the book. The basic nature of the control function, together with its key methods and techniques, is outlined in Chapter 28. This is followed by a short chapter (Chapter 29) outlining some of the key elements of a Quality Management system. In Chapter 30, the role of Information Technology is discussed, especially in terms of its impact on office routines and procedures.

CHAPTER 28

Controlling Performance

Introduction

1.   It was noted in the introduction to Organising for Management (p.84) that, if planning represented the route map for the journey, then organising represented the means by which one could arrive at the chosen destination. We can now add that controlling ensures that the travellers know how well they are progressing along the route, how correct their map is, and what deviations, if any, they need to make to stay on course.

2.   The basic elements of control are as follows:

•   Establish standards of performance

•   Measure performance

•   Compare actual results against standards

•   Take corrective action where required.

This sequence of events can be demonstrated diagramatically in a simplified form, as in Figure 28.1, which shows how each element is linked to form a continuous process ending *either* in the achievement of targets *or* the modification of plans as a result of feedback (see Figure 28.2).

3.   Several comments can be made about Figure 28.1. *Firstly*, standards of performance need to be verifiable and clearly stated, for example in units of production or sales volumes. Where standards are qualitative rather than quantitative, it is preferable for them to be expressed in terms of end-results rather than of methods. Budgets are a particularly useful vehicle for the expression of quantifiable results, and will be looked at more closely later in the chapter. *Secondly*, the measurement of performance depends heavily on the relevance, adequacy and timeliness of information. The supply of such information comes

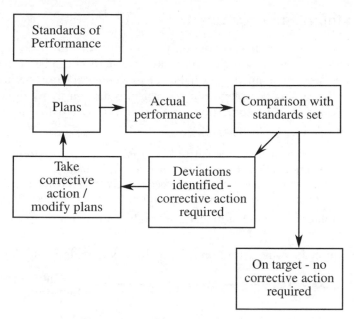

Figure 28.1. The control sequence.

from a variety of sources within the organisation. The single most important source is the Management Accounting department, which is responsible for the regular production of operating statements, expenditure analyses, profit forecasts, cash flow statements and other relevant control information. *Thirdly*, when comparing actual against target performance, most organisations only require action to be taken when the deviation against standards is significant. Otherwise no action is taken and no reference upwards is asked for. This is sometimes called the 'management by exception' principle. *Fourthly*, control is not just a matter of identifying progress, it is also a matter of putting right what may have gone wrong. Hence the importance of directing part of the control process to the implementation of appropriate corrective action.

4. The information generated by control systems is known as feedback. Feedback is usually produced on results ie on the outputs of the system. Actual performance is recorded and the information fed back to the managers responsible for achieving the target performance. Early feedback is essential for accurate control, especially where unexpected deviations have occurred. Where deviations occur, feedback may indicate the need for a change in the process or its inputs, or, possibly, a change in the basic plans or original standards (see Figure 28.2).

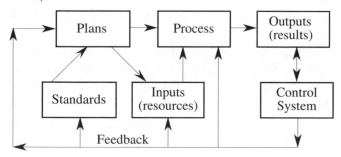

Figure 28.2. Feedback in the control system.

Management Information Systems

5.   The information necessary to carry out the control function effectively is produced from a variety of sources and often in a variety of forms. Information can be of the most detailed kind (usually processed by computer), or can be of a judgemental nature (usually in a written report). With the increasing complexity of control information many organisations have devised a formal Management Information System (MIS) to cope with this problem.

6.   Lucey (1991)[1] defines an MIS as follows:

'A system to convert data from internal and external sources into information and to communicate that information, in an appropriate form, to managers at all levels in all functions to enable them to make timely and effective decisions for planning, directing and controlling the activities for which they are responsible.'

This definition emphasises the use of management information for the purpose of decision-making.

7.   The model implied by this definition is basically as shown in Figure 28.3.

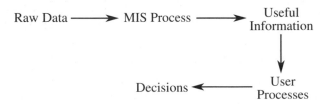

Figure 28.3

The raw data are the basic facts and figures of operational life, such as output figures, hours worked, invoice values, part numbers etc. These data may be stored on manual or computer systems. In themselves they may not have great meaning. Taken together and assembled into relevant groupings, they become *information*, which is basically data that has been analysed, summarised and interpreted for the benefit of the potential user, in this case a manager. The MIS processes are the various procedures and methods used to convert the data into useful information. This can be acted upon, for example to produce comparisons with expected standards and then take appropriate corrective actions (decision-making).

8.   It is possible to identify four types of formal MIS which are useful to management concerned with control at the tactical level. These are briefly:

❶   Control systems which monitor the organisation's activities and report on them, eg production output, sales revenue etc.

❷   Database systems which process and store information, which can be drawn upon as a kind of organisational memory bank.

❸   Enquiry systems, based on either internal or external databases, for carrying out investigations into the performance of departments, product lines, competitors etc.

❹   Decision support systems, providing computer-based facilities for conducting analyses, simulations etc.

9.   The application of an MIS to key management functions assists control in a variety of ways, as the following examples suggest.

Marketing/Sales

•   Clarify current order position

- Identify profitability of particular products
- Identify selling costs
- Produce customer analyses
- Provide surveys of markets.

Personnel

- Provide Wage & Salary analyses
- Identify sickness absence trends
- Analysis of manpower statistics
- Production of labour turnover reports.

Management Accounting

- Production of operating and budget statements
- Analyses of costs/expenditure etc
- Investment appraisal analysis
- Profit forecasts
- Cash flow projections/statements.

Ideally the MIS should be operated on the basis of 'management by exception', ie it should enable managers to delegate confidently in the sure knowledge that significant variances in actual performance compared with standard performance will be highlighted in timely fashion by the system.

Control Methods

10. The two major approaches to control are (a) those that focus on financial values, such as budgetary control, and (b) those that focus on physical values, such as quality control. By far the most widespread method of control is that of budgetary control, which will be considered first.

Budgets

11. A budget is a statement, usually expressed in financial terms, of the desired performance of an organisation in the pursuit of its objectives in the short-term (one year). It is an action plan for the immediate future, representing the operational and tactical end of the corporate planning chain. Budgetary control takes the targets of desired performance as its standards, then systematically collates information relating to actual performance (usually on a monthly or four-weekly period basis) and identifies the variances between target and actual performance. Thus, whereas budgets in themselves are primarily tools of planning, the process of budgetary control is both a planning device and a control device. The primary aims of a budgetary control system are to:

- establish short-term business plans (N.B. Budgets are sometimes referred to as business plans or profit plans),
- determine progress towards the achievement of short-term plans,
- ensure coordination between key areas of the organisation (eg between marketing and production),
- delegate measurable responsibilities to managers, without loss of control,
- provide a controlled flexibility for meeting change in the short-term.

12. The steps by which a budgetary control system is built up are basically as follows:

❶ **Forecasts** for key aspects of the business are prepared. These are statements of probable sales, costs and other relevant financial and quantitative data.

❷ A **Sales Budget** is prepared based on an analysis of past sales and a forecast of future sales in the light of a number of assumptions about market trends. The resulting budget is an estimate of sales for a given budget period.

❸ A **Production Budget** is prepared on the basis of the Sales Budget. This involves an assessment of the productive capacity of the enterprise in the light of the estimates of sales, and a consequential adjustment of either, or both, to ensure a reasonable balance between demand and potential supply. Production budgets will include output targets, and cost estimates relating to labour and materials.

❹ A **Capital Expenditure Budget** is drawn up to cover estimated expenditure on capital items (fixed assets) during the budget period.

❺ A **Cash Budget** is prepared by the accountant to ensure that the organisation has sufficient cash to meet the on-going needs of the business. This budget reduces the organisation's transactions to movements of cash and indicates shortfalls or excesses of cash at particular periods of time.

❻ **Departmental Budgets** are drawn up in the wake of the Sales and Production Budgets.

❼ Finally, the budgets are collected into one **Master Budget,** which is effectively a statement of budgeted Profit and Loss together with a projected Balance Sheet.

❽ Production of **Period Budget Statements**, which inform management about their performance against budget in the immediately preceding period and indicate any variances.

❾ **Action by management,** as appropriate.

13. In developing a system such as the one above, a number of points of good practice need to be considered. These are as follows:

• Budgets should be sufficiently detailed to set clear targets for the managers responsible for carrying them out, but should not be so complex that they defeat their purpose of providing planning and control aids at the operating levels of the enterprise;

• Budgets should not be kept to rigidly if conditions change significantly, but should permit reasonable flexibility. *They are a means to an end, not an end in themselves;*

• The responsibility for a particular budget should be clearly defined;

• Budgets should show variances between actual and budgeted performance (ideally in quantitative as well as financial terms, whenever possible);

• Managers responsible for carrying out budgets should participate in their formulation.

Break-even Analysis

14. Not all control information is expressed in statements and computer printouts. Some useful information can be made available in chart form, such as a 'break-even chart'. This is a chart which shows how costs and profits vary with the volume of production. The name is taken from the point on the chart where the total costs line crosses the sales revenue line ie at the point where neither a loss nor a profit is being made. An example of a simple break-even chart appears as Figure 28.4.

In the example given, total costs (ie total fixed costs plus variable costs) range from £20,000 to about £38,000. Total revenue ranges from nil to about £55,000. The break-

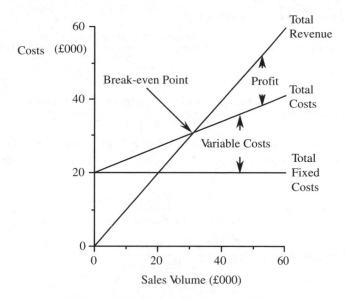

Figure 28.4 Simple break-even chart.

even point is achieved when a sales volume of about £32,000 is reached. Sales in excess of this figure begin to produce a profit.

15. Break-even charts are useful for their indication of the effects of marginal changes in sales volume or costs on profit figures. They are also useful for converting profit targets into production targets or sales targets. The major criticism of such charts is that they assume linear relationships between costs and output, and sales and revenue, whereas this is not always true. The straight lines on the charts may be over-simplified, therefore, and would need to be treated with some caution. Like many other information sources, break-even analysis should preferably be used as one of several devices for obtaining an accurate picture of the business.

Ratios

16. A key feature of all planning and control activities is the analysis of performance data. We have mentioned budgets and break-even charts above, but another useful form of analysis is by the use of financial (and other) ratios. Financial ratios are relationships that exist between accounting figures, and which are usually expressed in percentage terms. Such ratios can be grouped under a number of different categories, such as assessment of profitability, for example. Examples of typical financial ratios are as follows:

- Return on Capital Employed = $\dfrac{\text{Net Profit before Tax}}{\text{Net Capital Employed}} \times 100$

- Net Profit Margin = $\dfrac{\text{Net Profit}}{\text{Sales}} \times 100$

  The above are tests of profitability. Other ratios include tests of liquidity, cost ratios and Stock Exchange tests. Examples of each of these in turn are:

- Current ratio (liquidity) = $\dfrac{\text{Current Assets}}{\text{Current Liabilities}}$

(NB This should usually be a 2 : 1 ratio.)

- Selling/Distribution Costs to Sales = $\dfrac{\text{Selling \& Distribution Cost}}{\text{Sales}} \times 100$

- Earnings per share = Profit (after tax) in pence per share.

- Price – Earnings Ratio = $\dfrac{\text{Market (Stock Exchange) price per share}}{\text{Earnings per share}}$

17. Non-financial ratios indicate the relationship between quantifiable pieces of information, and may or may not be expressed in percentages. Examples of non-financial ratios are:

- Labour Turnover Index = $\dfrac{\text{No. of leavers in period}}{\text{Average No. employed during period}} \times 100$

- Days lost through Strikes = $\dfrac{\text{No. of Working Days lost}}{1{,}000 \text{ Employees}}$

- Sales/Volume of space = $\dfrac{\text{Total Sales of unit}}{\text{Square foot/metre}}$

18. Ratios can provide useful summaries of relative efficiency or progress. Single figures on their own can mean very little, but compared with other sets of figures, they can take on greater significance. Nevertheless, ratios themselves require standards of comparison if an organisation is to compare its performance with its competitors, and these standards are not always available. Also some ratios are fairly crude, eg Index of Labour Turnover, which shows the position in gross terms and gives no indication as to whether turnover is spread throughout the organisation or is heavily concentrated in one department or in one occupation. As with break-even analysis, ratios need to be treated cautiously, and should preferably be used in conjunction with other forms of performance analysis.

Quality Control

19. In the physical world of production, numerous control systems are in operation. One example is that of Quality Control. The control of quality rests on the assumption that in mass-production no two units are exactly identical, but that it is possible to mass produce vast quantities of *almost* identical units. These last-mentioned can be produced within certain tolerances, and a customer will accept variations between these tolerances, but not outside them. The role of Quality Control is to ensure that appropriate standards of quality are set and that variances beyond the tolerances are rejected. Thus Quality Control is basically a system for setting quality standards, measuring performance against those standards and taking appropriate action to deal with deviations outside permitted tolerances. Quality Control activities can be very costly, and since they represent an overhead cost in the production area, the degree of time and resources spent on them must be related to factors such as price, consistency, safety and legal requirements, for example. Products such as highly-priced porcelain will be subject to far higher quality controls than run-of-the-mill household earthenware. Pharmaceutical products are subject to health controls, backed by legislation, and thus require the highest standards of quality. By contrast, the solid fuel merchant can afford to vary the content of what goes into pre-packed bags of household fuel, provided the weight is correct.

20. Inspection is an important part of Quality Control. Usually a choice has to be made whether to carry out 100% inspection or some lesser amount on a sampling basis. Where perfect quality is required, for example in the construction of nuclear reactor plant, then 100% inspection will be applied. In batch or mass-production (for definitions, see Chapter 39), 100% inspection is not always necessary, nor is it always effective. Inspectors usually have to carry out their inspections in noisy and busy surroundings, which may affect their ability to concentrate. In fact several recent studies have shown that up to 15% of defective items have passed unnoticed in a 100% inspection. Better results than this can be achieved by sampling techniques in these circumstances. The most widely used techniques of inspection apart from 100% inspection are random sampling, where batches are concerned, or continuous sampling, in mass-production. Random sampling means that a batch is accepted or rejected on the basis of the number of rejects found after taking a random sample from the batch. Continuous sampling is used in mass-production systems, and entails an initial 100% inspection until a pre-determined number of correct items have passed in succession; then random sampling begins and continues until a further reject appears; 100% inspection is recommenced and the cycle is repeated if necessary. Further points relating to Inspection can be found in Chapter 38.

21. The benefits of Quality Control are primarily as follows:

- Reduction in costs of scrap or re-working
- Reduction in complaints from customers
- Enhanced reputation for company's products
- Feedback to designers and engineering staff about performance of products and the machines required to produce them.

Techniques for Control

22. The scope for detailed questions on quantitative techniques in the examinations covered by this book is very limited. However, in general questions about control in management, some reference ought to be made to the increasing number of mathematical and other techniques which are now available to management in the execution of their planning and controlling activities. This section of this chapter provides a summary of the principal techniques which examiners could reasonably ask of candidates. The object in this chapter is to convey something of the nature and application of these techniques without going into detailed descriptions. For those wishing to enquire further into the field of quantitative techniques, an extremely useful book in this series is 'Quantitative Techniques' by T. Lucey.

23. The techniques which will be outlined are Network Analysis (especially Critical Path Method and Programme Evaluation and Review Technique), Simulation and Inventory Control. Before going on to describe the basic features of these techniques, a few words are necessary about the general field of quantitative techniques.

24. The label given to such techniques varies considerably. Sometimes they are referred to as Management Science, sometimes as OR or Operational Research, and sometimes as Quantitative Techniques. In this Manual the expression OR will be utilised. The purpose of these techniques is to make quantitative data available to managers in order to aid decision-making, planning and control. The basic approach of OR techniques was referred to briefly in Chapter 19 (p. 167), dealing with the topic of decision-making. The approach, this time in slightly more detail, can be stated as follows:

- Analyse Data and Define Problem
- Develop a Mathematical Model of the Situation
- Select Inputs/Data required
- Develop Optimum Solution
- Test/Modify Solution
- Provide Controls/Feedback Mechanism
- Obtain Management Support for Solution
- Implement, Maintain and Review.

25. The distinctive approach of OR, according to the UK OR Society, is that it develops 'a scientific model of the system, incorporating measurements of factors, such as chance and risk, with which to predict and compare the outcomes of alternative decisions, strategies or controls. The purpose is to help management determine its policy and action scientifically.' The models of OR are symbolic, or abstract, representations of real life problems. They are usually expressed in mathematical terms (symbols, equations and formulae), and can be contrasted with other models in common use in business, such as budgets, profit and loss statements, sales charts, and numerous others.

26. The main advantage of OR models is that they provide a basis for the solution of *complex* problems in static or dynamic situations. Such models can be designed to take a large number of factors into account at any one time. They can reduce these factors to mathematical terms and experiment with them by introducing a variety of inputs to assess what effects they have. All this can be done without interfering with the operational or planning processes currently under way in the organisation. Thus the risks of a particular strategy can be evaluated in a relatively safe manner before being put to the test in a real life context.

27. The disadvantages of OR models are: (a) they take time to be developed, and are thus less useful for producing quick answers, (b) they can represent an over-simplified picture of a particular set of conditions, and therefore may suggest only partial solutions, and (c) they may be resisted by line managers on the grounds that such models are too theoretical to be put into practice. To some extent these criticisms are being offset by (a) the wider use of computers to handle complex calculations, and (b) the development of OR teams made up of managers from a variety of disciplines, and not just mathematics.

Network Analysis

28. Network analysis is the term used to embrace a number of techniques for the planning and control of complex projects. The basis of network planning is the representation of *sequential* relationships between activities by means of a network of lines and circles. The idea is to link the various activities in such a way that the overall time spent on the project is kept to a minimum. The optimum linking of the various stages is called the critical path. The two most frequently used forms of network planning are CPM – Critical Path Method – and PERT – Programme Evaluation and Review Technique. The major difference between these two forms is that CPM assumes that the time required to complete an activity can be predicted fairly accurately, and thus the costs involved can be quantified once the critical path has been identified, whereas PERT assumes that time has to be estimated in drawing up the critical path. CPM tends to be used in large or complex projects in construction and manufacturing. PERT tends to be applied to one-off projects of a complex nature or to projects where time or cost are of overriding importance.

29. The basic network is a combination of *events*, *activities* and *dummy activities*, as illustrated in Figure 28.5.

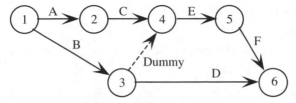

Figure 28.5 A simple network.

Events are the start or the end of an activity, eg kettle filled, tea poured out. Events are shown as a circle or node and are usually identified by a short description of the event or by a number (1, 2, 3 etc).

Activities are actions which take time, eg filling kettle, pouring tea. They are shown as straight arrows, and are usually designated by letters (A, B, C etc).

Dummy activities are actions which do not incur time, but need to be shown to ensure the logic of the network. They are shown as a dotted arrow.

30. Additional information can be added to the basic network as the exercise progresses. So, for example, times and costs can be included in the model which is being built up. The *critical path* through the network is the *longest* sequence of activities from the beginning of the network through to the end. In drawing up networks, estimating times and identifying critical paths, a number of rules and conventions have to be applied. Among these are that a complete network may have only one start event and only one finish event; that an event is not complete until all the activities leading to it are themselves complete; and that a network must always move forwards in time.

31. The advantages of using networks are chiefly:

• they provide a logical picture of the layout and sequence of a complex project

• they help to identify the activities and events which are critical to the entire project

• they provide a basis for working out times, costs and resources involved in the project

• they act as a focal point for action and coordination

• they make an enormous contribution to both the planning and, especially, the control of complex projects.

Simulation

32. Simulation is one of the most widely used quantitative techniques. It consists of developing a model of a process, eg corporate planning, which is then subjected to a series of trial-and-error experiments designed to predict the reactions of the process to variations in its inputs. For example, it would be possible to simulate the effects of differing volumes of sales on key factors in a corporate plan, such as production capacity, purchasing targets and manpower forecasts. Simulation tends to be used in problems where mathematical solutions are not possible, or where long time scales are involved (eg predicting population changes over a 30 year period), or where there is no other way of tackling the problem (eg charting space-satellite trajectories).

33. The basic steps in a simulation are as follows:

• Define problem to be simulated

• Construct a model

- Test the model
- Gather relevant data for experiments
- Run the simulation
- Analyse the results
- Re-run simulation in light of results
- Repeat testing and simulation.

For all practical purposes it is necessary to run simulations on a computer, on account of the number of times it is essential to re-run the model under different conditions.

34. The inputs to any model of a business operation will have to include probabilistic elements, if the model is to be a reasonable representation of reality. Every commercial business, in particular, is subject to chance or risk, and this is where probability comes in. Probability is the quantification of chance (uncertainty). It is an important feature of every business simulation, eg a corporate planning model or a production planning model. The rules of probability (p) state that the value of p ranges from 0 (zero) to 1 (one), where 0 indicates the lowest degree of probability and 1 indicates complete certainty. The values in between are usually expressed as decimals of 1. For example, the chances of your living to the age of 100 would be very small indeed, say 0.01. On the other hand your chance of dying before the age of 100 will be of the order of 0.99, ie a very high probability.

35. Probability is either objective or subjective. *Objective probability* applies to those events which have been tested previously and found to come up with consistent results. For example, if an ordinary coin is tossed, the probability that it will come down heads is 0.5. Where an estimate of probability has to rely on human judgement and experience, this is called *subjective probability,* and is the most widely used in business situations. An example of subjective probability is as follows: the Production Manager of a fast-growing microcomputer manufacturer, whose production has increased by 50% in the past year, without additional capital investment, now estimates the probability of repeating that 50% growth rate as 0.4, given no change in investment levels.

36. In the simulation of a corporate plan, for example, the probabilistic elements are selected on a random basis. This is sometimes known as a Monte Carlo simulation, due to the original gambling application of this approach. Random selection can be undertaken in several ways, but in this case the most likely methods will include the use of random number tables or computer-generated random numbers. A random number table consists of lists of randomly selected numbers in which there is no bias.

Inventory Control

37. The final example of a quantitative technique in this chapter is that of Inventory, or Stock, Control. The inventory of an organisation is its idle resources at any particular point in time. Taking a manufacturing organisation as an example, its inventory can be described as:

- Raw materials and purchased items
- Work in progress (partly-finished goods/sub-assemblies etc)
- Finished goods.

In many organisations, the inventory figure is their largest current asset, and is a key factor in their ultimate profit situation.

38. The reasons for maintaining inventory levels are chiefly as follows:

❶ Raw materials
  - to take advantage of bulk-buying
  - to smooth out irregularities in supply
  - to ensure internal supply to production

❷ Work in progress
  - to act as buffer between production processes

❸ Finished goods
  - to ensure availability of goods to meet demand
  - to smooth out fluctuations in demand.

39. The two basic questions of inventory control are:

- How much to order to replenish stocks?
- When to order?

Before these questions can be answered, organisations have to consider the costs involved. The two basic costs of inventory items are (i) *ordering costs*, ie wages, administration and transport costs etc, and (ii) *carrying, or holding* costs, ie interest on money invested in stock, storage costs, insurance costs etc. It is these two types of costs that inventory control aims to minimise in the light of the required inventory levels, referred to in the previous paragraph. The OR scientist applies mathematical and statistical formulae to models of an inventory so as to produce data on which buying and stockholding decisions can be taken. Inventory control is an important feature of Purchasing activities, and is referred to in more detail in Chapter 38, which also describes JIT (just-in-time) systems.

References

1. Lucey, T. (1991), *Management Information Systems*, (6th edition), DP Publications.
2. Lucey, T. (1992), *Quantititative Techniques*, (4th edition), DP Publications.

CHAPTER 29

Quality Standards and Management

Introduction

1. The subject of quality has been referred to in its traditional production sense in the previous chapter, and is further mentioned in the chapter on Production Planning & Control (Chapter 38). The concept of quality which these traditional applications have adopted has been overtaken in recent years by a broader, organisation-wide approach to quality known variously as Quality Management, Total Quality Control and Total Quality Management. The term Quality Management is intended to convey a vertical approach to quality in an organisation, ie quality is a matter of concern for everybody from the Board of Directors down to the humblest employee.

2.   What is 'quality'? It is difficult to find agreement on this, since much depends on the perspective of those concerned. For example, an engineer will tend to see quality in terms of how well the product or component fulfils its purpose, an accountant might judge the product in terms of its cost-effectiveness, whilst a customer may judge it in terms of its reliability. The point is, however, that 'quality' is seen as something good and worth having, whatever one's perspective. There is one useful way of distinguishing between different sorts of quality, and that is to separate out the quality of the original design from the quality of the conformance to that design. Much of traditional quality control has been directed towards the latter, ie to ensure that the production process produced components or finished goods which conformed to their specification (or within close tolerances). This has been described as the internal view of quality, and has been a feature of Western production systems for decades. In contrast to this approach the emphasis today is more on the former perspective, ie to focus on the original design, which the customer ordered or expressed a preference for. This has been described as the external view of quality, and has been typified in recent years as the Japanese approach to quality.

3.   Another distinction that can be made between approaches to quality lies in the different attitudes towards specifications. In traditional quality control systems, based on the internal view, there is an underlying assumption that there will always be faulty parts, components etc, and that allowance (tolerances) must be made in the production process. This viewpoint is not accepted in a total quality control approach, based on the external view, which expects that every part or component will be fit for its purpose, that everything will be 'right first time'. Such an approach places considerable responsibility on suppliers to provide exactly the right specifications. If, as in total quality systems, every person or unit in a production process is seen as a supplier of goods (or services) to others, then there is a clear pressure on all concerned to ensure that they pass on a perfect product or service to their colleagues (who are, in effect, their customers).

4.   A final general point that distinguishes the internal from the external view of quality lies in the attitude towards costs. In the internal view quality costs money and thus pushes up production costs, which leads to higher prices, which is unacceptable. On the contrary, according to this view, production costs must be minimised in order to reduce unit costs and achieve greater profitability. Therefore quality considerations must always be limited by their costs. The external view, by contrast, includes quality considerations as the core of the production process. Quality control in such circumstances means continuously improving the product and aiming for *prevention* of errors rather than relying on inspection to correct mistakes and/or to reject faulty components. The pay-off for such an approach is claimed to be increased productivity *and* lower costs together with increased customer satisfaction and profitability.

Deming, Juran and Ishikawa

5.   The greatest influences on the total quality approach to management have been exercised by two Americans and one Japanese. The first two, W. Edwards Deming[1] and Joseph Juran[2], applied and developed earlier techniques such as statistical process control (see Chapter 38) to the post-war industries of Japan. They showed that, by paying attention to the continuous improvement of production processes and gaining employees' commitment to the idea of quality at every stage of production, it was possible to achieve consistently high standards of finished goods at a price the customer was more than willing to pay in order to secure reliability and acceptable performance.

6.   Juran, in particular, has shown that at least 85% of failures in production can be laid at the door of management, and that much of this situation has arisen because managements have been prepared to accept that present performance could not be improved rather than thinking all the time of how improvements could be made. Given the day-to-day pressures of a production unit, it is not surprising that many managers are unable to move beyond short-term 'crisis' management. Juran argues, however, that it is essential to look further ahead in order to prevent problems occurring in the first place. Developing this attitude is what he terms 'management breakthrough', and it is a core feature of his ideas on total quality. In essence, he was urging managements to stop trying to cure the *symptoms* of production problems, and concentrate instead on identifying and tackling their *underlying causes*.

7.   W. Edwards Deming is probably the godfather of Japanese industrial success. In the immediate post-war period, after Japan had suffered great devastation of its industries, Deming persuaded the Japanese Union of Scientists and Engineers (JUSE) to try his approach of looking at products from the customer's point of view, and then meeting customer requirements in close collaboration with suppliers. A further key point in Deming's approach was to gain both managerial and employee commitment to engage in a process in which quality was paramount. Thus the total quality approach was born – an approach based not just on statistical process control but on a positive attitude towards quality at every level in the organisation.

8.   Deming's initial work led him to promote Fourteen Points for Total Quality Control. These give considerable insight into his arguments for a total quality approach, and can be summarised as follows:

❶   Create and publish for all employees a statement of the company's mission (aims and objectives) and ensure that managers constantly demonstrate their commitment to it.

❷   Everyone from top management down must learn the new philosophy
     (ie of continuously improving customer satisfaction).

❸   Employ inspection primarily for improving production processes rather than for detecting and correcting errors.

❹   Award business to suppliers on the basis of consistent quality and reliability of their product as well as on price (which is secondary).

❺   Continuously aim to improve the production system.

❻   Ensure adequate training both of employees and suppliers (so that all parties know what is expected of them).

❼   Introduce participatory leadership style in order to achieve employee cooperation.

❽   Develop climate of trust between management and employees, and between groups (including avoidance of approaches such as MbO, which is based on fear, according to Deming!).

❾   Develop an across-the-board approach to cooperation and teamwork.

❿   Cease all exhortations and slogans! Instead provide the *means* to improve customer satisfaction.

⓫   Eliminate numerical quotas for production in favour of instituting methods for improvement; eliminate MbO.

⓬   Remove barriers to workmanship by providing adequate training and equipment and encouraging pride in own work.

⓭   Encourage education and self-improvement at every level (including training in statistical control techniques).

⓮   Create a climate where quality improvement is embedded in the organisation's culture from top to bottom.

9.   In view of the above statements it is not surprising that Deming's approach emphasises top-management commitment, the development of a longer-term rather than short-term view towards quality, the need for managements to persist in the face of initial setbacks on the road to total quality, the encouragement of developing quality at source, and a ban on emphasising output at the expense of quality. Deming's approach tends to lead to a three-tier system of quality management with (1) the top management responsible for the quality of the aims, objectives and fundamental strategy of the organisation; (2) the middle management responsible for the implementation of those aims and objectives in accordance with the overall policy towards quality; and (3) the work group responsible for results within a continuous programme of improvements to production processes.

Ishikawa

10.   The Japanese influence on quality came especially from Professor Ishikawa, who in the early 1960's introduced the idea of Quality Circles (see Chapter 40). This idea arose from his interest in the training of supervisors in the quality process, where he realised that if the work groups themselves participated in the process it would provide a means of securing quality standards at the workplace, and provide a system for giving feedback to supervisors and managers on quality problems. The strongly participative nature of Quality Circles aids the process of gaining every employee's commitment to quality. However, such groups are not intended to be ends in themselves but are an integral part of a total quality control approach.

11.   In a total quality approach, especially where 'just-in-time' (JIT) systems are being implemented (see Chapter 38), an important lesson for quality circles is that their output is not passed on to the next process group until it is asked for. They in turn are not required to accept components, parts etc from their 'suppliers' until they are ready for them. Thus, each work group has to learn to react to the needs of their 'customers'. This idea of everyone being a supplier and a customer of someone else in the organisation, is a key feature of a total quality approach.

12.   Collard (1989)[3] reports a spokesman for JUSE stating that today in Japan quality control has the following principal features: quality control is company-wide, quality control audits are carried out both within the organisation and with suppliers, regular training is given in aspects of quality (and especially in statistical techniques) throughout the company, quality circles underpin the whole programme, statistical methods are applied to production processes, and nation-wide quality activities (conferences etc) are held for management and employees. This last point brings us neatly onto national encouragement for quality programmes in the UK. This is headed mainly by the development of British Standards for quality systems. The Standards do not go quite so far as total quality management in that they are aimed at encouraging frameworks for developing quality systems rather than being concerned, for example, with gaining employee commitment to total quality. The scope of BS5750 is described below. (BS5750 has been replaced by BS EN ISO 9001–9003, but the substance remains the same.)

British Standard 5750 (British Standard EN ISO 9001–9003)

13.   The Standard is not concerned with setting specific quality standards, but is a framework for the establishment of a quality management system. Organisations seeking to

obtain BS5750 have to demonstrate to the external assessors that they have the following key features of a quality system:

- A senior manager responsible for quality, who is charged with ensuring that BS5750 standards are met
- Documentation to support quality procedures, processes, organisation etc
- The system must be planned and developed across all other functions
- The planning of quality must address issues of updating techniques and ensuring adequate equipment, personnel and records
- Design and development planning must be adequately resourced and documented with adequate control of the interfaces between disciplines
- A coordinated system must be set up covering the total production process, in which all control functions are described and accounted for
- Control in writing of the quality system to be applied by suppliers, including reference to purchasing data, inspection of purchased products
- Establishment of procedures and work instructions, including customer specifications, in a simple form which covers every phase of manufacture, assembly and installation
- Procedures for inspection of, and tests on, incoming goods
- Procedures and records covering control etc of measuring and test equipment
- Written control procedures to establish quickly whether a product has not been inspected/been inspected and approved/been inspected and rejected
- System established to enable prompt and effective corrective action to be taken where non-conformance to specification is found
- Written procedures and instructions regarding the movement of the product as it passes through the plant
- Detailed records are available to demonstrate that customer quality requirements are being met (including audit reports etc)
- Effective internal quality audit systems are installed
- Adequate training is provided
- Clear statistical procedures for monitoring quality standards are operated.

The above standard might be described as representing the procedural approach to installing a quality management system. It enables the skeleton of a full-blown system to be established, but this requires fleshing out by means of a communication, motivation and training programme aimed at capturing the spirit of a total quality approach throughout the whole organisation.

Conclusion

14. Most of the ideas expressed above have been discussed in the context of manufacturing processes, since this is where the stimulus for total quality control has come. However, many of the ideas, and certainly the spirit, of total quality can be applied to services. Some of the techniques involved in production may not be transferable to services, but the basic ideas can be. Customers, wherever they are, want satisfaction. If they are buying a product they obviously want it to be fit for its purpose, and they want it to be safe, reliable and probably durable too. And they are influenced by price. For example, most people want a car, but not everyone wants a Rolls-Royce or an expensive

executive model. They are quite happy with a standard middle-range vehicle, but they want it to be reliable, safe and economical. In the past many manufacturers were unable even to guarantee these three features. Nowadays, all manufacturers have to provide these, and many other standard features, in order to maintain their sales against the competition. In the case of a service, people are looking for factors such as availability, reliability, effectiveness (fitness for purpose) and courtesy. They may also be influenced by price. Thus, in looking for a suitable dentist, they will probably want to book an early appointment (and not have to wait for weeks), they will want to be reassured that the dentist is capable, that he or she will carry out the necessary work to their satisfaction, that any fears they have will be dealt with sympathetically, and that the cost will not be excessive.

15. Quality management begins with a consideration of the customers, be they internal employees, other businesses or members of the public. Their wants and needs have to be translated into specifications of one kind or another. These specifications need to be developed and tested. Resources and operational plans have to be drawn up. Then production (or delivery, if a service) can begin. The process of production (or delivery of a service) must be assessed and monitored at every stage in order to see where improvements could be made. Once the customer has received the goods or service, procedures need to be in place to deal with after-sales problems or queries, and to assess the level of customer satisfaction. Then the quality process can begin all over again – in a total quality management system it is a cyclical process which never stops.

16. In the final analysis, a total quality management system should set out at least the following standards for itself:

❶ The aim of the system is *prevention* of errors, not their detection and correction

❷ Every person's motto should be 'Right first time!'

❸ Management must be totally committed to the total quality policy

❹ The ultimate purpose of the system is to meet customer requirements – quality is defined by the customer

❺ Each employee is a customer to every other employee

❻ Quality implies continuous improvement

❼ Quality assurance must be installed to review and measure performance, including all the quality processes involved as well as the delivery of the final product, or service

❽ Quality is everyone's responsibility (including suppliers).

References

1. W. Edwards Deming (1986), *Out of the Crisis*, MIT Press.
2. Juran, J. (1980), *Quality Planning and Analysis*, McGraw-Hill.
3. Collard, R. (1989), *Total Quality – Success Through People*, IPM.

CHAPTER 30

The Role of Information Technology

Introduction

1.   The advent of microelectronics has revolutionised the nature and scale of human communications. The ability to harness electrical power in miniature form has had a huge impact on everyday life both at home and in the workplace. Combined with the calculating possibilities of computers and the global reach of telecommunications facilities, microelectronics has transformed people's ability to acquire, store, use and disseminate information. This information may be in numeric, textual, pictorial or sound form, and can be applied in a wide range of contexts. In the workplace the impact of the information technology revolution (IT) is to be seen most powerfully in the huge range of computers and servers that now form part of the furniture or background of every office or factory. In manufacturing areas there is an increasing use of robots and other automated machinery (see Chapter 41). More generally, we are used to seeing such other applications as mobile phones, pocket calculators, lap-top computers, automated tills and bank cash machines. The possibilities of microelectronic applications are tremendous but, as with every other invention, such applications give rise to their own particular problems, which need to be addressed by the users.

Brief History of Computing and Microelectronics

2.   The three major components of IT are computers, microelectronics and telecommunications. The development of these three elements of the IT revolution is summarised in the next few paragraphs, which will be followed by a short assessment of the implications of IT for the office workplace.

Computers

3.   The earliest attempt to process large amounts of data (information) by means of an electro-mechanical device was made by Herman Hollerith in the USA in the 1890s. The context was the recording and analysis of the national census, and Hollerith needed to find a way of automating the process. He adapted the idea of a punched card from Charles Babbage, an English inventor, by designing a tabulator that could 'read' the information on a card. The application was successful and the tabulator cut the number of man-hours by some two-thirds. Eventually Hollerith machines went on to form the basis of commercial data processing for several decades.

4.   Processing data is one problem, but producing a machine that can itself solve problems is another. The first such machine emerged during the Second World War, when scientists and mathematicians developed a 'computer' that was able to interpret the enigma behind complicated enemy codes. The machine itself was powered by large numbers of valves, which produced so much heat that those working near them were obliged to shed most of their clothes to remain comfortable! After the war such computers, suitably cooled

in air-conditioned rooms, became commercially available. In Britain the Ferranti Mark I appeared, and in the USA the Leo computer. These machines were large, costly, rather unreliable and required a dedicated team to operate them.

5.   It was not until the late 1950s that valves were replaced by much smaller components known as transistors, enabling computers to become much smaller, more reliable, and cheaper to build and operate. Nevertheless even these machines filled a large room and required a dedicated team of systems analysts, programmers and operators to oversee their operations. The trend in computer development, however, was clearly towards enclosing greater power in a smaller machine. What was needed was to find some way of miniaturising the electrical power available in a transistor. Only when this was available would powerful computers be able to be placed on an office desk, or carried around in a briefcase.

The Silicon Chip

6.   The biggest single leap in the impact of IT came in the 1960s with the development in the USA of the first 'integrated circuits', known as 'chips'. Whereas a transistor is a small crystal-based component able to switch or amplify small amounts of electrical current between circuits, the silicon chip is manufactured as a complete circuit, built initially on microscopic layers of metal and silicon. The resulting chip is an immensely complex circuit. The first commercially produced chips were brought to market by the Intel Corporation in 1971. They each carried about 1,000 tiny components. Within ten years very large-scale integrated (VLSI) chips were being produced with more than 10,000 components on a single chip. Today new manufacturing techniques are producing state-of-the-art chips (ultra large-scale integration) with more than one million components on each. Such chips enable computers and other machines to store, process and output much more data, and in many more applications than in the past.

7.   There are three main classes of chips, as follows:

•   memory chips for storing information

•   CPU chips – microprocessors for carrying out the calculating and coordinating functions of a computer or other machine

•   Interface chips for handling the input/output functions of a system (eg printing, scanning, mouse operation).

In addition to such standard chips, which can be fitted and used in a wide variety of computers and other machines, there are custom-built chips, manufactured according to the precise specifications of the user. Standard chips can be mass-produced cheaply; custom-built chips are made to order and are costly.

8.   The following diagram (Figure 30.1) summarises the revolution in electronics over the last sixty years:

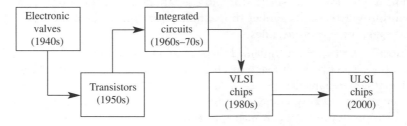

Figure 30.1. Developments in electronics.

Telecommunications

9.   The term 'telecommunications' means communicating over a distance. In technical terms this means transmitting information by means of electric cables (telephone and tele-graph) or by radio waves (using transmitters and satellites). Research in recent decades has focused on how to make transmissions faster, clearer and multifunctional. People now want to receive information in a variety of forms and simultaneously, and this requirement is being met ever more effectively. A major problem that has arisen is that of integrating analogue systems with digital (binary) systems.

10.   A telephone system is typically an analogue system, where the machine mirrors what is being fed into it (voice message) by means of variations in electrical current. Compared with a digital system, which relies on signals that are either on or off, an analogue system is much slower. A digital signal is a *binary* signal, that means it is transmitted at two levels only – for example 'on or off', '0 or 1', or 'yes or no'. The capacity of a modern computer is still referred to in terms of 'bytes', each of which represents eight binary digits, which is the smallest amount of information that a computer can store. Twenty years ago the maximum capacity was expressed in kilobytes, then megabytes, and today in gigabytes, demonstrating how the increased power of chips increases the storage and functional capacity of the average computer.

11.   In order to realise the benefits of binary forms of communication, all modern economies are now upgrading their telephone networks from analogue to digital systems. The advent of the mobile (cellular) phone has also hastened the move towards digitisation. The main improvements in telecommunications are a result of the following developments:

*   Fibre-optic cabling, which enables high-speed pulses of light to be transmitted at great speed along tiny strands of cable made of glass. This development enables many thousands more messages to be transmitted than when using conventional copper cable.

*   Microwave transmissions, from both land-based transmitters and fixed orbit satellites, which greatly increase the scope and speed of radio transmissions around the globe.

*   Infra-red systems, which enable the cordless switching of machines, such as televisions, home entertainment centres, and personal computers.

*   Radio telephones (the mobile phone), which are becoming increasingly complex, and are able to send and receive text messages, handle email in association with a laptop computer, and perform other functions.

The Internet

12.   The development of the Internet represents one of the most dazzling breakthroughs in world-wide communications. It is hard to believe that within the last decade of the twentieth century a revolution occurred in electronic communications that enabled people (a) to send messages almost instantaneously to others all over the world (email), and (b) to publish information that could be stored on one powerful computer and accessed readily by someone using another computer (the World Wide Web). The Internet originated in the USA as an attempt to link (network) a number of different computers in the Department of Defense in the ARPANET project. Then a number of US and European research institutions became involved as they sought to share research results between remote campuses. The first email message was sent in 1971 whereas the Internet proper began operating in 1983, and has grown hugely since that time. The Internet itself is an international network of computers, cables and satellite links that today enables millions of computer users to communicate with each other.

13. The first public, as opposed to academic or military, use of the Internet was to send mail electronically between computer users. This required the installation of appropriate software to enable the remote computers to 'talk' to each other. Email is essentially a private activity, involving the passing of messages between individuals, whether for personal or business reasons. Today such software is fitted as standard to every personal computer. However, it was not until 1989 that individuals were able to access the global reference library that is today called the World Wide Web.

14. In that year a British physicist, Tim Berners-Lee (2000),[1] devised a global hypertext system that enabled data from any source to be accessed by a remote computer using a common system. This development led directly to the World Wide Web, which is essentially a vast array of information in documentary, sound and video forms that can be accessed via the Internet. The Web could not exist without the Internet, but the Web gives tremendous added value to the Internet, because of the huge amount of information that it makes available. Today every business enterprise and government department has its Web pages, informing users about products and services. Other organisations, and private individuals too, are supplying Web pages about their activities. So-called 'e-commerce' is being transacted over the Internet, as sellers and buyers of goods and services conduct their business in the light of what they have seen on their computer screen.

15. Access to the Internet is provided by gatekeeper organisations known as Internet Service Providers (ISPs). They enable users to access their powerful computers cheaply using local telephone links and, once connected to the ISP's computer, users can access the rest of the Internet. Increasingly, ISPs are offering Web space to all their subscribers, so the amount of information potentially available is beyond imagination. In order to make use of the Internet ('surf the Net'), computer users need to have appropriate software installed. Separate programs are needed (a) to send and receive e-mail, and (b) to browse the Web. These are mostly pre-installed on new computers, or can be downloaded from the subscriber's ISP site. The widespread development of email and the Web has thrown up a number of security issues, as individuals and organisations seek to protect themselves against fraud, hackers, abusive emails and viruses. Hackers are individuals who aim to enter another person's computer system in order to create trouble. Viruses are computer programs designed to disrupt other computers by distorting and replicating their files, so that the system becomes inoperable. These unwelcome developments have caused users to give greater attention to the use and control of passwords, registration procedures, secure sites and anti-virus protection.

16. The success of the Internet has led many business organisations to conduct sales and other business via the Internet. This development, known as e-commerce, is in its infancy at present, but its potential is huge. Already book sales have been successfully achieved through companies such as Amazon.com, whose Web pages provide a catalogue of holdings and the means to order, using credit card facilities. Banks are also offering Internet accounts to their customers, enabling them to conduct real-time transactions on their accounts, such as paying bills, and transferring money between accounts, as well as checking balances and statements. Such activities can only grow in the future, especially in respect of retail services.

17. The success of the Internet has also led many organisations to establish their own internal 'intranets', enabling staff to access information on an organisation-wide basis using a powerful central server to store and re-route files, documents, statistics and other useful data. Access is restricted to employees and requires the use of a password and user name.

Information Technology in the Workplace

18. The impact of microelectronics on the workplace is immense. Every kind of organisation uses desktop computers, which can be found in such varied locations as offices, laboratories, factory production lines, warehouses, school classrooms, hospital reception areas, police stations and airport check-in desks. Particularly important applications of microelectronics include:

- data storage, retrieval and processing
- industrial process control
- robotics (see Chapter 41)
- computer-aided design and manufacture (see Chapter 41)
- worldwide electronic communication (via the Internet)
- scientific measurement
- medical diagnosis using miniaturised instruments
- electronic point of sale (especially in retail environments)
- electronic funds transfer (by financial institutions and individuals)

19. For the purposes of this chapter, we shall focus on the effects of information technology on offices, because the prime purpose of every office is to collect, process, store and despatch information. Typical office functions, once dealt with separately, often by specialised sections, can now be handled as a whole by flexible teams using comprehensive databases, which link previously separate documents. Now a clerk can call up, or process, a customer enquiry while at the same time checking the original invoice or purchase order and establishing the current state of the customer's account. A secretary can prepare a letter or email on behalf of a manager, add a relevant document stored on a computer, and print out for signing or despatch electronically.

20. This ability to integrate office functions easily and speedily is one of the great advantages of computers and associated office machinery, such as printers, copiers, scanners and facsimile machines. When the product of this integration can also be sent down a telephone line to someone on the other side of the globe in seconds, we indeed have a communications revolution! The benefits of this information technology revolution are bestowed on *people* – users, customers, suppliers and others – whose interactions are served by the combined powers of computers, microelectronics and telecommunications. Whereas robots, CNC machines and other industrial computers (see Chapter 41) serve materials and components, and data processing computers serve administration systems, information technology facilitates people's needs to communicate with their fellow human beings.

21. How then can we summarise the benefits and disadvantages of information technology? Perhaps to our surprise, the drawbacks have been fewer than first anticipated. It was forecast that the development of office technology would lead to a reduction in office jobs, and to boredom in the operation of standard office systems – neither of these things has happened. It was thought that there would be a loss of personal contact between people in offices, as more and more functions were assigned to computer software, but again this has not happened. Indeed, through office intranets people are able to maintain ready email contact with colleagues. Not only that, but computers have not destroyed the social interactions that continue to thrive in an office situation. There are potential health problems associated with the use of information technology, such as repetitive strain injuries, and eye problems, but these have not proved as frequent as at first suspected. Most offices provide guidance for their staff to help reduce any health difficulties.

22. The benefits of information technology have been considerable – secretarial, clerical and administrative workers have learned to handle integrated software, which has enabled them to write letters, reports and memos, access records, handle calculating tasks, and search relevant databases all from the one work-station. The speed at which information can be placed on a database, retrieved by a colleague, updated as required, and then forwarded to a customer, supplier or other recipient is altogether faster than in the pre-information technology era. Last but not least, the drafting of reports and other documents is greatly assisted by the powerful editing facilities of word-processing software, supported by the integrating facilities of combined software, enabling financial reports, statistics, charts, pictures and other items to be included in the final version.

23. The costs of equipping offices with the most appropriate hardware (computers, printers, scanners, digital telephones etc) have come down as prices have felt the impact of a mature market. The cost of software remains relatively high, as it is this that drives the hardware, and needs to be frequently updated to maintain the efficiency of office systems. Nevertheless, standard software programs are no more expensive than in recent years. It is only when a business needs a customised system to integrate its office functions that costs can be high. For these developments a proper project budget needs to be prepared, internal IT staff need to liaise closely with user departments and the external software consultants, and the senior team leaders need to be able to negotiate fair terms with the consultants at the outset.

Discipline in the use of Information Technology

24. Some aspects of the use of information technology require monitoring to prevent undesirable or unlawful use by staff, whether deliberate or accidental. The integration of so much information on any one individual's computer means that more and more staff are able to access personal data about customers, and other individuals, including other staff. Personnel staff need to be especially watchful in this regard. The subject of personal data, as opposed to numerical or statistical data, is covered by law in the UK. The relevant legislation is contained in the Data Protection Act, 1998, which sets out the rules for handling personal data, defined as 'data which relate to a living individual who can be identified from those data, or from those data and other information which is in the possession ... of the data controller.' Personal data could relate to more than one specific individual, for example a small group, but do not include data about corporate bodies. The data controller is the person (generally the employing organisation) responsible for determining the purpose for which, and manner in which, the personal data are processed (eg customer or staff records).

25. Essentially, the law is intended to ensure, so far as practicable, that data of a personal nature is used with appropriate safeguards against loss of privacy or personal abuse, and is only processed for lawful purposes. The law applies to manual records as well as electronic data. Many organisations have developed data protection policies to reduce the possibility of breaches of personal privacy. These policies are implemented through procedures that include reference to the following:

- identifying the managers/supervisors responsible for data security
- ensuring that only authorised persons have access to areas/work stations where personal data are being processed
- restricting password access to a database on a 'need-to-know' basis, and increasing levels of access, where necessary, to specified job-holders

- training staff in the procedures for handling personal data, including authenticating the identity of any person to whom information may be disclosed (eg over the telephone)

- selection of staff to work on personal data, and measures for removing people who do not show sufficient discretion in handling such data

- establishing a procedure for removing personal data from files, and/ or shredding personal data held in manual form

- ensuring guidance for staff on the disciplinary rules applying to the handling of personal data.

26. The proliferation of personal computers and work-stations in every type of office also means that most employees now have ready access both to electronic mail (email) and to use of the Internet (via the World Wide Web). Here, too, it is in everyone's interest that a clear policy on email and Internet use should be available. The possibility of email and Internet abuse, intended or accidental, affect all staff, and this is why it is important to establish proper disciplinary rules to cover this aspect of working life.

27. Email communication has the advantage of enabling written messages to be passed speedily between individuals and around organisational networks, and for responses to be returned just as quickly. The excessive use of email, however, can overload certain individuals, resulting in relatively trivial items being read, and replied to, as well as more important items. The ready facility for forwarding items to a number of colleagues simultaneously can also produce a situation where many individuals receive mail that is not strictly relevant to them. Such over-enthusiasm for using email could prepare the ground for an over-casual use, leading to the dissemination of offensive material which certainly would constitute misconduct. Material of a racial, religious or sexual nature, used to make fun of, bully or perhaps titillate colleagues is clearly a disciplinary matter. An advantage here is that unlike a telephone conversation, an email is captured in writing, and this makes it easier for an employer to produce evidence of misconduct. If an organisation has a policy of monitoring emails, it should state this openly, and be aware of possible breaches of individual privacy under the Human Rights Act (see Chapter 50).

28. Employee access to the Internet opens up an organisation's own network to abuse from external sources. Viruses may be imported unwittingly, junk mail included in email messages, and pornography downloaded, unless steps are taken to restrict the types of addresses accessible from the user's work station. The careless use of passwords by employees can lead to unauthorised 'hacking' into an organisation's database. These are serious issues for any employer. Add to these the possibility of copyright breaches in respect of downloaded material, and the sheer cost of time-consuming Web-browsing, it is not surprising that many employers are keen to set down clear and fair guidelines on use of IT communications.

29. A policy statement on Internet use is likely to include the following points:

- access – guidance on who should have access to email and use of the Web

- passwords – rules for allocating or changing passwords, as well as rules to minimise the unauthorised use of passwords

- Web use – guidance regarding legitimate sites for access, banning access to sites containing offensive or indecent material, and limiting the amount of time spent browsing; also rules clarifying who is permitted to make adaptations to the organisation's own Web site

- email – guidance concerning disclosure (and non-disclosure) of email addresses, limitations on private use of the organisation's email, restrictions on the content of emails (eg banning offensive or salacious gossip), and rules for email distribution

- disclaimers – guidance in respect of disclaimers to be attached to emails sent by employees (e.g. regarding any legal references made)

- monitoring – a statement to the effect that all, or some, emails and Web site access may be monitored on a routine basis

- disciplinary rules – a statement setting out the types of breach that constitute misconduct and/or serious misconduct, together with the sanctions that may be imposed on staff.

References

1. Berners-Lee, T (2000), *Weaving the Web*, Texere Publishing.

Questions for Discussion/Homework

1. What is the relationship between control and planning?
2. Discuss the role of feedback in a control system.
3. Write out a 'code of good practice' for an organisation about to install a budgetary control system for the first time.
4. Why do firms need to pay attention to quality control?
5. In what ways can an Operational Research specialist contribute to the effectiveness of line managers?
6. Why is it advisable for employers to establish clear ground-rules for employees who have access to email and the Internet?
7. How would you personally describe the term 'electronic office'?
8. Given the power and portability of modern lap-top computers and mobile telephones, why should business organisations continue to invest in offices?

Examination Questions

Questions on the control process in management are not among the most frequent questions in general management papers. Two fairly typical questions on this topic are included below. Outline answers may be found in Appendix 2.

EQ 26 In defining the basic principles of management, textbooks often list Planning and Control as two separate and distinct functions. How far can they be regarded as independent of one another?

(IOM Business Organisation)

EQ 27 What are the basic steps in the Control process? Identify and explain the key considerations in each step.

(IOB Nature of Mgt.)

Part Three

FUNCTIONAL MANAGEMENT: MARKETING, PRODUCTION, PERSONNEL AND FINANCIAL

Marketing is the one function of management which has to be more concerned with what is going on *outside* the organisation than with what is happening internally. Marketing activities are conducted mainly across the *external* boundaries of the organisational system, and they are undertaken by managers of all kinds, not only by marketing specialists. Marketing has been described in several different ways. A cross-section of definitions, which have appeared over the past twenty years or so, is as follows:

❶ 'Marketing is a social and managerial process by which individuals and groups obtain what they need and want through creating, offering, and exchanging products of value with others.' *(P. Kotler, Marketing Management – Analysis, Planning Implementation and Control, 8th Edition, 1994)*

This definition emphasises marketing as an issue of social and economic exchange.

❷ [Marketing is] … 'The management function which organises and directs all those business activities involved in assessing and converting customer purchasing power into effective demand for a specific product or services and moving the product or service to the final consumer so as to achieve the profit target or other objectives of the company.' *(Institute of Marketing, 1966)*

This definition is distinctly action-centred and managerial in approach.

❸ [Marketing is] … 'the whole business seen from the point of view of its final result, that is from the customer's point of view.' *(P. Drucker, The Practice of Management, 1954)*

This definition emphasises the *concept* of marketing and expresses a philosophical approach to marketing activities.

The idea of the 'marketing concept' is taken up in Chapter 31, and is compared with other approaches to marketing. The other chapters in the section deal with those aspects of marketing, which are the most frequent topics of examination for non-marketing specialists. These are: the marketing mix, market research, the organisation of a marketing department and consumer protection.

CHAPTER 31

The Marketing Concept, Competitiveness and the Global Dimension

Introduction

1.   Every business or public organisation has its market, that is to say the group of existing and potential buyers or users of its goods and services. A market may consist of a mere handful of people (eg specialist collectors of a certain type of antique porcelain), or it

may consist of millions (eg consumers of breakfast cereals). Clearly, relationships with the market are an important ingredient of corporate planning and policy-making. Organisations have developed several different ways of regarding their existing and potential customers. The most notable options are as follows:

- **Production** orientation – in this situation, the organisation concentrates its attention on production efficiency, distribution and cost in order to attract customers to its products. This works well when demand is well ahead of supply, and where lower costs will encourage people to buy. Engineering firms tend to have this orientation.

- **Product** orientation – in this case the organisation stands or falls by the quality of its products. The thinking behind this orientation is that customers buy products or services rather than solutions to problems. Examples of product orientation are to be found in education, the arts and journalism, where the inference often is that the supplier knows best what the customer needs.

- **Sales** orientation – here the dominant concept is that people will not buy until they are persuaded to buy by positive selling. Thus the focus of attention is more on the skills of selling, than on the needs of the buyer. Several life-insurance companies have adopted this approach over the years.

- **Market** orientation – a market-oriented organisation is one which focuses on the needs of its customers. Its primary concern is to find out what its customers' needs and wants are so as to meet them with the highest level of customer satisfaction. In this situation production responds to the demands of marketing rather than the other way round. This approach to marketing is called the 'marketing concept' and its perspective is radically different from the approaches of production, product and sales-oriented organisations. Examples of market-oriented attitudes can be found in supermarket chains and in numbers of travel agency operations and in motor-car manufacturing (eg 'Everything we do is driven by you').

2.   Few business organisations have total control over their markets. On the contrary, most businesses find that they are in fierce competition with others wanting to serve the same group of buyers. In recent times competition has become more widespread, as foreign competitors join domestic competitors in offering similar goods or services to the same market. Lower trade barriers, better worldwide transport systems (especially air travel), and access to high quality electronic technology mean that new competitors can enter markets previously the preserve of just one or two key players. Suddenly, the world seems a smaller place, and major firms decide on their marketing strategies in a global context, both in terms of markets and suppliers. Thus 'globalisation' and 'competitiveness', especially in terms of *competitive advantage*, become increasingly important concepts to modern companies.

The Marketing Concept

3.   The marketing concept takes the view that the most important stakeholders in the organisation are the customers. This does not necessarily mean that the customer is always right, but it does mean that the customer forms the starting point for the organisation's corporate strategy. Organisations that adopt the marketing concept also tend to see marketing as a very diffuse activity, shared by many, and not just the preserve of a specialist group called Marketing & Sales. This is a very important consideration, for, as we shall see shortly in the discussion of the marketing mix, there are certain key issues, such as pricing, which have to be considered and agreed on a *shared* basis.

4.   Reference was made earlier to customer needs and wants. What are the differences

between these two? One way of distinguishing between them is to define *needs* as basic physical and psychological drives arising from being human (eg need for food, clothing, self-esteem etc), and to define *wants* as specific desires directed towards fulfilling the basic needs. A need for food, for example, could be transformed into a specific desire (want) for curried chicken, or for bread and cheese or countless other variations of food. The point is that human beings have relatively few needs, but can generate an enormous number of wants. Not surprisingly, therefore, most marketing efforts concentrate predominantly on satisfying people's *wants*. In addition to this, some marketing is directed specifically at creating or changing people's wants.

5. The marketing role in an organisation is carried out by numerous individuals. In the first place all those senior managers, and their advisers, contributing to the organisation's corporate plan, are fulfilling, among other things, a marketing role by examining the marketplace and assessing the organisation's ability to meet current and future demands on its resources. Many middle managers also carry out a marketing role when dealing with issues relating to their public. For example, when a production manager meets a customer to discuss a quality problem, or a minor design change, he is fulfilling a marketing role; and so is a personnel manager who negotiates an agreement with union representatives that facilitates the flexible use of labour in producing customers' goods. Finally, there is the Marketing department. Its staff are specifically charged with marketing duties – assessing customer wants, gathering market intelligence, obtaining customer reactions, and organising sales and distribution. The other chapters in this Section concentrate mainly on the activities of these Marketing specialists, but before considering detailed aspects of marketing, it will be helpful to look briefly at the twin issues of competitiveness and globalisation, since they are of such significance in modern marketing practice.

Competitivenesss

6. As was noted in Chapter 16, Porter's (1980)[1] analysis of the competitive situation facing firms showed that current competitors were not the only competitive forces at work in the external environment. Suppliers and buyers also made an impact on the competitive situation, as did the actions of potential newcomers and the possibility of substitute products. Competitiveness, according to Porter and others (eg Kotler, 1996)[2] is primarily about delivering *enhanced value* to customers. Kotler, for example, defines competitive advantage as:

> 'An advantage over competitors gained by offering consumers greater value, either through lower prices or by providing more benefits that justify higher prices.' (p.256)

He defines value as follows:

> 'The consumer's assessment of the product's overall capacity to satisfy his or her needs ... [The total customer value is] ... The total of all the product, services, personnel, and image values that a buyer receives from a marketing offer.' (p.570)

7. Porter (1990)[3], in a later work on international competitiveness, comments that firms create competitive advantage

> 'by perceiving or discovering new and better ways to compete in an industry and bring them to market, which is ultimately an act of innovation.' (p.45)

He suggests that typical causes for such innovation include the following:

❶ New technologies (eg product design, production technologies, delivery systems etc)

❷ New or shifting buyer needs (eg need for fast-food services instead of sit-down restaurants for busy people)

③ Emergence of a new industry segment (ie a product or service that meets a new group of buyers or a regrouping of existing customers, such as the small fork-lift truck segment of the wider fork-lift truck industry)

④ Shifting input costs or availability of inputs (eg significant changes in labour costs or raw materials)

⑤ Changes in government regulations (eg trade tariffs, product standards, environmental controls etc).

8. Since any of the above five items is extremely likely to occur in the short to mid-term, it is necessary for business organisations to be responsive to these triggers for change in the external environment. Kotler's views on value indicate that being competitive implies much more than providing attractive product features. Businesses also have to pay attention to delivery and after-sales services, quality/competence of their own personnel, and the general reputation of their company. These are the reasons why many people will buy a BMW instead of a comparable model of motorcar, despite the former's relatively higher cost. Motorcar manufacturers, in particular, are selling products which frequently have a status appeal as well as functionality. Thus, value to a customer has to be seen in terms of the attractiveness of the car and its image as well as to features such as reliability and fuel economy. Japanese car firms realised early on that most customers wanted reliable servicing, and accordingly set up systems for training dealers' mechanics to a consistently high standard – an extension to the concept of after-sales service. Being competitive means being able to supply the range of customers needs in a way that they perceive as offering better value. This may mean providing similar products at a lower cost, but nowadays is more likely to imply providing some extra benefit at the same cost.

Globalisation

9. As mentioned earlier, the tendency for firms to operate in a global market, both for sales and supplies has accelerated over the past decade. It is no longer unusual for major manufacturing firms to be investing in substantial operations overseas, whilst maintaining similar facilities in their domestic market. Aircraft produced by the European aircraft industry may have their engines made in the United States, the wings in Sweden or the UK, the bodies in France or Germany, the electronics in the UK or France, the fittings in Italy or Belgium, and final assembly in the UK or France. Pharmaceutical companies, many of whom are based in Switzerland – one of the smallest nations in the world – have for many years manufactured in several countries, and marketed through a select number of offices in key capital cities, using local staff for sales and distribution.

10. Porter (1990)[4] defines a global strategy as:

'... one in which the firm sells its product in many nations and employs an integrated worldwide approach to doing so.' (p.54)

He suggests that adopting a global approach to marketing strategy provides two distinct ways in which firms can gain a competitive advantage, or at least off-set a domestic disadvantage. These are that:

① a global firm can spread activities among nations to serve the world, and this not only enables expansion of the business, but also helps to off-set poor returns in domestic or other select markets

② a global firm can coordinate dispersed activities, for example where marketing, distribution and after-sales are located in the buyers' nation, but manufacturing and supply can be located anywhere.

11. Porter thinks that competitive industries, when compared internationally, are those that improve and innovate by investing in such activities as R&D, learning, modern facilities and training. He acknowledges that this innovatory behaviour is conditioned by other key factors in determining national advantage, which are set out in a 'diamond' system as shown in Figure 31.1.

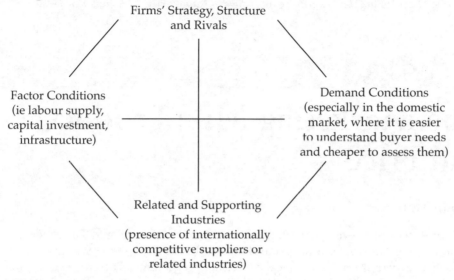

Figure 31.1 Determinants of national advantage (adapted from Porter).

12. Apart from firms' own strategic choices, including the structure of their organisation, the local competitive situation has to be taken into account. These aspects are themselves affected by conditions in the national economy – supply of labour, skills, adequate transport and communications infrastructure – together with the availablity of sufficient capital in firms to sustain innovation. The demand situation is critical, since this is the national marketplace. However, Porter considers that conditions in the home market need to be sufficiently promising to enable a firm to be able to study what customers really want before launching out into other nations, even though their needs may not be exactly the same. Finally, the existence of key suppliers and related industries is an important factor in the ability of a national industry to compete globally.

13. There are several alternatives open to companies wishing to globalise their operations, as follows:

❶ by exporting their goods and services to foreign countries, which is the easiest option

❷ by entering into joint ventures with companies in the target nation through licensing agreements or joint ownership, for example

❸ by direct investment in new plant and manufacturing facilities in the foreign country.

Worldwide operations will imply that the organisation's marketing mix (see following chapters) will probably have to be adapted to meet conditions in the foreign countries in which the firm is operating. It will also be necessary to have an appropriate marketing organisation to support its overseas activities, ranging from an export sales department (at the very least) through an international division to the establishment of a full international subsidiary company.

References

1. Porter, M. E. (1980), *Competitive Strategy*, The Free Press Collier Macmillan.
2. Kotler, P. & Armstrong, G. (1990), *Marketing: an Introduction*, (7th edition), Prentice-Hall.
3. Porter, M.E. (1990), *The Competitive Advantage of Nations*, The Free Press Macmillan.
4. Porter, M.E. (1990), *The Competitive Advantage of Nations*, The Free Press Macmillan.

CHAPTER 32

The Marketing Mix: Product and Price

Introduction

1. A vital element in every marketing strategy is the marketing mix. The concept was first expounded by Professor Neil Borden of Harvard University in the 1940s, when he identified twelve key variables in the typical marketing programme. These twelve variables have subsequently been reduced to four main headings by later writers. The mix may now be defined as 'the particular group of variables offered to the market at a particular point in time.' These variables are principally (1) product, (2) price, (3) promotion and (4) distribution. Each of these can be further sub-divided, as illustrated in Figure 32.1.

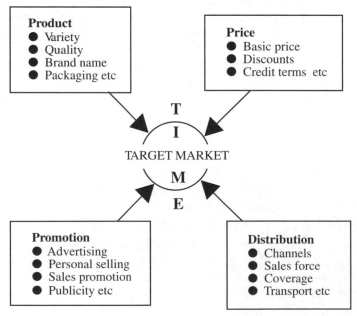

Figure 32.1. The marketing mix.

2. The marketing mix, as illustrated, is the central part of an organisation's marketing tactics. Once the market situation (customers, competitors, suppliers, middlemen etc) has

272

been identified and evaluated, and once the decision has been made to penetrate, or develop, a particular market, then the role of the marketing mix is crucial. This role will be amplified in the rest of this chapter, and in Chapters 33 and 34.

3.   Before moving on to consider the different variables, the question of timing should not be overlooked.

The element of time is a vital factor in assessing the particular mix to be offered to a market. Any market situation can change rapidly over even a short period of time, as can be the case when a major competitor is suddenly declared bankrupt. By using the marketing mix as a tactical tool of an organisation's marketing plans, it is possible to adapt speedily and profitably to changes in the marketing environment. Thus the development of the mix to meet conditions at a particular point or period in time is essentially a contingency approach to marketing management.

Product

4.   Any discussion about the marketing mix must begin with the product. The 'product', in this context, means anything that is offered to a market for its use or consumption. The product can be a physical object or a service of some kind. The product offered by a manufacturer consists of physical items, such as machine tools, television sets, loaves of bread or cosmetics. Products offered by service industries include hospital care, dental treatment, holiday arrangements and accountancy services, for example.

5.   The range of products offered by an organisation is called the product mix. Since most, if not all, of the organisation's revenue is going to be obtained from the sale of its products, it is clearly important that the range and quality of the product mix is frequently evaluated and amended. Examples of a product mix are as follows:

- Motor car manufacturer – cheap, basic family runabouts, medium-priced family saloons, estate cars, executive saloons, and sports cars. Within most of these product lines, various other refinements can be offered, eg two-door and four-door versions of the family saloons, hatchbacks as an alternative to the estate models, variations in engine sizes, and, of course, a range of colours.

- District hospital – surgical and medical services, diagnostic services, paramedical services, prenatal advice and others. Within each of the major 'product lines' various alternative services are offered, eg general surgical, accident services, coronary care, X-radiography, physiotherapy, pre-natal classes and so on.

6.   In considering products, it is important to note that people generally want to acquire the *benefits* of the product, rather than its *features*. For example, in buying a motor car a person is buying such things as luxury or speed or economy or status. The fact that these benefits are achieved by differences in engine size, suspension design or paintwork is really of secondary interest. Similarly, the reason why we want hospitals is for such aims as the preservation of life or the improvement of health or peace of mind. Whether these things are achieved by surgery, or by drugs, or by nursing care, or by modern diagnostic apparatus is, for many people, a matter of secondary importance.

7.   If we agree that customers are buying the benefits of a product, then equally organisations are *selling* the benefits of that product. The selling effort is not just confined to the Promotion element in the marketing mix. It begins by being designed into the product itself. So, for example, the very existence of a product range is, in itself, a selling point for a product. The same consideration applies to other aspects of the product, such as quality, brand, packaging and after-sales service, where applicable. Where quality is designed into

a product, the benefits can be long product life, absence of faults and subsequent break-downs, reliability, increase in value and many others. However, product quality may not be sought after at all. For example, the benefits of disposable goods are immediate and one-off. Such goods do not need to be durable or aesthetic, so long as they are hygienic and functional. Practically every airline traveller in the world has been introduced to plastic cutlery, and every nurse in training has been introduced to disposable syringes. Thus product quality may be high or low, depending on the wants or preferences of the market, and part of an organisation's product strategy is to decide the level of quality to be aimed at.

8.   One important method used to sell benefits is by branding products. This means applying the organisation's 'signature' to its product by the use of special names, signs or symbols. Branding has grown enormously during this century, and there is hardly a product in the Western world which does not have a brand name or designation of some kind. Famous brand names include Coca-Cola, Biro and Hoover, all of which have become synonymous with certain categories of products, whether produced by them or by their competitors. A ball-point pen is a 'biro' to many people, regardless of whether it is a Biro, or a Parker, or a Papermate, for example. In Britain, the Marks & Spencer company market their products under the brand-name of St Michael. These products are manufac-tured by other reputable companies to a standard approved by Marks and Spencer and sold under the St. Michael label. By comparison, other retailers, such as Boots, John Lewis, and Sainsbury's, market some goods under their own branding and some under the manu-facturers label. Branding also occurs in certain consumer services, such as transport – Blue Riband, Economy, Four Star, Ambassador are all titles that are, or have been, used to differentiate between levels of service. In general, branding is a feature of consumer prod-ucts. It is far less common in industrial products.

9.   Packaging is an important factor in the presentation of a product to the market. Not only does packaging provide protection for the product, but it can also reinforce the brand image and the point-of-sale attraction to the buyer. The protective aspect of packaging is vital in respect of items such as foodstuffs, dangerous liquids and delicate pieces of machinery. Goods such as soft toys and items of clothing may not need such protection, but here other considerations apply, such as the appearance of the goods on the shelf, or the possibility of seeing the contents through the packaging. Other aspects of packaging may emphasise the convenience of the pack, as for example in cigarette packets which may be opened and reopened several times, or beer cans, which can be opened safely by pulling a ring.

10. Some products are sold with a very strong emphasis on after-sales service, warranties, guarantees, technical advice and similar benefits. Mail-order firms invariably have an arrangement whereby, if customers are not satisfied with the goods received, they may return them at the firm's expense without any questions being raised. Computer suppliers frequently provide customer training as an integral part of their total product package. Car retailers sell vehicles with various kinds of warranties concerning replacement of faulty parts at the supplier's expense. This facility applies as much, if not more, to industrial and commercial buyers as it does to individual consumers. In recent years the growth of 'consumerism' or consumer protection lobbies has led to many organisations taking action to improve the service to the customer after the sale has been concluded.

11. Emphasis on the make-up of the product is not only vital because of the need to sell benefits to potential customers, but also to take account of another key factor, ie the 'product life cycle'. Studies have shown that most products pass through a series of stages – their life cycle – from the time they are introduced until the time they are withdrawn. A

product will typically pass through five major stages in its life. These are shown in Figure 32.2.

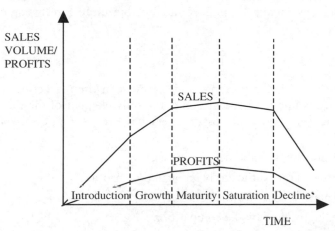

Figure 32.2. Product life cycle.

12. The consequences of these stages of the product life cycle are as follows:

- **Introduction**   Costs are high (because they include the development costs), sales and profits are low. Few competitors. Price relatively high.

- **Growth**   Sales rise rapidly. Profits at peak level. Price softens. Increasing competition. Unit costs decline. Mass market appears.

- **Maturity**   Sales continue to rise, but more slowly. Profits level off. Competition at its peak. Prices soften further. Mass market.

- **Saturation**   Sales stagnate. Profits shrink. Measures taken against remaining competition. Prices fiercely competitive. Mass market begins to evaporate.

- **Decline**   Sales decline permanently. Profits low or even zero. Product is withdrawn from the market.

13. The total length of time over which a product may decline depends on a variety of factors, such as its relevance to basic needs, its adaptability in the light of economic trends and whether it is the focus of short-term fads or of longer-lasting fashions. A basic foodstuff, such as the common loaf of bread or a packet of ground coffee, will have a relatively long life cycle. Conversely, in an economy where energy costs are high and fuel conservation is the fashion, the expensive motor car with a high petrol consumption will tend to have a short life cycle, but the economy car will continue for years. Fads breed products with a short life cycle, such as pop records and other leisure items; fashions tend to develop or reappear over the course of years, and the products which follow them tend to have a relatively long life cycle. In Britain the fashion for home ownership has developed gradually over three or four decades. Alongside this development have appeared key products such as estate agents services and mortgage facilities, which have established themselves firmly over the same period.

14. Taking into account the various stages of the product life cycle and the period of time concerned, it is possible to plan the product mix, plan the development and introduction of new products, plan the withdrawal of obsolete or unprofitable products, and set the revenue targets for each product within the total range. If the current position of any one product is plotted correctly on its life cycle, then it is possible to assess the potential growth

of sales, or the degree to which prices should be allowed to soften in order to maintain the market share, or whether the product should be superseded by another. Thus the concept of the product life cycle makes an important contribution to forecasting of sales and planning of products.

Price

15. If product is the most important single element in the marketing mix, then price is usually next. Price is important because it is the only element of the mix which produces revenue; the others all represent costs. Sellers have to gear prices to a number of key factors, such as:

- the costs of production (and development),
- the ability to generate sufficient revenue and/or profits,
- the desired market share for the product,
- the prices being offered by the competition.

16. Price is especially important at certain times. For example:

- when introducing new products
- when placing existing products into new markets
- during periods of rising costs of production
- when competitors change their price structure
- when competitors change *other* elements in their marketing mix (eg improving quality or adding features without increasing prices)
- when balancing prices between individual products in a product line.

17. When a new product is introduced, such as a video-cassette recorder or a home computer, the price tends to be high on account of the initial development and marketing costs. This sort of product tends to be directed, initially, to higher-income groups or specialist-interest groups. As the product begins to attract increasing sales, and initial costs begin to be covered, then prices can be reduced and production volume stepped up. However, it is also possible to introduce a product with a very low price in order to obtain a foothold in a new market, or an increased share of an existing market. A bargain price may well attract considerable sales and at the same time discourage competitors. The cheap trans-Atlantic air travel pioneered by Laker Airways is an example of this kind of market penetration. The danger is, of course, that the price may be so low that the business fails to generate sufficient revenue to cover its operating and/or capital costs.

18. Few products stand still in terms of their costs. Labour costs increase from year to year; materials costs and energy costs may be subject to less regular, but sharper, increases; interest rates may be extremely variable, and hence the cost of financing products fluctuates. Many costs can be offset by productivity savings. Therefore, the costs which are the most crucial are those which represent sudden and massive increases, which cannot be absorbed by improving productivity. In this situation price increases are practically inevitable, and the question is 'by how much should we increase them?'. In certain situations, it may be possible to gain a temporary advantage over competitors by raising prices by the lowest possible margin, and offering some other advantage such as improved after-sales service or credit terms. Examples of this kind of approach are common in the motor car retail trade in times of low demand, when one-year warranties are extended to two years, and interest-free credit may be offered for a limited period.

19. The activities of competitors have an important bearing on pricing decisions. The most obvious example is when a competitor raises or lowers his prices. If your product can offer no particular advantages over his, then if he drops his price, you will have to follow suit. If, on the other hand, you can offer other advantages in your marketing mix, there may be no pressure at all to reduce your price. If a competitor raises his price, perhaps because of rising costs, it may be possible to hold yours steady, provided you can contain your own rising costs. Pricing is a very flexible element in the marketing mix and enables firms to react swiftly to competitive behaviour.

20. Competitors may throw out a challenge by improving the product and offering a better distribution service, for example. This kind of behaviour, too, can be countered by price changes – in this case by easing prices and/or improving credit terms. Much will depend on the sensitivity of the market to price changes. If price is the dominant issue for buyers, then they will prefer lower price to slightly higher quality or improved distribution arrangements. If price is not the major factor in the buyer's analysis, then marginal extra quality and delivery terms may prove the more attractive.

21. Finally, price is important in determining the relative standing of one product or product line vis-à-vis another within the product mix. This issue applies particularly in highly differentiated products in the consumer area. It is important, for example, that a motor car manufacturer establishes appropriate differentials between different models within a product-line, eg between 1600cc and 2 litre models, between 2-door and 4-door versions, and between these and estate car versions. If 1600cc models are selling well but 2 litre models are not, it may be in the seller's interests to reduce the differential so as to attract more buyers to the 2 litre models. Otherwise a reasonable differential will be expected in order to justify the enhanced engine rating of the larger model.

22. The concept of a loss leader is often applied to internal price-differentials. This means that one product in a line is reduced to below-cost levels with the aim of attracting attention to the product line or range as a whole. So, for example, a new fibre-tipped pen, in a range of such pens offered by a newcomer to the market, may be sold at a loss in order to draw attention to the range as a whole, and to establish a share of the total market. Loss leaders naturally represent very good value for money to the buyer, and can be a very useful way of establishing a range in the marketplace.

CHAPTER 33

The Marketing Mix: Promotion

Introduction

1. Every product needs to be promoted, that is to say it needs to be drawn to the attention of the marketplace, and its benefits identified. The principal methods of promotion are: advertising, personal selling, sales promotion and publicity. It is in these areas that Marketing departments come into their own. They provide the bulk of the expertise, and carry the biggest amount of responsibility, in respect of these aspects of the marketing mix. Each of these methods will be looked at shortly.

2.   The aim of an organisation's promotional strategy is to bring existing or potential customers from a state of relative unawareness of the organisation's products, to a state of actively adopting them. Several different stages of customer behaviour have been identified. These have been described in several different ways, but in summary can be stated as follows:

- Stage 1   Unawareness of product

- Stage 2   Awareness of product

- Stage 3   Interest in product

- Stage 4   Desire for product

- Stage 5   Conviction about value of product

- Stage 6   Adoption/Purchase of product.

3.   The four different methods of promotion mentioned above are applied, where appropriate, to each of the stages of customer behaviour. Advertising and publicity have the broadest applications, since they can affect every stage. Personal selling and sales promotion activities, by contrast, tend to be more effective from Stage 3 onwards.

4.   Before describing each of the methods in greater detail, one further point can be made about them as a whole. This is that they have a different emphasis according to whether they are being applied to consumer markets or industrial markets. For example, whilst advertising is very important in reaching out to consumer markets, it is of relatively little significance to industrial markets, where personal selling is the most popular method. Publicity and sales promotion activities appear to rank equally between both types of market.

Advertising

5.   Advertising is the process of communicating persuasive information about a product to target markets by means of the written and spoken word, and by visual material. By definition the process excludes personal selling. There are five principal media of advertising, as follows:

- the press – newspapers, magazines, journals etc

- commercial television

- direct mail

- commercial radio

- outdoor – hoardings, transport advertisements etc.

To this list can be added advertising via Internet service providers and the World Wide Web.

6.   By far the most important medium, in terms of total expenditure on advertising and sales promotion, is the press. In Britain this has averaged about 70% in recent years. The second most important medium is commercial television, which has consistently maintained about 25% of the total.

7.   Whatever the medium a number of questions must be decided about an organisation's advertising effort. These are basically as follows:

- How much should be spent on advertising?

- What message do we want to put across?

- What are the best media for our purposes?

- When should we time our advertisements?

- How can we monitor advertising effectiveness?

Advertising Expenditure

8.   Decisions about advertising expenditure will usually be made in conjunction with assessments about the position of the product in its life cycle. If the product is at the introductory stage, a considerable amount of resources will be put into advertising. Conversely, if the product is in decline little or no expenditure on advertising will be permitted. If the product is at the saturation stage, advertising may well be used to score points off the competition, eg 'our vehicle does more miles per gallon than theirs, (naming specific competing models).

9.   There are various options open to an organisation in deciding how much to spend on advertising its products. It could decide to adopt a 'percentage-of-sales' approach, where advertising expenditure is related to sales revenue. This has the advantage of relating expenditure to sales, but it discourages innovative approaches to advertising expenditure and does not allow for distinctions to be made between products or sales territories. It is a relatively crude way of allocating such expenditure.

10.   Another approach to advertising expenditure is to base it on what the competition is spending. Organisations such as Media Expenditure and Advertising Ltd. in the UK provide regular information on media expenditure for subscribers, and other sources provide information on other key facts such as competitors' market share. The important point to note about this approach is that it is vital to compare like with like, otherwise the value of the exercise is rather wasted.

11.   The sales-task approach to advertising expenditure can be particularly useful in situations where it is possible to state clearly defined objectives for advertising, eg 'to increase awareness of product X in Y market from present levels to (say) 70%.' This approach has the merit of allocating advertising expenditure to specific targets, but relies heavily on the organisation's ability to define its objectives realistically.

The Advertising Message

12.   Probably the most important aspect of any advertising campaign is the decision about *what* to say to prospective customers, and *how* to say it. This is the message which aims to make people aware of the product and favourably inclined towards it. Advertising copy (ie the text) also aims to make people desire the product. The entire process is the fundamental one of turning customer needs into customer wants.

13.   Advertising aims to achieve on or more of the following:

- increase customer familiarity with a product (or variations of it, eg brand, product range etc)

- inform customers about specific features of a product

- inform customers about the key benefits of a product

- indicate distinctive features and/or benefits of a product (implicitly or explicitly by comparison with competing product).

- establish the credibility of a product

- encourage potential customers to buy the product

- maintain loyalty of existing customers.

In setting out to achieve such aims, an advertiser usually has to abide by a number of laws and codes of practice. Most countries exert some degree of State control over the content and form of advertising. Issues such as obscenity, blasphemy, racial prejudice and sheer misrepresentation figure high on the list of proscriptions.

14. The content of an advertisement should not, therefore, contain anything offensive to particular groups in society; nor should it contain information or suggestions which are misleading. Most advertisements tend to select one or two features of their products for treatment and aim to sell the benefits of these. In some cases, no specific product is mentioned, but a key aspect of the organisation's marketing policy is referred to, eg 'We'll Take More Care of You ...' or 'Shop at X, where the customer comes first ...' One way of drawing attention to a firm, or a brand, in general terms is to develop a symbol, or logo, by which everyone can recognise it. Well-known logos in the UK include those for ICI, Philips, and Lloyds Bank (firms) and for Guinness, Anchor Butter and Birds Eye (specific products or brands).

15. What is the best way of putting a message across? This is an important question at this stage. The content and the form of the advertisement have been dealt with, and now the key point is to get the message over to the customers. The choice of media depends on the organisation's requirements in terms of:

- the extent of coverage sought to reach customers
- the frequency of exposure to the message
- the effectiveness of the advertisement, ie is it making a relevant impact?
- the timing of the advertisement
- the costs involved.

16. If wide coverage is sought (eg for a new Do-it-Yourself product or a new consumer banking service), then a television advertisement put out at a peak viewing time would be the most effective. However, cost would preclude very frequent advertising via this particular medium, so for frequency of exposure it would be preferable to consider hoardings and transport advertisements (eg as with the famous Guinness advertisements). For effectiveness, then, magazines and journals tend to reach the most relevant markets, provided they are selected carefully in the first place. For example, advertisements for camping enthusiasts will tend to produce better results in camping magazines than in national newspapers or magazines aimed at other interest groups, such as collectors of antique furniture. One of the problems with magazine advertisements, however, is their relatively long lead-time before an advertisement appears. Newspapers are better media on this score. Direct mail scores high on relevance, ie it can be directed very specifically at certain markets, but because of the personnel costs, it can be expensive. In the final analysis, organisations have to weigh up the anticipated benefits of particular media against the costs involved. This brings us on to the question of how do organisations assess the effectiveness of their advertising?

Advertising Effectiveness

17. There are two main ways of looking at the question of advertising effectiveness – the first is to consider the results of the advertising in achieving target improvements in specific tasks, eg increasing brand awareness in a specific market; the second is to consider the impact of advertising on sales generally. It is extremely difficult to assess the impact of advertising on sales as a whole, because so many other factors, internal and external, are at work in the marketing process of an organisation. It is easier to assess the impact of specific advertising campaigns on sales in specific product areas.

18. The evaluation aspect of advertising is an element of marketing which is remarkably short of measurement devices. The limited aids that are available are as follows:

- Television audience measurement figures
- Information on the circulation figures for printed media

- Information concerning the readership of newspapers and periodicals
- Information on specific campaigns obtained by interviews and/or questionnaires.

The value of the first three items is restricted to quantifying or qualifying the market. They do not provide information about the effects of advertising, but point the way to relevant markets. The final item offers more genuine guidance about the effects of advertising. After a new series of newspaper advertisements, for example, a firm can test a sample of the readership to ascertain how many readers noticed the advertisement, how many recalled what it said and how many had actually bought the product since reading it.

19. Like any other aspect of management, if marketing activities can be made measurable, then it is much easier to assess their effectiveness in achieving their objectives. If they cannot be measured with any degree of objectivity, then effectiveness can only be judged in an incomplete way. At present the assessment of advertising effectiveness falls into the latter category.

Personal Selling

20. However vivid the message put over by advertising, there is no substitute for the final face-to-face meeting between the buyer and the seller or his representative. Advertising creates the interest and the desire, but personal selling clinches the deal. In industrial markets, as was noted earlier, personal selling plays an even more extensive role. For the moment, let us consider the basic sales process. This is generally understood to encompass five immediate aims, plus a follow-up, as shown in Figure 33.1.

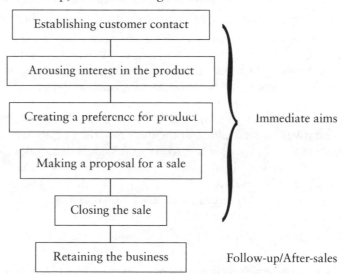

Figure 33.1 Personal selling

21. So far as *consumer* markets, and especially mass markets, are concerned, advertising must play a vital role in the first three stages of the process. After that, advertising becomes rapidly less important, and personal selling takes over. By comparison, advertising plays a much less important role in *industrial* markets, where even the first stage is dominated by personal selling.

22. Personal selling is the most expensive form of promotion. This is reflected in the marketing statistics, which show, for example, that in the United States in 1976 about $100 billion were spent on personal selling compared with $33 billion on advertising. Such

personal selling ranges from the mere taking of an order in a shop or a sales office, to the creation of new sales in a highly competitive market. Companies which utilise an aggressive sales policy, based on personal selling, are said to be adopting a *push* strategy. By comparison firms which rely more heavily on advertising are described as adopting a *pull* strategy.

23. The tasks of a sales representative, except in the routine order-taking role, include other duties than making sales. These other duties can comprise:

- after-sales servicing (dealing with technical queries, delivery matters etc)
- gathering information (feedback on customer reactions, competitors' activities etc)
- communicating regular information to customers and prospective buyers (new catalogues etc)
- prospecting (looking out for new selling opportunities).

24. In order to fulfil these duties a sales representative needs to have relevant information about:

- his or her own organisation (Customer policies, resources available, organisation structure etc)
- the products on offer (goods, services, ranges etc)
- sales and profit targets
- customers (size, type, location etc)
- sales plan for his/her territory
- promotional material (brochures, catalogues etc)
- techniques of selling (creating interest, dealing with objections, closing a sale etc).

25. Whilst many organisations still see the prime role of the sales representative as that of generating sales, there is an increasing trend which sees the representative in a wider marketing role, which emphasises the profit responsibility of the position. If sales are pursued regardless of costs, other factors, such as reputation and the value of the sales volume obtained, can be severely reduced, eg if costs have been excessive and/or the organisation's image has been tarnished by over-zealous representatives. If, on the other hand, representatives are trained to put themselves in their customers' shoes, ie develop a market-oriented approach, they are less likely to put immediate sales gains before the prospect of much larger market opportunities in the future. This, of course, assumes that they are rewarded on this basis as well. In a sales-oriented approach the sales representative is focusing on his or her needs as a seller. By comparison, a market-oriented approach to selling concentrates on the needs of the buyer.

26. In organising their sales force, organisations usually have three basic options open to them:

- they can organise their representatives on a geographical, or territory, basis
- they can organise on a product basis (eg where high technology products are involved)
- they can organise on a customer basis.

The most frequent option is the first one, sometimes with one of the others. A *territory* is normally allocated on the basis of workload and/or potential sales. The aim is to ensure a fair balance of work and earnings potential amongst the representatives. The use of territories helps to reduce the costs of travel, accommodation and related expenses, and also eases some of the administrative burdens of controlling the sales force.

Where the *product* provides the basis for allocating work, there are advantages in having specialist sales representatives who can deal with technical as well as general queries (eg as in computer sales). The main disadvantage is that there is a possibility, with large customers in particular, that several different representatives from the organisation will each be calling on the same customer. This increases sales costs considerably, and may possibly outweigh the advantage of specialist representation.

Sales forces organised on a *customer* basis have the advantage of a thorough knowledge of their customers' needs and sales records. They are thus in a good position to forecast potential needs as well. The drawback, as in the case of product centred sales forces, is that of overlapping – in this case an overlapping of sales journeys. Here again organisations have to weigh up the relative gains of this approach against the extra costs. One way of achieving economy here is to adopt a programme of telemarketing, ie using the telephone to sell direct to customers. This kind of service is becoming increasingly popular and can be provided over 24 hours a day, 7 days a week.

27. The effectiveness of sales representatives can be measured in a number of different ways. Typical evaluation criteria include:

- Net sales achieved (per product, per customer etc)
- Call rate (number of calls in a given period)
- Value of sales per call
- Number of new sales/new customers (compared with colleagues or with last year's figures)
- Sales expenses in proportion to sales achieved.

In the total marketing effort of the organisation, there are, of course, other activities than sales, and the performance of the sales force cannot be taken in isolation. As was noted at the beginning of this chapter, personal selling is *one* part of the promotional activities of the organisation, which brings us on to a consideration of the next item: sales promotion activities.

Sales Promotion

28. Sales promotion activities are a form of indirect advertising designed to stimulate sales mainly by the use of incentives. Sales promotion is sometimes called 'below-the-line advertising' in contrast with above-the-line expenditure which is handled by an external advertising agency. Sales promotion activities are organised and funded by the organisation's own resources. They can take a number of different forms, as, for example:

- Free samples
- Twin-pack bargains (two for the price of one) ⎫ Promotions directed
- Temporary price reductions ⎬ at consumers
- Point-of-sale demonstrations ⎭

- Special discounts
- Cooperative advertising ⎫ Promotions directed
- Bonus/prizes for sales representatives ⎬ at trade customers
- Provision of display material ⎭

29. Reference was made earlier to 'push' and 'pull' strategies. Sales promotion falls into the first category. It aims to push sales by offering various incentives at, or associated with, the point-of-sale. Its use is most frequent in the field of consumer products.

The objectives of a *promotion directed at consumers* could be to:

- draw attention to a new product or line

- encourage sales of slow-moving items

- stimulate off-peak sales of selected items

- achieve higher levels of customer acceptance/usage of a product or product-line.

  Objectives for a *trade-oriented promotion* could be to:

- encourage dealer/retailer cooperation in pushing particular lines

- persuade dealers/retailers to devote increased shelf space to organisation's products

- develop goodwill of dealers/retailers.

30. The evaluation of a sales promotion is never a clear-cut matter, mainly on account of other variables in the overall marketing mix. The most popular method of evaluation is to measure sales and/or market share before, during and after the promotion period. The ideal result is one which shows a significant increase during the promotion, and a sustained, if somewhat smaller increase *after* the promotion. Other methods of evaluation could include interviewing a sample of consumers in the target market (eg to check if they had seen the promotion, changed their buying habits etc), and checking on dealers' stock levels, shelf space etc.

Publicity

31. Publicity differs from the other promotional devices mentioned in this chapter in that it often does not cost the organisation any money! Publicity is news about the organisation or its products reported in the press and other media without charge to the organisation. Of course, although the publicity itself may be free, there are obvious costs in setting up a publicity programme, but, pound for pound, these are considerably lower than for advertising, for example. Publicity usually comes under the heading of public relations, which is concerned with the mutual understanding between an organisation and its public. In recent years several European football clubs have experienced acute problems of crowd behaviour at matches. One way of reassuring the thousands of well-behaved fans, who might well be turned away for ever, is to back up disciplinary action with a publicity campaign aimed at showing the better side of club football. Such a campaign could include articles and press releases about improvements in accommodation, the development of the Supporters Club and other club matters. It could also involve talks to youth groups and others by both players and staff.

32. Sponsorship events in the arts and sports are becoming an increasingly popular form of publicity. Concerts, both live and recorded, have been promoted jointly by the musical interests concerned and by industrial and commercial interests. Athletics meetings, tennis tournaments and horse races have all been the subject of sponsorship. Again, although the publicity itself is free, the costs of sponsorship are not. Nevertheless, such activities can contribute significantly to an organisation's public image. Organisations which are selling products that are the target of health or conservationist lobbies are often to be found sponsoring activities such as sporting events and animal welfare campaigns.

33. A final method of obtaining publicity, and one of the most costly, is by donating substantial sums of money towards an academic or research institution. In some cases the organisation's name is included in the title of the project or position etc (eg as in the XYZ Chair of Industrial Relations at X University).

Thus patronage of sports, the arts and learning are all useful means of gaining publicity in a manner which casts a favourable light on the organisation, and, ultimately, on its products.

CHAPTER 34

The Marketing Mix: Distribution

Introduction

1. Having looked at three major elements in the marketing mix – product, price and promotion – we can now turn to the fourth, and last, element: distribution. As the Institute of Marketing definition said earlier, one of the key functions of marketing is 'moving the product or service to the final consumer…'. This is the purpose of distribution.

2. Distribution is primarily concerned with (a) channels of distribution, and (b) physical distribution. We shall look at these in turn, commencing with channels of distribution. These channels are the marketing institutions which facilitate the movement of goods and services from their point of production to their point of consumption. Some channels are direct, as when a computer firm sells its products direct to the users. Others, the majority, are indirect. This means that there are a number of intermediaries between original producer and eventual buyer, as in the case of the box of foreign-made chocolates bought at a local retailer.

3. The choice of channels utilised by a producer is determined ultimately by the customer, and in recent years there has been a trend towards shorter channels, as customers, especially in consumer markets, realise that there are price advantages to be gained when middlemen, or retailers, are by-passed in the chain of distribution. Thus direct mail, cash and carry, and 'pick your own' (fruit, vegetables etc) operations are increasing in response to consumer interest in this approach.

4. What are the most common channels of distribution, and what role is played by the various intermediaries in them? Figure 34.1 illustrates the channel options, which are now described in greater detail.

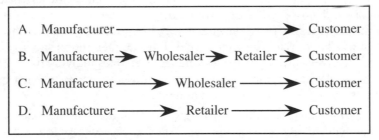

Figure 34.1. The most common channels of distribution.

5. Channel A represents a direct marketing channel. This is to be found more in industrial markets than in consumer markets. Manufacturers of goods such as machine tools, computers, ships and other large or expensive items tend to move them direct to the buyer without involving middlemen or intermediaries. However, this practice is becoming more frequent in consumer markets as well. For example, in mail order operations and in door-to-door selling (eg cosmetics, household wares and double glazing). The reasons for direct channels are basically as follows:

- **Industrial markets** – Relatively small number of customers; need for technical advice and support after the sale; possible lengthy negotiations on price between manufacturer and customer; dialogue required where product is to be custom built.

- **Consumer markets** – Lower costs incurred in moving product to consumer can lead to lower prices in comparison with other channels; manufacturers can exercise greater control over their sales effort when not relying on middlemen. Computer-based ordering and supply systems have had a major impact on telemarketing, which is now a major channel for many consumer goods from clothes to microcomputers.

6. Channel B represents the typical chain for mass-marketed consumer goods. Manufacturers selling a wide range of products over a wide geographical area to a market numbered in millions would find it prohibitively expensive to set up their own Highstreet stores, even if they were permitted to proliferate in this way. For such manufacturers (eg of foodstuffs, confectionery, footwear, clothing and soaps, to name but a few), middlemen are important links in the chain. Wholesalers, for example, buy in bulk from the manufacturers, store the goods, break them down into smaller quantities, undertake advertising and promotional activities, deliver to other traders, usually retailers, and arrange credit and other services for them. Their role is important to both manufacturer and retailer. The role of the latter is to make products available at the point-of-sale. Individual consumers need accessibility and convenience from their local sources of consumable products. They also need to see what is available, and what alternatives are offered. A retail store, whether owned by an independent trader or a huge supermarket chain, offers various advantages to consumers: stocks of items, displays of goods, opportunity to buy in *small* quantities, and convenient access to these services. So far as manufacturers and wholesalers are concerned the retailer is, above all, an outlet for their products, and an important source of market intelligence concerning customer buying habits and preferences.

7. Channel C represents one of the shorter indirect channels, where the retailer is omitted. This kind of operation can be found in mail-order businesses, and in cash-and-carry outlets. The former are usually composed of the larger mail-order firms, offering a very wide range of goods (and some services, too). They buy from manufacturers, store and subsequently distribute direct to customers on a nationwide basis. Their ability to attract custom in the first place relies heavily on (a) comprehensive, colourful and well-produced catalogues, and (b) the use of part-time agents, usually housewives, working on a commission basis. Whilst such an operation does not generally offer any price advantage over a retail business, it is a very convenient way of choosing goods and there is always extended credit available. With the wider use of Internet facilities in the home, mail-order can be pursued electronically. So-called 'e-commerce' enables individuals to buy goods on-line (e.g. books, weekend shopping), and to access services such as Internet banking. This form of distribution channel has enormous potential.

8. Cash-and-carry outlets usually deal in groceries, and many are open only to trade customers. They tend to rely on a rapid turnover of stock, to keep down inventory levels. Their main advantages for buyers are (a) price, which is significantly lower than in a retail operation, and (b) the opportunity to buy small bulk quantities. Unlike mail-order businesses, they serve relatively local and specialised markets.

9. Channel D is another version of a shorter, indirect channel. In this case, it is the wholesaler who is removed from the scene. Not surprisingly, the retailers who dominate this channel are powerful chains or multiples in their own right. Some such retailers, as in the footwear trade, concentrate on one range of goods only. They buy in bulk from manufacturers and importers, and distribute direct to their retail outlets. They usually offer a wide selection of lines, and are very competitively priced. Other large retail groups handle a diversity of goods, which are again competitively priced, and made available in prime shopping areas. The Woolworths chain was a pioneer in this field. Other examples include

Marks and Spencer, and British Home Stores, two chains which based themselves originally on the clothing trade, but which between them have diversified into footwear, foodstuffs, toys and books, amongst other items. One of the important features of chains such as Marks and Spencer is their use of private (ie own-name) branding, which is either used exclusively or at least predominantly. Other chains, such as Boots, supply a wide range of other brands in addition to their own. Invariably, the own-brand range is offered at lower prices than the competing brands. This is an advantage to the consumer, but not necessarily to the manufacturer, who may well have made both!

Market Segmentation

10. The above reference to large and powerful retail chains implies that they can exert a strong influence in the marketplace. This influence works in two directions:

- it enables them to demand standards of quality, and ranges of goods which fit into *their* market strategy, rather than accepting what the manufacturer might prefer;
- it enables them to cultivate a particular part, or segment, of a market. Some footwear chains are exclusively geared to meeting the demands of fashion conscious teenagers, for example. Others are aimed mainly at a middle-aged market, where comfort and quality are more important than the current fashion. In both examples, a conscious attempt has been made to segment the market.

11. The term 'market segmentation' is based on the concept that most, if not all, markets are made up of different types of customers, ie within each total market there exist sub-markets which express distinctive product preferences compared with each other. Market segmentation, therefore, can be defined as the sub-division of a market into identifiable buyer-groups, or sub-markets, with the aim of reaching such groups with a particular marketing mix. To take an example: in the private motor car market as a whole there are several different sub-markets, ranging from buyers who are looking for sports cars, through those interested in family saloons and estate cars to those requiring a small, economical second car. A manufacturer may decide to attempt to meet the needs of the entire market or may decide to specialise in, say, sports cars. Either way such a manufacturer and his distributors have to vary their marketing mix, if they are to attract the 'right' kind of customer. The product offered, the price range, the manner of promotion and the distribution arrangements must all be considered carefully in the light of the differing requirements of the different market segments.

12. Market segmentation is especially important in consumer markets, where the numbers of potential buyers can be measured in millions. The most frequent methods of segmenting a market are based on geographical, demographic and buyer-behaviour variables, as indicated in Figure 34.2.

13. Geographical variables, such as regions and populations, may be of the utmost significance to suppliers of such goods as delicatessen foods or skiing equipment, for example. Such goods are attractive to specialised segments of the markets for food and sports equipment, respectively. Attempts to achieve sales without segmenting these markets would result in a great deal of wasted effort. Large retail chains are usually only prepared to locate stores in areas of high population density, in order to gain the economies of scale that large local markets can stimulate. This is the result of a conscious decision to segment their markets in this way.

14. Demographic segmentation involves the sub-division of markets on the basis of variables such as age, sex, occupation and class, for example. Magazines and journals are

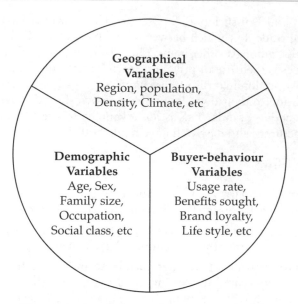

Figure 34.2. Market segmentation variables.

examples of products which are directed towards carefully segmented markets (readership). In addition to the basic reading material, the advertising contained in each edition reflects the segmentation. For example, a magazine aimed at mothers with young children will carry articles of interest to such mothers, and advertisements inserted by suppliers of mother-and-baby products. Age is a powerful basis for segmentation (a) because of the physical changes brought about by growth and ageing, and (b) because of frequently differing attitudes and preferences between age groups. In retail operations, particular stores or chains will focus on particular segments of the market (eg Mothercare), whilst others will aim to attract a wide range of customers into their shops, but will organise their shelf-displays to cater for segment needs. Thus W.H. Smith's shops offer a wide range of magazines, books and records as well as fairly standard ranges of stationery and similar items, in order to meet the needs of a wide range of tastes from a variety of ages and social classes.

15. Segmentation by social class is aided, in Britain, by the use of a social grading structure based on the occupation of the head of each household. The grades used are shown in Figure 34.3.

16. Whilst social class is a demographic factor, it is also a prime determinant of buyer-behaviour variables, since class background influences tastes, values and attitudes. For example, in beer advertisements there is a strong appeal to working class loyalty, often to particular, local brews. By comparison, pre-Christmas television advertisements for liqueurs are openly aimed at those who are, or would like to be, middle and upper middle class. These appeals to distinctive class values are not hit-and-miss affairs, but are based on careful research into class preferences for particular goods and services.

17. An important variable in buyer behaviour is usage rate. Some buyers are very light users of a product, whereas others use the same product frequently. For example, there are regular readers of a particular Sunday newspaper, and these represent the core of its readership, but there are also occasional and casual readers, who may buy because of its coverage of particular events. Taking usage rate as a variable essentially means segmenting on the basis of volume purchased. If a supplier decides to increase his market share by

Social Grade	Social Status	Occupation (Head of Household)
A	Upper Middle Class	Higher Managerial, administrative or professional
B	Middle Class	Intermediate Managerial, administrative or professional
C1	Lower Middle Class	Supervisory, clerical or junior managerial etc
C2	Skilled Working Class	Skilled manual workers
D	Working Class	Semi-skilled or unskilled manual workers
E	Subsistence Levels	Pensioners or widows on basic pension; casual and lowest paid workers

Figure 34.3. Social class grading structure: UK.

attracting higher usage by occasional users, he must first attempt to find out whether they buy competitors' goods or not, or where there is something about the present marketing mix which dissuades them from buying more frequently. Train operating companies, for example, conduct surveys amongst the travelling public to enquire why they do not make more use of trains. Clearly, the family motorcar is the biggest competitor for seats on a journey, and price is probably the biggest disadvantage of rail travel. Therefore, to increase the usage rate for non-business travellers, some special price arrangements are needed to encourage people to leave their cars at home and travel by train instead. The companies offer a wide range of economy fares for off-peak periods as a result of such surveys. The usage rate is an important aspect of marketing because of the high level of fixed costs involved in operating a railway network.

18. The approaches to market segmentation referred to above apply more naturally to consumer markets than to industrial markets, where an entire market may be made up of just a few customers. Industrial segmentation usually takes place on one or more of the following bases:

• Type of buyer – Government, public service, private firm etc.

• Customer size – Large, medium or small.

• Class of buyer – Insists on quality or economy or service, for example.

• Trade group – Standard Industrial Classification entry.

• End-use – Routine/non-routine, specialised/general etc.

• Usage rate – Regular or infrequent buyer.

• Location – Domestic or overseas, regional/national etc.

19. Industrial segmentation occurs when a microcomputer business applies differing marketing mixes to two markets, one of small private businesses, and the other of State secondary schools. The first market may be offered complete packages of equipment, including a printer and additional storage units in addition to the central processor and visual display unit. The package will be offered at a competitive rate in the medium price range for such a product. A regular follow-up servicing arrangement will be included as well as full training manuals. By comparison, the second market will be offered a cheaper price for a less comprehensive service. Instead of packages, it is more likely that options based on a central processor and visual display unit will be offered, to enable buyers to

spend more on input and output devices rather than on storage and printing facilities. A key consideration in this example is the end-use to which the customer wishes to put the product. In the case of a small private business, the use is primarily aimed at invoicing, accounting and stock control activities. The school's use is primarily aimed at familiarisation training for pupils.

20. The principal benefits of market segmentation from the point of view of sellers are that:

❶ they have a better idea of the total market picture, especially in relation to marketing opportunities between segments of that market,

❷ they can tailor their marketing mix to suit the needs of particular segments,

❸ by gaining familiarity with one or more segments, they are more likely to be able to assess the response from them, which is an invaluable asset for planning purposes.

21. The main benefit from the point of view of customers is that they are likely to have their needs met in a more appropriate way than if the market is not segmented, ie where the same product range and price are offered regardless of geographical, demographic and buyer-behaviour considerations.

Physical Distribution

22. Whereas channels of distribution are marketing *institutions*, physical distribution is a *set of activities*. The former provide the managerial and administrative framework for moving products from supplier to customer. The latter provide the physical means of so doing. Physical distribution is concerned with order processing, warehousing, transport, packaging, stock/inventory levels and customer service. In recent years a number of attempts to integrate and coordinate these functions has come to be called Physical Distribution Management. This aims to integrate the activities of marketing, production and other departments in this aspect of the organisation's marketing task.

23. The degree of attention paid to physical distribution depends considerably on the proportion of total costs taken up by distribution costs. If the product is a high-quality, high-cost item, then distribution costs will probably represent a small proportion of total costs of manufacturing and marketing it, and so physical distribution may be considered very much a secondary issue. Where the product is offered at a very competitive price, and hence where profit margins may be tight, all overhead costs will be carefully examined. In this situation distribution costs will form an important issue for the supplier. An important feature of such costs is that they tend to increase rather than decrease with sales volume. Whereas unit production costs tend to benefit from increased volume of production, distribution costs tend to worsen. A high level of customer service also tends to greatly increase distribution costs. For example, if a customer requires 100% delivery from stock within two days, this means carrying extra stock levels as a buffer against any shortfall in supplies to the warehouse. If that customer could be persuaded to reduce his requirements to, say, 80% delivery within two days, this might effect useful savings in distribution costs.

CHAPTER 35

Marketing Research

Introduction

1.   Marketing research is fundamentally about the acquisition and analysis of information required for the making of marketing decisions. The two basic areas in which the information is sought are (a) markets (existing and potential), and (b) marketing tactics and methods. The former is oriented towards what is happening *outside* the organisation, in the marketplace. The second is oriented towards the way in which the organisation is responding *internally* to its customers, present and future.

2.   There is an increasing need for marketing information, because of three important trends in marketing. These are:

❶   the shift from purely local to wider national and international markets,

❷   the changing emphasis from buyer needs to buyer wants,

❸   the trend towards competition based on non-price weapons.

The implications of these points are that wider markets are not as familiar to suppliers as local markets, and they must therefore seek out sources of information about distant markets. The move away from relatively predictable needs towards much less predictable wants requires much more research into buyer behaviour. The trend towards non-price competition requires firms to evaluate their own methods of assembling the marketing mix for their markets. Ought a better after-sales service be offered to hold off competitors? How effective are our advertising campaigns compared with our competitors? Should we put more effort into sales promotions? These are examples of the kind of questions which firms have to face. In order to answer them they need marketing research.

3.   The data which forms the raw material of marketing research can be placed under two categories: primary and secondary. *Primary data* is gathered directly from the persons concerned, be they customers, wholesalers, or even competitors, for example. Such data is usually collected by means of surveys and other formalised methods. *Secondary data* is information available from published sources externally, and from company records. The use of secondary material is cheaper than developing primary data, but may be less relevant or up-to-date.

4.   Kotler (1996)[1] distinguishes between market intelligence and market research. The former he refers to as the everyday information about developments in the market. The gathering of such information is reactive and managers cannot always wait for information to arrive in bits and pieces (p.114). Marketing research, by comparison, is a planned approach to information gathering.

5.   A marketing research study usually includes the following steps:

❶   Definition of problem and specification of information to be sought

❷   Design of study/project, with particular reference to data collection methods (surveys etc), instrumentation (questionnaires etc) and sample design (of target population)

❸   Field work (utilising questionnaires, structured interviews, consumer panels)

❹   Data analysis (using statistical and OR techniques)

❺ Presentation of report.

6. As was noted earlier, marketing operates on the *external* boundaries of the organisation. Its main object of attention is the customer (or marketplace), and it is the customer's response, or non-response, that gives rise to most of the problems which marketing research is applied to. A typical problem could be that of a falling market share for one or more of the organisation's product lines. In order to clarify the problem, and put it into perspective, a number of questions need to be asked. For example, 'Is the market expanding, declining or stable?'; 'What is the situation for competitors?'; 'Is the threat from UK competitors, or from overseas?'; 'What advantages, if any, are enjoyed by competitive products?'; 'What is the organisation's reputation with its existing customers?'; and so on. Some of these questions can be answered by analysing secondary data and others by analysing primary data.

7. Sources of secondary data are twofold: firstly, internal information from sales budgets, field sales reports and others; and secondly, external information from Government statistics, trade, banking and other reports, the press and marketing research agencies. The last-mentioned – marketing research agencies – play a significant role in the whole area of marketing research. They are employed not only by firms with no market research specialists of their own, but also by firms with large market research departments. Some agencies offer a comprehensive marketing research service, some offer a range of specialised services and others offer what is basically an information-selling service. Some well-known agencies include A.C. Nielsen, which provides regular data on sales, brand shares and prices etc in the retail trade, Gallup, which specialises in opinion research, and AGB (Audits of Great Britain), which is heavily involved in television audience measurement. Television and readership surveys in Britain are conducted under the umbrella of two national bodies – JICTAR (Joint Industry Committee for Television Advertising Research), which meters a representative sample of television sets throughout the nation, and JICNARS (Joint Industry Committee for National Readership Surveys), which conducts, and reports on, 30,000 interviews annually, covering over 100 different publications.

8. Primary data is most frequently collected by means of surveys, based on questionnaires or interviews. These surveys are invariably undertaken by specialist research organisations, since the construction and administration of questionnaires is a highly-skilled operation. Interviews are generally conducted in a structured form, so as to ensure consistency between interviewers. The agencies use trained interviewers, briefed about the objectives of each assignment. Both the questionnaires and the structured interviews tend to concentrate on *what* the customer likes and dislikes, rather than *why*. This last question is handled by means of a number of behavioural techniques, which form part of what has been called motivational research. The techniques include in-depth, and less-structured, interviews, discussion groups, role-playing and psychological tests. Motivation research is one of the newer aspects of marketing research, and since it concentrates on motives and attitudes, it relies heavily on the expertise of psychologists for the design of and interpretation of its surveys.

9. Some of the more important advantages and disadvantages of the three approaches described are highlighted in the table on the opposite page.

10. Some or all of the above approaches may be applied to consumer panels, which are permanent groups representing a cross-section of a particular market. These panels are used by individual companies and by specialised agencies, such as A.C. Nielsen. They receive regular samples of different products and lines, about which they complete questionnaires, diaries and similar records. They are usually well-disposed towards researchers

		Advantages	Disadvantages
❶	Questionnaires	Wide coverage. Low cost.	Difficult to construct. Low return rate.
❷	Structured Interviews	More flexible than questionnaires. Product etc can be shown to consumer. Target population can be controlled.	Costly and time-consuming. Permits interviewer and consumer bias.
❸	Motivational Research	Better understanding of consumer decisions.	Is only applied to small groups. Costly and time-consuming. Not easy to interpret results.

and are good subjects for interview as well as questionnaires. The main advantage of panels is that they provide feedback over a period of time, which increases the reliability of their responses compared with people who may have been stopped for a brief interview outside their local supermarket, for example. The main disadvantage is that panels tend to be influenced in their buying behaviour by the role they are playing in consumer research. On balance, the advantages to be gained from panels outweigh the disadvantages.

11. So far we have been concerned mainly with the *market* research aspects of marketing research. The other prime interest of marketing research, as was noted in paragraph 1 in this chapter, is the way in which the organisation responds to the demands of the market-place. The most important method of evaluating the organisation's total marketing effort is by employing a marketing audit. This is an independent examination of an organisation's marketing objectives, marketing activities and marketing environment, with the primary aims of assessing present effectiveness and of recommending future action. The audit needs to be carried out on a periodic rather than on an ad hoc basis, and, like any other rational evaluation, needs to be conducted in a systematic way. The audit may be carried out by the organisation's own staff or by external consultants. The requirements of the task call for objectivity, independence and suitable experience. Many firms feel that these requirements can best be found in external rather than internal sources.

12. A systematic audit would encompass the following aspects of the organisation's marketing system:

❶	The Marketing Environment	Economic and demographic trends Technological change Legal developments Social change Markets, Customers, Competitors, Suppliers, Middlemen, etc
❷	Marketing Strategy	Corporate objectives Marketing objectives Marketing plan (strategy) Marketing resources Strengths and weaknesses
❸	Marketing Plans and Control	Sales forecasting Market plans

		Product development
		Control procedures
		Marketing research
④	Marketing Mix	Evaluation of products, pricing policies, advertising and sales promotion, channels of distribution and sales force
⑤	Profitability and Cost-effectiveness	Profitability of products and markets
		Marketing costs
⑥	The Marketing Organisation	Management structure
		Staff motivation
		Efficiency
		Training
		Relationships with other departments

13. The advantage of such an audit lies in its ability to produce a critical assessment of the organisation's marketing strengths and weaknesses, whilst at the same time weighing up the threats and opportunities posed by the external environment. This critical assessment is valuable to the organisation's corporate planning process as well as to its marketing planning. The main disadvantages are those of time and cost. It takes a considerable amount of time to conduct an audit covering the points mentioned above, and this time is expensive in labour costs.

Reference

1. Kotler, P. & Armstrong, G. (1996), *Principles of Marketing*, (7th edition), Prentice-Hall.

CHAPTER 36

Marketing Organisation

Introduction

1. As was noted in Chapter 31, there are several ways of looking at marketing. Some organisations see it as an extension of their production process, others as the means by which their product or service is brought to the attention of the marketplace. Yet other organisations see marketing as essentially a selling activity, and finally, there are those who see marketing as an activity which begins and ends with the customer. Naturally, the particular group of values which are held will determine whether the organisation will have a marketing department at all, and, if it does have one, what kind of department it will be.

2. This chapter assumes that the organisation sees some definite role for a marketing department, even if it is not a *comprehensive* marketing role. The next few paragraphs outline (a) the major structural alternatives that are available to a marketing department, (b) the principal objectives of a marketing department, and (c) the differing perspectives between the marketing department and other departments in the organisation.

Marketing Structures

3.   Marketing grew out of sales activities. It eventually absorbed these activities into its own growth and development. This radical change of role for marketing led to a major change of organisation structure, at least for those organisations that adopted the marketing concept.

4.   The early process of change is as shown in Figures 36.1–36.4.

Figure 36. 1 – Stage one.

At this stage there is no specific marketing section or department. The Sales Manager is responsible for advertising and promotion as well as selling.

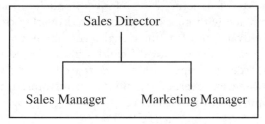

Figure 36.2 – Stage two.

Stage two introduces the first formal recognition of marketing as such, but places the marketing manager under the direction of the Sales Director. At this stage marketing is seen as an important provider of information to support the organisation's sales effort. The marketing section will probably be concerned with advertising, sales promotion, product development and marketing research.

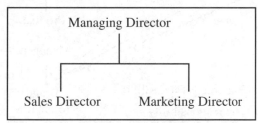

Figure 36.3 – Stage three.

By Stage three, marketing has moved up to a position of equality with sales. This situation probably produces the maximum amount of conflict between sales and marketing, as the former concentrate on their preoccupation with current sales and the latter concentrate on long-term market developments. Since marketing will see the sales effort as part of the total marketing mix, there will be a strong desire to tell sales what to do and why! The resolution of this built-in conflict has been achieved, in many companies, by giving predominance to marketing, as shown in Figure 36.4.

5.   Stage four presents a functional view of the marketing department. The separate specialisms of sales, research and advertising/promotions each have their own manager.

Figure 36.4 – Stage four.

This is a common form of structure for a marketing department. Organisations frequently add other specialist sections, such as customer services and product development. The main advantage of this type of structure is its relative simplicity, whereby identifiable divisions of labour can be made without causing unwanted overlap or competition between sections. The main disadvantage of a functional structure is its inability to cope with multiple products or markets, because of difficulties in allocating priorities amongst the specialist sections. In order to cope with the increased diversity of decision-making required in these circumstances, several companies have introduced a matrix-type of structure, incorporating a number of operational roles, as in Figure 36.5.

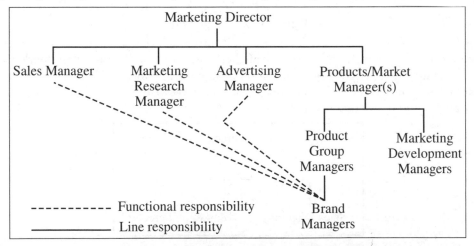

Figure 36.5. – Matrix organisation in marketing.

This structure allocates specific responsibility for individual products/product groups and for specific markets, whilst retaining all the key functional posts. As in every matrix structure, the operational roles have reporting responsibilities to functional managers as well as to their immediate line managers. So, for example, a Brand Manager's freedom to act is not only prescribed by his immediate Product Group Manager, but also by any one of the functional managers, in respect of his own speciality. Thus, advertising programmes for a brand would have to be agreed not only by the Product Group Manager, but also by the Advertising Manager.

6.   In very large organisations, where a divisionalised structure may have developed

because of product or geographical reasons, for example, a decision has to be made about splitting the marketing activities between the divisions and corporate headquarters. Here the underlying values of the organisation's top management come into operation. If the philosophy is to decentralise, in the way described in Chapter 22, that is to say by effectively delegating authority to the sub-units, then it is likely that little or no role will be available for a corporate marketing department. If, however, divisionalisation is seen as a way of delegating part, but only part, of the organisation's marketing effort, then a definite marketing role at corporate level will be established. A corporate role could just be confined to the provision of specialist services, such as marketing research and specialist advertising advice. Alternatively, there could be a strong corporate role, giving the staff concerned the right to direct key functional aspects of marketing in the divisions, eg in terms of product design, corporate image, and marketing control information systems.

The Marketing Department in the Organisation

7.   The question of conflict within the marketing function has already been touched on. We can now turn to the possible conflicts that can occur between the marketing department and other departments. In any organisation it is natural for each sub-division to have its own perspective concerning the ultimate goals of the organisation, and the best way of achieving them. The degree of conflict which may occur depends largely on the way in which departmental or functional objectives have been drawn up, and whether suitable conflict-resolution mechanisms exist (eg regular meetings between common interest groups, inter-departmental committees etc). Also, in the context of marketing vis-à-vis the others, a vital element is the extent to which the organisation as a whole is committed to the marketing concept. Obviously, where the marketing concept prevails, the likelihood of serious conflict is reduced, and vice versa.

8.   Before considering the points of possible friction between the marketing department and others, it will be useful to reflect on the objectives of the former. If we assume that the marketing concept is upheld in a particular organisation, then the key objectives of its marketing department could be as follows:

> 'To contribute to the organisation's corporate aims in respect of profitability, growth and social responsibility by
> a. Proposing, and seeking acceptance for, improvements in the organisation's marketing policies;
> b. Seeking out and identifying advantageous marketing opportunities;
> c. Preparing, in conjunction with other departments, suitable marketing strategies to meet opportunities identified;
> d. Selling and distributing the organisation's products;
> e. Developing new products in the marketplace;
> f. Designing and implementing approved marketing plans;
> g. Acquiring sufficient and suitable information, both internal and external, concerning the organisation's products, and their impact on customers, competitors, suppliers and others in the marketplace;
> h. Ensuring that the organisation's products are brought to the attention of existing and potential customers by means of suitable advertising and promotional methods;
> i. Promoting a reputable image for the organisation in the marketplace.'

9.   The opening sentence of the above list of objectives was included advisedly to indicate the contributive nature of the marketing department's efforts to corporate aims. Other departments, too, make their contribution to these overall aims. If the organisation's

strategy has been worked out in a thorough and collaborative way, there should exist a mutual understanding of roles as between departments. This will affect the manner in which problems of misunderstanding and conflict are handled. However, there is no practical way in which it is possible to *avoid* all such misunderstandings and conflict. Even within the marketing department, there are potential conflicts. For example, the conflicts between current sales effort and market development and between short-term profits and long-term growth.

10. There are similar tensions between short- and long-term gains in other departments, and, of course, between departments. Some of the most important sources of friction between the marketing department and other departments are as indicated below.

	Marketing Preoccupations	Others' Preoccupations
	Production	
a.	Short production runs	Long production runs
	Wide variety of models	Small range
	Tailor-made orders	Standardisation
	Purchasing	
b.	Broad product line	Narrow product line
	Ample stocks	Tight stocks
	Quality of stock	Price of stock
	R & D	
c.	Applied research	Pure research
	Sales benefits	Functional features
	Finance	
d.	Flexible budgets	Tight budgets
	Pricing to promote market development	Pricing to cover costs
	Easy credit terms	Tough credit terms

11. The overall conclusion to be drawn from the above list is that the marketing department, in particular, disturbs the routines that other departments like to set for themselves in order to achieve efficiency in their own organisation. This happens because marketing personnel are more concerned with what the customer desires, rather than whether it is practicable to give him what he desires. Marketing's task is to define the customer's needs and wants, but it is up to the other departments to convert those needs and wants into practical reality. In a truly market-oriented organisation there will be a greater willingness to respond positively to the varied demands of marketing than in an organisation whose orientation lies elsewhere, in production, for example.

CHAPTER 37

Customer Services and Consumer Protection

Introduction

1.   Commercial organisations spend a great deal of effort on assessing the needs and wants of their customers, and yet, as we saw in Chapter 31, there is a variety of possible orientations towards customers. Not all firms are 'market oriented' to the extent that they put the customers' needs and wants before all else. Even if firms were completely market oriented, they would still make errors of judgement from time to time. Therefore, even in the best-regulated circles, the customer may sometimes be badly treated. Over recent years consumers have become more vocal in reacting to shoddy products or poor service. As a result there are now Government, as well as private consumer, organisations whose purpose is to stand up for consumers' rights. The word 'consumerism' has been coined to describe the activities of pressure groups in this area, and the term 'consumer protection' used to describe the efforts made by Government and other bodies to provide rules and codes of conduct for relations between commercial organisations, public services and customers or users.

2.   A consumer may be defined as 'any person (including a corporate body) who buys goods and services for money.' A 'user' is used here to describe someone who uses a public service of some kind (eg a national health service). In the United Kingdom, there are several means by which consumer interests may be protected. These involve the application of one or more of the following:

* The Common Law
* Acts of Parliament
* Codes of 'Good Practice' or various Charters
* Trade Marks
* Independent Consumer Groups.

Each of these will be looked at briefly in this chapter, which will also examine some of the leading public and private pressure groups which help ordinary citizens to obtain redress against unfair trading in goods and services.

Common Law Rights

3.   Common law rights are acquired as a result of custom and practice over many years. In consumer matters these rights have not stood the test of time, and in modern economic conditions, Britain and other Western nations have had to introduce numerous statutory regulations to clarify and indeed strengthen the rights of individual consumers. However, there are still general rules which apply to those who provide goods and services to the community. For example, a person offering a service must carry it out in a proper and workmanlike way, or to a standard agreed with the customer. Providers also have a duty of care in relation to any property (eg motor vehicle, television set etc) which a customer leaves with them.

Statutory Rights

4.   By far the greatest protection for consumers in Britain is provided by parliament, which in several important pieces of legislation has set up a framework in which the respective rights and duties of consumers and suppliers can be identified and clarified.

The most important statutes concerning consumer affairs include the following:

- Sale of Goods Act, 1979
- Trade Descriptions Act, 1968
- Consumer Safety Act, 1978
- Consumer Credit Act, 1974
- Unfair Contract Terms Act, 1977
- Fair Trading Act, 1973
- Supply of Goods and Services Act, 1982

The key features of these Acts will be described briefly below.

5.   So far as the sales of goods are concerned, the current law is consolidated in the *Sale of Goods Act, 1979*. This emphasises that goods must fulfil three basic conditions:

❶   they must be of merchantable quality

❷   they must be fit for the purpose and

❸   they must be as described.

An example of how these conditions might be broken is as follows.

A person buys a new washing machine, and is unfortunate enough to discover that (a) the cabinet is badly scratched, and thus not of merchantable quality; (b) the machine ripped up the first batch of clothes and half-flooded the kitchen (ie it was not fit for the purpose); and (c) the model delivered by the suppliers was not the model agreed upon in the shop (ie the goods were not as described by the retailer). The remedies available to the consumer depend on the circumstances of the breach. For example, in the case of situation (b) above, there would be a right to a complete refund of the price paid together with compensation for loss and damage caused. In the case of (a) it is likely that the retailer would replace the machine, but his obligation would only be to offer a discount on the price in view of the damaged surface. In the case of (c), the customer is entitled to his money back. Note that suppliers are not obliged to offer anything more than cash compensation.

6.   The Sale of Goods Act, 1979, also contains provisions preventing consumers' rights from being eroded by exclusion clauses and special guarantees.

7.   Protection against being misled by false or inaccurate descriptions of goods on sale is provided by the *Trade Descriptions Act, 1968*. This Act has been used successfully by motorists, who have discovered that they had been deceived about the previous mileage covered by a second-hand car. The winding-back of car mileometers is a contravention of this Act. In such a case the dealer can be prosecuted and fined.

8.   The consumer's physical safety is considered in the *Consumer Safety Act, 1978*, which draws up regulations to minimise risks to consumers from potentially dangerous products, such as oil heaters, electric blankets and certain children's toys.

9.   Moneylenders have abounded in every society, and in recent years have achieved great importance in developed economies because of the stimulus that their services have given to trade. However, it has become increasingly important, too, that borrowers should not be exploited unknowingly. In Britain the *Consumer Credit Act, 1974*, requires that

borrowers should know the true rate of interest being charged, and, where an agreement is signed away from trade premises, the person is entitled to change his mind. There are also conditions preventing consumers from being unfairly penalised, if they get into arrears. The Act affects all transactions between £50 and £15000.

10. Another protection for consumers in their dealings with commercial organisations is provided by the *Unfair Contract Terms Act, 1977,* which protects individuals against possible loss of rights from exclusion clauses and disclaimer notices on posters, tickets etc. Under the Act a contractor cannot 'contract out' of his liability for death or personal injury arising from his negligence, for example by supplying a vehicle with faulty brakes. Nor can he supply goods or services in a substantially different way from those ordered, for example by providing a 1Mb microcomputer when a 10Mb version was what the customer ordered. The Act also stipulates that a *manufacturer's* guarantee cannot exclude liability for damage caused or loss suffered as a result of the manufacturer's negligence. Disclaimer notices, such as 'Articles left at owner's risk ... etc' are not valid unless the firm concerned can show in court that they were reasonable in the circumstances, and in any case would not protect the firm against any claim arising out of the negligence in respect of the articles.

11. One of the growing practices in modern legislation is to set up supervisory bodies, or 'watchdogs', to monitor the effects of the law in society. In the consumer rights arena the central watchdog is provided by the Office of Fair Trading, set up by the *Fair Trading Act, 1973*, to encourage voluntary codes of practice between sellers and their customers, and to provide a central reference point for doubtful cases and matters of principle. Currently codes of practice have been established in trades such as:

- motorcar servicing
- laundry services
- electrical repair work
- package holidays
- funeral services.

12. The Fair Trading Act, 1973, also set up the Monopolies and Mergers Commission to:

- investigate and report on references that relate to the existence of a monopoly situation, ie where 25% of a particular market is supplied by one supplier or supply group;
- investigate mergers between business organisations. The intention of these investigations is to ascertain if there could be any adverse effect on the public interest as a result of a particular monopoly or merger situation. Adverse effects could include: a restricted choice of products/services, and a lack of responsiveness to consumer pressure.

13. The *Supply of Goods and Services Act, 1982,* was introduced to improve the consumers' rights in relation to poor service or workmanship. The Act was needed to make up for the shortcomings of the Sale of Goods Act, 1979, which applied only to the transfer of goods from a seller to a buyer and not to a situation where goods were being provided as part of a service, such as building work and car repairs, for example. The new Act adopts a similar approach to the Sale of Goods Act in respect of description, merchantable quality and fitness for purpose of goods, but applies it to:

- contracts for work and materials
- part-exchange contracts (barter)
- 'free gifts'

- contracts for the hire of goods.

The new Act also codifies the Common Law requirements relating to three key aspects of service, ie skill, time and price. The Act requires suppliers of services to act with reasonable care and skill, and to complete the work within a reasonable time. The purchaser is required to pay a reasonable price for the service. The Act also tightens up the application of the Unfair Contract Terms Act, 1977, in respect of services and disclaimer clauses.

Codes of Practice and Charters

14. The Fair Trading Act, 1973, requires the Director General of Fair Trading to encourage trade associations to draw up codes of practice for fair trading. Codes do not have the force of law in their own right, but are nevertheless very influential when a court is determining the rights and wrongs of a situation. Codes are less formal, more easily amended and less time-consuming to operate than legal provisions. Codes of practice have been developed by associations such as the Association of British Travel Agents, the Motor Agents Association and the Mail Order Traders' Association.

15. Since advertising and promotion play such a significant part in the marketing of consumer goods, it is not surprising that consumer protection applies to these activities. The *Trade Descriptions Act, 1968*, has already been mentioned, but there are two very important voluntary bodies operating in this field – the *Advertising Standards Authority* and the *Independent Broadcasting Authority*.

16. The *Advertising Standards Authority* embraces press, poster, cinema advertising and direct mail. It has developed the *British Code of Advertising Practice* whose intentions are primarily to ensure that:

- advertisements are legal, decent, honest and truthful
- advertisements are prepared with a sense of responsibility to the consumer
- advertising conforms to the principle of fair competition
- advertisers do not bring the advertising industry into disrepute.

17. An example of how the industry maintains its standards can be seen in the treatment of a complaint against a Japanese motor manufacturer by a member of the public (ASA Case Report 119, 1985). In this case the advertisement said 'Let us lead you into temptation' and described one of its models as having 'A decidedly illegal top speed.' The complainant considered that the advertisement was likely to encourage drivers to drive in excess of the legal speed limit. The complaint was upheld, and the advertisement was withdrawn.

18. Advertisements on commercial radio and television are controlled by the Independent Broadcasting Authority, which has produced a code of practice for advertisers to ensure, so far as possible, the legality, truthfulness and reputation of broadcast advertising.

19. Recently in the UK, the Government has extended the concept of codes of practice to public services in the form of various public charters, such as the Patients' Charter and the Taxpayers' Charter.

Other Standards

20. Probably the most well-known body in Britain for establishing voluntary standards of quality and reliability is the *British Standards Institution*, whose famous Kitemark indicates that goods conform to the high standards set by the Institution. The BSI is an inde-

pendent non-profit making body incorporated by Royal Charter in 1929. Its principal objectives include the promotion of health and safety, the protection of the environment and the establishment of quality standards. Domestic examples of items for which British Standards are available include pushchairs, cots and motor cycle crash helmets.

21. Another body somewhat similar to the BSI is the *Design Council*, set up in 1944 to improve design standards in a wide range of manufactured goods. The Council tests products to see if, in their opinion, they are well-designed, well-made and of practical value. In suitable cases they award their distinctive triangular logo as a mark of their approval. By their work they are promoting the idea that goods should be of merchantable quality and fit for their purpose.

Trade Marks

22. Trade marks were originally established to protect manufacturers' products from being 'pirated' by their rivals. Once certain marks became well known, they also provided an advantage to consumers, who were able to associate particular trade marks with a particular quality goods. Famous trade marks include Coca-Cola, Guinness, Sellotape, IBM and WordStar. Persons buying products bearing those names are entitled to expect the particular standards associated with them.

Manufacturers' Liability

23. In England and Wales, a manufacturer has a common law duty of care to ensure that his products do not cause injury or damage to a person or to his property. Note that this duty does not extend to the *quality or performance* of the goods, but only to their causing injury or damage. In such a case, it is up to the complainant to show that the damage or injury was due to the manufacturer's negligence.

24. Statutory duties are imposed on manufacturers by the *Health and Safety at Work etc Act, 1974*. This Act, amongst other duties, requires designers, manufacturers and importers to ensure, so far as practicable, that any article is safe when properly used.

Independent Pressure Groups

25. There are a number of independent pressure groups in the United Kingdom working directly on behalf of consumers. These include:

- The Citizens' Advice Bureaux (including C.A.B. Consumer Advice Centres). These provide free advice for local citizens on a wide range of matters, including consumer affairs.
- The Consumers' Association. This body carries out independent tests on a wide variety of consumer goods and services. The results are published in a monthly magazine ('Which?').
- National Viewers' and Listeners' Association. This organisation monitors radio and television programmes with the aim of persuading programme planners to avoid excessive violence, sex and other issues which could be distasteful to family viewers.

Publicly-appointed Consumer Groups

26. Publicly appointed bodies representing consumers' interests are considerably more numerous than private groups. Local authorities have established services such as Trading

Standards Departments and Consumer Advice Centres, for example. There are also several bodies established by statute to represent the views of users of public services. Examples of such groups include:

- The Post Office Users Council
- The Transport Users' Consultative Committee
- Electricity Consultative Council
- Regional Gas Consumers' Councils
- National Consumer Council.

These Councils are composed of representatives from various user-groups, including local authorities, Citizens Advice Bureaux, welfare groups etc. They are independent of the industry concerned.

Questions for Discussion/Homework

1. What are the implications for a business organisation of adopting the marketing concept?

2 In what ways can marketing departments differ from other departments in terms of key objectives, main activities and system of values?

3. 'Promotion and Distribution are very much the second class members of the marketing mix.' Discuss this view of their role in the mix.

4. How true is it to say that customers look for benefits, not for features, when considering a product? Discuss in relation to some popular consumer item.

5. What advice would you give a manufacturer of robots concerning the promotion of his products in Britain?

6. How would you distinguish between 'push' and 'pull' strategies in selling?

7. Why do so many suppliers of goods and services still rely on the services of middlemen? What factors do you think could change their reliance on such services?

8. Discuss the impact on marketing of the growing use of the Internet to supply goods and services to customers (e-commerce).

9. What is 'consumerism', what forms can it take, and how can marketing managers and public service managers respond to it?

10. In what ways might the following seek to segment their markets:
   a. a manufacturer of beers and lagers.
   b. an estate agent in a suburban area.

11. Is marketing research a luxury? Discuss.

12. How might an organisation divide up the responsibility for marketing activities between its sub-divisions and head office?

Examination Questions

Most of the questions selected below are taken from the examinations of bodies other than the Institute of Marketing. In most cases, therefore, what is required is a good general grasp of the topic. Detailed answers, showing an in-depth knowledge of the subject-matter, would not normally be expected. Outline answers are supplied in Appendix 2.

EQ 28 'Without adopting the marketing concept a company cannot possibly hope to develop future plans.' Discuss this statement from the point of view of a manufacturer of capital goods.

(ICMA OMM)

EQ 29 In the concept of the 'marketing mix' what is meant by the term 'below-the-line' activities? Discuss the range of objectives likely to be set in using such activities.

(ICMA OMM)

EQ 30 What is the importance of the concept of the 'product cycle' for business planning and budgeting?

(ACCA Business Management)

EQ 31 In the development of new products, the marketing, design and manufacturing departments have a contribution to make. Discuss the areas of potential conflict between these departments, in finalising new product design, and suggest ways in which these conflicts might be resolved.

(IOM Business Organisation)

The production function of an organisation exists in order to make available the goods or services required by the customer. Production management, in particular, is concerned with the provision of goods. It is the central part of the manufacturing process. Its responsibility is to plan, resource and control the processes involved in converting raw materials and components into the finished goods required to satisfy the needs and wants of the organisation's existing and potential customers.

In a market-oriented organisation, production begins with the customer in the marketplace. An idea for a new product is generated, or assessed in marketing terms, by the market research section. If the idea seems viable, it will be turned over to the Research and Development (R&D) section, where any necessary research, design and development work can be carried out. The next stage forward is for early prototypes to be produced. If the prototypes are satisfactory, then the pre-production stage can commence. This stage aims to simulate, as far as possible, the actual conditions on the production line. Thus at this stage the customer's needs are being set against the cost of materials and labour, the manufacturing capacity of the production department, and issues such as quality levels. In the case of a firm manufacturing industrial goods, it is likely that at this stage, if not earlier, samples of the new product will be sent to the customer for testing and approval. If the pre-production runs have been successful, then the product can move forward again, this time to the manufacturing stage.

There are several key elements in the production process, and this section looks at those that are the most relevant for business and management students. Chapter 38 sets out the main features of a production planning and control system, Chapter 39 briefly outlines the principal methods of production available to organisations, Chapter 40 examines some of the leading aids to production, such as Work Study, whilst Chapter 41 summarises key aspects of new technology in manufacturing.

CHAPTER 38

Production Planning and Control

Introduction

1.   Modern production processes are complex and costly. Machines, computers, materials of all kinds, and labour all have to be blended together to enable the production system to carry out its operations in a cost-effective way. Thus production processes require careful planning and controlling.

Production Organisation

2.   Before we proceed further, it is helpful to consider the likely organisation structure of the production function in a manufacturing organisation. The organisation chart in Figure

38.1 illustrates the principal divisions of labour within the function and provides an example of the structural relationships between the different departments or subunits.

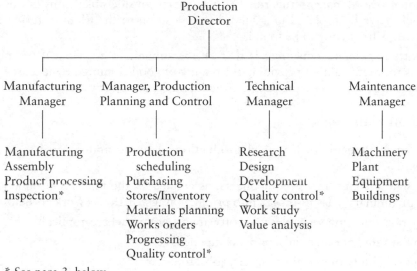

* See para 3. below

Figure 38.1 Organisation of the production function – manufacturing industry.

3.   The organisation chart in Figure 38.1 represents just one of several ways in which production could be organised. Much depends on the type of production, the relative standing of groups such as Quality Control, Purchasing and Maintenance, and the extent to which sophisticated computerised systems are in operation. In the example shown, Quality Control is shared among three subunits: Manufacturing (as Shopfloor Inspection), Production Planning & Control (as Quality Control of processes, materials and purchased items), and Production Engineering (responsible for quality of design and with overall responsibility for Quality Control standards in production).

4.   In the example given, the production function has been divided into four subunits or departments. There could have been a greater degree of specialisation, but this has been avoided here in order to emphasise the collaborative nature of many of the specialisms to be found in production. Brief observations that can be made about the four subunit management positions are as follows:

*   Manufacturing Manager – this person is responsible for the manufacturing and assembly processes, together with their associated product processes (heat treatment, painting etc); this work is carried out in accordance with Works Orders and schedules submitted by Production Planning & Control; inspection has been included here, although it could have been located separately to provide an independent inspection service; the Manufacturing Manager has a heavy responsibility for the recruitment, training, rewarding and retention of employees.

*   Manager, Production Planning and Control – this role is responsible for providing the framework and the impetus for production; the main activities of the role are described in the following chapter on this topic.

*   Technical Manager or Production Engineer – the latter title is the more popular of the two, in practice, although the former is probably a better description of the role. The role is the first major link between Marketing and Production, being involved at the earliest possible stages of transforming customer needs and wants into practical possi-

bilities. This role is particularly important in the development and application of computers in the production process.

- Maintenance Manager – this role has been given considerable status in this example; it could have been placed in a subordinate position to the Manufacturing Manager, where it is frequently to be found.

The important point to remember is that all the subunits are needed if the production function is to meet is aim of providing the quality of goods required by its customers, and to do so in a way that meets the profit, growth and other objectives of the organisation.

Production Planning

5. The basic elements of a typical production planning and control system can be summarised as follows:

- Translate the customer's requirements, as defined by the final pre-production design and preliminary sales forecasts, into production instructions (Works orders)
- Prepare production schedules and software programs (where applicable)
- Plan the supply of materials, parts, components etc
- Plan availability of machines, specify jobs, tools etc
- Allocate people/work-teams
- Set production and quality targets
- Maintain stock and purchasing records
- Progress orders throughout the factory
- Liaise with the marketing department
- Raise final production documents (delivery notes, invoices etc).

6. There are several important points arising from the above summary of a production planning and control system:

- The plans referred to are short-term plans for periods of from one week to one month. At the start of a new production process, these plans may be altered at frequent intervals.

- Production schedules are basically timetables, usually of a detailed nature. They specify the timetabled requirements for precise operations and jobs, and set out the sequence of priorities, including the setting up of appropriate software programs. The major aims of scheduling are to ensure, so far as possible, that the work is completed on time and within budgeted costs. Wide use is made of Gantt charts (see Chapter 3 para. 27 above) in production scheduling. These are particularly useful for the scheduling of relatively straightforward, routine projects.

- Plans for machines include the availability, capacity and loading of machines. Capacity and loading may vary considerably between different types and models of machines, and these facts have to be taken into account in planning the overall production effort. Carefully planned loading can reduce idle time and highlight machine utilisation. JIT – Just-in-Time – systems (see below) are increasingly being adopted in manufacturing.

- Labour requirements are a vital part of the production process. As well as detailing the numbers and types of employees required, there are questions of pay and incentives to be agreed before production commences. If new machines or new processes are to be employed, it will also be necessary to organise training in machine operations and safety.

- All plans should set targets. In this case targets, based on sales forecasts, will be set in collaboration with marketing or sales staff, as representatives of the customer, and will take into account considerations such as planned maintenance, product quality control and machine breakdowns.

- The progressing of orders through the production process is essentially a monitoring and reporting task, which also involves some 'chasing-up' of progress in situations where orders have fallen behind schedule. The main job of a progress chaser is to watch out for, and report, any deviations from schedule, and provide help in sorting out delays in production.

- Liaison with the marketing department is important to ensure that the productive effort is meeting the customer's needs, or where there are difficulties in production, ensuring that the customer is informed and/or is prepared to accept a slightly different standard or quality of product, for example.

- Finally, the outputs of the production system need to be accounted for, invoiced and delivered (to the customer or into stock). Thus the final step is to ensure that the appropriate paperwork is available and correctly completed. Many modern systems are facilitated by tailor-made software programs, designed to record and track items in progress, and enabling the appropriate staff member to match up customers' invoices with the progress of goods through the system, and to despatch the paperwork on their being supplied.

7. The process which has just been described is clearly a very complex affair, but most of the decisions involved in it are programmable types of decisions. It is possible, therefore, to apply the considerable power of a computer to the process. Computers have the ability to undertake masses of calculations very rapidly, they can perform a number of separate operations at one and the same time, and have the ability to store massive amounts of information.

8. The use of computers in production is extending all the time, as fully-automated plants and robots can bear witness. However, in a more conventional way, computers can be employed to store and develop works orders, schedules, machine loading, stock levels, progress documents and many other related examples of production information. The prime benefits of computer applications in these circumstances are:

- effective control over the processes concerned;
- the ability to adapt quickly to avoid difficulties;
- the ability to take advantage of opportunities arising from the speed and accuracy of feedback information received from the computer;
- the ability to coordinate all the various phases of production, including inventory control and customer documentation.

Purchasing (Procurement)

9. Purchasing is an important aspect of production management. Purchasing costs, for example, often represent a substantial part of the total costs of production. At a time of extreme competitiveness in the marketplace, an efficient and cost-effective purchasing section can make all the difference between a competitively priced product and one that is comparatively more expensive. The purchasing section, or department, usually maintains

close links with other units in the production function in addition, of course, to its links with external suppliers of goods and services.

10. The primary responsibility of the purchasing/procurement department is to secure sufficient and suitable raw materials, components, other goods, and services to ensure that the manufacturing process is fully supplied with all its materials, and to achieve this responsibility in a cost-effective manner. To this end the purchasing department can usually be expected to be responsible for the following:

- Appraisal and selection of suppliers.

- Collation of up-to-date information on suppliers, prices, distribution methods etc.

- Negotiating the purchase of goods and services at prices which represent the best value to the business in the long-term (ie not necessarily the lowest prices at a given time).

- Ensuring that suppliers are familiar with, and adhere to, relevant quality standards operated by the company.

- Maintenance of adequate stock/inventory levels.

- Establishing and maintaining effective working relationships with relevant departments (Production, Marketing and Finance).

- Developing effective links with existing suppliers, and maintaining good relationships with potential suppliers.

11. The above description clearly denotes an extremely important function. Purchasing ought not to be seen as mainly a question of routine paperwork. Purchasing decisions can sometimes be quite risky, and can involve an organisation in carrying considerable costs. It has been estimated that a 5% excess in purchasing costs can lead to a 25% reduction in profits. By contrast, a small saving in purchasing costs can be worth considerably more in terms of equivalent sales value.

12. The Purchasing Manager in charge of a purchasing department exercises his responsibilities in close collaboration with other colleagues. For example, most purchasing decisions can only be taken after due agreement with financial, production or marketing colleagues. Where the Purchasing Manager's particular expertise comes into its own is in the presentation and evaluation of purchasing alternatives, or in the assessment of whether to make or buy a particular product or component. It is in these discussions that the knowledge of materials, their quality, prices, availability etc enables the Purchasing Manager to contribute significantly to the ultimate decision to buy, or not to buy.

13. If a decision is made to proceed with a purchase, then the sequence of events could follow these lines:

1. Purchasing receives a requisition from an appropriate authority.

2. Purchasing approaches a selected supplier to negotiate quantity, quality, price and delivery of goods.

3. The next stage will be to seek an alternative supplier if a satisfactory agreement cannot be reached, or to place an order with the supplier. This could be a one-off, or spot, order, or a contract order over a period of time.

4. Purchasing maintains records of orders made, orders fulfilled, delivery dates, invoices etc.

5. Purchasing arranges for the originating requisition to be met, either directly from the supplier or via stores, and amends its stock or delivery records as appropriate.

14. In the purchase of material goods, issues of quantity, quality, price and delivery are crucial in several respects. These could be described as the key elements of the '**purchasing mix**'. The negotiating skills required of those in the purchasing function are likely to be crucial elements in a company's ability to produce quality goods at a competitive price.

The 'Purchasing Mix' – Quantity

15. The quantity of goods to be ordered, and the time at which they need to be ordered, are major considerations. On the one hand insufficient quantities at a particular point in time will cause costly delays in production. On the other hand, the larger the quantity ordered, the more will have to go into stock as temporarily idle resources, also a costly business. The ideal to be aimed at is to find the optimum way of balancing the costs of insufficient stock against the costs of holding stock (eg tied-up capital, storage space, insurance costs, damage, deterioration etc). Techniques have been devised by Operational Research scientists to enable organisations to work out the Economic Order Quantity (EOQ) for individual stock items, and to aid them in setting optimum re-order levels (ie the levels at which stock needs to be replaced). In some cases, the decision about quantity (and indeed time) may be dictated by considerations of future supply, particularly where these may be threatened by economic or political pressures. Decisions may also be influenced by favourable trends in short-term prices.

The 'Purchasing Mix' – Quality

16. The quality of the goods purchased needs to be suitable (a) for the manufacturing process, and (b) for the customer's wants. In seeking decisions about quality, the purchasing department have to work closely with both production and marketing staff to arrive at a suitable compromise. Inspection of goods received is vital to check that the supplier is fulfilling the order to the correct specification.

The 'Purchasing Mix' – Price

17. Purchasing should ideally aim for a price which gives the best value to the organisation, taking quality, delivery and relative urgency into account. This may not always be the lowest price available, but the one which represents the best value over a period of time.

The 'Purchasing Mix' – Delivery

18. One of the factors which needs to be considered by the purchasing department in the appraisal and selection of suppliers is the reliability of deliveries. The lead time between an order and a delivery is an important aspect of stock control. Where lead times are certain, they can be allowed for in stock calculations. Where they are uncertain, it makes stock control much more difficult. Not only is stock affected by the delivery situation, so is production. The latter is particularly vulnerable to delays in deliveries for items which are used continuously, and for which minimum buffer stocks are held. Buffer stocks are reserve stocks held for emergency shortages.

19. Several aspects of stock control have already been mentioned above, and these can be drawn together in a simplified graph of stock levels. Such graphs have a typically saw-tooth pattern, reflecting the **outputs** (usage) and the **inputs** (deliveries) to stock, as in Figure 38.2.

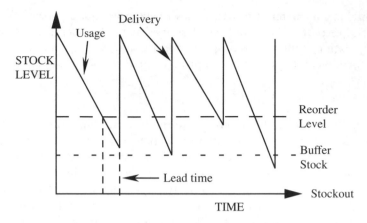

Figure 38.2 Simple stock control graph.

Figure 38.2 indicates how usage reduces stocks over a period of time, and invariably absorbs some of the buffer stock unless planned deliveries are made on time. The lead time, as shown, is the time taken between the order being made and delivery taking place. As soon as the delivery is made stocks shoot up again, until further usage reduces them, and this produces the saw-tooth effect on the graph. Should planned deliveries not take place, and should usage continue, then eventually a 'stockout' situation will be reached, where, in the short-term, the goods in question will be out-of-stock.

Material Requirements Planning (MRP)

20. MRP is an internal production process designed to ensure that materials (ie raw materials, components, sub-assemblies and parts) are available when required. The process is closely linked both to production planning and purchasing, which provide the context for MRP decisions. The starting point for MRP is the master schedule of production plans from which the process works backwards to develop both a timetable for deliveries and an optimum quantity of the required materials. By adopting MRP manufacturing plants hope to achieve a relatively low levels of stocks (inventory), a reduction in warehousing and associated costs, and a faster turnaround time for finished goods. Once set up, the process lends itself to computerisation, which in turn enables other functions such as ordering and purchasing to be linked into the system. Such a system presupposes the existence of adequate production schedules, the support of a purchasing section and agreement about the quality aspects of materials.

Just-in-time (JIT) Systems

21. JIT systems represent a good step forward from MRP, since, unlike the latter, they aim to coordinate the supply of materials so that they arrive just when they are needed – not before, not afterwards, but just in time! This approach to materials planning and inventory management has been used with great success by a number of large Japanese companies, and is increasingly being considered by a number of other manufacturing organisations. In theory, the system should lead to no stocks (buffer stocks/reserves) being held; in practice, it *minimises* them (in contrast to MRP which aims to *optimise* stock levels). An obvious example of the difference between JIT and other approaches towards stock levels can be seen in the differing requirements of steam locomotives compared with electric. The former requires to carry its own limited stocks of wood, coal and water en route; it may also

require further water as it gets further from its starting point; and it will certainly require fairly substantial stocks of wood, coal and water at one or both of its termini. By comparison, an electric train picks up its current from the overhead wires *as it needs it*. The manner in which the electric locomotive gets its power is just-in-time.

22. Like the rigorous approach to quality embodied in total quality control (see Chapter 29), JIT systems require total commitment from the workforce and its suppliers – there is no room for errors such as faulty components, delays in delivery etc. The JIT approach is based on the twin assumptions of (1) uninterrupted production flows, and (2) fully acceptable quality of materials. It works best in a stable production environment, and, of course, relies heavily on the efficiency of suppliers and their dedication to total quality. The benefits claimed for JIT systems include:

- challenges management to consider why buffer stocks are thought to be needed and thus to analyse the production process with a view to making improvements (a total quality management approach)
- reduction in manufacturing time
- increased equipment utilisation
- simplified planning and scheduling
- improved quality
- reduced scrap and wastage.

However, the system is basically inflexible, as well as rigorous. It makes considerable demands on the planners, the workforce and suppliers, and it is therefore not an easy system to introduce. Where it can be employed the results seem to be extremely successful.

Inspection

23. In addition to the purchasing and stock control aspects of production planning and control, there is the question of the control of quality. This control begins with inspection of the raw materials and other items purchased from suppliers, continues with inspection during production, and ends with a final inspection before delivery to the customer. The responsibility for checking quality on the shop-floor is usually that of the Inspection department, whose main task is to ensure adherence to the organisation's quality standard. These standards are normally set with several objectives in mind:

① to produce products which are satisfactory to the customer (quality, reliability, variety etc).

② to produce products that are consistent with the organisation's responsibility to its workforce, shareholders, and other stakeholders, (safety in the production area, ethically acceptable products etc)

③ to attain the above within agreed levels of inspection costs.

24. The costs of ensuring quality are twofold: *direct* costs, such as the wages and salaries of designers and inspectors, and *indirect* costs, such as the loss of orders, wastage and rectification costs. Some of these costs are directed towards preventing faults and errors, other are directed towards curing faults and errors.

25. In inspection there are basically three main reasons for inspecting work:

- to accept or reject items
- to control the process of producing the items
- to improve the process itself, if necessary.

There are two main methods of dealing with these issues, and these are **Process Control** and **Acceptance Sampling**, which are examples of what has been called '**Statistical Quality Control**'.

26. Process Control consists of checking items as they progress through the production process, comparing them with the relevant standards, and taking any immediate corrective action to prevent further faults. Process Control may be expedited by the use of control charts, which can show in graph form actual performance against standard performance, and the amount of any deviation. Another form of process control is automatic process control, where sensing and other measuring devices are built into the machine concerned to provide immediate information and immediate corrective action. Automatic inspection of this kind is more feasible than human inspection in cases where (a) accurate measurement is possible, (b) where continuous inspection is highly desirable and (c) where reliability of inspection is important. Objective measurement in inspection is called checking by variables, which contrasts with checking by attributes, which is a subjective method.

27. This leads us on to Acceptance Sampling. This is where the customer samples a batch of newly delivered goods, and either rejects or accepts the batch on the basis of an acceptable quality level, usually a small percentage of rejects per batch. If the number of rejects in the sample is in excess of the agreed percentage, the whole batch is returned to the supplier. The sampling may be checked by variables, or by attributes (eg 'satisfactory' or 'unsatisfactory'). The latter calls for a human judgement instead of a 'scientifically' measured fact. Human inspection is most suited to instances where (a) objective standards are not available, and (b) where discretion is required in analysing and assessing faults and errors. This approach is most likely to apply to the more complex issues of quality control, and to the improvement of processes, where machine functioning and location, materials used and other factors need to be seen in context, if changes are to be made in the process.

Maintenance

28. The role of maintenance in a production planning and control system is to so organise maintenance activities that production has the optimum availability of plant and machinery in the conduct of its operations, and that, if an unexpected breakdown occurs, it will be dealt with in the minimum possible time.

29. According to the British Standards Institution, maintenance is '*work undertaken in order to keep or restore every facility*'. There are several different kinds of maintenance, as follows:

- Preventive maintenance, which aims to prevent breakdowns.
- Corrective maintenance, to repair faults.
- Breakdown maintenance, to rectify breakdowns and prepare contingency plans for possible breakdowns (provision of important spare parts etc).
- Running maintenance, carried out whilst plant or machinery is operating.
- Shutdown maintenance, carried out when plant or machinery is taken out of service.

30. The above forms of maintenance can be combined into a planned programme of maintenance for each major piece of plant or machine. Planned maintenance means that routine servicing and overhaul arrangements are scheduled in advance and contingency plans drawn up for unexpected breakdowns. The effect of having planned maintenance is to minimise unforeseen faults or breakdowns. Thus maintenance can make an important contribution to containing machine running costs as well as ensuring optimum machine availability.

CHAPTER 39

Types of Production

Introduction

1.   The most common method of distinguishing between production systems or types of production is to separate them into the three categories of jobbing, batch and mass production. This is the approach which will be used in this short chapter. The three categories are very broad, as Joan Woodward and her researchers[1] discovered in the 1950s during their work on industrial organisation in Essex (see Chapter 10). In the Essex research, it was felt necessary to subdivide these broad categories further so as to produce eleven distinguishable categories. A comparison between the Woodward list and the three common categories will be made towards the end of this chapter.

2.   The jobbing, batch and mass production categories each have their own distinctive systems of operation, and their own problems of production planning and control. Each will be examined in turn with the aim of highlighting the most important factors.

Jobbing Production

3.   Jobbing production may also be called job production or unique production. The essential feature of jobbing production is that it produces single articles or 'one-off' items. These products may be small, tailor-made components, huge pieces of equipment or large single items, such as a ship. Most products are made for a particular customer or to a particular order. Jobbing production is to be found in industries such as heavy engineering (eg production of electricity generating plant), shipbuilding and civil engineering (eg bridge construction). It is also to be found in most other industries, where it is employed to produce prototype models, spare parts, modifications to existing plant and countless other 'one-off', tailor-made pieces. There is hardly a factory in existence which does not have a jobbing department somewhere or other.

4.   Because of the unique or individual nature of each article or item to be produced, planning is not easy in jobbing production, neither is control. Efficiency of operations has to give way to inventiveness and creativity. This can be illustrated by considering some of the key characteristics of jobbing production. These are as follows:

- A wide variety of different operations to be performed under varying circumstances, ie no standardisation.
- Varying sequences of operations, also subject to varying circumstances.
- General-purpose machinery and equipment.
- Varied work layouts, depending on process and/or operation.
- Unpredictable demands on stores.
- Workforce skilled in wide range of skills.
- Adaptable and equally skilled supervision.

Many of the above conditions make it extremely difficult to plan, integrate and control the types, sequence and timing of operations. It is difficult to avoid idle time for both men and machines. Thus the entire manufacturing process tends to be relatively expensive compared with other forms of production. Against this can be weighed the advantages of producing an article or item which is made especially to the customer's own specification.

Batch Production

5.   Batch production is the production of standardised units, or parts, in small or large lots (batches). It represents a halfway position between jobbing production and mass production, and is mostly to be found in the light engineering industry. The main distinction between batch and jobbing production lies in the standardised nature of the former. Unlike the varied operations and sequences of the unique 'one-off' products of jobbing production, the products of batch production are dealt with systematically in lots, or batches, only moving on to the next operation when each lot has been machined or processed in the current operation.

6.   Batches may be produced to order and forwarded direct to the customer, as in the production of subcomponents for another manufacturer, or they may be made for stock. One of the major problems associated with batch production is to determine the optimum size of batches, particularly where a generalised, rather than specific, demand for a product exists. If too many units are produced, stocks will lie idle or go to waste; if too few are produced, the item will go out of stock, and it may be difficult to fit in further batches in the short-term.

7.   The key characteristics of batch production are as follows:

* A standardised set of operations, carried out intermittently, as each batch moves from one operation to the next.
* General purpose machinery and plant, but grouped in batteries of the same type.
* Heavy shop-floor stores requirement.
* Narrower range of skills required.
* Emphasis on production planning and progressing.
* Relatively short production runs.

These characteristics lead to a generally well-controlled and efficient method of production, whose main disadvantage is the time-delay caused by the queuing effect of individual units waiting for the batch to be completed before moving on to the next operation. This problem can be overcome by changing to an assembly line operation which is a prominent feature of flow production, or mass production, as it is commonly called.

Mass Production

8.   Mass production dates from the time of Henry Ford, who was the first man to adopt the principle of the production line, when he used this approach to produce a restricted range of motor cars put together in a flow-line process. In a unit mass production system, a small range of products is produced in large quantities by 'flowing' uninterruptedly from one operation, or process, to the next until completion. This type of production requires careful and lengthy planning of plant and processes. The capital costs are high on account of the specialised nature of the machines required for the production line. However, once the line has been set up, control is relatively simple. Mass production systems are dependent on the high demand created by mass markets, for it is only by making the fullest use of the capital equipment involved that a manufacturing organisation can achieve its target profit levels.

9. The key features of mass production are as follows:

- Rigid product specifications, previously tested.
- Specialised machines and equipment, set out in a line formation.
- Highly-standardised methods, tools and materials.
- Long production runs for individual products.
- Narrow range of skills, and specified range of operations required by workforce at any one point in the line.

In purely rational terms, mass production is the most efficient way of producing large quantities of articles or items. Control can be exercised to a sophisticated level because of the standardised nature of the entire process. Its greatest drawback is that it requires human beings to adapt themselves to the production process, and in most Western countries, there has been a reaction against this requirement. Employees are seeking to counteract the tedium and monotony of the highly specialised work patterns in mass production by pressing for more integrated roles, requiring a wider range of skills and operations. In some cases this has led to the complete break up of production lines into autonomous circuits, each operated by teams of employees using their skills on a shared or flexible basis.

10. Another form of mass production, usually called flow production or process production, can be seen in continuous process industries such as steel-making, paper-making and cement production. In such industries the products literally flow from one process to the next, but, unlike in the mass production of individual products, this process is continuous for weeks or months on end. In flow processes, the supply of raw materials has to be planned to the highest standards in order to avoid complete plant shutdown owing to unforeseen shortages. In these situations shortages have a much more serious effect than in unit mass production. Fortunately, the control mechanisms and procedures for flow processes are usually so sophisticated that the processes become automatically self-regulating. Another important difference between this form of mass production and unit mass production is that the former invariably requires a lower labour force than the latter.

Sub-dividing the Categories

11. As was noted above (in paragraph 1), the three common categories are very broad. Even our analysis has had to distinguish between two forms of mass production, and the use of batch methods was applied to small and medium sized lots, which omits the possibility of large batches. Clearly it would be better to have a more detailed picture, which more accurately represented the number of options available. This is all the more reasonable if one considers that very few, if any, manufacturing concerns engage solely in one type of production.

12. The list which follows compares the much more detailed analysis of Woodward's researchers with the broader one that has been applied above. The Woodward list is taken from the published account of the research.

Broad Categories	Woodward Categories
a. Jobbing Production	i. Production of units to customer's requirements
	ii. Production of prototypes
	iii. Fabrication of large equipment in stages
b. Batch Production	i. Production of small batches to customer's orders

		ii.	Production of large batches
		iii.	Production of large batches on assembly lines
		iv.	Intermittent production of chemicals in multi-purpose plant
c.	Mass Production – Flow Production	i.	Mass production
		ii.	Continuous flow production of liquids, gases and crystalline substances

13. It can be seen that the Woodward analysis of jobbing production corresponds to the description given in paragraph 3 above, but by giving each of the main types of jobbing production its own title, the Woodward analysis provides for a more accurate representation of the range of options. Where batch production is concerned, the Woodward analysis distinguishes four types of batch production compared with the one type we have described. The Woodward team not only distinguished between small and large batches, as described in paragraph 5 above, but also between large batches produced by single machines or batteries of machines and large batches produced on assembly lines. (The latter, in our definition, would fall under 'mass production'.) They also included the intermittent production of chemicals as a separate batch process. Thus their range of batch options is much more comprehensive and distinctive than the broad category we have used. Finally, the Woodward breakdown of mass production into two categories makes explicit the distinction made in our analysis between mass production and flow or process production.

14. On balance, it is probably helpful to think firstly in terms of the three broad categories, so as to separate the main production options, and secondly in terms of the more detailed breakdown in order to draw a truer picture of what may be possible.

Summary

15. This brief chapter has sought to describe the main features of the basic types of production systems – jobbing, batch and mass production. Jobbing production refers to the production of unique or 'one-off' items, made to order. These items may be small or large, and they are produced under conditions of what is appropriate at a given time, rather than conditions which are standardised. Both planning and control are difficult to achieve in this form of production.

16. Batch production refers to the production of standardised units in batches, or lots. Only when a batch has completed one process can it be moved to the next. Batches may be produced to order, or for stock. Batch production can be relatively well planned and controlled, but queuing problems may arise when batches are ready to move on to the next operation. These problems can be overcome by utilising assembly lines, ie moving over to a mass production method.

17. Mass production refers to the production of vast quantities of product units in a flow-line process, where each flows smoothly from one operation, or process, to the next until completion. Where the mass production of continuous processes is concerned, the method is called flow production or process production. Mass production methods call for detailed planning and sophisticated control procedures. There is very little scope for the exercise of skills by the workforce, and the flowline layout has been challenged in several quarters.

Reference

1. Woodward, J (1965), *Industrial Organisation: Theory and Practice*, OUP.

CHAPTER 40

Aids to Production

Introduction

1.   This chapter outlines the key features of three aids to production management – Work Study, Value Analysis or Value Engineering, and Quality Circles. They may all have applications elsewhere, but in the paragraphs which follow they are considered in terms of their contribution to production.

Work Study

2.   Work Study was developed in American industry in the 1920s. The first known attempts to make a rational assessment of work and tasks were made by F.W. Taylor and the other 'Scientific Managers', whose ideas were described earlier, in Chapter 3. Since their time, Work Study has become an established part of the industrial scene.

3.   Work Study has been defined in a British Standard (B.S. 3138) as follows:

> 'A generic term for those techniques, particularly method study and work measurement, which are used in the examination of human work in all its contexts, and which lead systematically to the investigation of all the factors which affect the efficiency and economy of the situation being reviewed, in order to effect improvement.'

The two basic techniques, Method Study and Work Measurement, are complementary to each other, and are rarely utilised in isolation from each other. The usual practice is for a method study of some kind to precede a work measurement activity. Each technique will be described in outline shortly.

4.   The reasons why Work Study techniques are utilised in production include the following:

- To eliminate wasteful work.
- To improve working methods.
- To increase production.
- To achieve cost savings.
- To improve productivity of workers and machines.

5.   **Method Study.** This technique is itself composed of a collection of techniques, all of which systematically examine and record all the methods, existing and proposed, utilised in an operation or process, with a view to increasing efficiency. It could be said that Method Study attempts to answer the questions What? When? How? Who? and Where? in contrast to Work Measurement's emphasis, which asks How long? and When? The scope of Method Study, therefore, is considerably wider than that of Work Measurement.

6.   Method Study is used to aid solutions to a variety of production problems. These problems include those of workplace layout, materials handling, tool design, product design and process design for example. The basic approach of a method study is illustrated in a simplified diagram (Figure 40.1).

7.   The procedures noted in the diagram are the vehicle for a rational analysis of working methods. Firstly, the target operation or process is selected. If a choice has to be

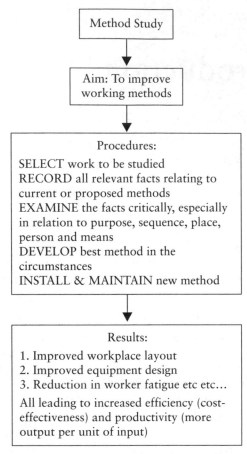

Figure 40.1. Method Study: an outline.

made between priorities for attention, the likelihood is that the activity having the biggest impact on costs will be selected, since if this can be improved, some real savings will be achieved. Secondly, a thorough examination of all the pertinent facts is made. Much of the data collected for a method study is presented in a flowchart form, which utilises a standard set of symbols for all the basic activities and operations. The symbols are as shown in Figure 40.2.

A simple flowchart records the activities in the order in which they occur, assigns the appropriate symbol to each activity, notes the elapsed time taken for each activity and adds any comments that may be useful. Thus the recording of facts for a method study is a very detailed business. The third step in the procedure is to examine critically the data obtained, even to the extent of questioning the very purpose of an activity. 'Is this activity necessary?' 'Is this the most economical sequence of events in the process?' 'What are the alternative ways of conducting this operation?' These and other questions can help the person conducting the study to eventually produce a best method of working, taking all the circumstances into account. If this new method is approved, the final stages are implementation and subsequent maintenance and review.

8.   It was mentioned in the previous paragraph that much of the data for a method study is present in flowchart form. Other charts and diagrams used in method study are as follows:

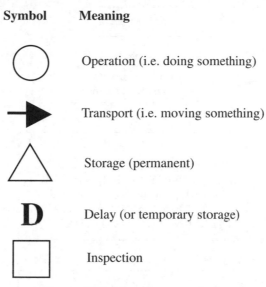

Symbol	Meaning

Operation (i.e. doing something)

Transport (i.e. moving something)

Storage (permanent)

D   Delay (or temporary storage)

Inspection

Figure 40.2. Flowchart symbols.

- Multiple activity charts – these are charts where the activities of more than one subject (eg workers, machines etc) can be recorded against a common time-scale, and where Time is registered on the vertical axis, and Subjects on the horizontal;

- Flow diagrams – these are scale drawings of the workplace which indicate where each activity takes place;

- String diagrams – these are similar to flow diagrams, but where movements between activities are recorded by means of string, or thread, connecting pins inserted into all the activity points on the diagram; they enable the paths of all the movements taking place to be recorded with clarity, and can highlight short-cuts;

- Chronocyclegraph – this is a photographic record, which traces the path of movement onto a photographic plate; in principle, it is similar to the string diagram, and is most effective when recording short, rapid movements.

- Therbligs – these are the basic units of work activity, originated by Frank Gilbreth in the United States (see Chapter 3); they are used in so-called micromotion studies, which are detailed studies of repetitive work.

9.   **Work Measurement.** This is a collection of techniques, particularly Time Study, aimed at establishing the time taken by a qualified worker to complete a specified job at a defined level of performance. As mentioned above, Work Measurement techniques set out to answer the questions How long? and When? They usually follow or overlap with a method study, and are employed not only to improve methods of working, but also to develop costing systems, production schedules and incentive schemes, as well as to establish machine capacities and manning levels.

10. Like Method Study, Work Measurement has a systematic set of procedures to be followed, and these are set out below. When work measurement is linked into a method study, it is introduced at the 'DEVELOP best method' stage, as shown in Figure 40.1. The basic steps in work measurement are as follows in Figure 40.3.

11. It can be seen from Figure 40.3 that the aim of Work Measurement is significantly different from that of Method Study. The latter aims to improve working methods; the former aims to measure, or assess, the performance of people. In pursuing its aim, Work

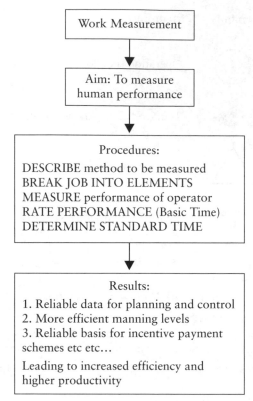

Figure 40.3. Work Measurement: an outline.

Measurement has to rely on the exercise of a greater degree of *subjective* judgement than is required for Method Study. In particular, the rating of performance and the determination of the standard time rely heavily on the judgement of the person conducting the measurement.

12. The procedures of Work Measurement require the method (or job) to be described. This has usually been done as part of a Method Study. The point is, that if someone is to measure an operation, he must be clear what the operation is! Once the job or method of operation has been described, logically, from beginning to end, then it is broken down into very small elements based on time taken. These elements typically last no more than 30 seconds. Having broken the job down in this way, the person conducting the study then measures the performance of the employee concerned, generally using a stop-watch for the purpose. This is usually known as *direct* Time Study, in contrast to indirect Time Study (see below). Once sufficient numbers of elements have been timed, we can arrive at the elapsed or observed time, for the job.

13. The next step in the procedure – rating – is the one which is the most vulnerable to mistakes or errors on the part of the investigator. The latter is required to 'rate' the employee, ie to decide how quickly (or slowly!) the employee is working compared with a standard. This is usually the Standard Rating of 100 in the British Standard 3138 which is equivalent to the 'average rate at which qualified workers will naturally work at a job, provided they know and adhere to the specified method and provided they are motivated to apply themselves to their work.' Thus if an employee is adjudged to be working at a slower pace, he may be rated at, say, 80; by comparison an employee adjudged to be working at a faster pace than average may be rated at 115 for example. Clearly, if the

person conducting the measurement is relatively inexperienced in Work Study and is unfamiliar with the job being rated, the probability of reaching a mistaken rating is quite high. Rating the job enables a Basic Time to be established, using the following formula:

$$\text{Basic Time} = \frac{\text{Observed Time} \times \text{Rating}}{\text{Standard Rating}}$$

For example, if an employee's time for a particular element is observed to be 0.30 minutes, and he is rated as 115, then his Basic Time will be as follows:

$$\text{Basic Time} = \frac{0.30 \times 115}{100}$$

$$= 0.345 \text{ minutes}$$

14. In order to reach a Standard Time for the job, a number of allowances are added to the Basic Time. These allowances are designed to accommodate such contingencies as relaxation, collection of materials or tools, and unavoidable delays, for example. This is another area of Work Measurement where subjective judgements have to be made, and where the person conducting the study may come under strong pressure from employees to allow more, rather than less, time for these allowances.

15. Where indirect time study is carried out – that is where times are worked out on paper without observing employees – the following techniques are the most commonly employed: Synthetic Timing, Predetermined Motion Time Study (PMTS), and Analytical Estimating. Briefly these may be described as follows.

Synthetic Timing

This is a technique for obtaining Basic Times for new jobs, which have not been time-studied previously and where it is impracticable (eg because of time constraints) to conduct direct Time Studies. In developing synthetic (or made-up) times, a job is broken down into elements, following a study of the drawings involved. Element times are assigned on the basis of past experience by utilising records from previous studies. The key to Synthetic Timing, therefore, is the existence of adequate past records of earlier *direct* studies. It has proved to be a reliable and consistent method for many businesses.

Predetermined Motion Time Study (PMTS)

This is a technique which according to British Standard 3138, is one in which 'times established for basic human motions (classified according to the nature of the motion and the conditions under which it is made) are used to build up the time for a job at a defined level of performance'. PMTS differs from Synthetic Timing in that it is concerned not with job elements but with the basic motions that underlie every job element. PMTS is concerned with the lowest common denominators of work carried out by human beings. The most important method, to date, of PMTS is known as Methods Time Measurement (MTM). MTM is based on a small number of basic hand, eye and other movements, for which *universal* times have been established for skilled workers.

Analytical Estimating

As its title suggests, Analytical Estimating is a form of calculated guesswork. It is the most subjective technique employed in Work Measurement, and consequently the least reliable. It involves breaking a job into larger than usual elements and allocating Basic Times on the basis of the estimator's knowledge of the operations and skill in estimating times. This method tends to be used for one-off jobs.

Value Analysis (Value Engineering)

16. This is another analytical technique which is widely used, especially in engineering, hence the alternative title. It is very like Method Study in its approach. The purpose of Value Analysis is to examine critically the function of a product with a view to fulfilling that function at the least cost consistent with reliability of the function. Thus Value Analysis is concerned with identifying the relationship between costs and reliability of function.

17. The stages of a value analysis are typically as follows:

• Select product to be studied.

• Determine function, design and cost of product (including components).

• Develop alternative designs for product in order to achieve same function at less cost, ie designs of 'higher' value.

• Evaluate the alternative designs.

• Adopt optimum design, ie the one able to perform the required function reliably but at least cost.

• Implement design and review results.

This process is usually carried out by a multi-disciplinary team composed of the following: value analyst/engineer, product designer, cost accountant, production representative and purchasing manager.

18. Value Analysis is applied most frequently in mass production or assembly line production processes, where large numbers of items are being produced, and where marginal cost savings can lead to substantial savings overall. Figure 40.4 provides an illustration of this point, indicating the effects, in terms of *quantity* savings, of unit savings of a few pence or even a fraction of a penny.

	Cost per item	Best cost Saving	%	Volume per annum	Total Savings
Item A	£1.00	£0.15	15	50,000	£7,500
Item B	£0.25	£0.01	4	4 millions	£40,000

Figure 40.4. Value Analysis: examples of cost savings.

19. The benefits of Value Analysis are that it encourages cost consciousness and the search for alternative designs and materials etc, and also permits more competitive pricing. However, it does tend to require large-scale production to show it off to the greatest advantage, and must, to a certain extent, duplicate work carried out at the design stage of a product.

Quality Circles

20. The development of so-called 'Quality Circles' is a recent phenomenon. Quality Circles are small groups of about eight to ten employees, meeting together on a regular basis to discuss day-to-day issues such as quality, productivity and safety, with the object of (a) making improvements, and (b) organising their implementation. The second object is significant, as it implies a degree of grass-roots decision-making which is new to most shop-floor situations. In the past employee involvement in initiating changes on the shop floor could only arise via formal productivity committees or via the firm's suggestion

scheme. With Quality Circles, there is an attempt to delegate real power to ordinary employees not only to make suggestions regarding quality etc, but also to implement those suggestions.

21. Membership of Quality Circles is voluntary, but usually consists of a number of shop-floor employees and a foreman or supervisor, or may consist of a mixture of skilled and unskilled employees together with one or two shop-floor specialists such as Quality Engineers and Inspectors. Each Circle selects its own leader, and usually the organisation concerned provides training for such leaders in appropriate subjects (discussion leading, quality control etc).

22. Typically, a Quality Circle will adopt the following approach to its task:

• Identify and clarify problems in the local work situation,

• Select a problem for solution (eg wastage rates),

• Set a realistic target for improvement (eg to reduce wastage rates by 15% over next 12 months),

• Establish a plan, together with a timetable, for achievement of the target,

• Propose plan to local management,

• Implement and test plan,

• Revise plan, where necessary, and monitor results.

23. Those organisations which operate Quality Circles claim to see them as a practical means of achieving employee participation on the shop-floor. They are not primarily instruments of cost-reduction exercises, even though costs may well figure in their discussions. Surveys in Japan, for example, where Quality Circles are widely employed, indicate that whilst costs are one of the major topics of discussion in the Circles, there are several others of equal importance, such as quality, use of equipment, efficiency and safety.

24. The benefits of Quality Circles are:

• greater awareness of shop-floor problems by Circle members,

• greater confidence in tackling problems and generating solutions on the part of Circle members,

• improved productivity and/or quality, and

• improved motivation on the shop-floor.

CHAPTER 41

New Technology in Manufacturing

Introduction

1. What is the new technology in manufacturing? It can best be summarised as 'the selective application of computing and microelectronics to the planning, resourcing and

controlling of the manufacturing process, from the design stage to the completion of the product'. In practice this means the development and application of one or more of the following:

- computers for production control
- computer-aided design (CAD)
- computer-aided manufacture (CAM)
- robots
- process measurement and control devices.

2.   The above applications can be combined in various ways to form:

- computer-integrated manufacturing (CIM)
- computer-aided engineering and
- flexible manufacturing systems (FMS).

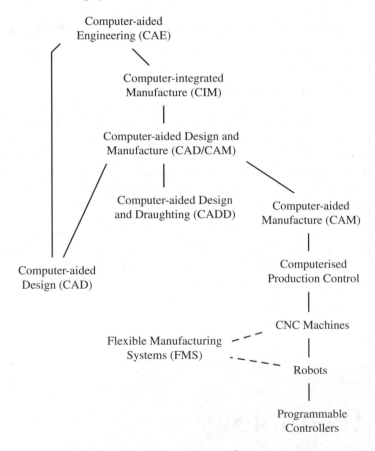

Figure 41.1 Hierarchy of manufacturing systems.

There is a certain amount of confusion currently as to what these integrated manufacturing systems should be called. In this chapter they will be taken to have the following relationship to each other (see Figure 41.1).

Each of the items will be described briefly in the following paragraphs. The chapter will end with a summary of the overall impact of the new technology on industrial nations.

Computers and Production Control

3.   Over 70% of the computers currently in use in Britain's factories are microcomputers, and several of their principal applications are described in this chapter. Perhaps the most orthodox use of computers in manufacturing is to be found in the processing of information for production planning and control. Typical production control programs handled by computers include stock control, sales orders, purchase orders, machine scheduling, capacity planning, tooling lists and work scheduling.

4.   The main benefits of these applications are:

*   they improve control of the production process
*   they enable more efficient utilisation of plant and equipment
*   they enable fewer items to be held as stock or as work in progress
*   they reduce labour costs
*   they speed up deliveries by reducing the waiting time between processes.

Overall, firms using computers for production planning and control can expect to see marked gains in productivity through better machine utilisation and reduced overheads.

Computer-aided Design

5.   Computer-aided design (CAD) refers to the use of a computer-based system for translating engineering concepts into engineering designs by means of programs incorporating data on (i) design principles and (ii) key variables (eg product size, shape etc). CAD programs are capable of providing *3-dimensional* representations on a screen. These representations can be rotated through a number of different perspectives. This form of computer modelling is extremely useful in the design process, as it enables detailed changes to be made, and their effects measured, with speed and accuracy.

6.   Associated with CAD is computer-aided draughting, which is a computer-based system for translating engineering concepts and designs into *2-dimensional* drawings for use in the manufacturing process. At present computer-aided draughting systems are very costly and can only be justified where either (a) there is a chronic shortage of skilled draughtsmen, or (b) where the system produces such greatly increased output that work previously turned away can now be tendered for.

7.   Computer-aided design and draughting systems make it possible for firms to compensate for the shortage of skilled personnel by combining a computer with a small number of people to achieve a much greater workload than is possible when traditional methods are used. A further advantage of such systems is that they produce useful information resulting from the design/draughting process such as data on parts lists, materials requirements, wiring schedules and other relevant manufacturing data.

Computer-aided Manufacture

8.   Computer-aided manufacture (CAM) is a general term which refers to any production system in which manufacturing plant and test equipment are controlled by computer. CAM is more than just metal-cutting. It embraces important engineering processes such as welding, assembling and painting. CAM is particularly applicable to processes where parts are complex and accuracy is vital. A CAM system can be expected to achieve:

*   more speedy production of parts;

- a consistently high level of product quality;

- replication to within very close tolerances;

- ability to achieve high production levels even when skilled craftsmen are in short supply.

9.   An important feature of CAM is that its software generates numerical control (NC) tapes for the computer control of machines (CNC machines) and robots. Numerical control of machine tools is not new. What is new is the ability of a computer program to introduce far greater flexibility into the way the numerically controlled machine can be operated. In the past this had to be done on a step-by-step process, but now several processes can be woven together by the computer. Another advantage is that programs can be amended very easily under a computer-controlled system. Typical work handled by CNC machines (Computerised Numerical Control) includes turning, drilling, milling and sheet metal working. The use of such machines has been found to lead to greatly improved productivity on account of the reduced requirement for toolsetting. One example of CAM is the Flexible Manufacturing System which we shall describe briefly.

Flexible Manufacturing Systems

10.   A Flexible Manufacturing System (FMS) is one where a small group (or cell) of CNC machine-tools is used in a coordinated way for producing components without manual intervention in a small batch operation. The objective in this case is to mirror the productivity possible on large-scale, fully-automated systems. A typical FMS would consist of the following:

- a group of NC machines each with the capacity to manufacture a range of parts

- a number of robots and/or wire-controlled work-carriers

- a computer control station

11.   Such systems are costly to introduce, but where justified can lead to:

- reduced work-in-progress

- reduced stock-levels

- faster throughput times

- quicker change-over times

- lower unit costs

Robots

12.   The expression 'robot' derives from the Czech word for 'work'. In modern usage 'robot' means *a programmable machine that can replicate a limited range of human actions*. Most of the robots in use in the world are so-called 'first generation' machines, which are basically mechanical arms used for repetitive tasks such as machine-loading, spot-welding, injection-moulding and paint spraying. In 1984 there were about 2,500 industrial robots in the UK. By the year 2001 this figure had increased to nearer 19,000 (source: British Automation & Robot Association). Major growth in robot use is typical of all the advanced economies. What has not changed is the application of robots, which is substantially the same now as it was 15 years ago. The biggest users of robots are still motor manufacturers and suppliers of car parts, and their applications are dominated by spot-welding, arc welding and material handling. Other industries tend to use robots for material handling, automated palletising and packaging operations, machine loading, and

sealing/gluing operations. One well-known military application is the use of robots to identify and deactivate car bombs.

13. More sophisticated robots ('second-generation' models) can be used for more complex operations than those mentioned above. This is because they are supplied with improved sensing abilities, especially 'sight', 'smell' and 'touch'. In the automotive industry, for example, such robots are deployed to fit windscreens on cars and to locate test leaks from completed vehicle bodies. In a recent United Nations Economic Commission for Europe report[1] on world robotics, it was stated that the world-wide stock of robots was at least 760,000, of which 360,000 were located in Japan, 220,000 in the European Union, and just under 100,000 in North America. In Europe the leading user by far was Germany with the UK at the bottom of the list. The report also showed that the price of robots had fallen by more than 40% over the period 1990–2000, whereas their performance and efficiency had improved substantially in such aspects as repetition accuracy, number of variants that can be supplied, and RAM capacity (a 400% increase).

14. The principal reasons why firms introduce robots into their manufacturing plants are as follows:

- competitors are installing them;
- they can be employed on work which employees are reluctant to undertake, because it is repetitive or dirty or noisy;
- they can be employed on dangerous tasks such as handling radioactive materials or dangerous viruses;
- they help to reduce production costs, for, once programmed, they are tirelessly accurate and thus free skilled employees for other tasks;
- they are a necessary prerequisite for any firm intending to work towards the adoption of highly-automated systems such as FMS and CIM (see below).
- they can make up for a shortfall in skilled technicians, which is an increasingly likely prospect as the populations in industrialised nations decline, and fewer younger people are available to support an ageing population.

Process Measurement and Control Devices

15. Microprocessor-based process measurement and control devices are used mainly in situations where the measurement and analysis of chemicals, gases, liquids and solids are important. The devices can monitor and record such variables as flow, pressure, temperature and constituent levels. In the cement-manufacturing process, for example, a controller known as a fluorescent spectrometer can analyse samples of the product and produce a complete chemical analysis of seven elemental oxide constituents of the material.

16. Process measurement devices tend to be relatively easy to use, do not require highly qualified operators and can carry out a wide range of monitoring and testing activities. A new device for checking telephone equipment can automatically perform over 40 tests on the equipment in a few hours. Using earlier methods such a test would have taken several days.

Programmable Controllers

17. Programmable controllers are microprocessor-based devices capable of performing a wide range of switching, monitoring and signalling functions. Fitted to a particular

machine or part of a process plant, they are linked to a host computer and can carry out a variety of monitoring and reporting functions during operations. In a large plant several such controllers may be fitted to control various stages of the process. These controllers are frequently to be found in such industries as petrochemicals, brick-making and food processing.

CAD/CAM Systems

18. The computer-aided manufacturing systems that have just been described have close links with the computer-aided design and draughting referred to in paragraphs 5 and 6 above. Where such systems are combined they are usually referred to as a CAD/CAM system, and undoubtedly this will become the standard for the future.

19. The benefits of CAD/CAM can be summarised as follows:

- greatly improved productivity of designers and draughtsmen (eg drawings produced in a quarter of the time previously taken using traditional methods);
- reduction in waiting list of projects to be tackled by the design department;
- ability to tender for work which previously would have been turned away for lack of skilled personnel;
- development of uniform design standards throughout the organisation;
- consistency of specifications, and the elimination of inconsistencies between drawings;
- ability to amend designs/drawings to take account of modifications or improvements;
- shorter production times leading to lower optimum batch sizes and more rapid changes of product lines;
- improved quality and consistency of finished products;
- simplified quality control through automatic testing and inspection using the specification already held in a computer.

20. Given the substantial benefits of CAD/CAM, it is surprising that many British firms have not yet taken it up. The answer appears to lie in one or more of the following reasons given by firms as to why they have not introduced CAD/CAM:

- such systems are extremely costly to install, and may not produce enough sizeable benefits for small and medium-sized companies;
- many firms are unaware of the advantages of CAD/CAM;
- industrial managements often lack the confidence to incorporate such sophisticated systems into their production areas;
- the personnel implications of introducing CAD/CAM can be daunting, requiring firms to recruit additional, qualified staff, retrain many grades of existing staff and develop new payments systems to cope with all the job changes.

Computer-integrated Manufacture

21. Computer-integrated manufacture (CIM) refers to the integration and coordination of all aspects of manufacturing from the design and layout of plant, product and component design, through processing and production control to quality assurance and final despatch. Currently examples may be seen in modern motor manufacturing plants, where dealer-orders for specific models are fed into a master-computer, and subsequently passed down to production for manufacturing in accordance with the dealers' requirements as to colour,

engine size and so on. Such a system incorporates despatch and delivery procedures, as well as monitoring stock levels and a host of other production and marketing data. CAD/CAM systems, in themselves, are advanced systems, but on an altogether smaller scale than CIM. CAD/CAM equipment could be used in a piecemeal way and fail to reap the full benefits of the new technology. By integration of the total manufacturing system the greatest result will be possible, and for large-scale manufacturing will probably become the norm in future.

Computer-aided Engineering

22. This is another general term which encompasses not only computer-integrated manufacture but also the analysis of design and other software used in computer-aided systems. In our original figure (Figure 41.1) this item comes at the head of the hierarchy of computer-based manufacturing systems.

The Impact of the New Technology

23. In sheer economic terms, the impact on manufacturing of the new microelectronic technology is likely to produce as many threats as it does opportunities, especially for advanced industrial nations. There are several reasons why this may be so:

- microelectronic technology is as available to the emergent economies of the East as it is to the powerful economies of the USA, Japan and Western Europe
- the emergent economies have far lower labour costs than the advanced nations and will therefore be able to compete more keenly for world trade in a wide range of manufactured goods
- whereas in the emergent economies new technology is likely to lead to greater employment opportunities, the reverse is likely in the advanced nations, where employment levels in manufacturing are falling in any case
- yet any nation that does not adopt the new technology will fail to compete in world markets for manufactured goods, and is likely to end up as a museum of industrial history
- generally speaking the biggest gains from the new technology will come from increased productivity and improved product quality.

24. The application of microelectronics technology to the economic life of advanced industrial nations is more likely to be successful in the exploitation of information processing. Figure 41.2 illustrates the declining role of industry and the increasing role of information processing in an advanced economy, in this case the United States. The figure shows that since the 1950s, industry has been in decline in the USA, whereas by contrast information processing activities have been increasing sharply since the 1940s (the advent of the computer). The challenge for advanced nations will undoubtedly be to maintain a viable, though much smaller, manufacturing industry based on the best of the new technology.

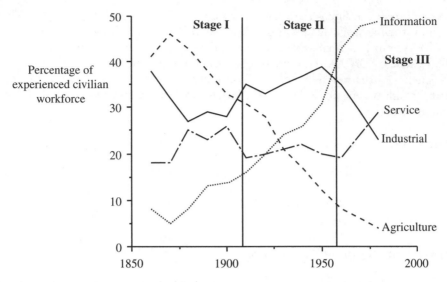

The chart shows that almost half of America's civilian workforce are already employed in the information field. Things are similar in Western Europe, where a considerable proportion of the service sector's workforce are also involved in generating, recording, processing and transmitting information in one form or another.

Stage I has been described as the agricultural economy; Stage II the industrial economy. Stage III the information economy.

Source: Bureau of Labor Statistics – USA

Figure 41.2. Towards the information economy – the changing pattern of employment in the USA, 1860–1980.

References

1. United Nations Economic Commission for Europe (2002), *World Robotics 2002*, United Nations, Geneva.

Questions for Discussion/Homework

1. In what ways can the use of computers be advantageous in the production planning and control process?

2. It could be said that a typical Purchasing Manager is under pressure from suppliers to order to the maximum, and under pressure from colleagues to keep prices to the minimum. Discuss to what extent this is a fair view of the Purchasing Manager's role?

3. What is the role of Inspection in Quality Control?

4. How far can maintenance be planned? What kinds of maintenance would you expect to find in a planned maintenance programme for a continuous process plant?

5. How can batch production be distinguished from mass production? Give an example of each type of production.

6. What, basically, is Work Study and what benefits are claimed for it?

7. What alternative ways exist for collecting or presenting Method Study data?

8. What is a Standard Rating and what significance can this have for Work Measurement?

9. Where is the value in Value Analysis?

10. How do Quality Circles approach shop-floor problems, and what is considered to be distinctive in this approach?

11. What problems do you foresee for production managers considering the introduction of an integrated manufacturing system in a mass production plant?

12. What, in your opinion, are the most convincing arguments for extending the application of microelectronics to manufacturing processes?

Examination Questions

The subject of Production Management only appears infrequently in the examination papers at which the main emphasis of this manual is directed. However it is a frequent enough topic in the Business Organisation paper of the Institute of Marketing, so the majority of questions selected are taken from that particular paper. It should be sufficient to show that you have grasped the essentials of the subject matter of the questions concerned. Suggested answers appear in Appendix 2.

EQ 32 Describe briefly the main activities within a Production Planning and Control system.

(IOM Business Organisation)

EQ 33 Describe the circumstances which would justify the adoption of (a) jobbing, (b) batch, and (c) flow/mass patterns of production.

(ACCA Business Management)

EQ 34 Briefly describe the sequence of necessary activities for the purchasing department of a manufacturing company to carry out, in purchasing a raw material not previously required.

(IOM Business Organisation)

There are nine chapters in this section on Personnel or Human Resource Management. The emphasis throughout is on the activities of specialists in Personnel and Training Management, since the expression 'Human Resource Management' (HRM) encompasses a wider range of activities, including aspects of team leadership such as grievance handling and employee counselling. Chapter 42 introduces the Personnel Management function. Chapter 43 deals with recruitment and selection. Chapter 44 focuses on employee development. Chapters 45 and 46 examine key aspects of performance appraisal, grievances, disciplinary matters and management development. Chapter 47 outlines the topic of workplace stress and summarises some of the ways in which this can be avoided or at least minimised. Chapter 48 briefly outlines key aspects of job evaluation, whilst Chapters 49 and 50 deal with the legal consequences of employment, firstly at the collective level, and secondly at an individual level.

CHAPTER 42

Human Resource Management

1.   Personnel management, in the sense of human resource management, can be said to be part of the role of every person who is responsible for the work of others. However, the HRM approach implies a very broad meaning of 'personnel management' and does not tell us anything about the particular areas of work in which personnel specialists make a distinctive contribution to an organisation. In this chapter, the expression 'Personnel Management' refers to the duties and activities of personnel specialists.

2.   What then is Personnel Management? It is that specialist function of management which has the prime responsibility for the following:

*   formulating, proposing and gaining acceptance for the personnel policies and strategies of the organisation,

*   advising and guiding the organisation's managers on the implementation of personnel policies and strategies,

*   providing personnel services for the organisations to facilitate the recruitment, motivation and development of sufficient and suitable employees at all levels,

*   advising the organisation's managers of the human consequences of change.

3.   The policy-making and strategic responsibilities are carried out by senior Personnel Managers; advisory and guidance responsibilities are carried out both by senior and middle ranking Personnel Managers; the provision of personnel services is very much a middle-management responsibility; finally, the management of change is primarily a senior Personnel role.

4.   By virtue of their specialist function, all Personnel Managers, regardless of seniority, are able to concentrate exclusively on personnel (HRM) matters, unlike their colleagues in other departments (line or functional) who are only able to give a proportion of their time to such matters. How other managers see their personnel colleagues depends on several factors such

as the organisational climate, the managerial styles of the managers concerned and the extent to which the Personnel department is able to be helpful. Personnel Managers sometimes have to tread a delicate path between offering constructive, and sometimes unpopular, advice to their colleagues and appearing to tell them how to handle their own staff. Under modern conditions of employment, the needs and wishes of staff are fairly well protected, and, as a result, many issues which, formerly, could have been dealt with solely by a manager acting on his own, now have to tackled jointly with the Personnel department.

5. Personnel policies, like any other corporate policies, are not just the preserve of a particular group of Managers. Such policies have to be agreed by the top management team as a whole, and approved by the Board. The role of the senior personnel staff is to formulate draft personnel policies and to argue the case for their acceptance. In many instances it will be the personnel department which provides the initiative for the introduction of new policies and the revision or rejection of existing policies. Key areas of personnel policy can include the following:

- Recruitment and Selection
- Pay and Benefits (Pensions etc)
- Relations with Trade Unions or Staff Associations
- Career Development
- Training
- Safety and Health
- Employment Legislation.

As in other policy areas, personnel policies are guidelines for behaviour stating what the organisation will do, or positively will not do, in relation to its employees and employee affairs.

6. Examples of personnel policies are as follows:

- Every job vacancy will be advertised within the organisation before any external advertising takes place,
- The Company will encourage employees to pursue training and education opportunities, where this might qualify them for promotion or career development moves within the organisation,
- The organisation will always negotiate in good faith with the representatives of recognised independent trade unions,
- The Company will always endeavour to obey the spirit as well as the letter of laws relating to employment; it will actively discourage any activities which might cause a breach of the law.

7. Strategic advice on personnel matters is directed towards the fulfilment of the organisation's corporate plan, and covers issues such as the manpower plan, the development of harmonious and mutually respectful relationships with trade union representatives, the maintenance of employee motivation by means of fair and equitable payment systems and of adequate personal and career development opportunities, and, finally, the organisation's actions in relation to new developments in employment legislation.

8. Personnel services represent the operational or production aspect of Personnel Management. Personnel services include the following:

- recruitment services (eg advertising, preparing candidate specifications, shortlisting candidates, arranging interviews and handling the correspondence)

- pay procedures and associated procedures, such as the provision of job evaluation services

- appraisal procedures (ie appraisal forms, timetable for appraisals, maintenance of records etc)

- employment services (ie conditions of service procedures – informing managers and employees, recording employee details, handling enquiries etc)

- employee relations – especially organising arrangements for management–union meetings, taking records, providing relevant information on pay rates, recent agreements, legal aspects etc; monitoring grievance and disciplinary procedures etc

- training services (ie providing information about training, handling arrangements for courses, maintaining training records etc)

- safety, health and welfare services (eg organising safety committees, maintaining safety records, provision of welfare and canteen facilities etc).

9. In addition to the policy-making, strategic and personnel services roles, most modern Personnel departments are expected to have something useful to say about the implications of change for the employees of the organisation. In some organisations this is specifically referred to as the Organisation Development function of Personnel. Whether it has a title or not, the activity itself is directed towards the recognition of change, from whichever quarter, and the assessment of the likely impact of that change on personnel affairs in the organisation. The introduction of new technology, for example, could reduce the demand for certain categories of employee, whilst increasing the demand for other categories. This, in turn, could lead to difficult negotiations with unions over redundancies, re-training opportunities, pay arrangements for the introduction of the new technology and other personnel issues.

10. Ultimately the role of Personnel will be determined by the attitudes of the top management of the organisation. Where Personnel is recognised as having a major part to play in the renewal and maturation processes of the organisational system, then the Personnel Manager will be given a key role in the corporate development of the organisation. Where, by contrast, Personnel is seen mainly as a provider of services to other managers, then the Personnel Manager will be given a routine administrative role, enlivened at intervals by 'fire-fighting' responsibilities whenever there is a crisis.

The Organisation of Personnel

11. The type of structure which may be found in a Personnel department will be a reflection of the role it is expected to play in the organisation. For example, in an organisation where Personnel is held to be of vital importance to the future of the organisation as well as to its present, the Personnel department is likely to be structured along the lines of the example shown in Figure 42.1. Some junior posts have been ignored in the interests of simplicity.

12. In Figure 42.1, the senior Personnel Manager is shown as an executive director, to emphasise the Board level role which is expected of Personnel in this organisation. The Personnel Services' Manager is responsible for recruitment and personnel administration, and would also have other responsibilities not indicated on the chart (eg welfare, canteen, office services etc). The Employee Relations Manager is responsible for industrial relations matters, including job evaluation, job grading and industrial relations intelligence. The Training & Development Manager is responsible for all aspects of training, including job training, management development and related matters. The Organisation Planning Manager is responsible for assessing manpower requirements, organisation design projects, management succession planning and career planning. He would probably share some of

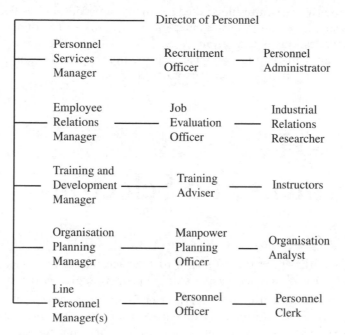

Figure 42.1. Personnel function with wide-ranging role.

the responsibility for appraisals with the Training & Development Manager. Several options are open to the Personnel Director concerning the allocation of responsibilities between the Training Manager and the manager responsible for organisation planning. In the final analysis, the decision would probably be made on the basis of experience and personality.

13. In an organisation where little is expected of Personnel apart from the provision of services, and where line managers are expected to bear the brunt of dealing with the personnel matters raised by their own employees, then the structure shown in Figure 42.2 is likely to be met. In this form of structure, the emphasis is entirely on the provision of services. Each of the jobs referred to is intended to pursue a routine, here-and-now path. There is no intention of including Personnel in any strategic activity, nor in any corporate advice-giving, except for routine information.

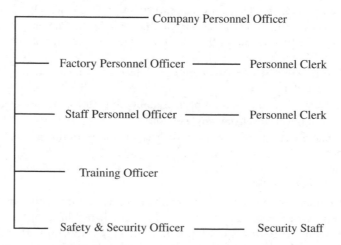

Figure 42.2. Routine-oriented Personnel department.

14. In between the two structures illustrated are many other options, as Personnel departments grow or wane in stature, as top management attitudes to Personnel change, and as external conditions (especially legislation) make labour more, or less, important. The rest of this section assumes an organisation which has the full range of Personnel activities, and which assumes a corporate role for the Personnel function.

CHAPTER 43

Recruitment and Selection

Introduction

1. This chapter outlines the typical stages of the recruitment and selection process in organisations, and considers certain aspects of the process in greater detail.

2. It will be helpful to distinguish 'recruitment' sub-processes from 'selection' sub-processes. The aim of recruitment is to ensure that the organisation's demand for employees is met by attracting potential employees (recruits) in a cost-effective and timely manner. The aim of selection is to identify, from those coming forward, the individuals most likely to fulfil the requirements of the organisation. To put it another way, recruitment is concerned with assembling the raw materials, and selection is concerned with producing the right blend for the organisation, at a particular point in time.

Recruitment: Policies and Procedures

3. Recruitment policies constitute the code of conduct which the organisation is prepared to follow in its search for possible recruits in the marketplace. Some examples of reputable policies in this field are as follows.

'In matters of recruitment, this Company *will*:
- advertise all vacancies internally before making use of external sources,
- always advertise under the Company name when advertising externally,
- endeavour to ensure that every applicant for a position in the Company is informed in advance about the basic details of the vacancy, and the basic conditions of employment attached to it,
- endeavour to ensure that applicants are kept informed of their progress through the recruitment procedures,
- seek possible candidates on the basis of their ability to perform the job required.'

'In matters of recruitment, this Company *will not*:
- knowingly make exaggerated or misleading claims in recruitment literature or job advertisements,
- discriminate unfairly against possible candidates on the grounds of sex, race, age, religion or physical disablement.'

4. The recruitment activities of an organisation are carried out mainly by Personnel staff. These activities represent the marketing role of Personnel, reaching out across the organisation's external boundaries into the labour market. It is important, therefore, that such activities are conducted in a manner that sustains or enhances the good reputation of the

organisation. People who are treated well when they seek employment with the organisation are potential ambassadors for the organisation, whether they are successful in their application or not. Conversely, those who are treated badly in this situation are quick to spread their criticism. Examples of bad treatment of applicants include omitting to reply to a letter or form of application, keeping applicants waiting for an interview, and failing to inform applicants who have been unsuccessful.

5. Well-organised Personnel departments work to a checklist of recruitment procedures designed to minimise errors and thus avoid marring the organisation's image externally and Personnel's reputation internally. A typical checklist is shown in Figure 43.1. It helps to ensure a rational and logical approach to the recruitment of employees throughout the organisation.

Item	Question to be considered
1	Has the vacancy been agreed by the responsible manager?
2	Is there an up-to-date job description for the vacant position?
3	What are the conditions of employment (salary, hours, holidays etc) for the vacant position?
4	Has a candidate specification been prepared?
5	Has a notice of the vacancy been circulated internally?
6	Has a job advertisement been agreed? Have details of the vacancy been forwarded to relevant agencies?
7	Do all potential candidates (internal or external) know where to apply and in what form?
8	What arrangements have been made for drawing up a shortlist of candidates?
9	Have the interviewing arrangements been agreed, and have shortlisted candidates been informed?
10	Have unsuitable candidates, or candidates held in reserve, been informed of their position?
11	Have offer letters been agreed and despatched to successful candidates? Have references been taken up, where necessary?
12	Have suitable rejection letters been sent to unsuccessful shortlisted candidates, thanking them for their attendance?
13	Have all replies to offer letters been accounted for?
14	Have the necessary procedures for placement, induction and follow-up of successful candidates been put into effect?

Figure 43.1. Recruitment checklist.

6. The job description referred to in item 2 would usually contain at least the following information about the job concerned:

- Title of Job
- Grade/Salary Level of Job
- Title of Immediate Superior's Job
- Number of Subordinates
- Overall Purpose of the Job
- Principal Responsibilities of the Job
- Limits of Authority
- Location of Job.

In most organisations this information is contained in a formal document, completed following an analysis of the job. In some cases it may be less formally expressed, but nevertheless covers the points noted above.

7. The candidate specification, or personnel specification, as it is frequently called, is a

summary of the knowledge, skills and personal characteristics required of the jobholder to carry out the job to an acceptable standard of performance. This is an extremely important feature of the recruitment process, because it sets down a standard by which candidates for interview may be tested. There are two very well-known classifications for personal requirements: the Seven-Point Plan, developed by Professor Rodger of the National Institute of Industrial Psychology in the 1950s, and the Five-Point Plan produced by J. Munro Fraser at about the same time. These two attempts to produce general profiles of candidates for selection are compared in Figure 43.2.

Seven-Point Plan (A. Rodger)	Five-Point Plan (J. Munro Fraser)
1. Physical make-up	1. Impact on others
2. Attainments	2. Acquired Qualifications
3. General intelligence	3. Innate abilities
4. Specialised aptitudes	4. Motivation
5. Interests	5. Adjustment
6. Disposition	
7. Circumstances	

Figure 43.2. Personal classifications.

8.   It can be seen that are many common features between the two classifications. In practice, the Seven-Point plan tends to be the most popular, and individual firms often model their own personnel specifications on it. A formal layout for a specification is shown in Figure 43.3. Note that the form enables a distinction to be drawn between points that are essential in order to fulfil the job requirements and those that are desirable, but not essential, for adequate performance.

	Essential	Desirable
Formal Qualifications		
Knowledge		
Experience		
Skills – Manual – Social – Other		
Personality/Motivation		
Physical Requirements		
Interests		
Circumstances		

Figure 43.3. Personnel specification.

9.   In cases where a tight specification is drawn up, ie where the emphasis is on the essential requirements of the job, the job market is being effectively segmented, and the response will be specialised. Where a loose specification is drawn up, the emphasis will be more on what is desirable than on what is essential, and the response will tend to be proportionately

larger. When skilled manpower is plentiful, specifications will tend to be tight, and vice versa in times of manpower shortages.

10. To illustrate the use of such a document as shown in Figure 43.3, we could take the example of a Chief Accountant's position in a medium-sized engineering company employing, say, 1500 people. In this case a formal accountancy qualification would be regarded as essential, as would a practical knowledge of the accounting systems used in engineering companies. Experience of deputising for the chief accountant in an accountancy department would be desirable. Any reference to skills would tend to relate to social skills (eg ability to work with line colleagues) and intellectual skills (eg ability to see opportunities for developing computer-based control systems).

The requirements for personality/motivation would probably include an ability to work under pressure and a willingness to adapt accountancy procedures to meet the needs of marketing and production, where existing systems are not working effectively enough. Physical requirements would probably be omitted, and interests might be related only to work interests. The circumstances of the position might require the Chief Accountant to live within a reasonable travelling distance of the company's head office, and might require him to be away from home for short periods on company business.

11. The job advertisement referred to in item 6 in Figure 43.1 is the external advertisement in the Press and trade or professional journals. The basic principles of an effective job advertisement (ie one that attracts sufficient numbers of the right kind of candidates) can be summarised as follows:

- Provide brief, but succinct, details about the position to be filled,
- Provide similar details about the employing organisation,
- Provide details of all *essential* personal requirements,
- Make reference to any *desirable* personal requirements,
- State the main conditions of employment, especially the salary indicator for the position,
- State to whom the application or enquiry should be directed,
- Present the above information in an attractive form.

12. Short-listing arrangements are necessary to select from the total number of applicants those who appear, from their application form, to be worthy of an interview. If an external advertisement has hit the target segment correctly, then only relatively small numbers of applications will be forthcoming, and most of these will be strong candidates for interview, and the difficulty will be to decide who *not* to invite. If the advertisement has been drawn up rather loosely, or has deliberately sought to tap a large segment of the labour market, then large numbers of applications can be expected, many of whom will be quite unsuitable. In drawing up a short-list, it is common practice to divide the applications into three groups as follows:

❶ **Very suitable** – must be interviewed.

❷ **Quite suitable** – call for interview if insufficient numbers in category (1), or send holding letter.

❸ **Not suitable** – send polite refusal letter, thanking them for their interest in applying.

If there are numbers of very suitable candidates, then it may be necessary to have two or more sequential interviews, until only the best two or three candidates remain. This whole procedure may sound quite long-winded, but when purchasing the *human* assets of the organisation it is worthwhile spending time over the selection of these the most valuable assets of all.

Selection Processes

13. In the overall process of tapping the labour market for suitable skills and experience, recruitment comes first and is followed by selection. Recruitment's task is to locate possible applicants and attract them to the organisation. Selection's task is to cream off the most appropriate applicants, turn them into candidates and persuade them that it is in their interests to join the organisation, for, even in times of high unemployment, selection is very much a two-way process – the candidate is assessing the organisation, just as much as the organisation is assessing him. The main objective of selection, therefore, is to be able to make an acceptable offer to the candidate who appears, from the evidence obtained, to be the most suitable for the job in question.

14. The most widely-used technique in the selection process is the interview. Well behind the interview, in terms of popularity, comes psychological testing, and both interviews and tests will be considered shortly. However, before turning to them, it is important to reflect on the role of application forms and letters of application in the selection process.

Application Forms

15. An application form or a letter of application tells an organisation whether or not an applicant is worthy of an interview or a test of some kind. This initial information constitutes the bedrock of the selection process, ie prima facie evidence of an applicant's suitability or unsuitability for the position in question. An applicant who is deemed suitable on this evidence, then becomes a candidate for interview. Many organisations require applicants to write a letter explaining why they are interested in the vacant post and how they propose to justify the role they think they could play in it. This approach enables the organisation to see how well applicants can argue a case for themselves in a letter, but it has the disadvantage that the information provided is controlled by the applicant – he can leave out points which may not help his case, and build on those which do. Thus most organisations prefer to design their own application forms, so as to require applicants to set out the information about themselves in a standardised way.

16. Application forms vary considerably in the way they are set out. Some, for example, as in Figure 43.4, require prospective candidates to answer routine questions in a form that gives them no opportunity to discuss their motives for applying or to talk about themselves in a general way. Others, as in Figure 43.5, are very open-ended in their format, and require applicants to expand at some length on themselves and on how they see the job. In between the two forms illustrated are several compromise versions, which aim to establish some kind of balance between closed and open questions. The answers to the closed questions supply the organisation with routine information in a standardised form; the answers to the open questions provide a clue to the motives, personality and communication skills of the applicants.

The Selection Interview

17. The selection interview is far and away the most common technique used for selection purposes. Unlike most other management techniques, it is employed as much by amateurs as by professionals. Whereas in Work Study, for example, only a trained work study

Post Applied For:	
Surname:	First Names:
Address:	Telephone No.:
Date of Birth:	Place of Birth:
Marital Status:	Children:

Education:
     School:
     College:
     University:
 	
 Training:
     Course Attended/Qualifications Obtained:
	Examinations Passed:

Work Experience:
     Present Post (Title, length of service, current salary):
 	
     Previous Posts Held:
 	
 Employer Job Title Dates Reasons for Leaving	

Interest/Hobbies	

Referees: (One from current employer
            one personal referee)
    1.
 	
    2.	

Notice Required by Current Employer:	weeks/months
Signed:	Date:

Figure 43.4. Form to obtain routine information.

analyst will generally be permitted to conduct method studies and work measurement exercises, in the selection of staff everybody is deemed capable! Few managers and supervisors carry out selection interviews regularly; many of them have received no formal training in the technique either, so it is not surprising to learn that research has shown that such interviews are frequently neither reliable nor valid. The measure of the reliability of an interview is the extent to which conclusions about candidates are shared by different interviewers; the measure of the validity of an interview is the extent to which it does measure what it is supposed to measure, ie the suitability of a particular candidate for a particular job.

18. The main reasons why so many poor interviews are carried out are two-fold:

❶ lack of training in interviewing technique, and

❷ lack of adequate preparation for an interview.

Training designed to enable appropriate staff to conduct competent interviews generally involves two major learning methods: firstly, an illustrated talk/discussion; and, secondly,

Post Applied For:
Surname: First Names:
Address: Telephone No.:
Date of Birth: Marital Status:
Details of Examinations Passed/Qualifications Obtained:
Current Post:
Last Three Posts (starting with the latest):
What attracts you to this post?
How do you think you can contribute to the post?
What has given you the greatest satisfaction, to date, in your current or previous employment?
How do you see your career developing over the next ten years or so?
How soon could you start work if appointed?
Please supply the names of two persons who could speak on your behalf.
Signed: **Date:**

Figure 43.5. Open-ended application form.

the process that is taking place during an interview, and to acquire a method for harnessing that process (ie an interview plan). The second method helps trainees to *experience the process* by means of role-playing exercises, and to understand how they may need to adapt their behaviour in order to meet the aims of this kind of interview.

19. Much has been written about selection interviewing, but most of the points made can be condensed into the following guide to good practice (Figure 43.6). This highlights the sort of issues which busy managers need to know about if they are to make optimum use of their own, and the candidates', time in the short period available for the interview.

20. There are a few points arising from the guide in Figure 43.6, which particularly ought to be stressed. The first is the question of preparation. As with so many tasks, the better the preparation, the better the final result. It is very important to be properly prepared before an interview. It enables the interviewer to feel confident in himself about his key role in the process, and enables him to exploit to the full the information provided by the candidate. It also helps to minimise embarrassment caused by constant interruptions, inadequate accommodation and other practical difficulties.

Be Prepared	Obtain available information, eg job details, candidate specification & application form.
	Arrange interview room. Ensure no interruptions.
	Plan the interview.
Welcome the Candidate	After initial courtesies, thank candidate for coming.
	Explain **briefly** what procedure you propose to adopt for the interview
	Commence by asking relatively easy and non-threatening question.
Encourage Candidate to talk	Ask open-ended questions.
	Prompt where necessary.
	Indicate that you are listening.
	Briefly develop points of interest raised by candidate.
Control the Interview	Direct your questions along the lines that will achieve your objectives.
	Tactfully, but firmly, clamp down on the over-talkative candidate.
	Do not get too involved in particular issues just because of your own interests.
	Keep an eye on the time.
Supply Necessary Information	**Briefly** add to information already made available to candidate.
	Answer candidate's questions. Inform candidate of the next steps in the selection procedure.
Close Interview	Thank candidate for his/her responses to your questions.
	Exchange final courtesies.
Final Steps	Write up your notes about the candidate.
	Grade, or rank, him/her for suitability.
	Operate administrative procedures regarding notifications etc.

Figure 43.6 Selection interviewing – guide to good practice.

21. Questioning plays a vital role in a selection interview, as it is the primary means by which information is obtained from the candidate at the time. Questions have been categorised in a number of different ways. For our purposes, it is enough to distinguish between *closed questions* and *open questions*. The major differences between them are as follows:

Closed questions

These are questions which require a *specific* answer or a Yes/No response. For example: 'What course of study led to your qualification?' (specific); 'How many people were you responsible for in your previous job?' (specific); 'Were you personally authorised to sign purchase orders?' (Yes/No); 'Have you had experience of ...?' (Yes/No).

Open questions

These are questions that require a person to reflect on, or elaborate upon, a particular point in his own way. Examples of open questions are: 'What is it that attracts you about this job?' 'Why did you leave ... Company?' 'How would you tackle a problem of this kind, if you were the manager?' Open questions invariably begin with What? or How? or Why?

22. It is usual to ask closed questions to check information which the candidate has already partly supplied on his application form, and to re-direct the interview if the candidate is talking too much and/or getting off the point. Open questions tend to be employed once the interview has got under way, with the object of getting the candidate to demonstrate his knowledge and skills to the interviewer.

23. Controlling the interview is sometimes a problem for interviewers. Lack of control can be manifested in the following ways:

- the candidate takes over the interview, dominating the talking, following his own interests and interrupting the interviewer,
- the candidate is allowed to spend too long over his replies, and to repeat things he has already mentioned,
- the interviewer appears to be tentative in asking questions, and appears to accept whatever the candidate says,
- the candidate patronises the interviewer.

24. Interviewers can help themselves to maintain control in a firm, but diplomatic way by:

- proper preparation, especially the preparation of key questions to be put to the candidate,
- returning to questions which they feel have not been adequately answered by the candidate, ie they are showing that they will not be fobbed off by a plausible non-answer,
- politely, but firmly, cutting short a response which has gone on too long,
- taking an opportunity themselves to supply information to the candidate, thus requiring him to listen,
- using the application form as a map of the interview, on which progress can be plotted,
- resisting the temptation to get involved in an interesting, but time-consuming, issue raised by the candidate,
- allocating the time available for the interview between the key phases to be covered.

25. It is usual for interviewers to supply a certain amount of information to candidates. It is better not to treat the candidate to a ten-minute account of the job and its conditions right at the beginning of the interview, when he or she is feeling tense and wants to get started. If possible, it is better to feed in information as the interview progresses and to round off the final stage of the interview with any routine information about conditions of service. Candidates' questions may be left to the end or dealt with during the course of the interview. In general, the more information that can be supplied *before* the interview, the better.

26. Ideally, the time available for the interview should be spent in assessing the candidate as a person, and adding a feedback dimension to the information obtained from the application form, references and any other previous data about the candidate. Thus the hallmark of a good interview is a lively exchange of relevant facts and impressions between the interviewer and the candidate, which enables the interviewer to decide if the candidate is suitable, and which enables the candidate to decide if he or she still wants the job.

27. Interviews are usually conducted on a one-to-one basis, but a two-to-one situation is also widely favoured, and there is still a lot of support for panel interviews, especially in the public services. In a two-to-one situation, the two interviewers usually agree amongst themselves as to how they will share the questioning and information supplying during the interview. Frequently, in medium and large organisations, one of the two organisation-

representatives is a Personnel specialist, and the other is the 'client', seeking to fill the vacancy in question. The advantages of this type of interview are that whilst one interviewer is asking a question, or pursuing a point, the other can observe the candidate's reactions and make an independent evaluation of this response; and that each interviewer can specialise in his own areas of interest in the selection process, the 'client' concentrating on technical capability and the ability to fit into his team and the Personnel member concentrating on the wider aspects of having such a person as an employee of the organisation. The slight disadvantage of this approach is that the candidate may be less forthcoming if there are two people present to interview him.

28. The panel interview is an altogether different prospect for a candidate. In this case the individual candidate is faced by several interviewers – at least three and possibly as many as eight or ten. In the case of a panel interview, it is of greatest importance to decide who is going to ask which questions, and how the panel is to be chaired. In some public sector panels, there are members who do not ask any questions and who do not comment either – they are there simply as observers, until after the interviewing process is over, when they contribute their impressions to the final decision-making discussion. Generally, however, panel members agree beforehand how they will allocate questions, and then they rely on the discretion of the chairman to deal with the allocation of supplementary issues. The advantage of this type of interview is that it ensures the fairness of the proceedings. There are several disadvantages, however – the candidate will find it difficult to feel at ease in such a formal atmosphere; the individual panel members may be more concerned about being cued for their questions than being concerned to listen to what the candidate is saying; and there is also the problem that the interviewers are often not able to follow up points with the candidate because they are under pressure from their chairman or their colleagues to move on to the next question.

29. Taken as a whole, interviews are most useful for assessing the personal qualities of an individual. They help to answer questions such as 'Is this candidate likely to be able to fit into our team or our environment?' and 'Has this particular candidate any special personal characteristics which give him an advantage over his rivals?' Interviews are not so useful for assessing technical ability or the value of *past* experience. This is one of the reasons why organisations may consider using psychological tests to supplement information gained during interviews.

Psychological Tests

30. Psychological tests, or selection tests as they are often called, are standardised tests designed to provide a relatively objective measure of certain human characteristics by sampling human behaviour. Such tests tend to fall into four categories as follows:

❶ intelligence tests
❷ aptitude tests
❸ attainment tests and
❹ personality tests.

31. Intelligence tests and others are standardised in the sense that the same set of tasks have been given to many other people over a period of many years, and bands of typical results have been developed to provide standards against which subsequent results can usefully be compared. Publishers of tests invariably insist that only trained personnel should administer their material so that the standard conditions of each test are adhered to strictly, and so that the scoring of tests can be relied upon. All reputable tests have been

carefully checked for their validity and their reliability. Checks for validity are designed to ensure that any given test measures what it sets out to measure, eg an intelligence test should be able to measure intelligence, and a manual dexterity test should be able to measure manual dexterity. Checks for reliability are designed to ensure that tests produce consistent results in terms of what they set out to measure. Thus, if a test which is carried out on an individual at a particular point in time is repeated, the results should be similar.

32. The different categories of tests are as follows:

•   **Intelligence tests**

    These tests are designed to measure thinking abilities. The word 'intelligence' has no generally accepted definition, as yet, and has to be defined in terms of a number of different interpretations of its meaning. It is enough for our purposes to understand that general intelligence can be manifested by verbal ability, spatial ability or numerical ability, or a combination of these. Popular tests in use for personnel selection are often composed of several different sections, each of which aims to test candidates on the key ability areas just referred to.

•   **Aptitude tests**

    These are basically tests of innate skills. They are widely used to obtain information about such skills as mechanical ability, clerical and numerical ability, and manual dexterity. Several standard tests are available for the use of organisations, and it is also possible to have tests specially devised, although this is a much more expensive business, since the tests have to be validated before they can be implemented with any confidence.

•   **Attainment tests**

    These tests measure the depth of knowledge or grasp of skills which has been learned in the past – usually at school or college. Typical attainment tests are those which measure typing abilities, spelling ability and mental arithmetic, for example.

•   **Personality tests**

    The use of personality tests derives from clinical situations. Their application to personnel selection is rather restricted, because of the problems associated with the validity of such tests. Where they are employed in work situations, they usually take the form of personality inventories – lists of multiple choice questions in response to theoretical situations posed by the test designers – or of projection tests – where the candidate is required to describe a series of vague pictures or a series of inkblots. The aim of personality tests is to identify an individual's principal personality traits or dimensions, eg introverted or extroverted, sociable or isolate etc.

33. The arrival of the Internet has provided an opportunity for widespread organisations to conduct selection tests remotely. Multinationals, in particular, can benefit from 'e-testing' of new recruits, or promotion prospects, without having to incur all the costs involved in bringing individual candidates into a recruitment centre or personnel office. Other organisations might find a benefit in e-testing if there is a large number of candidates to be tested at any one time, or where it is not easy to set up the appropriate facilities in-house (eg obtaining the services of a qualified psychologist or tester). Online testing of candidates does raise issues of security and confidentiality, which are unlikely to occur in face-to-face testing. This means that such tests need to be adapted to online applications, so that both tester and test taker are properly identified, and that the results will be dealt with via a secure Web site. Data protection legislation will apply to any records of tests kept by the tester.

34. The advantages and disadvantages of e-testing can be summarised as follows:

Advantages	Disadvantages
• Reduction in costs of organising tests	• Lack of control over the test environment
• Flexibility of timing of tests	• Difficulty in ensuring consistency of treatment for all candidates
• Faster scoring of tests as results produced electronically	• Possibility of candidates getting unauthorised help in responding to questions
• Convenience and privacy for test takers	• No immediate advice or support available to candidates who may be having difficulties understanding what they are being asked to do
	• Possible lack of security of personal data

35. Psychological tests can provide useful additional or confirming information about a candidate for a position. They can supplement the information obtained from application forms and from interviews, and are particularly useful where objective information would be illuminating. They are probably most economically applied in situations where reasonably large numbers of recruits are needed every year eg school-leavers, college-leavers and other younger employees. Apart from attainment tests, most of the categories still remain relatively unpopular with employers, and there is no question of psychological tests ousting the need for application forms and interviews.

CHAPTER 44

Employee Development and Training

Introduction

1.   Human resources are the most dynamic of all the organisation's resources. They need considerable attention from the organisation's management, if they are to realise their full potential in their work. Thus motivation, leadership, communication, work restructuring, payments systems and training/development may all be included in the issues which have to be faced by management today. Most of these issues have already been considered, but now it is time to consider the role of training and development activities in the organisation. This short chapter highlights the principal features of a training and development sub-system within the Personnel function.

2.   A question frequently raised by examiners is 'what is the difference, if any, between 'training' and 'development'?' Another question which is sometimes asked is 'what is the difference between 'education' and 'training'?' Given the continuing interest in the implications of such concepts as the 'learning organisation' and competence-based training (see

below), it would also be useful to consider what is meant by the expressions 'learning' and 'competence'. We can thus compare the core meanings of each of these five concepts, as follows:

- **Education** – this is usually intended to mean basic instruction in knowledge and skills designed to enable people to make the most of life in general; it is personal and broadly based.

- **Training** – this usually implies preparation for an occupation or for specific skills; it is more narrow in conception than either education or development; it is job-oriented rather than personal.

- **Development** – this usually suggests a broader view of knowledge and skills acquisition than training; it is less job-oriented than career-oriented; it is concerned more with employee potential than with immediate skill; it sees employees as adaptable resources.

- **Learning** – this is the process of acquiring knowledge, understanding, skills and values in order to be able to adapt to our environment; it underpins all of the above three; the amount, quality and rate of take-up of learning depends mainly on (a) the innate intelligence and motivation of the learner, (b) the skills of the teacher, and (c) the conditions in which the learning takes place (especially the use of relevant learning aids).

- **Competence** – this refers primarily to a person's ability to demonstrate to others that they can perform a task, process or function to a predetermined standard; competence is all about putting learning into practice; it is about the difference between 'knowing how' and 'doing' to a satisfactory level; using predetermined standards in this way is called 'competence-based' training.

3.   Generally, education is a matter for the community to sort out. Training and development are matters for individual organisations to sort out. Learning is the responsibility of all. The rest of this chapter looks at how organisations set about meeting their training and development needs.

Training and Development: Basic Framework

4.   The scope of training and development activities, as in most other activities in an organisation, depends on the policy and strategies of the organisation. There are many organisations in the commercial field that carry out the minimum of staff training and development, because, as a matter of policy, they prefer to recruit staff who are already trained or professionally qualified. These organisations are prepared to pay the top market-rates for skilled staff, and what they put into recruitment, selection and pay and benefits they do not put into training and development. In fact, one of the reasons for the establishment of Industrial Training Boards in Britain was precisely to ensure that *all* organisations in their scope contributed to total training costs, even if they carried out little or no training themselves.

5.   The majority of organisations, however, do have a positive policy on training and development. In some cases, this may be no more than to state that 'The Company will provide resources to ensure that key skills are maintained within the organisation'; in other cases, the policy may refer comprehensively to the various actions it will take to ensure not only a regular supply of skills, but also a high degree of personal motivation through development opportunities provided by the Company. For the purposes of this chapter, it will be assumed that organisations see an important role for training and development in the provision of skills and the improvement of employee motivation.

6.   A term frequently used to describe well-organised training (and development) is 'systematic training'. This can be illustrated diagramatically as a cycle of events, which is initiated by the organisation's policy, and sustained by its training organisation, as shown in Figure 44.1.

Figure 44.1. Systematic training: the basic cycle.

7.   Once the training organisation has been set up, the first priority is to establish what the training and development needs of the organisation are. This will involve the use of job descriptions, employee appraisal records and other data which may indicate such needs. The next step is to plan the training required to meet the needs identified. This entails such matters as setting budgets and timetables, and deciding on the objectives, content and methods of training to be employed. The implementation of plans is usually a joint affair between the training specialists and their line and functional colleagues. Having implemented the required training, it is important to evaluate the results, so far as possible, so that subsequent changes to content and methods can be made, if necessary. Events then move on to the identification of new needs, which re-starts the cycle afresh.

8.   The benefits of systematic training include:

- the provision of a pool of skilled personnel for the organisation,
- the improvement of existing skills,
- an increase in the knowledge and experience of employees,
- improvements in job performance with resulting improvement in productivity overall,
- improved service to customers,
- greater commitment of staff (ie increased motivation),
- increased value of individual employees' knowledge and skills, and
- personal growth opportunities for employees.

The Role of the Trainer

9.   The role of training staff in the organisation, ie the part they are expected to play, as well as the part they themselves expect to play, depends considerably on the style or culture of the organisation. If the organisation actively encourages training and development activities, then trainers will have an exciting and important role to play; if, however, the organisation wishes only to pay lip-service to training, then the role for trainers will be severely limited. The other major factor in deciding what kind of role can be played is that of the training staff's own competence and professionalism. Where trainers are highly skilled both politically and professionally, they will tend to enjoy a good reputation within the organisation; where their skills and ambitions are of a lower order, then so will their reputation and effectiveness be proportionately lower.

10.   The range of roles that can be played out by training staff is strongly influenced by the requirements of their jobs. In a Report on the Training of Trainers, published by the Manpower Services Commission in 1978[1], four key areas for training-specialist jobs were identified. These were as follows:

❶   Planning and organising activities,

❷   Determining and managing activities,

❸   Direct training activities, and

❹   Consulting and advisory activities.

From these four areas of activity it is possible to see several alternative roles, for example: planner of training, training organiser, training manager, instructor, consultant and adviser. Clearly, the more senior the job, the wider the range of possible roles, and vice versa for less senior jobs. A Training Manager, for example, would encompass all the above mentioned roles, although with an emphasis on determining, managing, consultancy and advisory activities. By comparison, a Job Instructor would only be concerned with direct training or instructional activities, and with some organising.

11.   In performing their direct training roles, training specialists are intimately concerned with (a) the identification or assessment of training needs, and (b) the design, content and methods of training to be employed, and (c) the evaluation of training. These three key aspects of training will be looked at in the next few paragraphs.

Identifying Training Needs

12.   A training need is any shortfall in terms of employee knowledge, understanding, skill and attitudes against what is required by the job, or the demands of organisational change. In diagramatic form this can be expressed as shown in Figure 44.2.

13.   All jobs make some demands on their job-holders. Simple jobs will require only a little knowledge with no need for any deeper understanding of what is involved; such jobs will also require little in the way of skill, but may demand more in terms of attitude, ie attention to detail, acceptance of routine and lack of discretion etc. Complex jobs, by comparison, will demand not only a specialist knowledge, but also a real understanding of the basic principles or underlying concepts of the work involved; such jobs will probably require a high level of specialist skill, and attitudes that foster an awareness of the importance of teamwork and the necessity for first-rate quality, for example.

14.   When training staff conduct a comprehensive training needs analysis in their organisation, they will focus on four main sources for their information:

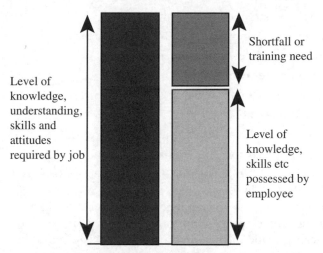

Figure 44.2. Training need.

- **organisation-level data** (eg about the management structure, communication channels, products/ services offered, personnel requirements)
- **job-level data** (eg about individual jobs/roles, and skill requirements)
- **individual data** (eg performance appraisal data, training records)
- **competence standards** (i.e. occupational standards agreed nationally for different levels of responsibility – see Chapter 46 for an example).

15. The data obtained in this way enables the training staff to draw a comprehensive picture of the areas of current, and potential, shortfall in requirements. The collection of information for a training needs analysis is carried out by one or more of the following methods:

- Analysing recorded data relating to the organisation, to jobs and to individuals.
- Analysing questionnaires and attitude surveys issued to employees.
- Interviewing managers and supervisors about their own or their subordinates' training and development needs.
- Observing the job performance of individuals.
- Monitoring the results of group discussions relating to current work problems etc.
- Analysing self-recording diaries etc kept by managers, specialists and others.

16. The most popular of the above methods are those which utilise *existing* records, and those which involve interviewing managerial and supervisory staff. One particularly important document which contributes to the analysis of training needs is the appraisal form. This is the record of an employee's job performance, usually completed following an annual interview with his superior. Appraisal interviews, and the documentation which accompanies them, are the formal mechanisms by which organisations can assess or evaluate their human assets. In a well-managed organisation, this formal appraisal merely rounds off, in a relatively standardised way, the frequent informal appraisals carried out regularly by the organisation's managers as a normal part of their job.

17. The objectives of the formal system of appraisals are various. They include some or all of the following:

- To identify the current level of job performance,

- To identify employee strengths and weaknesses,
- To enable employees to improve on current performance,
- To identify training and development needs,
- To identify potential performance,
- To provide the basis for salary reviews,
- To encourage and motivate employees,
- To provide information for manpower planning purposes.

18. The document on which formal appraisal records are held may take one of several forms. A simple appraisal form is illustrated in Figure 44.3. This example could be used with junior retail staff, for example.

The document is relatively easy to complete, and does cause the manager or supervisor concerned to consider the employee's performance in a number of different work areas. Such a document can provide the basis for a constructive appraisal interview between the employee and his superior.

Name:	Job Title:		
Department:	Appraised by:		
	Date:		
Present Performance:	Unacceptable	Barely acceptable	Perfectly acceptable
Appearance and Manner			
Relationships with Customers			
Relationships with Staff			
Cash Handling			
Documentation Handling			
Enthusiasm			
Reliability			
Timekeeping			

Figure 44.3. Simple appraisal form.

19. An example of a more complex appraisal form is provided in Figure 44.4. In this case the document asks the employee's superior to assess performance against previously agreed targets or objectives, and is the kind of appraisal one would expect to find in an organisation where Management by Objectives was installed.

Name:			Job Title:	
Department:			Appraised by:	
			Date:	

Current Performance			Date:	

Objectives set for the period	Achieved?			Reasons for any shortfall	Comments
	Yes	No	Partly		
1.					
2.					
3.					
4.					

Overall Assessment: Outstanding/Fully Satisfactory/Satisfactory/
Unsatisfactory

Training, Development or Guidance Needs

Potential Performance

Ready for Promotion Now
Ready for Promotion in One/Two years
No Promotion Potential
Move to another Department

Figure 44.4. Objective appraisal form.

20. A document such as the one illustrated in Figure 44.4 can provide a substantial amount of relevant information about training and development needs. Not only is current performance assessed, in terms of specific and measurable parts of the employee's job, but also potential performance is considered. Thus it is possible to consider training and development needs in terms of future job performance as well as in terms of improving current performance.

Planning Training

21. Once training needs have been identified by means of the training needs analysis, the training staff can begin the tasks of sorting training priorities, drawing up initial plans, costing them and then submitting their draft plans for approval by the senior management. These draft plans spell out the key areas for training, the numbers and categories of employees concerned, the nature of the training proposed, the preliminary time-tabling of the training programmes contained in the proposals, and an estimate of the costs which are likely to be incurred.

22. Training programmes can be formal or informal, and can take place on-the-job or off-the-job. The latter can mean in-company, or in-service, training or it can refer to externally provided training. Figure 44.5 illustrates some of the different methods of on-the-job and off-the-job training, and indicates some of the advantages and disadvantages of each approach.

On-the-job Training Methods	Advantages	Disadvantages
On-the-job instruction	Relevant; develops trainee-supervisor links	Noise, bustle and pressure of workplace
Coaching	Job-related; develops boss-subordinate relationship	Subject to work pressures; may be done piecemeal
Counselling	Employee needs help and boss provides it	Counselling skills have to be developed
Delegation by boss	Increases scope of job; provides greater motivation	Employees may make mistakes or may fail to achieve task
Secondment	Increases experience of employee; creates new interest	Employee may not succeed in new position
Guided Projects/Action Learning	Increases knowledge and skills in work situation, but under guidance	Finding suitable guides and mentors

Off-the-job Training Methods	Advantages	Disadvantages
(a) **In-company**		
Lectures/Talks	Useful for factual information	One-way emphasis; little participation
Group discussions	Useful for generating ideas and solutions	Requires adequate leadership
Role-playing exercises	Useful for developing social skills	Requires careful organising; giving tactful feedback is not easy
Skills development exercises eg: manual operations, communication skills etc	A safe way to practise key skills	Careful organisation required
(b) **External**		
College courses (long)	Leads to qualification; comprehensive coverage of theory; wide range of teaching methods	Length of training time; not enough practical work
College courses (short)	Supplement in-company training; independent of internal politics	May not meet client's needs precisely enough
Consultants/Other training organisations	Clients' needs given high priority; fills gaps in company provision; good range of teaching methods	Can be expensive; may rely heavily on 'packages'

Figure 44.5. Summary of training methods.

23. Training plans are designed to encompass the following:

* *what* training is to be provided,
* *how* it is to be provided,
* *when* it is to be provided,
* *by whom* it is to be provided,

- *where* it is to be provided, and
- at *what* cost it is to be provided.

For many companies the resources put into training and development represent a considerable investment in time, money and manpower. This investment needs to be evaluated from time to time to ensure, so far as possible, that it is being deployed wisely.

Evaluation of Training

24. The evaluation of training is part of the control process of training. Evaluation methods aim to obtain feedback about the results or outputs of training, and to use this feedback to assess the value of the training, with a view to improvement, where necessary. Like any other control process, training evaluation is firstly concerned with setting appropriate standards of training. These may take the form of policies, objectives, adherence to external standards, and standards of trainer-training and qualifications. Clearly, the more precise the standards set, the easier it is to evaluate the success of training. This brings us on to the next key point, which is the collection of relevant feedback data about training.

25. Two British contributions to this important issue are those of Hamblin (1970)[2] and of Warr, Bird & Rackham (1970)[3]. Hamblin takes the view that evaluation can take place at a number of different levels, ranging from immediate to long-term results. Each level requires a different evaluation strategy, as indicated in Figure 44.6, which is based on Hamblin's ideas.

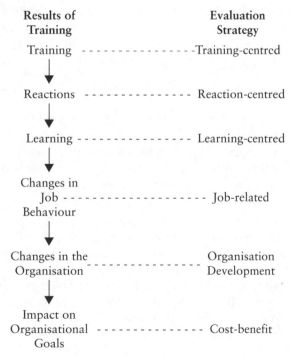

Figure 44.6. Training and evaluation.

26. *Training-centred* evaluation aims to assess the inputs to training ie whether we are using the right tools for training. *Reactions-centred* evaluation, which is probably the most widely-used strategy for evaluation, seeks to obtain and assess the reactions of trainees to the learning experiences they have been put through.

Learning-centred evaluation seeks to measure the degree of learning that has been achieved. This is usually achieved by testing trainees following the training, as in a driving test. *Job-related* evaluation is aimed at assessing the degree of behaviour change which has taken place on-the-job after returning from a period of training. It is, of course, a measure of learning, but learning which has been applied in the workplace. It is not an easy task to evaluate the degree to which learning has been applied, especially in cases where training in social skills, such as leadership, are concerned. Organisation changes can be brought about by training, and here the evaluation strategy is linked to an *Organisation Development* programme.

Finally, there is the impact on organisational goals to be considered, ie what has training done for profitability or company image, for example? This is a favourite question asked by top management, but is extremely difficult to evaluate on account of the many other variables which have an impact on these goals.

27. Warr, Bird and Rackham have produced a somewhat different framework for evaluating training. This takes four major dimensions, and suggests what information should be sought to enable evaluation to become an on-going process in the organisation. In summary these four dimensions are as follows:

- Context evaluation – information required about training needs and objectives.

- Input evaluation – information required about training resources (staff, training aids etc).

- Reaction evaluation – information required about trainees' reactions to training.

- Outcome evaluation – information about immediate, intermediate and ultimate results of training.

28. It was said earlier that, where training standards are laid down precisely, it is easier to assess the value of the training. One of the ways in which organisations attempt to set clear standards is by

- establishing the overall purpose of a particular programme, and

- setting specific objectives for the kind of behaviour expected of trainees at the end of the training.

It is obviously easier to set specific objectives for measurable features of behaviour, than it is for those features which are difficult to measure. A typical example of an attempt to set standards for a training programme is set out in Figure 44.7.

29. The overall purpose stated above is put in rather general terms, eg 'improve key skills...' What the objectives try to do is to specify *how* a supervisor can indicate that he has gained an improved grasp of this topic. In each case, the objective aims to describe *behaviour* (ie what the trainee is expected to do) at the end of the course. If few members of a supervisory course were able to demonstrate that they *could* now do the things that the course had set out to achieve, the organisers would know that they had failed to achieve their training objectives, and would have to change any further courses in the light of this feedback. This approach is sometimes known as training validation, ie assessing if training achieves what it is supposed to achieve. Validation is one facet of the overall evaluation process.

The Learning Organisation

30. Senge (1990)[4] describes learning organisations as 'organisations where people continually expand their capacity to create the results they truly desire, where new and expansive patterns of thinking are nurtured, where collective aspiration is set free, and where people are continually learning how to learn together' (p.3).

Course:	Recruitment and Selection for Supervisors.
Overall Purpose:	To improve key skills needed in the recruitment and selection process, and to assist in the application of these skills in the workplace.
Objectives:	At the end of the course, a supervisor should be able to: i. Describe the key stages in the recruitment and selection process, ii. Prepare acceptable job descriptions and personnel specifications, iii. State the role of the Personnel department in recruitment and selection, iv. Apply the Seven-point Plan as an assessment tool in an interview, v. Conduct a systematic interview of a prospective employee, vi. Complete correctly all the Company's selection documents, which apply to his/her role as a supervisor.

Figure 44.7. Training objectives.

The last point is a key one, for the mark of an organisation that is really committed to learning is the openness of its employees to the learning opportunities that occur daily in their work environment. Learning in this context, means that all levels and grades of staff are developing their capacity to acquire new skills and insights into the way their duties must be fulfilled. This, it should be noted, means accepting that mistakes and errors of judgement are as much sources of learning as successes and achievements. Indeed, Hamel and Prahalad (1994)[5] argue that 'creating a "learning organisation" is only half the solution. Just as important is creating an "unlearning organisation" ... To create the future, a company must unlearn at least some of its past.' (p.60)

31. A learning organisation is one that sees that learning, training and development are best achieved by collaborative efforts. Every employee from top to bottom is expected to reflect on present practices, suggest better ways of doing things, and collaborate with others to achieve improvements. Teams are effective sources of learning – leaders stimulate actions and provide models of behaviour (good and bad!); team members contribute their own particular talents and also provide models of behaviour; individuals are both beneficiaries of, yet challenged by, the behaviour of the others. Where the culture of the organisation stresses the need for learning from each other, teams become the greatest source of creative and constructive thinking. Newcomers are more easily assimilated into a group that is committed to learning, as they are encouraged to seek help from others. Yet their perspectives as newcomers are also welcomed by the group, which may see a better way of achieving a particular task. It is no surprise that Senge (op. cit.) considers that team learning, and having a shared vision, are two of the dominant elements of a learning organisation.

References

1. MSC (1978), *First Report – The Training of Trainers*, HMSO.
2. Hamblin, A.C. (1970), *Evaluation and Control of Training*, McGraw-Hill.

3. Warr, P.B., Bird, M.W. and Rackham, N. (1970), *Evaluation of Management Training*, Gower Press.

4. Senge, P. (1990), *The Fifth Discipline – the Art and Practice of the Learning Organisation*, Doubleday (British edition, 1992, by Century Business).

5. Hamel, G. & Prahalad, C. (1994), *Competing for the Future*, Harvard Business School Press.

CHAPTER 45

Performance Appraisal, Discipline and Grievances

Introduction

1.   Only a minority of activities in personnel management are concerned with evaluating employees as individuals. These activities are primarily selection and appraisal, but also include grievance and disciplinary matters. In all other cases, the focus of attention is not on individuals but on jobs, structures, procedures or people in groups. Thus, for example, job evaluation focuses on jobs, not on job-holders; job design and organisation development focus on job/task structures; wage and salary administration focus on procedures; whilst manpower planning and collective bargaining focus on people in groups.

2.   This chapter considers the evaluation of individuals in terms of their job performance. This is a task requiring a quality of managerial judgement which places a considerable responsibility on the managers involved. It is a task that is delicate as well as complex. This chapter examines the key features of performance appraisal and suggests a code of good practice in this area.

Performance Appraisal

3.   At its simplest, the appraisal process can be depicted as in Figure 45.1.

Any systematic approach to performance appraisal will commence with the completion of an appropriate appraisal form. This preparatory stage will be followed by an interview, in which the manager discusses progress with the member of staff. The result of the interview is some form of agreed action, either by the staff member alone, or jointly with his manager. The action generally materialises in the shape of a job improvement plan, promotion to another job or to a salary increase, for example.

4.   The expression 'performance appraisal' usually relates to the assessment of staff or managerial performance, and not to that of manual workers. There are two main categories of appraisal, as follows:

-   Informal appraisal, which is the continual day-to-day assessment of an employee's progress by his or her manager, and which is ad hoc in nature, and as much determined by intuitive feelings as by objective evidence. It is a natural by-product of the ongoing relationship between employee and manager.

-   Formal appraisal, which is a planned event based on performance evidence, at which an employee's progress is discussed with his or her superior, usually in the context of job targets and priorities.

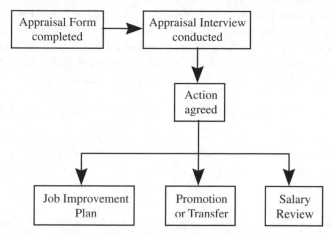

Figure 45.1 The appraisal process.

Most appraisals are conducted by superiors on the staff who report to them, and so an element of formal authority is invariably present in the appraisal interview. However, in recent years so-called 360° appraisals have been introduced by organisations that are keen to improve the appraisal of managerial staff. This form of appraisal requires that the manager's own staff are formally encouraged to comment on their leader's performance. Peer group managers are also consulted, so that appraisal in this case becomes all-round rather than just top-down. The success of such appraisals depends on the dominant culture in the organisation. In a mature culture, where collaboration is accepted as the norm, and where mistakes are seen as opportunities rather than threats, 360° appraisals are more likely to produce authentic results than in a culture still dominated by the hierarchy.

Reasons for Appraisal

5.   There are several reasons why appraisals are carried out in organisations. These may be summarised as follows:

- to identify an individual's current level of job performance
- to identify employee strengths and weaknesses
- to enable employees to improve their performance
- to provide a basis for rewarding employees in relation to their contribution to organisation goals
- to motivate individuals
- to identify training and development needs
- to identify potential performance
- to provide information for succession planning.

6.   The most likely reason for the adoption of staff appraisal is to draw attention to present performance in the job in order to (a) reward people fairly, and (b) to identify those with potential for promotion or transfer.

7.   Writers such as Drucker (1954)[1] are enthusiastic about appraisal:

'To appraise a subordinate and his performance is part of the manager's job. Indeed, unless he does the appraising himself he cannot adequately discharge his responsibility for assisting and teaching his subordinates.'

Drucker's view as a whole is that managers are responsible for achieving results. These results are obtained from the management of human, material and financial resources, all of which should be monitored. Monitoring means setting standards, measuring performance and taking appropriate action. In respect of people this entails taking action to improve performance by means of training and help, ie 'management development' (see Chapter 46).

8.   Other writers such as McGregor (1960)[2] are critical of formal appraisals:

> 'Appraisal programs are designed not only to provide more systematic control of the behaviour of subordinates, but also to control the behaviour of superiors...'

He thus sees them as promoting the cause of Theory X, ie a management style that assumes that people are unreliable, unable to take responsibility and therefore require close supervision and control.

9.   Whenever the argument is more about practicalities than managerial philosophy, the main issue is not whether performance appraisal, in itself, is justified but whether it is fair and accurate. McBeath & Rands (1976)[3], in discussing salary administration, comment:

> '...equitable salary relationships depend on sound job classification, periodic salary surveys of competitive levels, employee appraisal and effective salary planning.'

For them appraisal is part and parcel of an important personnel activity–salary planning and administration. They are keen to acknowledge, however, that 'it is clearly essential to make some attempt at accurate measurement of performance if the appraisal is to be taken seriously into account as a factor which will influence salaries.'

10.   If we accept that staff performance appraisal *is* a legitimate activity in organisations, what are the difficulties concerning both accuracy and fairness? Briefly, they boil down to:

• the construction of the appraisal documents
• the style in which the appraisal is approached
• the culture of the organisation.

Taking the last point first, the 'culture', or value-system, of the organisation will act as the major determinant of both the appraisal scheme adopted and the way it is introduced. For example, if the culture is one which favours control and measurement of people then it is likely that a system will be imposed on the participants, but that it will at least contain some measurable criteria against which to judge performance. In another situation, where openness and participation are encouraged, any system will be discussed first with those involved, with the result that appraisals are more likely to be joint problem-solving affairs rather than a 'calling to account' by a superior.

Appraisal Forms

11.   There are various ways in which appraisal forms can be devised. The key elements, however, are the following:

❶   the focus of the appraisal, ie the job or the person
❷   the performance criteria to be selected
❸   the performance ratings to be used.

Where the appraisal focuses on the job, the appraisal form is more likely to ask the appraiser to look for success in achieving job targets or objectives than to comment on the job-holder's personal attributes. Where the focus is on the person rather than on the job, the reverse is true, ie the appraiser is expected to give an account of the jobholder's qualities and attitudes rather than of his or her relative success in achieving results. Thus, the focus of the appraisal will determine the nature of the criteria against which individual performance will be judged, as well as of the ratings or measures to be used.

12. Forms which seek information about the person rather than about their performance in the job are typified by an emphasis on:

- generalised criteria
- generalised ratings of performance
- individual qualities rather than results
- box-ticking as method of describing performance.

Figure 45.2 provides an illustration of such a form, employed originally by a medium-sized manufacturing company.

Personal Attributes		
Leadership	1	Always at the centre of activity
	2	Capable of leading smallish groups
	3	Has no real leadership qualities
Initiative	1	Always acts on own initiative
	2	Will act on own initiative in minor ways
	3	Never acts unless instructed
Judgement	1	Assesses a situation with cool discernment
	2	Sometimes confused by strong counter arguments, but generally makes sound assessment
	3	Totally lacks any critical faculty
Decision-making Ability	1	Makes sound decisions at all times
	2	Cannot always foresee the outcome of his decisions
	3	Decisions are more like guesses
Customer Awareness	1	Aware of need for quality, timeliness and price
	2	Only partially aware of the importance of the customer during the working day
	3	Customers' needs are seen as secondary to his own
Self-discipline	1	Has well-balanced attitude towards work and leisure
	2	Concentrates on work he prefers
	3	Needs constant instruction and supervision
Technical Attributes		
Technical Knowledge	1	Wide technical knowledge of Company's products with specialist knowledge of some
	2	Limited technical knowledge but useful practical ability
	3	Very little knowledge required
Quality of Work	1	Always careful, rarely makes mistakes
	2	Sometimes makes mistakes
	3	Work characterised by carelessness
Diligence	1	Consistently hard worker
	2	Occasionally needs reminding about time-wasting
	3	Makes no great effort when working
Cost Consciousness	1	Fully appreciates the importance of cost control
	2	Give some thought to costs
	3	Tends to be wasteful, rarely considers costs

Figure 45.2 Appraisal form emphasising individual qualities.

13. The first difficulty with the above approach is that of measurement. How can a manager fairly assess qualities of leadership or judgement, for example? The second difficulty is that of relevance. How central to success are diligence and cost consciousness, for example? Hard work is not synonymous with *effective* work; awareness of costs may be disadvantageous if it discourages initiative or decision-making. The third difficulty is that the managers completing the form have to rely on subjective impressions instead of concrete evidence. Fortunately, the senior management of the company concerned found it too difficult to operate such a generalised instrument and eventually substituted a results-oriented system.

14. The approach just described does not provide a sound basis on which to take decisions about pay and promotion, for example. It clearly deserves the comment made by McGregor[2] that:

> 'If we then take these somewhat questionable data and attempt to use them to make fine discriminations between people for purposes of salary administration and promotion, we can create a pretty picture, but one which has little relation to reality.'

The way forward to reality for many organisations is to take the *job* duties and responsibilities as the focal point of appraisal. In this approach the emphasis is placed on results achieved against standards set, and after taking circumstances into account.

15. In any situation what is 'real' depends partly on the perceptions of those concerned, ie how they 'see' things, and partly on objective evidence, ie information that can be verified by a third party. To build such elements into an appraisal form requires a document such as the one illustrated in Figure 45.3.

Company:	**Office Equipment Sales**				
Position:	**Managing Director**				
Key Result Areas	Targets set for the period*	Achieved?	Evidence	Notes	
Profitability	Increase profit:sales ratio by 2%	Yes	Annual accounts		
Market Share	Maintain present market share at 15%	No (13%)	Industry statistics	Price-cutting by all competitors	
Sales	Achieve gross sales of £150m	No (£148m)	Annual accounts		
Delivery	Reduce average delivery time to four weeks	Yes	Customer accounts		
Staff Performance	Ensure staff costs do not exceed 55% of total expenditure	Yes	Annual Budget Summary		

* Financial year

Figure 45.3 Results-oriented appraisal form.

16. In an appraisal form set out as in Figure 45.3, it is possible to identify the relevant aspects of the job and to set measurable targets against which to assess the individual jobholder's performance in a fair and accurate manner. Humble (1967)[4] sees a performance standard as a statement of the conditions which exist when the required result is expressed in terms of:

- Quantity (How much?)

- Quality (How well?)
- Time (By what time?)
- Cost (At what cost?)

17. The example of a results-oriented appraisal as in Figure 45.3 illustrates the kind of approach suggested by Humble and other advocates of Management by Objectives. In the example all the potential criteria of performance are measurable in quantitative terms. Qualitative standards can also be utilised. Indeed, theorist-managers such as Wilfred Brown (1960)[5] insist that they are inescapable:

> 'I cannot wholly assess the work of a general manager... on figures of output... etc. I must come to difficult intuitive judgements on the relationship of actual to optimum performance.'

When such judgements have to be made, they should be based on criteria which, though general, are sufficiently assessable to enable a reasonable manager to judge the extent to which due standards of performance had been met.

18. An example of a general criterion of managerial behaviour could be:

> 'To achieve a major shift in employee attitudes regarding labour flexibility.'

Reddin (1970)[6] dislikes this latter example:

> 'If no measurement method is available... some expression such as 'subjective judgement' is added. Try and avoid this.'

Brown's (1960)[5] rebuff to this advice is to comment:

> '...the results obtained in any manager's command are a function not only of his own decisions but also of those of his superior manager, and of the policy operated by the Company...'

Thus, to return to the example above, to achieve a major shift in employee attitudes requires the joint efforts of various managers. It also requires meshing together such factors as pay structures, job design, redundancy arrangements and shop-floor supervision in order to achieve any real prospects of change.

Rating Scales in Performance Appraisal

19. We have just seen that appraisal criteria are generally either personality oriented or results oriented. Within each of these orientations appraisers still have to 'measure' individual performance. They do so by using one or more scales for rating performance. The principal options available are:

- **Linear or Graphic Rating Scales,** in which the appraiser is faced with a list of characteristics or job duties and is required to tick or circle an appropriate point on a numerical, alphabetical or other simple scale. Examples are given in Figure 45.4.
- **Behavioural Scales,** in which the appraiser has a list of key job items against which are ranged a number of descriptors, or just two extreme statements of anticipated behaviour. One example is shown in Figure 45.2 above. Another scale, dealing with customer relations, could demonstrate a range of possible behaviour from the *best*, eg 'Deals politely and efficiently with customers at all time', to the *worst* 'is barely civil to customers, is inefficient.'
- **Results/Targets Set,** as in Figure 45.3 above.
- **Free Written Reports,** in which appraisers write essay-type answers to a number of questions set on the appraisal document.

	EXCELLENT				NON-EXISTENT
Initiative	A	B	C	D	E

	EXCELLENT				POOR
Relationship with customers	A	B	C	D	E

	LOW				HIGH
Initiative	1	2	3	4	5

	POOR				EXCELLENT
Relationship with customers	1	2	3	4	5

Figure 45.4 Linear rating scales.

20. The most common scales currently in use are linear scales although both results-oriented measures and written reports also have their advocates among several companies. One other approach, which has not been mentioned so far, is that of self-appraisal, where the employee either writes an 'annual report' on their work or answers questions set out in an appraisal document. In a survey carried out by the IPM in 1977, over a quarter of firms questioned mentioned that they were making use of self-appraisal forms as part of their appraisal procedures.

21. We noted in paragraph 10 above that one of the difficulties in achieving accuracy and fairness in appraisals concerns the style in which the appraisal is approached. Having considered the effects of (a) the organisation culture, and (b) the appraisal documentation, we can now turn to the appraisal interview conducted by the job-holder's manager.

22. The appraisal interview is the formal face-to-face meeting between the job-holder and his manager at which the information on the appraisal form is discussed and after which certain key decisions are made concerning salary, promotion and training, for example. Judging from research studies into appraisal, the majority of managers do not like conducting annual appraisals of their staff. McGregor (1957)[7] in an article on appraisal interviews commented that

> 'Managers are uncomfortable when they are put in the position of playing God'.

23. In a study of six British firms it was found that:

- appraisers were reluctant to conduct appraisals, finding ways of evading full completion of the appraisal forms
- appraisers were extremely reluctant to carry out face-to-face interviews
- there was inadequate follow-up to the appraisals, in terms of their effect on transfers etc.

Thomason (1981)[8] summarises the situation as follows:

> '... the appraiser feels ... put on the spot in carrying out plans of this type. He is required, whatever his own perception of the subordinate's expectations, to confront the individual in an authoritarian setting and to prescribe courses of action on the basis of judgements which he may or may not understand or accept.'

24. The manner in which managers approaches an appraisal interview will be strongly influenced by their understanding of the purpose of the interview. Appraisal interviews can serve several purposes:

1 to evaluate the subordinate's recent performance

2 to formulate job improvement plans

3 to identify problems and/or examine possible opportunities related to the job

4 to improve communication between superior and subordinate

5 to provide feedback on job performance to the employee

6 to provide a rationale for salary reviews

7 to identify potential performance/possibilities for promotion or transfer

8 to identify training and development needs

Clearly some of the above purposes involve the manager and his or her team members in a in joint discussion of common issues, with only a hint of remedial work for the appraisee. A few involve a 'top-down' emphasis in which the manager, as representative of the senior hierarchy passes judgement on those lower down the pyramid. Other appraisal interviews fall somewhere between these two extremes.

Appraisal Styles

25. Maier (1958)[9] identified three basic approaches to the appraisal interview. These were as follows:

1 TELL AND SELL approach, in which the manager tells his or her team members how they are doing, and endeavours to persuade them to accept what has already been decided in terms of improvement.

2 TELL AND LISTEN approach, where the manager tells the team member how he or she is how he is doing, but then sits back and listens to the individual's point of view both about the appraisal and about any follow-up action required.

3 PROBLEM-SOLVING approach, in which the manager effectively puts aside the role of judge in order to join the team member in mutual reflection on progress and mutual discussion about required action.

Maier has in effect described a continuum of interviewer behaviour ranging from a relatively autocratic style to one that is fully participative. The continuum may be described graphically as in Figure 45.5.

26. The likely success of the varying styles, judging from research into appraisals, can be summarised as follows:

- 'TELLING' can be counterproductive. It has been found that praise has little effect one way or the other on appraisees. Criticism, however, has a *negative* effect on subsequent achievement. At least this approach does give the employee some idea of his or her progress.

- 'TELLING/SELLING'. Unless the manager is very persuasive, it is unlikely that the employee will accept his version of what is required to be done.

- 'TELLING/LISTENING'. This approach has the merit of informing employees of their progress, but then goes further by actively involving them in the process of deciding what ought to be done, which is much more likely to produce a positive response.

- 'SHARING'. This is generally considered to provide the best basis for an appraisal owing to its joint problem-solving approach, in which the manager and his or her team member work together more or less as equals. This approach is closer to coaching than anything else.

367

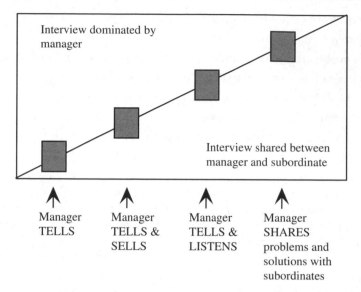

Manager
TELLS

Manager
TELLS &
SELLS

Manager
TELLS &
LISTENS

Manager
SHARES
problems and
solutions with
subordinates

Figure 45.5 A continuum of appraisal interview styles (after Maier).

27. The importance of Maier's appraisal model lies in its use as a device for managers to identify their preferred approach and consider how they could improve upon it. The range of approaches in the model can also be applied in other situations, such as disciplinary and grievance interviews.

Disciplinary and Grievance Procedures

28. Disciplinary and grievance interviews are more likely than appraisal interviews to be encompassed within a set of procedures that are explicitly stated as part of the organisation's culture. An important part of any personnel policy is to establish appropriate standards of managerial conduct in respect of:

*   unacceptable behaviour on the part of employees (ie disciplinary matters)
*   grievances raised by employees in the course of their employment.

Disciplinary matters, in particular, have to be handled with fairness and credibility. Employees should be given a fair hearing when their behaviour falls well short of expectations by breaking important rules of conduct. It is also necessary for organisations to be able to take appropriate sanctions against employees who break the rules, so as to retain the credibility of the disciplinary system. Similar considerations apply to the handling of grievances brought to management by employees.

Discipline

29. A typical preamble to a policy statement on discipline could be as follows:

'In matters of alleged employee misconduct, the Company will ensure that each case is thoroughly and fairly investigated before any action may be taken against the employee concerned. Every employee in a disciplinary situation will be given ample opportunity to state his case. Any disciplinary action that may be taken will be applied fairly and consistently, in accordance with the Company's disciplinary procedure'.

30. Good practice in disciplinary matters is set out in an ACAS Code of Practice[10] on disciplinary procedures. In summary this proposes that disciplinary procedures should:

- be in written form,
- specify to whom they apply (ie all, or some, of the employees),
- be capable of dealing speedily with disciplinary matters,
- indicate the forms of disciplinary action which may be taken (eg dismissal, suspension or warning),
- specify the appropriate levels of authority for the exercise of disciplinary actions,
- provide for individuals to be informed of the nature of their alleged misconduct,
- allow individuals to state their case, and to be accompanied by a fellow employee (or union representative),
- ensure that every case is properly investigated before any disciplinary action is taken,
- ensure that employees are informed of the reasons for any penalty they receive,
- state that no employee will be dismissed for a first offence, except in cases of gross misconduct,
- provide for a right of appeal against any disciplinary action, and specify the appeals procedure.

31. A model disciplinary procedure should aim to *correct* unsatisfactory behaviour, rather than to *punish* it. It should specify as fully as possible what constitutes 'misconduct' and what constitutes 'gross misconduct'. It should then state what is the most likely penalty for each of these categories. In cases of proven 'gross misconduct', this is most likely to be immediate (or summary) dismissal, or suspension, followed by dismissal. In cases of less serious misconduct, the most likely consequence is that a formal warning will be given. For *repeated* acts of misconduct, it is likely that the employee concerned will be dismissed. So far as appeals are concerned, a model procedure should aim to ensure that these are dealt with quickly, so that the employee involved can be informed of the final decision without undue delay.

32. Because of the serious implications of disciplinary action, only senior managers are normally permitted to carry out suspensions, demotions or dismissals. Other managers are normally restricted to giving warnings of one kind or another, and the same applies to supervisors.

Grievances

33. When it comes to handling grievances, however, all managers and supervisors have an important role to play, for one of the key features of every effective grievance procedure is that it should aim to settle the grievance as near a possible to the point of origin. In the UK, legislation requires employers to inform their employees, within 13 weeks of commencing employment, about the main terms and conditions of their employment, including specific references to disciplinary and grievance procedures.

34. A grievance, unlike a disciplinary matter, is first raised by the employee. The onus is on the employee to state what is the nature of the grievance, and what if anything he or she wants done about it. In a work team where the manager or supervisor is in close touch with the members, issues that might lead to a grievance tend to be dealt with in the course of day-to-day problem-solving. Where, however, an issue is still not satisfactorily resolved from the employee's point of view, then a formal application may be made to raise the issue under the appropriate procedure.

35. What is a typical grievance procedure? It is likely to follow the stages set out below:

- **Preamble**
  'Management recognises the right of every employee to seek redress for any grievances they may have relating to their conditions of employment. The procedure which follows aims to provide a fair and speedy settlement of grievances, as near as possible to their point of origin.'

- **Stage 1**
  'The employee should first raise the matter with his or her immediate supervisor or manager, and may be accompanied by a fellow employee. The manager or supervisor will endeavour to resolve the grievance without delay.'

- **Stage 2**
  'If the employee is not satisfied with the response of his or her immediate manager or supervisor, the matter may be referred to the departmental manager or other appropriate senior manager, who will hear the grievance within five working days of it being referred to him. At the meeting the employee may be accompanied by a fellow employee, and the Company Personnel Manager will be present.'

- **Appeal**
  'If the employee is still dissatisfied after the second stage, he or she may appeal to a director, who will arrange to hear the appeal within five working days. The employee, any accompanying employee, and the Company Personnel Manager will be present at the appeal hearing. The results of the appeal will be recorded in writing and distributed to all the parties concerned.'

36. When dealing with a grievance interview, a manager or supervisor is usually unable to prepare in advance for it. An employee, however, may have been storing up a particular grievance for weeks. In order, therefore, to help them cope with the demands of what is often an extremely emotional situation, many managers and supervisors are trained in the tactics of grievance interviewing. The fundamental point is that no hasty judgements or solutions should be made until all the facts of the case are clear, and all third parties have been consulted and, where appropriate, have agreed to the proposed solution. The key points to be noted can be summarised as in Figure 45.6

Objectives	1.	Obtain the facts
	2.	Arrive at an acceptable solution
Strategy	Aim for a 'win/win' conclusion	
Tactics	a.	Listen carefully to the employee's side of the story
	b.	Ask probing questions to elicit relevant facts and feelings
	c.	Summarise from time to time to ensure mutual understanding
	d.	Attempt to unravel cause(s) of grievance
	e.	Check facts obtained and meet any other parties involved
	f.	Consider actions that could be taken and assess their consequences
	g.	Reply to the aggrieved employee and record actions taken

Figure 45.6 Planning a grievance interview

37. Whether or not a grievance turns out to have any substance, after due investigation, it has still been a source of upset feelings for an employee. It is important, therefore, that managers and supervisors aim for a mutually beneficial result at the end of a grievance interview. The employee concerned should be able to go away feeling reassured that, either he or she has no problem, or, if they have, it is being tackled constructively by the imme-

diate superior. The manager or supervisor concerned should be able to feel that the grievance has been handled correctly, and that both parties have 'won'. As with disciplinary cases, the ideal is that the outcome of a grievance includes appropriate learning by all those concerned.

References

1   Drucker, P. (1954), *The Practice of Management*, Heinemann.
2. McGregor, D.(1960), *The Human Side of Enterprise*, McGraw-Hill.
3. MacBeath, I. & Rands, D. (1976), *Salary Administration*, Gower.
4. Humble, J. (1967), *Improving Business Results*, McGraw-Hill.
5. Brown, W. (1960), *Exploration in Management,* Heinemann.
6. Reddin, W. (1970), *Managerial Effectiveness*, McGraw-Hill.
7. McGregor, D. (1957), 'An Uneasy Look at Performance Appraisal', in *Harvard Business Review 35* No. 3 (May–June).
8. Thomason, G. (1981), *Textbook of Personnel Management*, IPM.
9. Maier, N. (1958), *The Appraisal Interview*, Wiley.
10. ACAS, *Code of Good Practice in Disciplinary Procedures*, HMSO.

CHAPTER 46

Developing Managerial Competencies

Introduction

1.   In the field of training and development, management development has become an important activity in its own right. It has developed its own techniques, practices and literature. This chapter reviews the subject of management development, commencing with some definitions, continuing with an assessment of typical management development techniques and practices, and concluding with a consideration of the relationship between management development and corporate policies and culture.

Management Development – Some Definitions

2.   The following definitions of management development indicate some of the differences of emphasis that exist:

> '... manager development must embrace *all* managers in the enterprise. It must aim at challenging all to growth and self development. It must focus on performance rather than on promise, and on tomorrow's requirements rather than those of today.'
>
> *Drucker (1955) The Practice of Management*[1]

In this statement Drucker was well ahead of his time, especially in terms of seeing management development as self-development within the total management structure, and of recognising the importance of preparing for change in the organisation.

'… any attempt to improve managerial effectiveness through a planned and deliberate learning process.'   *MSC (1978) Policy paper on Management Development.*[2]

This general statement emphasises the wide range of options facing organisations wishing to undertake management development, and stresses the need for a systematic approach.

'… development is a continuing improvement of effectiveness within a particular system, which may be a person, but in the case of management development is within the management function of an organisation …'

Morris (1978) Management Development and Development Management[3]

Professor Morris sees management development as part of the process of organisational renewal, with the implication that a variety of approaches are possible.

'In some organisations the focus of management development will primarily be upon the training and education of managers. In other(s) … (it) … may be seen to be aiming to change the managerial style … In yet others…the main focus will be on formalised systems…associated with performance appraisal and career planning …'

Easterby-Smith et al (1980) Auditing Management Development[4]

Easterby Smith and colleagues found a variety of approaches to management development in their studies of several hundred managers' experience of management development.

3.   Although by no means the majority of management development systems are formalised, the structure of activities implicit in such an approach can be illuminating. Figure 46.1 indicates the range of features likely to be present in a formal system.

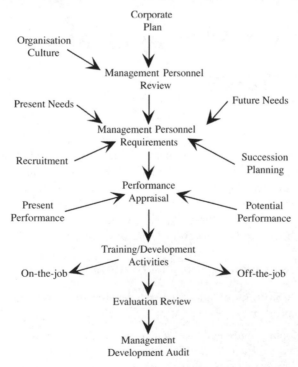

Fig 46.1 Formal management development system.

In a formal system, management development arises from needs expressed in plans and personnel reviews, as influenced by the corporate culture, or value system. Present and future needs for managers imply recruitment and succession planning measures.

Performance of managers is formally appraised in terms of present and potential level of achievement. Improvements in performance are dealt with by a variety of training and development activities, which are evaluated individually, and, in some cases, may also be subjected to a management development audit as a whole.

4.   Three underlying trends can be discerned in the variety of possible approaches to management development, and these are as follows:

❶   the improvement of individual manager effectiveness, ie 'The extent to which a manager achieves the output requirements of his position.' (Reddin, 1970)[5]

❷   the improvement of management performance as a whole

❸   the improvement of organisational effectiveness (ie the achievement of corporate objectives by means of collaborative efforts throughout the enterprise).

5.   In practice the first of these three trends results in specific educational and training activities provided to meet individuals immediate and short-term needs. The second trend is directed more towards common, medium-term needs of *groups* of managers. The third trend emphasises the medium and long-term needs of the organisation as a whole in adapting to the pressures of its environment. If we take the first two trends, a key question is 'What do managers need to know and need to perform to be effective?' This question will be considered in the next few paragraphs. The third trend will be considered towards the end of the chapter.

Management – Knowledge and Skills

6.   In his classic definition, Fayol (1949)[6] saw the task of management as follows:

'To manage is to forecast and plan, to organise, to command, to coordinate and to control.'

Such a definition is always limited by its generality. It does not tell you what managers need to know or do in order to be able to carry out the functions described. In recent years there has been an emphasis on examining what managers actually do in practice (eg Mintzberg, 1973[7], and Stewart, 1982[8]). This approach has led to other developments, where attempts have been made to identify specific areas of knowledge and skill in managerial positions.

7.   A useful example of this last development is provided by Pedler et al (2001)[9] in their list of attributes of 'successful' managers. Their list comprises the following features of an effective manager:

❶   Command of basic facts

❷   Relevant professional knowledge

❸   Continuing sensitivity to events

❹   Analytical, problem-solving, decision-making and judgement-making skills

❺   Social skills and abilities

❻   Emotional resilience

❼   Proactivity, ie the inclination to respond purposefully to events

❽   Creativity

❾   Mental agility

❿   Balanced learning habits and skills

⓫   Self-knowledge.

Whilst the list reads rather like a prosaic version of Kipling's 'If', nevertheless it does provoke other questions, as the authors themselves are aware, and these questions can help to direct managers' thinking about their effectiveness as managers.

8.   Pedler and colleagues raise several questions under each of their eleven features to enable managers to assess themselves at the start of a series of self-development exercises built around their list. Rosemary Stewart (1982)[8] took a rather different approach to analysing managers' jobs. She looked at managers' jobs in terms of the demands, constraints and choices that are present. Jobs were described along these lines and then managers were encouraged to consider how they could extend their range of choices, as well as learning to cope with those aspects that could not be changed.

9.   Another view of managerial jobs was expressed by Simmons & Brennan (1981)[10]

> '...managing well means:
> 1. Having frequent reviews of performance as a group...
> 2. ...listening to each individual's views on the situation and how things can be improved...
> 3. Proposing and getting commitment to a solution ... which is in line with the goals ... of the system.'

This particular viewpoint emphasises the team leadership aspects of a managerial position.

10.   Taking all these views about the nature of managerial jobs as a whole, four key elements can be discerned in terms of what managers might need to know or be able to do. These are as follows:

- Managerial knowledge – what the manager needs to know about the organisation, the job, the procedures involved etc

- Managerial skills – what problem-solving, social and other skills the manager needs to be able to practise

- Managerial attitudes – what the manager is required to accept in terms of coping with stress, dealing with clients etc

- Managerial style – the expectations that people have concerning the way the manager exercises leadership.

These four elements can be found in most management development programmes, whether for individuals or for groups.

Benchmarks for Management

11.   Over the last decade the principal benchmarks for management practice in the United Kingdom have been those drawn up by the Management Standards Centre, which is the standards-setting body for national occupational standards in management. The benchmarks, known as management standards, have been widely used in work organisations in the UK and abroad, and have been incorporated into all nationally recognised qualifications in management. The standards were developed with the assistance of thousands of practising managers in all types of organisations, and represent 'best practice' for all levels of management. They thus provide a very credible basis for assessing the kind of knowledge and skills required by managers, and the level of performance, which ought to be expected from a competent person.

12.   The standards are set out in series of flowcharts and guidance notes, using headline phrases such as 'key purpose', 'key role', 'unit of competence', 'element of competence',

and 'performance criteria'. An example of the logic and content of typical standards are given in Figures 46.2 and 46.3 :

Key purpose	Key roles
	Key role A:
	Manage activities
	Key role B:
	Manage resources
	Key role C:
	Manage people
To achieve the	Key role D:
organisation's	Manage information
objectives and	
continuously	Key role E:
improve its	Manage energy
performance	
	Key role F:
	Manage quality
	Key role G:
	Manage projects

Figure 46.2 Management standards: key roles

13. The initial logic identifies seven key roles required to achieve the overall purpose. These roles are expressed in very general terms, which are unpacked as one reads further into the process. So, for example, the key role of managing people is broken down into seventeen 'units of competence', each of which has a number of specified elements, which are expressed in ever greater detail. Figure 46.3 gives some examples of units of competence for this role, and Figure 46.4 shows the elements relevant to Unit C10 (Develop teams).

Key role C: **Unit of competency**
Manage people ---------- C1   Manage yourself
                     C2   Develop your own resources
                                 ....
                     C4   Create effective working relationships
                                 ....
                     C8   Select personnel for activities
                                 ....
                     C10 Develop teams and individuals to enhance performance
                                 ....
                     C14 Delegate work to others
                                 ....
                     C17 Redeploy personnel and make redundancies

Figure 46.3 Management standards: units of competency

Interestingly, the managing people role commences with a consideration of managing oneself before going on to identify the other key aspects of managing people.

14. At the unit of competence level the standards become ever more explicit, as the required performance elements focus on specific requirements for competency in that unit. Figure 46.4 shows the six elements related to Unit C10 (Team development):

Unit of competence	Required elements
C10 – Develop teams ---------	Identify the development needs of teams and individuals
	Plan the development of teams and individuals
	Develop teams to improve performance
	Support individual learning and development
	Assess the development of teams and individuals
	Improve the development of teams and individuals

Figure 46.4 Management standards: Elements of performance

At this stage of the breakdown, managers are given guidance on the personal competencies they will require to undertake this unit, such as acting assertively and applying team-building skills. Each element is then provided with relevant performance criteria to enable managers to assess how well they are executing their role. They are also given guidance on the knowledge requirements of the element. Finally, for assessment for 'best practice', managers are given guidance on the sort of evidence that will be required to convince a third party of one's competence.

15. As currently presented, the standards contain a considerable amount of detail.

This has both advantages and disadvantages. The advantages include the following:

• the detail arises out of authentic day-to-day requirements of the different facets of the manager's job, and is therefore relevant

• managers are given a large number of competence options to consider, especially in relation to personal competencies

• a wide range of performance criteria are supplied to help managers and assessors to select appropriate criteria for particular cases

• considerable guidance is given concerning the nature of the evidence that can be produced to show that the relevant criteria have been achieved.

The disadvantages of having so much detail are primarily (1) that individuals and organisations may find the process too daunting to implement, and (2) that the level of job analysis gives management the appearance of being a collection of discrete skills rather than a holistic function in which the whole is greater than the sum of its parts. Nevertheless, for the purposes of developing vocational qualifications, the detail in the standards is helpful in devising appropriate training and assessment activities.

Management Development Methods

16. The various methods employed in management development can be placed into four main categories, as follows:

❶ Management education: qualification-bearing courses run by universities or public-sector colleges, for example MBA degrees, Diplomas in Management Studies, and various professional examinations, such as the Institute of Personnel Management; the level of work is regarded as post experience, and the emphasis is on acquiring knowledge and theory.

❷ Management training: internal and external courses, off-the-job and focusing on acquiring specific knowledge and relevant job skills; some experiential learning via course exercises.

❸ Experiential learning: 'learning by doing'; on-the-job experience usually with guidance from superior or colleague.

❹ Continuing professional development (CPD): activities designed to update knowledge and learn new skills flexibly, using one or more of the previous three methods; also used to enable individuals to upgrade their membership of a professional body (e.g. to obtain chartered manager/engineer etc status); online personal profiling and assessment questionnaires increasingly available from a range of professional bodies.

Experiential Approaches to Management Development

17. The most widely used experiential methods are as follows: coaching/guided experience, delegation, projects, secondments/job rotation. In Figure 46.5, we briefly examine each of these, and highlight their key points and advantages.

METHOD	SALIENT FEATURES	ADVANTAGES
• Coaching/Guided Experience	Planned involvement of the manager in advising and aiding subordinate manager to develop effective job performance. Involves discovery learning with support.	Relevant to learner. Improves collaboration between parties. Good feedback for junior manager.
• Delegation	Superior gives manager specific responsibility, authority and resources. Performance is monitored.	Individual able to exercise real responsibility for results.
• Projects	A specific problem or opportunity is worked on by an individual or a team with the object of producing concrete proposals in a given time span.	May generate a high degree of commitment. Utilises problem-solving, negotiating skills.
• Secondments/Job Rotation	A manager is assigned to a post in another department/unit for a limited period.	Valuable experience based on doing the job assigned. Tests individual.
• Continuing professional development	Personal development plan Performance benchmarks Assessment tools On-the-job development	Linked closely to individual needs Keeps professionals up to date

Fig. 46.5 Experiential methods in management development.

18. The emphasis in these experiential approaches is on learning whilst doing the job. In some cases off-the-job training will be required to enable the manager concerned to understand important concepts or to carry out initial practice in a 'safe' environment. Such off-the-job training, however, is only employed in a supporting role. Nevertheless, there are several well-tried methods for employing experiential learning in a 'safe' off-the-job environment. Some of the leading methods will be described below.

Off-the-job Methods and Experiential Learning

19. The majority of experiential methods used in management courses are directed at social skills development, eg leadership, influencing skills, negotiating, assertiveness etc. A

few are directed at cognitive skills development, eg problem-identification, problem-analysis etc. Perceptive use of such methods by trainers can overcome many of the problems of lack of relevance to the job levelled at off-the-job training by its critics. The point here is that skills development in these particular areas extends the range of an individual's competence in his whole life, not just in his present job. These particular skills are in fact 'context-free', that is they do not depend on any one situation in order to be of use to the learner, unlike the on-the-job activities mentioned in para. 17 above. An example of one such method is the use of the so-called 'Managerial Grid'. The Grid (see Figure 46.6) represents a matrix of potential management styles of leadership, and was first devised as an aid to management development. Using the basic Grid model, managers can identify their current style and, if appropriate, learn what to do to achieve a 'better' style. Learning is achieved by means of structured questionnaires and a combination of group discussion and practical exercises. The basic Grid is set out as shown in Figure 46.6.

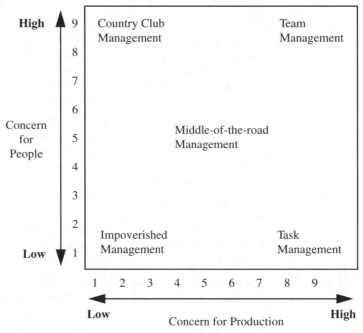

Fig. 46.6 The Managerial Grid (after Blake & Mouton, 1964).[13]

The Grid uses two dimensions: *concern for people* and *concern for production (or task)*. By measuring responses to questionnaires, for example, managers can identify what preferences they have when faced with certain 'context-free' situations. They can then plot their initial positions on the Grid, and begin to see a picture of themselves emerging. The Country Club style is very considerate to people, but shows little concern for the task. By comparison, the Task Management style emphasises getting the task completed, more or less regardless of people's feelings or views. Of the five styles, the Team Management style is seen to be the 'best' style, in that it emphasises both the task and people's needs. As a management development device, the Grid has proved very useful. As a theory of leadership, it has not received much support.

20. Typical methods used in courses are described briefly in Figure 46.7. These methods try to overcome the problem stated by Schein (1970)[14] that:

'The typical training effort therefore faces the problem not only of how to teach a new employee the specifics of a complex job for today, but how to create a learning situation in which that employee can develop other capacities by way of preparing for an uncertain future. In management training the latter factor is paramount.'

METHOD	SALIENT FEATURES	ADVANTAGES
Group exercise	Groups are given a task and certain limits; the results achieved and the process by which they were achieved are examined by the group and a tutor	Definable focus for activities; task provides peg on which discussion can take place; useful for leadership and team-building
Role-playing	Individuals take on a role and experience the nature of an interpersonal encounter; may be tightly or loosely-scripted	Participants learn to think on their feet; experience genuine emotions so long as role is authentic
Sensitivity training	Group exercises in which processes taking place in the group are examined; the focus is on the 'here and now' interactions; requires careful guidance by trainer	Enables groups to explore interpersonal relations and to share feelings
Case study	A real or imaginary account of an organisational problem is studied by an individual or a small group with a view to diagnosing a situation or proposing solutions	Provides focal point for developing analytical and problem-solving skills
Brainstorming	A group are asked to suggest ways of dealing with an issue/problem; no discussion or criticism of suggestions is made until after the list has been completed	Has proved to be an effective means of stimulating new ideas and creative suggestions
Simulation exercise	This is a combination of a case-study with role-play; participants are given a fairly detailed scenario and are asked to undertake a number of decisions within a time limit	As a kind of enlarged role-play, this can reproduce many real-life situations; useful for developing negotiating and decision-making skills
Workshops	These are practical exercises in which participants work on particular work-based problems as a group	Provide opportunity to share ideas on real day-to-day problems; useful when devising plans/systems

Fig 46.7 Experiential methods (courses).

21. Whilst it is by no means easy to measure the effects of management training courses and on-the-job development, the outcomes that senior management might expect from 'successful' management development activities will include:

- individual managers performing at a fully satisfactory level
- improved performance from work teams as a result of better leadership
- pool of managers ready and able to take up promotion or stand in for absentees
- managers working collaboratively together
- improved communication between managers and their staff and between managers and colleagues
- improved problem-solving capacity throughout the organisation

Succession Planning

22. One of the key features of a structured management development system is a succession plan. This is basically a plan for identifying who is currently in post and who is available and qualified to take over in the event of retirement, voluntary leaving, dismissal or sickness, for example. As Figure 46.8 indicates, a typical succession chart includes details of key management jobholders and brief references to their possible successors.

Department:				Manager:		Date:	
Present Jobholders				Possible Successors		Ready	
Post	Jobholder	Age	Performance	First choice:	Second choice:	Now	6–12 months

Fig. 46.8 Management succession chart.

Auditing Management Development

23. Some important outcomes of management development were referred to in paragraph 21 above. However, the assessment of the effects of management development activities is a complex matter, as the Durham University Business School team discovered when conducting their study into management development in a number of British companies.

Part of the Durham remit was to produce an instrument for evaluating management development, and this is described in Easterby-Smith et al (1980)[4]. The so-called Management Development Audit aims 'to ensure that the provisions adopted by any organisation for developing its managers do produce the intended results.' The essence of the Audit approach is 'to ask individual managers to describe their own experiences of, and views about, management development, and then to reflect the collective view back to those responsible for making decisions about the development of managers.'

24. The Audit, which is intended to be a neutral instrument, not preferring any particular approach to management development, attempts to portray a picture which contrasts:

❶ the formal view of what is intended to happen

❷ managers' perceptions of what is happening in fact

❸ what managers would like to see happening in management development.

The Audit seeks answers to questions such as the following:

• What are the main objectives of management development, and how well are they being achieved?

• What are the main forms of training available for managers, and what emphasis is placed on them?

• How is self-development encouraged?

• What discussion takes place before a manager goes on a course, and what happens on his return?

- What kind of appraisal system exists?
- Is there a formal system of career development, and is this related to appraisal?
- For what levels of management is succession planning carried out?
- What internal and external resources are made available for management development?
- What are the main problems confronting management development in the organisation at the present time?

25. The Audit represents a thorough review of management development activities, enabling senior management to pinpoint strengths and weaknesses of the current system as well as obtaining a 'feel' for the way the system is operating. Many of the responses to the audit will undoubtedly reflect the various cultural influences at work in the organisation, and these will be considered briefly next.

Management Development and Corporate Culture

26. The approach to management development in an organisation will tend to reflect the dominant value-system of the senior management. They are the persons who, above all, are charged with building a management team and developing their successors. If the top management is centralist and bureaucratic, then its view of management development is likely to produce a logically structured system such as that shown in Figure 46.1 above. In such a system, job descriptions, appraisal forms, succession charts and the like are vital items in the analysis of needs and in decisions about how they are to be met. Such a system would probably favour structured efforts, both on and off-the-job to supply individual manager needs. Where top management believes in delegation and devolution, then the emphasis in management development will be on self-development on-the-job. Where management is considered an elite group, then features such as 'accelerated promotion' and graduate trainee programmes tend to predominate. Such systems provide selective support for manager development by concentrating on so-called 'high fliers', ie persons with outstanding potential. The modern trend is to implement management development within work-teams, with an emphasis on leadership and team-building skills.

References

1. Drucker, P. (1955), *The Practice of Management*, Heinemann.
2. MSC (1978), *Policy Paper – Management Development*, HMSO.
3. Morris, J. (1978), 'Management Development and Development Management' in Burgoyne, J. & Stuart, M. (eds), *Management Development: Context and Strategies*, Gower Press.
4. Easterby-Smith, M. (1980), *Auditing Management Development*, Gower Press.
5. Reddin, W. (1970), *Managerial Effectiveness*, McGraw-Hill.
6. Fayol, H. (1949), *General and Industrial Management*, Pitman.
7. Mintzberg, H. (1973), *The Nature of Managerial Work*, Harper & Row.
8. Stewart, R. (1982), *Managerial Choice*, McGraw-Hill.
9. Pedler, M. et al (2001), *A Manager's Guide to Self-development*, (4th edition), McGraw-Hill.
10. Simmons, J. & Brennan, R. (1981) in Nixon, B. (ed), *New Approaches to Management Development*, Gower/ATM.
11. Humble, J. (1967), *Improving Business Results*, McGraw-Hill.
12. Hague, H. (1974), *Executive Self-development*, MacMillan.
13. Blake, R. & Mowton, J. (1964), *The Managerial Grid*, Gulf Publishing.
14. Schein, E. (1970), *Organisational Psychology*, (2nd edition), Prentice-Hall.

CHAPTER 47

Stress Management and Employee Counselling

1.   Increasingly, employers are paying greater attention than in the past to the effects of stress on their staff, especially on their key management personnel. What is 'stress'? It can best be described in lay terms *as the adverse psychological and physical reactions that occur in individuals as a result of their being unable to cope with the demands being made on them.* Stress is triggered not by the external problems faced by individuals, but by the way they cope (or fail to cope) with those problems. Thus, most people can cope with a variety of pressures in their life, and many seem to thrive on 'pressure', especially at work. However, once individuals fail to deal adequately with pressure, then symptoms of stress appear. In the short-term these can be manifested in such conditions as indigestion, nausea, headaches, back-pain, loss of appetite, loss of sleep and increased irritability. In the longer-term, such symptoms can lead to coronary heart disease, stomach ulcers, depression and other serious conditions. Clearly the effects of stress, whether triggered by work problems or domestic/social problems, will eventually lead to reduced employee performance at work, increased sickness absence and even to an early death.

2.   In a widely reported study of stress carried out in the 1960s (Holmes & Rahe)[1], most of the life-events referred to as potentially leading to stress occur in a person's domestic and social life, not at work. Critical events include death of spouse, divorce, death of close relative, personal injury or illness, marriage, loss of job, retirement and change in financial state. However, since individuals bring their problems with them to work, it scarcely matters in one sense whether the trigger for stress is work-related or not, for the effect on the individual is just the same and his or her work performance is likely to be adversely affected.

Sources of Stress at Work

3.   The main sources of stress at work are located in a number of groupings. They may arise from environmental factors, job and organisational factors (including the organisation culture), workplace relationships, domestic situation, or personality factors. These potential sources of stress depend for their effect on:

❶   the attitude of the individual towards what is perceived as the problem

❷   the uncertainty and perceived importance of the outcomes for the individual

❸   the individual's level of self-confidence/assertiveness.

4.   Examples of factors that have been found to contribute to stress include the following:

Factor Group	Examples of Factors
❶ External environment	• **Economic situation** for the industry – especially where the industry is in decline and redundancies are commonplace • **Development of new technology** – may lead to fewer jobs and/or skill requirements; and pressure to acquire new knowledge and skills

- **Political changes** may affect organisations vulnerable to political influence – eg state-owned businesses, key industries in energy, military equipment etc.

② Organisational factors

- **Organisation structure** – especially where the pattern of jobs, roles, rules and regulations, constrain the individual's range of choices in how to do the job
- **Communications** – where these do *not* facilitate communication with colleagues
- **Organisation culture** – especially if the dominant ethos is one of internal competition for resources, rewards etc, or where a 'hire and fire' policy operates
- **Management style** – especially where the individual finds it difficult to adapt to a superior's management style because it is too autocratic, or too participative
- **Career development** – especially where individuals' efforts are unrecognised by promotion, or further training, or where a flatter structure limits prospects.

③ Job characteristics

- **Physical conditions** – where the individual finds these uncomfortable and/or dangerous to health
- **Job demands** – where the task is seen as boring, repetitive, or offering insufficient challenge; or even simply too excessive for one person
- **Degree of autonomy** – where this is insufficient to meet either the demands of the job and/or the expectations of the job-holder
- **Role conflict** – ie where the organisation's expectations of the role either (1) lead to confusion with related roles, or (2) do not meet the job-holder's expectations.

④ Work relationships

- **Superiors** – especially where individuals fail to achieve a reasonable working relationship with their immediate superior
- **Colleagues** – an inability to get on reasonable terms with fellow team-members or colleagues from other sections can be source of considerable unhappiness; women, in particular, may suffer from male patronage or sexual harassment (Davidson & Cooper, 1983)[2]
- **Own staff** – many people appointed to a leadership role in the organisation find it stressful to deal with the demands of their own staff
- **Customers/suppliers/other outside people** – these stakeholders can be a source of stress, especially for those dealing with customer services.

⑤ Domestic situation

- **Home life** – upheavals at home due to family illness, care of elderly parents, unhappy marriage, debt problems etc are problems that can overflow into the workplace and adversely affect an individual's performance and attitude
- **Outside social life** – individuals with a rich social life may find that work and leisure clash, especially if their work requires unsocial hours or availability at short notice.

⑥ Personal factors

- **Individual perception of role/job etc** – as noted above, the individual's perceptions of tasks etc and their difficulty is a key factor in the stress formula
- **Personality type** – research suggests that certain types (eg Type A personalities) are much more vulnerable to stress symptoms than others (eg Type B)
- **Ability to adapt to change** – adaptable individuals are less prone to stress than those who are inflexible
- **Motivation** – ie where a person is deeply committed to his or her work, they are more likely to find ways of coping with potentially stressful situations than someone with a low commitment
- **Tolerance for ambiguity** – where an individual can tolerate uncertainty (eg role/task ambiguity), stress is less likely.

5.   Given that stress is essentially related to personality and personal perceptions, the reference above to Type A and Type B personalities is important. Friedman & Rosenman (1974)[3], in a famous study, identified what they termed the Type A personality in their researches into coronary patients. Type As were people who were identified as at great risk of heart disease. They were characterised by excessive competitiveness, a chronic sense of urgency of time, a constant search for achievement, and behaviour that tended to be aggressive, impatient and restless. Such personalities were constantly engaged in activity, and expressed guilt feelings when they tried to relax. Type B personalities had none of these characteristics, and were altogether calmer and more relaxed.

The Symptoms of Stress

6.   These were mentioned briefly above. Symptoms of stress are typically analysed under three headings – physiological, psychological and behavioural. Common symptoms are as follows:

Physiological – in addition to short-term reactions such as increased heart beat, tensed muscles and extra adrenalin secretion which are a human being's instinctive reaction to danger, the chronic (ie longer term) effects of stress are associated with such unhealthy conditions as coronary heart disease, high blood pressure, indigestion, gastric ulcers, back pain and even cancer. Stress is also likely to be manifested in less serious infections, allergies and physical disorders.

Psychological – in chronic situations the psychological symptoms of stress tend to become manifest in anxiety states (phobias, obsessions etc) and depression. In less serious cases, stress emerges in the form of tension, irritability, boredom and job dissatisfaction.

Behavioural – ultimately the physiological and psychological symptoms lead to generalised changes in behaviour such as loss of appetite, increased cigarette smoking and alcohol consumption, and sleeplessness. In the workplace behaviour may take the form of increased absences (flight), aggression towards colleagues (fight), committing more errors than normal and taking longer over tasks. In utterly intolerable conditions individuals may leave the organisation and seek work elsewhere or sink into despair at home. The loss to the community resulting from stress-related conditions is estimated to be substantial.

Coping with Stress

7.   Strategies for coping with stress can best be analysed under two headings – personal strategies and organisational strategies. The former include actions that individuals can take

at work and outside of work to increase their ability to cope with sustained pressure and thus avoid the symptoms of stress. The latter include a number of organisational steps that can be taken to reduce the likelihood of stress due to structural and style problems.

Personal Coping Strategies

8.   In their study of women managers, Davidson and Cooper[2] asked their respondents to give their answers to a number of questions relating to 'positive coping strategies'. These included such questions as 'How often do you use the following to relax?' on a 1 (Never) to 5 (Always) scale:

- relaxation techniques?
- exercise?
- talking to someone you know?
- using humour?
- leaving the work area?

These questions provide some clues as to the sort of actions at a physiological and psychological level that individuals themselves can take to reduce the effects of stress in their lives. However, the responses implied by these particular questions are more concerned with external aspects of stress. What is especially important in becoming more stress-free is to examine one's own attitudes towards personal strengths and weaknesses, and this is more a matter of assertiveness and personal planning.

9.   A good deal of stress could be avoided if people paid more attention to their own rights. Assertiveness, as noted earlier (Chapter 27) is a question of standing up for your own rights, but in a way that does not violate another person's rights. Assertiveness is also concerned with expressing (ie making known) personal wants, feelings and opinions in honest and appropriate ways. This latter point is important because, if other people do not know how we are feeling about a particular action, or decision, made on our behalf, how can they appreciate our problem and how can they begin to address it? Stress, according to Back & Back (1992)[4], will result '...*if there is a continuing conflict between what you want or would like and what is actually happening to you*' (p.141). The addition of the word conflict to the stress equation is significant. Stress is not just about excessive pressures and individual self-image, but also about personal conflicts of interest. Thus, a young and ambitious manager with a young family and a wife or husband at home is likely to find a conflict of interests if frequently asked to be away on business overnight or at weekends.

Organisational Responses to Stress Avoidance

10.   What can employers do to help employees who are suffering from stress? Firstly, and this applies only if the causes of the stress are work-related, they can investigate the source and take appropriate action, such as:

- change individual's job responsibilities (give more or reduce)
- provide greater opportunity for personal autonomy in job
- set agreed job targets for employees (see Chapter 18)
- provide appropriate training (eg in time management, assertiveness etc) (see Chapter 27)
- permit flexible hours, reduce time spent away from home etc

- put a stop to any bullying and sexual/racial harassment
- improve physical working conditions
- relocate employee to another office or work-base
- provide counselling facilities
- provide fitness centres/programmes for their employees.

  NB Many Japanese employers insist on employees doing physical exercises before their daily work

11. Secondly, and this applies in *all* cases of employee stress, employers can help support employees' ability to cope with the stress. Steps that could be taken, in addition to or instead of those mentioned above, include the provision of:

- counselling services (see below)
- team/workgroup workshops on stress
- sports and social facilities
- relaxation classes
- adequate canteen and rest-room facilities.

12. Managers may sometimes wonder why they have to spend time dealing with employees whose problems are domestically-related, but the fact of the matter is that employees cannot help but bring their personal problems with them to work. Most people are usually too embarrassed to admit that they are having acute problems with their spouse, teenage children or elderly parents. Thus they tend to suppress their anxieties when they come to work, and all too often the first that a manager learns of a problem is either when the employee begins to take increased amounts of sick leave, or when confronted by requests for time off to attend a solicitor's, or a juvenile court or a funeral!

13. Most managers are not, and probably do not want to become, trained counsellors. However, it is important for the well-being of a team that the leader should take sufficient time out to listen to a stressed employee's story, agree that the immediate situation should be taken into account in respect of performance, work-load etc, and propose that the employee seeks professional help. In other words, the manager's job in such circumstances is to reassure himself/herself that the employee's situation is not being allowed to drift, but is being managed, both by the individual concerned and the manager.

14. Before looking more closely at counselling at work, it will be useful to consider one of the known, and unfortunately growing, causes of stress that is work-related – sexual and racial harassment

Harassment in the Workplace

15. Developments in equal opportunities have been one factor in focusing attention on harassment at work, since much of the harassment is sexually or racially motivated. What is harassment? Clearly, it has to do with the individual's right to privacy and dignity at work. If workmates, colleagues or superiors bring excessive pressure to bear on an individual, which is clearly distressing to that person, then prima facie this could constitute harassment. The European Commission puts it this way in its Recommendation on the protection of the dignity of women and men at work (November 1991):

> '... Member States should take action to promote awareness that conduct of a sexual nature, or other conduct based on sex affecting the dignity of women and men at work, including conduct of superiors and colleagues, is unacceptable if:

a) such conduct is unwanted, unreasonable and offensive to the recipient,

b) a person's rejection of, or submission to, such conduct … is used explicitly as a basis for decision which affects that person's access to vocational training … employment … promotion … or any other employment decisions,

c) such conduct creates an intimidating, hostile or humiliating work environment for the recipient…'

16. Any person who is perceived by work colleagues as being different or somehow vulnerable is liable to harassment. The greatest attention has been focused on harassment of a sexual nature, mainly, but not exclusively, inflicted on women by men. However, harassment can be triggered by racial or religious prejudice, membership or non-membership of a trade union, and attitudes towards young persons, the disabled and other minority groups. Harassment can take forms such as : unwanted physical contact, suggestive propositions or language, public jokes, offensive posters and graffiti, isolation or non-cooperation at work, shunning an individual at work and socially ('sending to Coventry'), and pestering a person.

17. The consequences for employers in the UK of not taking action against harassment are primarily two-fold: firstly, they stand to be taken to an industrial tribunal (eg under Sex Discrimination/Race Relations legislation) or to a civil court (eg for breach of contract), and the costs of such procedures are high; secondly, the work performance of their organisation is likely to suffer adversely due to workplace tension, higher staff turnover, increased absenteeism and generally lower morale. What steps could an employer take in order to minimise the possibility of harassment? The most important are as follows:

❶ Produce and publish a clear policy statement on this issue to include examples of harassment and its likely effects, and to make clear the standards expected of employees and the penalties available for those who breach them

❷ Ensure that appropriate communication systems exist to enable employees to report harassment in confidence

❸ Ensure that appropriate disciplinary measures are in operation to deal fairly with offenders

❹ Ensure that allegations of harassment are investigated and dealt with without delay

❺ Provide appropriate counselling for recipients and offenders

❻ Through internal communications to give wide publicity to the organisation's intentions regarding the harassment of fellow employees.

Counselling at Work

18. In several earlier paragraphs above we have referred to 'the provision of counselling services' for employees. This might sound as though 'counselling' is something that is done to people or given to them, but this would be false. In essence counselling is *a joint activity in which a person seeking help, support or advice in dealing with personal problems (a 'client') shares his or her dilemma with a trained helper (a 'counsellor')*. The Institute of Personnel Management Statement on Counselling in the Workplace (1992)[5] sees workplace counselling as a situation where *'one individual uses a set of techniques or skills to help another individual take responsibility for and to manage their own decision-making whether it is work related or personal.'* The clear implication is that counselling, from the point of view of the counsellor, is a skilled activity. Of course, work colleagues can and do provide a level of informal counselling to workmates in the course of their daily work. At the very least this boils down to listening to the other person and giving them the opportunity to share their

anxieties and fears. However, it may also involve the passing on of quite unhelpful remarks from the one acting as informal counsellor! As the IPM statement notes *'Only a minority of managers are trained counsellors...(and most therefore)...need information to enable them to be aware when a counselling situation exists, have the confidence to stay with that problem, but ... recognise their own limitations ...'*. The message for managers and others in supervisory positions is 'Recognise when a problem may require employee counselling, provide immediate support but then facilitate professional counselling arrangements'.

19. The goals of counselling are effectively to enable an individual to handle stress by making better use of their own strengths, insights and resolve. Gerard Egan, in his seminal book 'The Skilled Helper' (1990)[6], puts it this way:

> 'Helpers are effective to the degree that their clients, through client–helper interactions, are in a better position to manage their problem situations and/or develop the unused resources and opportunities of their lives more effectively.'

It is of prime importance to recognise that counselling is not intended to *do* anything to individuals; its role is to enable *them* to get their problems into perspective and to see what *they themselves* can do to solve them.

20. Essentially, counselling is a process in which the counsellor helps the client to:

❶ identify the problem,

❷ agree what would be the ideal, or preferred, outcome,

❸ consider ways by which the client might achieve that outcome.

Thus, if a male employee seeks help because his marriage has broken down and he cannot concentrate on his work or cope with many of the usual pressures of his work, how might a trained counsellor help such a person? Firstly, it is likely that the counsellor would try to get the client to name the particular issues that are worrying him, both at work and in his domestic situation. Then the counsellor would try to draw out from the client what it is that he now wants from the counselling process, eg repair his marriage/accept the inevitability of divorce or separation/contribute fully to his work role once again etc. The next stage is for the counsellor and client between them to investigate the range of possibilities that could be drawn on to help bring about the desired outcomes. Counsellors can be very helpful at this stage by extending the range of possibilities for their clients, eg 'Have you considered so-and-so?', 'What about going to a priest, marriage guidance counsellor, solicitor etc'? 'How do you think your own manager might be able to help you?' In each case, however, the counsellor leaves the *client* to decide what he may do and in what order of priority.

21. Organisations which provide counselling services for their employees may provide an in-house service using their own trained counsellor(s), or may hire the services of an external counselling organisation. One British approach which relies on external assistance is the Employee Assistance Programme, in which an employer contracts a specialist counselling service to provide counselling support for its employees. This usually takes the form of a **telephone** counselling service which employees can ring at any time of the day or night to seek help for work problems or personal problems. There is usually a limit to the number of occasions that the service can be used by any one employee. Where appropriate the counselling can be of a face-to-face kind in an off-the-job location. Client confidentiality is guaranteed, and the only information that is fed back to the contracting employer is the rate of calls, the type of problems raised and other general information which does not identify individuals in any way, but which does provide important evidence as to the use and costs of the service.

22. Why should employers provide such a service for their employees? The answer is primarily one of enlightened self-interest, ie unhappy, anxious or over-stressed employees are not going to be able to achieve high performance in their jobs, they may take more time off work for sickness and may even decide to change their job, leading to increased turnover. It is therefore in an organisation's interests to avoid such uneconomic use of their human resources, and the provision of counselling services may be one way of sustaining employee performance, achieving business targets and showing commitment to employees as individuals.

23. In the final analysis an organisation must weigh up the costs (both direct and indirect) of providing such a service against the perceived benefits. It is also important to consider the costs (mostly indirect) of *not* providing the service. In organisations where the performance of particular individuals is crucial to results, or where there are high levels of sickness absence or accidents on the job, the costs of *not* providing access to counselling could be substantial.

References

1. Holmes, T & Rahe, R. (1967), 'The Social Readjustment Scale' in *Journal of Psychosomatic Research*, 11. Pergamon Press.
2. Davidson, M. & Cooper, C. (1983), *Stress and the Woman Manager*, Martin Robertson.
3. Friedman, M. & Rosenman, R.H. (1974), *Type A Behaviour and your Heart*, Alfred Knopf.
4. Back, K. & Back, K. (1994), *Assertiveness at Work*, BCA/McGraw-Hill.
5. Institute of Personnel Management (1992), *Statement on Counselling in the Workplace*, IPM (now IPD).
6. Egan, G. (1990), *The Skilled Helper*, (4th edition), Brooks/Cole.

CHAPTER 48

Job Evaluation

Introduction

1. Job evaluation is the name given to a set of methods designed to compare jobs systematically with a view to assessing their relative worth. Job evaluation produces a rank order of jobs based on a rational, and reasonably objective, assessment of a number of key factors taken from a representative cross-section of all the jobs in a particular job hierarchy. Job evaluation sets out to answer such questions as 'Is the Company Secretary's job as demanding as the Chief Accountant's?' and 'Should specialised, but in-depth jobs, be placed in the same grade as broader, but shallower jobs?'

2. The purpose of job evaluation is to produce a defensible ranking of jobs which can be used as the basis for a rational pay structure. Following job evaluation, pay can be based on a rational estimate of the contribution made by individual jobs to the organisation in terms of skill, responsibility, length of training and other factors. There are several key points which need to be noted about job evaluation. These are as follows:

• Job evaluation deals in relative positions, not in absolutes,

- Job evaluation assesses *jobs*, not the individuals in them, ie it is not a performance appraisal exercise,
- The evaluation process is usually carried out by groups (job evaluation committees) rather than by individuals,
- Job evaluation committees utilise concepts such as logic, fairness and consistency in their assessment of jobs,
- There will always be *some* element of subjective judgement in job evaluation,
- Job evaluation by itself cannot determine pay scales or pay levels, it can only provide the basic data on which decisions about pay can be taken.

3.   Job evaluation is clearly not the only basis for settling pay. Collective bargaining between unions and management is often the dominant method of determining pay, and this, in the final analysis, boils down to who has the strongest bargaining position at a particular point in time. 'Custom and practice' is another common method for arriving at pay structures and pay levels. This tends to produce a haphazard structure derived from a variety of ad hoc and often conflicting pressures from employee groups at the grass-roots. In other cases, management attempt to determine pay in the light of the 'going rate' for their industry or their local market. Whilst this may work reasonably well for the overall level of pay, it does nothing to sort out differentials in pay between different groups of employees. The advantage of a job-evaluated pay structure is that it does provide a defensible basis for allocating pay differentials between groups. Where such a structure is developed in a unionised situation, the job evaluation results enable both management *and* trade union representatives to defend the gradings which are drawn up. The major effect of collective bargaining in this situation is to maintain or increase the *overall* level of earnings, but without interfering with differentials.

Job Evaluation Methods

4.   Most job evaluation methods can be divided into two categories:

❶ Non-analytical methods, and

❷ Analytical methods.

Non-analytical methods take whole jobs, compare them and then rank them. The two most common examples of such methods are:

- **Job Ranking** – in this method, basic job descriptions are written up for a representative sample of jobs in the total population; evaluators compare the descriptions and then make an initial ranking of the jobs in order of perceived importance, ie this is their subjective view of relative importance; the rankings are discussed in an evaluation committee, and eventually a final rank order is agreed; the remaining jobs in the population are then slotted in to the rank order. The advantage of this method lies in its simplicity; the main disadvantage is that, because of the high degree of subjective judgement required, it can only be effective in a relatively simple and clear-cut organisation structure.

- **Job Grading/Job Classification** – in this case, the usual procedure is reversed, for in job grading the pay/salary grades are worked out first, then the broad characteristics of each grade are defined (eg in terms of knowledge, skill etc expected for each grade); a representative sample of jobs, known as benchmark jobs, is selected as typical of each grade; full job descriptions are written for these jobs; the remaining jobs (usually written up in outline) are then compared with the benchmarks and allocated to the appropriate grade. Like Job Ranking, this is also a simple method to operate, but it relies heavily on the credibility of the initial salary grades, and does not permit sufficient distinctions to be made between jobs, especially in a relatively complex organisation with a wide variety of specialist roles.

5.   In a phrase, non-analytical methods are simple, but crude. In complex organisations it is essential to use analytical methods, as these are the only way of discriminating fairly between jobs which are not at all similar. For example, they could be used to distinguish the relative importance of a systems analyst compared with, say, a management accountant, or of a chief architect compared with a head brewer.

6.   Analytical methods break jobs down into their component tasks, responsibilities and other factors, and assess the jobs factor by factor, sometimes allocating points for each factor and sometimes allocating monetary sums to them. A group of benchmark jobs is evaluated in this way, and ranked according to the scores. The remaining jobs in the population are slotted in to this benchmark rank order. Then all the jobs are either allocated to a salary grade, or, if monetary sums were allocated, are allotted a specified total salary. The most commonly used analytical method is *Points Rating*, where points are allocated to job factors; the method where monetary sums are allocated to the factors is known as *Factor Comparison*, and is not widely used nowadays.

7.   The most commonly used factors in analytical methods are as indicated in Figure 48.1.

SKILL
- Education and training required
- Experience
- Initiative and creativity

RESPONSIBILITY/DECISION-MAKING
- Complexity of work
- Supervising work of others
- Equipment or process
- Material or product

EFFORT
- Mental demands of job
- Physical demands of job

WORKING CONDITIONS
- Pressures in the job
- Difficult or hazardous conditions

Figure 48.1 Analytical methods – typical job factors.

8.   In a Points Rating Method, each factor is broken down into degrees or levels, which are allocated points in accordance with an agreed weighting. In evaluating manual jobs, a greater weighting may be given to factors such as Effort and Working Conditions, whereas in evaluating white-collar jobs, the greater weighting will tend to be given to Skill and Responsibility. In a situation where trade unions are involved, the weightings given to each factor are usually a matter for negotiation. The important point to be borne in mind is that, whatever is eventually agreed, the same treatment will be applied to every job. There is no question of applying different criteria to different jobs in the same population, apart, that is, from the manual/white-collar differential. An example of a possible Points Rating matrix for the evaluation of manual jobs is shown in a simplified form in Figure 48.2. In terms of degrees of each factor, 1 represents a *minor* requirement in the job, whilst 8 represents a *major* requirement.

Job Factor	Degree							
SKILL	1	2	3	4	5	6	7	8
1. Education	15	30	45	60	75	90	–	–
2. Experience	20	40	60	80	90	100	–	–
3. Initiative	15	30	45	60	75	90	105	120
EFFORT								
4. Physical	10	20	30	40	50	–	–	-
5. Mental	5	10	15	20	25	30	35	40
RESPONSIBILITY								
6. Supervisory	5	10	15	20	25	30	35	40
7. Equipment	5	10	15	20	25	–	–	–
8. Safety	5	10	15	20	25	–	–	–
WORK CONDITIONS								
9. Hazards	5	10	15	20	–	–	–	–
10. Noise/dirt	10	20	30	40	50	–	–	–

Figure 48.2 Manual jobs – points rating matrix.

9. The matrix in Figure 48.2 weights the points in favour of the skill factors, physical effort and noisy/dirty working conditions. These are typically the most important factors to be considered in establishing the comparative value of manual jobs. If an example for managerial or senior white-collar jobs had been chosen, there would still have been an emphasis on skill factors, but then responsibility factors would have outweighed effort and working conditions. To help make evaluations as consistent as possible, the various degrees of each factor are described in an accompanying document. For example, if we take Education: 1st degree could equate to 'basic secondary education', 3rd degree could equate to 'GCSE in 4 subjects' and 6th degree could equate to 'HNC equivalent'; the other two degrees are not required for manual jobs.

10. Some points rating methods are available in proprietary form. A notable example is the Hay-MSL Guide-chart System, which is particularly popular with organisations composed of a wide variety of specialist, professional and managerial occupations, although it can also be applied to junior clerical and to manual grades of work. The Hay-MSL system is a points system based on three key factors – Know-how, Problem-solving and Accountability – all of which can be broken down into several important sub-factors or dimensions as follows:

- Know-how: can be scored in terms of *depth* as well as *breadth* of Knowledge and Skills required; it can also be scored in terms of Human Relations Skills.

- Problem-solving: can be scored in terms of the thinking *environment* (eg routine or broadly defined etc) and in terms of the thinking *challenge* (eg repetitive, variable or creative etc).

- Accountability: can be scored in terms of *freedom to act, impact* on the organisation/ department (ie remote, contributory, shared or prime) and in terms of the money involved in the business (eg turnover of business, size of annual budget etc).

Clients pay for the use of the Hay-MSL Guide-charts, the services of their consultants, and for a salary guidance service which enables them to keep up-to-date in the marketplace for labour. The Guide-charts form a standardised system of job evaluation, and it is thus possible to see what other organisations are paying for jobs of a particular points total. This feature overcomes one of the major drawbacks of most points methods, which is that whilst they can solve the problem of internal differentials, they cannot link the results into the external labour market or the 'going rate' for the jobs they have evaluated.

11. Taking a broad view of job evaluation, as a technique for facilitating management decision-making in an important area of personnel relations, namely pay, the advantages are:

- it provides a rational and defensible basis on which to decide pay in general, and differentials in particular, because it focuses on *job content*,
- it provides a rational basis for devising, or improving, grading structures,
- it reduces the effects of ad hoc or traditional arrangements for pay or grading,
- it encourages management and employees alike to think of jobs in terms of key components.

The full range of advantages can only come from the use of analytical methods, nevertheless there are certain disadvantages of job evaluation. These are:

- implementation of even quite simple methods can be a costly and time-consuming business,
- analytical methods, in particular can give the impression that they are completely objective and scientific, but they still rely considerably on human judgement, ie subjective influences cannot be ruled out,
- whilst job evaluation can provide a rational basis for grade differentials based on job content, it is usually unable to link the resulting pay grades into the labour market itself.

CHAPTER 49

Employee Relations and Collective Rights

Introduction

1. The expression *'employee relations'* generally describes all those activities which contribute both formally and informally to the organisation of the relationships between employers and their employees. In some instances these relationships are predominantly formalised as a result of collective bargaining between employers and trade unions as to the role, status and working conditions of employees. This aspect of employee relations is often called 'industrial relations'. However, employee relations can refer just as easily to arrangements worked out less formally between local managements and their work teams, whether unionised or not. Because of its importance to national economies, employee relations has tended to be the focus of legislation. Thus, procedures such as balloting for possible strike action or the election of union representatives, or for the announcement of redundancies, are contained within legal parameters.

2.   The cornerstone of employee relations is the contractual relationship that exists between an employee and his or her employer, even where aspects of the relationship are subject to collective agreements. The individual employment contract is more than just a written document; it also encompasses unwritten or implied terms, and can include custom and practice as well as formal matters. The contract is subject to common law in Britain, as well as to the terms of various statutes. When differences of opinion occur between the parties to an employment contract, the courts or tribunals then have to decide one way or another.

3.   In Britain over the last thirty years there has been a marked shift in employee relations away from the more combative stance of collective bargaining towards a more unified approach to management–employee relationships. This change has been accompanied by a strengthening of individual rights in the workplace, both in respect of the individual's relationships with management, and in respect of union members' rights vis-à-vis their union. The change has come about for a variety of reasons, including:

*   the increased competitive pressures on commercial organisations, leading to cost-cutting exercises

*   substantial reorganisation of businesses in industry and commerce

*   privatisation of many public sector organisations

*   organisation structures have been made flatter, thus changing work responsibilities and expectations

*   flexibility of working has become an integral element of job design in both private and public sectors.

4.   At the present time, trade unions as such have little say in the way work is organised, and their role in collective bargaining has been weakened. ACAS (1994)[1], reviewing changes over its first twenty years of operation, reported that:

> 'In 1974, one half or more of workers were members of trade unions and the terms and conditions of more than two-thirds of the labour force were determined to some extent through collective agreements … By 1994, fewer than two-fifths were union members; and collective bargaining covered a much reduced part of the whole economy and notably fewer issues were dealt with by collective bargaining. Similarly, in 1974 much collective bargaining was conducted via industry-wide procedures, while by 1994 all but a few of these had disappeared.'

Nevertheless, trade unions still have an important watchdog role to perform, supported by law, to prevent managements from acting in a purely arbitrary fashion. Nowadays it is more likely that groups of employees themselves – as empowered work teams – will contribute to the control of work and its key processes.

5.   Employee relations in Britain today is dominated by company/organisation-wide relationships rather than by industry-wide collective arrangements made between trade unions and employers' bodies on behalf of their respective constituents. The legal system now acts to support *individuals* in the workplace as well as collective groups represented by a union. The emphasis now is less on producing joint procedures and rules of behaviour, and more on gaining mutual commitment to organisational success within the framework of the law.

Perspectives in Employee Relations

6.   In view of the number of groups having an interest in employee relations, it is not surprising that differences of viewpoint should arise concerning both the subject matter and the ultimate goals of this major element of relationships at work. The subject matter of

employee relations can be seen quite differently by the parties concerned, as the following examples can illustrate:

Managers may see employee relations as one or more of the following:

- creating and maintaining employee motivation
- achieving higher levels of efficiency and service by cooperation with employees and their representatives
- establishing workable and credible channels of communication with employees
- negotiating with trade union representatives
- sharing power with employee representatives (not necessarily trade unions) in an organised way.

Employees may see employee relations as one or more of the following:

- management's efforts to win them round to their way of thinking
- a genuine attempt by management to adopt a benevolent approach to employees
- a 'them-and-us' situation involving management–union meetings and frequent wranglings
- an opportunity to participate in shop-floor decision making, and possibly even at Board level.

Third parties, such as Government ministers, conciliators, arbitrators and judges, may see employee relations as one or more of the following:

- attempting to achieve mutually harmonious relationships between employers and employees
- Laying down rules of conduct (ie fair play) for employer–employee relations
- regulating the power struggle between owners and managers on the one side, and employees and organised labour on the other
- establishing peace-making arrangements between the two sides referred to above, and the protection of the interests of the rest of the community.

7.   An approach to employee relations where managers see their role as motivating employees by means of *'good human relations'*, and adopt a collaborative or perhaps a paternalistic style of management, is described as a *unitary approach*. This assumes that the organisation is one large, happy family with a generally agreed sense of its common purpose. There are organisations which take this approach, and, where the employees are happy to accept it, the end result seems to be harmony and success. Where, however, employees feel dissatisfied with a paternalistic management (ie in Argyris's terms, they want to become more mature, more independent, at work), then conflict is likely to ensue, unless management can adapt its style. Where the existence of separate interests is openly admitted, and where arrangements are made to resolve possible conflicts, then this is called a *pluralistic approach* to employee relations.

Rules and Agreements

8.   An important implication of employee relations is that rule-making is essential if the parties concerned are to contain any conflict within manageable bounds. The main body of rules in employee relations is drawn from the following:

- **company/organisation rules** – these are usually generated by, and enforced by, managers;

- **collective agreements** – jointly agreed rules or practices made by management representatives and employee representatives;

- **custom and practice** – these are the informal rules which arise from the behaviour of managers and employees over a period of time; unlike the other rules just mentioned, these rules are not usually written down;

- **legal sources** – these are the rules arising from statute, judicial precedent, and the Common Law, so far as they relate to employee relations;

- **codes of practice** – these may be the codes of professional bodies, or those of bodies such as ACAS (the Advisory, Conciliation and Arbitration Service).

Collective Agreements

9. Collective agreements between employers and employees are usually divided into two categories: **procedural** agreements and **substantive** agreements. Procedural agreements constitute the foundation stones of collective bargaining. They lay down the rules of behaviour which the parties should adhere to in their relationships with each other. Matters covered by procedural agreements include:

1. negotiating rights for unions
2. scope of subjects for collective bargaining (ie what is negotiable)
3. union membership (eg categories of employees to be covered)
4. numbers and rights of union representatives
5. procedure to be followed in the case of a dispute between the parties
6. grievance and disciplinary procedures.

The concluding of a procedural agreement is the first union aim in a situation where it has just been recognised by the employer for bargaining purposes.

10. Substantive agreements, by comparison, deal with the substance of employee relations, ie actual terms and conditions of employment. Topics to be found in such agreements include:

1. pay, ie wages and salaries
2. hours of work, including shift work etc
3. holiday entitlements
4. benefits, such as pension schemes, accident insurance, profit-sharing etc
5. staffing arrangements, establishments etc,
6. arrangements in case of redundancy or dismissal.

Substantive agreements are usually re-negotiated every one or two years, but procedural agreements are negotiated only as and when the parties feel the need to change or clarify the rules. Most procedural agreements require either side to give several months' notice of variation or termination of the agreement, whereas most substantive agreements run out automatically at the end of the period concerned.

Negotiations

11. In conducting a negotiation both sides engage in a considerable amount of prior preparation. This invariably includes:

- Deciding objectives, ie what improvements or changes to seek
- Assessing relative bargaining power vis-a-vis the other side

- Deciding the tactics to be employed, eg the level of starting offer, concessions, exploiting own strengths and others' weaknesses
- Assessing the impact of external influences, eg cost-of-living, competitive rates etc.

An objective for the management side could be *'to obtain acceptance of flexible rostering/shift-working at minimum cost to the organisation'*; an objective for the trade union side could be *'to achieve pay parity with XYZ group of workers in the industry'*.

12. The relative bargaining power of each side depends on several issues, of which typical examples include:

- the general economic situation (boom time, stagnation or recession?)
- company's ability to pay (profitable, just surviving, loss-making?)
- company's need for particular skills
- extent of any changes to mainstream production or services processes
- pay deals struck elsewhere in comparable industries
- the negotiating ability of union officials.

13. Much depends on the particular circumstances of a negotiation. For example, when the demand for particular skills is high, the union has the advantage; when the demand for labour is low, then management have the stronger position. This latter situation can be offset to a certain extent by a union that is well-organised and not afraid to employ sanctions (ie strikes, overtime bans etc). The immediacy of the impact of possible sanctions is an important factor here. For example, where union sanctions can bring immediate chaos, or disruption of a service, then clearly the union is in a stronger bargaining position than one whose sanctions have no immediate effect whatsoever. In recent years the number of days lost through strikes in the UK is but a mere fraction of what it was twenty years ago, reflecting changed economic circumstances and a less indulgent legal framework.

14. The tactics employed by each side are those actions which, in the course of the negotiations, can contribute to the achievement of their respective objectives. The issue of tactics can be illustrated by considering a substantive matter – the negotiation of a pay increase. As Figure 49.1 shows, each side in the negotiation has its idea of the ideal settlement – ie the *lowest* possible increase from the management side, and the *maximum* possible increase from the trade union side. Recognising the relative bargaining strength of the other side, plus the influence of external factors, each side also has its *fall-back position*. This represents the point beyond which each side is not prepared to retreat. When this

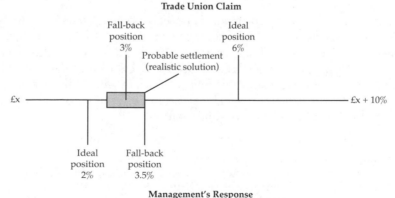

Figure 49.1 Anatomy of a pay claim.

point is reached, the likelihood of a breakdown in negotiations is very great, especially if it has not been recognised until too late. One of the skills of experienced negotiators is to be able to recognise when the other side is close to its fall-back position, and settle before it is too late, hopefully somewhere near the realistic solution. In the example shown (Figure 49.1), the likely increase will be in the 3%–3.5% range.

The likely outcome in Figure 49.1 reflects the tight fall-back position of the management side, probably set in the light of other settlements, the desire to contain labour costs in a highly competitive situation, and yet wanting to provide some incentive to employees. The union side, in accepting this level of increase, are probably bowing to general economic conditions, in which their members are lucky to be employed.

Disputes Procedures

15. A key element in most procedure agreements is the disputes procedure, which in a few cases, such as in engineering, may be a separate agreement. The aim of a disputes procedure is to settle disputes speedily, and as near to the original source as possible. Disputes can arise from a failure to agree during the course of negotiations, or from a differing interpretation of an existing agreement, or from an issue which has arisen as the result of the implementation of an agreement (eg concerning redundancies or dismissals). When they arise, disputes have to be tackled at once, for it is generally in everyone's interests that disputes should be short-lived. Most organisations have two or three stages of an internal procedure, involving progressively more senior managers and union officers. If the dispute cannot be solved internally, then, but only then, can external sources be called in. These external sources may be in the shape of an ACAS conciliation officer, a mediator or an arbitrator. The difference between these three alternatives is as follows:

❶ conciliation is essentially a peace-making service, in which the outsider helps the parties to reach their own decision

❷ arbitration is a settlement-making service, in which the arbitrator makes the decision for the parties

❸ mediation is a halfway approach between conciliation and arbitration, in which the third party makes active suggestions to the disputing parties as to how they might reach a compromise.

Trade Unions in Britain

16. Essentially, a trade union is an organisation of workers, which aims to protect and promote their interests in the workplace, mainly by means of collective bargaining and consultation with employers. Although the last decade has seen a major change in the emphasis of British employment law from collective rights to the rights of individuals in the workplace, there is still a considerable body of law affecting collective activities, especially those of trade unions. The principal legislation on trade unions is contained in the Trade Union and Labour Relations (Consolidation) Act, 1992.

17. The legal definition of a 'trade union' is stated in the 1992 Act as follows:

> '...an organisation (whether permanent or temporary) which either –
> (a) consists wholly or mainly of workers of one or more descriptions and is an organisation whose principal purposes include the regulation of relations between workers...and employers or employers' associations; or
> (b) consist wholly or mainly of –
>   (i) constituent or affiliated organisations ... or

(ii) representatives of such ... organisations;

and in either case is an organisation whose principal purposes include the regulation of relationships between workers and employers or between workers and employers' associations ...'

18. The same Act defines an *independent* trade union as follows:

'...a trade union which –
(a) is not under the domination or control of an employer or a group of employers or one or more employers' associations; and
(b) is not liable to interference by an employer...'

In assessing whether a trade union is independent, the Certification Officer (see below) applies a number of guiding principles. These can be summarised in the form of a number of key questions, as follows:

- is the union financially independent?
- what assistance does it receive from the employer (eg premises, offices, extra time off etc)
- how much employer intervention is present?
- what is the union's history (eg always independent or started out as a staff association established by the employer)?
- what rules are established to run the union?
- is this a single-company union (and therefore more liable to employer interference)?
- how is the union organised and financed?
- what is the union's attitude towards negotiations, and what is its record?

Certification Officer

19. The Certification Officer is appointed by the Secretary of State to supervise the registration and overall conduct of trade unions in Britain. Among his duties are:

- maintaining a list of trade unions
- certifying whether trade unions are independent
- certain functions regarding trade union amalgamations
- administering the scheme for financial contributions to trade union ballots (eg on strike action, election of senior union officers, amending rules etc)
- dealing with various complaints made by union members (eg regarding the union's political fund etc)
- the investigation of a trade union's financial affairs where fraud or some breach of the rules is suspected.

Each year the Certification Officer is required to make a public report on his activities.

20. Trade union membership in Britain has fallen quite substantially in recent years. In 1995, the Certification Officer reported[2] that the number of trade union members stood at 8.2 million from a total of 256 listed unions. This compared with 10.5 million members from 354 unions in 1988. By 2001 membership had dropped to 7.9m from 218 listed unions.[3] The decline in membership has been due to several factors, including:

- fewer people employed in industries with strong tradition of union membership
- where employment growth has occurred, it has been in white-collar areas not usually known for their interest in trade union representation

- demise of the 'closed shop' and similar agreements, whereby individuals had to join an appropriate trade union

- removal of state encouragement for collective bargaining

- less enthusiasm for trade union membership amongst employees, whose fate is now more in the hands of the market place than in the outcome of collective bargaining

The number of trade unions has declined mainly as a result of mergers. Like their counterparts in management, unions have had to seek mergers in order to survive, in this case in order to sustain their role as viable negotiating and representational bodies.

Types of Trade Union

21. Trade unions have typically been placed into four categories, as follows:

- **Manual Workers' Unions** – nowadays these are principally the large general workers' unions, although there are still a few craft-based and industrial unions. An example of a general union is the Transport & General Workers Union with 872,000 members, making it the largest such union. Examples of craft unions include the Amalgamated Engineering & Electrical Union (727,000) and the Graphical Paper & Media Union (201,000). An example of an industrial union is the Union of Construction Allied Trades & Technicians (123,000).

- **White-collar Unions** – these are mostly general unions for clerical, administrative and technical workers, although there are still some specific to certain occupational groups, especially in the public sector. An example of a general white-collar union is Unison (1.27 million), which resulted from the merger of three unions representing local government officers, public employees and health workers. It is now the largest of all trade unions. An example of a public sector union is the Public and Commercial Services Union (258,000). An example of a large white-collar union in the private sector is the Manufacturing Science & Finance Union (405,000).

- **Managerial/Professional Unions** – these tend to recruit from those employed in middle-management and professional occupations. Examples include the Engineers' and Managers' Association (EMA), the Association of University Teachers (AUT), which have fewer than 100,000 members, and other larger unions, such as the Royal College of Nursing (RCN) with 327,000 members and the National Union of Teachers (NUT) with 295,000 members.

- **Staff Associations** – these are unions representing the employees of a single employer, usually in the white collar sector. Such staff associations, whilst tied to a single employer, are nevertheless sufficiently independent to obtain a certificate of independence from the Certification Officer. Several have merged with related unions/associations as a result of widespread takeovers in the banking and insurance sector.

22. As mentioned earlier, trade union membership has fallen in Britain over the last decade. Not only that, but the overall profile of trade unionism is changing from one dominated by manual workers to one distinguished by a major proportion of white-collar technical and professional occupations. Of the top 16 trade unions (in terms of size) in 1999–2000 some 35% of the membership is now to be found in the white-collar sector.

Most trade unions are affiliated to the Trades Union Congress (TUC), which is the central confederation of unions in Britain. With the decline in both national collective bargaining and direct government intervention in industrial relations, this body has lost much of its former power, and this is reflected in its corresponding employer bodies, at least so far as their industrial relations influence is concerned.

The TUC

23. The role of the TUC (Trades Union Congress) today is primarily to represent the interests of employed people in debates and policy discussions on employment and social security matters (eg pensions policy) at national, European Community and international levels. The organisation's policies are derived from the annual congress of the TUC, whilst the day-to-day operations are administered by a General Secretary and staff directed by a General Council composed of a cross-section of independent trade union leaders, who are elected every year. Most union members are represented at the TUC, which currently has more than 70 affiliated organisations with a membership totalling nearly 8 million.

Employers' Associations

24. The approximate employers' equivalent to the TUC is the Confederation of British Industry (CBI), which represents all the major industries in Britain. Its aims include acting as a national reference point for those seeking industry's views (eg governments, foreign investors etc) on a range of economic, social and commercial matters. The CBI also operates a number of important information, advisory and training services for its members.

25. Employers' associations are primarily intended to handle employee relations issues, including, where applicable, collective bargaining on behalf of a group of employers. In this role their main objectives are as follows:

❶ represent employers in collective bargaining

❷ develop industry-wide procedures for the avoidance of disputes

❸ provide information and advice to members on employee relations matters

❹ represent members on national employee relations issues.

Employers' associations must be distinguished from *trade associations*, which are only concerned with furthering their members interests in commercial and competitive matters (eg the Publishers' Association).

Workplace Representatives

26. Whilst some collective issues are still handled by national bodies, such as unions and employers' associations, the majority of collective matters are dealt with in the workplace. In organisations where one or more trade unions are recognised for the purposes of bargaining and/or consulting on behalf of the employees, it is usual for workplace representatives to be appointed by the union members. These may be called 'shop steward', 'staff representative' or some other agreed term. Such representatives are employees of the organisation who fulfil unpaid work on behalf of their trade union colleagues within a framework of rules agreed between the two parties – employer and union members.

27. The work of a representative usually includes the following responsibilities:

- negotiating local conditions, where appropriate agreements exist for enabling them to do so
- dealing with members' problems in respect of pay, hours and other relevant conditions of employment
- representing members in the course of a grievance
- monitoring the implementation of agreements with employers
- acting as a communication channel between members and the employer on relevant matters

- contributing to joint discussions on workplace safety, efficiency etc
- acting as a link between the trade union and its members.

28. Whereas some twenty years ago the average workplace representative would have had a considerable amount of power to influence both employment conditions and working methods, the situation today is very different. The combined effects of increased competition, legal restrictions on arbitrary trade union sanctions, and more flexible working methods have substantially weakened the power once held by shop stewards and staff representatives.

Employee Participation

29. Broadly speaking, employee participation is about involving employees in the affairs of the organisation. However, the extent to which they should be encouraged or indeed permitted to do so is a matter of considerable debate. Figure 49.2 indicates some of the leading alternatives that have been proposed over the last twenty years. The options are shown on a continuum, since this helps to reflect the various degrees of participation that can be available to employees. They range from participation in the ownership of the organisation by means of shareholdings to total employee control through worker cooperatives. Each alternative is described briefly below.

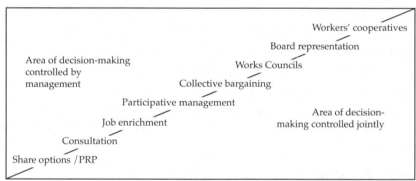

Figure 49.2 Range of alternatives for employee participation

30. **Share options/profit-related pay.** This option was promoted in the UK as part of the drive to extend the scope and spirit of private enterprise in the economy. The intention was to offer relevant employees the chance to own shares in their company, and thus participate in its financing. There was also an intention to link employee effort to profitability by permitting profit-related elements in total pay. Part of the encouragement to employees lies in the tax benefits that operate for those who participate in such schemes. This option does give employees the chance to take a stake in their employer's business, but is scarcely relevant if one considers 'participation' to involve sharing in decisions.

31. **Consultation.** This can be seen as 'participation' only in the sense that employees are consulted about decisions affecting their working lives. This does not imply that employers need take any notice of employees' views. However, there have been efforts in recent years to give communications with employees a higher profile. Companies that make use of workplace consultative groups (eg Quality Circles) are not only engaging in a management–employee dialogue, but in many cases are actively encouraging such consultation in order to improve working methods, quality standards and productivity. This form of consultation comes much closer to real participation in decision-making.

32. At a wider level, the Companies Act, 1985, for example, places a requirement on companies with over 250 employees to show in their Directors' Report what steps they have taken to inform or consult with their employees on issues that affect them. Certain other Acts also contain consultation requirements (eg the duty on employers to disclose relevant information during collective bargaining/or consultation regarding redundancies in the Trade Union & Labour Relations (Consolidation) Act, 1992, and certain of the requirements to consult under the Health & Safety at Work etc Act, 1974).

33. **Job enrichment.** This is 'participation' in the sense that the employee is given greater discretion over immediate work decisions. It can certainly add to employee motivation by increasing responsibility and job interest. However, it does not offer any opportunity to participate in the major, strategic decisions affecting the organisation.

34. **Participative management.** A participative management style implies that all employees will be encouraged to play a part in the decisions affecting their work. However, in practice this may be no more than a paternalistic attempt to involve employees in day-to-day affairs. Where a radical approach to participation is adopted, then it is likely that employees will be enabled to share in the decision-making process at all levels, including the strategic level.

35. **Collective bargaining.** As stated above, collective bargaining is less common now than it was a decade ago. This is not difficult to understand, for when managements are in a strong negotiating position due to external economic circumstances, then they are less likely to want to engage in negotiations with their employees, since this restricts their freedom of discretion. Should labour again become a scarce commodity, then union members will be in a more powerful position to insist on joint negotiations before agreeing to major changes in policies or practice. Bargaining by its very nature is adversarial, and its outcomes, therefore, depend on the relative power of the parties, and the extent to which compromises can be reached. Consultation by comparison is essentially a passive form of participation.

36. **Works Councils.** These are joint bodies of managers and employees established to consider and agree key matters affecting employment within the organisation. They are not for union-only employees, as would be the case in collective bargaining, but must be open to all grades and groupings of employees regardless of any union membership. They originated in Western Europe, and now form the model for European Union states. An EU Directive on Works Councils (1994) required all members states to ensure the establishment of such councils (or similar arrangements) in all organisations employing more than 1000 staff throughout the EU (or more than 150 in at least two of the states) by September 1996. Britain, having originally opted out of the Social Chapter of the Maastricht Treaty, was not obliged to follow this Directive. Several multinational companies have nevertheless set up such bodies in the belief that they represent 'good practice' in employee relations. The issue of employee involvement will arise again in the UK, as Britain has signed up to the Social Chapter, and is consulting employers, trade unions and others on how to implement a new Directive on this topic.

37. **Board representation.** This option usually means appointing rank-and-file employees to non-executive directorships on the company's board. Where there is a two-tier board, as in Germany, the employee-directors sit on the Supervisory Board, but not on the smaller Executive Board. A few large corporations in the UK have experimented with employees on the board, and undoubtedly this approach enables employees views to be heard on key policy issues. However, such employee directors are invariably in a minority, and are hardly likely to be able to effect radical policies against the wishes of their colleagues from

management. The trend in the future is likely to be to encourage more employee–directors to sit as non-executive directors.

38. **Workers' cooperatives.** This option is the nearest to workers' control. Effectively it means that the business is run by the employees in a totally collaborative way. It has never been a widespread form of business management. Probably the most successful example of this model of participation has been the Mondragon experience in the Basque region of Spain, where thriving cooperatives have been established over several years.

39. Organisations considering establishing some form of increased employee participation in decision-making need to ask themselves a number of important questions, such as:

- should participation be confined to operational processes or extended to include strategic issues?

- what topics/issues should be the subject of shared decision-making?

- how should individuals be selected for participation in relevant bodies?

- what part should trade union representatives play in any arrangements?

- how should statutory obligations be dealt with (eg disclosure on redundancies/ communication on safety matters etc)?

- what standards of behaviour may need to be established for participants?

- what employee training and other resources may need to be provided?

- how can participative groups contribute to the needs of other stakeholders, especially customers?

In the current climate of intense competition, reduced public expenditure and the need to create flexible, responsive organisations, it would seem that both private and public sector organisations could gain much from increasing the extent of their employees' participation in the decision-making processes of the corporation.

Collective Employment Law

40. The remaining paragraphs of this chapter outline the main features of current legislation regulating the collective relationships between trade unions and employers. There have been considerable changes to the law on trade unions in the thirty years since the passing of the Industrial Relations Act, 1971. The overall effect of the changes has been to reduce the power of trade unions to influence decisions about employment conditions, and especially working methods, in the workplace. The changes have also enhanced the rights of individuals in the workplace, protecting them from arbitrary behaviour on the part of trade union officials as well as of their employers. Individual rights are contained mostly in the Employment Rights Act, 1996 (see Chapter 50). Collective matters are the concern of the Employment Relations Act, 1999 and the Trade Union and Labour Relations (Consolidation) Act, 1992 (TULRCA). These last two pieces of legislation deal with such key issues as the status of collective agreements, trade disputes, strikes and other employee sanctions, picketing, and balloting. These will be outlined in turn, commencing with collective agreements.

Collective Agreements – Legal Status

41. The law in the UK currently assumes that collective agreements are *not* intended by the parties to be legally binding, unless certain conditions apply. These are:

❶ the agreements are in writing

❷ it is stated that they are intended to be enforceable contracts.

Most collective agreements are still voluntary (ie non-binding). However, the terms of all collective agreements may be incorporated into individual contracts of employment, in which case they then become legally binding. This applies especially to the terms agreed in a substantive agreement (ie pay, holidays, hours of work etc). However, any reference to a 'no-strike' clause in a collective agreement is *excluded* from an individual contract, unless the agreement states in writing that this condition will be incorporated into the contract. There are other conditions that have to be met before such a clause can be so absorbed into individual contracts. The situation in practice is that few such clauses have been agreed between unions and managements.

Trade Dispute

42. The definition of a trade dispute is important because it give certain immunities to the unions and individual members in respect of action they might take during a dispute. Normally, any action taken by one person to induce others to break their contract will be considered a civil wrong (a tort). However, such an action will not necessarily be held to be a tort in the circumstances of a 'trade dispute', which is defined (TULRCA) as follows:

> 'a dispute between workers and their employer which relates wholly or mainly to one or more of the following ...:
> (a) terms and conditions of employment ...;
> (b) engagement or non-engagement, or termination or suspension of employment ... of one or more workers;
> (c) allocation of work or the duties of employment as between workers or groups of workers;
> (d) matters of discipline;
> (e) a worker's membership or non-membership of a trade union;
> (f) facilities for officials of trade unions ...;
> (g) machinery for negotiation or consultation, and other procedures relating to any of the above matters, including the recognition by employers ... of the right of a trade union to represent workers ...'

The above clauses effectively mean that trade unions and their members can generally be protected from legal liability for tort when involved in a dispute with the relevant employer on matters which are crucial to the conditions under which members are employed. It should be noted, however, that the law restricts the meaning of 'worker' to a worker employed by the employer with whom he is in dispute. It thus precludes action against someone who is not your employer (previously called 'sympathy action').

43. In order to gain the necessary protection, a union or its members in a dispute have to fulfil the following obligations:

❶ the employees involved must be employees of the employer at the centre of the dispute

❷ the action must not be designed to pressure an employer into recognising a trade union, or forcing employees to take up union membership, or to exclude suppliers or others on the grounds that they do not recognise or consult with trade unions

❸ so far as trade unions themselves are concerned, they must ballot their members *prior* to any action; such a ballot must conform to laid down conditions, and the union may only take action freely if there is a majority in favour of the specific questions put in the ballot.

44. There will be no protection for unions or members taking action to support individuals who have been dismissed as a result of unofficial strikes. There are also certain groups

of employees who are forbidden by law to strike. These are basically the armed services and the police force.

Picketing

45. Picketing refers to actions taken to persuade a person to support a strike by not attending for work. Trade unions and union members will be immune from civil action when picketing so long as certain conditions are fulfilled (TULRCA):

'A person acts lawfully if he attends

(a) in contemplation or furtherance of a trade dispute...

(b) at a specified place, namely

(i) at or near his own place of work...

(ii) if he is unemployed and either his last employment was terminated in connection with a trade dispute or if the termination was one of the circumstances giving rise to a trade dispute, at or near his former place of work...

(iii) if he does not ... normally work at any one place ... at any premises of his employer...

(iv) if he is an official of a trade union, at or near the place of work or former place of work of a member of that union whom he is accompanying and whom he represents...

(c) for the purpose only of peacefully obtaining or communicating information or peacefully persuading any person to work or abstain from working.'

46. It is important to note that picketing is only permissible at the place of work, and not, for example, at the private residence of an employer. Also the law only protects peaceful actions by the pickets in pursuit of their strike. An official Code of Practice on Picketing is in force, which recommends that there should be no more than six pickets at any one entrance. Such a code does not have the force of law in itself, but may be taken into consideration in any legal proceedings. Action outside what is permitted by the TULRCA may lead to criminal charges against individuals, including fines or imprisonment.

Ballots

47. In order to encourage the use of secret ballots on proposals for strike action or other important trade union purpose (eg the election of officers), the Secretary of State is empowered to provide payments towards the costs of a ballot. Qualifying ballots include the following:

1. strike ballots (or other industrial action) in respect of specific actions not general union policy development

2. ballots for the election of a union's key officers (General Secretary etc)

3. ballots on amendments to union rules

4. ballots on decisions about amalgamation with another union

5. ballots on whether to hold a political fund on behalf of members

6. ballots to obtain the views of members concerning proposals made by an employer regarding their pay, hours of work, holidays etc.

48. Ballots should be conducted in secret, and proper arrangements made for the correct counting of voting papers. Employers, subject to certain conditions being fulfilled, are obliged to provide facilities on their premises to enable voting to take place properly. Part of the reasoning behind such legal support for ballots is to ensure that trade unions are

made accountable to all their members rather than just to their activists. However, the present system of refunding ballot costs to the trade unions is about to be phased out over a three year period.

References

1. Advisory, Conciliation and Arbitration Service (1995), *Annual Report 1994*, ACAS.
2. *Annual Report of the Certification Officer* (1995), HMSO.
3. *Annual Report of the Certification Officer* (2001), HMSO.

Further Reading

Trades Union Congress – Annual Reports.
Individual Trade Union Reports.

CHAPTER 50

Legal Aspects of Employment – Individual Rights

Introduction

1.   It is important for managers at any level of responsibility to be aware of the legal framework that applies to the workplace. This chapter outlines some of the key features of employment law as likely to be experienced by a practising manager. When more detailed information is required, managers may refer to specific guides to the legislation as published from time to time by the appropriate government department or statutory body (eg ACAS, Health & Safety Commission etc).

2.   There are four sources of employment law in England and Wales as follows:

❶   The **common law** – ie the 'unwritten law' arising from custom and practice, especially in relation to (a) the contract of employment, and (b) the law of torts (civil wrongs) affecting workplace incidents.

❷   **Statute law** – ie the written law arising from the numerous Acts of Parliament passed by the nation's law-makers, and which is the most far-reaching of the legal influences on the workplace.

❸   **Case law** – ie the decisions of courts and tribunals (in the European Union as well as in Britain itself) in interpreting statutes in particular.

❹   **European Community law** – ie legislation arising from the Treaty of Rome,1957, and from **regulations** (directly binding on member states) and **directives** (not directly binding but requiring domestic legislation within a stated period) made under the treaty; also from decisions of the European Court of Justice.

3.   The chapter will begin with a short consideration of the all-important question of what is, and what is not, employment, and outlines the principal features of the employment contract. The remaining sections of the chapter focus on the following:

- human rights
- individual rights in the workplace
- anti-discrimination measures in employment
- health and safety at work
- role of Employment Tribunals.

The Employment Contract

4.   A person employed by an organisation is either employed under a *contract of service*, and is therefore an employee, or under a *contract for services*, and is then an independent contractor. It is only the former which is referred to as the contract of employment. The distinction is important because legal rights granted to individuals under current legislation, such as the right not to be unfairly dismissed, are only applicable to employees, and not to independent contractors.

5.   Several legal cases have helped to clarify what is, and what is not, a contract of employment. At the present time there are three main tests applied by the Courts to establish whether a contract of employment exists in a given situation. These are as follows:

❶   **The control test** – this asks where the control lies in the situation; if the individual is told *what* to do and how to do it, he is an employee; if not, then he is an independent contractor;

❷   **The organisation test** – this asks whether the individual is integrated into the organisation; if he is, then he is an employee; if not, he is an independent contractor;

❸   **The multiple test** – this takes several circumstantial factors into account as well as both the control and organisation factors; this is the most comprehensive test to date; where an individual appears, in all the circumstances, to be carrying out the role of an employee, then he is an employee; where there is sufficient doubt about the role being performed, it is more likely that he is an independent contractor.

6.   As mentioned above, the difference between an employee and a contractor is important. For example if a person is an employee, his employer is liable vicariously for any civil wrongs that the employee may commit in the course of his employment. A civil wrong, or tort, could occur when an employee steals from a customer or injures a member of the public when driving in the course of his or her duties. An employer bears no such responsibility in respect of independent contractors. Another reason why the difference is important is that only *employees* are granted certain rights or protection in legislation, such as rights to minimum periods of notice, and to a written statement of the main terms and conditions of employment, and to protection such as the right not to be unfairly dismissed, and the right to pursue trade union activities without being penalised. Another distinction between employees and independent contractors is made in matters relating to benefits. For example only *employees* are permitted to claim unemployment benefit and industrial injuries benefit.

7.   Where an individual *is* employed under a contract of employment this need not necessarily be written, except in the case of an apprenticeship. Most employment contracts are in fact a mixture of written and unwritten terms, and of express and implied conditions. The written elements of the contract can be contained in a formal document, in a letter of appointment and in the statement of main terms of employment required by statute (Employment Rights Act, 1996); these written terms constitute the *express* conditions of the contract although they are not the contract itself. The unwritten, and therefore *implied*,

terms of the contract arise from the common law duties of the parties, from custom and practice in the organisation, and from the operation of collective agreements and codes of practice.

Variations to a contract should normally be subject to a period of notice not less than that to which the employee is entitled by virtue of his length of service, unless, of course, the employee agrees to a shorter period.

8.   The common law duties of the respective parties can be summarised briefly as follows:

The Employer has an obligation to:

- pay wages,
- provide work (but only for those who are paid by results eg salesmen on commission),
- take reasonable care of the employee,
- indemnify the employee where he necessarily incurs expenses and liabilities in the performance of his duties,
- treat the employee with courtesy.

The Employee has an obligation to:

- render a personal service, and be willing and able to do so,
- take reasonable care in the performance of his duties,
- obey reasonable and lawful instructions from his employer,
- act in good faith towards the employer, eg not to work for two competing employers at one and the same time,
- not to impede his employer's business.

As can be seen from the above lists, the common law duties of the parties to each other are set out very generally, and have to be related to the circumstances of each situation in order, for example, to assess what is reasonable. Where statute law and common law appear to conflict, then it is the statute which prevails. Where aspects of a contract are not clear, and where no statutory rule applies, then the common law rules are applied.

Human Rights Act, 1998

9.   This Act came into force in October 2000 and is derived directly from the European Convention on Human Rights. It enables British citizens to obtain redress on human rights matters in UK courts and tribunals, instead of having to refer to the European Court of Human Rights. The Act is an over-arching law, which means that other relevant pieces of legislation must be interpreted in the light of its principles. The Act applies *prima facie* to public bodies, such as government departments and local authorities, but its implications stretch much further. In respect of employment matters, it is inconceivable that the Act will not affect all organisations that employ people. There are sixteen basic rights protected in the Act, including the right to life, and to liberty and security.

10.   The rights most relevant to employers and employees are as follows:

- **Right to a fair trial** – everyone is entitled to a fair and public hearing within a reasonable time by an independent and impartial tribunal established by law. Disciplinary rules within organisations should make clear provision for a right of appeal to an employment tribunal
- **Right to respect for private and family life** – everyone has the right to respect for their private and family life, their home and their correspondence. Managers need to be

aware of possible abuses of this right when monitoring employees' personal telephone calls or emails whilst at work. Clear guidelines will be needed to show staff where the limits are to be set. This is especially important when company rules require behaviour to conform to security and other restrictions on personal communications. Employers do not have an absolute right to contact employees at their home, unless such arrangements form part of the employees' contract of employment.

- **Freedom of thought, conscience and religion** – this right includes the right to change one's beliefs. For employers this right has to be considered in relation to the Race Relations Act, and clearly any exercise by individuals of the basic right must not contravene legislation designed to restrict racial or religious abuse. Managers now need to take more notice of religious beliefs than in the past and ensure that employees are not *expected* to work on their Sabbath days and major religious festivals. With the increasing provision of retail and other services for twenty-four hours a day seven days a week, such considerations must be taken into account in setting employment conditions.

- **Freedom of expression** – individuals have the right to hold opinions and receive and impart ideas without interference by a public authority. This right extends to dress codes and personal appearance. Managers now have to review disciplinary rules to ensure that any restrictions on an employee's right of expression are reasonable in the circumstances (eg for safety and health reasons).

- **Freedom of assembly and association** – this includes the specific right to join, or not to join, a trade union, and to hold union meetings during working hours. The right to take industrial action is not explicit, but is strongly implied. Most of the implications of this basic right are already well catered for in UK businesses and public sector organisations.

- **Prohibition of discrimination** – access to the rights available under the Act should not be denied on any discriminatory grounds unless they can be justified objectively. The effect of this right is to extend the scope of anti-discriminatory measures to religious and political issues as well as those already in force regarding sex, race and disability discrimination. Any such prohibitions in the workplace have to be seen to be lawful and reasonable.

11. As a consequence of the Act, all managers in the workplace will have to review their existing grievance, disciplinary and other codes of behaviour. They will also need to review their agreements with recognised trade unions in order to ensure that they conform to the spirit of the human rights legislation. The Act does not give carte blanche to individuals to do or say what they want without any consideration of public unrest or outrage caused by their behaviour. When everyone has rights there have to be arrangements for deciding what is fair when one person's rights conflict with another's. The UK's existing laws affecting employment are still very much in force. The chief difference now is the way in which they are likely to be interpreted by courts and tribunals.

Employment Legislation – Individual Rights

12. Until the 1960s, employment legislation in England and Wales was directed at *collective* rights arising out of the bargaining between employers and trade unions, and was contained principally in a number of Trade Union Acts passed between 1871 and 1927. It was only in the 1960s that statutes dealing with *individual* rights began to appear on the scene. The trend towards individual rights received a massive boost in 1971, with the

passing of the Industrial Relations Act, and since then numerous statutes defining such rights have been passed, covering issues such as redundancy payments, notice periods, unfair dismissal and maternity rights. The current legislation is embodied in the Employment Rights Act, 1996.

13. The individual rights that are most likely to be of concern to the practising manager are as follows:

1. the provision of written particulars of employment
2. the obligation to pay a minimum wage
3. the right to a mimimum period of notice
4. the right to a redundancy payment
5. the right not to be unfairly dismissed
6. provision of maternity rights for women employees
7. provision of appropriate health, safety and welfare measures
8. the right not to be unfairly discriminated at work on grounds of sex, race or disability.

Written Particulars of Employment

14. The law requires employers to provide all their employees with a written statement of specified particulars of employment. These particulars should include the following:

1. date when employment and continuous employment began,
2. the scale or rate of remuneration, or the method of calculating remuneration (eg piece-rates, over-time rates etc),
3. the intervals at which remuneration is paid, ie weekly, monthly etc,
4. the hours of work,
5. holiday entitlement, holiday pay, sickness arrangements and sick pay, pensions arrangements,
6. the length of notice to be given on either side,
7. the title of the job the employee is employed to do and the place of work,
8. the disciplinary rules which apply to the employee, or a reference to a reasonably accessible document (eg a Company handbook) which specifies the disciplinary rules and procedure,
9. the grievance procedure applicable to the employee.

The above particulars have to be given to the employee within one month after the commencement of employment. The intention of the legislation is to provide employees with a written statement of their main terms of employment, and not to provide them with a written contract.

National Minimum Wage

15. The UK government has now introduced enabling legislation to provide for a national minimum wage, the National Minimum Wage Act, 1998, which can be amended from time to time by secondary legislation (ie by regulations). The intention is to set minimum hourly rates of pay for (1) younger employees (in the 18–21 age-range), and (2) for all employees over 22 years. The rates as at October 2002 were £3.60 per hour for the younger group, and £4.20 for those over 22. The Act also established a Low Pay

Commission to deal with claims arising under this legislation. Many employers already pay rates well in excess of the statutory minima as a result of negotiations with trade unions or their need to maintain competitive wages in the marketplace.

Minimum Period of Notice

16. The Employment Rights Act, 1996, gives employees the right to a minimum period of notice of termination of employment. Currently, these minima are as follows:

- at least one weeks' notice if employed for between one month and two years
- one additional weeks' notice for each further complete year of service up to a maximum of twelve weeks' notice
- not less than twelve weeks' notice if employed for twelve years or more.

These rights may be extended or waived by agreement, and an employer may offer pay in lieu of notice. Contracts can, of course, be terminated without notice, if the conduct of either parties justifies it (see unfair dismissal notes below).

Redundancy Payments

17. The provisions relating to redundancy originated in the Redundancy Payments Act, 1965. The current position is that an employee, with at least two years' continuous service with an employer, is entitled to a redundancy payment from the latter, if his services are no longer required as a result of the cessation or diminution of the business at the place where he works. This right does not apply to those over the normal retiring age at the time of the redundancy.

18. The provisions for redundancy pay represent the minimum standard, and many organisations pay substantially more mainly as a result of collective agreements. The legal minima are as follows:

- For each year of service from age 41   ... $1\frac{1}{2}$ weeks' pay
- For each year of service from age 22 to age 40   ...   1 weeks' pay
- For each year of service below 22   ... $\frac{1}{2}$ weeks' pay

The maximum number of weeks' pay that can be claimed is 30 weeks, and there is a statutory limit on weekly pay (£250 in 2002).

Right not to be Unfairly Dismissed

19. The concept of unfair dismissal was introduced by the Industrial Relations Act, 1971, and has remained firmly entrenched in subsequent legislation. It now forms an integral part of the Employment Rights Act, 1996 (S. 94) as follows:

> 'An employee has the right not to be unfairly dismissed by his employer.'

Dismissal occurs when an employee has had his contract of employment terminated by his employer, with or without notice; it also refers to the non-renewal of a fixed term contract; and it applies in a situation when, because of the employer's conduct, the employee himself terminates the contract, with or without notice, in circumstances where he is entitled to terminate it without notice (known as 'constructive dismissal').

20. A dismissal may be justified on the following grounds:

- for reasons of the lack of capability or qualifications of the employee
- for reasons relating to the employee's conduct

- where continuation of the employment would contravene a legal duty or restriction
- some other substantial reason which could justify dismissal.

21. A dismissal for reasons of lack of capability usually revolves around questions of ill-health or incompetence, and the Courts will invariably want to know whether other, more suitable, work has been offered to an employee in one of these situations, for, even if the grounds for dismissal are considered as fair, the employer must still show that it was reasonable to dismiss in the circumstances. A dismissal for reasons of misconduct is very much an issue where 'reasonableness' must be taken into account. The ACAS Code on this topic (see Chapter 49) provides useful guidance as to how misconduct should be dealt with. It especially advises against dismissal for a first offence, except in cases of gross misconduct. What constitutes 'reasonable behaviour' by the employer depends on how tribunals interpret the difference between 'misconduct', 'repeated misconduct' and 'gross misconduct'; it also depends on what is stated in Company rule-books, how previous cases have been dealt with by the Company, and the extent to which the ACAS Code has been adhered to. A dismissal on the grounds of redundancy requires the employer to show that there is no longer any need for that job in the organisation. The job becomes redundant and the employee is dismissed—this at least is the logic of the situation. Such a dismissal can be unfair, however, if the employee is unfairly selected for redundancy in a situation where some jobs are redundant, but other similar jobs are not.

22. The grounds on which a dismissal will usually considered to be *unfair* can be summarised as follows.

Dismissal will be unfair:

- if the employee was dismissed solely or mainly for reasons of pregnancy
- where the employee was not permitted to return to work after childbirth, even though she had given due notice of her intention to return
- where the employee was selected for redundancy on grounds related to her pregnancy or childbirth
- if dismissal was on grounds of taking part in trade union activities
- if the dismissal is for membership or non-membership of a trade union
- where the dismissal was on grounds of redundancy, but where usual selection for redundancy procedures were not followed, and/or where the employer failed to provide adequate warning or consider providing alternative employment
- where dismissal took place during an official industrial dispute.

23. It is up to the individual employee to show that they were dismissed, but if they are able to do so, then the employer must show that the reason for the dismissal was an admissible reason. Normally a person can only claim unfair dismissal after being continuously employed for 1 year.

24. The remedies for unfair dismissal are as follows: (a) an award for compensation, (b) reinstatement (ie in the employee's original post), (c) re-engagement (ie in some other post). Most applications relating to unfair dismissal do not reach a tribunal for decision. About two-thirds are conciliated, ie withdrawn or settled out of court. Of the one-third which do reach a tribunal, the results are generally as follows:

- about two-thirds are dismissed
- a little over ten percent are upheld
- the remainder are referred back for further conciliation.

The conclusion to all this is that, despite the apparent legal safeguards against dismissal, the employee continues to be extremely vulnerable to the unilateral termination of the employment contract by his employer.

Maternity Rights

25. Maternity rights stem directly from the Employment Protection Act, 1975, which contained Britain's first such provisions for women employees. The present rights are included in the Employment Rights Act, 1996, as amended by the Employment Relations Act, 1999. In summary the basic rights are as follows:

❶ Paid time off (at the appropriate hourly rate) to receive antenatal care regardless of length of service

❷ Maternity leave of 18 weeks, subject to due notice being given by the employee

❸ Statutory Maternity pay (introduced by the Social Security Act, 1989), subject to a number of conditions (eg must have been continuously employed by her employer for at least 26 weeks preceding the 14th week before her confinement, and have stopped work because of the pregnancy etc); maternity pay is for a period of 18 consecutive weeks from when the woman stops work

❹ Return to work after maternity leave (applicable only to those who have at least 26 weeks' continuous service with the employer) up to 29 weeks after the baby has been born, on terms and conditions no less favourable than previously; the employee must give at least 21 days' written notice of her intention to return to work

❺ Protection from dismissal by reason of pregnancy or childbirth; a woman who is dismissed for any of the following reasons will be deemed to be unfairly dismissed:

- on grounds of pregnancy
- where her maternity leave period is ended by her dismissal on grounds of her childbirth
- where the woman is selected for redundancy on any of the grounds associated with pregnancy or childbirth

There is no qualifying period for a complaint by the employee of unfair dismissal in the above instances

❻ Where a woman is suspended on maternity grounds because of a health or safety requirement/recommendation (code of practice), she is entitled to be offered alternative work of a suitable kind, and on terms not substantially less favourable than her own; she is also entitled to remuneration on such suspension at the rate of a week's pay for each week of suspension, unless she has unreasonably refused alternative work.

Parental leave

26. A parent is entitled to a total of 13 weeks leave for the purpose of caring for a child up to its fifth birthday. This section applies especially to fathers. The employee has to supply evidence of his responsibility for the child, and has to have been employed by the employer for one year. The law permits employers and employees to agree local arrangements for taking this leave in individual cases. Where no such agreement is in force a fall-back scheme provides as follows:

- leave must be taken in blocks or multiples of one week
- the maximum amount of leave in any one year is four weeks

414

- twenty-one days notice must be given to the employer
- leave can be postponed by the employer for up to six months, in situations where the employee's absence would be disruptive, except for the leave taken immediately after childbirth.

Time Off Work

27. The Employment Rights Act, 1996, allows employees time off work for specified reasons. In some cases, the employer is also bound to pay the employee his normal remuneration during the time off. Apart from certain trade union activities, the principal rights to time off work for individuals include performing certain public duties (eg JP, school governor, local councillor), performing safety duties and attending relevant training if a safety representative and attending for antenatal care. The employer is not obliged to pay employees their normal pay where public duties are concerned.

Unfair Discrimination at Work

28. In recent years the very word *'discrimination'* has come to have a pejorative meaning, implying that it is always a bad thing or, in our context, unfair. This is not always the case. Discrimination means selecting between alternatives or making judgements about comparative attributes. Where this applies to physical objects or to alternative courses of action, there is no problem. The problem only comes about when we are dealing with people. Managers have to discriminate between employees when deciding which person should be offered promotion or redeployed, for example. However, they may only do so legally on the grounds of the *individual's performance or ability*. The so-called 'anti-discrimination' laws of numerous countries, Britain included, are in fact directed against arbitrary or unfair discrimination against individuals, usually on the grounds of their sex, marital status, race, nationality, disability or religion.

29. In Britain the principal statutes dealing with unfair discrimination are as follows:

1. Equal Pay Act,1970 (as amended by the Equal Pay (Amendment) Regulations, 1983)
2. Sex Discrimination Act,1975 (as amended by the Sex Discrimination Act,1986)
3. Race Relations Act, 1976
4. Fair Employment (Northern Ireland) Act, 1989 (dealing with unlawful discrimination on grounds of religion)
5. European Community Law (eg Article 119 on principle of equal pay).

30. The Equal Pay Act, 1970, applies to all the main contractual terms and conditions of employment, not just pay. It applies as much to men as to women, although its effect has been primarily to improve the relative position of women at work. The Act establishes the right of an individual woman (man) to equal treatment in respect of the terms of her (his) contract of employment when employed

1. on work of the same, or broadly similar, nature to that of a man (woman), and
2. in a job, which, although different from that of a man (woman), has been rated as equivalent under job evaluation.
3. on work of equal value to that of a man (woman) in the same employment in terms of the demands made by the work in terms of skill, effort etc (this amendment was brought into effect on 1 January 1984).

The implications of item 3 are firstly, that women (or men) who feel that the demands of their job are equal in value to other jobs in the organisation may claim equal pay, and secondly, that any employer intending to rebut such a claim will have to utilise an analytical method of job evaluation, since only such methods are considered as 'proper' job evaluation.

It is worth noting that 'equal pay' does not mean the same as 'identical pay', which can depend on many other factors such as age, length of service and performance. What is important is that the same terms or opportunities should apply regardless of sex.

31. The Sex Discrimination Acts, 1975 and 1986, and the Race Relations Act, 1976 can be considered in tandem since the last named is shaped on the first. In contrast to the Equal Pay Act which is concerned with the *contractual terms of employment* (pay, hours, holidays etc), these other Acts are concerned with the *context of the employment* (promotion, training etc). The Acts define two kinds of discrimination: *direct* discrimination and *indirect* discrimination. The former occurs in situations where an employer treats a person less favourably than others on the grounds of sex, marital status or race. The latter occurs where the effect of a condition of employment is discriminatory, even though on the surface it appears to apply equally to all employees. For example, in a leading case on sex discrimination, it was held that a Civil Service requirement, that applicants for a post should be under 28 years of age, operated indirectly against women, because in practice fewer of them would be able to meet this requirement than men. It is important to notice that whereas direct discrimination is intentional, indirect discrimination is usually not so.

32. The Sex Discrimination Acts forbid unfair discrimination at every stage of employment. Thus, in recruitment advertising, for example, the employer may not show any intention to discriminate unlawfully. Selection procedures (ie interviews, terms of offers, selection decisions etc) must also be even-handed in their treatment of applicants. Once employees are in their job they should be offered the same opportunities for promotion, training and any other benefits regardless of their sex or marital status. There are occasional exceptions to such rulings, however, when training may be offered positively to encourage applicants in situations where no one (or very few) of a particular sex is employed. Where dismissals are involved, employers may not fairly select an individual on grounds of their sex. It is also no longer lawful for employers to offer differing compulsory retirement ages to men and women, even though the pensionable age for the state pension is still based on an unequal distinction between them (65 for men and 60 for women).

33. The Race Relations Act,1976, follows very much in the steps of the Sex Discrimination Act,1975, and most of the points made above apply equally to cases of discrimination on grounds of a person's race, nationality or ethnic origin. As noted in the previous paragraph, there are always some exceptions to the rule. So, for example, in the Race Relations Act, it is not unlawful for a Chinese restaurant to recruit only Chinese waiters! In a similar way, under the Sex Discrimination Act, it is not unlawful to discriminate in favour of women in respect of pregnancy or childbirth, nor to discriminate on grounds of 'genuine occupational qualification', eg where acting or modelling calls for men (or women) for reasons of physiology or credibility!

34. The general intention behind the anti-discrimination laws is to create a framework which can deal with the worst abuses of employers, but without being particularly punitive, and which can educate employers to adopt a more genuinely fair approach to those who are liable to be discriminated against unfairly because they are women, or married, or a member of an ethnic minority.

Disability Discrimination

35. Until the recent Disability Discrimination Act, 1995, the main legal requirements in Britain for dealing with the employment of disabled persons were contained in the Disabled Persons (Employment) Act, 1944. The requirements were very modest, but represented an example of what would now be called 'positive discrimination'. This took the form of (a) requiring employers of more than 20 employees to employ a quota of disabled persons up to 3% of the total staff – a figure that was generally well in excess of the total number of registered disabled persons in the population, and (b) identifying certain work as being particularly suited to disabled persons who should be given such work ahead of other employees. The 1944 Act is now repealed by the new Act, which introduces some major changes.

36. The 1995 Act introduces a longer, more searching definition of 'disability', and relates it to the ability to carry out the normal day-to-day activities of the employment. The quota provision is repealed, and is replaced by a requirement not to discriminate against a disabled person at any stage of employment, thus giving disabled employees some of the rights available under sex and race discrimination laws. Discrimination against a disabled person may take three forms:

❶ direct discrimination, ie where the disabled person is treated less favourably than other persons on the grounds of his disability, when such treatment cannot be justified by the employer

❷ discrimination by failure of the employer to make reasonable adjustments to working conditions and procedures to ensure that a disabled person is not substantially at a disadvantage compared with other employees

❸ discrimination by victimisation, ie where a disabled person has brought evidence or made a complaint against an employer, and is treated less favourably on account of his complaining.

The employment provisions of the Act do not apply to organisations of less than 50 employees.

Health and Safety at Work

37. An employer has a *common law duty* to provide a safe place of work for his employees, and is liable at common law for accidents caused by his employees in the course of their employment. The principal *statutory* duties of employers (see below) arise from the following:

• Factories Act, 1961

• Offices, Shops and Railway Premises Act, 1963

• Health and Safety at Work Act, 1974

• Regulations made under the above legislation.

The statutory duties include specific duties towards members of the public affected by the employer's activities and employees of other employers working on his premises, as well as towards his own employees. Every employer is obliged by law to take out employers' liability insurance to cover accidents and injury to his employees.

38. The employer's *common law duties* are usually categorised under the following headings:

❶ the provision of a safe place of employment, so far as is reasonable in all the circumstances

417

2 the provision of safe means of access to work

3 the provision of safe systems of working

4 the provision of adequate equipment, materials and clothing to enable employees to carry out their work safely

5 the provision of competent fellow workers

6 duty of care to ensure that employees are not subjected to any unreasonable risks in the workplace.

In each category the courts are likely to assess what is reasonable in the circumstances of a particular employer's safety provision.

39. The employer's *statutory* duties under the Factories Act, 1961, can be summarised as follows:

1 to keep the factory clean and prevent overcrowding

2 maintain a reasonable temperature, and adequate ventilation and lighting

3 to securely fence (ie guard) machinery

4 maintain floors, passages and stairs

5 provide safe means of access to and from work.

The Offices, Shops and Railway Premises Act, 1963 imposes similar duties on employers.

40. These statutory duties do not supplant common law duties, but rather supplement them. Thus, a breach of a duty could result both in a common law claim by the employee and a criminal prosecution by the Health and Safety Inspectorate. Where an employee makes a common law claim for damages as a result of injury at work, he may be liable to a counter claim of contributory negligence, which may reduce any damages awarded by the court.

41. The general principles to be followed by employers in matters of health and safety at work are contained in the Health and Safety at Work etc. Act, 1974, which is the principal Act for health and safety at work. This Act contains the administrative and enforcement arrangements for supporting safety in the workplace. The Act is essentially an enabling Act, under which all kinds of relevant issues can be dealt with by means of additional Regulations without the need for further Acts of Parliament. The Act established a uniform enforcement agency in the shape of the Health and Safety Commission (the governing body), and the Health and Safety Executive (HSE) – (its executive arm).

42. The purposes of the principal Act can be summarised as follows:

1 to secure the health, safety and welfare of persons at work

2 to protect persons other than employees against risks to health and safety arising from work activities

3 to control the keeping and use of explosives or highly flammable or otherwise dangerous substances

4 to control the emission into the atmosphere of noxious or offensive substances from prescribed premises (eg factories).

The task of the Commission and its Executive is basically to provide a visible framework within which employers and others (eg self-employed, occupiers, employees, manufacturers) may fulfil their health and safety obligations. This is broadly achieved by means of (1) statutory regulations, proposed by the Commission but passed by Parliament, (2) Codes of Practice approved by the Commission, (3) HSE inspections backed up by substantial powers, and (4) research and advice on health and safety issues by the HSE.

43. The powers of HSE inspectors are considerable. For example, they can:

- enter any premises with good reason to investigate conditions, take samples and measurements

- take statements from relevant persons in the course of their investigations

- serve notices on employers (and other persons) requiring them to remedy breaches of the relevant statutory provisions

- serve prohibition notices where there is a serious risk of personal injury at work

- conduct summary prosecutions in a magistrates court for failure to discharge health and safety duties.

44. The European Community has also added to health and safety legislation at work by means of Directives (eg the 'Framework Directive') which require the member states to introduce appropriate legislation. Typical issues that have occurred, and for which new statutory regulations have been introduced in Britain, include noise at work, management of health and safety regulations (including making assessments of risks), and the use of visual display screens.

The Role of Employment Tribunals in Enforcing Employment Rights

45. Where individuals think they have a case against their employer in respect of the various rights available to them under the employment protection and anti-discrimination laws, they may make an application to an employment tribunal for financial compensation or other remedy (eg re-instatement, re-engagement etc). Tribunals provide for a speedier, cheaper and less complex approach to legal disputes than the ordinary courts. Such tribunals have been active in Britain since the 1960s, and their jurisdiction has been substantially increased over the last forty years. The typical tribunal is presided over by a legally qualified chairman and two other approved persons, usually one an experienced manager and the other an experienced employee representative. Procedures are considerably less formal than in other courts, and legal representation is not necessary, although it is increasing. Appeals on a point of law only may be made to the Employment Appeal Tribunal, which is presided over by a High Court Judge supported by two lay-members, one representing employers and the other trade unions. Further appeals lie to the Court of Appeal, the House of Lords and the European Court of Justice.

46. When an application is made to a tribunal, it is usual for ACAS – the Advisory, Conciliation and Arbitration Service – to attempt to conciliate between employee and employer. ACAS, in fact, has a duty to conciliate in respect of several of the rights referred to earlier such as:

- unfair dismissal (including the right to return after maternity leave)

- equal pay claims

- sex discrimination

- race discrimination

- unfair selection for redundancy

- time off for antenatal care, etc.

47. ACAS conciliation officers help to establish facts and clarify issues between the parties, whilst facilitating communication between them. They help to identify the options available to each party, and explain the procedural and legal features of the tribunal to them. Most claims are made under the following headings, based on figures taken from the ACAS Annual Report for 2000–2001:

Type of claim	No. of cases (rounded)
Unfair dismissal	50,000
Equal pay	4,900
Sex discrimination	9,100
Race relations	4,100
Protection of wages	39,000
Breach of contract	29,000
Disability discrimination	4,400
Other	26,000

(Source: ACAS Annual Report 2000–2001)

Note: the largest number of complaints were those connected with unfair dismissal, closely followed by wage-related items. This has been so for many years. The high number of wage-protection cases in the year were largely a result of the minimum wage legislation. ACAS reported that its clear-up rate (where conciliation was successful) was 43%. Of the remaining cases, 28% were withdrawn and 29% went to tribunal.

Questions for Discussion/Homework

1. 'The role of the Personnel department is mainly to provide routine personnel services to line managers.' Discuss this assertion.

2. Devise a personnel classification plan of your own, but based on the Seven-Point Plan. Under each heading write one question you might ask of a potential applicant for a job of your choice.

3. In a selection interview, what are the marks of an effective interviewer?

4. Using your own words, distinguish between the terms 'training' and 'development'.

5. What sources of information are likely to prove the most fruitful for a person undertaking a training needs analysis in an office environment?

6. What are the essential features of an analytical method of job evaluation?

7. How might **managers** view employee relations in a different light from other employees in the same organisation?

8. What rules operate at the place of work? Comment on the most important of these.

9. Why is the role of the workplace representative, or shop steward, important in employee relations?

10. In what ways in the past decade has legislation granted additional rights to employees? Do you see any groups who may appear to have benefited more than others from these additions?

Examination Questions

The following are a cross-section of questions about various aspects of Personnel Management which have been set over the years. Suggested answers are given in Appendix 2.

EQ 35 Comment on the usefulness of the Seven-Point Plan as a framework for the preparation of person specifications in the selection process. To what extent are alternative frameworks available, and how do they compare with the Seven-Point Plan?

(ICSA PPP)

EQ 36 Identify the essential features of: (a) an ideal disciplinary procedure; (b) an ideal grievance procedure. Evaluate the role of each in industrial conflict.

(IOB Nature of Management)

EQ 37 What is the difference between 'training' and 'development'? To what extent can these processes occur through the medium of courses?

(ICSA PPP)

EQ 38 Discuss the possible ways in which employees can participate in decision-making at work.

(ACCA Business Management)

EQ 39 What do you understand by the term 'collective bargaining'? How far may it be considered a problem solving, decision-making process?

(IOB Human Aspects of Management)

The final section of this book focuses mainly on the needs of small and medium sized enterprises for adequate financial controls. It is not intended to say anything new to accountancy and other students taking examinations in various aspects of financial management, but should be used as background information for those wishing to understand the basics of financial reporting and control as part of general management.

Chapter 51 sets out briefly the statutory financial statements required by companies in order to fulfil their accountability to shareholders and other key stakeholders.

Chapter 52 looks at accounts whose prime purpose is to inform and guide the management of the enterprise, ie budgets, cash-flow forecasts and business plans.

CHAPTER 51

Company Accounts

Introduction

1.   Formal company accounts are essentially financial statements presented by the directors of a company to the annual general meeting of its shareholders. The information that has to be made public in this way is governed by statute, viz the Companies Acts 1985 & 1989. The main purpose of such formal accounts is to enable the directors (both executive and non-executive) to demonstrate their accountability to the shareholders' meeting. (See Chapter 12.)

2.   The principal statements of the accounts must be made in specified ways. They comprise the following:

- The Directors' Report
- The Auditors' Report
- The Profit and Loss Account
- The Balance Sheet
- Notes to the Accounts.

(Although not required by statute, a Cash Flow Statement is usually given at the same time.)

3.   The Directors' Report is usually a quite short piece of narrative which outlines the company's principal activity, summarises the financial results for the year, lists all the directors (executive and non-executive) holding office during the year, highlights particular events during the year, and includes a note confirming that the auditors have expressed their willingness to act for the company in the coming year.

The Auditors' Report is the formal statement – a few lines – made by the external auditors (chartered or certified accountants) to confirm that they have examined the financial statements and found them to be in order. Very occasionally auditors will qualify their report in some way, where they have been unable to check a particular aspect of the accounts. The object of the exercise is to ensure the correctness of the accounts submitted to share-holders, and to dissuade the directors from masking certain issues from the public (eg concealing large debts or improper use of pension fund monies). As cases such as the Enron Scandal in the USA have shown, there is never an absolute guarantee that auditors will uncover malpractices. Indeed, in the Enron case, the auditors themselves collapsed after being found guilty of shredding vital evidence. The issue of corporate governance is impor-tant here. All company boards need to demonstrate integrity and transparency in the way they conduct, and report on, their responsibilities. Chapter 12 above listed some of the practical ways by which these standards can be achieved.

The Profit & Loss Account

4.   The Profit & Loss statement presented in the Annual Accounts is a historical review of the revenue and expenditure activities of the company for the previous financial year. These statements may also be called Income & Expenditure or Revenue Accounts. They may be produced at other intervals during the year (eg monthly or quarterly) but in these circumstances the purpose is not to account to shareholders but to provide useful informa-tion to management. The conventional way of producing the Profit & Loss statement is to show gross sales' income (or turnover) less the cost of sales (materials, wages and other direct costs) to produce a gross profit figure, which is further reduced by the deduction of overheads (all the indirect costs of the business – rents, administration, salaries etc) to produce a net profit or surplus before tax. It is also usual to include items such as Interest received and payable during the year, and Exceptional Items (which need to be explained in the Notes to the Accounts). Non-manufacturing companies omit the cost of sales step in the presentation of their accounts.

5.   An example of a Profit & Loss Account, in this case an Income & Expenditure Account, is given in Figure 51.1. The company is a not-for-profit organisation limited by guarantee (ie it has no share capital like public and private limited companies, but is limited by a nominal sum guaranteed by its members. The statutory requirements for presenting the profit and loss accounts only require that the annual figures are consoli-dated. However, all company accounts supply detailed notes explaining various features of the results, and some companies additionally provide a full breakdown of the profit and loss account under its principal income and expenditure headings, as shown in Figure 51.2.

	£' 000s
Income	1,152
Administration expenses	<u>1,919</u>
	(767)
Other operating income	<u>316</u>
Operating deficit	(451)
Interest receivable	<u>537</u>
Surplus before taxation	86
Tax	<u>(22)</u>
Surplus for year	64

Figure 51.1 A small not-for-profit company – income and expenditure Account (year ending 31 March 2002)

Notes: The figures in brackets are negative amounts or deductions. The overall picture here shows that administration expenses are greater than income from the company's operations, but that because in this case the company holds large sums of undistributed royalties in a deposit account on behalf of its members, the interest receivable more than makes up for the operating deficit. Indeed at the year end corporation tax is due on the surplus. As the company is not for profit the excess of income over expenditure is described as *surplus* rather than *profit*.

6.   By supplying a full breakdown of its consolidated management accounts for the year, and presenting them in its annual report after the statutory accounts, the company enables its members to see exactly where the main sources of income and expenditure arise, as shown in Figure 51.2:

	£'000s	£'000s
Fee revenue		1,152
Operating expenditure		
Wages and salaries	800	
Social security costs	76	
Pensions	56	
Other staff costs	45	
Directors' fees	62	
Rent and services	397	
Travel costs	30	
Publishing and PR	164	
Computer facilities	54	
Telephone, insurance and other administrative costs	76	
Legal and audit fees	39	
Depreciation	98	
Projects written off	22	
		(1,919)
		(767)
Other income		
Rents received	244	
Subscriptions received	52	
Interest	537	
Sundry income	20	
		853
Surplus before tax		86
Corporation tax		(22)
Surplus for year		64

Figure 51.2 A small not-for-profit company – consolidated management accounts (year ending 31 March 2002)

The Balance Sheet

7.   Unlike the Profit & Loss Account, the Balance Sheet does not serve to review activity over a year (or some other period), but presents a snapshot view of the company at a particular point in time. A Balance Sheet attempts to state what a company is worth at that time, rather than showing how much money it is attracting over a period of time, which is the role of the Profit & Loss Account.

8.   A typical Balance Sheet is divided up into two main elements – (1) assets and (2) liabilities. An asset is something of value to the company and is conventionally separated into Fixed Assets and Current Assets. The former relate to tangible items such as land, buildings, furniture and equipment owned by the company; the latter refer to items that are readily realisable in cash terms, and include stock, cash at the bank and debtors (sums due to be paid within one year by purchasers of the company's products or services). Liabilities represent the debts of the company and may be divided into current or short-term liabilities (ie to be paid within one year) or longer-term liabilities (to be paid after more than one year). Liabilities include trade creditors (those to whom the company owes money), banks and other financial institutions who have made loans to the company, and corporation tax.

9.   A typical example of a Balance Sheet is given in Figure 51.3 for a public utility in the UK. The figures are based on the company's position as at 31 March 1996. The company shown is a public limited company (ie a company with a minimum share capital of more than £50,000, and whose shares are offered to the public).

An Electricity Company Plc Balance Sheet as at 31 March 1995	
FIXED ASSETS:	£m
Tangible assets	525
Investments	55
	580
CURRENT ASSETS:	
Stocks	10
Debtors	220
Investments	15
Cash and short term deposits	36
	281
CREDITORS: (Amounts falling due within one year)	251
NET CURRENT ASSETS:	30
TOTAL ASSETS LESS CURRENT LIABILITIES	610
CREDITORS: (Amounts falling due after more than one year)	15
PROVISION FOR LIABILITIES & CHARGES	40
NET ASSETS	555
CAPITAL AND RESERVES:	
Called up share capital	122
Profit and Loss account	425
Other	8
	555

Figure 51.3

NB The tangible assets referred to in the accounts include the electricity network, land, buildings, vehicles and equipment. The provisions for liabilities and charges include sums set aside for restructuring following privatisation, and pensions.

Cash Flow Statements

10. A cash flow statement is not required by company law but is required by the Accounting Standards Board, a quasi-statutory body established in 1990 from earlier developments promoted by the accounting professions. What a cash flow statement indicates is where the company's cash and funds came from and where they were spent. It is summarised as net cash inflow or outflow. An example of a cash flow statement is given at Figure 51.4, which is based on the reported accounts of a large public transport undertaking.

	£m
Net cash flow from operating activities	718
Returns on investments and servicing of finance	
Interest received	27
Interest paid	(150)
Net cash outflow from returns on investments etc	(123)
Capital expenditure	
Purchase of tangible fixed assets	(2,189)
Sale of tangible fixed assets	55
Capital element of finance lease receipts	14
Capital grants received	63
Loans to joint ventures	(32)
Net cash outflow from capital expenditure	(2,089)
Equity dividends paid	(124)
Management of liquid resources	
Disposal of short-term investments	474
Financing	
Issue of ordinary share capital	3
New loans	1,165
Net cash inflow from financing	1,168
Increase/(decrease) in cash	24

Figure 51.4 Large transport Plc – group cash flow statement (year ending 31 March 2001)

Notes: Any enterprise involved in large-scale infrastructure projects, such as here, requires considerable purchases of fixed assets. It needs to raise substantial sums from loans and share issues, and is likely to receive government grants for certain activities with a strong element of social responsibility. In the present example, where the company was once in public ownership, it can be seen that income from operating activities is greatly out of step with the capital requirements of the business. It will take years to build up the contribution made to the business by the income it receives from operations. At the year end the company showed an increase of £24m in its cash holdings compared with a net decrease of £15m reported in the previous year.

Conclusion

12. Whilst the Balance Sheet tends to remain somewhat of a mystery to those who are not accountants, the Profit & Loss Account and the Cash Flow Statement can be useful for many people in management as an indication of how well a business is progressing over the course of a year. Most managers, however, are more accustomed to dealing with finance at an operational level, ie at the level of department and section budgets, and it is to these aspects of finance that we turn in the next chapter.

CHAPTER 52

Budgets, Forecasts and Business Plans

Introduction

1. The process of budgeting was referred to briefly in Chapter 28. For the purposes of this chapter some examples of budgets and forecasts are given to illustrate points of interest arising from the development and use of budgets as part of management's control of a business. Today practically every type of organisation practises some form of budgetary control. Thus voluntary bodies, not-for-profit businesses, small and medium-sized enterprises, public sector organisations and local councils are just as likely to be involved in budget setting as large commercial undertakings.

2. We noted earlier (Chapter 28) that a budgetary control system is laid on the foundations of forecasts, sales and production budgets, capital expenditure and cash budgets, and departmental/unit budgets. All these subsidiary budgets are put together to form a Master Budget for the organisation, which becomes in effect a projected Profit and Loss statement and Balance Sheet. Budgets, as noted earlier, are statements of desired performance expressed in financial terms. They represent the tactical or operational end of business activities, and can be applied to different organisational contexts in which individual managers are given responsibility for a particular unit of operation, which typically may be a revenue centre, cost centre or profit centre.

3. The essential features of these three responsibility centres are as follows:

❶ A **revenue centre** is a unit such as a sales section whose outputs are measured in monetary terms but are not compared with the costs incurred in operating the unit. In such a case the budget becomes essentially a series of sales targets to be achieved – by territory, region and nationally. Regular (eg monthly) comparisons of actual sales against targets can then be made and appropriate action taken. One disadvantage of such a centre is that it may cause sales staff to press ahead with their targets regardless of the costs involved.

② A **cost centre** is usually a unit which serves other parts of the organisation (eg personnel department, accounts etc) and which is allocated a budget based on the costs of operating the service at an agreed level. Whilst it is clearly important to control costs, especially the indirect or overhead costs incurred by such units, one disadvantage of such a budget centre is that the individuals working in it tend to develop an overly cost-conscious attitude in order to keep within their budget.

③ A **profit centre,** in contrast to the above two centres, is an operating unit whose targets are based on the difference between its revenues and its expenditure. Thus, a profit centre has both revenue-earning targets and cost levels to take into account. For example, in a retailing business, individual shops could be identified as profit centres. Sometimes internal sections of an organisation can be considered as notional profit centres by allowing them to charge out their services to other departments.

Budgets

4.   All budgets should be prepared against the backcloth of wider organisational plans. They are, after all, a means to an end, which is the achievement of the organisation's business or service objectives. In overall terms the process of developing budgets can be summarised as follows:

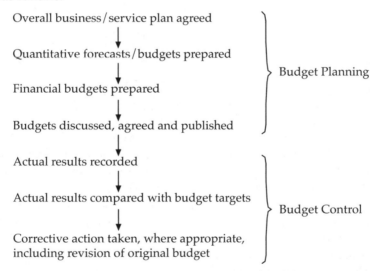

5.   In the process described above, the overall plan is the corporate plan or intention of the organisation. The quantitative forecasts and budgets refer to the volume of business or service to be aimed for, eg new house sales over the next 12 months (building firm); number of housing enquiries satisfactorily completed (local authority housing department). The financial budgets are the statements of revenue and/or expenditure which are aimed for in the light of the level of activity set out in the quantitative budgets/forecasts. As mentioned above (para 2), the financial budgets are all drawn together into one Master Budget or Operating Statement, which becomes, in effect, the projected Profit and Loss Account and Balance Sheet.

6.   Most budget planning embraces a period of one year or less, and some budgets are of a 'rolling' nature, ie they are amended each month or quarter in the light of what has transpired during the previous monthly or quarterly period. This ability to amend and adapt budgets, as well as to take other corrective action, is the essence of budgetary control.

When managements discuss performance against budget they usually work from what are called Management Reports, which have been prepared by their accountants (or Management Accountant in a large organisation). Such reports show **budgeted** revenues and costs for the period or year to date (YTD), **actual** revenue and costs to date, and the variances between them. This gives management the opportunity to judge whether the variances are significant, and if so, what to do about them.

7. An example of such a Management Report is given in Figure 52.1, which is based on a fee-earning service industry in publishing. A feature of these particular accounts is the column dedicated to the revised forecast for each item.

	YTD actual £	YTD budget £	YTD variance £	Full Yr budget £	Revised forecast £
Report for 9 months ending 31 December 1996					
Income and Expenditure Account					
Income:					
Fee revenue	175,000	160,000	15,000	335,000	240,000
Member subscriptions	3,000	3,000	–	11,000	11,000
Publications sales	500	300	200	500	750
Gross interest-members' fund	180,000	120,000	60,000	160,000	220,000
less Provision for Tax	(45,000)	(30,000)	(15,000)	(40,000)	(55,000)
Total Income	313,500	253,300	60,200	466,500	416,750
Expenditure:					
Salaries etc	145,000	135,000	(10,000)	185,000	190,000
Rent etc	60,000	60,000	–	80,000	80,000
Administration expenses	34,000	32,000	(2,000)	42,000	42,000
Computer	12,000	15,000	3,000	20,000	18,000
Legal and accountancy fees	10,000	10,000	–	14,000	14,000
Directors fees	7,500	10,000	2,500	13,500	12,000
Contingency item	–	–	–	5,000	5,000
Depreciation (at year end)	–	–	–	50,000	50,000
Total Expenditure	268,500	262,000	(6,500)	409,500	411,000
Operating Surplus	45,000	(8,700)	53,700	57,000	5,750

Figure 52.1

8. In the above report it is clear that budgeted fee income for the year as a whole will not be realised, even though the year to date figure exceeds budget. The revised forecast is substantially lower than budgeted and this fact should be the focus of management questions. Why the shortfall? Why the absence of the expected high revenue for the final quarter of the year? There may be quite acceptable reasons for the situation, in which case these can be put forward. If there are no satisfactory explanations, then management will need to take some fairly strong corrective action by the start of the next financial year, given that overall expenditure is forecast to be slightly higher than budget and the operating surplus considerably lower than originally budgeted. The point is, that by having regular reviews of actual progress against budget targets, the management of an organisation is in a position to take corrective action, where necessary, before the situation gets out of control.

Cash Flow Forecasts

9. Trading businesses, whether selling goods or services, need to know that they have enough cash available to fund their immediate operating expenses such as wages/ salaries, rent, telephone charges etc. If sufficient funds are not available from internal sources, then borrowings must be made – usually in the form of a bank overdraft (ie credit on the firm's current account). The most usual way of keeping track of the cash position is to prepare a cash flow forecast. This is essentially a budget which sets out the estimated receipts and payments of the business on a month-by-month basis over a period of one financial year. The net cash flow figure and balance for each column is expressed as a positive or negative sum. Thus it is easy to see at what stages of the year it may be necessary to borrow in order to finance the operating costs of the business. An outline example of a cash flow budget is shown at Figure 52.2.

	Outline of a Cash Flow Budget					
Month	Jan		Feb		Mar	
	Budget	Actual	Budget	Actual	Budget	Actual
	£	£	£	£	£	£
Cash sales						
Cash from debtors						
Sale of assets						
Loans received						
Total Receipts (a)						
Payments:						
Cash purchases						
Payments to creditors						
Wages/Salaries						
Rent/rates						
Repairs etc						
Insurance						
Telephone						
Postage						
Stationery						
Transport						
Loan repayment						
Interest						
Bank charges						
Professional fees						
Other						
VAT payable (or refunded)						
Total Payments (b)						
Net Cash Flow (a – b)						
Opening Bank Balance						
Closing Bank Balance						

Figure 52.2

10. In preparing a budget for cash there are a number of important conventions to bear in mind. The key ones are as follows:

❶ Each entry should relate to an expected receipt or payment for the period in question (ie in Figure 52.2 monthly).

② Where items are sold on credit terms, it is important to forecast in which month actual payment is likely to be made. (In Figure 52.2 this is the Cash from debtors item)

③ Regular payments are entered according to when they are actually paid, eg weekly in the case of wages, monthly for salaries, quarterly for telephone/other utilities etc

④ VAT is normally payable quarterly and sometimes produces a net refund to the business (expressed as a deduction from payments in Figure 52.2)

⑤ The Net Cash Flow is one crucial figure to watch, since this identifies whether expected cash flow is negative or positive for the period.

⑥ A Cash Flow Budget also shows the Opening and Closing Bank Balances, of which the latter is another crucial figure.

11. The Cash Flow Budget in Figure 52.2 is a working document, unlike the Cash Flow Statement referred to in the previous chapter, which is an end-of-year summary of the total cash position in the company concerned. As a working document the Cash Flow Budget is intended to provide a detailed (eg month-by-month) picture of the movement of funds in and out of the organisation. A sufficiency of cash is vital for every business – it is literally the life's blood of the system. Even if a business is actually and potentially profitable, it cannot survive without sufficient cash (liquidity), and there have been numerous businesses which have collapsed because, even though profitable and with a good product, they have experienced a 'cash crisis' and have been unable to meet their debts.

Business Plans – Small & Medium-sized Businesses

12. The budgets and forecasts that have been described above are, of course, examples of business plans, and those principally interested in using them are the managers of the business. However, the expression 'Business Plan' has particular meaning for small and medium-sized enterprises, and here the main interested parties are (a) owners and (b) lenders (usually banks). It is estimated that in recent years in Britain alone some 250,000 new businesses have been created every year. Many of these are destined to fail within the first two years, and one of the key reasons is that they have failed to produce a viable business plan for their operation. Whether we are considering a business start-up or, possibly, a management buy-out (where the managers of a failed company attempt to resuscitate it by bidding for ownership via the receivers), there are a number of crucial questions to ask before being committed to a decision.

13. For a new business the potential owner has some important questions to ask of him/herself, such as:

- Am I mentally prepared to work for myself and accept all the risks?
- Am I willing to give up a regular salary and hours of work?
- Have I got the support of my spouse/partner/family etc?
- Can I cope with setbacks and disappointments?
- Am I sufficiently single-minded about running this kind of business?
- What are my strengths and weaknesses when it comes to running my own business?
- Am I prepared to sell myself and my product or service?
- Am I confident that there is a viable market for the business?
- What kind of business will be best for me – sole trader? partnership? limited company? cooperative? (see Chapter 12)
- What help can I get in drawing up a business plan?

14. Most lenders will insist that a small businessman/woman presents and defends an initial business plan before agreeing even to consider lending money for a business start-up. Typically, such a plan will set out evidence under a number of key headings as follows:

Personal and/or Business objectives	Broadly, what do you want to achieve?
Product/Service	How well do you know your product/service?
	How much experience have you in this field?
	What advantage does your product/service have over competitors?
	What are the possibilities of diversifying the product/ service?
Market	What is your evidence that there are sufficient numbers of people who might be willing to buy your product/ service?
	Who are the competition?
	How do you intend to reach your customers?
Pricing	How will you arrive at a price for your product/ service?
	Will that price adequately cover your costs?
	How will the price compare with the competition?
Supplies	Can you obtain sufficient and suitable supplies for your product?
	What prices can you expect/afford to pay?
Physical assets	What premises will you need?
	How much are they likely to cost?
	What about maintenance/repair?
	What equipment are you likely to need, at what cost?
Personnel	What staff/workers will you need to provide your goods/services?
	What wages/salaries bill are you likely to incur?
	Will new employees require training?
	What legal aspects do you need to consider?
Finance	Have you prepared an initial Profit & Loss Account/ Cash Flow Forecast etc?
	How much will you need to borrow?

15. On the basis of answers to the above questions, the small business will be able to prepare a draft profit budget for discussion with its business advisers (bankers, accountant etc). Such a budget will be set out along the following lines:

Sales less Direct Costs (eg cost of materials and wages) = Gross Profit

Gross Profit less Overheads (eg salaries and rent) = Trading Profit

Trading Profit less Depreciation* = Net Profit (Before Tax)

* Depreciation is an allowance made for the loss in value of an asset over a given period of time.

16. An example of a small-business profit budget forecast is shown at Figure 52.3, which is based on a manufacturing business. The section of budget illustrated covers the first six

months of trading, and looks for a doubling of sales revenue after a settling in period of three months. Depending on whether the product is a seasonal one, which in this case we assume it is not, sales would be expected to increase steadily over the second half of the year as those concerned gained in confidence and experience. As the level of business activity increases, so will direct costs which are linked directly to levels of production. Gross profits, therefore, are likely to increase less dramatically. In the example, indirect costs or overheads, as they are usually called, are shown as fixed for each month. These costs tend *not* to vary with the level of business activity and will be incurred whether any sales take place or not. It makes sense for a new business to allocate overheads month by month rather than, say, quarterly in order to keep each item in mind as the first year of trading progresses. The figures show a trading loss for the first three months followed by a very modest profit, which would be expected to grow more strongly throughout the second half of the year. As this is a manufacturing operation, an allowance for depreciation is especially important, and must be deducted from Net Profit or Loss right from the start of the business.

Profit Budget Forecast – Small Business							
(first six months only)							
	Jan	Feb	Mar	Apr	May	Jun	etc
SALES	4000	4000	4000	8000	8000	10000	
less: Buy or Make	3000	3000	3000	6000	6000	7000	
Packaging	500	500	500	1000	1000	1250	
Total Direct Costs	3500	3500	3500	7000	7000	8250	
GROSS PROFIT	500	500	500	1000	1000	1750	
less Overheads:							
Salaries	350	350	350	350	350	350	
Rent, rates etc	200	200	200	200	200	200	
Insurance	50	50	50	50	50	50	
Transport	100	100	100	100	100	100	
Heating etc	75	75	75	75	75	75	
Postage	30	30	30	30	30	30	
Telephone	40	40	40	40	40	40	
Printing/stationery	25	25	25	25	25	25	
Professional fees	50	50	50	50	50	50	
Interest charges	0	0	0	0	0	0	
TOTAL OVERHEADS	920	920	920	920	920	920	
TRADING PROFIT/(LOSS)	(420)	(420)	(420)	80	80	830	
less: Depreciation	50	50	50	50	50	50	
NET PROFIT/(LOSS)	(470)	(470)	(470)	30	30	780	

Figure 52.3

17. The example is of a fictitious manufacturing company in a start-up situation. Only the first six months' figures are shown for the sake of simplicity.

18. In planning a budget, managers or owners have to make a number of assumptions about each item. Sales revenue, for example, can only be estimated on (a) the number of units likely to be sold, and (b) the sale price per unit, and these factors in turn depend on others such as anticipated demand for the product and the prices being charged by competitors. Direct costs are variable depending on the level of production, and so assumptions have to be made about the size of output in order to reach some estimate of the likely additional direct costs for given levels of production. Overheads are more

predictable, but still depend on assumptions about the number of staff, size of premises and other resources thought to be required to sustain the business as a whole. With the advent of computer spreadsheets, it is easier for firms to consider different scenarios for their business, asking 'what if?' questions, eg 'What would be the effect on Gross Profit if we increased production by 1000 units per month?' 'What would be the effect on overheads of an increase in full-time clerical staff by two?'.

19. Once a new business has gone through the difficult but necessary process of preparing draft budgets and forecasts, it will have achieved a number of important benefits:

- the owners or managers will have a number of performance indicators against which to pit their resources

- these indicators will set the parameters for profitability and cash flow on a month by month basis for the first year

- the very process of trying to estimate likely sales and costs (both direct and indirect) enables owners and managers to think through their assumptions and test them in discussion

- the resulting draft budgets will form the basis for discussion with the banks and other financing bodies about funding support, overdraft facilities etc.

- the owners can be satisfied that they have a viable basis for their new business.

A1 Examination Technique

Introduction

1.   It is rarely easy to write a good narrative answer to an examination question. This is particularly true in the field of Management Studies where the *quality* of your discussion of a topic is as important, if not more important, than the quantity of facts you can raise to support your arguments. It is also worth recognising that in most cases there is no one correct answer. The important thing for you is to convince the examiner of the reasonableness of your own particular solution.

2.   Nevertheless, it is possible with practice to develop a technique to enable you to improve the way *you* tackle the more popular questions that occur in examinations.

3.   Part of the aim of this book is to help you with both the technique and the practice.

At the Start of the Examination

4.   Read the instructions on the paper and follow them. Make quite sure how many questions you must answer.

5.   Mark off the questions that seem to be the easiest, ic those which trigger off plenty of ideas the moment you look at them.

6.   Make an appropriate allocation of time for each question. Then select your first question.

Tackling the Questions

7.   Read each question carefully. It will be worth it! Ask yourself, 'Is there more than one question?' 'What is the examiner getting at?' 'What issues are raised by the question?'

8.   Now make a rough answer plan, jotting down key points that come to mind, and re-arranging them into some kind of order. This will take perhaps five minutes, but will enable you to proceed with confidence to write a satisfactory answer. If the question is set out in a particular sequence, answer it in the same sequence.

9.   Where opinion or comment is asked for by the examiner, don't be afraid to say what you think, *so long* as you can point to some evidence or other source of opinion to back up your assertions.

10.   Always try to keep to the point. Identify the issues raised in each question and build your answer around them. Do not go off at a tangent, for there will be precious few marks awaiting you at the end.

11.   Remember that neat writing and tidy layout always create a good impression with examiners. It helps them in their task, and may earn you an extra mark or two.

12.   Your final task is to read quickly through your answer and make any amendments or last-minute additions.

Towards the End of the Examination

13. Make sure you have moved on to your final question even if the previous one is incomplete. You will tend to earn more marks at the beginning of an answer than towards the end, so it is wise to make a start, however brief. If you are desperately short of time (as a result of bad planning) then write down brief notes or headings for the examiner.

14. If you do have time to spare at the end of the examination, it is worth looking to see if you can add any further relevant points to your completed answers.

At the End of the Examination

15. Check that your answer sheets are correctly numbered and collated.

Final Notes

16. The above techniques can be thoroughly practised in this book by working through the Practice Questions, making use of the Outline Answers and getting your tutor or lecturer to comment on what you have written.

A2 Outline Answers to Examination Questions

EQ1

Comments: *This is a general question which can be handled in a general way. Note that there are two parts to the question, ie to first discuss the role and then to assess it.*

Key points:

i.   Fayol's definition (to manage is to forecast and plan, to organise etc).

ii. More up-to-date variations of Fayol eg Drucker's inclusion of motivation, staff development etc.

iii. Management is the dynamic element of organisations, enabling (a) the processing of resources and inputs to provide goods and services to clients in efficient and profitable way, and (b) the development of appropriate change.

iv. The discussion so far could be summed up by reference to Mintzberg's managerial roles (entrepreneur, resource-allocator etc).

v.   The importance of management as a resource itself can be illustrated in terms of organisational control, efficient use of materials and manpower, level of employee morale, ability to promote and control change (innovation).

EQ2

Comments: *This question requires some explanation of the terms management and scientific methods before commencing any discussion of the topic.*

Key points:

i.   Management is a process of planning, coordinating, motivating and controlling.

ii. The use of scientific methods involves searching systematically for evidence to prove or disprove some theoretical proposition.

iii. Early examples of attempts to apply the methods of science to management were provided by F.W. Taylor and the Scientific Managers, who observed and measured work in order to establish more efficient ways of working.

iv. Those such as Fayol, Urwick and Brech who attempted to define certain laws or principles of management also may be included amongst the users of scientific or rational methods.

v. In more recent times the scientists are generally social scientists, interested in the study of human behaviour in organisations. Their methods are based on observation and analysis of people as individuals and in groups.

vi. Management has also been described as 'getting things done through people'. The application of scientific methods has shown that it is easier to record, measure and evaluate information about things, and much more difficult to make consistent sense of human behaviour.

vii. Scientific methods have made management more exact in terms of measuring and predicting things, but have done much less to prove that management is a science rather than an art.

EQ3

Comments: *The first step here is to identify who were the classical/traditional school and what their ideas were, before proceeding to assess their contribution to organisation theory.*

Key points:

i. The leading exponents of classical theory were Henri Fayol, F.W. Taylor (and the scientific managers), L.F. Urwick and E.F.L. Brech.

ii. The scientific managers concentrated on improving the organisation and efficiency of work at the workplace.

iii. Fayol, Urwick and Brech were concerned with the organisation as a whole, especially in terms of its structure and the principles required to maintain that structure.

iv. Important principles were the Principle of Specialisation or Division of Work, the Principle of Authority, the Span of Control etc.

v. The classical theorists showed that it was possible to study management and organisations and to isolate key aspects of them. They provided us with a basic definition of management which has proved useful as a general guide to the scope of the function. They showed that attention to organisation structures was a vital element in establishing healthy operations.

vi. They also demonstrated that an organisational hierarchy is almost unavoidable for most enterprises. Their ideas illustrated the bureaucratic type of organisation as described by Max Weber.

vii. Overall they have indicated the importance of considering structure as one of several factors in developing a successful organisation.

EQ4

Comments: *Firstly give an outline of Taylor's approach to the study of work and then apply it to a marketing context.*

Key points:

i. Taylor's approach to work was essentially as follows: study the job, determine a time and a method for it, set up a management organisation to plan and control it, select and train the worker to perform it. The pay-off for management was to be increased productivity and profits; for the workers it was to be increased pay.

ii. Taylor's ideas have given rise to Work Study ie work measurement and method study techniques. Work measurement is concerned with the time taken by a qualified (trained) worker to complete a particular task at a specified level of performance. Method Study involves the systematic recording and critical examination of job methods with the aim of improving them.

iii. These ideas can be applied to modern marketing management in the following ways: applying clerical work study (O & M) to sales office etc to improve form design, office procedures etc; using work measurement to establish performance standards for field sales staff; set up training programmes to enable staff to achieve/exceed measured standards of performance.

EQ5

Comments: *Most of the answer will be taken up with a description of the major features of the Studies. The examiner is also looking for some evaluation and comment from you concerning the impact of Hawthorne on social psychology.*

Key points:

i. The Hawthorne experiments were conducted at the Western Electric Company's Chicago plant during the period 1927–1932. The researchers consisted of company personnel and members of Professor Elton Mayo's Industrial Research Department at Harvard Business School.

ii. The first stage of the experiments was to study the effects of lighting on output. Two groups of workers were selected for study – one group had no variations in its level of lighting, whilst the other had several variations from better to worse. The significant result was that the output of *both* groups increased. Obviously some factor other than purely physical conditions was at work in the situation. At this stage Mayo's staff were invited in by the company.

iii. The next stage was called the Relay Assembly Test Room. A group of women were made the subject of various studies into the effects of changes in working conditions, especially in relation to rest periods, meal breaks etc. As before, regardless of whether the conditions were improved or worsened, productivity always increased. The women were responding to the attention of the researchers, and saw themselves as a special group. This form of behaviour has been called the Hawthorne Effect. Awareness of this effect has helped subsequent researchers to make allowance for it, or obviate it, in the design of their programmes.

iv. The third stage consisted of a major interview programme to establish employee attitudes towards working conditions, jobs and supervision. This recognition of the importance of work attitudes represented a complete break from the ideas of scientific management, and laid the foundation for later developments in understanding employee motivation at work.

v. Stage three established the importance of social relationships in the work situation. The findings led to a greatly increased interest in 'human relations' at work. This idea was furthered by the results of the fourth stage – the Bank Wiring Observation Room. In this case the group concerned set their own standards of work and work behaviour. The importance of *groups* with their informal or unofficial standards was seen to be a key factor in workplace productivity.

vi. The final stage took the form of personnel counselling, in which employees were able to discuss their work problems. The result was an improvement in personal relationships, especially with supervisors. Here again the importance of taking account of employee needs as individuals was recognised by the Company.

vii. The main significance of the Hawthorne Studies was in its impact on subsequent social research methods. For managers it indicated the vital importance of groups and social relationships at work.

EQ6

Comments: *First it is necessary to establish who were the respective theorists and what were they saying. In this question the examiner has referred to alternative descriptions for both groups. The important point is that the reference to human resources theorists means discussing the work of later social psychologists as well as that of the human relations school.*

The second step is to compare the approaches of the two groups.

Key points:

i. The classical/traditional theorists focused their attentions on the structure and activities of the formal organisation at work. By contrast, the human relations/resources theorists focused on people in organisations.

ii. The major theorists of the classical/traditional school were Fayol, Taylor, Urwick and Brech. Each of these attempted to lay down principles of organisational behaviour, which, if adopted, would open the way to 'effective' organisation, ie capable of achieving its goals and objectives. For example Fayol's Principles of Management referred to the importance of the division of work, the scalar chain (or chain of command), and unity of direction etc. Urwick's principles referred to issues such as the importance of the overall purpose or objective of the organisation, and the clear definition of duties, the span of control etc.

iii. F.W. Taylor focused his attention on organisation at the workplace with his ideas of scientific management, ie the application of rational and systematic methods to tasks. His emphasis was on work rather than on the worker.

iv. The theorists of human relations/resources originated with the Hawthorne experiments and the writings of Elton Mayo in the mid-1920s. They were initially concerned at the effects of scientific management on the worker in terms of fatigue and absenteeism, for example. However, their researches took them into a study of people as part of the *social* fabric of the organisation. At first, social relationships and the importance of groups were the focus of attention. Subsequently, from the 1940s onwards, interest broadened into factors other than physical conditions, pay and social needs to questions of personal growth and fulfilment at work.

v. The label 'human resources' has been applied to the social psychologists who took up these self-fulfilment needs. This line of approach relies considerably on the work of Maslow in identifying a hierarchy of needs in which a person moves up from satisfying basic needs to situations where higher needs are activated. Theorists who have utilised this approach include Frederick Herzberg, Douglas McGregor and Rensis Likert. Herzberg's motivation-hygiene theory, for example, has become well-known for its distinction between intrinsic job factors such as achievement possibilities, recognition and job interest, and external factors such as pay, company policy and administration etc. The former tend to produce high motivation, the latter can only serve to prevent demotivation.

vi. The two approaches described are different in their emphasis, but they have one thing in common – neither is sufficient to explain fully the complex nature of organisations.

EQ7

Comments: *This question is about the motivation to work, and invites you to discuss the truth or otherwise of the assertion which has been made.*

Key points:

i. People do come to work for money, ie they have economic motives. It is unlikely that they come *only* for money. The reasons why people work have been studied by various writers and researchers. In several cases, assumptions about people's behaviour have been considered as important as research evidence.

ii. In the first twenty-five years of this century the assumptions made by owners and managers were that people come to work primarily to fulfil economic needs. Therefore pay and monetary incentives are the key to employee motivation. Examples of this concept are F.W. Taylor and the Scientific Managers.

iii. By the 1930s it was becoming evident, on the basis of research studies such as the Hawthorne experiments, that people have other needs, especially needs relating to personal relationships. In other words, whilst money is still an important factor, it is by no means an over-riding one.

iv. Since the period following World War II, a number of theorists and research workers have concluded that people have a variety of needs at work. In particular, there is strong evidence, from the work of social scientists such as Herzberg and Likert, that people seek self-actualisation at work, ie they seek to realise their full potential.

v. The implications of self-actualisation are that people seek more than financial returns from work. They seek more than friendly relationships. What they are looking for are opportunities to exercise responsibility, to obtain a sense of achievement and to develop new ways of doing things.

vi. In the final analysis people come to work for a variety of motives. Each person has his or her own set of priorities. The challenge for modern management is to be aware of these needs and to meet them in an adaptable manner.

EQ8

Comments: *This is a question of practical motivation. It does not require lengthy statements of motivation theory, but a practical approach, especially to the second part.*

Key points:

i. Most people are motivated by money to the extent that they come to work to fulfil economic needs. It is very debatable whether people are motivated to work harder by the lure of money. Even where money is seen as a real incentive, the evidence seems to be that it is not a lasting form of motivation.

ii. Most people are also motivated by the social contacts they make at work. There is plenty of evidence to suggest that the formation of social relationships and the need to belong to groups, is a very important motivator. The building of supportive work teams can therefore be a powerful motivator to people.

iii. A person's standing or reputation at work are important motivators, whether he receives then from his peers or from the organisation. Opportunities to achieve and to receive recognition for that achievement are also significant factors in the work needs of most people. On balance, the evidence seems to suggest that motives associated with the job itself are the most likely to encourage people at work. Nothing succeeds like success!

iv. A manager could take the following steps to motivate his or her subordinates:

    a. ensure adequate level of pay etc.

    b. train the individual so as to enable him to master the job, and eventually move to a bigger one.

    c. develop a team spirit in which the members feel that they can support the others and yet be supported by them as well.

    d. provide means whereby the employee can measure his progress in the job.

    e. take an interest in the person and thank him when he has worked well.

    f. ensure that the person's job was a challenging one, however modest the level.

    g. keep the employee well-informed about matters that may concern him.

EQ9

Comments: *This question is about the meaning and nature of leadership. The examiner has provided a few prompts to stimulate the discussion.*

Key points:

i. The concept of 'leadership' is open to several different meanings – there is no ideal definition, as yet.

ii. Among the various definitions that have been attempted are:

    a. those that see leadership mainly as a matter of personal qualities – the so-called 'trait theories' of leadership;

    b. those that identify leadership with the tenure of a particular position (eg manager) in an organisation – the bureaucratic-type of leader; and

    c. those that see leadership in terms of behaviour, ie what the person *does* to fulfil a leadership role.

iii. Research has shown that there are difficulties in attempting to rely on trait theories. The main difficulty is that remarkably few *common* characteristics of personality have been identified. Reliance on personal qualities, therefore, is no sound foundation for an analysis of what constitutes leadership.

iv. There are situations where leadership is identified with position-power, ie appointed leaders such as managers and supervisors. In these cases, job-holders receive delegated authority commensurate with their position. Their leadership responsibilities are thus built into their work roles. However, it is quite obvious that, whilst many such appointed leaders are able to respond to the demands of team-management, there are many others who fail in this respect. The appointment clearly does not make the leader – being a leader must imply other factors.

v. The most promising research into leadership suggests that leadership consists of performing certain functions in relation to tasks and to people. Leadership is seen as an aspect of human behaviour, and human behaviour can be observed and, to some extent, measured.

vi. Important contributions to a behavioural analysis of leadership have been made by so-called 'style theories'. These have attempted to define key dimensions of leadership behaviour such as:

   a. Authoritarian versus Democratic styles of management; (eg D. McGregor and R. Likert). These suggest that a democratic style is more productive in terms of team commitment, but more recent studies suggest that this is not necessarily so, and there will be times when an authoritarian approach represents the optimum style.

   b. Task-orientation versus People-orientation; examples of these dimensions have been provided by the Ohio Studies, the Michigan Studies and by the so-called 'Managerial Grid'. The Ohio studies identified two distinct forms of leader-behaviour: 'consideration' (ie considerate of employees' feelings) and 'initiating structure' (ie organising task processes). It was possible for a manager to score high on *both* dimensions. By contrast the Michigan Studies concluded that leader-behaviour was an either/or matter, viz. either employee-centred *or* production-centred. The Managerial Grid devised by Blake & Mouton followed the Ohio view by concluding that it was possible for leaders to behave in two dimensions at once – in this case the variables were 'concern for people' and 'concern for production'. The optimum style according to Blake & Mouton is one which is high on both dimensions.

vii. Another important contribution to behavioural theories of leadership is Adair's functional model of leadership. This sees leadership as behaviour designed to balance the needs of people (as groups and as individuals) and the needs of the task in pursuit of team goals. The clear implication of this model is that effective leadership depends on the leader's ability to adapt his behaviour in the light of circumstances, ie essentially a contingency view of leadership. This latter approach is the one most likely to provide the best definition of leadership.

EQ10

Comments: *Note that the question asks you to discuss the evidence concerning a flexible managerial style. To date there is more speculation than evidence available to answer such a question.*

Key points:

i. There is not a great deal of evidence on this issue, although there is considerably more untested speculation.

ii. An early attempt to suggest a range of leadership styles, as opposed to one or two mutually exclusive styles, was made by Tannenbaum and Schmidt in the 1950s. Their continuum of leadership styles ranged from authoritarian behaviour at one extreme to democratic behaviour at the other with several alternative styles in between. Like most of their contemporaries, Tannenbaum and Schmidt were more concerned with identifying a 'best' style rather than an 'appropriate' style (ie the best *in the circumstances*).

iii. Professor John Adair's functional model of leadership goes some way towards an appropriate style by suggesting that a leader's aim is to achieve the task set for him by paying sufficient attention to task needs, group needs and the needs of individuals within the group. Depending on the circumstances, the leader may need to pay more or less attention to each of the three variables, but he must direct some attention to all of them. The approach suggested by Adair has been used as the basis for training leaders.

iv. The most influential theory on the issue of flexible leadership style, however, is that of F.E. Fiedler. His researches were first written up in 1967 in a volume entitled 'Theory of Leadership Effectiveness', in which Fiedler referred to a 'contingency' approach to leadership. His conclusions were that group performance was dependent, or contingent upon, the leader adopting an appropriate style in the light of the relative favourableness of the situation. Fiedler found that the most important variables in determining the relative favourableness of the situation were as follows:

a. the quality of leader–member relationships,

b. the degree of structure in the task, and

c. the power and authority of the leader's position.

v. The most favourable combination of variables for the leader appeared to be when (i) he had good leader–member relations, (ii) the task was highly structured, and (iii) his position was powerful. By comparison, the least favourable combination was when (i) the leader was disliked by the members, (ii) the task was relatively unstructured, and (iii) the leader had little position power.

vi. In considering the issue of style flexibility, a number of important factors appear to be emerging from the theories and researches carried out so far. These factors are as follows:

a. there is no 'one best way' of arriving at an optimum leadership style,

b. the most practicable approach is to aim for the 'best fit' between the leader and his situation,

c. the situation usually comprises the following variables:

- the requirements of the task
- the needs of the team
- the needs of individuals within the team
- the relations between the leader and the team
- the authority granted to the leader as part of his appointed role
- the power of the leader to act.

d. meeting the demands of the situation requires leaders to select an appropriate style from a range of styles, depending on the circumstances.

EQ11

Comments: *This is the sort of question which lends itself to a neat and concise answer.*

Key points:

i. The principal factors which influence effective teamwork are as follows:

a. Leadership.

b. Nature of tasks required to be performed.

c. The knowledge, skills and motivation of the team members.

    d.   The size of the group.

    e.   The group's stage of development.

    f.   Extent to which group sticks together (group cohesiveness).

    g.   Group norms and organisation norms.

    h.   The roles played by individuals.

    i.   The environment in which the group has to work.

ii.   **Leadership:** Every group needs adequate leadership. An effective leader can meet the team needs of the group (eg fair treatment, adequate resourcing, development of team spirit etc). He or she can also meet the needs of individuals (eg counselling, practical assistance etc) and of the task (eg allocating work, arranging resources, scheduling events etc). Ideally, an effective leader will have a dominant style which suits the team for most of the time, but which can be adapted to meet contingencies arising from outside task pressures or from within the group (ie conflict). Conflict is not a bad thing in itself but it does require carefully handling by the leader to prevent the team from disintegrating.

iii.   **Stage of development:** The effectiveness of a team, ie its ability to fulfil its tasks competently and with satisfaction, depends considerably on the relative state of development of the group who make up the team. A newly formed team will spend a good deal of their time in finding out what is expected of them, what the rules are, and where they can obtain information and resources. In other words, they will be inward looking during this formative stage. As the team begins to settle down, the first conflicts and doubts tend to appear. Here again a good deal of the team's energy will be taken up resolving these internal issues. As internal conflicts and doubts are settled, the team will find new levels of cooperation and standards of operation. At this stage team spirit will be very high, and the group will be outward looking. As success with the task is experienced, and individual collaboration is achieved in practice, the team will be performing at about its optimum level.

iv.   **Group cohesiveness:** This is the extent to which the members of a team stick together, and also the extent to which they can attract new members. Highly cohesive groups demonstrate a strong loyalty to individual members and a strong adherence to group norms (standards of behaviour). Cohesiveness tends to be high in groups where there is similarity of work, close physical proximity, common social factors (eg age, sex, social status etc) and where the group size is smaller rather than bigger than average. Cohesiveness is important in the development of teams as collaborative groups of workers, but it does have the disadvantage that it puts the needs of the group before all else.

v.   **Roles in groups:** In a team, as in any other human group, a variety of roles can be played out by the members. Roles are an aspect of the way in which jobs are performed by the job-holders. Roles are affected considerably by the expectations of job-holders, their colleagues and others, concerning the way the jobs should be carried out. Typical roles in a team are as follows: spokesman, expert, ideas person, willing helper, humorist and devil's advocate. Some of these roles are defined by the work, others by the group itself and others by the organisation's rules.

EQ12

Comments: *This question is in two parts. The first part seeks a description of the major* *features of the Trist-Bamforth studies, while the second part requires some comment about the significance of these studies.*

Key points:

i. The main purpose of the research carried out by Trist and Bamforth of the Tavistock Institute was to assess the effects of mechanisation upon social and work organisation at the coalface.

ii. Prior to mechanisation the coal had been extracted by small, closely knit teams of men, working at their own pace and in their own way. Loyalty to the group was intense, both during and after work. Conflict between groups was settled in ways determined by the men themselves. The control of work was basically in the hands of the teams.

iii. The introduction of a mechanised coalface required a different social system. The small teams were broken up and replaced by much larger groups, each with their own supervisor. More than that, the larger groups were no longer responsible for the whole operation, but only for a specialised part of it.

iv. The outcome of these changes in production methods was that the men were unhappy, petty disputes persisted, absenteeism increased and productivity fell.

v. Eventually, a compromise situation was arrived at, where the working arrangements were altered to enable groups to tackle a range of tasks, and to do so by agreement within their groups. The revised situation improved employee morale and productivity.

vi. The prime significance of the research was that it identified the interdependence between technical factors and social factors at work. Changes in either set of factors would inevitably bring about changes in the other.

vii. Effective work organisation, therefore, depended on attention to social as well as technological needs in the workplace.

viii. The description 'socio-technical system' was given to the situation described above. This concept helped to advance the ideas of theorists about organising for change.

EQ13, EQ14

Comments: *These two questions are seeking the same answer, ie comment on the contingency approach to organisation structures. Allowing for the slightly different emphasis in each question, the following points should be noted.*

Key points:

i. The contingency approach to organisation structures is based on the concept that there is no one best way to design an organisation. It all depends on a variety of circumstances, or contingencies.

ii. For many years theorists held the view that an organisation could be structured according to certain principles, and the implication was that the principles applied to most, if not all, situations. In recent years, researchers such as Joan Woodward have shed considerable doubt on the validity of such 'principles'.

iii. In the 1960s other theorists felt that the most important factor in considering how to structure an organisation was to take account of the needs of people. The main focus of their attention was on issues such as group behaviour, individual motivation, leadership and self-fulfilment. This approach has been criticised on the grounds that it does not pay sufficient attention to the realities of other key factors, such as technology, environmental conditions and the handling of conflict.

iv. The conclusion to be drawn from the most recent research is that organisation design depends not on one or two major variables, but on several. Structures may be relatively mechanistic (highly structured) or relatively organic (less structured) depending on the kind of environment in which the organisation exists, the technology it has to utilise, the size of the organisation and the nature of its personnel.

v. The contingency approach suggests that all these variables must be considered in attempting to find the optimum form of organisation structure. Burns and Stalker, for example, found that firms facing a situation of change were better adapted if they took on an organic structure. Firms in situations of stability tended to benefit more from a mechanistic type of structure.

vi. Lawrence and Lorsch, in another study, found that successful firms were those that adapted best to their environment in terms of coping with (a) issues of specialisation, and (b) issues of integration. A key point in this study was that even where less specialisation was required, there was always a need for *integrating* activities.

vii. The net result of the influence of the 'no one best way' approach is that organisations in future can only be studied in various dimensions. No other way can make adequate sense.

EQ15

Comments: *Note that this question does not ask for discussion or comment. It would be reasonable to infer, therefore, that the examiner is looking for a full rather than partial description of the principal factors.*

Key points:

i. The most important factors that have a bearing on the design of the structure of an organisation are as follows: size, technology, environment, people, tasks, goals and values.

ii. Size is one of the most significant factors in determining structure. Small organisations require little or no formal structure. As organisations grow, they have to differentiate or specialise, and the more they differentiate, the more pressure there is for integration. The end result is a high degree of formal structuring.

iii. Technology refers not just to machines, but also to production or operational methods. The degree of sophistication of machinery is not as significant in itself as the impact it makes on the organisation of work activities. Studies carried out by the Tavistock group in British coalmines, and by Joan Woodward's team in Essex, showed that there was an important relationship between technology and structure.

iv. The environment of an organisation is made up of a variety of social, economic and political elements, all of which may have some bearing on the way an organisation is structured. Research studies have suggested that where the environment is relatively stable, a more formalised structure is advantageous. By contrast, turbulent environments require a less formalised and more flexible structure.

v. A further point is that the environment may affect one part of an organisation differently from another part. In such cases, part of the organisation, eg production, could be formally structured while another part, eg research and development, could be organised much less formally.

vi. People's needs and aspirations are also influential in the design of organisations. As the Tavistock studies in the mines showed very clearly, it is not enough to just consider production issues. People have their views about how their work should be organised, and this has to be taken into account when designing the structure. Argyris's views concerning people's needs to move towards maturity are relevant here. Formal organisation, he says, treats people as being immature by prescribing their duties and controlling their activities. People who wish to take an active, less dependent role will rebel against formality.

vii. Tasks are important in that complex tasks have to be broken down into sub-tasks and the higher the degree of differentiation, the greater the need to integrate activities. Goals and values will often be associated, as part of the philosophy or culture of the organisation. A market-oriented firm, for example, will adopt a more flexible structure in order to be responsive to customer needs.

EQ16

Comments: *The issue of bureaucracy has been looked at earlier. This particular question, however, asks you to assess the response to change in the environment, which is an extremely relevant issue for this section.*

Key points:

i. The main features of a bureaucratic organisation are as follows:

   a. a high degree of specialisation of jobs.

   b. a hierarchical arrangement of jobs where one level is controlled by the next higher level.

   c. a system of rules and procedures.

   d. impersonal roles filled by professional managers and administrators.

ii. These features have been developed in response to the increasing size and complexity of organisations, ie to *internal* considerations. In a bureaucracy the structure itself becomes all-important. Other factors, such as technology and environment, have to comply with the demands of a bureaucratic structure.

iii. Bureaucracy, therefore, is adapted to stable conditions. It is not adapted to changing conditions, least of all in its environment. Research such as that carried out by Burns and Stalker indicated that formal, ie 'mechanistic', structures appeared unsuited to conditions of change.

iv. The existence of formal rules of conduct both in relation to internal staff as well as customers and clients, means that there is insufficient discretion in the power of employees to amend their behaviour towards colleagues or members of the public. Rules are fine for achieving consistency and fairness in routine situations, but they are frequently ineffective for dealing with new needs and new demands.

v. The hierarchical structure of a typical bureaucracy is another obstacle to adaptability. Decisions have to be referred to higher levels in the hierarchy before new precedents may be set to meet changing conditions externally.

vi. Finally, the very fact that jobs are highly specialised means that they must automatically become redundant in the face of radical change. People with broad roles encompassing a variety of skill and knowledge requirements will invariably be better able to cope with the effects of change in the environment of their organisation.

EQ17

Comments: *The question is looking for an understanding of some of the pros and cons of typical business enterprises, ie limited companies, partnerships, sole traders and cooperatives.*

Key Points:

i. Recognised types of business enterprise include:

    a. public limited companies

    b. private limited companies

    c. partnerships

    d. sole traders

    e. cooperatives

ii. All to a greater or lesser degree are in business for profit.

iii. State-owned enterprises in industries such as steel, rail transport and coal-mining have not usually had to meet profit targets, and are excluded from this analysis.

iv. Limited companies are endowed with separate corporate status and thus exist independently of the members and directors. The key advantage to managers who are investors is that they are only liable for the debts of the company up to the level of their share-holding. Managers employed by limited companies are able to check on company progress as reports have to be made regularly by the directors to shareholders. Details of companies have to be made available to a central Registrar, where they are open to public inspection. There are few disadvantages to managers. Perhaps the most important are the legal requirements to set up and operate a business.

v. Partnerships, usually two but not more than twenty people, have the advantage to the partners (proprietors) of relatively little legal fuss to start trading, no obligation to publish accounts, and the chance of sharing talents and stresses with others. The disadvantages are that the partners may not get on well personally, and that each partner is personally liable for the debts of other partners.

vi. A sole trader is a person working on his own. The main benefits are freedom to run the business as he wishes, few legal restrictions and the opportunity to retain all the profits of the business. The disadvantages are mainly that he is responsible for all the debts of the business, works in isolation and has to carry out all the usual management roles.

vii. Cooperatives are set up on the basis of one person–one vote and operate on an openly democratic basis. The advantages to managers are that they do have limited liability and they share in the decision-making process as well as sharing profits. The disadvantages are that profits are normally modest, decision-making processes can be frustratingly slow, and that long-term progress depends heavily on members' ability to work together.

EQ18

Comments: *This is a straightforward question designed to test your understanding of the basic decision-making process.*

Key points:

i. The major steps in the decision-making process are as follows:

a.   Define the problem.

b.   Collect relevant data.

c.   Develop alternative solutions.

d.   Assess the consequences of proposed solutions.

e.   Select optimum solution and implement.

f.   Measure results.

ii.   Key considerations in each step include the following:

Defining the problem: this is a matter of asking the right questions, and of isolating the *crucial* problem from subsidiary issues; it is important to identify underlying problems and not to confuse them with the overt effects of such problems.

Collecting data: the important point here is to collect information which is relevant to the problem concerned, and which involves the staff associated with the problem; seeking information and points of view from the staff concerned helps decisions to be accepted in a positive spirit.

Developing solutions and assessing their consequences: solutions depend not only on their technical ability to solve a problem, but also on their acceptability to the parties involved and other factors (cost, legality etc); the use of quantitative techniques may help to develop solutions and assess some of the consequences; assessing consequences is vital because most decisions can produce negative as well as positive results.

Selecting and implementing optimum solution: the final selection of a solution will be based on a number of factors, ie optimum implies the best solution *in the circumstances;* the implementation of the solution is the responsibility of management.

Measuring results: this step implies some ability to monitor and evaluate the end results of a decision; this final step also enables decisions to be modified or even revoked in the light of experience.

EQ19

Comments: *Although it is not stated in the question, it is reasonable to assume that the weight of the answer should be given to the second part of the question, ie to setting out the objectives of a business.*

Key points:

i.   The main reasons why it is necessary for companies to establish and periodically review their objectives are as follows:

a.   a statement of objectives gives substance to the overall goals of the organisation, which are usually stated in very general terms, eg 'meet customer requirements for high-quality goods in a profitable and cost-effective way'; objectives can clarify how the organisation intends to achieve profitability etc;

b.   a statement of objectives gives managers and other employees a focal point for their efforts;

c.   a review of objectives helps to ensure that existing objectives are still relevant, and that new objectives are added as required in response to changing conditions.

ii.   In addition to the overall goals, which are objectives in themselves, companies need to set long-term, or strategic, objectives and short-term, or tactical, objectives.

iii.   Strategic objectives are usually set for five years or so ahead in all the major functional areas of the business, ie marketing, sales, production, research and development, personnel, finance and other resourcing functions. Examples of strategic objectives are:

Marketing: 'to develop export sales to Third World nations so that 25% of total sales is represented by these markets five years from now';

Personnel: 'to ensure that the company's needs for skilled and professionally qualified manpower are met over the next five years'.

iv. Other strategic objectives are set with stakeholder groups in mind, eg customers, employees, suppliers etc. Examples are:

Customers: 'to introduce measures designed to reduce customer complaints, about the level of service provided, by at least two-thirds over the course of the next three years'.

Employees: 'to develop, in close collaboration with employees and employee representatives, a system of employee participation in decision-making, which can be installed throughout the company in the next three to four years'.

v. In setting strategic objectives, companies have to make some statements about the manner in which these objectives shall be pursued, ie they must develop policy guidelines for the guidance of management and other employees.

vi. In achieving strategic objectives, companies have to set short-term, or tactical, objectives. These are usually prepared by individual departments for endorsement by senior management and set out in specific and quantifiable terms the particular targets to be aimed at in pursuit of strategic aims.

EQ20

Comments: *The question seeks to establish your familiarity with the concept of MbO by asking for a description of the system and some appraisal of its advantages and disadvantages. The answer can be divided neatly into (i) the description, (ii) the advantages, and (iii) the disadvantages.*

Key points:

i. Management by objectives (MbO) is a system of management which attempts to integrate individual goals, such as job satisfaction and personal growth, with organisational goals, such as profitability and expansion.

ii. The vehicle of this integration is the organisation's strategic plan, from which are developed operating or tactical plans, unit objectives and individual manager objectives. Thus MbO is operated at the tactical end of the business, where detailed results are expected in pursuit of organisational goals.

iii. MbO assumes that managers have personal objectives or goals which are closely linked to success at work. Thus if a job can be seen as challenging, as providing responsibility and as relevant to organisational aims, then managers will be motivated to cooperate in achieving these aims in a purposeful manner.

iv. In keeping with these assumptions, MbO assumes that knowledge of results is an important factor in managerial motivation, and as such concentrates on the outputs or end-results of management activities.

v. A typical MbO programme begins with establishing management job descriptions, isolating key task areas and setting mutually agreed performance standards for the key tasks. It continues with the development of a job improvement plan, which is essentially a list of short-term targets to be achieved in a three or six month period. Control data are identified for both Key Tasks and Targets to enable progress to be monitored by the individual manager and his superior. The programme concludes with reviews of performance – current performance and, frequently, potential performance. Where MbO is part of a management development programme, succession planning may also be a feature of MbO.

vi. The advantages of MbO are mainly that:

    a. it enables managers to see their priorities clearly,

    b. it provides specific targets to work for,

    c. it keeps managers and their superiors informed of progress in the job,

    d. it can help to identify obstacles in the way of effective performance,

    e. it provides a sound basis for measuring management performance,

    f. it provides useful material for assessing the training and development needs of managers.

vii. The disadvantages are mainly that:

    a. it can become an end in itself, with individuals going through the motions to satisfy the company's bureaucrats,

    b. it requires time, effort and a considerable amount of inevitable paperwork to be successful,

    c. it can be used by superiors to exert pressure on their subordinates to accept targets which are not fully acceptable, ie it is just another way of increasing managerial productivity.

viii. On balance, the advantages would seem to outweigh the disadvantages considerably.

EQ21

Comments: *The major part of this answer will need to be taken up with a description of manpower planning, leaving the second part of the answer in a subsidiary role.*

Key points:

i. Manpower planning is the name given to the systematic approach to the recruitment, retention, utilisation, improvement and disposal of an organisation's human resources.

ii. Manpower planning is not just a matter of obtaining the right numbers of particular categories of employee; it is also a matter of obtaining the right blend of skills and experience in the organisation's current and planned workforce.

iii. The major stages of the manpower planning process are as follows:

    a. analysis of existing manpower situation

    b. forecast of future demands for manpower,

    c. assessment of external labour market (ie external manpower supply)

    d. establishment of manpower plans in detail.

iv. Activities involved in (a) above include: an analysis of current employment categories and the numbers of employees currently in post; an analysis of the knowledge and skills available; an analysis of the employee turnover rate; an assessment of the training/development potential of existing employees.

v. The forecast of future demands for labour is closely linked with the organisation's long-term corporate plans ie the quantity and quality of employees required will depend on marketing intentions, new product development, new production processes (technology, robotics) and other key variables in the organisation's total plans.

vi. The assessment of the external labour market has to take account of questions such as what changes in the national employment situation are forecast and how these might affect the organisation.

vii. Detailed manpower plans are laid with time-horizons of about one year. These plans encompass intentions in respect of recruitment, internal promotion, training and development, pay and productivity, and retirement and redundancy.

viii. As in the case of every other planning activity, the final stage of all is the review. Manpower reviews may be carried out monthly (in line with budgets) or annually (or any suitable review period).

ix. The reasons why manpower planning is necessary are:

    a. to ensure that the organisation can fulfil its *existing* commitments to customers,

    b. to ensure that suitable manpower is available *in the future* to meet changes in the organisation's circumstances,

    c. to enable the organisation to audit its human resources,

    d. to enable the organisation to develop an *integrated* approach to the recruitment, retention, development and disposal of its human resources.

EQ22

Comments: *This is a very straightforward question, which does not even ask for any comment on OD.*

Key points:

i. Organisation Development (OD) is the name given to any strategy for improving organisational effectiveness by means of behavioural science approaches involving the diagnostic and problem-solving skills of an external consultant or change-agent.

ii. An OD programme is directed towards improving an organisation's effectiveness, ie its ability to achieve its various corporate objectives. It is designed to enable the organisation to become sufficiently adaptable in the face of changing circumstances.

iii. The phases of a typical OD programme are as follows:

Preliminary: Discussion of aims of programme between top management and the external consultant(s), and the respective roles of the parties concerned.

Analysis and Diagnosis: The consultant designs and implements appropriate methods for obtaining relevant information about the organisation – problems, employee attitudes etc. The information obtained is used to diagnose problem areas and to confirm certain facts about the organisation.

Agreement about Aims: With a clear picture of the organisation and its problems in front of them, the top management team and the consultant agree the objectives of the programme, eg 'to introduce and maintain an open and participative style of management in all departments' and 'to re-structure the production departments to permit greater delegation by senior management'.

Action Planning: Planning the content and sequence of the activities designed to put agreed changes into effect. Such activities could include briefing meetings, training programmes, job analysis, organisation-planning committees and so on.

Evaluation and Review: Once action plans have been put into operation, measures must be taken to check their progress, obtain feedback, and make preparations for corrective actions, if required.

Completion: The third party – the consultant – leaves the scene, and the management team continue with the task of leading a more effective organisation.

EQ23

Comments: *The danger in a question such as this is that you will not be able to include sufficient material in your answer. It is very much a 'thinking' question. A useful way to start the thinking process is to define what you understand by delegated authority and responsibility.*

Key points:

i.   Delegated authority usually refers to the power to act which is conferred on managers by other, more senior managers, or by shareholders. All authority of this kind is prescribed in some way, ie limits are set over the power to act.

ii. Responsibility refers to a person's accountability for certain tasks or duties. The degree of responsibility is usually prescribed by written job duties, custom and practice, and rules of various kinds.

iii. Ideally an individual manager should be given sufficient delegated authority to enable him or her to execute their responsibilities fully. Authority, as the classical writers put it, should be commensurate with responsibility.

However, the ideal situation does not always obtain, and there is a mismatch between delegated authority and responsibility.

iv. The results of this mismatch can be as follows:

   a.   managers are unable to fulfil their responsibilities because they have insufficient authority to effect changes or improvements,

   b.   managers who have insufficient power to act feel demotivated by their powerlessness,

   c.   in cases where too *much* authority is granted, an individual manager may find that he or she has exceeded their responsibilities, and this means someone else has to bear the consequences,

   d.   in bargaining or negotiating situations, a mismatch between delegated authority and responsibility can easily lead to a loss of credibility on the part of the manager concerned on the grounds that he or she is unable to substantiate his or her side of the bargain,

   e.   managers are unable to delegate authority to their own subordinates, if they have insufficient to carry out their own personal responsibilities.

EQ24

Comments: *This question can be answered in three parts: (i) definition of matrix organisation, (ii) description of where such organisation structures are to be found, and (iii) why* *they are found there. The first part of the question is probably the most important. An illustration is helpful in this answer.*

Key points:

i. A matrix organisation is one whose structure is based on a combination of lateral as well as vertical lines of communication and authority. The lateral lines enable a project-based organisation to be formed; the vertical lines enable this project-based organisation to be superimposed on the functional organisation. This can be illustrated as shown in the diagram.

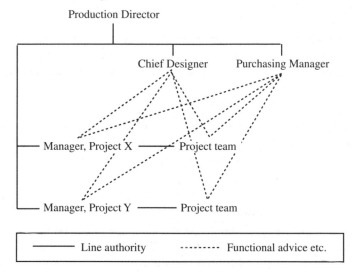

ii. In this situation the functional managers and the Production Director provide technical expertise and organisational stability, whilst the Project Managers provide leadership and control of the individual, and rather temporary, projects. While a project is under way, the client has only to deal with one manager – the Project Manager – for routine monitoring of progress instead of having to deal with several specialist and line managers.

iii. A distinct advantage of a matrix organisation is that it enables individual project managers to identify strongly with their projects, their clients and their project teams in a way that is not always possible in a typical functional organisation. A further advantage is that the matrix approach helps to put functional specialisms in perspective ie they are there to provide line managers with advice, guidance and expertise. This is especially highlighted in the role of specialist members of a project team. Their first priority is to put their knowledge and skills at the disposal of their team, rather than to beat them over the head with functional rules and procedures. Nevertheless, this situation does cause conflicts of loyalty for some team members, who may be torn between adhering to their own functional standards and cutting corers in order to satisfy the demands of their project manager.

iv. Matrix organisations are most likely to be found in complex industries, such as aerospace and electronics, which are often widely differentiated in terms of processes, skills and production methods, but which require careful coordination in order to meet customer requirements and to ensure adequate resourcing from corporate funds etc. They are not always applied to the entire organisation, but may be limited to certain complex units within it.

v. The reasons for adopting a matrix organisation are mainly that:

    a. the matrix approach enables a high degree of collaboration between line managers and functional specialists,

    b. it is possible to hold one person – the project manager – responsible for the success of the project, for the link with the customer and for the motivation of the project team,

    c. it enables complex contracts to be broken down into a number of separate projects without losing overall control, and without losing the benefits of considerable functional involvement.

EQ25

Comments: *This question is about the reasons for delegating work, and about some of the difficulties involved.*

Key points:

i. The factors that would influence my decision to delegate work to a subordinate would be as follows:

    a. The degree to which I was under pressure in carrying out my duties, as a result of volume of work or of complexity of work,

    b. the degree to which I felt able to cope with the risks associated with delegation,

    c. the capabilities and experience of the subordinate,

    d. my assessment of how much benefit he might obtain from being given increased responsibilities,

    e. the degree of cost involved in the work to be delegated (financial cost, reputation with customer etc),

    f. the amount of help available to the subordinate from colleagues,

    g. my intention to use the opportunity to delegate as part of his planned development at work.

ii. The major barriers to delegation are:

    a. Unwillingness on the part of superiors to delegate work through desire to retain personal control over work or through fear that subordinates may be so successful that the superior's own job may be threatened,

    b. inability of busy superiors to (i) see the need to delegate, or (ii), if they do see the need, the inability to make time to brief subordinates, allocate additional tasks and provide some form of feedback, ie planned delegation,

    c. unreadiness of subordinates to carry additional responsibilities,

    d. insufficient training available to enable subordinates to be adequately prepared to accept greater responsibilities,

    e. complexity of work, which limits the number of people who are able to carry it out safely and correctly,

    f. uncertain nature of work, eg technical or scientific research and development requires experienced staff.

EQ26

Comments: *In this case an early explanation of terms is necessary before going on to discuss the links between the two functions.*

Key points:

i. In management the term planning is given to those activities which define the various objectives of the organisation and the means by which they are to be achieved. Planning encompasses policy-making, for policies are the behavioural guidelines which must be followed in seeking to achieve objectives. Plans lead to actions, and these actions need to be monitored to check if they are in accordance with the results expected. This is where the control function of management comes in.

ii. Control rounds off the process of managing the organisation's resources by measuring results, checking them against previously agreed standards of performance, and then indicating any corrective action that may be required. Planning and control are inextricably linked together, even though, for the purposes of analysis, they are often treated separately.

iii. One of the major distinctions that can be drawn between the two is that planning is a decision-making activity, while control is a monitoring process which depends on the existence of the former – control serves no useful purpose in its own right.

iv. Another distinction, arising from the first, is that planning is concerned with ends and means, whereas control is concerned with results and feedback.

v. Common features between planning and control include the following:

    a. they are both concerned with identifying and quantifying standards of performance.

    b. the measures used for planning purposes are frequently the same as those used for control purposes (eg budget targets, financial and other ratios etc).

    c. they both make use of quantitative techniques such as Network Analysis and Inventory Control.

vi. To sum up, planning and control cannot be regarded as independent functions of management. Some distinctions can be made between them, but in reality they are intimately linked together with control following planning in a cyclical fashion.

EQ27

Comments: *This is a straightforward question with a definite focal point, ie the steps in the Control process.*

Key points:

i. The basic steps in the Control process are as follows:

    a. Set standards of performance.

    b. Measure performance.

    c. Compare results obtained with standards.

    d. Initiate corrective action, where required.

ii. The key considerations to be taken into account in setting performance standards are:

    a. standards need to be demanding, but not out of reach, otherwise the employees involved become disheartened;

    b.   standards should be clear and measurable, preferably quantitatively, but if not, then qualitatively;

    c.   qualitative standards should ideally be expressed in terms of end results, otherwise standards may become confused with methods;

    d.   quantitative techniques may help in the establishment of suitable standards, and managers should be aware of appropriate techniques.

iii.   The key considerations in respect of measuring performance are:

    a.   to ensure that performance is rated against the appropriate standards;

    b.   to ensure the flow of information about results to the management; this is crucial if the control process is to act as a feedback mechanism;

    c.   to ensure that the information obtained is relevant, adequate for the purpose and timely, otherwise inappropriate action may be taken or, worse still, action may be too late to be effective;

    d.   budgetary systems are probably the single most important source of information about performance results, and should play the key role in any control system.

iv.   The key points to be considered when comparing actual performance with standard performance are:

    a.   the process must allow for variances to be identified and notified without delay to the appropriate manager, for this, after all, is the raison d'être of the Control process;

    b.   action should only be taken on the 'exception principle', ie only significant variances should be dealt with, otherwise managers can spend fruitless hours reviewing systems which are working perfectly well.

v.   The key considerations in respect of corrective action are:

    a.   the responsibility for taking corrective action should be clearly allocated to the appropriate managers; the control process is only a tool of management and, to be effective, its results must be put into effect in a systematic way by those in authority;

    b.   as the control process is essential a regulatory process, corrective action should be taken without delay, otherwise the system concerned will continue to malfunction until attended to.

EQ28

Comments: *The answer needs to explain what is the marketing concept and then to illustrate its significance for planning, using a manufacturer of capital goods as an example.*

Key points:

i.   The marketing concept is an approach to business which looks at the needs and wants of the customer before all else, and then directs the energies of the business towards the fulfilment of those needs and wants.

ii.   Other approaches to business are those which concentrate firstly on production efficiency or product quality, before the needs of the customer. This is not to say that the customer is ignored, but only that he has a somewhat lower priority than these other issues.

iii.   A manufacturer of capital goods, ie goods for use by other manufacturers, could use any one of the three alternative approaches mentioned. The best approach for the development of future plans would almost certainly be the adoption of the marketing concept, but the others would also have considerable relevance too.

iv. The advantages of utilising the marketing concept are that the manufacturer would:

    a.   be aware of his existing customers' needs in the short-term, and possibly further ahead;

    b.   be developing new or revised products with customer requirements firmly in mind;

    c.   be consulting with existing customers about new developments in the field concerned, eg computer controls, robots etc;

    d.   be flexible about adapting his products to compete with new features offered by competitors;

    e.   be sensitive to the needs of potential customers, and able to discuss their requirements with them;

    f.   be able to produce goods to a specification agreed by an individual customer to meet particular needs;

    g.   generally be able to offer a marketing mix which was closely geared to customers' requirements.

v. The adoption of the marketing concept would give the manufacturer a very good idea of what his customers – existing and potential – are seeking from him, and his competitors. This would certainly provide him with a confident base on which to build his future plans. Nevertheless, he could still plan ahead with a fair degree of confidence, if he used one of the other alternative approaches.

vi. For example, if he were to adopt a production-oriented approach, he would certainly be concerned to ensure that every modern facility was available to support the production of his goods. He would be concerned with developing a high reputation for his goods, on the assumption that if his goods are reputable, customers will buy them. He would also be concerned with efficiency of production with a view to offering his goods at a more competitive price than his competitors. All these contingencies could be planned for, and there is no question of the marketing concept being the only way to develop future plans in this situation.

vii. If he adopted a product-orientation, much of what was mentioned in paragraph vi would also apply. In this case, however, it would be the products themselves which would be the centre of attention for the future. The aim would be to develop a range of products which were so technically brilliant that potential customers would be bound to be attracted by them. This approach implies a considerable degree of confidence in the products and their future prospects in terms of sales. However, this is a risky approach since, if customers do change their minds, the manufacturer is left high and dry with excellent products that nobody wants! Nevertheless, many firms successfully adopt this approach in planning for the future.

viii. If the manufacturer was producing fast-moving consumer goods in a competitive market, then it would be easier to demonstrate that the marketing concept was the best approach. In this case, however, the issue is not at all so clear-cut.

EQ29

Comments: *This is a two-part question, requiring an introductory definition of the term* *'below-the-line' activities followed by some discussion of the objectives of such activities. A brief description of the 'marketing mix' should also be included.*

Key points:

i. The term 'below-the-line' activities refers to sales promotion activities which are organised by a firm's own staff out of its general marketing budget. Such activities can be contrasted with 'above-the-line' activities, which are those undertaken by external advertising agencies on behalf of the firm, and separately accounted for.

ii. Below-the-line activities form part of the Promotion element in the marketing mix, which is the group of variables assembled by the firm for presentation to its customers at a particular point in time. The other variables are the Product, the Price and the Distribution arrangements.

iii. Below-the-line activities may be directed at consumers or to the trade. They usually consist of measures such as special offers, free samples, point-of-sale demonstrations, (for consumers) and special discounts and the provision of display material (for trade customers).

iv. The objectives likely to be set for sales promotion activities directed at consumers include the following:

    a. to draw customers' attention to a new product,

    b. to encourage sales of slow-moving items,

    c. to stimulate off-peak sales of seasonal items,

    d. to achieve higher level of customer acceptance of a product.

v. The objectives mentioned fall into two main categories: firstly, those aimed at encouraging sales among items that are stagnating; and, secondly, those aimed at promoting new or recently-introduced items. In each case, incentives of one kind or another are being offered to consumers to tempt them into buying.

vi. Objectives likely to be set for a promotion aimed at trade customers could include the following:

    a. to stimulate retailer or dealer cooperation in pushing selected items,

    b. to persuade retailers to increase shelf-space devoted to the company's products,

    c. develop goodwill amongst retailers and dealers.

vii. These objectives fall into the categories of (i) those that are designed to encourage retailers and dealers to play their part in pushing sales of particular items; and (ii) those that are designed to promote good relationships between the suppliers or manufacturers and the dealers or retailers selling their products to the consumer. As in the case of consumer-oriented promotions, those directed at dealers and retailers also contain incentives.

viii. The particular objectives set in any one sales promotion campaign will depend mainly on whether the supplier wants to shift old stock or encourage new products. The principal overall purpose will always remain to increase sales by positively pushing, or promoting, them.

EQ30

Comments: *The first step is to describe the concept of the 'product cycle' before relating it to planning and budgeting.*

Key points:

i.   The concept of the 'product cycle' has been developed from studies of the life-cycles of individual products. These studies suggest that any product tends to pass through a number of common stages, which are as follows: Product introduction, Growth, Maturity, Saturation and Decline.

ii.   Each of the stages has its dominant features, for example:

Product introduction: Production costs are high, partly as a result of development costs; price is also high; competitors are few, if any, but sales and profits are low at this stage.

Growth: Sales rise rapidly; prices ease; unit costs decline and profits are at their peak; mass market appears but competition increases.

Maturity: Sales continue to rise, but less rapidly; competition is fierce and prices ease further; profits begin to level off.

Saturation: Sales stagnate; prices become very competitive and profits begin to shrink; mass market begins to evaporate.

Decline: Sales take a permanent downturn; profits low or non-existent; product is eventually withdrawn.

iii.   The implications for business planning and budgeting are various, as the following examples indicate:

a.   At the introductory stage pricing can be geared at least to the recovery of costs, and possibly to what the market will bear. As there is little or no competition, this is a time to be bold about prices.

b.   From the budgeting point of view, targets for sales and profits should not be set too high at the introductory stage, but need to set at a demanding level for the subsequent stage of growth.

c.   When the product reaches the growth stage, production needs to be planned at peak levels to meet increasing sales; distribution needs to be geared up to moving goods to the point-of-sale as efficiently as possible. From the planning point of view, this is the period of peak activity to ensure that the product realises the benefits of maximum availability to the consumer at a time of minimum competition from rival products.

d.   As sales increase, and competition begins to appear this is the time to take advantage of the flexibility of pricing, by reducing prices just at the moment when competitors are having to bear their own development costs. Budgets at this stage can set maximum profit targets with confidence.

e.   During the maturity stage competition will tend to be at its highest, and this is a time for utilising advertising to help beat off the worst effects of this competition. It is also a time to consider further reductions in prices. At this stage both sales and profits will need to be budgeted at a lower level.

f.   At the saturation stage, as sales begin to stagnate, efforts can be directed towards a variety of sales promotion activities to boost flagging sales and demoralise competitors by offering special offers to both consumers and dealers etc. At this stage, earnings from the growth period can be used to support some of the costs incurred in subsidising sales. Profit targets should continue to be set, but at a nominal level. By now production resources should be curtailed considerably in the face of the slow-down in sales.

g. As the decline stage approaches, budgeted costs should be set at the lowest possible levels, as the whole product cycle begins to wind down for good. By now replacement products should be well under way and another cycle about to begin.

EQ31

Comments: *This is an interesting question which raises the important issue of how business organisations can cope with the conflicting priorities between key departments such as marketing, design and production. The question is looking for some explanation of these different priorities, together with some suggestions as to how conflict may be resolved.*

Key points:

i. In organisations which have adopted the marketing concept, there will tend to be a lesser chance of serious conflict since every department's priorities will include some direct reference to the needs of the customer. The reverse will apply in organisations that have not adopted the marketing concept, but have opted for another approach, eg product-orientation.

ii. Nevertheless, whatever approach is adopted, certain underlying causes of conflict will be present. These arise out of the differing priorities of the three departments concerned. These priorities include the following:

Product design: Marketing departments seek primarily the designs that meet the customers expressed wishes, whereas design departments are primarily motivated to produce designs that are technically satisfying and/or innovatory, and production departments prefer designs that can be translated readily into production terms.

Product costs: Marketing departments usually want the costs to be low enough to enable attractive prices to be quoted, whereas design departments may not be interested in costs so much as product quality. Production departments may well prefer costs to be kept to a minimum consistent with product reliability.

Product features: Marketing departments usually look for a variety of product features as a way of boosting sales, whereas design departments look for purely functional features and production departments look for simplicity of production, ie the maximum amount of standardisation.

Pricing: Marketing departments look for prices that are flexible and have the effect of stimulating sales. Design departments are not usually so sensitive to price, since they are more interested in assembling the most suitable product in the light of their interpretation of marketing's wishes. Production departments are traditionally concerned with pricing only to the extent that it covers the costs of production.

iii. Given these underlying differences of priorities between the groups in question, what are the ways in which potential conflict may be resolved or at least contained within reasonable limits? Possible answers are as follows:

a. by establishing regular review meetings between the three departments concerned to build up mutual understanding and ensure a regular flow of information between them;

b. by ensuring that regular meetings are held during the product development stage of any product to enable potential problems to be ironed out as soon as possible;

c. by ensuring that each department's objectives refer to their contributory role in relation to other key departments, ie as opposed to a competitive role;

d. by endeavouring to achieve acceptance throughout the organisation of the marketing concept, ie ensuring that every department is market-oriented so far as practicable.

EQ32

Comments: *This is a straightforward question requiring a descriptive answer.*

Key points:

i. The role of production planning and control is central to the production process, and consists of planning, acquiring, scheduling and controlling all the resources and facilities required to transform customer requirements into acceptable end-products.

ii. In fulfilling this role, production planning and control can be divided up into a number of different activities. These are described below.

iii. The first activity is to translate the final pre-production design into production instructions, so that those responsible for the manufacturing know what they are expected to make and how.

Secondly, production schedules, or timetables, need to be prepared in some detail, using Gantt charts among other devices.

This step is followed by the planning of the various resources (labour, materials, parts etc) and facilities (machine tools etc). Labour requirements have to be discussed with the Personnel department, who will be responsible for the initial recruitment; materials supply and parts etc, have to be discussed with the Purchasing department, who have the responsibility of purchasing at prices, and in quantities, that represent the best interests of the organisation. Plans for facilities include the allocation of machines and plant in accordance with technical requirements, machine availability and capacity, and machine loading.

The next step is to set production targets for the various work groups involved, and this has to be done in conjunction with either marketing or sales, as representatives of the customer.

Once production is under way, part of the control function will be to ensure that work is progressing as scheduled and in accordance with job standards. This aspect of production planning and control is usually called 'progress chasing'.

Another aspect of control is that all appropriate records are maintained, eg work completed, work delayed, stock levels etc.

The final step is to ensure that the outputs of production are properly accounted for, invoiced and delivered – either to the customer or into stock.

iv. Today computers are utilised to handle the complex paperwork of the production planning and control process. Their advantage is that they can cope with vast amounts of record-keeping and at great speed, which are important factors in the control process.

EQ33

Comments: *The answer requires a brief definition of each of the production patterns referred to in the question, before going on to discuss the circumstances that would justify them.*

Key points:

i. **Jobbing production** is the production of single items usually to order. The circumstances which would justify the adoption of jobbing patterns of production include the following:

a. where large items such as ships are to be built;

b. where single large pieces of equipment such as electricity generating plant are to be manufactured;

c. where large individual items such as a major bridge are to be constructed;

d. where small one-off parts or components are to be produced to the order of the production department in a factory;

e. where prototype models are required for design and/or planning processes in a manufacturing or construction organisation.

ii. **Batch production** is the production of standardised units in lots, where each lot has to be processed at each operation before moving forward to the next operation. The circumstances which would justify the adoption of batch patterns of production include the following:

a. where items such as standard components are to be produced for stock, eg to support production in due course;

b. where standardised items are being manufactured on a sub-contracted basis for another manufacturer;

c. where production requires a variety of quantities and types of items, which cannot be produced under a flow-production process, because of the interruptions to the flow of operations.

iii. **Flow/mass production** is the continuous production of items which move, or flow, from one operation to the next until completion without break. The circumstances which would justify the adoption of flow or mass patterns of production include the following:

a. where large quantities of a narrow range of goods are required to meet the demands of mass markets;

b. where standardised units can be moved *individually* from one operation or process to the next without requiring any break in operations;

c. where the returns from mass production are more than able to meet the expensive start-up costs of an assembly-line form of production;

d. where large quantities of liquids, powders or gases are to be processed, as in the case of paper production, the manufacture of cement or the production of petroleum spirit, for example.

EQ34

Comments: *The question is seeking no more than a brief set of descriptive statements about the key steps in a purchasing operation.*

Key points:

i. The necessary activities which the purchasing department would need to carry out in purchasing a raw material not previously required would be as follows

a. seek out suppliers of the new raw material;

b. appraise suppliers in terms of how they propose to meet the potential purchase order in respect of quantity, quality, price and delivery;

c. select supplier who appears on the evidence to represent the most cost-effective source of the raw material;

d. negotiate contract with supplier, so as to achieve sufficient quantities of a suitable quality of the material required for the manufacturing process; and so as to obtain price and delivery arrangements which are acceptable;

e. prior to negotiating (d) above, the purchasing department would need to know the details of quantity, quality and delivery times from the user departments (production, stores, and inspection etc);

f. place order with supplier and maintain all necessary records (purchase orders, delivery notes, invoices etc);

g. arrange routine follow-up checks with user departments to ensure that the order is being met satisfactorily, and to iron out with the supplier any problems that may arise;

h. review the contract, as necessary, after a suitable period, and be prepared to either submit further orders or to change supplier.

EQ35

Comments: *This question is in three parts – first you are asked to comment on the Seven-Point Plan (having previously described it); next you are asked to discuss what alternatives are available; and, finally, you are asked to compare these alternatives with the original Plan.*

Key points:

i. The Seven-Point Plan is the name given to a classification of personal requirements produced by Prof. Alec Rodger of the National Institute for Industrial Psychology (NIIP) in the 1950s in Britain. The classification is as follows:

- Physical make-up (Build, height, colouring etc)
- Attainments (Exams passed etc)
- General Intelligence
- Specialised aptitudes (particular skills)
- Interests
- Disposition (Character or personality)
- Circumstances (Domestic and personal situation).

ii. The usefulness of this Plan lies in its application to employee assessment, especially in the area of selection. The range of factors in the Plan covers most of the attributes that could be looked for in an employee. If it is applied to an individual employee or candidate, then at least the right sort of questions are going to be asked about that person's suitability for a particular job. Such a Plan also enables personnel specifications to be written up for job vacancies in order to clarify what kind of person is to be sought.

iii. The Plan is not intended to be a tightly-drawn measuring device able to identify an ideal candidate with precision, and this it could not do in any case. Nevertheless it can and does provide a useful frame of reference for those seeking to describe the 'ideal' candidate in a general way.

iv. Alternative frameworks are available mainly as versions of the Seven-Point Plan. However, there is one well-known alternative, which was produced in its own right. This is the so-called Five-Point Plan of J. Munro Fraser, which also dates back to the 1950s.

v. The Munro Fraser Plan consists of five points, and is rather more condensed than the Rodger Plan in that it does not refer to General Intelligence and specialised aptitudes, which can hardly be measured in an interview, but refers instead to Innate abilities, which places the emphasis on skills generally rather than on reasoning power. The full Munro Fraser list is as follows:

- Impact on others (Presence, dress etc)
- Acquired qualifications (Exams etc)
- Innate abilities (What the person can do)
- Motivation (Personal drive)
- Adjustment (Temperament)

This list does not take specific account of circumstances, although these can be covered under the item of Adjustment, which seeks among other things to assess how well a person might adjust to a new situation.

vi. Organisations frequently use their own versions of one or other of the above-mentioned Plans. The Seven-Point Plan seems to be generally more attractive as a starting point, since it enables personnel selectors to specify a more narrowly-defined set of standards for potential candidates. A typical example of such a personnel specification could include the following:

- Formal qualifications
- Manual skills
- Physical requirements
- Personality requirements
- Interests/Hobbies
- Experience (work)
- Social skills
- Personal circumstances
- Motivation
- Experience (other than work)

vii. The list in paragraph vi. above could be incorporated into an interview plan to ensure that all interviewers covered approximately the same ground, and that each candidate had to prove himself against each of the items.

viii. Greatly reduced versions of these Plans can be found in job advertisements under the title of 'The Person Sought' or some similar wording.

ix. To sum up, the use of the Seven-Point Plan, and its derivatives, is an extremely important means for assessing personnel, especially in an employment interview situation.

EQ36

Comments: *The first two parts of the question are straightforward, but the third part requires some reflection before answering.*

Key points:

i. The essential features of an ideal disciplinary procedure are as follows:

a. it should be written down and made known to all those involved;

b. it should specify clearly to whom the procedure applies, ie *all* employees or only some?

c. it should be capable of dealing swiftly with disciplinary matters;

d. it should indicate what is meant by misconduct and gross misconduct, and what are the likely forms of disciplinary actions which may be taken against those found guilty;

e. it should clearly specify who has the authority to enforce disciplinary actions, and to what extent, eg power of dismissal etc;

f. it should ensure that every disciplinary case is fully investigated, and that the employees concerned are given every opportunity to state their case and to be accompanied by a fellow employee if they wish;

g. it should ensure that employees are informed of the reasons for any action taken against them, permit them the right of appeal and ensure that no person is dismissed for a first offence, except in cases of gross misconduct.

ii. The essential features of an ideal grievance procedure are as follows:

a. it should recognise the right of every employee to seek redress for grievances at work;

b. it should aim to provide for the fair and speedy settlement of grievances as near to the source as possible;

c. it should provide, initially, for the employee to raise the grievance with his immediate superior; if this does not produce a satisfactory conclusion, the employee should be permitted to refer the issue to the next higher level of management, and if he is still dissatisfied, to a senior manager or director, on appeal;

d. at each stage the employee should be allowed to take a fellow employee with him;

e. it should provide for time limits to be set for each stage, so as to ensure that no delays occur;

f. it should make arrangements for the results of grievances to be recorded in writing and distributed to the parties concerned.

iii. The aim of the two procedures described above is to ensure, so far as possible, that employees will receive fair and just treatment if ever they are involved with these procedures. The effect of this overall aim is to minimise conflict. After all, employees do not seek confrontations with their employers if they feel well treated at work.

iv. Of course, the aim of a particular procedure may not be realised because of some misunderstanding about it. For example, if a manager believes, incorrectly, that he has the power to suspend an employee without pay in a situation of alleged gross misconduct, he is likely to spark off a major conflict with employee representatives if he proceeds to enforce his supposed power. To avoid such conflict, it is essential to make every manager and supervisor absolutely clear about the extent of his authority to impose disciplinary action on employees.

v. So far as grievances are concerned, the most likely cause of conflict with employees is delay on the part of management in dealing with the issues raised by the person with the grievance. Time limits are an important means of ensuring that such delays do not occur, and open conflict is avoided.

vi. Provided the above procedures are clear, and are fairly operated, there is no reason at all why they should not be supported by employees just as much as by managers, as a means of reducing conflict and ensuring fair treatment for all, regardless of position.

EQ37

Comments: *This is a question that is popular with examiners. It is in two parts, the second of which asks you to consider how much training and development takes place in training courses.*

Key points:

i. Training usually implies preparation for a specific occupation or for specific skills, and aims primarily to ensure that organisations have sufficient skills and experience available to fulfil their business objectives. Training is thus job-oriented rather then aimed primarily at the personal development of individuals.

ii. Development, by contrast, is more concerned with enabling individuals to grow in skills and experience in order to be of greater potential use to the organisation at some later date. Development is broader in scope than training and is career-oriented rather than job-oriented. Development tends to contribute to personal growth as much as it does to securing future resources for the organisation. Development may include activities such as management by objectives and succession planning as well as traditional training type activities, such as courses.

iii. Courses are an important feature of most training and development activities. In some respects, courses lend themselves more to training than to development. A course can provide a few hours or a few days of instruction and/or practice opportunities in closely specified skills, such as learning how to operate a till or learning how to conduct an employment interview. At the end of the course, whether it was organised internally or arranged by an external provider, the organisation can expect to see some noticeable improvement in the way knowledge or skill is applied in the workplace. However, this assumes that the course was appropriate for the trainee, and that the trainee was thought to be capable of benefiting from the training. If these conditions are not met, no effective training will have taken place.

iv. Some courses, a minority, are not designed with specific skills or knowledge in mind. These are the more broadly developmental courses that key employees are sent on to widen their horizons, increase their self-confidence and improve their ability to think in strategic terms. On such courses what takes place is development rather than training. Organisations that send their key personnel on such courses are always faced with the risk that these employees will make use of their more marketable position by moving to a competitor before making any further contribution to the business. The pay-off in developmental courses is medium to long-term, rather than immediate as in the case of most training events.

EQ38

Comments: *This is a general question about employee participation, and allows scope for a wide-ranging answer to take in the various options available at different levels in the organisation.*

Key points:

i. There are several different ways of enabling employees to participate in the decision-making processes of their organisation. In some organisations the senior management regard employee participation in decision-making as no more than allowing employees, or their representatives, access to a number of joint consultative bodies. Many organisations utilise their collective bargaining machinery to provide employee participation in decision-making. In such cases, joint negotiations between management and trade unions produce compromises which are jointly agreed and implemented.

ii. The drawbacks of the first two options referred to above are that, in the case of joint consultation, there is no real employee participation in the sense of joint decision-making; and that, in the case of collective bargaining, this involves only union members and excludes non-members and managerial staff.

iii. Another option which is currently much in favour is that of job enrichment, ie restructuring an individual's job so that he is able to exercise greater discretion over the way the job is done. This is a genuine form of employee participation, but only at the level of the individual job. Naturally, this may have an enormous impact on employee motivation, but it is stretching a point to suggest that this can ever be considered to represent employee participation in the sense of joint decision-making with management.

iv. An extremely important and significant form of employee participation is that installed in many German companies, ie the works council system. This system, which in the Federal Republic, is supported by the force of law, produces one or more workers' councils which have certain rights to co-determination (joint decision-making) on matters affecting a wide range of employment conditions. A few organisations in Britain have experimented with this form of participation on a voluntary basis. In these cases, the council is usually at company level and is a *joint* council but which has a majority of employee-representatives on it. Decisions are usually taken by consensus, rather than by a vote, and can include vital strategic decisions as well as routine and local decisions. This is a genuine form of participation in the sense of joint decision-making.

v. Another important option is that of appointing or electing employee directors to the boards of companies. This is another feature of the German system mentioned above. In Germany the law requires most organisations to arrange for the election of employee directors onto Boards. In some situations the employee directors are only entitled to one-third of the Board seats; in others, half the members must be employee representatives. So far, in Britain, only a few attempts have been made to put workers on the Board. The difficulty in Britain is that, unlike German companies which have a two-tier Board (a Supervisory Board and a much smaller Executive Board), British companies have only one Board – the unitary Board. In this situation it is difficult to reconcile the conflicts inherent in having day-to-day executive decisions mixed up with long-term and/or strategic decisions. In the Federal Republic, day-to-day decisions are left firmly with the Executive Board and the works councils, while strategic decisions are left with the Supervisory Board.

vi. The final option which is available is that of workers' control. This way suggests that workers should take over the ownership and general management of organisations. The experiment has been tried successfully in Spain, at Mondragon, for example, where workers are shareholders in their companies, and elect the Board, but where the day-to-day task of running the business is left to a professional manager reporting to the Board. A key feature of the Mondragon experiment is that all organisations have to be less than 400 strong. Small size, therefore, is seen as crucial to the success of this kind of partnership.

EQ39

Comments: *This is a two-part question. The first part is straightforward: the second part requires some thinking about the extent to which collective bargaining is a problem-solving, decision-making exercise.*

Key points:

i. The term 'collective bargaining' means, principally, bargaining between employers and employee organisations about terms *and* conditions of employment and about the nature of the relationship that shall exist between the two parties.

ii. Collective bargaining is more than just the collective version of individual bargaining between an employee and his employer; it is also a mechanism for regulating relationships between employees and their employers.

iii. The products of collective bargaining are collective agreements – procedural agreements and substantive agreements. The former deal with the rules of behaviour that shall be applied to the consenting parties, and cover such issues as:

- trade union membership and recognition.
- facilities for union representatives (shop stewards etc).
- negotiating machinery (number and composition of committees etc).
- grievance procedures (individuals' disputes).
- disputes procedures (collective disputes).

iv. Substantive agreements deal with terms and conditions of employment, and cover such issues as pay, hours of work, holidays and job grading. These agreements usually operate for one year and then are re-negotiated, unlike procedural agreements which are intended to be relatively permanent. Where one party wishes to amend or revoke a procedural agreement, they are obliged to give due notice, eg six months, one year etc.

v. There are several grounds for stating that collective bargaining is a problem-solving, decision-making process. These include the following:

a. collective bargaining helps to solve the problem about how much of the organisation's income should be made available to employees in the form of wages and other employee benefits;

b. it helps to produce decisions relating to employee productivity, which are acceptable to both employees

c. it helps to deal with potential sources of conflict between employers and employees over issues such as pay, changes in working arrangements and discipline by establishing jointly agreed rules and conditions;

d. it provides a framework for the regulation of collective representation of the employees by establishing procedure agreements designed to control the extent of bargaining and the behaviour of people within it;

e. it helps to solve many of the problems arising from the need for organisational change, and produces jointly agreed decisions which can enable changes to be put into effect without either side resorting to punitive action.

vi. Collective bargaining may also be considered as part of a power struggle between management and workers, and in this sense it is not primarily a problem-solving, decision-making process. However, in practice, this is not the attitude of the parties concerned in the majority of organisations in Britain. There are differences of aims, but collective bargaining sets out to find acceptable compromises between the parties.

vii. There is also a sense in which collective bargaining can be considered more of a bureaucratic process to organise the collective relationships between employers and employees. In the public sector, the machinery which has been set up ensures that there is a well organised structure of collective bargaining and consultation. Too much emphasis on machinery, however, can lead to a neglect of many of the problems and decisions which it is intended to deal with.

A3 Examination Questions for Practice

There are suggested answers for Lecturers/Tutors only, available separately on application (see Preface).

PQ1   List some advantages and disadvantages of decentralising decision-making in large organisations.   *(ICSA MPP)*

PQ2   How might the practical assistance of a psychologist help a group of people to work together effectively as a team?   *(ICMA OMM)*

PQ3   Describe what you understand by the phrase 'matrix management'.   *(ICSA MPP)*

PQ4   'Marketing does not merely take over where production leaves off, but is concerned with determining the nature and scale of production...' (L.W. Rodger). Discuss this view of the marketing concept for:

    a. a large manufacturer of breakfast cereals, and

    b. a small commercial printer.   *(ICMA OMM)*

PQ5   Identify and discuss the distribution alternatives available to a manufacturing company in the distribution of its products to consumer markets. Illustrate by reference to any particular industry with which you may be familiar.   *(ACCA)*

PQ6   a. What are the objectives of sales promotion activities?

    b. At whom are the sales promotion activities aimed, what forms can they take and how can their success be evaluated?   *(ICMA OMM)*

PQ7   Assess the role of pricing as an element in the marketing mix.   *(ICMA OMM)*

PQ8   Traditionally, your organisation has been non-unionised but you are becoming increasingly aware of pressure from the employees to gain union recognition. From your management view point, what are likely to be advantages and disadvantages of recognising trade union representation?   *(ICSA MPP)*

PQ9   'Management always gets the shop stewards it deserves.' To what extent do you regard this as an adequate analysis of the industrial relations climate in an organisation?   *(ICSA PPP)*

PQ10 Discuss the role of a formal committee structure within an organisation. Make particular reference to the importance and content of written records as an integral part of committee activity.   *(ACCA)*

PQ11 'The reliability and validity of the selection interview is usually so low as to render it practically useless as a selection technique.' To what extent is this true?

(ICSA PPP)

PQ12 To what extent is the Points Method of job evaluation useful in establishing the basis for factory pay scales?   *(ACCA)*

PQ13 Examine and assess the problems you see for the personnel manager in devising, implementing and controlling a dismissals procedure.   *(ICSA PPP)*

PQ14 In what major ways has British legislation attempted to pursue social fairness in employment over the past years?   *(ACCA)*

PQ15 What are the likely consequences of a manager introducing an element of competition

    a. between individuals, and

    b. between work groups, in order to increase organisational efficiency?

(ICMA OMM)

PQ16 Describe and discuss the requirements for an effective grievance procedure.

(ICSA PPP)

PQ17 a. State the different types of pricing policy open to a manufacturer.

b. Discuss the reasons why the pricing policy of a manufacturer of pet foods should be different from that of a manufacturer of scientific measuring equipment.

(ICMA OMM)

PQ18 What do you understand by the term 'market segmentation'? Select two from the following:

i. a manufacturer of machine tools;

ii. a supplier of office cleaning services;

iii.a manufacturer of PVC pipes; and describe the likely bases on which each might segment his market.

(ICMA OMM)

PQ19 Comment critically on the contribution made to contemporary personnel policies by any *one* of the following behavioural theorists:

Abraham Maslow

Frederick Herzberg

Douglas McGregor

Rensis Likert

(ICSA PPP)

PQ20 You have been appointed as the first manager of a new department. Your first task is to establish the objectives of the department, to establish the departmental organisation structure and to decide on staffing levels. What steps will you take and what information will you require? The new department can be any ONE of the following: (a) production; (b) personnel; (c) accounts; (d) marketing.

(ICSA MPP)

PQ21 Outline and comment on the stages involved in managerial decision-making.

(IAM Dipl.)

PQ22 What would be the major factors you would wish to consider when drawing up the corporate plan for ONE of the following organisations:

a. a nationalised industry;

b. a manufacturing company;

c. a college or university;

d. a water authority.

(ICSA MPP)

PQ23 What difference in structure would you expect to find between:

a. a company manufacturing and selling chemical plant worldwide,

b. a company manufacturing and distributing fastmoving domestic appliances in its home market,

c. a company operating a chain of retail supermarkets? (IOM Business Orgn.)

PQ24 Outline the role of committees and examine their importance as part of an organisation's management structure. (IAM Dipl.)

PQ25 What do you understand by the term 'functional relationship' in an organisation? Choose one example of a functional executive and describe his work and method of operation. (ICMA Orgn. of Production)

PQ26 Outline the main theories relating to individual motivation to work and show how leadership styles may be adapted to accommodate the aspirations of employees.

(IOB Human Aspects of Mgt.)

PQ27 Explain the phrase 'leadership style'. Discuss the strengths and weaknesses of the various types of leadership style, illustrating your answer by reference to any banking organisation with which you are familiar. *(IOB Nature of Mgt.)*

PQ28 How might the organisation of production into work teams: (a) help, and (b) hinder the efficient running of the enterprise? *(ICMA OMM)*

PQ29 You have been asked to investigate the effectiveness of the use of 'budgetary control' in your organisation. Set out and discuss the problem areas you would expect to find. *(IAM Approach to Office Admin.)*

PQ30 a. What is advertising?

　　　 b. What range of objectives might be set for an advertising campaign?

　　　 c. How might their success be evaluated? *(ICMA OMM)*

PQ31 Outline the main sequence of events of a Work Study programme. In what ways have recent changes in the attitude of workers and management towards the working environment affected the usefulness of this technique?

(IOM Business Orgn.)

PQ32 What factors determine the maximum number of subordinates who can be effectively managed by one person? *(ACCA Business Mgt.)*

PQ33 Identify the similarities and differences between 'organisation development' and 'management development' programmes. *(ICMA OMM)*

PQ34 How can the role of the personnel manager be distinguished from that of any manager with responsibility for the supervision of personnel? *(ICSA PPP)*

PQ35 a. What is meant by Job Evaluation, and for what purpose is it used?

　　　 b. Briefly describe three methods of Job Evaluation. *(IOM Business Orgn.)*

PQ36 What are the main features of the Employment Protection Act, 1975?

(ACCA Business Mgt.)

PQ37 How far, in your view, can industrial relations be regulated or improved by means of legislation? *(ICSA PPP)*

PQ38 Discuss what is meant by the term 'two-tier Board of Directors', and suggest plausible functions for each tier. *(ACCA Business Mgt.)*

BIBLIOGRAPHY

ACAS, *Code of Good Practice in Disciplinary Procedures*, HMSO.

Alderfer, C. (1972), *Existence, Relatedness and Growth*, Collier Macmillan.

Annual Report of the Certification Officer, HMSO.

Argyris, C. (1957), *Personality and Organisation*, Harper & Row.

Atkinson, P.E. (1988), *Achieving Results through Time Management*, Pitman.

Back, K. & Back, K. (1994), *Assertiveness at Work,* 2nd edition, Pitman.

Berners-Lee, T. & Fischetti, M. (2000), *Weaving the Web*, Texere Publishing.

Boyatzis, E. (1982), *The Competent Manager: A Model for Effective Performance,* Wiley.

Brech, E.F.L. (1975), *Principles and Practice of Management*, 3rd edition, Longman.

Brown, W. (1960), *Exploration in Management,* Heinemann.

Burns, T. & Stalker, G.M. (1961), *The Management of Innovation*, Tavistock.

Clutterbuck, D. (1994), *The Power of Empowerment*, Kogan Page.

Cole, G.A. (1995), *Organisational Behaviour*, Continuum.

Coulson-Thomas, C. (ed) (1994), *Business Process Re-engineering: myth and reality*, Kogan Page.

Covey, S. (1992), *Principle-Centred Leadership*, Simon & Schuster UK.

Covey, S.R. (1989), *The Seven Habits of Highly Effective People*, Simon & Schuster.

Davidson, M. & Cooper, C. (eds) (1993), *European Women in Business and Management*, Paul Chapman.

Davidson, M. & Cooper, C. (1983), *Stress and the Woman Manager*, Martin Robertson.

Drucker, P. (1954), *The Practice of Management*, Heinemann.

Eagly, A. & Johnson, B., 'Gender and leadership style: A meta-analysis', in *Psychological Bulletin* Vol. 108, No. 2 (1990), p.233–256.

Egan, G. (1990), *The Skilled Helper*, 4th edition, Brooks/Cole.

Emery, F.E. & Trist, E.L. (1965), 'The Causal Texture of Organisational Environments', in *Human Relations, Vol. 18 No. 1.*

Fayol, H. (1949), *General and Industrial Management*, Pitman.

Flanders, M. (1994), *Breakthrough – The career woman's guide to shattering the glass ceiling*, Paul Chapman.

Follett, M.P. (1941), *Dynamic Administration*, Harper Bros.

Fowler, B. (ed) (1994), *MCI Personal Competence Model: Uses and Implementation.*

French, J. & Raven, B. (1958), 'The bases of social power', in Cartwright, D. (ed), *Studies in Social Power*, Institute for Social Research.

Friedman, M. & Rosenman, R.H. (1974), *Type A Behaviour and your Heart*, Alfred Knopf.

Goldsmith, W. & Clutterbuck, D. (1984), *The Winning Streak*, Penguin.

Gouldner, A. (1955), *Patterns of Industrial Bureaucracy*, The Free Press.

Graham, P. (ed) (1995), *Mary Parker Follett – Prophet of Management: A Celebration of Writings from the 1920s*, Harvard Business School Press.

Hamel, G. & Prahalad, C.K. (1994), *Competing for the Future*, Harvard Business School Press.

Hammer, M. & Champy, J. (1993), *Reengineering the Corporation – a Manifesto for Business Revolution*, Nicholas Brealey.

Hammer, M. & Champy, J. (1994), *Reengineering the Corporation – A Manifesto for Business Revolution*, revised edition, Nicholas Brealey.

Handy, C. (1993), *Understanding Organizations*, 4th edition, Penguin Business.

Herzberg, F. (1968), *Work and the Nature of Man*, Staples Press (GB).

Herzberg, F. (1959), *The Motivation to Work*, 2nd edition, John Wiley.

Hickson, D.J. & Pugh, D.S. (1995), *Management Worldwide – The Impact of Societal Culture on Organisations around the Globe*, Penguin.

Hofstede, G. (1980), *Culture's Consequences: International Differences in Work-related Values*, Sage Publications.

Hofstede, G. et al (1990), 'Measuring Organisational Cultures: A Qualitative and Quantitative Study across Twenty Cases', in *Administrative Science Quarterly 35/2*.

Hofstede, G. (1997), *Cultures and Organisations*, McGraw-Hill.

Holmes, T. & Rahe, R. (1967), 'The Social Readjustment Scale' in *Journal of Psychosomatic Research*, 11. Pergamon Press.

Humble, J. (1967), *Improving Business Results*, McGraw-Hill.

Humble, J. (1971), *Management by Objectives*, Management Publications/BIM.

Institute of Management Checklist No. 028, *Codes of Ethics*, Institute of Management Foundation.

Institute of Personnel Management (1992), *Statement on Counselling in the Workplace*, IPM (now IPD).

Jaques, E. (1961), *Equitable Payment*, Heinemann.

Jaques, E. (1964), *Time-Span Handbook*, Heinemann.

Katz, D. & Kahn, R.L. (1966), *The Social Psychology of Organisations*, Wiley.

Korth, Christopher M. (1985) *International Business, Environment and Management*, 2nd edition, Prentice-Hall.

Kotler, P. & Armstrong, G. (1996), *Principles of Marketing*, 7th edition, Prentice-Hall International.

Kotter, J.P. (1996), *Leading Change*, Harvard Business School Press.

Lawrence, P.R. & Lorsch, J.W. (1967), *Organisation and Environment*, Harvard University Press.

Lewin, K. (1951), *Field Theory in Social Science*, Harper.

Likert, R. (1961), *New Patterns of Management*, McGraw-Hill.

Locke, E. & Latham, G.P. (1988), *A Theory of Goal-setting and Task*.

MacBeath, I. & Rands (1976), *Salary Administration*, Gower.

Maier, N. (1958), *The Appraisal Interview*, Wiley.

Marshal, J. (1993), 'Patterns of Cultural Awareness: Coping Strategies for Women Managers', in Long, C. & Kahn, S. (eds), *Women, Work and Coping*, McGill-Queens University.

Maslow, A. (1954), *Motivation and Personality*, Harper & Row.

Matsumoto, D. (2002), *The New Japan*, Intercultural Press/ Nicholas Brealey Publishing.

Mayo, E. (1933), *The Human Problems of an Industrial Civilisation*, Macmillan.

McClelland, D. (1961), *The Achieving Society*, Van Nostrand.

McDougall, M. & Briley, S. (1993), *Developing Women Managers*, HMSO.

McGregor, D. (1960), *The Human Side of the Enterprise*, McGraw-Hill.

Mintzberg, H. (1973), *The Nature of Managerial Work*, Harper & Row.

Mintzberg, H. (1979), *The Structuring of Organisations – a Synthesis of the Research*, Prentice Hall.

Mintzberg, H. (1983), *Structure in Fives: Designing Effective Organisations*, Prentice-Hall.

Mintzberg, H. (1994), *The Rise and Fall of Strategic Planning*, Prentice-Hall.

Morgan, G. (1986), *Images of Organisation*, Sage.

Moss Kanter, R. (1984), *The Change Masters – Corporate Entrepreneurs at Work*, Allen & Unwin.

Ohmae, K. (1982), *The Mind of the Strategist*, McGraw-Hill.

Ouchi, W. (1981), *Theory Z: How American Business can meet the Japanese Challenge*, Addison Wesley.

Pascale, R, & Athos, A. (1986), *The Art of Japanese Management*, Penguin Books.

Pascale, R, (1991), *Managing on the Edge*, Penguin Books.

Peters, T. & Waterman, R. (1982), *In Search of Excellence: Lessons from America's Best-Run Companies*, Harper & Row.

Peters, T. (1988), *Thriving on Chaos: Handbook for a Management Revolution*, Macmillan.

Porter, M.E. (1980), *Competitive Strategy*, The Free Press.

Porter, M.E. (1985), *Competitive Advantage: Creating and Sustaining Superior Performance*, The Free Press.

Porter, M.E. (1990), *The Competitive Advantage of Nations*, The Free Press.

Pugh, D. & Hickson, D. (1976), *Organisational Structure in its Context*, Gower.

Pugh, D.S. & Hickson, D.J. (1976), *Organisational Structure in its Context: The Aston Programme I*, Gower Publishing.

Reddin, W. (1970), *Managerial Effectiveness*, McGraw-Hill.

Rice, A.K.(1958), *Productivity and Social Organisation*, Tavistock.

Rice, J. (1995), *Doing Business in Japan*, Penguin Books.

Robbins, S.P. (1993), *Organizational Behaviour*, 6th edition, Prentice-Hall.

Roethlisberger, F.J. & Dickson, W.J. (1939), *Management and the Worker*, Harvard University Press.

Schein, E. (1951), 'The Mechanics of Change', in Bennis, W.G. et al (eds), Interpersonal Dynamics, Dorsey Press.

Schein, E. (1992), *Organisational Culture and Leadership*, 2nd edition, Jossey-Bass.

Schein, E.H. (1988), *Organisational Psychology*, 3rd edition, Prentice-Hall.

Sell, R. (1983), *The Quality of Working Life*, WRU Paper, Department of Employment.

Senge, P. (1990), *The Fifth Discipline*, Century Business.

Skinner, B.F. (1974), *About Behaviourism*, Random House.

Slade, E.A. (1995), *Tolley's Employment Handbook*, Tolley Publishing.

Stewart, R. (1994), *Managing Today and Tomorrow*, Macmillan.

Taylor, F.W. (1947), *Scientific Management*, Harper & Row.

Thomason, G. (1981), *Textbook of Personnel Management*, IPM.

Trist, E.L. & Bamforth, K. (1951), 'Some Social and Psychological Consequences of the Longwall method of Coal-getting', *Human Relations, Vol 4. No 1*.

Trompenaars, F. & Hampden-Turner, C. (1997), *Riding the Waves of Culture* 2nd edition, Nicholas Brealey Publishing.

Urwick, L.F (1952), *Principles of Management*, Pitman.

Urwick, L.F. (1947), *The Elements of Administration*, Pitman.

Vinnicombe, S. & Colwill, A. (1995), *The Essence of Women in Management*, Prentice-Hall.

Vroom, V.H. & Deci, E.L. (1992), *Management and Motivation*, 2nd edition, Penguin.

Vroom, V. (1964), *Work and Motivation*, Wiley.

Weber, M. (1947), *The Theory of Social & Economic Organisation*, The Free Press.

White, G.C. (1982), *Technological Change and Employment*, WRU Occasional Paper.

Woodward, J. (1965), *Industrial Organisation – Theory and Practice*, OUP.

Work Research Unit (1984), *Learning from Japan*, WRU.

USEFUL WEB SITES

The following Web sites contain much useful information for students of management. In many cases these sites are the best sources for gaining an up-to-date picture of current economic and employment matters in the UK. Much of the material is in the public domain and can be downloaded freely; some sources can only be accessed via membership, or by the payment of a fee for use. Many of the sites supply helpful links to related Internet sites. The potential list of relevant sites is so huge that students may waste time trawling the Internet, and this list aims to identify some of the major gateways into sites of interest to management theory and practice. Students should be prepared to quote Web sites which are subject to copyright, just as much as books and journals, even where downloading without charge is permitted.

www.acas.org.uk	Advisory Conciliation and Arbitration Service (ACAS)
www.bara.org.uk	British Automation and Robot Association
www.britcoun.org	British Council
www.cac.gov.uk	Central Arbitration Committee
www.cbi.org.uk	Confederation of British Industry
www.cedefop.eu.int	Centre Europeen pour le Developpement de la Formation Professionnelle (Vocational Training)
www.cib.org.uk	Chartered Institute of Bankers
www.cii.co.uk	Chartered Insurance Institute
www.cipd.co.uk	Chartered Institute of Personnel Management
www.cre.gov.uk	Commission for Racial Equality
www.dataprotection.gov.uk	Information Commissioner
www.dfes.gov.uk	Department for Education and Skills
www.dti.gov.uk	Department of Trade and Industry
www.dwp.gov.uk	Department for Work and Pensions
www.eoc.org.uk	Equal Opportunities Commission
www.europa.eu.int	European Union information service
www.gateway.gov.uk	UK Government departments' pathway
www.hmso.gov.uk	Her Majesty's Stationery Office (HMSO)
www.hse.gov.uk	Health and Safety Executive
www.ibe.org.uk	Institute of Business Ethics
www.icaew.co.uk	Institute of Chartered Accountants of England and Wales
www.ifsis.org.uk	Institute of Financial Services
www.iipuk.co.uk	Investors in People
www.imi.ie	Irish Management Institute
www.instam.org	Institute for Administrative Management
www.iod.com	Institute of Directors

www.ilo.org	International Labour Organisation
www.incomesdata.co.uk	Incomes Data Services
www.indsoc.co.uk	The Industrial Society
www.ismstowe.com	Institute for Supervision and Management
www.learndirect.co.uk	LearnDirect
www.lifelonglearning.co.uk	UK Lifelong Learning
www.lsc.gov.uk	Learning and Skills Council
www.management-standards.org	The Management Standards Centre
www. managers.org.uk	The Institute of Management
www.open.gov.uk	Open Government site
www.rospa.co.uk	Royal Society for the Prevention of Accidents
www.statistics.gov.uk	Office for National Statistics
www.tiger.gov.uk	Tailored Interactive Guidance on Employment Rights (DTI)
www.tuc.org.uk	Trades Union Congress

INDEX